Management Information Systems

FOR THE INFORMATION AGE

NINTH EDITION

Stephen Haag

DANIELS COLLEGE OF BUSINESS

UNIVERSITY OF DENVER

Maeve Cummings

KELCE COLLEGE OF BUSINESS

PITTSBURG STATE UNIVERSITY

McGraw-Hill
Irwin

McGraw-Hill
Irwin

MANAGEMENT INFORMATION SYSTEMS FOR THE INFORMATION AGE
Published by McGraw-Hill/Irwin, a business unit of The McGraw-Hill Companies, Inc., 1221 Avenue
of the Americas, New York, NY, 10020. Copyright © 2013, 2010, 2008, 2007, 2005, 2004, 2002, 2000,
1998 by The McGraw-Hill Companies, Inc. All rights reserved. Printed in the United States of America.
No part of this publication may be reproduced or distributed in any form or by any means, or stored in
a database or retrieval system, without the prior written consent of The McGraw-Hill Companies, Inc.,
including, but not limited to, in any network or other electronic storage or transmission, or broadcast for
distance learning.

Some ancillaries, including electronic and print components, may not be available to customers outside the
United States.

This book is printed on acid-free paper.

1 2 3 4 5 6 7 8 9 0 DOW/DOW 1 0 9 8 7 6 5 4 3 2

ISBN   978-0-07-131464-0
MHID   0-07-131464-4

www.mhhe.com

For my wife Pam: Conqueror of cancer
in 2011. My hero.
Stephen Haag

To Don Viney who showed
me in my darkest hour that
there can be life after death.
Maeve Cummings

BRIEF TABLE OF CONTENTS

TABLE OF CONTENTS

The Ninth Edition of *Management Information Systems for the Information Age* provides you the ultimate in flexibility to tailor content to the exact needs of your MIS or IT course. The nine chapters and thirteen Extended Learning Modules may be presented in logical sequence, or you may choose your own mix of technical topics and business/managerial topics.

The nine chapters form the core of material covering business and managerial topics, from strategic and competitive technology opportunities to the organization and management of information using databases and data warehouses. If you covered only the chapters and none of the modules, the focus of your course would be MIS from a business and managerial point of view.

The thirteen Extended Learning Modules provide a technical glimpse into the world of IT, covering topics ranging from building a Web site, to computer crimes and digital forensics, to how to use Microsoft Access. If you chose only the modules and none of the chapters, the focus of your course would be on the technical and hands-on aspects of IT.

At the beginning of each chapter (and in the Instructor's Manual for each chapter), we include our recommendations concerning which modules to cover immediately after covering a given chapter. For example, Module H on computer crime and digital forensics follows logically after Chapter 8 on protecting people and information. But you can cover Chapter 8 and omit Module H—that's completely up to you. On the other hand, you can omit Chapter 8 and cover Module H—you have flexibility to do what suits your needs and the needs of your students.

You can easily select a course format that represents your own desired blend of topics. While you might not choose to cover the technologies of networks, for example, you might require your students to build a small database application. In that case, you would omit Module E (Network Basics) and spend more time on Module C (Designing Databases and Entity-Relationship Diagramming) and Module J (Implementing a Database with Microsoft Access).

On the facing page, we've provided a table of the chapters and the modules. As you put your course together and choose the chapters and/or modules you want to cover, we would offer the following:

- Cover any or all of the chapters as suits your purposes.
- Cover any or all of the modules as suits your purposes.
- If you choose a chapter, you do not have to cover its corresponding module.
- If you choose a module, you do not have to cover its corresponding chapter.
- You may cover the modules in any order you wish.

Please note that your students will find Modules F, G, I, K, L, and M on the Web site that accompanies the textbook at www.mhhe.com/haag. Also, to better serve a large and diverse market, we have provided two versions of Module D (Decision Analysis with Spreadsheet Software) and two of Module J (Implementing a Database with Microsoft Access). In the book, these two modules cover Office 2010 Excel and Access. However, if you're using a previous iteration of Microsoft Office, you can teach Excel and Access using the versions of Modules D and J found on the Web site, as they teach Excel and Access using Office 2007.

The unique organization of this text gives you **complete flexibility** to design your course as you see fit.

THE CHAPTERS	THE EXTENDED LEARNING MODULES
CHAPTER 1 The Information Age in Which You Live	**Extended Learning Module A** Computer Hardware and Software
CHAPTER 2 Major Business Initiatives	**Extended Learning Module B** The World Wide Web and the Internet
CHAPTER 3 Databases and Data Warehouses	**Extended Learning Module C** Designing Databases and Entity-Relationship Diagramming
CHAPTER 4 Decision Support Analytics, and Artificial Intelligence	**Extended Learning Module D** Decision Analysis with Spreadsheet Software
CHAPTER 5 Electronic Commerce	**Extended Learning Module E** Network Basics
CHAPTER 6 Systems Development	**Extended Learning Module F*** Building a Web Page with HTML
CHAPTER 7 Infrastructure, Cloud Computing, Metrics, and Business Continuity Planning	**Extended Learning Module G*** Object-Oriented Technologies
CHAPTER 8 Protecting People and Information	**Extended Learning Module H** Computer Crime and Digital Forensics
CHAPTER 9 Emerging Trends and Technologies	**Extended Learning Module I*** Building an E-Portfolio
	Extended Learning Module J Implementing a Database with Microsoft Access
	Extended Learning Module K* Careers in Business
	Extended Learning Module L* Building Web Sites with FrontPage
	Extended Learning Module M* Programming in Excel with VBA

*The complete text for Modules F, G, I, K, L, and M are on the Web site (www.mhhe.com/haag) that accompanies this text. (On the Web site also are versions of Modules D and J using Office 2007.)

- Management focus—By focusing on the chapters, your class will take a managerial approach to MIS.
- Technical focus—If hands-on, technical skills are more important, focus your MIS course on the modules.

Organization—The Haag Advantage

The separation of content between the chapters and the Extended Learning Modules is very simple. We can sum it up by saying:

- The **chapters** address what you want your students **to know.**
- The **modules** address what you want your students **to be able to do.**

Together, both combine to provide a well-balanced repository of important information aimed at developing a prospective business professional equipped with both foundational knowledge and application experience, ready to take on today's highly competitive job market.

Each chapter and module contains full pedagogical support:

- Student Learning Outcomes
- Summary
- Key Terms and Concepts
- Short-Answer Questions
- Assignments and Exercises

ing in some way that information. Of course, what it contains is really up to you and your needs.

DATA WAREHOUSES SUPPORT DECISION MAKING, NOT TRANSACTION PROCESSING In an organization, most databases are transaction-oriented. That is, most databases support online transaction processing (OLTP) and, therefore, are operational databases. Data warehouses are not transaction-oriented: They exist to support decision-making tasks in your organization. Therefore, data warehouses support only online analytical processing (OLAP).

ure 3.8

ltidimensional
Warehouse
Information from
ple Operational
ases

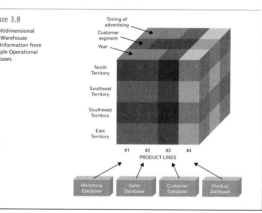

The chapters focus on the *business and managerial* applications of MIS and information technology.

ure C.3

ding an Entity-
tionship (E-R)
ram

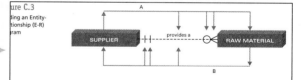

The **modules** focus on giving your students real *hands-on-knowledge* they can apply in both their personal and professional experiences.

Once you determine that a relationship does exist, you must then determine the numerical nature of the relationship, what we refer to as "minimum and maximum cardinality." To describe this, you use a | to denote a single relationship, a O to denote a zero or optional relationship, and/or a crow's foot (<) to denote a multiple relationship. By way of illustration, let's consider the portion of your E-R diagram in Figure C.3 above. To help you read the symbols and diagram, we've added blue lines and arrows. Following the line marked A, you would read the E-R diagram as:

"A *Supplier* may not provide any *Raw Material* (denoted with the O) but may provide more than one *Raw Material* (denoted with the crow's foot)."

So, that part of the E-R diagram states that the logical relationship between *Supplier* and *Raw Material* is that a *Supplier* may provide no *Raw Material* currently in inventory but may provide more than one *Raw Material* currently in inventory. This is exactly what business rule 4 (on page 373) states.

Student Engagement and Enrichment— the Haag Advantage

Your students exhibit three different learning styles:

1. Auditory (hearing)
2. Visual (seeing)
3. Tactile (doing and experiencing)

To be at your best in the classroom, you need engagement and enrichment support that fosters learning within each of the three different learning styles. *Management Information Systems for the Information Age,* Ninth Edition, provides you with a vast array of engagement and enrichment support for all learning styles, including:

- High-quality, relevant videos
- "Study to Go" material downloaded to electronic handheld devices
- An opening case study (now with questions) and two closing case studies per chapter
- 24 electronic commerce projects
- 22 group projects requiring your students to use technology to solve a problem or take advantage of an opportunity
- Over 175 assignments, exercises, homework, and in-class breakout activities. You can find these great assignments in the Instructor's Manual.

Use high-quality videos covering such topics as Hurricane Katrina, Motley Fool, Spawn.com, and Digital Domain to challenge your students to define the role of IT and MIS in real-life situations.

SDLC STEP						
PLANNING	ANALYSIS	DESIGN	DEVELOPMENT	TESTING	IMPLEMENTATION	MAINTENANCE
Business process expert						
Liaison to the customer						
Quality control analyst						
Manager of other people						

4. CONSTRUCTION AND THE SDLC The systems development life cycle is often compared to the activities in the construction industry.

Fill in the following chart listing some of the activities performed in building a house and how they relate to the different SDLC steps.

SDLC	Activities for Building a Home
Planning	

Engage your students in active participation by assigning any of the over 175 assignments, exercises, homework, and in-class breakout activities. Some can be used in class and others require outside class work.

Case Studies

OUTRAGEOUS INDUSTRY TRANSFORMATION

Each chapter begins with a one-page Outrageous Industry Transformation and an accompanying graph, highlighting how technology is transforming online industries.

CHAPTER ONE

The Information Age in Which You Live
Changing the Face of Business

OUTRAGEOUS INDUSTRY TRANSFORMATION: CELL PHONES DOOM PHONE REVENUES FOR HOTELS

Think about the title of this case. It's not the typical opening case study you've come to expect in textbooks. This is about the outrageous, yes, literally outrageous, transformations that are being caused by information technology. Newspaper subscriptions are declining rapidly, as is revenue for print advertising in magazines; people are building homes without land-based phone lines; movie rentals largely happen online, not at a local video

newspapers and magazines, music, movies, the local news, education, financial services. The list goes on and on.

As a future business leader, you don't need to focus on how cell phones work. Rather, you need to focus on how and why people use cell phones. The same is true for all the new technologies. You don't really need to "pop the hood" and learn all about the engine of technology. Rather, you need to focus on the personal and business uses of technology. That's the knowledge you need to effectively build business strategy that incorporates technology.

CHAPTER TWO

Major Business Initiatives
Gaining Competitive Advantage with IT

OUTRAGEOUS INDUSTRY TRANSFORMATION: DEATH OF A TRAVEL AGENT

In Chapter 1, we explored the extent to which cell phones are transforming (i.e., wiping out) in-room phone revenues for hotels. Hotels are often considered broadly within the context of the travel and leisure industry segment. So, let's stay within that industry and explore another technology-enabled transformation.

Up through the mid-1990s, airline reservations systems were closely guarded barriers to entry. If you wanted to book a flight, you had one of two options: (1) call an airline directly, or (2) call or visit a travel agent. The travel agency industry flourished during this time. By offering hotel reservations, rental cars reservations, cruise bookings, and much more, the local travel agent became a friendly, one-stop shop for many people's vacationing needs.

Will there be a need for travel agents? Sure. Some will survive and even thrive by focusing on the personal touch, what many people call *customer experience management.* Others will also survive by focusing on specific niches, say perhaps excursions to the north and south poles. (This is a form of *focus* as described in Porter's three generic strategies from Chapter 1.) It's rather like hotels losing in-room telephone charge revenue; they figure out how to make up that lost revenue elsewhere.

Technology is certainly a game changer. Some businesses will win, others will lose. The winners work diligently to build strategies and major business initiatives around the use of technology. That's our focus in this chapter.[1]

CLOSING CASE STUDY TWO

Google and Apple Know Where You Are, Maybe

In April 2011, some interesting discoveries were made regarding location tracking by Apple iPhones and iPads and Google Android smartphones. Pete Warden and Alasdair Allan, British researchers, discovered a file on Allan's iPhone that provided a detailed list of places Allan had visited in the U.S. and United Kingdom over a 300-day period. The file included a time stamp of each location.

Similarly, Duke and Penn State student researchers, with the help of Intel, found that 15 of 30 popular Android apps systematically communicated location information to a variety of ad networks. Those researchers found that some of the apps transmitted location data only when displaying specific ads, while others did so even while the app was not running. On some Android smartphones, the location data was transmitted as often as every 30 seconds.

Well, as you can imagine, this sent the public into an uproar. Google and Apple (if you're using one their smartphones) are tracking my every movement? Those organizations know exactly where I was and when I was there? The outcry was unbelievable.

subcommittee on privacy for May 10, 2011. According to Franken, "People have the right to know who is getting their information and how (it) is shared and used. Federal laws do far too little to protect this information. . . . No one wants to stop Apple or Google from producing their products, but Congress must find a balance between all of those wonderful benefits (from devices) and the public's right to privacy." After getting little or no response from either Apple or Google, Franken went on to say, "I have serious doubts those rights are being respected in law or in practice."

At the time, Steve Jobs, CEO of Apple, was on medical leave, and he came back from medical leave to defend Apple's location tracking technology. According to Jobs's right-hand executive Guy Tribble, Apple vice president of software technology, Apple iPhones and iPads only gather location data about nearby cell towers and Wi-Fi hot spots. As he explained, "[Apple] does not share personally identifiable information with third parties for their marketing purposes without customers' explicit consent . . .

CLOSING CASE STUDIES

To help your students apply what they have just learned, you'll find two closing case studies at the end of each chapter. Each case has a set of questions that are great for class discussion.

Interactive Learning Pedagogy

Student Learning Outcomes open and close each chapter and module. We summarize the learning content by revisiting each Student Learning Outcome—"tell them what you're going to tell them, tell them, and then tell them what you told them."

CHAPTER FOUR OUTLINE

STUDENT LEARNING OUTCOMES

Compare and contrast decision support systems and geographic information systems.

Describe the decision support role of specialized analytics like predictive analytics and text analytics.

Describe the role and function of an expert system in analytics.

Explain why neural networks are effective decision support tools.

Define genetic algorithms and the types of problems they help solve.

■ SUMMARY: STUDENT LEARNING OUTCOMES REVISITED

1. **Compare and contrast decision support systems and geographic information systems.** A *decision support system (DSS)* is a highly flexible and interactive IT system that is designed to support decision making when the situation includes nonstructured elements. A *geographic information system (GIS)* is a decision support system designed specifically to analyze spatial information. So, they both are designed to support decision-making efforts. While traditional DSSs mainly use text and numeric data, GISs represent many types of information in spatial or map form.

2. **Describe the decision support role of specialized analytics like predictive analytics and text analytics.** *Predictive analytics* is a highly computational data-mining technology that uses information and business intelligence to build

---

EACH CHAPTER AND MODULE CONTAINS COMPLETE PEDAGOGICAL SUPPORT IN THE FORM OF:

1. Summary of Student Learning Outcomes
2. Closing case studies and discussion questions (chapters only)
3. Key terms and concepts
4. Assignments and Exercises

Broadband router (home router), 411	Intrusion prevention system (IPS), 428	Virtual private network (VPN), 429
Cable modem, 418	Local area network (LAN), 414	Virus, 429
Cat 5 (Category 5), 410	Malware, 429	Voice over IP (VoIP), 421
Coaxial cable (coax), 423	Metropolitan area network (municipal area network, MAN), 414	Wide area network (WAN), 414
Communications media, 422		
Communications satellite, 425		Wi-Fi (wireless fidelity), 424
Computer network, 409	Microwave transmission, 424	Wi-Fi hotspot, 424
Denial-of-service (DoS) attack, 428	Network interface card (NIC), 410	Wired communications media, 422
Digital Subscriber Line (DSL), 417	Optical fiber, 423	Wireless access point (WAP), 410
DS3, 419	Repeater, 425	
Encryption, 429	Router, 413	Wireless communications media, 422
Ethernet card, 410	Satellite modem, 419	Worm, 429
Firewall, 427	Spyware, (sneakware, stealthware), 430	
Infrared, 424	Switch, 412	

■ SHORT-ANSWER QUESTIONS

1. What are the four basic principles that apply to all networks?
2. What is an Ethernet card?
3. What does a network switch do?
4. What is bandwidth?
5. What do you need to have a dial-up connection to the Internet?
6. How is a DSL Internet connection different from a telephone modem connection?
7. What impact does Frame Relay have on a metropolitan area network?
8. What is Cat 5 cable used for?
9. What is Bluetooth?
10. What does Wi-Fi do?
11. How does a VPN protect confidentiality?
12. What are the four principles of computer security?

ASSIGNMENTS AND EXERCISES

1. **WHAT ARE THE INTERNET ACCESS OPTIONS IN YOUR AREA?** Write a report on what sort of Internet connections are available close to you. How many ISPs offer telephone modem access? Is DSL available to you? Is it available to anyone in your area? Does your cable company offer a cable modem? If your school has residence halls, does it offer network connections? Compare each available service on price, connection speed, and extras like a help line, list of supported computers and operating systems, and people who will come out to your home and help you if you're having difficulties. What type of Internet connection do you currently use? Do you plan to upgrade in the future? If so, to what type of connection? If not, why not?

2. **INVESTIGATE BUILDING YOUR OWN HOME NETWORK** Build your own home network on paper. Assume you have the computers already and just need to link them together. Find prices for switches and routers on the Web. Also research Ethernet cards and cables. If you were to get a high-speed Internet

4. **CONSIDER THE IMPORTANCE OF NETWORK SECURITY** Write a report about the importance of computer and network security in your daily life, in terms of the four principles of computer security. If you have a job in addition to being a student, write about computer security in your workplace. If you don't work outside the classroom, write about how computer security affects you at school and in your personal life. You may be surprised at how many things you do that depend on some aspect of secure computer records and communications, like banking, grades, e-mail, timesheets, library and movie rental records, and many more.

5. **FIND OUT ABOUT FIREWALLS** Go to the Web and find out about software and hardware that protect your computer and home network, respectively.

   If you have only one computer connected to the Internet, then a software firewall like Zone Alarm will most likely be enough protection from intruders. Find three different firewall software packages on the Web. A good place to start looking would be the sites that sell

---

■ ASSIGNMENTS AND EXERCISES

1. **FINDING FREE IMAGES AND BACKGROUNDS ON THE WEB** To insert and use images and backgrounds, you don't necessarily need to scan them yourself. Literally thousands of Web sites provide free images and backgrounds. Below, we've listed two.

   • Animated GIFs—www.webdeveloper.com/animations/

   • Free Graphics—www.freegraphics.com

   Connect to the sites above as well as three others that you can find and answer the following questions:

   A. How do you download an image?
   B. Do you have to register at the site first before downloading images?
   C. What categories of images can you find?
   D. Because there are so many sites offering free images, why would anyone want to scan their own?

2. **BUILD A NUMBERED LIST OF LINKS** In this module, we demonstrated to you how to

many ways in which you can combine HTML tags to create a powerful presentation. One such way is to create a list (either numbered or unnumbered) of useful links. Go to the Web and find five job databases (Monster.com is one). Now create a small Web site that provides links to those five Web sites. You are to present those links in the form of a list.

3. **MAKE MODIFICATIONS TO FIGURE F.1** Figure F.1 on page F.3 contains some very interesting information, but it does not include any links to other related Web sites and it contains only one image. You have two tasks here. First, connect to NASA's site at www.nasa.gov, download another astronomy image, and insert it into Figure F.1. To download an image, simply right click on the image and choose *Save Picture As . . .*. Your second task is to provide links to the main Web site for each of the six listed states. So, the state names of Arizona, California, Kansas, Oregon, Nevada, and Georgia should all be links that will take

---

PROJECTS

Group PROJECTS

CASE 1:
ASSESSING THE VALUE OF CUSTOMER RELATIONSHIP MANAGEMENT

TREVOR TOY AUTO MECHANICS

Trevor Toy Auto Mechanics is an automobile repair shop in Phoenix, Arizona. Over the past few years, Trevor has seen his business grow from a two-bay car repair shop with only one other employee to a 15-bay car repair shop with 21 employees.

Trevor wants to improve service and add a level of personalization to his customers. However, Trevor has no idea who his best customers are, the work that is being performed, or which mechanic is responsible for the repairs. Trevor is asking for your help. He has provided you with a spreadsheet file, **TREVOR.xls**, that contains a list of all the repairs his shop has completed over the past year including each client's name along with a unique identifier. The spreadsheet file contains the fields provided in the table below.

Column	Name	Description
A	CUSTOMER #	A unique number assigned to each customer
B	CUSTOMER NAME	The name of the customer
C	MECHANIC #	A unique number assigned to the mechanic who completed the work
D	CAR TYPE	The type of car on which the work was completed
E	WORK COMPLETED	What type of repair was performed on the car
F	NUM HOURS	How long in hours it took to complete the work
G	COST OF PARTS	The cost of the parts associated with completing the repair

---

Electronic Commerce PROJECTS

BEST IN COMPUTER STATISTICS AND RESOURCES

For both personal and professional reasons, you'll find it necessary to stay up with technology and technology changes throughout your life. Right now, knowing about technology—the latest trends, new inventions, processor speeds, wireless communications capabilities, and the like—can help you support technology infrastructure recommendations for a company in one of your term papers. That same kind of information can help you determine which personal technologies you need to buy and use.

As you progress through your career, you'll make numerous business presentations and recommendations, most of which will contain some sort of discussion of the best uses of technology from an organizational point of view. Indeed, if you plan to move up the corporate ladder to the C-level (CEO, CFO, CIO, etc.), a knowledge of the organizational uses of technology is essential. Connect to several Web sites that offer computer statistics and resources and answer the following questions for each.

A. What categories of personal technologies are covered?
B. What categories of organizational uses of technology are covered?
C. To what extent is time-based (e.g., year-by-year) numerical data provided?
D. Who supports the site? Is the site for-profit or not-for-profit?
E. Are the various types of research reports free or do you have to pay a fee?
F. How helpful is the site from a personal point of view?
G. How helpful is the site from an organizational point of view?

Electronic commerce projects require your students to learn through Web exploration. Group projects require your students to use technology to solve a problem or take advantage of an opportunity.

The electronic commerce projects appear immediately following Chapter 9. These projects each have a singular focus and can be applied to many different chapters and modules. Each chapter starts by identifying which electronic projects are most appropriate to use. The Instructor's Manuals for the modules identify the most appropriate ones as well. As a quick reference, please refer to the table below.

	CHAPTER								
	1	2	3	4	5	6	7	8	9
1. Best in Computer Statistics and Resources			X	X		X	X		X
2. Consumer Information		X	X	X					
3. Interviewing and Negotiating Tips	X								X
4. Meta Data		X	X	X		X	X		
5. Bureau of Labor and Statistics		X	X	X					
6. Demographics		X	X	X					
7. Free and Rentable Storage Space					X				X
8. Gathering Competitive Intelligence		X			X				
9. Ethical Computing Guidelines	X							X	
10. Exploring Google Earth			X		X			X	
11. Financial Aid Resources	X		X						X
12. Finding Hosting Services						X	X		
13. Global Statistics and Resources	X	X	X		X	X			X
14. Gold, Silver, Interest Rates, and Money		X		X	X				
15. Privacy Laws and Legislation								X	
16. Protecting Your Computer	X							X	
17. Learning About Investing				X	X				
18. Locating Internships									
19. Small Business Administration		X			X				
20. Stock Quotes				X					
21. Researching Storefront Software					X	X			
22. Searching for Shareware and Freeware						X	X	X	
23. Searching Job Databases	X		X			X	X		X
24. Searching for MBA Programs									X

In the text, you'll find 22 Group Projects. These require your students to use technology to solve a problem or take advantage of an opportunity. A quick warning to instructors: Some of these take an entire weekend to solve. Be careful not to assign too many at one time. These projects can be applied to many different chapters and modules. As a quick reference, please refer to the table below.

	CHAPTER/MODULE										
	1	2	3	4	5	6	7	8	9	D	C/J
1. Assessing the Value of Information	X			X				X		X	
2. Analyzing the Value of Information	X							X		X	
3. Executive Information System Reporting		X		X		X				X	
4. Building Value Chains			X		X						X
5. Using Relational Technology to Track Projects			X							X	X
6. Building a Decision Support System				X						X	
7. Advertising with Banner Ads				X	X	X	X			X	
8. Assessing the Value of Outsourcing Information Technology				X		X	X			X	
9. Demonstrating How to Build Web Sites											
10. Making the Case with Presentation Software	X										
11. Building a Web Database System			X		X						X
12. Creating a Decision Support System				X		X	X			X	
13. Developing an Enterprise Resource Planning System		X		X			X	X	X	X	
14. Assessing a Wireless Future					X				X		
15. Evaluating the Next Generation		X			X				X		
16. Analyzing Strategic and Competitive Advantage	X			X						X	
17. Building a Decision Support System				X						X	
18. Creating a Financial Analysis				X						X	
19. Building a Scheduling Decision Support System		X		X						X	
20. Creating a Database Management System			X						X		X
21. Evaluating the Security of Information								X	X		
22. Assessing the Value of Supply Chain Management		X		X			X			X	

The Support Package

We realize that no text is complete without a well-rounded and value-added support package. Our support package is designed to ease your teaching burden by providing you with a Web site full of valuable information, a test bank with more than 2,000 questions and easy-to-use test generating software, an Instructor's Manual that walks you through each chapter and module and provides value-added teaching notes and suggestions, and PowerPoint presentations.

ONLINE LEARNING CENTER AT WWW.MHHE.COM/HAAG

As in previous editions, the Web site for the Ninth Edition contains a wealth of valuable information and supplements for both the instructor and the student.

INSTRUCTOR'S MANUAL

The Instructor's Manual is provided to you in an effort to help you prepare for your class presentations. In its new format, you will find a separate box for each PowerPoint slide. In that box, you will find an overview of the slide and a list of key points to cover. This presentation enables you to prepare your class presentation by working solely with the Instructor's Manual because you also see the PowerPoint slide presentations. We've also provided embedded links within each Instructor's Manual document to the various in-text pedagogical elements.

- **The Global** and **Industry Perspectives boxes**—how to introduce them, key points to address, possible discussion questions to ask, etc.

At the beginning of each Instructor's Manual document you'll find other useful information including the appropriate author to contact if you have questions or comments, a list of the Group Projects that you can cover, and a list of any associated data files.

We've provided the Instructor's Manual files in Word format and placed them on the text's Web site.

TEST BANK

For each chapter and module, there are approximately 125 multiple-choice, true/false, and fill-in-the-blank questions aimed at challenging the minds of your students. McGraw-Hill's EZ Test is a flexible and easy-to-use electronic testing program. The program allows instructors to create tests from book-specific items. It accommodates a wide range of question types and instructors may add their own questions. Multiple versions of the test can be created and any test can be exported for use with course management systems such as WebCT, BlackBoard, or PageOut. The program is available for Windows and Macintosh environments.

POWERPOINT PRESENTATIONS

The PowerPoint presentations are ready for you to use in class. In preparing to use these, you simply work through the Instructor's Manual which includes thumbnails of each slide and important points to cover. Of course, we realize that you'll probably want to customize some of the presentations. So, we've made available to you most of the images and photos in the text. You can find these on the text's Web site at www.mhhe.com/haag.

VIDEOS

Videos will be downloadable from the instructor side of the OLC. Selections from our archive of videos from previous years will be delivered upon request.

MBA MIS CASES

Developed by Richard Perle of Loyola Marymount University, these 14 comprehensive cases allow you to add MBA-level analysis to your course. Visit our Web site to review a sample case.

ONLINE LEARNING CENTER

Visit www.mhhe.com/haag for additional instructor and student resources.

ONLINE COURSES

Content for the Ninth Edition is available in WebCT, Blackboard, and PageOut formats to accommodate virtually any online delivery platform.

USE OUR EZ TEST ONLINE TO HELP YOUR STUDENTS PREPARE TO SUCCEED WITH APPLE IPOD® IQUIZ.

Using our EZ Test Online you can make test and quiz content available for a student's Apple iPod®.

Students must purchase the iQuiz game application from Apple for 99¢ in order to use the iQuiz content. It works on the iPod fifth generation iPods and better.

Instructors only need EZ Test Online to produce iQuiz ready content. Instructors take their existing tests and quizzes and export them to a file that can then be made available to the student to take as a self-quiz on their iPods. It's as simple as that.

McGraw-Hill *Connect MIS*

LESS MANAGING. MORE TEACHING. GREATER LEARNING.

McGraw-Hill *Connect MIS* is an online assignment and assessment solution that connects students with the tools and resources they'll need to achieve success.

McGraw-Hill *Connect MIS* helps prepare students for their future by enabling faster learning, more efficient studying, and higher retention of knowledge.

MCGRAW-HILL *CONNECT MIS* FEATURES

Connect MIS offers a number of powerful tools and features to make managing assignments easier, so faculty can spend more time teaching. With *Connect MIS*, students can engage with their coursework anytime and anywhere, making the learning process more accessible and efficient. *Connect MIS* offers you the features described next.

SIMPLE ASSIGNMENT MANAGEMENT

With *Connect MIS*, creating assignments is easier than ever, so you can spend more time teaching and less time managing. The assignment management function enables you to:

- Create and deliver assignments easily with selectable end-of-chapter questions and test bank items.
- Streamline lesson planning, student progress reporting, and assignment grading to make classroom management more efficient than ever.
- Go paperless with the eBook and online submission and grading of student assignments.

SMART GRADING

When it comes to studying, time is precious. *Connect MIS* helps students learn more efficiently by providing feedback and practice material when they need it, where they need it. When it comes to teaching, your time also is precious. The grading function enables you to:

- Have assignments scored automatically, giving students immediate feedback on their work and side-by-side comparisons with correct answers.
- Access and review each response; manually change grades or leave comments for students to review.
- Reinforce classroom concepts with practice tests and instant quizzes.

INSTRUCTOR LIBRARY

The *Connect MIS* Instructor Library is your repository for additional resources to improve student engagement in and out of class. You can select and use any asset that enhances your lecture.

STUDENT STUDY CENTER

The *Connect MIS* Student Study Center is the place for students to access additional resources. The Student Study Center:

- Offers students quick access to lectures, practice materials, eBooks, and more.
- Provides instant practice material and study questions, easily accessible on the go.
- Gives students access to the Personalized Learning Plan described next.

STUDENT PROGRESS TRACKING

Connect MIS keeps instructors informed about how each student, section, and class is performing, allowing for more productive use of lecture and office hours. The progress-tracking function enables you to:

- View scored work immediately and track individual or group performance with assignment and grade reports.
- Access an instant view of student or class performance relative to learning objectives.
- Collect data and generate reports required by many accreditation organizations, such as AACSB.

LECTURE CAPTURE

Increase the attention paid to lecture discussion by decreasing the attention paid to note taking. For an additional charge, Lecture Capture offers new ways for students to focus on the in-class discussion, knowing they can revisit important topics later. Lecture Capture enables you to:

- Record and distribute your lecture with a click of a button.
- Record and index PowerPoint presentations and anything shown on your computer so it is easily searchable, frame by frame.
- Offer access to lectures anytime and anywhere by computer, iPod, or mobile device.
- Increase intent listening and class participation by easing students' concerns about note-taking. Lecture Capture will make it more likely you will see students' faces, not the tops of their heads.

MCGRAW-HILL CONNECT PLUS MIS

McGraw-Hill reinvents the textbook learning experience for the modern student with *Connect Plus MIS*. A seamless integration of an eBook and *Connect MIS*, *Connect Plus MIS* provides all of the *Connect MIS* features plus the following:

- An integrated eBook, allowing for anytime, anywhere access to the textbook.
- Dynamic links between the problems or questions you assign to your students and the location in the eBook where that problem or question is covered.
- A powerful search function to pinpoint and connect key concepts in a snap.

In short, *Connect MIS* offers you and your students powerful tools and features that optimize your time and energies, enabling you to focus on course content, teaching, and student learning. *Connect MIS* also offers a wealth of content resources for both instructors and students. This state-of-the-art, thoroughly tested system supports you in preparing students for the world that awaits.

For more information about Connect, go to **www.mcgrawhillconnect.com**, or contact your local McGraw-Hill sales representative.

Tegrity Campus: Lectures 24/7

Tegrity Campus is a service that makes class time available 24/7 by automatically capturing every lecture in a searchable format for students to review when they study and complete assignments. With a simple one-click start-and-stop process, you capture all computer screens and corresponding audio. Students can replay any part of any class with easy-to-use browser-based viewing on a PC or Mac.

Educators know that the more students can see, hear, and experience class resources, the better they learn. In fact, studies prove it. With Tegrity Campus, students quickly recall key moments by using Tegrity Campus's unique search feature. This search helps students efficiently find what they need, when they need it, across an entire semester of class recordings. Help turn all your students' study time into learning moments immediately supported by your lecture.

To learn more about Tegrity watch a 2-minute Flash demo at **http://tegritycampus. mhhe.com**.

Assurance of Learning Ready

Many educational institutions today are focused on the notion of *assurance of learning,* an important element of some accreditation standards. *Management Information Systems for the Information Age* is designed specifically to support your assurance of learning initiatives with a simple, yet powerful solution.

Each test bank question for *Management Information Systems for the Information Age* maps to a specific chapter learning outcome/objective listed in the text. You can use our test bank software, EZ Test and EZ Test Online, or in *Connect MIS* to easily query for learning outcomes/objectives that directly relate to the learning objectives for your course. You can then use the reporting features of EZ Test to aggregate student results in similar fashion, making the collection and presentation of assurance of learning data simple and easy.

AACSB Statement

The McGraw-Hill Companies is a proud corporate member of AACSB International. Understanding the importance and value of AACSB accreditation, *Management Information Systems for the Information Age* recognizes the curricula guidelines detailed in the AACSB standards for business accreditation by connecting selected questions in the test bank to the six general knowledge and skill guidelines in the AACSB standards.

The statements contained in *Management Information Systems for the Information Age* are provided only as a guide for the users of this textbook. The AACSB leaves content coverage and assessment within the purview of individual schools, the mission of the school, and the faculty. While *Management Information Systems for the Information Age* and the teaching package make no claim of any specific AACSB qualification or evaluation, within *Management Information Systems for the Information Age* we have labeled selected questions according to the six general knowledge and skills areas.

McGraw-Hill Customer Care Contact Information

At McGraw-Hill, we understand that getting the most from new technology can be challenging. That's why our services don't stop after you purchase our products. You can e-mail our Product Specialists 24 hours a day to get product-training online. Or you can search our knowledge bank of Frequently Asked Questions on our support Web site. For Customer Support, call **800-331-5094,** e-mail **hmsupport@mcgraw-hill.com**, or visit **www.mhhe.com/support.** One of our Technical Support Analysts will be able to assist you in a timely fashion.

McGraw-Hill Higher Education and Blackboard have teamed up. What does this mean for you?

1. **Your life, simplified.** Now you and your students can access McGraw-Hill's Connect® and Create® right from within your Blackboard course—all with one single sign-on. Say goodbye to the days of logging in to multiple applications.

2. **Deep integration of content and tools.** Not only do you get single sign-on with Connect and Create, you also get deep integration of McGraw-Hill content and content engines right in Blackboard. Whether you're choosing a book for your course or building Connect assignments, all the tools you need are right where you want them—inside of Blackboard.

3. **Seamless Gradebooks.** Are you tired of keeping multiple gradebooks and manually synchronizing grades into Blackboard? We thought so. When a student completes an integrated Connect assignment, the grade for that assignment automatically (and instantly) feeds your Blackboard grade center.

4. **A solution for everyone.** Whether your institution is already using Blackboard or you just want to try Blackboard on your own, we have a solution for you. McGraw-Hill and Blackboard can now offer you easy access to industry leading technology and content, whether your campus hosts it, or we do. Be sure to ask your local McGraw-Hill representative for details.

Craft your teaching resources to match the way you teach! With McGraw-Hill Create, www.mcgrawhillcreate.com, you can easily rearrange chapters, combine material from other content sources, and quickly upload content you have written, like your course syllabus or teaching notes. Find the content you need in Create by searching through thousands of leading McGraw-Hill textbooks. Arrange your book to fit your teaching style. Create even allows you to personalize your book's appearance by selecting the cover and adding your name, school, and course information. Order a Create book and you'll receive a complimentary print review copy in 3–5 business days or a complimentary electronic review copy (eComp) via email in about one hour. Go to www.mcgrawhillcreate.com today and register. Experience how McGraw-Hill Create empowers you to teach *your* students *your* way.

Acknowledgments

As we present our Ninth Edition of this text, we remember how things began and the people who have helped us along the way. In 1995, the Web was very much in its infancy, cell phones were used only in case of an emergency, and terms such as phishing and pharming had yet to be invented. It's been a fast 17 years and we have many people to thank.

McGraw-Hill's strategic management is simply second to none. We gratefully acknowledge the dedicated work and leadership of Brian Kibby and Doug Hughes. Their guidance is invaluable.

EDP includes all those people who take our thoughts on paper and bring them to life in the form of an exciting and engaging book. This wonderful group of people includes Mary Conzachi (the book's project manager), Peter de Lissovoy (our manuscript editor), Jeremy Cheshareck (photo research coordinator), and Cara Hawthorne (cover and interior design specialist).

The editorial group comprises those people who determine which projects to publish, and they have guided us every step of the way with a wealth of market intelligence. Brent Gordon (editor-in-chief) leads the editorial group that includes Paul Ducham (our editorial director), Anke Weekes (*senior sponsoring editor*), Trina Hauger (the book's developmental editor) Jonathan Thornton (editorial coordinator). We are indebted to them for leading the way.

We would also like to acknowledge the dedicated work of the following people at McGraw-Hill: Alpana Jolly (media project manager) and Amee Mosley (marketing manager). Without Alpana, our text would be just a text, with no supplements or great supporting Web site. Without Amee, you might never know we created this text.

We wish to acknowledge the wonderful efforts of our contributor team: Dan Connolly, David Cox, Jeff Engelstad, Syl Houston, and Keith Neufeld. Each has brought to the table unique talents and knowledge indispensable to the success of this text.

Last, but certainly not least, we offer our gratitude to our reviewers, who took on a thankless job that paid only a fraction of its true worth. We had the best. They include

Anil Aggarwal
University of Baltimore
John Aje
University of Maryland University College
Ihssan Alkadi
University of Louisiana at Lafayette
Dennis M. Anderson
Bentley University
Stephen Anderson
CUNY - Baruch College
Noushin Ashrafi
University of Massachusetts–Boston
Jack D. Becker
University of North Texas
Ashley Bush
Florida State University

Jerry Carvalho
University of Utah
Teuta Cata
Northern Kentucky University
Casey Cegielski
Auburn University
Syama Chaudhuri
University of Maryland University College
Michael Chuang
Towson University
David J. Cohen
University of Maryland University College
Vance Cooney
Eastern Washington University
Mohammad Dadashzadeh
Oakland University
Roy Dejoie

Purdue University-Krannert School of Management
Frederick Fisher
Florida State University
Mark E. Goudreau
Johnson & Wales University-College of Business
Richard Harris
Columbia College
Shaoyi He
California State University-San Marcos
Fred Hughes
Faulkner University
Wade M. Jackson
Fogelman College
Ted Janicki
Mount Olive College
Bomi Kang
Coastal Carolina University
Howard Kanter
DePaul University
Jack T. Marchewka
Northern Illinois University
Ali Mir
William Paterson University
Ram Misra
Montclair State University
Lawrence S. Orilia
Nassau Community College
Leslie Pang
University of Maryland University College
Craig A. Piercy
University of Georgia
Leonard Presby
William Paterson University
Sachidanandam Sakthivel
Bowling Green State University
Aaron Schorr
Fashion Institute of Technology
Keng Siau
University of Nebraska-Lincoln
Andrew Targowski
Western Michigan University
Jyhhorng Michael Tarn
Haworth College of Business, Western

Michigan University
Sameer Verma
San Francisco State University
Haibo Wang
Texas A&M International University
Robert Wurm
Nassau Community College
James E. Yao
Montclair State University
Bee Yew
Fayetteville State University
David Bahn
Metropolitan State University
Raquel Benbunan-Fich
Baruch College
Richard Christensen
Metropolitan State University
David DuBay
Metropolitan State University
James Elwood
Utah State University
Roger Finnegan
Metropolitan State University
David Gadish
California State University–Los Angeles
Frederick Gallegos
California State Polytechnic -University
Yujong Hwang
DePaul University
Curtis Izen
Baruch College
Jeffrey Johnson
Utah State University
Brian Kovar
Kansas State University
Subodha Kumar
University of Washington
Al Lederer
University of Kentucky
Ron Lemos
California State University–Los Angeles
Jay Lightfoot
University of Northern Colorado
Wenhong Luo

Villanova University
Gloria Phillips-Wren
Loyola College
Sharma Pillutla
Towson University
Alexander Pons
University of Miami
Daniel Rice
Loyola College
Sherri Shade
Kennesaw State University

Richard Turley
University of Northern Colorado
Craig Tyran
Western Washington University
William Wagner
Villanova University
Bee Yew
Fayetteville State University
Enrique Zapatero
Norfolk State University

FROM STEPHEN HAAG To the entire author team—coauthors and contributors alike—I commend you for all your efforts. I am also grateful to the many people who helped me along the career path of writing books. They include Peter Keen, Dr. L. L. Schkade, JD Ice, Rick Williamson, and a host of people at McGraw-Hill.

My colleagues in the Daniels College of Business at the University of Denver also provide support. I wish I could name all of you, but there isn't enough room. To James Griesemer (Dean Emeritus), Christine Riuplan and Glyn Hanbery (Senior Associate Dean), I thank you all.

And my writing efforts would not be successful nor would my life be complete without my family. My mother and father live just a few minutes away from me and give me unending support. My two sons—Darian and Trevor—make me smile after long nights of working. My four-legged son—Zippy—doesn't really care that I write books; he offers me unconditional love. And I have two beautiful daughters from Ukraine. We adopted Alexis in the summer of 2007 and Katrina in the winter of 2009. I cannot put into words how much happiness they have brought into our lives. The latest addition to our family is another four-logged child, Princess. She reminds us everyday that happiness is the key to life.

FROM MAEVE CUMMING My sincere thanks go to the many people who helped directly and indirectly with this edition and the previous ones. Thanks to Steve, who is every bit as good a friend as he is a lead author. Thanks to all the people at McGraw-Hill who put in long hours and lots of work to bring this project to completion.

A special thanks is due to Don Viney who helped with the section on ethics. Keith Neufeld is an expert on networks and was generous with his knowledge. Lanny Morrow keeps me in touch with the fascinating world of computer forensics. My thanks to you all.

Thanks to the Holy Faith and Loreto nuns who gave me an excellent early education, which served as a solid foundation on which I was able to build. These were exceptionally dedicated teachers and I learned much more from them than the basics of reading, writing, and arithmetic. Much credit for what I have been able to accomplish goes to Pittsburg State University and the unusually talented and caring faculty who nurtured and guided a penniless foreigner terrified to the point of paralysis into becoming a contributing member of society.

As always, I want to thank my great family: My parents (Dolores and Steve), sisters (Grainne, Fiona, and Clodagh), brother (Colin), and their families for their support and love. And a final thank you goes to Slim who always believed in me even when I didn't.

STEPHEN HAAG is a Professor in Residence of Business Information and Analytics in the Daniels College of Business at the University of Denver. Previously, Stephen has served as Chair of the Department of Information Technology and Electronic Commerce, Director of the Master of Science in Information Technology program, Director of the MBA program, and Associate Dean of Graduate Programs. Stephen holds a B.B.A. and M.B.A. from West Texas State University and a Ph.D. from the University of Texas at Arlington.

Stephen is the author/coauthor of numerous books including *Computing Concepts in Action* (a K-12 textbook), *Interactions: Teaching English as a Second Language* (with his mother and father), *Information Technology: Tomorrow's Advantage Today* (with Peter Keen), *Excelling in Finance*, *Business Driven Technology*, and more than 40 books within the *I-Series*. He has also written numerous articles appearing in such journals as *Communications of the ACM, Socio-Economic Planning Sciences,* the *International Journal of Systems Science, Managerial and Decision Economics, Applied Economics,* and the *Australian Journal of Management*. Stephen lives with his family in Highlands Ranch, Colorado.

MAEVE CUMMINGS is a Professor of Information Systems at Pittsburg State University. She holds a B.S. in Mathematics and Computer Science and an M.B.A from Pittsburg State and a Ph.D. in Information Systems from the University of Texas at Arlington. She has published in various journals including the *Journal of Global Information Management* and the *Journal of Computer Information Systems*. She serves on various editorial boards and is a coauthor of *Case Studies in Information Technology,* the concepts books of the *I-Series,* entitled *Computing Concepts* and *Information Systems Essentials,* now in its second edition. Maeve has been teaching for 25 years and lives in Pittsburg, Kansas.

Management Information Systems

FOR THE INFORMATION AGE

CHAPTER ONE OUTLINE

STUDENT LEARNING OUTCOMES

1. Define management information systems (MIS) and describe the three important organizational resources within it—people, information, and information technology.

2. Describe how to use break-even analysis to assess the financial impact of information technology.

3. Describe how to use Porter's Five Forces Model to evaluate the relative attractiveness of and competitive pressures in an industry.

4. Compare and contrast Porter's three generic strategies and the run-grow-transform framework as approaches to the development of business strategy.

PERSPECTIVES

WEB SUPPORT

www.mhhe.com/haag

- Searching job databases
- Interviewing and negotiating tips
- Financial aid resources
- Protecting your computer
- Ethical computing guidelines
- Global statistics and resources

SUPPORTING MODULES

XLM/A: Computer Hardware and Software
Extended Learning Module A is a comprehensive tour of technology terminology focusing on personal technologies including application software, system software, input devices, output devices, storage devices, CPU and RAM, and connecting devices such as cables and ports.

XLM/K: Careers in Business
Extended Learning Module K is an overview of job titles and descriptions in the fields of accounting, finance, hospitality and tourism management, information technology, management, marketing, productions and operations management, and real estate and construction management including what IT skills you should acquire to be successful in each field.

The Information Age in Which You Live
Changing the Face of Business

OUTRAGEOUS INDUSTRY TRANSFORMATION: CELL PHONES DOOM PHONE REVENUES FOR HOTELS

Think about the title of this case. It's not the typical opening case study you've come to expect in textbooks. This is about the outrageous, yes, literally outrageous, transformations that are being caused by information technology. Newspaper subscriptions are declining rapidly, as is revenue for print advertising in magazines; people are building homes without land-based phone lines; movie rentals largely happen online, not at a local video store. The impact of technology is definitely profound, and it is transforming entire industries.

Consider hotels. They rely on a number of sources of revenue to make a profit. These sources include room rentals (the largest), restaurant food charges, the use of banquet and conference facilities, parking lot fees, and charges for the use of in-room telephones. But the latter is quickly going away. With the proliferation of personal cell phones, fewer and fewer hotel guests are picking up the in-room hotel phone to make local and long distance calls.

Take a look at the accompanying graph. In 2000, a typical hotel received $1,274 annually per available room for in-room phone charges. So, for a hotel with 500 rooms, it could budget approximately $637,000 annually in phone revenue. Not anymore. In 2009, that annual revenue per room for phone charges had dropped to $178. That's a decline of almost 86 percent. For a hotel with 500 rooms, $637,000 in revenue had dropped to $89,000 in a hurry.

This truly demonstrates the "outrageous" corrective and transformative nature of technology. And it's happening in most every industry—travel, newspapers and magazines, music, movies, the local news, education, financial services. The list goes on and on.

As a future business leader, you don't need to focus on how cell phones work. Rather, you need to focus on how and why people use cell phones. The same is true for all the new technologies. You don't really need to "pop the hood" and learn all about the engine of technology. Rather, you need to focus on the personal and business uses of technology. That's the knowledge you need to effectively build business strategy that incorporates technology. And that's why we wrote this book. Welcome to the wonderful and outrageous world of technology.[1,2]

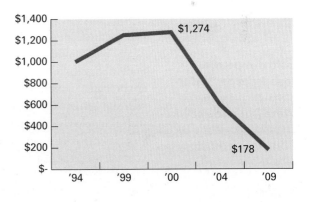

Questions

1. When was the last time you used a pay phone? How often have you used a pay phone in the last year?

2. If you needed to use a pay phone, would you know immediately where one was located?

3. When was the last time you used your cell phone? How often have you used your cell phone in the last *day*?

Introduction

As you just read in the opening case study (appropriately titled "Outrageous Industry Transformation"), the way in which people use technology can and, in fact, does radically change the competitive landscape of business. Hotels have traditionally relied on making roughly $1,200 per room per year in phone charges. That annual per room telephone revenue, because people use their cell phones instead of the in-room fee-based phone, is now less than $200 and may soon vanish altogether. In some way, this is an *unintended consequence of technology.* No one set out to invent the cell phone for the sole purpose of helping people lower their in-room hotel phone service charges. Indeed, the original architects of the cell phone never envisioned the extent to which cell phones (now more appropriately referred to as *smartphones*) would become such an integral part of our lives through delivering so much functionality.

You live in the "digital age." You live, work, learn, play, drive, network, eat, and shop in a digital world. The influence of technology permeates everything you do. The average American relies daily on more than 250 computers. Every part of your life depends on technology. Your TV, Kindle Fire, iPod, iPad, DVD player, car, and cell phone are all technology enabled and—more important—not "able" without technology. Technology is so pervasive in your life it is often considered "invasive." Here's a wild statistic: According to a worldwide survey conducted by *Time* magazine in 2005, 14 percent of cell phone users stated they had stopped having sex to take a phone call.[3] Hmmm . . .

Your generation, specifically the group of people born in the mid-to-late 1980s and early 1990s, was born into the digital age. Society refers to you as *digital natives,* while those of us born earlier are referred to as *digital immigrants.* In the early 1990s, few people had yet heard of the Internet, "surfing" was a term identified only as a water sport, and Microsoft was not the dominant software publisher for word processing, spreadsheet, presentation, or DBMS applications. Viruses were seen only under a microscope, worms were used for fishing, and "spam" was just a canned meat. Back then, teachers of grammar and spelling would have corrected you for using the term "unfriend." But all this changed in your first years on earth.

As you moved through your early teens, e-commerce exploded and then quickly imploded, transforming overnight Internet millionaires into overnight Internet paupers. You are probably more than familiar with unique and interesting IT terms such as podcasting, wiki, avatars, emoticons, spoofing, acorns, tweeting, retweeting, sexting, and phishing (now with a completely different kind of bait). Technology has been so much a part of your life that you may consider it more of a necessity than a convenience. Can you actually imagine what your life would be like if you didn't have a cell phone? What would you do for a week without text messaging? What if Facebook's Web site went down? How often would you check to see if it was up and running again?

Not only that, the pace at which technology is changing (and thus, transforming your life and the way business works) is far faster now than for previous technologies and generations of people. Consider these statistics regarding the years to penetrate a market audience of 50 million people.

- Radio—38 years
- Television—12 years
- Internet—4 years
- iPod—3 years
- Facebook—2 years[4]

The **Did You Know?** video series on YouTube (www.youtube.com) is an exellent resource for learning fascinating facts about how technology is transforming our lives.

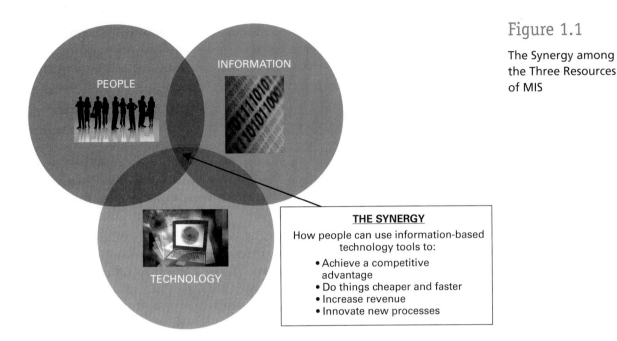

Figure 1.1

The Synergy among
the Three Resources
of MIS

Interesting stuff, huh? This book and the course you're in are about the dynamic mix of information technology and how people use that technology, whether in their personal lives, their careers in an organization, or perhaps for just making the world a better place to live. Specifically, this book is about *management information systems.* Formally, we define management information systems as follows:

- *Management information systems (MIS)* deals with the planning for, development, management, and use of information technology tools to help people perform all tasks related to information processing and management.

LEARNING OUTCOME 1

So, MIS deals with the coordination and use of three very important organizational resources—information, people, and information technology. Stated another (and perhaps more simple) way, *people* use *information technology* to work with *information.*

Think of MIS as you would your other business courses. You take a course in finance, perhaps called financial management. The focus of that course isn't really the money itself (what it looks like, its color, etc.); rather it's about how organizations can use money as a resource. The same is true for a course in supply chain management. You won't spend the entire course studying trains, planes, and trucks. You'll learn how to define and build effective supply chain management systems—that include some combination of trains, planes, and trucks—to meet the distribution, shipping, and warehousing needs of an organization.

The same is true of MIS. While we explore numerous aspects of many different technologies like databases and artificial intelligence, our real focus is on how people can use those technologies to work with and massage information to help an organization achieves its goals. So, there's a real synergy among the three resources of MIS, that is, the people, the information, and the information technology (see Figure 1.1).

MIS Resource No. 1: Information

While we have called it the digital age, we are also in the *information* age, and what that means is knowledge is power. And information can take on many forms depending on the context in which it is used. To shed some light on the often elusive term information let's first define *data* and *information* and briefly look at *business intelligence.*

- ***Data*** are raw facts that describe a particular phenomenon such as the current temperature, the price of a movie rental, or your age. (Actually, the term data is plural; datum is singular.)
- ***Information*** is data that have a particular meaning within a specific context. The current temperature becomes information if you're deciding what to wear; in deciding what to wear, the data describing the price of a movie rental are not pertinent information (and therefore only data in that context).

Consider Figure 1.2. In the left is a single Excel workbook containing the number 21; let's assume that's your age. That is a piece of data, some sort of fact that describes the amount of time you have been alive. Now let's create a list of customers for a business that contains the age of each customer (the right portion of Figure 1.2). This is potential information since

Figure 1.2

Data and Information

In an Excel cell, you can store a single piece of data. Here, the cell contains the number 21, which we're assuming to be your age.

Data become information when they take on meaning. Here, information is a list of ages of all customers, which starts to provide insight into your customers.

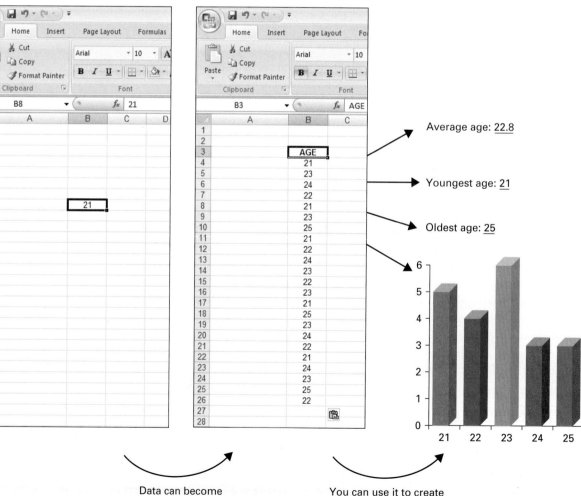

Data can become information when . . .

You can use it to create meaningful intellectual assets.

your business can use it. Notice that you can create an average, find the ages of the youngest and oldest customers, and build a frequency distribution of customers by age.

Now, look at Figure 1.3. There you'll see an Excel workbook containing many groups of information for each customer. From these multiple sources of customer information, we can start to derive business intelligence. **Business intelligence (BI)** is collective information—about your customers, your competitors, your business partners, your competitive environment, and your own internal operations—that gives you the ability to make effective, important, and often strategic decisions. Let's explore a few BI examples.

Notice coupon use by gender. Clearly, women use more coupons than men. That sort of business intelligence leads to some interesting questions. Can we encourage women to buy more by offering them more coupons? Does it even make sense to continue to offer coupons to our male demographic? Take a look at total sales by sales plan. Clearly, Plan A generates more revenue ($6,600) than Plan B ($2,650). This raises even more questions. Does your growth opportunity lie in hoping to expand the number of customers on Plan B? Or should you focus your marketing efforts on getting more customers to spend even more money on Plan A, clearly the more popular plan?

Notice that data, information, and business intelligence all build on each other. Information is a more complete picture of multiple data points; in our example, an age was a single piece of data while information was the collective ages of all customers. Business intelligence extends that information to include gender behavior, the use of coupons, preferred salespersons, and total purchases.

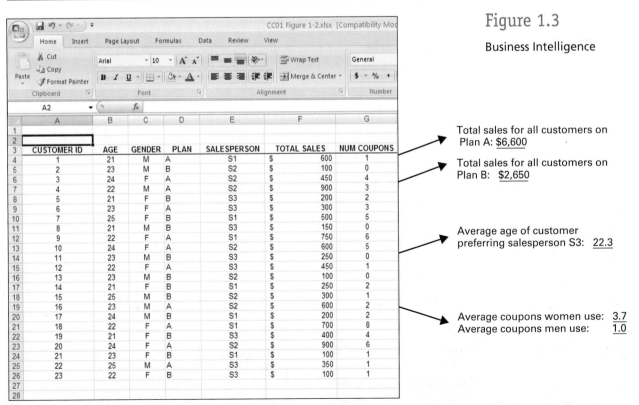

Figure 1.3

Business Intelligence

When you start to combine multiple sets of information, you can generate a considerable amount of business intelligence. Business intelligence helps you make effective strategic business decisions.

A critical characteristic of data, information, and business intelligence is that of *quality*. Quality is another one of those often elusive terms that can mean different things in different contexts. (In our discussions of quality to follow, we'll be using the common term *information* generically to refer to all intellectual assets—data, information, and business intelligence. We don't want you to forget the distinctions we've just described, but the fact is that the term *information* is used by business people and academics alike in a shorthand fashion in this way to cover all grades of intelligence.)

DEFINING INFORMATION QUALITY

Information exhibits high quality only if it is pertinent, relevant, and useful to you. Unfortunately, in today's information age, information is not exactly at a premium; you are bombarded daily with information, much of which is not really important to you in any way. Below are some information attributes that help define its quality.

- **Timeliness**—There are two aspects here. Do you have access to information *when you need it?* If you're preparing to make a stock trade, for example, you need access to the price of the stock right now. Second, does the information describe the time period or periods you're considering? A snapshot of sales today may be what is relevant. Or for some important decisions, you really need other information as well—sales yesterday, sales for the week, today's sales compared to the same day last week, today's sales compared to the same day last year, and so on.

- **Location**—Information is of no value to you if you can't access it. Ideally, your location or the information's location should not matter. IT can definitely create information quality here with technologies that support telecommuting, workplace virtualization, mobile e-commerce, and so on, so you can access information at or from any location.

- **Form**—There are two aspects here also. Is the information in a form that is most useful to or usable by you—audio, text, video, animation, graphical, or other? Depending on the situation, the quality of information is defined by its form and your ability to make use of it. Second, is the information free of errors? Think of information as you would a physical product. If you have a defective product, it lacks quality in that you cannot use it. Information is the same. This is the concept of ***garbage-in garbage-out (GIGO)***. If the information coming into your decision-making process is in bad form (i.e., garbage-in), you'll more than likely make a poor decision (i.e., garbage-out).

- **Validity**—Validity is closely related to the second aspect of form above. Validity addresses the credibility of information. Information is all over the Internet, but does it come from a credible source? Much of the information on the Internet has not gone through any sort of quality control or verification process before being published, so you have to question its validity.

CONSIDERING INFORMATION FROM AN ORGANIZATIONAL PERSPECTIVE

Organizations must treat information as any other resource or asset. It must be organized, managed, and disseminated effectively for the information to exhibit quality. Within an organization, information flows in four basic directions (see Figure 1.4):

1. **Upward.** Upward information flows describe the current state of the organization based on its daily transactions. When a sale occurs, for example, that information

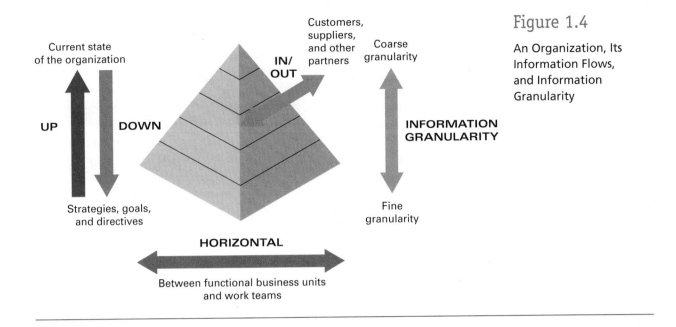

Figure 1.4

An Organization, Its Information Flows, and Information Granularity

originates at the lowest level of the organization and is passed upward through the various levels. Along the way, the information takes on a finer level of *granularity*. **Information granularity** refers to the extent of detail within the information. At lower organizational levels, information exhibits fine granularity because people need to work with information in great detail. At the upper organizational levels, information becomes coarser because it is summarized or aggregated in some way. That is, strategic managers need sales by year, for example, as opposed to knowing the detail of every single transaction.

2. **Downward.** Strategies, goals, and directives that originate at a higher level are passed to lower levels in downward information flows. The upper level of an organization develops strategies; the middle levels of an organization convert those strategies into tactics; and the lower levels of an organization deal with the operational details.

3. **Horizontal.** Information flows horizontally between functional business units and work teams. The goal here is to eliminate the old dilemma of "the right hand not knowing what the left hand is doing." All units of your organization need to inform other units of their processes and be informed by the other units regarding their processes. In general, everyone in a company needs to know everything relevant in a business sense (personal, sensitive data not included).

4. **Outward/Inward.** Information is communicated from and to customers, suppliers, distributors, and other partners for the purpose of doing business. These flows of information are really what electronic commerce is all about. Today, no organization is an island, and outward/inward flows can yield a competitive advantage.

Another organizational perspective on information regards what information describes. Information is internal or external, objective or subjective, and various combinations of these.

- *Internal information* describes specific operational aspects of an organization.
- *External information* describes the environment surrounding the organization.
- *Objective information* quantifiably describes something that is known.
- *Subjective information* attempts to describe something that is unknown.

EMPLOYMENT INFORMATION HAS GONE SOCIAL

Social media tools and Web sites are all the rage. LinkedIn, Facebook, Twitter, and hundreds of other social media sites get millions of visitors per day, many of whom spend several hours perusing those sites, watching videos, catching up with friends, and creating relationships.

And now, social media is quickly becoming the preferred marketplace of employers and job seekers. In 2009, UPS hired 29 employees using the latest and greatest Web 2.0 technologies such as videos and mobile-friendly Web content for those job seekers using a smartphone to find and apply for a job. One year later, UPS hired 955 employees using the same techniques. That represents a 3200 percent increase.

Over 40 percent of surveyed employers stated they would use different recruiting tactics to attract the best Generation Y job seekers. Over 60 percent of those employers identified social media sites as being the preferred places to meet Generation Y job seekers.

According to Matt Lavery, Managing Director of Corporate Talent Acquisition for UPS, "Our reason for using social media is because that's where we think the candidates are." And he's right. Almost 28 percent of surveyed college students plan to use LinkedIn (www.linkedin.com) to find a job. That's up from 5 percent the previous year. LinkedIn is a professional version of Facebook. At LinkedIn, you develop "relationships" for business. Only 7 percent of college graduates planned to use Facebook for job searching.

Savvy graduating students are using social media sites to gather valuable information about potential employers. They read Facebook and Twitter updates about potential companies. They read comments posted by current and previous employees of those same companies.

As you move forward through your studies and prepare to enter the job market, you need to develop a social media strategy—actually two strategies: The first is in regard to using social media like LinkedIn to review potential employers and make contacts. Do you have a LinkedIn account? The second is in regard to what information the Internet holds about you. Do you want potential employers to see everything on your Facebook wall? That's a good question to ponder.[5]

Consider a bank that faces the decision about what interest rate to offer on a CD. That bank will use *internal* information (how many customers it has who can afford to buy a CD), *external* information (what rate other banks are offering), *objective* information (what is today's prime interest rate), and *subjective* information (what the prime interest rate is expected to be in the future). Actually, the rate other banks are offering is not only external information (it describes the environment surrounding the organization) but objective information (it is quantifiably known). Information usually has more than one aspect to it.

MIS Resource No. 2: People

The single most important resource in any organization is its people. People set goals, carry out tasks, make decisions, serve customers, and, in the case of IT specialists, provide a stable and reliable technology environment so the organization can run smoothly and gain a competitive advantage in the marketplace. So, this discussion is all about *you*.

In business, your most valuable asset is *not* technology but rather your *mind*. IT is simply a set of tools that helps you work with and process information. Technology really is just a mind support tool set. Technology such as spreadsheet software can help you quickly create a high-quality and revealing graph. But it can't tell you whether you should build a bar or a pie graph, and it can't help you determine whether you should show sales by territory or sales by salesperson. Those are *your* tasks, and that's why your business curriculum includes classes in human resource management, accounting, finance, marketing, and perhaps production and operations management.

Nonetheless, technology is a very important set of tools for you. Technology can help you be more efficient and can help you dissect and better understand problems and opportunities. So, it's as important for you to learn how to use your technology tool set as it's important that you understand the information to which you're applying your technology tools.

TECHNOLOGY LITERACY

A *technology-literate knowledge worker* knows how and when to apply technology. The "how" aspect includes knowing which technology to purchase, how to exploit the many benefits of application software, and what technology infrastructure is required to get businesses connected to each other, just to name a few. From your personal perspective, we've provided extended learning modules in this text to help you become a technology-literate knowledge worker.

We encourage you to read all the extended learning modules, especially *Extended Learning Module K (Careers in Business).* That module covers career opportunities in a variety of business disciplines including finance, marketing, accounting, management, and many others. Reading *Extended Learning Module K* will help prepare you for whatever career you choose. You'll find a discussion there of key technologies for each business discipline that will help you succeed in your career.

A technology-literate knowledge worker also knows "when" to apply technology. Unfortunately, in many cases, people and organizations blindly decide to use technology in a desperate effort to solve a business problem. What you need to understand is that technology is not a panacea. You can't simply apply technology to a given process and expect that process instantly to become more efficient and effective. Look at it this way—if you apply technology to a process that doesn't work correctly, then you'll only be doing things wrong millions of times faster. There are cases when technology is not the solution. Being a technology-literate knowledge worker will help you determine when and when not to apply technology.

INFORMATION LITERACY

An *information-literate knowledge worker*

- Can define what information is needed.
- Knows how and where to obtain information.
- Understands the information once it is received (i.e., can transform the information into business intelligence).
- Can act appropriately based on the information to help the organization achieve the greatest advantage.

Consider a unique and real-life example of an information-literate knowledge worker. Several years ago, a manager of a retail store on the East Coast received some interesting information: diaper sales on Friday evenings accounted for a large percentage of total sales of that item for the week. Most people learning this would have immediately jumped to the decision to ensure that diapers were always well stocked on Friday evenings or to run a special on diapers Friday evenings to increase sales even further, but not our information-literate knowledge worker. She first looked at the information and decided that she needed more information in order to create business intelligence. She simply needed to know more before she could act.

She decided the business intelligence she needed was *why* a rash of diaper sales (pardon the pun) occurred on Friday evenings and *who* was buying the diapers. That intelligence was not stored within the computer system, so she stationed an employee in the diaper aisle on Friday evening to record any information pertinent to the situation (i.e., she knew how and where to obtain the information). The store manager learned that young businessmen purchased the most diapers on Friday evenings. Apparently, they had been instructed to buy the weekend supply of diapers on their way home from work. The manager's response was to stock premium domestic and imported beer near the diapers. Since then, Friday evening has been a big sales time not only for diapers but also for premium domestic and imported beer.

There are a couple of important lessons you can learn from this story. First, as we've stated, technology is not a panacea. Although a computer system generated the initial report detailing the sales of diapers on Friday evenings, our retail store manager did not make any further use of technology to design and implement her innovative and highly effective solution. Second, this story can help you distinguish between information and business intelligence. In this case, the information was the sales of diapers on Friday evening. The business intelligence, however, included:

- *Who* was making diaper purchases on Friday evening.
- *Why* those people were purchasing diapers on Friday evening.
- *What* complementary product(s) those people might also want or need. (This last point might also illustrate the manager's special *knowledge*.)

As a good rule of thumb, when you receive information and need to make a decision based on it, ask yourself questions that start with who, what, when, why, where, and how. Answers to those questions will help you create business intelligence and make better decisions.

YOUR ETHICAL RESPONSIBILITIES

Your roles as a technology-literate and information-literate knowledge worker extend far beyond using technology and business intelligence to gain a competitive advantage in the marketplace for your organization. You must also consider your social responsibilities: This is where ethics become important. *Ethics* are the principles and standards that guide our behavior toward other people. Your ethics have consequences for you just as laws do. But ethics are different from laws. Laws either clearly require or prohibit an action. Ethics are more subjective, more a matter of personal or cultural interpretation. Thus, ethical decision making can be complex. A decision or an action in some cases might have—or be expected to have—an outcome that is actually right or wrong according to different people's ethics. Consider the following examples of actions:

1. Copying software you purchase, making copies for your friends, and charging them for the copies.
2. Making an extra backup of your software just in case both the copy you are using and the primary backup fail for some reason.
3. Giving out the phone numbers of your friends and family, without their permission, to a telecom provider of some sort of calling plan so you can receive a discount.

Each of these examples is either ethically (according to you or some people) or legally (according to the government) incorrect or both. In the second example, you might be ethically okay in making an extra backup copy (because you didn't share it with anyone), but according to some software licenses you're prohibited by law from making more than one backup copy. What do you think about the first and third examples? Illegal? Unethical? Both?

To help you better understand the relationship between ethical acts and legal acts, consider Figure 1.5. The graph is composed of four quadrants, and the complexity of ethical decisions about behavior is suggested by quadrant III (legal but unethical). Do any of the three examples above fall in quadrant III? Perhaps you can think of some other actions that although legal might still be unethical (how about gossiping?). You always want your actions to remain in quadrant I. If all your actions fall into that quadrant, you'll always be acting both legally and ethically and thus in a socially responsible way. Clearly, technology has further increased the complexity of ethics in our society because of the speed and casual ease with which people can access, distribute, and use information.

Being socially and ethically responsible in the information age involves not only the actions you initiate yourself but also what you do to protect yourself and your organization against the actions of others—that is, protecting yourself and your organization against cyber crimes. There are many types of cyber crimes—such as promulgating viruses or worms, committing identity theft, and engaging in Web defacing—performed by a variety of hackers such as black-hat hackers and cyberterrorists, and it is your responsibility to guard against them. It might even be considered an ethical lapse not to do so. We cannot stress enough how important it is for you to protect yourself and your organization's assets in cyberspace. We'll talk more about these issues in Chapter 8 (Protecting People and Information) and *Extended Learning Module H (Computer Crime and Forensics)*.

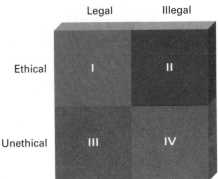

Figure 1.5

Acting Ethically and Legally[6]

MIS Resource No. 3: Information Technology

The third key resource for management information systems (MIS) is ***information technology (IT)***, any computer-based tool that people use to work with information and support the information and information-processing needs of an organization. IT includes a cell phone or tablet PC that you use to obtain stock quotes, your home computer that you use to write term papers, large networks that businesses use to connect to one another, and the Internet that almost one in every six people in the world currently uses.

KEY TECHNOLOGY CATEGORIES

One simple—yet effective—way to categorize technology is as either *hardware* or *software* (see Figure 1.6 on the next page). **Hardware** is the physical devices that make up a computer. **Software** is the set of instructions that your hardware executes to carry out a specific task for you. So, your Blackberry is the actual hardware; and it contains software that you use to maintain your calendar, update your address book, check your e-mail, watch videos, obtain stock market quotes, and so on.

All hardware technology falls into one of the following six basic categories:

1. An ***input device*** is a tool you use to enter information and commands. Input devices include such tools as keyboard, mouse, touch screen, game controller, and bar code reader.

2. An ***output device*** is a tool you use to see, hear, or otherwise recognize the results of your information-processing requests. Output devices include such tools as printer, monitor, and speakers.

3. A ***storage device*** is a tool you use to store information for use at a later time. Storage devices include such tools as thumb drive, flash memory card, and DVD.

4. The ***central processing unit (CPU)*** is the hardware that interprets and executes the system and application software instructions and coordinates the operation of all the hardware. ***RAM***, or ***random access memory***, is a temporary holding area

Figure 1.6

Information Technology
Hardware and Software

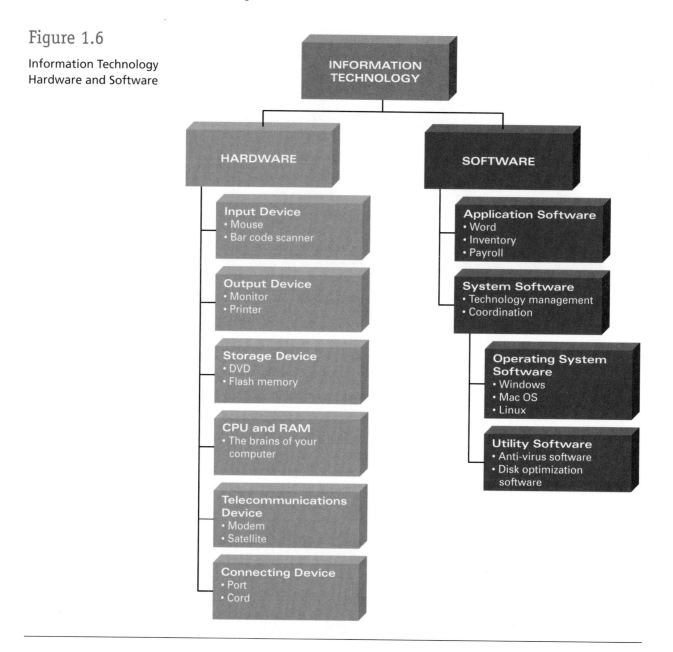

for the information you're working with as well as the system and application software instructions that the CPU currently needs.

5. A ***telecommunications device*** is a tool you use to send information to and receive it from another person or computer in a network. If you connect to the Internet using a modem, the modem is a telecommunications device.

6. *Connecting devices* include such things as a USB port into which you would connect a printer, connector cables to connect your printer to the USB port, and internal connecting devices on the motherboard.

There are two main types of software: *application* and *system*. **Application software** is the software that enables you to solve specific problems and perform specific tasks. Microsoft Word, for example, can help you write term papers. From an organizational point of view, payroll software, collaborative software, and inventory management software are all examples of application software.

System software handles tasks specific to technology management and coordinates the interaction of all technology devices. System software includes network operating system software, drivers for your printer and scanner, operating system software such as Windows XP and Mac OS, and utility software such as anti-virus software, uninstaller software, and file security software.

If this is your first exposure to technology hardware and software, we suggest you explore *Extended Learning Module A (Computer Hardware and Software)*.

As we have seen, *management information systems* really is all about three key organizational resources—the people involved, the information they need, and the information technology that helps them. MIS is about getting the right technology and the right information into the hands of the right people at the right time.

Financial Impact of IT: Break-Even Analysis

When considering the use of any resource in an organization, you must ask questions like, "What sort of financial impact will this have on the organization? What's the return on our investment (ROI)? Is this going to help reduce costs or increase revenue, or perhaps both?" All these questions address the financial impact of a resource. Technology is no different; you must be able to financially justify the use of technology.

A simple, and yet very powerful, tool for assessing the financial impact of a resource is called "break-even analysis." In break-even analysis, you consider and chart the following financial information (see Figure 1.7):

- **Fixed cost**—the total of all costs that you incur whether or not you sell anything. For example, rent for office or retail space is a fixed cost; even if you don't sell a single thing, you still have to pay the monthly rent. Other fixed costs might include utilities, insurance, employee salaries, and so on.
- **Variable cost**—the amount it costs to acquire/produce one unit that you will eventually sell to your customers.
- **Revenue**—how much you sell that one unit for.

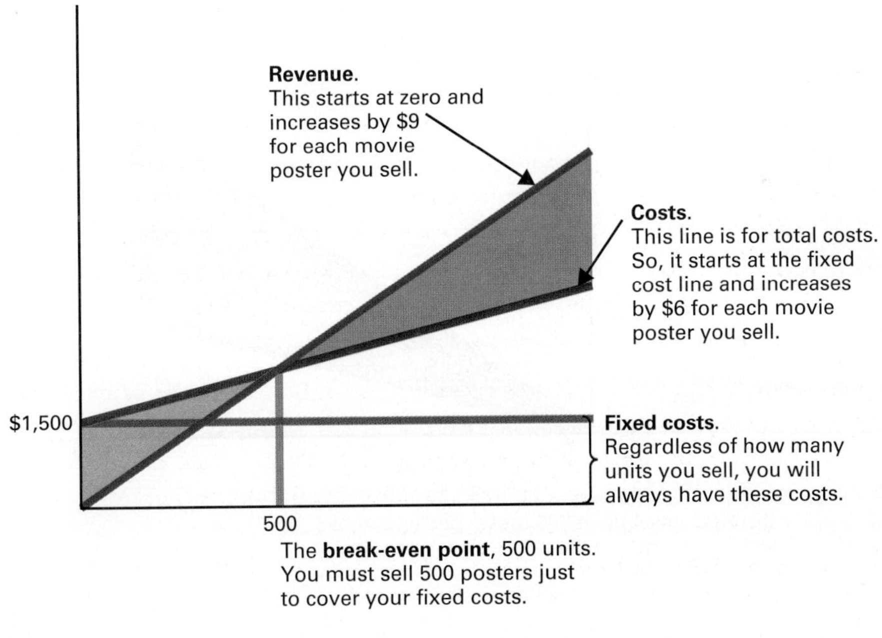

Figure 1.7

Break-Even Analysis

Let's assume that you've worked a deal with all the major movie studios to sell movie posters. You can buy each movie poster for $4 and sell it in your online store for $9. It costs you $2 to ship a movie poster to a customer. Your online store, product catalog, credit card processing, domain name registration, and search engine placement are all provided by GoDaddy (www.godaddy.com) at a cost of $1,500 per year. Your financial information then is this:

- **Fixed costs**—$1,500 per year for GoDaddy services. Whether you sell no posters or 10,000 posters, this cost remains fixed.
- **Variable costs**—$6, which represents $4 when you buy a movie poster from a studio and $2 when you ship that poster to a customer.
- **Revenue**—$9, or the price at which you sell a movie poster.

Using break-even analysis, you answer an important question, "How many movie posters do you have to sell to break even?" Graphically, it looks like Figure 1.7 (on the previous page). The logic is simple: You make a net profit of $3 per poster ($9 sales price minus $6 variable cost). To cover your $1,500 of fixed costs, you have to sell 500 posters ($1,500 divided by $3). What happens in a given year if you sell less than 500 posters? Right, you lose money. So, 500 is the break-even point. And what's your net profit if you sell 700 posters in a year? The answer is $600, which is your net profit per poster ($3) times 200. We derive 200 by subtracting the break-even point of 500 from total units sold of 700.

Why is this important from a technology point of view? Because technology can help you and your organization do one or any combination of the following three: reduce fixed costs, reduce variable costs, and/or increase revenue.

REDUCING FIXED COSTS

One financial and operational goal of any organization is to have no fixed costs. That is, in the business world you should strive to incur a cost only when you generate revenue. Why? Because when you have no fixed costs, your break-even point moves to zero (see Figure 1.8). So, you actually begin generating a profit with the very first unit you sell because the only costs you have are variable costs.

Figure 1.8

Driving Fixed Costs to Zero

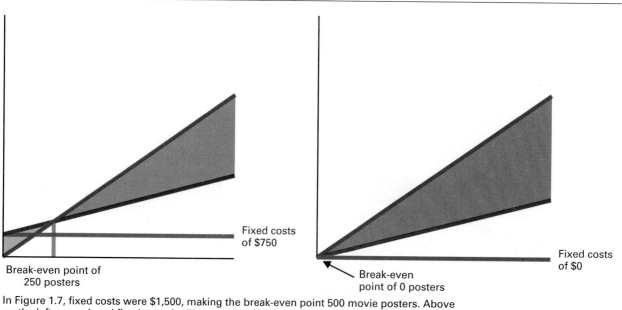

In Figure 1.7, fixed costs were $1,500, making the break-even point 500 movie posters. Above on the left, we reduced fixed costs by 50 percent to $750, making the break-even point 250 movie posters. Above on the right, we reduced fixed costs to $0, making the break-even point 0 movie posters. In the latter case, you start making a profit on the very first poster you sell.

Technology can definitely play a part in helping you reduce fixed costs. Below are some examples.

- **Digital storefronts**—Companies like Amazon and eBay that only have a presence in the virtual world have significantly lower fixed costs in terms of retail space than companies that have to pay for retail space, like retail stores you would find in a mall.
- **Telecommuting**—This is a popular trend in most industries. If you can create a technology infrastructure that allows your employees to work from home (or anywhere for that matter, as long as it's not in the office), you can reduce your expenses related to office space, which would also include utilities, insurance, parking, etc.
- **VoIP, or Voice over IP**—Again, this is another one of those initiatives gaining in popularity. VoIP allows you to use the Internet for making phone calls instead of leasing traditional telephone lines from the phone company. A popular variation on VoIP is Skype. (Here we go again—traditional phones are really getting hammered by technology. Remember the opening outrageous industry transformation.)
- **Cloud computing**—One of the hottest topics in the business world right now and one that we'll explore in great detail in Chapter 7. With cloud computing, you don't buy hardware infrastructure like servers or perhaps software site licenses. Instead, you rent them on an as-needed basis "in the cloud."

Throughout this text, we'll alert you to IT-enabled opportunities for reducing fixed costs.

REDUCING VARIABLE COSTS

Variable costs basically define your profit margin. That is, the smaller the variable cost the higher the profit margin (and vice versa). Your break-even point is smaller (moves to the left) as you increase your profit margin by reducing variable costs (see Figure 1.9). A couple of the really interesting IT-enabled variable cost reduction initiatives are listed on the next page.

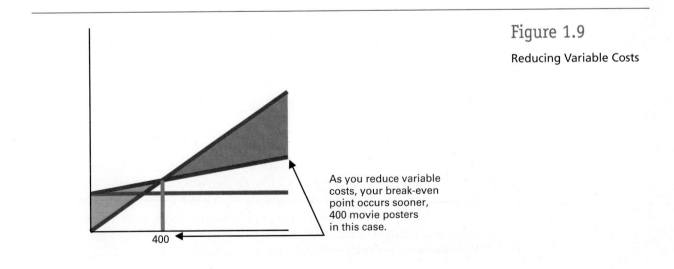

Figure 1.9

Reducing Variable Costs

400

As you reduce variable costs, your break-even point occurs sooner, 400 movie posters in this case.

SPENDING MONEY TO SAVE CUSTOMERS

Sometimes, it's not about spending money to make money. It may very well be about spending money to keep your customers from jumping ship and going over to the competition. When NetFlix exploded onto the video rental market with its model of allowing you to keep movies as long as you want with no late fee, Blockbuster reluctantly responded by eliminating its late fees. Unfortunately, Blockbuster waited too long to undertake the initiative and is suffering dearly for it.

Home Box Office (HBO) hopes to avoid sliding down the same slippery slope as Blockbuster. HBO, just like Blockbuster, is feeling "the pinch" of competing against NetFlix. Using one of NetFlix's current models, for $8 per month you can connect your TV to the Internet and download and watch as much NetFlix content as you want. Many people are taking advantage of that, even to the point of cancelling their HBO subscription and even going so far as to cancel their cable programming altogether.

In response in mid-2011, HBO introduced HBO Go. HBO Go is a completely free service to HBO subscribers that allows you to watch HBO shows and movies on your smartphone. Included in the HBO selection are over 1,400 movie titles. In the first week of its release, the HBO Go app (available for the Apple iPhone and Google Android) was downloaded more than a million times. That may very well be 1 million HBO customers who won't jump ship and go to NetFlix.

And there's another reason for HBO's move to mobile media. You can only use HBO Go if you're a subscriber to HBO through traditional cable or satellite programming. Non-HBO customers can't use it. HBO is hoping that more people will subscribe to HBO just so they can use HBO Go.[7]

- **Virtual goods**—Virtual goods are as their name implies; they don't exist in the physical world. These are the best types of goods to sell in financial terms because you have no variable costs. Think about Farmville, Habbo Hotel, or even World of Warcraft. In any of those environments, you can buy virtual goods—a better tractor for farming, cool clothes for going dancing, or better weaponry. What you get is a virtual good that has no variable cost associated with it because it's purely digital. So, the organization may have charged you $1 and that $1 was pure profit.

- **Crowdsourcing**—This is a great way to create value for free. Using crowdsourcing, you get non-paid non-employees to do your work. Think about eBay. eBay doesn't employ anyone to buy or sell in its marketplace. Instead, crowds of people (whom eBay doesn't have on the payroll) do all the work of listing items, taking photos, bidding, and even shipping goods and merchandise. Likewise, YouTube doesn't hire people to post videos. Instead, you do all the work to capture and upload a video, for free.

Virtual goods and crowdsourcing are two of the many IT-enabled methods for reducing variable costs. We'll cover more of them throughout the book.

INCREASING REVENUE

Finally, you can impact your break-even point by increasing revenue. That is to say, when you increase revenue or price per unit, your break-even point comes earlier. In our movie poster example, if you increased the price from $9 to $11 for a poster, your break-even point would be 300 units. Of course, if you raise prices too much, your competition will undercut you, and then you're in real trouble.

Technology can definitely help increase revenue. Below are a couple of ways.

- **Recommendation engines**—These engines make recommendations to you based on your likes, dislikes, and past purchases. You're very accustomed to these. Apple's Genius tool for iTunes recommends additional music selections based on your purchases. Amazon uses a recommendation engine to offer you additional books based on the book(s) you're considering buying.

- **Long-tail economics**—Technology can help your organization overcome the 80/20 rule, which basically states that only 20 percent of the total available products are worth selling. These are the big hits that everyone wants and that all physical retail stores carry. But there is money to be made in niche products too. That's why iTunes offers millions of songs. (Compare that to the rather sparse inventory of a brick-and-mortar music store.) It's also why Amazon has over 1 million book titles for sale and most brick-and-mortar book stores carry in the neighborhood of 25,000 to 50,000.

Industry Impact of IT: Porter's Five Forces Model

Simply put, *business strategy drives technology decisions, not the reverse.* In your personal life, you may choose to buy the latest piece of technology because it's cool. Not so in the business world. Businesses carefully scrutinize their technology purchases, seeking to find and justify a competitive advantage. A ***competitive advantage*** is providing a product or service in a way that customers value more than what your competition is able to do.

LEARNING OUTCOME 3

To assess technology and the competitive advantage it can yield, many people choose to use Michael Porter's Five Forces Model.[8] The ***Five Forces Model*** helps business people understand the relative attractiveness of an industry and the industry's competitive pressures in terms of the following five forces (see Figure 1.10):

1. Buyer power
2. Supplier power
3. Threat of substitute products or services
4. Threat of new entrants
5. Rivalry among existing competitors

BUYER POWER

Buyer power in the Five Forces Model is high when buyers have many choices from whom to buy, and low when their choices are few. Providers of products and services in

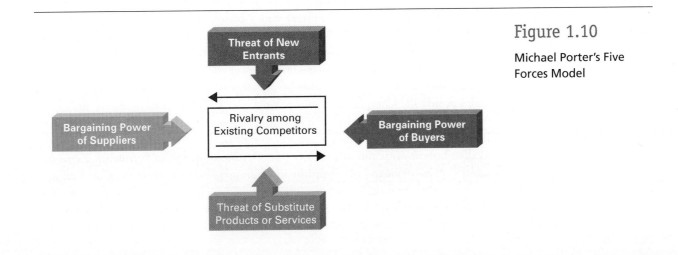

Figure 1.10

Michael Porter's Five Forces Model

a particular industry wish to reduce buyer power. They create a competitive advantage by making it more attractive for customers to buy from them than from their competition. Below are a few of the many companies using IT-enabled processes to reduce buyer power.

- NetFlix—Set up your movie list. After you watch a movie and return it, NetFlix will send you the next movie on your list. You can also rent videos through the mail, stream them to your computer, or stream them to your TV.
- United Airlines (or almost any airline for that matter)—Enroll in the *Mileage Plus* program. As you travel using United (or perhaps make purchases using your United credit card), you accumulate miles for free air travel, upgrades, and hotel stays. Programs like this one, which reward customers based on the amount of business they do with a particular organization, are called ***loyalty programs***.
- Apple iTunes—Create an iTunes account and buy and download whatever music you want. Then, you can organize and manage your music, move it to your iPod, and burn CDs. You can also store all your music (and photos and much more) in Apple's iCloud.
- Dell Computer—Completely customize your computer purchase. It will be delivered to your doorstep within a few business days.

What's interesting about each of these examples (as well as all the others you can think of) is that the competitors in those industries have responded by creating similar programs. This simply means that no competitive advantage is ever permanent. NetFlix was the first to offer movie rentals (with a profitable business model) using the Internet as the primary platform. Therefore, it had ***first-mover advantage***, a significant impact on gaining market share by being the first to market with a competitive advantage. Every major airline has a loyalty program similar to that of United Airlines. There are many places on the Internet where you can buy and download music. Almost every major computer vendor allows you to customize your computer purchase. The lesson learned here—and for all strategies that result in a competitive advantage—is that a competitive advantage is only temporary and your organization must constantly innovate to find new competitive advantages.

SUPPLIER POWER

Supplier power in the Five Forces Model is high when buyers have few choices from whom to buy, and low when their choices are many. Supplier power is the opposite of buyer power: As a supplier organization in an industry, you want buyer power to be low and your supplier power to be high.

In a typical supply chain (see Figure 1.11), your organization will probably be both a supplier (to customer organizations) and a buyer, or customer (of other supplier organizations). As a customer of other supplier organizations, you want to increase your buyer power. As a supplier to other organizations, you want to increase your supplier power, thus reducing your customer's buyer power.

In the quest for increasing supplier power, organizations use many tools at their disposal, not just IT. Companies obtain patents and trademarks to minimize the extent to which products and services can be duplicated and offered by other organizations. The De Beers Group for many years has fought fiercely to tightly control the supply and distribution of diamonds. OPEC (the Organization of the Petroleum Exporting Countries) has organized 11 oil-producing nations to better control the distribution of the world's most popular energy resource (supposedly to ensure the stabilization of oil prices).

Figure 1.11

Evaluating Buyer and Supplier Power for Your Organization

THREAT OF SUBSTITUTE PRODUCTS OR SERVICES

The ***threat of substitute products or services*** in the Five Forces Model is high when there are many alternatives to a product or service, and low when there are few alternatives from which to choose. Ideally, your organization would like to be a supplier organization in a market in which there are few substitutes for the products and services you offer. Of course, that's seldom possible in any market today, but you can still create a competitive advantage by increasing *switching costs.* **Switching costs** are costs that make customers reluctant to switch to another product or service supplier. What you need to realize is that a switching cost does not necessarily have to be an actual monetary cost.

As you buy products at Amazon.com over time, for example, Amazon develops a unique profile of your shopping and purchasing habits through such techniques as collaborative filtering. When you visit Amazon, products are offered to you that have been tailored to your profile. This is only possible through the use of sophisticated technologies. If you choose to do your shopping elsewhere, there is a switching cost of sorts because the new site you visit will not have a profile of you or a record of your past purchases. (This is an effective variant of a loyalty program.) So, Amazon has reduced the threat of substitute products and services, in a market in which there are many substitutes, by tailoring offerings to you, by creating a "cost" to you to switch to another online retailer.

Switching costs can of course be real monetary costs too. You've probably been introduced to a switching cost when you signed up for the services of a cell phone provider. All the options and plans sound really great. But there is a serious switching cost in that most cell phone providers require you to sign a long-term contract (as long as two years) in order to receive a free phone or unlimited night and weekend calling minutes. The very successful substitute to this is disposable cell phones that you buy and which contain a certain number of minutes for your use.

THREAT OF NEW ENTRANTS

The ***threat of new entrants*** in the Five Forces Model is high when it is easy for new competitors to enter a market, and low when there are significant entry barriers to entering a market. An ***entry barrier*** is a product or service feature that customers have come to expect from organizations in a particular industry and that must be offered by an entering organization to compete and survive. Such barriers are erected, and overcome, and then new ones are created again. This is that vicious business cycle of build a competitive advantage, enjoy first-mover advantage, and then watch your competition develop similar initiatives thereby nullifying your competitive advantage.

For example, if you're thinking of starting a bank, you must offer your customers an array of IT-enabled services, including ATM use, online bill paying and account monitoring, and the like. These are significant IT-based entry barriers to entering the banking market because you must offer them for free (or a very small fee). If you consider our previous example of cell phone providers, a significant entry barrier in the past had to

The average person was expected to spend $116 for merchandise for Valentine's Day in 2011. Total spending was expected to exceed $15 billion.

To capture a portion of that money, and perhaps even more than previously, many companies went virtual in 2011 with Valentine's Day stories, messages, flowers, and even food (although the food is real).

Mattel, the toy giant, created a campaign to ask people if Barbie should reunite with Ken. (Ken and Barbie split on Valentine's Day 2004.) Mattel used Facebook and Twitter to have Ken post his love and affection for Barbie. The purpose was to create "social" noise so that Ken and Barbie lovers would log on to BarbieandKen.com and vote one way or the other. Of course, the site included a link to Barbie's Facebook page, where people could buy Barbie and Ken merchandise.

Victoria's Secret created sexy e-valentine cards that people could send through a social network. Victoria's Secret posted photos and messages which people could choose to include in a card. Women even had the option of including a photo of a gift they wanted from Victoria's Secret.

Rovio Mobile, the creator of the ultra-popular Angry Birds game, created a Valentine's Day version of the game. Of course, you had to pay 99 cents to download it, but 99 cents is nothing to the millions of fanatic fans of Angry Birds.

Mulberry, a British apparel maker, created virtual flower seeds you could send via e-mail. When the recipient clicked on the seeds, Valentine's Day flowers bloomed right before their eyes.

Even Lenny's Sub Shop got into the social media game for Valentine's Day. It gave away subs (you had to send them to someone as a Valentine's Day gift) on its Facebook page. According to George Alvord, Lenny's CEO, "The quickest way to win someone's heart is through their stomach."

The lesson learned: Each of these gave some company a competitive advantage, if only for a day.[9]

do with your phone number. Previously, if you wanted to change cell phone providers, you couldn't take your telephone number with you (i.e., you had to get a new cell phone number). This created a significant entry barrier because new cell phone providers entering the industry were mainly limited to obtaining new customers who did not currently have a cell phone. But that has all changed with *LNP, Local Number Portability*, your ability to take your cell phone number with you to a new provider.

RIVALRY AMONG EXISTING COMPETITORS

The ***rivalry among existing competitors*** in the Five Forces Model is high when competition is fierce in a market, and low when competition is more complacent. Simply put, competition is more intense in some industries than in others, although the overall trend is toward increased competition in just about every industry. Rarely can you identify an industry that exhibits complacent competition. (One example might be mortician and burial services. Solely because of the nature of the services offered, you don't see mortician and burial service organizations actively advertising on TV, offering reduced rates, and so on.)

The retail grocery industry is intensely competitive. While Target and Walmart in the United States compete in many different ways, essentially they try to beat or match the competition on price. Since margins are quite low in the grocery retail market, grocers build efficiencies into their supply chains, connecting with their suppliers in IT-enabled information partnerships. Communicating with suppliers over telecommunications networks rather than using paper-based systems makes the procurement process much faster, cheaper, and more accurate. That equates to lower prices for customers—and increased rivalry among existing competitors.

As you can see, Porter's Five Forces Model is extremely useful in helping you better understand the positioning of your organization within its industry and in helping you better understand the competitive forces affecting your organization. With this knowledge in mind, your organization now needs to develop specific business strategies to remain competitive and profitable.

Strategy Impact of IT: Porter (Again) and RGT

LEARNING OUTCOME 4

The development of business strategies is a vast and wide discipline. There are literally hundreds of methodologies and approaches to the development of business strategy. There are even more books on the subject. (One such book with a particularly innovative approach is *Blue Ocean Strategy* by Kim and Mauborgne. Be sure to put it on your wish list of business books to read.) Here, we'll focus on Michael Porter's three generic strategies and two other approaches.

Michael Porter identified three approaches or strategies to beating the competition in any industry (see Figure 1.12). They are

1. Overall cost leadership
2. Differentiation
3. Focus

OVERALL COST LEADERSHIP

Overall cost leadership is defined by Porter as offering the same or better quality product or service at a price that is less than what any of the competition is able to do. Examples of organizations focusing on overall cost leadership are numerous and change almost daily, with the most well-known example being Walmart. Walmart's slogans of "Always Low Prices!" and "Every Day Low Prices" accurately describe the strategy of overall cost

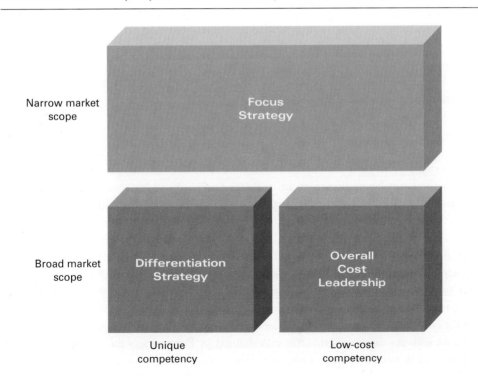

Figure 1.12

Michael Porter's Three Generic Strategies

leadership. For everything from women's lingerie to car batteries, Walmart's focus is on offering the same products as the competition but at a lower price. Walmart relies on an IT-enabled tight supply chain management system to squeeze every penny possible out of the procurement, distribution, and warehousing of its products. It uses sophisticated business intelligence systems to predict what customers will want and when.

Dell Computer works in similar fashion. Its famous sell-source-ship model of customizing computer purchases is the envy of the industry. Automobile makers Hyundai and Kia similarly attempt to sell reliable low-cost vehicles to a wide audience, in contrast to Hummer and Mercedes-Benz which have no overall cost leadership strategy.

IT can be a particularly effective tool if your organization chooses an overall cost leadership strategy. IT can tighten supply chain systems, help you capture and assimilate customer information to better understand buying patterns in an effort to better predict product inventory and shelf placement, and make it easy (efficient) for customers to order your products through Web-enabled e-commerce systems.

DIFFERENTIATION

Differentiation is defined by Porter as offering a product or service that is perceived as being "unique" in the marketplace. Hummer is an excellent example. Its differentiation strategy is reinforced by the unique design and eye-appeal of its H1, H2, and H3 vehicle lines. Even its slogan—"Like Nothing Else"—clearly attempts to differentiate Hummer vehicles from anything on the road. Another example is Lunds & Byerly's (usually just referred to as Byerly's) in the grocery retail industry. While other competitors compete mainly on price, Byerly's focuses on the shopping experience for differentiation. All of the Byerly's stores offer cooking classes and in-store restaurants for lunch and dinner. Many Byerly's stores have carpeted floors instead of tile and some even have chandeliers instead of fluorescent lighting.

Apple Computer also focuses on differentiation as a business strategy. Not only do Apple computers look different, they have a different screen interface and focus more on nontextual information processing such as photos, music, and videos than any of the competition. Both Audi and Michelin have successfully created a differentiation strategy based on safety. To be sure, differentiation is not about being different based on lower price—that's the strategy of overall cost leadership—but the two are interrelated. While many people are willing to pay extra for grocery products at Byerly's, they are not willing to pay too much extra. Organizations focusing on differentiation must still be concerned about price in relation to the competition.

FOCUS

Focus as a strategy is usually defined as focusing on offering products and services (1) to a particular market segment or buyer group, (2) within a segment of a product line, and/or (3) to a specific geographic market. Focus is the opposite of attempting to be "all things to all people." Many restaurants focus on only a certain type of food—Mediterranean, Mexican, Chinese, and so forth. Stores such as the Vitamin Cottage Natural Foods Market sell only natural and organic food and nutrition supplements (one form of focus on products within a product line) to a specific buyer group (another form of focus on a particular market segment). Many doctors focus on only a particular type of medical help—oncology, pediatrics, and so on; similarly, many law offices focus on a particular legal venue—workman's compensation, living trusts, patents and trademarks.

As with the other generic strategies defined by Porter, focus cannot be practiced in isolation. If your organization chooses a particular buyer group on which to focus, you

INNOVATE, OR GO HOME

The brief history of technology has moved through four major cycles, with society now squarely in the fourth. The first occurred in the 1950s and 1960s as the birth of commercial technology automated routine tasks like payroll and basic inventory management. The second occurred in the early 1980s with the advent of the PC, placing computing power and capability on the desktop. The third occurred in the late 1990s with the explosion of the Internet. It connected all of us together.

What's the fourth? You're in it—mobile. With powerful, yet inexpensive, devices such as smartphones and tablet PCs you can carry the Internet with you wherever you go. And that means it's time for companies to innovate in how they use technology. Consider these examples.

- Auto Insurance—With the proliferation of sensors that communicate wirelessly, auto insurers will gather driving information in real-time and can adjust insurance rates in the same real-time. Already, insurers like Allstate and Progressive have implemented versions of pay-as-you-go insurance. These programs are designed to reward safe drivers, who agree to have their driving monitored, with cheaper insurance rates. Some insurers are toying with the idea of sending a text message to Mom and Dad when a son or daughter is driving too fast or in an unsafe area.

- Retail Stores—Red Laser and other bar-code reading apps have created the necessity of transparency. It used to be that, if you could get a customer into your store through advertising via newspaper, magazine, of TV, you could be fairly well assured of a sale. Not so today. Smart shoppers are using smartphones and bar-code reading apps to compare prices. Many are opting to go to a different store for a cheaper price. Still others are approaching store employees and asking for a price match (or they will go to that other store). There may even come a time when Amazon could offer a 5 percent discount to shoppers browsing its site while in a Walmart.

- Utilities—"Smart" meters are now being installed in residential homes. These meters can adjust the price of the utility in real time based on peak-period usage. The meter may even notify the home owners, giving them the opportunity to turn off appliances to avoid higher prices.

Smart companies innovate; the others . . . well, you know.[10]

can bet that other competitors will do so as well, so you'll also have to compete on price (overall cost leadership) and/or differentiation too.

RUN-GROW-TRANSFORM FRAMEWORK A helpful conceptual framework for viewing the bigger organizational picture and determining the use of IT in it is the *run-grow-transform (RGT) framework*, an approach in which you allocate in terms of percentages how you will spend your IT dollars on various types of business strategies. For example, if you're only interested in "business-as-usual" but cheaper and faster than the competition, you would focus a great percentage of your IT dollars on a "run" strategy. If you wanted to transform your business in some way, you would allocate a certain percentage of your IT dollars to a "transformation" strategy. The following are the aspects of the RGT framework:

- *Run*—optimize the execution of activities and processes already in place. Seek organizational growth through offering products and services faster and cheaper than the competition.
- *Grow*—increase market reach, product and service offerings, expand market share, and so on. Seek organizational growth by taking market share from the competition (i.e., get a bigger piece of the pie).

Figure 1.13

Historical Spending
in Run, Grow,
and Transform[11]

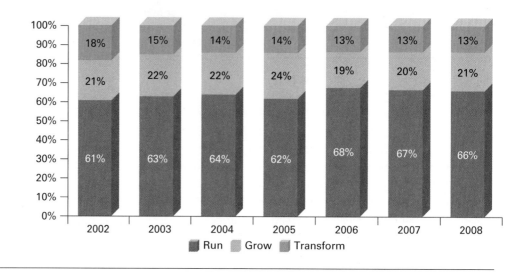

• *Transform*—innovate business processes and/or products and services in a completely new way, move into seemingly different markets, and so on. Seek organizational growth through new and different means.

As you can see, the RGT framework is similar in many ways to Porter's three generic strategies:

• Run = overall cost leadership
• Grow = focus and differentiation
• Transform = (new) differentiation

The application of the RGT framework occurs in almost all industries. In Figure 1.13 you can see RGT data gathered by The Gartner Group over a seven-year period. Note the general trend toward allocating more IT dollars to run initiatives and less to transform initiatives. Is this good or bad? It's hard to say with absolute certainty, but it's not a favorable trend. All organizations must focus to some extent on the transformation aspect. In the business world, as is often said, if you're standing still, you're falling behind. It's a simple fact—your competition is always trying to do something better than you are. Therefore, your organization must constantly seek to evolve and, in most cases, to transform itself.

Many times, your organization can take a proactive approach to using technology to transform itself. Apple is perhaps the most widely discussed organization that is constantly in a state of transformation. Apple, a personal computer company, launched itself into the music business with Apple iTunes in early 2001. Since then, Apple has added games, books, music videos, and movies to iTunes. Apple has successfully held its first-mover advantage in the music space because of its continuing focus on transformation.

■ SUMMARY: STUDENT LEARNING OUTCOMES REVISITED

1. **Define management information systems (MIS) and describe the three important organizational resources within it—people, information, and information technology.** *Management information systems (MIS)* deals with the planning for, development, management, and use of information technology tools to help people perform all tasks related to information processing and management. People, as an organizational resource within MIS, are the most

important of the three. To be successful in their use of technology, people must be both *information-literate* and *technology-literate.* Information in various forms goes by many names such as *data, business intelligence,* and *knowledge.* All are intellectual assets but exhibit subtle differences. *Information* is data that has meaning within a specific context. *Information technology (IT)* is any computer-based tool that people use to work with information and support the information and information-processing needs of an organization.

2. **Describe how to use break-even analysis to assess the financial impact of information technology.** Break-even analysis considers and charts three pieces of financial information: fixed costs, variable costs, and revenue. You can use break-even analysis to determine the financial impact of information technology by assessing (1) how technology can help reduce fixed costs, (2) how technology can help reduce variable costs, and (3) how technology can help increase revenue. Each of those ultimately focuses on how technology can be used to impact the break-even point, the point at which an organization has covered its fixed costs and begins to make a profit.

3. **Describe how to use Porter's Five Forces Model to evaluate the relative attractiveness of and competitive pressures in an industry.** Porter's Five Forces Model focuses on industry analysis according to five forces: (1) *buyer power*— high when buyers have many choices and low when choices are few; (2) *supplier power*—high when buyers have few choices and low when choices are many; (3) *threat of substitute products and services*—high when many alternative are available and low when alternatives are few; (4) *threat of new entrants*—high when it is easy to get into a market and low when it is difficult to get into a market; and **(5)** *rivalry among existing competitors*—high when competition is fierce and low when competition is more complacent.

4. **Compare and contrast Porter's three generic strategies and the run-grow-transform framework as approaches to the development of business strategy.** Porter's *three generic strategies* are: (1) *overall cost leadership*—the same or better quality products at a price less than that of the competition; (2) *differentiation*—a product or service that is perceived as being "unique;" and (3) *focus*—products or services for a particular buyer group, within a segment of a product line, and/or a specific geographic market. The *RGT framework* requires that you allocate in terms of percentages how you will spend your IT dollars among running the organization, growing the organization, and transforming the organization.

CLOSING CASE STUDY ONE

The Social Media Megaphone: Transparent Life Intensified

It's a story that's been told before. Twenty-Five-year-old Stacy Snyder was in her last semester of teacher-in-training at Millersville University School of Education. On her MySpace page, she posted a photo of herself at a party with a pirate hat and a cup in her hand. The caption read, "Drunken Pirate." Her school decided that the photo promoted drinking to her underage students at Conestoga Valley High School and denied her teaching degree. She sued citing her first amendment rights, and a federal district court judge dismissed her suit because she was a public employee and therefore her public speech (i.e., "Drunken Pirate") was not protected.

You may believe that Stacy's story is an unfortunate one, but the Internet, specifically social media tools and sites, has made it far too easy to share all types of information. If you're not careful, your use of social media may expose your life in the most transparent of ways to literally millions and millions of people. According to one survey, 75 percent of recruiters and HR professionals in the United States stated that their organizations required them to research applicants online. Some of the most commonly visited places for that research included search engines, social networking sites, photo and videoing sharing sites, personal Web sites, blogs, Twitter, and gaming sites. In the same survey, over 70 percent of the recruiters stated that they had rejected applicants based on the information they found online.

Of course, all the examples of life transparency on the Internet are not necessarily "bad." Some have a good ending, and others are simply interesting to consider.

WEBCASTING FUNERALS

According to John Reed, past president of the National Funeral Directors Association and current owner of two Virginia-based funeral homes, 20 to 30 percent of all funeral homes in the U.S. now provide webcasting funeral services. "I can honestly say that in the past three years we've gone from absolute zero to the point where we now do 50% of our funerals on the Web," stated Reed. For Cliff Reedy, whose son tragically died in a car accident, the webcast service was essential in reaching out to all friends and family. His son's funeral was webcast across the U.S. and in 10 countries. The webcast funeral had more than 700 views.

MILITARY BAGS FLY FREE AFTER VIDEO GOES VIRAL

Army Staff Sergeants Robert O'Hair and Fred Hilliker were upset that airlines were charging baggage fees to military service personnel returning from Afghanistan. The two made a video in which they stated that 36 military personnel from Oklahoma were charged more than $2,800 for excess baggage fees. The two sergeants posted the video on YouTube, and many people commented to express their outrage. Even congressman Bruce Baley from Iowa demanded that the airline reimburse the soldiers for the fees. Now, all airlines allow military personnel to check more bags of greater weight for free.

MAN RETRIEVES STOLEN LAPTOP AFTER TWEETING PHOTOS

Joshua Kaufman had his laptop stolen from his apartment. Fortunately, he had activated his theft-tracking software which sent to Kaufman's e-mail periodic photos of the person using it taken from the computer's Web cam and screen shots of the laptop while in use. He posted the photos through Twitter and instantly began receiving retweets of support and leads of who the person might be in the photos. One of the screen shots included the name of the business for which the suspect worked. Within days, the police had arrested the suspect and returned Kaufman's laptop.

RASHARD MENDENHALL FIRED BECAUSE OF OSAMA BIN LADEN TWEETS

Rashard Mendenhall, Pittsburgh Steelers' running back, had a lucrative endorsement contract with Champion. But Champion fired Rashard over tweets he sent regarding the death of Osama Bin Laden. In his tweets, Rashard questioned why people would celebrate the death of Bin Laden. In other tweets, Rashard also questioned the September 11th attacks. He tweeted that he had "a hard time believing a plane could take a skyscraper down demolition style."

POLICE STANDOFF LIVE ON FACEBOOK

Jason Valdez took a woman hostage at a motel in a 16-hour standoff with SWAT teams. During the ordeal, he constantly updated his Facebook page, letting friends and family know of his situation. Valdez even posted two photos of himself and the hostage with the caption, "Got a cute 'Hostage' huh." Family and friends responded with over 100 comments to his Facebook page. One friend even posted a comment regarding the location of SWAT personnel stating, "gunner in the bushes stay low." Valdez thanked him for the information.[12, 13, 14, 15, 16, 17]

Questions

1. What do you think of Stacy Snyder's story? Should she be denied a degree for publicly endorsing drinking to her underage students? To what extent do you believe that potential employers should explore social networking sites to validate the "goodness" of potential employees? Is there anything on your Facebook page that might turn off potential employers? If so, are you going to take any action?

2. The webcasting of funerals is an interesting example of the flatness of the world. Is this an invasion of privacy or do next-of-kin have the right to make such a decision? What other significant events in a person's life might

be suitable for webcasting? Identify at least three such events and then do some research to determine if webcasting of those events is already taking place.

3. Osama Bin Laden represents a very dark image for most Americans. His participation in the planning of the September 11th attacks will forever mark him as evil. Should people, like Rashard Mendenhall, who make positive or perhaps even neutral comments about terrorists like Bin Laden be fired from endorsement contracts? Can making such comments be considered grounds for termination of employment? Maybe dismissal from your school as a student?

4. Very few people would question the service and commitment of military personnel to our country. The two sergeants who created the YouTube video openly criticized Delta Airlines for its charging of baggage fees to military personnel. Is this open form of criticism of businesses and their practices acceptable? Will it help businesses be more accountable to customers?

5. The use of Facebook (or any other social networking site) can truly make a person's life transparent, available for the whole world to see. Should there be legislation regulating the openness of your life on the Internet? Can we expect society somehow to regulate this without any laws?

CLOSING CASE STUDY TWO

Google and Apple Know Where You Are, Maybe

In April 2011, some interesting discoveries were made regarding location tracking by Apple iPhones and iPads and Google Android smartphones. Pete Warden and Alasdair Allan, British researchers, discovered a file on Allan's iPhone that provided a detailed list of places Allan had visited in the U.S. and United Kingdom over a 300-day period. The file included a time stamp of each location.

Similarly, Duke and Penn State student researchers, with the help of Intel, found that 15 of 30 popular Android apps systematically communicated location information to a variety of ad networks. Those researchers found that some of the apps transmitted location data only when displaying specific ads, while others did so even while the app was not running. On some Android smartphones, the location data was transmitted as often as every 30 seconds.

Well, as you can imagine, this sent the public into an uproar. Google and Apple (if you're using one their smartphones) are tracking my every movement? Those organizations know exactly where I was and when I was there? The outcry was unbelievable.

Apple and Google went silent on the subject for several days, with neither returning phone calls or e-mails or posting any information on their Web sites or blogs.

Senator Al Franken, Democrat from Minnesota, quickly scheduled a hearing of the Judiciary Panel's subcommittee on privacy for May 10, 2011. According to Franken, "People have the right to know who is getting their information and how (it) is shared and used. Federal laws do far too little to protect this information. . . . No one wants to stop Apple or Google from producing their products, but Congress must find a balance between all of those wonderful benefits (from devices) and the public's right to privacy." After getting little or no response from either Apple or Google, Franken went on to say, "I have serious doubts those rights are being respected in law or in practice."

At the time, Steve Jobs, CEO of Apple, was on medical leave, and he came back from medical leave to defend Apple's location tracking technology. According to Jobs's right-hand executive Guy Tribble, Apple vice president of software technology, Apple iPhones and iPads only gather location data about nearby cell towers and Wi-Fi hot spots. As he explained, "[Apple] does not share personally identifiable information with third parties for their marketing purposes without customers' explicit consent . . . [and] Apple does not track users' locations. Apple has never done so and has no plans to ever do so." Apple intends to continue sending nearby cell tower and Wi-Fi hot spot location data but will only store that data for 7 days.

Google's long-awaited explanation was similar, with a few twists. Google did admit that Android devices do harvest location data for marketing campaigns. But Google stated that the location-tracking information is not traceable to individual users. Google went on to defend its action in stating that Google does ask Android device owners if they want to turn off the location-tracking feature. According to Alan Davidson, Google's director of public policy for the Americas, "If they opt in, all data is made anonymous."[18, 19, 20]

Questions

1. Location-based tracking is common to all smartphones, for good reason or bad. The popular location-based service company Foursquare has an app so you can check in at various locations to receive discounts, become Mayor, and see who else might be there. DealLeak, which aggregates deals from the likes of Groupon and Living Social, needs your location in order to offer local discounts on products and services to you. How many location-based service apps do you have on your smartphone? How often do you use them and why?

2. Apple and Google defended their processes by stating that their privacy policies very clearly stated what information would be gathered, how that information would be used, and how and with whom that information might be shared. When was the last time you read the privacy policy of any technology tool, such as a Web browser or app? Do you think very many people actually read these? Do the disclaimers in these privacy policies give the offering organization the right to do anything with your information?

3. What about location-based tracking in car systems like GM's OnStar? Those systems know the car's location to give you driving directions and perhaps identify local restaurants or other venues. Are you comfortable with this? When was the last time you bought a paper map? How much do you rely on your car's GPS system?

4. What about smartphone tracking for parents who want to know where their children are and where they've been? Minors under the age of 18 have very few privacy rights, especially when it comes to parents' knowledge of where they are. Are parents going too far in wanting to know where their children are? What are the benefits of such systems for parents? For the children? What does the term "helicopter parent" refer to?

■ KEY TERMS AND CONCEPTS

Application software, 14
Business intelligence (BI), 7
Buyer power, 19
Central processing unit (CPU), 13
Competitive advantage, 19
Data, 6
Differentiation, 24
Entry barrier, 21
Ethics, 12
External information, 9
First-mover advantage, 20
Five Forces Model, 19
Focus, 24
Garbage-in garbage-out (GIGO), 8
Hardware, 13
Information, 6
Information granularity, 9
Information-literate knowledge worker, 11
Information technology (IT), 13
Input device, 13

Internal information, 9
Loyalty program, 20
Management information systems (MIS), 5
Objective information, 9
Output device, 13
Overall cost leadership, 23
RAM (random access memory), 13
Rivalry among existing competitors, 22
Run-grow-transform (RGT) framework, 25
Software, 13
Storage device, 13
Subjective information, 9
Supplier power, 20
Switching cost, 21
System software, 14
Technology-literate knowledge worker, 11
Telecommunications device, 14
Threat of new entrants, 21
Threat of substitute products or
    services, 21

SHORT-ANSWER QUESTIONS

1. What is the relationship between management information systems (MIS) and information technology (IT)?
2. What are some relationships among data, information, business intelligence (BI), and knowledge?
3. How does the granularity of information change as it moves from lower to upper organizational levels?
4. What is the difference between a technology-literate knowledge worker and an information-literate knowledge worker?
5. How do ethics differ from laws?
6. What are the three financial elements of break-even analysis?
7. What role does the Five Forces Model play in decision making?
8. Why are competitive advantages never permanent?
9. What are the three generic strategies according to Michael Porter?
10. How are Porter's three generic strategies and the RGT framework similar?

ASSIGNMENTS AND EXERCISES

1. **USING PORTER TO EVALUATE THE MOVIE RENTAL INDUSTRY** One hotly contested and highly competitive industry is the movie rental business. You can rent videos from local video rental stores, you can order pay-per-view from the comfort of your own home, and you can rent videos from the Web at such sites as NetFlix. Using Porter's Five Forces Model, evaluate the relative attractiveness of entering the movie rental business. Is buyer power low or high? Is supplier power low or high? Which substitute products and services are perceived as threats? Can new entrants easily enter the market? What are the barriers to entry? What is the level of rivalry among existing competitors? What is your overall view of the movie rental industry? Is it a good or bad industry to enter?

2. **REVIEWING THE 100 BEST COMPANIES TO WORK FOR** Each year *Fortune* magazine devotes an issue to the top 100 best companies to work for. Find the most recent issue of *Fortune* that does this. First, develop a numerical summary that describes the 100 companies in terms of their respective industries. Which industries are the most dominant? Pick one of the more dominant industries (preferably one in which you would like to work) and choose a specific highlighted company. Prepare a short class presentation on why that company is among the 100 best to work for.

3. **BREAK-EVEN ANALYSIS** Perform a break-even analysis for the following scenario. Assume you sell widgets. You have total fixed costs of $12,000. Your manufacturing and shipping of widgets costs $7 per widget. You sell each widget for $22. What is your break-even point? How many widgets do you have to sell to realize a net profit of $15,000?

4. **BUSINESS STRATEGY FOR ENTERING THE CELL PHONE SERVICE INDUSTRY** Assume that you run a start-up and have decided to enter the cell phone service industry. Which of the three generic strategies would you choose as your primary business strategy—overall cost leadership, differentiation, or focus? Explain your choice by elaborating on the product and service features you would offer to lure customers from the competition.

5. **RESEARCHING YOUR CAREER AND INFORMATION TECHNOLOGY** To position yourself in the best possible way to succeed in the business world, you need to start researching your career right now. Here, we would like you to focus on the IT skills your career requires. First, consider what career you want to have. Second, visit Monster.com (www. monster.com) and search for jobs that relate to your career. Read through several of the job postings and determine what IT skills you need to acquire.

■ DISCUSSION QUESTIONS

1. The three key resources in management information systems (MIS) are information, information technology, and people. Which of these three resources is the most important? Why? The least important? Why?

2. We often say that hardware is the *physical* interface to a technology system while software is the *intellectual* interface. How is your hardware your physical interface to your computer? How is your software your intellectual interface to your computer? Do you see technology progressing to the point that we may no longer distinguish between hardware and software and thus no longer perceive differing physical and intellectual interfaces?

3. In a group of three to four students, consider eBay in the context of Porter's Five Forces Model. How does eBay reduce the threat of new entrants? If necessary, you may want to explore eBay's site (www.ebay.com) and determine the role of buyer and seller ratings, its integration with PayPal, and how it helps buyers and sellers resolve disputes.

4. In this chapter, we discussed the use of loyalty programs in the travel industry as a mechanism for reducing buyer power. What is another industry that also uses loyalty programs to reduce buyer power? How does that industry use loyalty programs to do so?

5. As an information-literate knowledge worker for a local distributor of imported foods and spices, you've been asked to prepare a customer mailing list that will be sold to international cuisine restaurants in your area. If you do so, will you be acting ethically? Suppose you don't consider the proposal ethical. What will you do if your boss threatens to fire you if you don't prepare the list? Do you believe you would have any legal recourse if you didn't prepare the list and were subsequently fired?

■ CHAPTER PROJECTS

GROUP PROJECTS

- Assessing the Value of Customer Relationship Management: Trevor Toy Auto Mechanics (p. 286)

- Analyzing the Value of Information: Affordable Homes Real Estate (p. 287)

- Making the Case with Presentation Software: Information Technology Ethics (p. 296)

- Analyzing Strategic and Competitive Advantage: Determining Operating Leverage (p. 303)

E-COMMERCE PROJECTS

- Interviewing and Negotiating Tips (p. 311)
- Ethical Computing Guidelines (p. 314)
- Financial Aid Resources (p. 315)
- Global Statistics and Resources (p. 316)
- Protecting Your Computer (p. 317)
- Searching Job Databases (p. 321)

CHAPTER TWO OUTLINE

STUDENT LEARNING OUTCOMES

1. Define supply chain management (SCM) systems and describe their strategic and competitive opportunities.

2. Define customer relationship management (CRM) systems and describe their strategic and competitive opportunities.

3. Explain the significance of enterprise resource planning (ERP) software as the integration of functional software systems.

4. Define social media and describe a few of its many dimensions that make it important in the business world.

WEB SUPPORT

www.mhhe.com/haag

- Consumer information
- Demographics
- Bureau of Labor and Statistics
- Gathering competitive intelligence
- Meta data
- Gold, silver, interest rates, and money
- Small Business Administration
- Global statistics a nd resources

SUPPORTING MODULES

XLM/B The World Wide Web and the Internet
Module B is a fast-paced tour of the Web and Internet. The first focus is on learning just enough about the Web to be an effective surfer. Then, explore the technology infrastructure behind the Web that makes it all possible. Finally, conclude with an overview of the options for connecting to the Web and the emerging life of Web 2.0.

CHAPTER TWO

Major Business Initiatives
Gaining Competitive Advantage with IT

OUTRAGEOUS INDUSTRY TRANSFORMATION: DEATH OF A TRAVEL AGENT

In Chapter 1, we explored the extent to which cell phones are transforming (i.e., wiping out) in-room phone revenues for hotels. Hotels are often considered broadly within the context of the travel and leisure industry segment. So, let's stay within that industry and explore another technology-enabled transformation.

Up through the mid-1990s, airline reservations systems were closely guarded barriers to entry. If you wanted to book a flight, you had one of two options: (1) call an airline directly, or (2) call or visit a travel agent. The travel agency industry flourished during this time. By offering hotel reservations, rental cars reservations, cruise bookings, and much more, the local travel agent became a friendly, one-stop shop for many people's vacationing needs.

You know what happened next. (In fact, you can probably tell this story without reading any further.) Along came the Web and with it, beginning in 1996, sites like Priceline, Travelocity, and Expedia. The accompanying graph shows the transformation. At the peak in 1999, there were 171,600 travel agents in the United States. By 2004, that had dropped to 115,000. And in August 2009, only 95,000 travel agents still survived, just barely half the peak total in 1999.

Today, many, but not most, people book their travel needs online. Consider these percentages booked online.

- 57%—car rentals
- 43%—airline reservations
- 28%—hotel reservations
- 8%—cruises

Will there be a need for travel agents? Sure. Some will survive and even thrive by focusing on the personal touch, what many people call *customer experience management*. Others will also survive by focusing on specific niches, say perhaps excursions to the north and south poles. (This is a form of *focus* as described in Porter's three generic strategies from Chapter 1.) It's rather like hotels losing in-room telephone charge revenue; they figure out how to make up that lost revenue elsewhere.

Technology is certainly a game changer. Some businesses will win, others will lose. The winners work diligently to build strategies and major business initiatives around the use of technology. That's our focus in this chapter.[1]

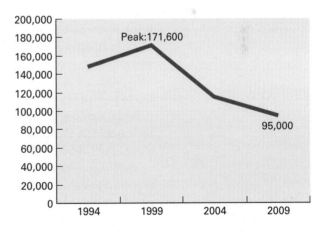

Questions

1. When you last flew, did you use a travel agent or go directly to the Web to book your tickets?

2. What is your preferred travel site for traveling? What features of it do you like best?

3. Why are airlines fully supportive of moving reservation systems to the Web and allowing consumers to make reservations for free?

Introduction

In almost any study you care to read, research shows that as competition intensifies in an industry, companies must develop innovative products, services, and business processes to compete and survive. Further, most of these studies point to the use of information technology as a way to help companies separate from the competition and develop a significant competitive advantage. In Chapter 1, we explored how a company can use tools such as Porter's Five Forces Model and Porter's three generic strategies and the run-grow-transform framework to develop business strategy to address the ever-intensifying competitive environment. In this chapter, we focus on four of the most important IT implementations of business processes companies can use to support their business strategies:

- Supply chain management
- Customer relationship management
- Enterprise resource planning
- Social media

Supply Chain Management

LEARNING OUTCOME 1

Dell Computer's supply chain management system is the envy of the industry. Its direct model gives the company a huge advantage over any competitor still using a traditional model of selling through retailers. Traditional computer manufacturers build computers and ship them to wholesalers, distributors, or directly to retailers. The computers sit in a warehouse or on the retailers' shelves until somebody comes in and buys them. If you took a look at a typical distribution chain, you would see that there are too many computers in inventory. A ***distribution chain*** is simply the path a product or service follows from the originator of the product or service to the end consumer. Holding onto inventory in a distribution chain costs money, because whoever owns the inventory has to pay for the operation of a warehouse or stores while waiting for someone to buy it. In the retailing of computers, not only does excess inventory cost money to hold, but the computers themselves can become obsolete, requiring retailers to slash prices in an effort to sell older models before the newer ones arrive.

Dell's model is different. Dell sells computers directly from its Web site so there is no inventory in its distribution chain. Dell has enhanced its *supply chain* as well. It uses i2 supply chain management software to send orders for parts to suppliers every two hours, enabling it to manufacture and deliver exactly what its customers want with little or no inventory in its supply chain.[2] The differences between Dell's "sell, source, and ship" model and the traditional "buy, hold, and sell" model are illustrated in Figure 2.1.

For a company the size of Ford Motor Company, with operations all over the world and tens of thousands of suppliers, supply chain management and IT-based supply chain management systems are critical necessities to ensure the smooth flow of parts to Ford factories. ***Supply chain management (SCM)*** tracks inventory and information among business processes and across companies. A ***supply chain management (SCM) system*** is an IT system that supports supply chain management activities by automating the tracking of inventory and information among business processes and across companies.

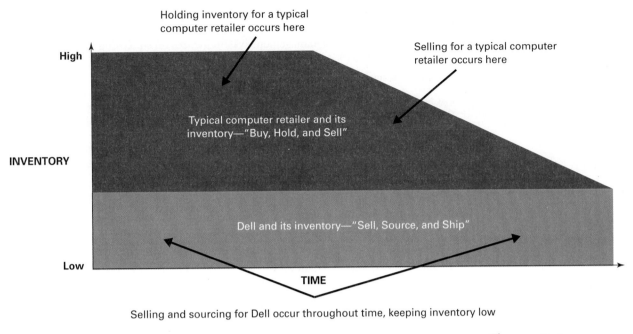

Holding inventory for a typical computer retailer occurs here

Selling for a typical computer retailer occurs here

Typical computer retailer and its inventory—"Buy, Hold, and Sell"

Dell and its inventory—"Sell, Source, and Ship"

Selling and sourcing for Dell occur throughout time, keeping inventory low

High

INVENTORY

Low

TIME

Figure 2.1

Buy-Hold-Sell versus Sell-Source-Ship

Most large manufacturing companies use *just-in-time* manufacturing processes, which ensure that the right parts are available as products in process move down the assembly line. ***Just-in-time (JIT)*** is a method for producing or delivering a product or service just at the time the customer wants it. For retailers, such as Target, this means that products customers want to buy are on the shelves when the customers walk by. Supply chain management systems also focus on making sure that the right number of parts or products are available, not too many and not too few. Too many products on hand means that too much money is tied up in inventory and also increases the risk of obsolescence. Too few products on hand is not a good thing either, because it could force an assembly line to shut down or, in the case of retailers, lose sales because an item is not in stock when a customer is ready to buy.

Consider snow blowers in Michigan around the month of November. If a store like Home Depot has too many, it may not be able to sell them all early in the snowy season when most customers buy them. Snow blowers are large and bulky and also cost a considerable sum of money. Having too many is an expensive proposition for Home Depot. Likewise, if Home Depot has too few snow blowers on hand and runs out early in the snowy season, a customer looking for a snow blower won't wait for new Home Depot inventory; instead, the customer will go to another store.

Companies with suppliers around the globe often employ inter-modal transportation. ***Inter-modal transportation*** is the use of multiple channels of transportation—railway, truck, boat, and so on—to move products from origin to destination. This further complicates the logistics of SCM because companies are required to carefully schedule, monitor, and track parts and supplies as they move among different modes of transportation. Consider that a given train may be carrying 50 or more truck trailers that will each eventually be connected to different trucks. Even purely domestic supply chains often employ inter-modal transportation such as railway lines and carrier trucks.

STRATEGIC AND COMPETITIVE OPPORTUNITIES WITH SCM

Overall, a tight supply chain management system focuses on squeezing every penny possible out of the supply chain process. Thus, the primary focus of supply chain management may be described in terms of our discussion in Chapter 1 as

- Overall cost leadership (from Porter's three generic strategies)
- Running the organization (run-grow-transform framework)

Of course, lower costs in the supply chain lead to lower prices for consumers, which in turn increase market share and top-line revenue. Consider Walmart's slogan, "Save Money. Live Better." Its operational model includes buying for less by creating a tight and extremely efficient supply chain management system (see Figure 2.2). That leads to selling for less and thus growing sales. This exhibits the characteristics of overall cost leadership. Walmart buys for less and passes the savings on to consumers, which encourages more consumers to buy more at Walmart than at the competition.

A well-designed supply chain management system helps your organization by optimizing the following specific supply chain activities:

- *Fulfillment*—ensuring that the right quantity of parts for production or products for sale arrive at the right time.
- *Logistics*—keeping the cost of transporting materials as low as possible consistent with safe and reliable delivery.
- *Production*—ensuring production lines function smoothly because high-quality parts are available when needed.
- *Revenue and profit*—ensuring no sales are lost because shelves are empty.
- *Cost and price*—keeping the cost of purchased parts and prices of products at acceptable levels.

Cooperation among supply chain partners for mutual success is another hallmark of modern supply chain management systems. For example, many manufacturing

Figure 2.2

Walmart's Approach to Buying for Less, Selling for Less, and Growing Revenue

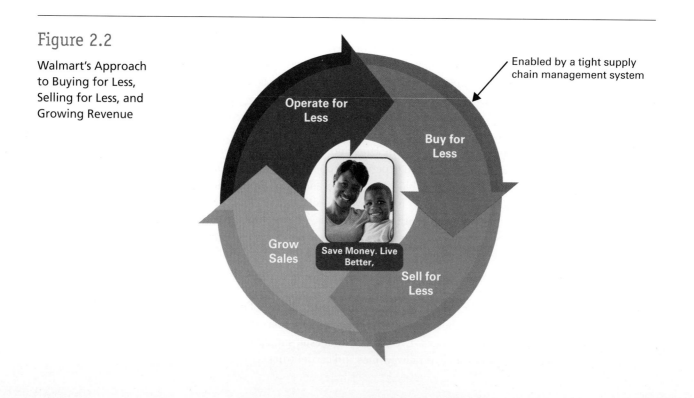

FRITO LAY GOES GREEN WITH ITS SUPPLY CHAIN MANAGEMENT INITIATIVES

Frito Lay Canada (FLC) is the nation's largest snack food manufacturer. Daily, its extensive supply chain network delivers millions of bags of snack foods to retailers all over the country.

For the last 10 years, FLC has focused extensively on optimizing its supply chain management system to cut costs at every corner. But more importantly, FLC has focused on making its supply chain management network *green*. Green initiatives focus on the environment such as by lowering pollution, minimizing carbon footprints, maximizing how many miles tires can be used before needing to be changed, minimizing fuel consumption, and so on. For its existing trucks, FLC created green efficiencies by:

- Improving anti-idling mechanisms.
- Creating more efficient cabin heating systems.

- Installing skylights in trailers to reduce the need for artificial light.

As trucks needed to be replaced, FLC introduced lighter-weight and more efficient trucks called *Sprinter vehicles*. It also began optimizing driving routes to reduce kilometers driven. Despite total revenue and units delivered all increasing from 2005 to date, FLC has been able to reduce its fleet size by 55 vehicles.

In 2010, FLC announced its latest green supply chain initiative of using fully electric vehicles. These new trucks, which produce zero emissions, have a daily range of approximately 60 kilometers, the needed range for a typical truck on the majority of routes from distribution centers.[3]

companies share product concepts with suppliers early in the product development cycle. This lets suppliers contribute their ideas about how to make high-quality parts at a lower cost. Such an arrangement is enabled through IT and is usually referred to as an *information partnership*—two or more companies cooperating by integrating their IT systems, thereby providing customers with the best of what each can offer.

IT SUPPORT FOR SUPPLY CHAIN MANAGEMENT

While the SCM market was pioneered by specialist companies such as i2 and Manugistics, it is now dominated by ERP software providers such as SAP, Oracle/PeopleSoft, SSA Global, and Microsoft (more on ERP later in this chapter). If your career choice takes you into industries that focus on the manufacturing of products and/or the distribution and use of those products (such as hospitality, resort, and tourism management), you will have a great deal to do with SCM software. To learn more about SCM software, we encourage you to visit the sites for some of the best SCM software vendors:

- Consona—www.consona.com
- Epicor—www.epicor.com
- IQMS—www.iqms.com
- NetSuite—www.netsuite.com
- CDC Software—www.cdcsoftware.com
- Sage—www.sageerpsolutions.com
- Microsoft Dynamics—www.microsoft.com/dynamics
- Oracle—www.oracle.com
- Solarsoft—www.solarsoft.com
- SAP—www.sap.com/usa

- HighJump Software—www.highjump.com
- TECSYS—www.tecsys.com
- JDA—www.jda.com
- Manhattan Associates—www.manh.com
- Intelex—www.intelex.com

Customer Relationship Management

Wells Fargo Bank's customer relationship management system tracks and analyzes every transaction made by its 10 million retail customers at its branches, at its ATMs, and through its Web-based online banking systems. Wells Fargo has become so good at predicting customer behavior that it knows what customers need even before many of them realize they need it. Wells Fargo's CRM system collects every customer transaction and combines it with personal information provided by the customer. The system is able to provide tailored offerings that will appeal to individual customers (a money-saving second mortgage, for example) at just the right time. As a result, Wells Fargo sells four more banking products or services per customer than the industry average of 2.2.[4]

Acquiring customers and then retaining them are the basic objectives of any organization, and thus, *customer relationship management* systems have become one of the hottest IT systems in business today. A ***customer relationship management (CRM) system*** uses information about customers to gain insights into their needs, wants, and behaviors in order to serve them better. Customers interact with companies in many ways, and each interaction should be easy, enjoyable, and error free. ***Multi-channel service delivery*** is the term that describes a company's offering multiple ways in which customers can

Figure 2.3

Customer Relationship Management (CRM) System

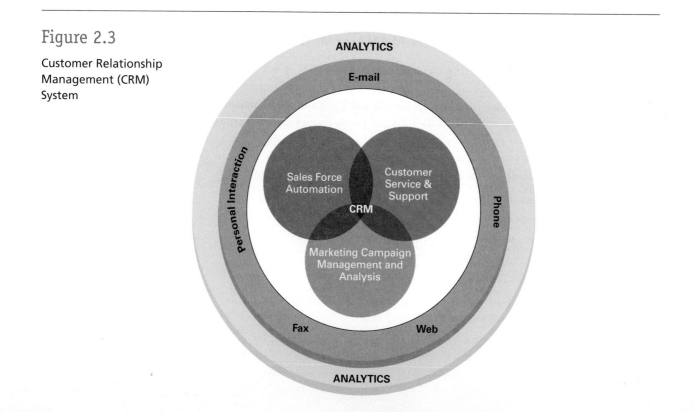

interact with it. E-mail, fax, phone, and the Web are all ways in which most companies interact with their customers. A fundamental goal of a CRM system, then, is the management and tracking of all these interactions. The communications within the various channels must be organized and carefully recorded for each customer. If that doesn't happen, then your experience with the company may be less than optimal and you may choose to change companies or perhaps return the product for a refund. It's not uncommon for a customer to change companies after having a negative experience. Thus, the overriding goal of CRM is to limit such negative interactions and provide customers with positive experiences (even delightful ones).

CRM systems (see Figure 2.3) typically include such functions as

- Sales force automation
- Customer service and support
- Marketing campaign management
- Analytics

It's important to note that CRM is not just the software. It is a total business objective which encompasses many different aspects of a business including software, hardware, services, support, and strategic business goals. The CRM system you adopt should support all these functions and should also be designed to provide the organization with detailed customer information.

In many cases, companies begin with a sales force automation application and then progress to other functions. ***Sales force automation (SFA) systems*** automatically track all the steps in the sales process. The sales process contains many steps, including contact management, sales lead tracking, sales forecasting and order management, and product knowledge. SFA systems empower sales representatives with information and business intelligence focused on customer buying patterns and needs. They help people at all levels of the organization to forecast future sales. That information is then fed into a supply chain management system to ensure that the right amount of products is available in the right location at the right time. Some of the more robust CRM systems and methodologies, such as at General Motors (see Figure 2.4), focus on creating repeat customers. It is far more expensive to acquire a new customer than it is to retain an existing customer, especially in the automotive retail industry.

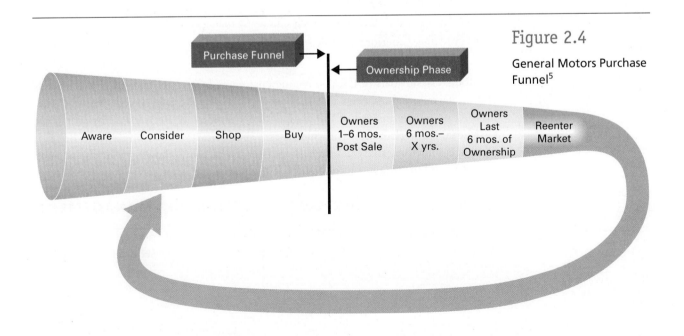

Figure 2.4

General Motors Purchase Funnel[5]

Customer service and support are functions that support CRM after the sale. These vitally important subsystems of a CRM system enable businesses to provide prompt and effective customer service and accurate and timely product support. Customer service and support functions are definitely *multi-channel,* attempting to meet the service needs of customers by phone, e-mail, Web, text message, Facebook presence, and so on.

Marketing campaign management helps people within the organization in regard to the marketing campaign life cycle. So, these subsystems help people design campaigns, identify target audiences and their preferred media, create campaign budgets, and deliver marketing campaign assets. Most important, these subsystems help marketing managers measure the extent to which a marketing campaign is successful.

Finally, tightly interwoven into any effective CRM system is analytics. Analytics (the focus of Chapters 3 and 4) are hard-core, numerical data that allow people to analyze operations and processes and make better decisions. "Seat of the pants" or "gut feeling" approaches to the development of CRM activities and processes simply will not work. Businesses today act on quantifiable data that allow them unique insight into the success or failure of their initiatives.

STRATEGIC AND COMPETITIVE OPPORTUNITIES WITH CRM

Overall, a well-designed customer relationship management system focuses on increasing revenue by providing delightful experiences for the customer in a variety of ways—tailored product and service offerings, seamless interaction, product knowledge, and so on. Thus, the primary focus of customer relationship management is

- Differentiation and focus (Porter's three generic strategies)
- Growing the organization (run-grow-transform framework)

Of course, customers are willing to pay only so much for these "delightful" interactions and product selections, so your organization must have a tight supply chain management system in place to ensure an acceptable price.

One of the rewards of CRM is competitive advantage through superior performance in CRM functions, in particular:

- Devising more effective marketing campaigns based on more precise knowledge of customer needs and wants.
- Assuring that the sales process is efficiently managed.
- Providing superior after-sale service and support, for example, through well-run call centers.

All the classic goals of CRM—treating customers better, understanding their needs and wants, tailoring offerings in response—are likely to result in buyers choosing your product or service instead of the competition's. Predicting the amount by which the CRM-enabled organization will gain market share, however, can be difficult. But certainly, it is something that can be measured after the fact, thus allowing your organization to understand the true results of better CRM in terms of customers' buying decisions.

IT SUPPORT FOR CUSTOMER RELATIONSHIP MANAGEMENT

Figure 2.5 shows a sample CRM system infrastructure. The ***front office systems*** are the primary interface to customers and sales channels; they send all the customer

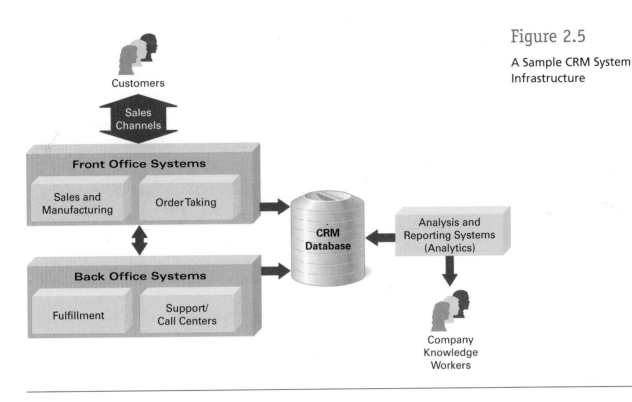

Figure 2.5

A Sample CRM System
Infrastructure

information they collect to the database. The **back office systems** are used to fulfill and support customer orders and they also send all their customer information to the database. The CRM system analyzes and distributes the customer information and provides the organization with a complete view of each customer's experience with the business. A typical back office function such as order fulfillment would have direct ties to the supply chain management system, creating synergy between the customer relationship management system and the supply chain management system.

There are many systems available today that a company can use that offer CRM functionality. CRM is actually one of those industry transformation areas for the IT industry. Originally, organizations bought CRM software systems, brought them in-house, created a hardware infrastructure for them to run on, installed the software, and provided tech support. Not so today. Most CRM systems are hosted by the software publishers. This is known as SaaS, or software-as-a-service. **Software-as-a-service (SaaS)** is a delivery model for software in which you pay for software on a pay-per-use basis instead of buying the software outright.

Using SaaS, often associated with cloud computing which we introduced in Chapter 1 and will explore more fully in Chapter 7, your organization doesn't buy a site license; instead you typically pay by the month per user for use of the software. Salesforce.com (www.salesforce.com) was one of the first to offer such a model for CRM software, as was NetSuite (www.netsuite.com). As you can see in Figure 2.6 on the next page, the enterprise version of Salesforce.com's CRM software is $125 per month per user.

Why do organizations choose to use a hosted or SaaS software model? The answer lies in the break-even analysis technique you learned in Chapter 1. All the associated costs of having software in-house—hardware infrastructure, training, maintenance,

Figure 2.6

Salesforce.com's Hosted
or SaaS CRM Software
Model

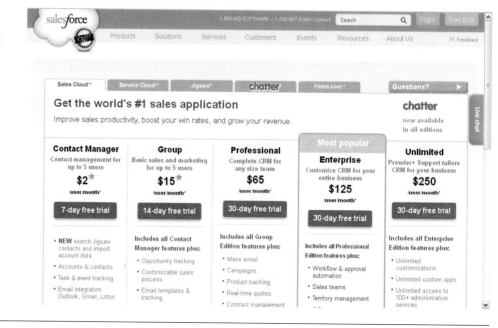

security, tech support, and the like—represent fixed costs. Whether you have 1 or 10,000 customers, those costs remain the same. With SaaS, you pay based on how many sales representatives you have, which to a large extent is determined by how many customers you have. If your customer base grows and you have to add additional sales reps, then you pay by the month for those new people, making your costs *variable*.

Most all CRM software providers now offer two access methods to their software. Your organization can still buy the software license outright and host it in-house. Many large organizations with thousands of sales reps may choose to do this because it's more economical than the SaaS model. Second, you can use a SaaS model. You sign up and pay for the software as a service. To learn more about some of the better CRM software providers, we encourage you to visit the following (all of these offer a SaaS model:

- InsideSales—www.insidesales.com
- Infusionsoft—www.infusionsoft.com
- Aplicor—www.aplicor.com
- SAP—www.sap.com
- CDC Software—www.cdcsoftware.com
- NetSuite—www.netsuite.com
- Zoho—www.zoho.com
- Microsoft Dynamics—www.microsoft.com/dynamics
- SugarCRM—www.sugarcrm.com
- Salesforce.com—www.salesforce.com
- SalesBoom—www.salesboom.com
- Sage Software—www.sagecrm.com
- RightNow Technologies—www.rightnow.com
- Oracle—www.oracle.com

AMERICAN RED CROSS AND CRM

The American Red Cross (usually referred to as just the Red Cross) does indeed have customers, perhaps not in the traditional business sense of selling products and services to them, but the people who depend on the Red Cross and its offerings during times of need and disaster.

Recently, the Red Cross chose Salesforce.com's hosted CRM solution to manage information related to its U.S.-based chapters, external partners, and inquiries for assistance worldwide. First and foremost, the software allows the Red Cross to track and manage information related to its thousands of volunteers all over the world. Second, the software helps the Red Cross manage and organize the tens of thousands of inquiries and requests for help it receives on an annual basis. Even after the earthquake in Haiti, Salesforce.com's CRM system was able to handle the large spike in requests without any interruption in service.

Within its 35 chapters in the U.S., the software has been deployed to help the chapters organize and manage information related to their volunteers, training events for volunteers, and all back-office functions. The software and information for each chapter is literally rolled up into a master system at Red Cross headquarters so that planners on a national and international scale can continually assess and identify locations of excess capability.

For organizations large or small and for organizations trying to make money or simply save the world, hosted software solutions are often the way to go. Hosted solutions ease the infrastructure and technical burden for many organizations. For the Red Cross, it's about spending more money on disaster relief because it spends less money maintaining in-house software.[6]

Enterprise Resource Planning—Bringing IT All Together

To this point, we've considered the major business initiatives supply chain management and customer relationship management individually, focusing on the key strengths and advantages of each. But in the business world, you will deal with the issue of integrating them and making them work together. Consider supply chain and customer relationship management. They must work together, sharing information. To create tight supply chains that provide the right products and services at exactly the right time, you must know what customers want and when they want it (the province of customer relationship management). That brings us to enterprise resource planning systems, also known as enterprise software. An *enterprise resource planning (ERP) system* is a collection of integrated software for business management, accounting, finance, human resources management, project management, inventory management, service and maintenance, transportation, e-business, and—yes—supply chain management, customer relationship management, and e-collaboration. It may sound like a long list (and it is), but the central notion behind an ERP system is that it includes all technology systems and software in your organization.

ERP systems are big business. At the top of the IT spending list is the ERP market. For instance, the U.S. federal government spent about $7.7 billion on ERP products and services in fiscal year 2009, up about 37 percent from 2004 spending of $5.6 billion. More than 60 percent of the Fortune 1000 companies have installed or are

LEARNING OUTCOME 3

Figure 2.7

ERP Vendors

Vendor/Web Address	ERP Specialties/Characteristics	Target Market
SAP www.sap.com	Customer relationship management, financial management, human resource management, and supply chain management	Large business
Oracle/PeopleSoft www.oracle.com	Financial management, human resource management, and supply chain management	Large business
Infor www.infor.com	Customer relationship management, financial management, human resource management, and supply chain management	Large business
Microsoft (Great Plains) www.microsoft.com	Financial management, distribution, manufacturing, project accounting, human resource management, and business analytics	Small-to-medium business

in the process of implementing ERP systems to support their business activities. These packages implemented by the Fortune 1000 companies run well over the IT budgets for most small-to-medium-size enterprises, and ERP vendors are targeting this untapped market with scaled-back systems suitable for smaller firms by offering simple, cheaper, preconfigured solutions easy to install within budget and time constraints. For instance, Microsoft now offers an ERP solution (called Microsoft Great Plains) geared toward the small-to-medium-size company.[7,8]

The dominating ERP software suppliers are SAP, Oracle/PeopleSoft, Infor, and Microsoft (see Figure 2.7). Together they control more than 70 percent of the multibillion-dollar global market. Each vendor, for historical reasons, has a specialty in one particular module area such as SAP in logistics, Oracle/PeopleSoft in financials, Infor in manufacturing, and Microsoft in retail management.

There are also about 50 established and a few more newly emerging smaller and mid-size ERP vendors including third-party developers competing for the very lucrative ERP market. There is stiff competition and overlapping products that are difficult to differentiate. The vendors are continually updating their products and adding new technology-based features. Long-term vision, commitment to service and support, specialty features, experience, and financial strength for research and development are considered the major vendor qualities for product selection and implementation.

The ERP market has been growing at a rate of more than 30 percent per year and most forecasts predict more of the same. The growth of the ERP market has been boosted by both business and technical factors. With respect to business, the most cited reason is globalization, which has fostered mergers and stimulated the creation of big corporations with high information requirements that the former individual information systems were not able to fulfill. Another factor is general market maturity in developed countries, which has fostered competition among all companies and increased the power of consumers, thus forcing enterprises to upgrade the efficiency of their business processes.

Finally, advances in information and communication technologies have made the development of ERP systems possible by allowing the database centralization to integrate with a distributed ERP environment.

THE EVOLUTION OF ERP SYSTEMS

ERP systems replace "islands of information and processes" with a single, packaged software solution that integrates all the traditional enterprise management functions such as financials, human resources, and manufacturing and logistics. Knowing the history and evolution of ERP is essential to understanding its current application and its future developments. To help give you a better perspective, let's review the evolution of ERP systems (see Figure 2.8).

The early stage of ERP was carried out in the 1970s through a system called *Materials Requirement Planning (MRP)*. The focus of the MRP software was on internal production planning, calculating time requirements components, procurement, and materials planning. The MRP software did not focus on any type of service orientation, but rather was developed to provide the right materials at the right time.

MRP, or "little MRP," represented a huge step forward in the planning process. For the first time, based on a schedule of what was going to be produced, which was supported by a list of materials that were needed for that finished item, the computer could calculate the total needed and compare it to what was already on hand or committed to arrive. This comparison could suggest an activity—to place an order, cancel orders that were already placed, or simply move the timing of these existing orders. The real significance of MRP was that, for the first time, management was able to answer the question "when?"

The next generation of these systems was introduced by the early 1980s under the name *Manufacturing Resources Planning* or *MRPII*. MRPII did not mean that MRP was done incorrectly the first time, but rather that it had evolved. MRPII closed the loop with the accounting and financial management systems. MRPII systems crossed the boundaries of the production functionality and started serving as decision support systems (DSS) as well as executive information systems (EIS) (in the modern day many people refer to implementations of these as *digital dashboards*).

For the first time, a company could have an integrated business system that provided visibility for the requirements of material and capacity. Good information leads to good decisions, and therefore these integrated IT systems provided a competitive advantage.

By the time each functional area of a company had developed its own software program, the need for tightly integrating them became obvious. The next major shift during the late 1980s and early 1990s was that "time to market" was becoming increasingly

Figure 2.8

Evolution of Enterprise Resource Planning Systems

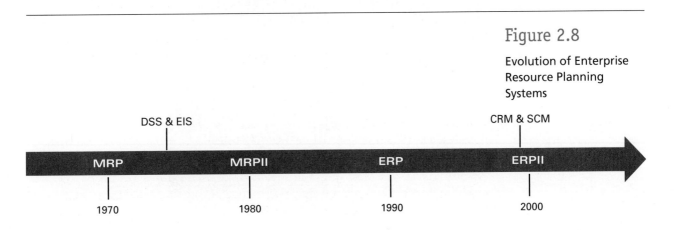

short. Lead times expected by the market continued to shorten and customers were no longer satisfied with the service level that was considered world class only a few years earlier.

The need to develop a tightly integrated system that would use data stored in common databases and would be used enterprisewide became the highest priority for IT professionals. No longer was it tolerable to submit a request to the IT department and wait several months to obtain this critical information. This common-database, companywide integrated system appeared at the beginning of the 1990s and was named *enterprise resource planning (ERP)*.

ERP encompasses all the resource planning for the enterprise including product design, warehousing, material planning, capacity planning, and communication systems. ERP systems help companies become leaner and more agile by integrating the basic transaction programs for all departments, allowing quick access to timely information.

ERP FUNCTIONALITY

In Figure 2.9, an ERP system allows transparent integration of functions, providing flows of information among all areas within the enterprise in a consistently visible manner. ERPs allow companies to implement a single integrated system replacing their *legacy* information systems. A ***legacy information system (LIS)*** represents a massive, long-term business investment in a software system with a single focus; such systems are often brittle, slow, and nonextensible. ERP systems are configurable information systems packages that seamlessly integrate all the information processes in the company within and across all functional areas—financial, accounting, human resources, supply chain, and customer information. The result is (1) integrated information across the board

Figure 2.9

Overview of ERP System

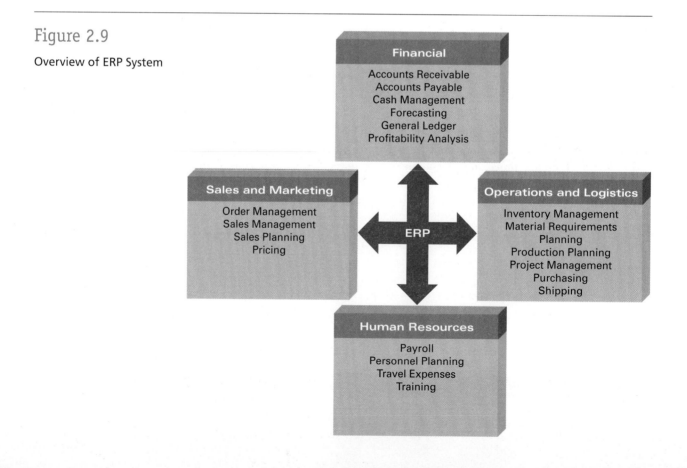

(data, information, and business intelligence), (2) one suite of applications, and (3) a unified interface across the entire enterprise. An ERP system is required to have the following characteristics:

- Modular design comprising many distinct business functions such as financial, manufacturing, and distribution.
- A centralized database that organizes and manages information.
- Integrated functions that provide seamless information flow among them.
- Flexible best practices.
- Functions that work in real time.
- Internet-enabled.[9]

Different ERP vendors provide ERP systems with some degree of specialty, but the core functions are almost the same for all of them. Some of the core ERP functions found in the successful ERP systems are the following:

- Accounting
- Financials
- Manufacturing
- Production
- Transportation
- Sales and distribution
- Human resources
- Supply chain
- Customer relationship
- E-business

You need to realize that ERP systems will not improve organizations' functionalities overnight. The high expectation of achieving cost savings (below-the-line initiative) and service improvements (leading to above-the-line revenue increases) is very much dependent on how good the chosen ERP system fits the organizational functionalities and how well the tailoring and configuration process of the system matches with the business culture, the IT culture, the strategy, and the structure of the organization. Overall, an ERP system is expected to improve both back-office and front-office functions simultaneously. Organizations choose and deploy ERP systems for many different benefits and reasons. In many cases the calculation of return on investment (ROI) is weighted against the many benefits expected.

It may be a challenge for you to wrap your brain around the concept of an ERP system without first-hand experience in using one. But consider your school for example, which to a greater or lesser degree, has some form of an ERP system. When you register for classes, for instance, you may not be able to do so because of outstanding parking tickets, overdue library books, an unpaid tuition balance, or a host of other reasons. And if you can register for classes, when you receive your tuition bill, it already includes allowances for government loans, scholarships, and the like. This is all possible because your school's individual IT systems—that each handle a different function such as registration, parking, tuition financials, and loans and scholarships—are tied together in the form of an ERP system. Businesses in the private sector (and some public sector ones as well) attempt to do the same thing on a grander scale (see Figure 2.10 on the next page). These organizations integrate predictions of customer demands (customer relationship management) into an ERP system to drive other functions such as finance, manufacturing, inventory, transportation, and distribution (with the latter

Figure 2.10

The Integration within an
ERP System

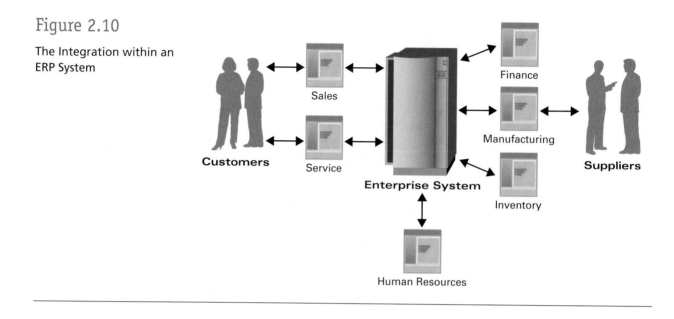

four being an integral part of supply chain management). Organizations even attempt
to predict the acquisition of human resource talent in light of existing human resource
attrition and the need for increased human resource capacity based on predicted customer demands.

ERP SOFTWARE FOR MARKET SIZE

ERP software is "big" software, and by that we mean that it can cost an organization
millions of dollars to acquire, install, and operate. But that doesn't mean that small businesses can't take advantage of the power and capability of ERP software. Many ERP
vendors choose niches in this expansive market based on the number of seats or users
in an organization that will be using an ERP system. Below is a list of ERP software by
number of seats.

- **Small businesses—less than 100 seats**
  - Microsoft Dynamics SL (http://www.microsoft.com/en-us/dynamics/
    products/sl-overview.aspx)
  - SAP Business One (http://www.sap.com/sme/solutions/businessmanagement/
    businessone/index.epx)
  - Sage ERP X3 (http://www.sageerpx3.com/)
  - Exact Software EXACT ONLINE Solution (www.exact.com)
  - Intuit QuickBooks Enterprise (http://enterprisesuite.intuit.com/)
- **Medium-size businesses—100–500 seats**
  - Microsoft Dynamics GP or NAV (http://www.microsoft.com/en-us/
    dynamics/products/gp-overview.aspx)
  - SAP Business All-In-One (http://www.sap.com/sme/solutions/
    businessmanagement/businessallinone/index.epx)
  - Infor ERP Solution (http://www.infor.com/solutions/erp/)
  - Epicor ERP Solution for Mid-Sized Businesses (http://www.epicor.com/
    pages/default.aspx)
  - SYSPRO (http://americas.syspro.com/)
  - Sage MAS 90 ERP, MAS 200 ERP, or Accpac Extended Enterprise Suite
    (http://www.sagemas.com/)

EBAY OFFERS END-TO-END SOLUTION FOR INTERNET RETAILERS

Many businesses, large and small, want end-to-end solutions for Internet retailing. They simply want to hook up with an Internet giant offering basically a full-fledged ERP system that will allow them to run the Web-based portion of their business. Amazon has always been that giant but eBay is growing taller.

According to John Donahoe, eBay CEO, "The number of retailers, large and small, that have come to us saying 'We are grappling with how you deal with mobile commerce, we are grappling with how to deal in a social-commerce world, we are grappling with how to do global' has been striking." In response, eBay recently purchased GSI Commerce for $2.4 billion.

GSI has created an ERP infrastructure specifically designed for Web-based commerce. It assists more than 180 top brands and retailers including Aeropostale, Timberland, Mattel, Zales, and Major League Baseball. GSI's services include order management, fulfillment, and shipping.

Electronic commerce is growing rapidly. In the U.S. alone last year, e-commerce was expected to top $176 billion with forecasted growth to $279 billion in 2015. But eBay's auction-style business revenue growth has been slower, up only 4.9 percent in 2010. John realized that eBay growth was not sustainable to the level of overall e-commerce growth. So, eBay is paying $29.25 a share for GSI, or a 50+ percent premium, to acquire a competitive position against Amazon.[10]

- **Large businesses (Enterprise Editions)—more than 500 seats**
  - Microsoft Dynamics AX (http://www.microsoft.com/en-us/dynamics/products/ax-overview.aspx)
  - Oracle (http://www.oracle.com/us/products/applications/ebusiness/index.html)
  - SAP (http://www.sap.com/solutions/business-suite/erp/index.epx)
  - Agresso Business World ERP Solution (http://www.unit4.com/products/agresso-business-world)

Social Media

LEARNING OUTCOME 4

No one can escape the reality, or the hype. Social media is all the rage right now, and probably will be for several years. Your technology-based life has most likely been spent largely within social media. Most people your age visit Facebook numerous times a day, watch several YouTube videos, text messages, and send tweets. These are all examples of social media.

Social media is a collection of Web-based and mobile technologies that create true interactivity among users, most usually allowing users to be both creators and consumers of content. Social media is fueled by Web 2.0 technologies. The ***Web 2.0*** is the so-called second generation of the Web and focuses on online collaboration, users as both creators and modifiers of content, dynamic and customized information feeds, and many other engaging Web-based services. In Figure 2.11 on the next page, you can see the progression of the Web using push versus pull technologies and static versus dynamic information. The early Web, what some people have retrospectively called *Web 1.0*, was characterized by pulling static information. That is, you started your Web browser and searched for (i.e., pulled) information you wanted. Most of that information was built into the Web page you found, making it static.

Figure 2.11

The Evolution of the Web

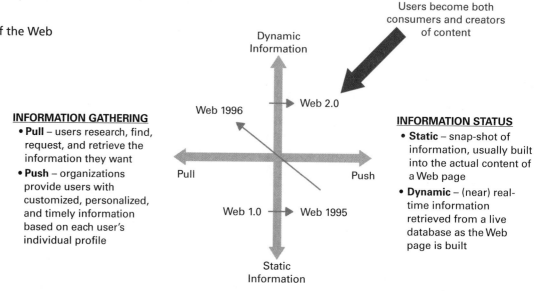

The Web moved quickly then into a short-lived environment of pushing static information. This ushered in one of the dirtiest four-letter words in Web terminology, *spam.* In those days, your e-mail box was littered with spam, or junk mail, for everything ranging from phony lottery winnings, to sexual performance–enhancing drugs, to diapers, to pet food. The senders had no idea if you needed any of those, but your e-mail address made a list and you were forever on it.

Shortly thereafter, the Web moved into the upper-left quadrant (probably the mid to late 1990s), characterized by pulling dynamic information. This ushered in the explosion of, for example, stock-trading Web sites like E*TRADE and Scottrade (online) and travel sites like Expedia and Travelocity. Then, you could search for (i.e., pull) real-time information about flights and stock quotes. This was the real birth of e-commerce on the Web.

Today, we are in Web 2.0, a time of active participation by consumers. It's also a time when businesses are getting good at pushing dynamic information to you, and it's information tailored to your needs. These include things like RSS feeds, recommendation engines on Amazon and iTunes, and even Facebook alerting you to people you might want to friend.

It would be impossible to cover every aspect of social media and how the world is using it in this book. Hundreds of books have been written on the subject. Thousands of conferences will be held this year in the United States alone focusing on social media. So, let's briefly explore a few of the many dimensions of social media.

SOCIAL NETWORKING

This is your world, namely that of social networking sites like Facebook. Broadly defined, a ***social networking site*** is a site on which you post information about yourself, create a network of friends, read about other people, share content such as photos and videos, and communicate with people. According to its own site, Facebook has more than 750 million users. Of those, 50 percent are on Facebook at least once a day. The average Facebook user has 130 friends. In total, users spend over 700 billion minutes per month on Facebook. In any given minute of any day, there are more than 16 million people on Facebook.[11] If you've never been on Facebook (a slim chance),

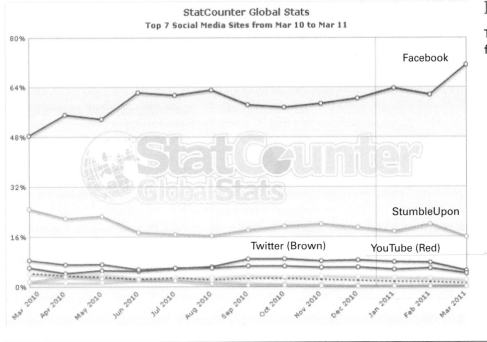

Figure 2.12

The Competitive Space
for Social Socializing[14]

ask the student next to you to show you his or her Facebook page. Chances are that he/she has one. On Facebook, you basically share everything you want about your life (stories, videos, photos, thoughts), make friends and get rid of friends (called *unfriending*), connect with other people who have similar interests, follow artists, musicians, and the like, and even visit the Facebook pages of retailers where you can buy merchandise.

Facebook has only a few competitors but they are not nearly so big (see Figure 2.12). StumbleUpon, the closest, is a form of social networking that recommends videos, photos, and Web pages to people based on their likes and the likes of other people similar to them. Then you have YouTube, a very popular site for sharing and commenting on videos. YouTube boasts over 15 billion videos and over 200 million viewers (in the U.S.). Twitter gets a small mention here, although it did announce in mid-2011 that it was handling over 200 million tweets per day.[12] A "tweet" is a form of a microblog and allows you to send and receive text messages of roughly 140 characters or fewer.

Google, in mid-2011, announced its rival to Facebook called *Google+*. While still in its beta stage when we wrote this text, Google has announced a few important features. Google+ will have Sparks, a referral system designed to offer you highly customized content based on your interests. It will also include a feature called Hangouts, which lets you connect with your Circles (groups of people you've identified) via live video chat. Finally, it will have Huddle, a group messaging service that allows you and multiple friends to have a conversation on your phone. We'll have to wait and see if Google can successfully compete against Facebook.

The only real legitimate competitor to Facebook is LinkedIn. LinkedIn is the professional equivalent of Facebook. While you use Facebook to share your personal life, you would use LinkedIn to share your professional life, including making contacts for potential employment, joining interests groups like international finance, making connections to other companies for sales purposes, and so on. In early 2011, LinkedIn announced that it had surpassed 100 million users.[13]

SOCIAL SHOPPING

Shopping, for a lot of people, has always been a social experience—to see what other people are buying and wearing, try to find the same, and perhaps inform others of where the best deals are. Within social media, those are still the same, only greatly amplified and augmented by other activities. Almost all retailers now sell their products and services on Facebook. On a user's Facebook page, he or she can talk about purchases and even send recommendations to a friend. These are typical shopping activities, but now you can perform them with hundreds or even thousands of friends watching your every move.

Pepsi has developed a unique social shopping experience with its social vending machines.[15] Using one of these machines, you can enter another person's information—cell number, name, and optional message—and then buy them a beverage. The other person receives a code via text message that he or she can use at a Pepsi social vending machine to redeem a beverage. Senders of beverage gifts can even participate in what Pepsi calls "Random Acts of Kindness." In this, the sender sends a beverage to an unknown person, for example, in an area struck by bad weather.

Bartab, an initiative of Webtab, offers a similar service for purchasing an alcoholic drink for a person at a bar or restaurant. As the sender of the drink gift, you pay $1 and provide the person's information. That person receives a coupon via e-mail through Facebook that he or she can then show the wait staff at a bar or restaurant to receive the drink. The receiver of the gift drink must pay the establishment $1 when redeeming the coupon.

And then there are social shopping services like those of Groupon. Groupon, and many other daily-deal type social shopping services, offers 50 percent to 90 percent discounts on products and services from a business for a short period of time. The goal is to get hundreds or thousands of people to take advantage of the deal. Groupon takes a cut of the money, the business gets tremendous exposure within Groupon's membership, and the business drives a lot of traffic to its location (virtual or physical).

SOCIAL PLAYING

Playing games within social media has been a strong trend for several years, and no doubt gaming mechanics and concepts will find their way into traditionally nongame environments such as education. We refer to these game systems as ***MMORPGs,*** or ***massively multiplayer online role-playing games,*** games in which thousands or perhaps millions of people play and interact in a robust virtual world. World of Warcraft and Second Life are two well-known examples.

World of Warcraft boasts over 11 million users and is the largest MMORPG.[16] In it, each player controls an avatar in a fantasy world of science-fiction type monsters, uberwarriors, and other types of mythical creatures. Each player completes quests, a series of tasks or steps in a mission. What truly makes these games "social" is the fact that it's more than just a game. Users can virtually gather and meet in groups; they can trade treasures they've earned in the game; they can spend real dollars to buy WoW gold and then use that gold in the game to buy better equipment for an avatar. This truly is a robust virtual world, complete with the characteristics of a free-enterprise economy.

Second Life is similar in many respects. Second Life isn't a game but rather a virtual world in which you can live a virtual life. You have an avatar. You can buy and sell property, both residential and commercial. You can open a business to sell products and services. Like WoW gold, Second Life has currency called Linden dollars. You use these in the game and can convert them into real cash.

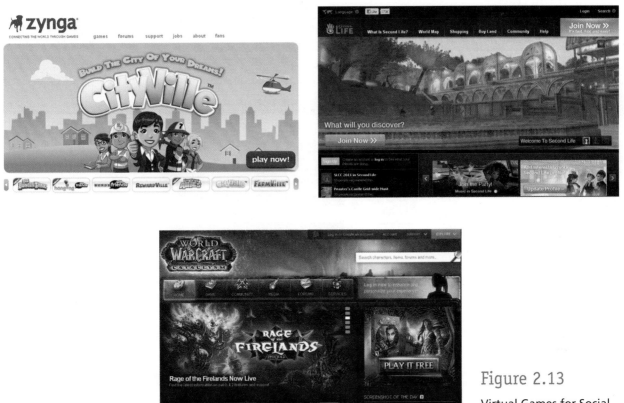

Figure 2.13

Virtual Games for Social Playing

Finally, there is Zynga, a social network game developer. Its portfolio of popular social network games includes:

- Cityville
- Empires & Allies
- Farmville
- Frontierville
- Mafia Wars
- Zynga Poker
- Words with Friends

Like World of Warcraft, Second Life, and most other social gaming environments, each of Zynga's games offers a virtual world, complete with an economy for buying, selling, and trading virtual goods. Zynga offers a total of 58 different games, many exclusively through Facebook. As of June 2011, over 270 million people were playing Zynga games via Facebook.[17]

SOCIAL "SAVING THE WORLD"

Sustainability and the triple-bottom-line are both important in today's business environment. Just as you read about Frito Lay Canada earlier and its desire to be more eco-friendly with its fleet of trucks in supply chain management, all organizations are seeking ways to build sustainable practices and processes that address the needs of the three Ps: People, Plant, and Profit. (These are the "triple" in triple-bottom-line and considered to be the three pillars of sustainability.)

Figure 2.14

Help Save the Planet at Volkswagen's Fun Theory

To achieve this, there is an emerging aspect to social networking that encourages people to create sustainable ideas. Many organizations have turned these into games, complete with prize money for the top innovators. Some of the more popular are:

- **The Pepsi Refresh Project**—contests in the areas of education, arts and music, and communities. Pepsi provides funding for the winners to implement their ideas.

- **Toyota Ideas for Good**—contests that require entrants to apply existing Toyota technologies to other environments (nonautomotive) for the betterment of people or the planet. For example, one contest winner applied Toyota's crash-test dummy technology to the head injuries that can occur in football to design better helmets and shoulder pads.

- **Volkswagen Fun Theory**—contests to change the behavior of people for the betterment of society in general (See Figure 2.14.) One entrant overlaid a piano keyboard on a set of stairs, with each step playing a musical note when stepped on. This encouraged people to take the stairs instead of a nearby escalator.

- **TOMS One-for-One**—buy a pair of shoes and TOMS will give away a pair to a person in need. Also, buy a pair of sunglasses and TOMS will pay for the surgery to repair the sight of an individual in a third-world country.

- **Epic Win**—a proposition by Jane McGonigal that all the world's problems should be converted into social-media type games. Gamers would compete to solve a problem, just as they compete in World of Warcraft, for example, to complete a quest.

SOCIAL LOCATIONING

Social locationing is an interesting phenomenon. Also called **location-based services, social locationing** is the use of a mobile device and its location (as determined by GPS) to check into locations such as businesses and entertainment venues, find friends and their locations, and receive rewards and take advantage of "specials" based on location. Popular social locationing systems include Geoloqi, Facebook Places, SCVNGR, Google Latitude, Foursquare, and Gowalla.

I'M ON FACEBOOK; SELL YOUR PRODUCTS THERE

Over 750 million people have Facebook pages. And many of them think it inconvenient to leave their Facebook world and go shop on a retailer's Web site. Many social media gurus believe that shopping on retailer Web sites will soon become a thing of the past. According to Janet Fouts, a social media coach, "Expecting people to come to your Web site is expecting them to make an extra effort. They're already on Facebook." Fouts goes on to explain, "It's social networks like Facebook that are the center of people's lives. It's where their friends are. It's where they play games. And it's increasingly becoming where they shop."

Retailers have not ignored this trend. In droves, retailers are beefing up their Facebook pages to include more than content; they are building entire stores on Facebook. Express, an apparel chain, is a good example. On its Facebook page it sells its entire line. Inventory calculators keep counts up-to-date and can inform customers of stockouts and backorders.

Think of selling on Facebook as the ultimate in convenience for a generation glued to their mobile devices and their Facebook pages. The old adage of "location, location, location" still holds true but with a slight difference. Now, retailers are setting up shop at the customer's location, and that's Facebook to a great extent. In the physical world large retail malls are located in densely populated areas. Well, Facebook has 750 million people. It makes sense to build your shop there.[18]

Foursquare is the most popular. In it, you check into a location (i.e., business, school, etc.) using your smartphone. If you check in more consistently than anyone else, you become the Mayor, which may entitle you to discounts and other special deals. You can create a circle of friends, enabling them to see where you always are.

Most social locationing systems allow you to explore the area around you. You can search for different types of restaurants, read others' reviews of entertainment events, and explore the physical world around you in many other ways via your smartphone.

These types of systems have come under close scrutiny because of the amount of information they provide about a person. Other people can see instantly when you check in at a location. Well, if you're there, you're not at home. And there have been reported stories of criminals using locationing systems to determine when a home is empty (by knowing that you have checked in someplace else). You can easily figure out the rest of that scenario. Still others are concerned that companies like Foursquare are gathering too much information about a person, namely their locationing habits. To be sure, we will probably see more and more legislation aimed at limiting the amount of private information these systems capture and share.

Again, these are just a few of the many dimensions of social media and social networking. No doubt, you use social media to network in other ways we haven't mentioned here. You probably visit social media sites like shopkick, IMVU, Café World, Mall World, and Yelp. Almost every commercial on TV is uploaded to YouTube to get more views. Many companies, in TV commercials and other media assets, now advertise their Facebook pages instead of their own Web sites. You may have used social media to gather information on potential colleges and universities to attend. The business world is frantically moving into the social media space hoping to avoid *FOMO,* the fear of missing out.

■ SUMMARY: STUDENT LEARNING OUTCOMES REVISITED

1. **Define supply chain management (SCM) systems and describe their strategic and competitive opportunities.** A *supply chain management (SCM) system* is an IT system that supports supply chain management by automating the tracking of inventory and information among business processes and across companies. Strategic and competitive opportunities for SCM systems include:

   - Overall cost leadership (Porter), running the organization (RGT framework)
   - Fulfillment—right quantity of parts or products at the right time
   - Logistics—low cost of transporting materials
   - Production—ensuring production lines run smoothly
   - Revenue and profit—no sales are lost
   - Cost and price—keeping part costs down and product prices at acceptable levels

2. **Define customer relationship management (CRM) systems and describe their strategic and competitive opportunities.** A *customer relationship management (CRM) system* uses information about customers to gain insights into their needs, wants, and behaviors in order to serve them better. Strategic and competitive opportunities for CRM systems include:

   - Differentiation and focus (Porter) and growing the organization (RGT framework)
   - Devising more effective marketing campaigns
   - Assuring the sales process is efficiently managed
   - Providing superior after-sale service and support

3. **Explain the significance of enterprise resource planning (ERP) software as the integration of functional software systems.** An *enterprise resource planning (ERP) system* is a collection of integrated software for business management, accounting, finance, project management, SCM, e-collaboration, and a host of other business functions. The basic goal of an ERP system is to provide (1) integrated information (data, information, and business intelligence), (2) one suite of applications, and (3) a unified interface across the enterprise. An ERP system replaces legacy systems and seamlessly integrates all functional software systems within an organization.

4. **Define social media and describe a few of its many dimensions that make it important in the business world.** *Social media* is a collection of Web-based and mobile technologies that create true interactivity among users, most usually allowing users to be both creators and consumers of content. A few of its dimensions include:

   - Social networking—gathering with friends and family on *social networking sites* like Facebook and sharing everything about your life.
   - Social shopping—technology-enabled shopping through sites like Groupon and buying other people gifts through the likes of Bartab and Pepsi social vending machines.
   - Social playing—participating in large, multi-user games or *MMORPGs,* which provide a large robust economy complete with a variety of commerce activities.

- Social "saving the world"—competing in contests to address important issues regarding the environment and the betterment of people and their behavior.
- *Social locationing,* or *location-based services*—using a mobile device and its location (as determined by GPS) to check into locations such as businesses and entertainment venues, find friends and their locations, and receive rewards and take advantage of "specials" based on location.

CLOSING CASE STUDY ONE

Coca-Cola Is Everything: SCM, CRM, ERP, Social Media, You Name It

If we told you that Coca-Cola had operating units in 50 countries around the world, you probably wouldn't be surprised. If we told you that Coca-Cola had been in business for almost 125 years, you probably wouldn't be surprised. So, you tell us . . . how many different beverages does Coca-Cola produce? 100? 500? 2,000? Are you surprised yet? Worldwide, Coca-Cola produces an amazing 2,800 different beverages.

When an organization is that big, has that sort of worldwide presence, and boasts what is perhaps the most well-known brand ever, you can bet that a multitude of IT systems are constantly churning in the background, not only keeping the organization running, but also keeping it running ahead of the competition.

To support internal collaboration efforts, Coke created something it calls its Common Innovation Framework, a Web-based system that combines project management capabilities with business intelligence. Using the Innovation Framework, anyone from any of the operating units worldwide can search for, find, and apply concepts, strategies, development successes, and marketing approaches that have been used elsewhere in the organization. For example, when introducing Georgia teas in Australia, the Coke people Down Under can research what marketing strategies worked well in related countries such as New Zealand. As Jean-Michel Ares, Coke CIO, explains it, "Once you've aggregated that pipeline of innovation, the object is to assess and prioritize the best allocation of resources in the organization."

Beyond internal employees, Coke is reaching out with new and innovative IT steps. Recently, it rolled out a new line of software services based on hundreds of business processes to its extended family of bottlers. These software services each perform a specific common business function and run within SAP's ERP software and are delivered by Coke's IBM-hosted data centers. The goal is to create a standardized business and technology platform across all Coke bottlers, most of which are independent franchises. (There are some partly owned by Coke.) If Coke and all its bottlers are speaking the same language, so to speak, and using the same technology, then supply chain management applications will be the more efficiently streamlined. Standardization in this case equates to saving money by reducing expenses associated with supply chain activities.

And even beyond its extended family of bottlers, Coke is using social media technology to create loyalty and engage more with its customers. Its award-winning Web site, My Coke Rewards at www.mycokerewards.com, is the second most popular consumer packaged-goods site, behind only www.kraftfoods.com. My Coke Rewards attracts some 300,000 visitors per day. Offering everything from magazine subscriptions to electronics as prizes (just look under your bottle cap), My Coke Rewards has reconnected Coke with its loyal drinkers. The site has teamed up with pop culture crazes such as *American Idol,* soccer, and auto racing to bring even more consumers into the fold. You can even find Coke-labeled songs through iTunes. Over 32 million people "like" Coke on Facebook.[19]

Questions

1. Why is standardization so important in supply chain management? Coke is developing its own set of software services for bottlers to use. Do you think Coke charges the bottlers for these software services? Why or why not?
2. How is My Coke Rewards an example of a switching cost? How can a switching cost not have a monetary penalty associated with it?

3. What sort of business intelligence could Coke gather from its My Coke Rewards Web site? How could it use this information for customer relationship management activities?

4. Visit Coca-Cola's Facebook page. Can you buy Coke products there? What social media tools are present that allow you to communicate with Coca-Cola?

5. Now, visit Pepsi's Facebook page. Compare and contrast it to Coca-Cola's Facebook page. Which has more eye appeal? Which seems to have more activity? Why do you think this is true?

CLOSING CASE STUDY TWO

The Business of Social Media and Making the ROI Case

So, what does social media mean for a business? How can a business take advantage of social media? How can a business measure the benefits of its social media strategy and quantify its return on investment (ROI)? These are the very questions with which businesses are wrestling. Social media as a business tool is still very much in its infancy. Some businesses, oddly enough, haven't yet taken the leap into the social media space. However, by 2012, eMarketer predicts that 88 percent of all businesses with at least 100 employees will use social media within their marketing strategies.

Let's look first at how to measure the ROI of a social media strategy. Return on investment (ROI) is another great financial tool for you to learn; it simply compares benefit to cost. There are definitely costs associated with a social media strategy. Just a few of those would include hiring a person to keep content fresh on a Facebook page, hiring a person to provide timely responses on a company blog, hiring a *Twitter jockey* (a person who focuses on the use of Twitter to communicate with customers, sponsors, business partners, and the like) to send company tweets about specials and new products/services, and so on. Below are some ways to measures the benefits of a social media strategy.

1. **Bottom Line Revenues**—This is a key indicator. After implementing a social media strategy, can you tie increases in revenue to that strategy? If you create a Facebook page for selling your products/services, what revenue are you now driving through your Facebook page? Have revenues through other outlets (your Web site and your physical store) stayed the same or declined by the amount you now receive through your Facebook page?

2. **More Analytics**—Social media represents another customer touch point. At each touch point, you can gather invaluable information for making better decisions. After visiting your company blog, to what sites do your customers go? How long do your customers spend on your Facebook page looking at but never buying your products? For those who have friended you on Facebook, how many have subsequently purchased something? How many are repeat customers? How many people tweet "bad" things about your company? Is that increasing or decreasing?

3. **Increased Traffic**—An important goal of social media is to drive traffic to your organization. After starting an extensive Twitter campaign (with tweets including your Web site or Facebook address), how much more traffic are you now seeing? After creating a Facebook presence, how many people are going from your Facebook page to your Web site to buy merchandise?

4. **More and Better Relationships**—Business is about relationships. Has your social media strategy allowed your organization to create relationships with new customers, suppliers, and business partners? How often do you use social media to engage these people in conversations? (This is a surrogate measure for the quality of the relationship. The more you talk to someone the better the relationship.)

5. **Increased Brand Awareness**—Brand awareness growth can be an important focus for social media efforts. How many new customers did you gain after creating a social media

presence? How many people are talking about your organization via Twitter? How many views on YouTube are you getting for your infomercials?

For your social media efforts to be successful, you must carefully determine your social media strategy. Now, strategy will be different for each organization, but below we list a few steps to success using social media that any organization can follow.

1. **Clearly Identify Goals and Objectives**—Of course, this is true for any business initiative. As Yogi Berra once said, "If you don't know where you're going, you might end up someplace else." Explicitly identify your goals; don't say "increase in sales," but rather say "increase in sales by 10 percent."

2. **Think Quality, Not Quantity**—Again, another solid truism for any business initiative. Quality will create deep and meaningful relationships with customers and business partners, and that translates into long-term, sustainable profits.

3. **Build Compelling Social Media**—Present important information in eye-appealing and eye-catching ways. Use images to tell your story. Don't blog or tweet if you have nothing new to say; find something new to say and reach to your audience in a compelling way with your message.

4. **Use Social Media as a Market Research Tool**—Gather feedback using the many Web 2.0 technologies. If you're the only one talking, the communication is a one-way street. Enable your customers to talk back and share their experiences, likes, and dislikes.

5. **Take Advantage of Analytics**—Gather hard data on every social media communication. Even if your organization doesn't currently use some of that data, store it for future use. Data is king—don't ever throw it away.[20, 21]

Questions

1. Let's suppose your current annual sales are $1 million. You implement a social media strategy and begin generating $200,000 in revenue through your Facebook page. At the end of the year, your sales are still $1 million. Was your social media strategy successful? Why or why not?

2. Every social media strategy costs money to implement, and we listed a few of those costs in this case study. Create a more comprehensive list of social media strategy costs. Briefly describe each cost and identify it as either a fixed cost or a variable cost.

3. Suppose you have a successful business with a well-liked product. One day something goes wrong and you ship 100,000 defective products. Almost the entirety of your customer base is disgruntled. What social media strategy would you employ to help? Why? Would you be better off just "waiting for it to blow over" or even "sticking your head in the sand"?

4. In the case study, we listed five steps to success. Identify two others and briefly describe them.

KEY TERMS AND CONCEPTS

■ SHORT-ANSWER QUESTIONS

1. Why is the traditional buy-hold-sell inventory model an expensive and potentially risky one?
2. What is the role of a supply chain management (SCM) system?
3. How does SCM fit into Porter's three generic strategies?
4. What are the typical functions in a CRM system?
5. How does CRM fit into the RGT framework?
6. What is the difference between front-office and back-office systems?
7. What is an enterprise resource planning (ERP) system?
8. What is software-as-a-service? What are its advantages?
9. What is the relationship between social media and Web 2.0?
10. What are massively multiplayer online role-playing games (MMORPGs)?
11. What are some popular social locationing systems?

■ ASSIGNMENTS AND EXERCISES

1. **WALMART'S SCM SYSTEM** Walmart is famous for its low prices, and you may have experienced its low prices first-hand. At least, you have probably seen its motto, "Always Low Prices— Always." One of the biggest reasons Walmart is able to sell at prices lower than almost everyone else is that it has a superefficient supply chain. Its IT-enabled supply chain management system is the envy of the industry because it drives excess time and unnecessary costs out of the supply chain. So, because Walmart can buy low, it sells low. As a matter of fact, if your company wants to sell items to Walmart for it to sell in its stores, you will have to do business with it electronically. If your company can't do that, Walmart won't buy anything from you. Log on to Walmart's Web site (www.walmart.com), search for supplier information, and find out what Walmart's requirements are for its suppliers to do business with it electronically. Prepare a brief summary of its requirements for presentation in class.

2. **REAL WORLD APPLICATIONS** In the chapter we mentioned that many CRM installations have been less than successful. On the other hand, there are many satisfied users of CRM applications. Log on to the Internet and find at least three examples of companies that are getting real business benefits from their CRM systems. Prepare a report on the results they are getting and the ways they achieved them. One place to start your search is at www.searchcrm.com. Another good source is the Web sites of CRM application software vendors Siebel and Salesforce.com (www.siebel.com and www.salesforce.com). At least one of your examples must be from a site other than the three mentioned.

3. **ERP FOR THE SMALL BUSINESS** Most major ERP vendors have been focusing on selling multimillion dollar installations of their software to very large organizations. That is shifting in focus somewhat as ERP vendors realize that the small-to-medium-size business market is probably just as large. Search the Internet for ERP vendors that focus on small-to-medium size businesses. Also, search for open-source ERP software. Prepare a short report for class presentation and offer the vendors that you found and their Web site addresses.

4. **SET UP A BLOG** Connect to any of the many sites that offer blog services and create a blog. The content doesn't really matter; simply go through the steps to create a blog. Which blog site did you choose to use and why? What is the registration process? How can you advertise your blog to other people? Why must blogs be constantly updated with new content?

5. **START LOCATIONING WITH FOURSQUARE** Sign up for the services of the social locationing service Foursquare. (After completing this assignment, you can delete your account immediately.) Do some playing around to learn the features of the system, check in at a few places, and wander around (virtually). What deals or specials did you find near your location? What is the concept of a Mayor? What privileges do Mayors have? How can you add friends? Do you have to upload a photo? What's your overall view? Is social locationing good or bad?

■ DISCUSSION QUESTIONS

1. Do you think your school would benefit from installing a customer relationship management (CRM) system? How might it benefit you as a student? How could it benefit your school?

2. In the run-grow-transform (RGT) framework, the third component is transformation, or enabling your organization to operate in entirely new ways. Of the three major business IT applications we discussed in this chapter (supply chain management, customer relationship management, and social media), which one(s) do you believe most support organizational transformation? Justify your answer.

3. We noted that it is extremely difficult to measure the success of a CRM system prior to its implementation and use. Why do you believe this is so? What can organizations do to develop measures of success before implementing a CRM system?

4. In 10 years, will Facebook still be so popular and so dominant? What competitors might overtake it? What are substitute products to social networking sites like Facebook?

5. Do you think ERP software is available through the software-as-a-service (SaaS) model? Do some research and find out? What were the results of your research? If ERP is available through SaaS, who are the leading providers in this space? Who benefits more from SaaS-delivered ERP, small businesses or large businesses? Justify your answer.

■ CHAPTER PROJECTS

GROUP PROJECTS

- Executive Information System Reporting: Political Campaign Finance (p. 288)
- Developing an Enterprise Resource Planning System: Planning, Reporting, and Data Processing (p. 299)
- Evaluating the Next Generation: Dot-Com ASPs (p. 301)
- Building a Scheduling Decision Support System: Airline Crew Scheduling (p. 306)
- Assessing the Value of Supply Chain Management: Optimizing Shipments (p. 309)

E-COMMERCE PROJECTS

- Consumer Information (p. 310)
- Meta Data (p. 311)
- Demographics (p. 312)
- Bureau of Labor and Statistics (p. 312)
- Gathering Competitive Intelligence (p. 313)
- Gold, Silver, Interest Rates, and Money (p. 316)
- Global Statistics and Resources (p. 316)
- Small Business Administration (p. 319)

CHAPTER THREE OUTLINE

STUDENT LEARNING OUTCOMES

1. List and describe the key characteristics of a relational database.
2. Define the five software components of a database management system.
3. List and describe the key characteristics of a data warehouse.
4. Define the five major types of data-mining tools in a data warehouse environment.
5. List key considerations in information ownership in an organization.

PERSPECTIVES

WEB SUPPORT

www.mhhe.com/haag

- Searching job databases
- Exploring Google Earth
- Financial aid resources
- Consumer information
- Demographics
- Bureau of Labor and Statistics
- Best of computer resources and statistics
- Global statistics and resources

SUPPORTING MODULES

XLM/C Designing Databases and Entity-Relationship Diagramming
Module C presents step-by-step instructions concerning how to design the optimal structure of a database including defining entity classes and primary keys, the relationships among the entity classes, and the information to be contained in each entity class.

XLM/J Implementing a Database with Microsoft Access
Module J presents hands-on instructions concerning how to implement a database using Microsoft Access including building tables, creating queries, building simple reports, creating customized reports, and creating input forms.

CHAPTER THREE

Databases and Data Warehouses
Supporting the Analytics-Driven Organization

OUTRAGEOUS INDUSTRY TRANSFORMATION: DID YOU KNOW CDS COME FROM DEAD DINOSAURS?

This outrageous industry transformation is a no-brainer. In 2001, Apple launched iTunes and *outrageously* transformed music retail sales. The graph at the bottom of the page makes perfect sense. In two years, the split of the music market by distribution between physical and digital went from 4-to-1 to 2-to-1. More recently, the Recording Industry Association of America (RIAA) has said that at the end of 2010, the split was almost exactly 50 percent each. Moving forward from today, there will never again be a time when the sale of physical music (CDs, etc.) is greater than that of digital downloads.

Music is an interesting "thing." Music defines generations. Music is integral to the fabric of most cultures. In history, music has been the rallying cry around which people gathered to fight tyranny and injustice. But to a computer music is just data. Each piece of sound on each track within a song is treated by a computer as one more piece of data, something that can be easily changed, deleted, augmented (e.g., made louder), and combined with other pieces of the same type of data to make new data.

As it turns out, music and its distribution are ideally suited to be handled by computers, with their storage capacity and the speed with which they can transfer data. When technology changed (ever heard of "records"?) and society began to buy music mostly on a new physical medium such as cassettes (do you even remember when that was the most popular medium?) or CDs, the music was still music, only the distribution media had changed. The same is true today. The music hasn't really changed, but we're now transferring it around, storing it, and listening to it as a collection of bits and bytes. All other data-oriented products are following similarly—books, newspapers, movies.[1, 2]

Questions

1. How many different digital music services do you use?
2. How many music CDs do you own that you bought from a retail store?
3. When was the last time you bought music on a physical medium such as a CD?

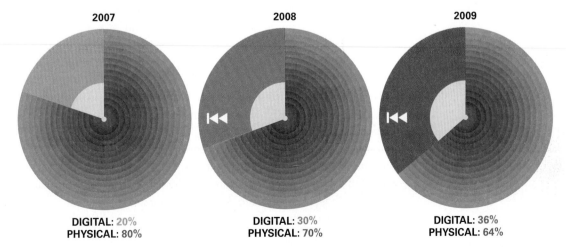

2007	2008	2009
DIGITAL: 20% PHYSICAL: 80%	DIGITAL: 30% PHYSICAL: 70%	DIGITAL: 36% PHYSICAL: 64%

Introduction

In the first two chapters, we briefly touched on a couple of important terms—*business intelligence* and *analytics*. We define them as follows:

- **Business intelligence (BI)**—collective information—about your customers, your competitors, your business partners, your competitive environment, your own internal operations—that gives you the ability to make effective, important, and often strategic business decisions.
- *Analytics*—the science of fact-based decision making. Analytics is a growing field of study, research, and career opportunities that focuses on the integrated use of technology tools and statistical techniques to create real-time, high-quality, fact-based business intelligence in support of decision making.

So, business intelligence is a resource/component of the overall framework or field of analytics.

Analytics has been and continues to be a strong focus for the business world. According to an April 2009 BusinessWeek Research Services survey, 83 percent of C-level executives agreed that the importance of using information to run their businesses has never been greater.[3] Further, according to a Gartner Group study, business intelligence has been the top technology priority in the business world for the last three consecutive years.[4]

Of course, to create business intelligence you need *data* and *information* (don't forget the distinction but we'll defer to the common practice of referring to both as just information in this chapter). Business intelligence doesn't just magically appear. You must first gather and organize all your data and information. Then, you have to have the right IT tools to define and analyze various relationships within the information. In short, knowledge workers such as you use IT tools to create business intelligence from information. This is what analytics is all about. The technology, by itself, won't do it for you. However, technology such as databases, database management systems, data warehouses, and data-mining tools can definitely help you build and use business intelligence.

As you begin working with these IT tools (which we'll discuss in great detail in this chapter), you'll be performing the two types of information processing: online transaction processing and online analytical processing. **Online transaction processing (OLTP)** is the gathering of input information, processing that information, and updating existing information to reflect the gathered and processed information. Databases and DBMSs are the technology tools that directly support OLTP. Databases that support OLTP are most often referred to as **operational databases.** Inside these operational databases is valuable information that forms the basis for business intelligence.

As you can see in Figure 3.1, you can also query operational databases to gather basic forms of business intelligence, such as how many products individually sold over $10,000 last month and how much money was spent last month on radio advertising. While the results of these queries may be helpful, you really need to combine product and advertising information (with several other types of information including customer demographics) to perform online analytical processing.

Online analytical processing (OLAP) is the manipulation of information to support decision making. At Australian P&C Direct, OLAP within a data warehouse is a must. P&C has created a data warehouse that supports its customer relationship management activities, cross-selling strategies, and marketing campaigns. By creating a data warehouse with customer information (including census data and lifestyle codes), its wide array of insurance and financial products, and its marketing campaign information, P&C agents can view all the products a given customer has purchased and more accurately determine cross-selling opportunities and what marketing campaigns a given customer is likely to respond to.[5]

A data warehouse is, in fact, a special form of a database that contains information gathered from operational databases for the purpose of supporting decision-making tasks. When you build a data warehouse and use data-mining tools to manipulate the data warehouse's information, you are actively engaging in analytics. As you can see in Figure 3.1, you can perform more in-depth queries to gather business intelligence from a data warehouse than you can with a single database. For example, "What new advertising strategies need to be undertaken to reach our customers who can afford a high-priced product?" is a query that would require information from multiple databases. Data warehouses better support creating that type of business intelligence than do databases.

As we first look at databases and database management systems in this chapter, we'll be exploring their use by Solomon Enterprises in support of customer relationship management and order processing. Solomon Enterprises specializes in providing concrete to commercial builders and individual homeowners in the greater Chicago area. Solomon tracks detailed information on its concrete types, customers, raw materials, raw materials' suppliers, trucks, and employees. It uses a database to organize and manage all this information. As we discuss Solomon Enterprises and its use of a database, we'll focus mostly on CRM and ordering processing. In *Extended Learning Module C,* we look at how to design the supply chain management side of Solomon's database.

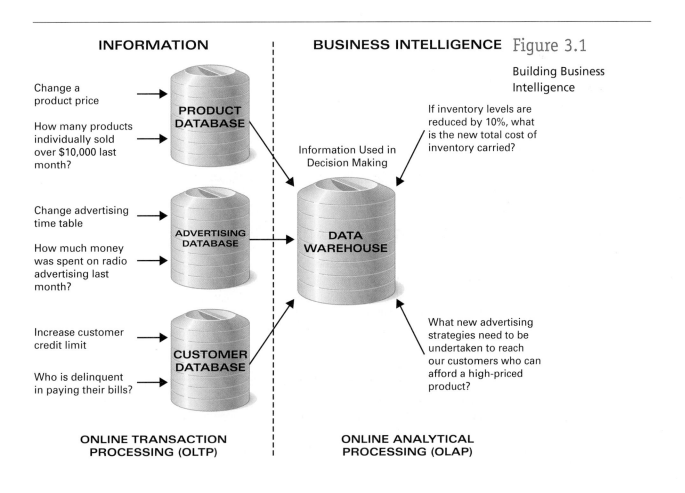

INFORMATION   **BUSINESS INTELLIGENCE**   Figure 3.1

Building Business Intelligence

Change a product price

How many products individually sold over $10,000 last month?

PRODUCT DATABASE

Information Used in Decision Making

If inventory levels are reduced by 10%, what is the new total cost of inventory carried?

Change advertising time table

How much money was spent on radio advertising last month?

ADVERTISING DATABASE

DATA WAREHOUSE

Increase customer credit limit

Who is delinquent in paying their bills?

CUSTOMER DATABASE

What new advertising strategies need to be undertaken to reach our customers who can afford a high-priced product?

ONLINE TRANSACTION PROCESSING (OLTP)   **ONLINE ANALYTICAL PROCESSING (OLAP)**

The Relational Database Model

For organizing and storing basic and transaction-oriented information (that is eventually used in analytics to create business intelligence), businesses today use databases. There are actually four primary models for creating a database. The object-oriented database model is the newest and holds great promise; we talk more about the entire object-oriented genre in *Extended Learning Module G.* Right now, let's focus on the most popular database model: the relational database model.

As a generic definition, we would say that any **database** is a collection of information that you organize and access according to the logical structure of that information. In reference to a **relational database,** we say that it uses a series of logically related two-dimensional tables or files to store information in the form of a database. The term **relation** often describes each two-dimensional table or file in the relational model (hence its name *relational* database model). A relational database is actually composed of two distinct parts: (1) the information itself, stored in a series of two-dimensional tables, files, or relations (people use these three terms interchangeably) and (2) the logical structure of that information. Let's look at a portion of Solomon's database to further explore the characteristics of the relational database model.

COLLECTIONS OF INFORMATION

In Figure 3.2, we've created a view of a portion of Solomon's database. Notice that it contains five files (also, again, called tables or relations): *Order, Customer, Concrete Type, Employee,* and *Truck.* (It will contain many more as we develop it completely in *Extended Learning Module C.*) These files are all related for numerous reasons—customers make orders, employees drive trucks, an order has a concrete type, and so on. And you need all these files to manage your customer relationships and process orders.

Within each file, you can see specific pieces of information (or *attributes*). For example, the *Order* file contains *Order Number, Order Date, Customer Number, Delivery Address, Concrete Type, Amount* (this is given in cubic yards), *Truck Number,* and *Driver ID.* In the *Customer* file, you can see specific information including *Customer Number, Customer Name, Customer Phone,* and *Customer Primary Contact.* These are all important pieces of information that Solomon's database should contain. Moreover, Solomon needs all this information (and probably much more) to effectively process orders and manage customer relationships.

CREATED WITH LOGICAL STRUCTURES

Using the relational database model, you organize and access information according to its logical structure, not its physical position. So, you don't really care in which row of the *Employee* file Allison Smithson appears. You really need to know only that Allison's *Employee ID* is 984568756 or, for that matter, that her name is Allison Smithson. In the relational database model, a **data dictionary** contains the logical structure for the information in a database. When you create a database, you first create its data dictionary. The data dictionary contains important information (or logical properties) about your information. For example, the data dictionary for *Customer Phone* in the *Customer* file would require 10 digits. The data dictionary for *Date of Hire* in the *Employee* file would require a month, day, and year, as well.

This is quite different from other ways of organizing information. For example, if you want to access information in a certain cell in most spreadsheet applications, you must

ORDER FILE

Order Number	Order Date	Customer Number	Delivery Address	Concrete Type	Amount	Truck Number	Driver ID
100000	9/1/2004	1234	55 Smith Lane	1	8	111	123456789
100001	9/1/2004	3456	2122 E. Biscayne	1	3	222	785934444
100002	9/2/2004	1234	55 Smith Lane	5	6	222	435296657
100003	9/3/2004	4567	1333 Burr Ridge	2	4	333	435296657
100004	9/4/2004	4567	1333 Burr Ridge	2	8	222	785934444
100005	9/4/2004	5678	1222 Westminster	1	4	222	785934444
100006	9/5/2004	1234	222 East Hampton	1	4	111	123456789
100007	9/6/2004	2345	9 W. Palm Beach	2	5	333	785934444
100008	9/6/2004	6789	4532 Lane Circle	1	8	222	785934444
100009	9/7/2004	1234	987 Furlong	3	8	111	123456789
100010	9/9/2004	6789	4532 Lance Circle	2	7	222	435296657
100011	9/9/2004	4567	3500 Tomahawk	5	6	222	785934444

CUSTOMER FILE

Customer Number	Customer Name	Customer Phone	Customer Primary Contact
1234	Smelding Homes	3333333333	Bill Johnson
2345	Home Builders Superior	3334444444	Marcus Connolly
3456	Mark Akey	3335555555	Mark Akey
4567	Triple A Homes	3336666666	Janielle Smith
5678	Sheryl Williamson	3337777777	Sheryl Williamson
6789	Home Makers	3338888888	John Yu

CONCRETE TYPE FILE

Concrete Type	Type Description
1	Home foundation and walkways
2	Commercial foundation and infrastructure
3	Premier speckled (concrete with pea-size smooth gravel aggregate)
4	Premier marble (concrete with crushed marble aggregate)
5	Premier shell (concrete with shell aggregate)

EMPLOYEE FILE

Employee ID	Employee Last Name	Employee First Name	Date of Hire
123456789	Johnson	Emilio	2/1/1985
435296657	Evaraz	Antonio	3/3/1992
785934444	Robertson	John	6/1/1999
984568756	Smithson	Allison	4/1/1997

TRUCK FILE

Truck Number	Truck Type	Date of Purchase
111	Ford	6/17/1999
222	Ford	12/24/2001
333	Chevy	1/1/2002

Figure 3.2

A Portion of Solomon Enterprises' Database for Customer Relationship Management and Ordering Processing know its physical location—row number and column character. With a relational database, however, you need only know the field name of the column of information (for example, *Amount*) and its logical row, not its physical row. As a result, in Solomon's database example, you could easily change the amount for an order, without having to know where that information is physically stored (by row or column).

And with spreadsheet software, you can immediately begin typing in information, creating column headings, and providing formatting. You can't do that with a database. Using a database, you must clearly define the characteristics of each field by creating a data dictionary. So, you must carefully plan the design of your database before you can start adding information.

WITH LOGICAL TIES WITHIN THE INFORMATION

In a relational database, you must create ties or relationships in the information that show how the files relate to each other. Before you can create these relationships among files, you must first specify the primary key of each file. A ***primary key*** is a field (or group of fields in some cases) that uniquely describes each record. In Solomon's database, *Order Number* is the primary key for the *Order* file and *Customer Number* is the primary key for the *Customer* file. That is to say, every order in the *Order* file must have a unique *Order Number* and every customer in the *Customer* file must have a unique *Customer Number*.

When you define that a specific field in a file is the primary key, you're also stating as well that the field cannot be blank. That is, you cannot enter the information for a new employee in the *Employee* file and leave the *Employee ID* field blank. If that were possible, you could potentially have two employees with identical primary keys (blank), which is not possible in a database environment.

Again, this is quite different from working with spreadsheets. Using a spreadsheet, it would be almost impossible to ensure that each field in a given column is unique. This reinforces the notion that, while spreadsheets work with information according to physical location, databases work with information logically.

If you look back at Figure 3.2, you can see that *Customer Number* appears in both the *Customer* and *Order* files. This creates a logical relationship between the two files and is an example of a foreign key. A ***foreign key*** is a primary key of one file that appears in another file. Now look at Figure 3.3. In it, we've provided the logical relationships among all five files. Notice, for example, that *Truck Number* is the primary key for the *Truck* file. It also appears in the *Order* file. This enables Solomon to track which trucks were used

Figure 3.3

Creating Logical Ties with Primary and Foreign Keys

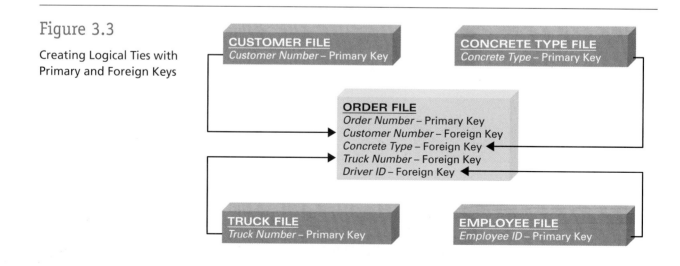

THE VALUE OF ANALYTICS? MORE EFFICIENT SUPPLY CHAIN MANAGEMENT AND MORE EFFECTIVE CUSTOMER RELATIONSHIP MANAGEMENT

The business world now understands that decisions need to be made based on verifiable data, information, business intelligence, or whatever you choose to call it. Competition is so fierce, so much is at stake, and the degrees of separation in distinguishing one competitor from another are so small that businesses cannot afford to make decisions that are not based on good, solid data.

Such is the case for Amway China, and the outcomes of its implementation of analytics demonstrate why analytics is important. Amway China ships more than 1,000 products through 229 stores, 29 home delivery centers, 22 warehouses, and a huge logistics center in Guangzhou. Annually, the company's fleet of trucks travels over 8.4 million miles, equal to circumventing the globe almost 350 times.

- **Demand prediction**—The analytics system uses time series forecasting in conjunction with data on 70 million orders placed in the previous three years. The system can even take into account regional differences for product demand.

- **Replenishment frequency**—Using data related to various transportation modes—vehicle type, cost of operation, capacity, speed, estimated maintenance and down time—the system can schedule exactly when and which products have to move from one place to another to guarantee minimum-required inventory levels.

- **Basic reporting**—The reporting capabilities of the system include being able to tailor analytics reports to the unique needs of each employee. Some reports include daily inventory management, procurement proposal analysis, inventory stock-out alarm, and transport no-load rate charges.

The net result of Amway China's analytics system? First, it has significantly cut costs related to inventory management, which of course is a primary goal of any supply chain management effort. Second, it has increased customer satisfaction to 97 percent.[6]

to deliver the various orders. So, *Truck Number* is the primary key in the *Truck* file and is also a foreign key that appears in the *Order* file. There are other examples of foreign keys as well in Figure 3.3.

Foreign keys are essential in the relational database model. Without them, you have no way of creating logical ties among the various files. As you might guess, we use these relationships extensively to create business intelligence because they enable us to track the logical relationships within many types of information.

WITH BUILT-IN INTEGRITY CONSTRAINTS

By defining the logical structure of information in a relational database, you're also developing *integrity constraints*—rules that help ensure the quality of the information. For example, by stating that *Customer Number* is the primary key of the *Customer* file and a foreign key in the *Order* file, you're saying (1) that no two customers can have the same *Customer Number* and (2) that a *Customer Number* that is entered into the *Order* file must have a matching *Customer Number* in the *Customer* file. So, as Solomon creates a new order and enters a *Customer Number* in the *Order* file, the database management system must find a corresponding and identical *Customer Number* in the *Customer* file. This makes perfect sense. You cannot create an order for a customer who does not exist.

Consumer Reports magazine has rated the Ritz-Carlton first among luxury hotels.[7] Why? It's simple: Ritz-Carlton has created a powerful guest preference database to provide customized, personal, and high-level service to guests of any of its hotels. For example, if you leave a message at a Ritz-Carlton front desk that you want the bed turned down at 9 P.M., prefer no chocolate mints on your pillow, and want to participate in the 7 A.M. aerobics class, that information is passed along to the floor maid (and others) and is also stored in the guest preference database. By assigning to you a unique customer ID that creates logical ties to your various preferences, the Ritz-Carlton transfers your information to all of its other hotels. The next time you stay in a Ritz-Carlton hotel, in Palm Beach for example, your information is already there, and the hotel staff immediately knows of your preferences.

For the management at Ritz-Carlton, achieving customer loyalty starts first with knowing each customer individually (the concept of customer relationship management). That includes your exercise habits, what you most commonly consume from the snack bar in your room, how many towels you use daily, and whether you like a chocolate on your pillow. To store and organize all this information, Ritz-Carlton uses a relational database, and employees use it to meet your needs (or whims).

Database Management System Tools

LEARNING OUTCOME 2

When working with word processing software, you create and edit a document. When working with spreadsheet software, you create and edit a workbook. The same is true in a database environment. A database is equivalent to a document or a workbook because they all contain information. And while word processing and spreadsheet are the software tools you use to work with documents and workbooks, you use database management system software to work with databases. A ***database management system (DBMS)*** helps you specify the logical organization for a database and access and use the information within a database. A DBMS contains five important software components (see Figure 3.4):

1. DBMS engine
2. Data definition subsystem
3. Data manipulation subsystem
4. Application generation subsystem
5. Data administration subsystem

The DBMS engine is perhaps the most important, yet seldom recognized, component of a DBMS. The ***DBMS engine*** accepts logical requests from the various other DBMS subsystems, converts them into their physical equivalent, and actually accesses the database and data dictionary as they exist on a storage device. Again, the distinction between logical and physical is important in a database environment. The ***physical view*** of information deals with how information is physically arranged, stored, and accessed on some type of storage device such as a hard disk. The ***logical view*** of information, on the other hand, focuses on how you as a knowledge worker need to arrange and access information to meet your particular business needs.

Databases and DBMSs provide two really great advantages in separating the logical from the physical view of information. First, the DBMS engine handles the physical tasks. So you, as a database user, can concentrate solely on your logical information needs. Second, although there is only one physical view of information, there may

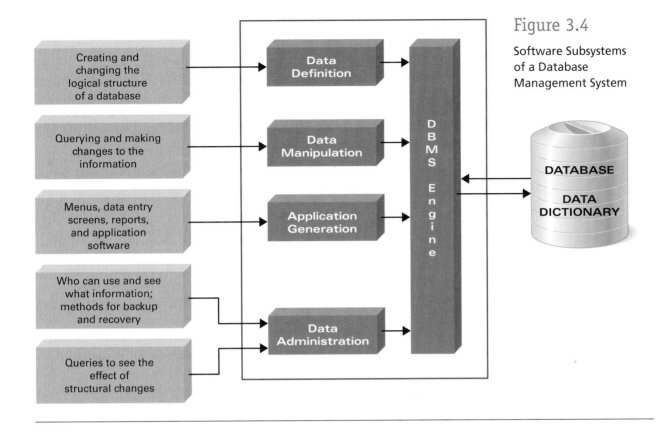

Figure 3.4

Software Subsystems
of a Database
Management System

be numerous knowledge workers who have different logical views of the information
in a database. That is, according to what business tasks they need to perform, different knowledge workers logically view information in different ways. The DBMS
engine can process virtually any logical information view or request into its physical
equivalent.

DATA DEFINITION SUBSYSTEM

The *data definition subsystem* of a DBMS helps you create and maintain the data dictionary and define the structure of the files in a database.

When you create a database, you must first use the data definition subsystem to create
the data dictionary and define the structure of the files. This is very different from using
something like spreadsheet software. When you create a workbook, you can immediately begin typing in information and creating formulas and functions. You can't do that
with a database. You must define its logical structure before you can begin typing in any
information. Typing in the information is the easy part. Defining the logical structure
is more difficult. In *Extended Learning Module C,* we take you through the process of
defining the logical structure for the supply chain management (SCM) side of Solomon
Enterprises' database. We definitely recommend that you read that module—knowing
how to define the correct structure of a database can be a substantial career opportunity
for you.

If you ever find that a certain file needs another piece of information, you have to use
the data definition subsystem to add a new field in the data dictionary. Likewise, if you
want to delete a given field for all the records in a file, you must use the data definition
subsystem to do so.

As you create the data dictionary, you're essentially defining the logical properties of the information that the database will contain. Logical structures of information include the following:

Logical Properties	Examples
Field name	*Customer Number, Order Date*
Type	Alphabetic, numeric, date, time, etc.
Form	Is an area code required for a phone number?
Default value	If no *Order Date* is entered, the default is today's date.
Validation rule	Can *Amount* exceed 8?
Is an entry required?	Must you enter *Delivery Address* for an order or can it be blank?
Can there be duplicates?	Primary keys cannot be duplicates; but what about amounts?

These are all important logical properties to a lesser or greater extent depending on the type of information you're describing. For example, a typical concrete delivery truck can hold at most eight cubic yards of concrete. Further, Solomon may not accept orders for less than four cubic yards of concrete. Therefore, an important validation rule for *Amount* in the *Order* file is "must be greater than or equal to 4 and cannot be greater than 8."

DATA MANIPULATION SUBSYSTEM

The ***data manipulation subsystem*** of a DBMS helps you add, change, and delete information in a database and query it for valuable information. Software tools within the data manipulation subsystem are most often the primary interface between you as a user and the information contained in a database. So, while the DBMS engine handles your information requests from a physical point of view, it is the data manipulation tools within a DBMS that allow you to specify your logical information requirements. Those logical information requirements are then used by the DBMS engine to access the information you need from a physical point of view.

Figure 3.5

A View in Microsoft Access

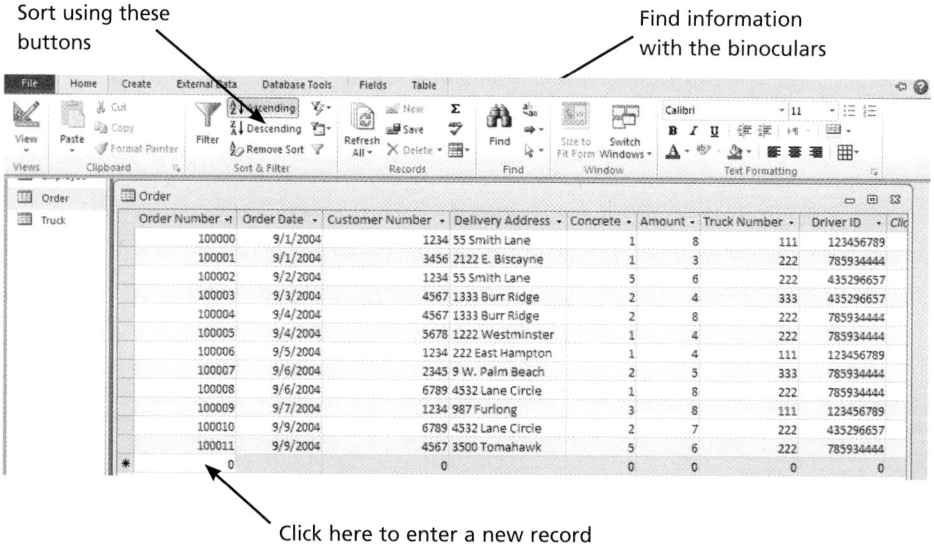

Sort using these buttons

Find information with the binoculars

Click here to enter a new record

Order Number	Order Date	Customer Number	Delivery Address	Concrete	Amount	Truck Number	Driver ID	Clie
100000	9/1/2004	1234	55 Smith Lane	1	8	111	123456789	
100001	9/1/2004	3456	2122 E. Biscayne	1	3	222	785934444	
100002	9/2/2004	1234	55 Smith Lane	5	6	222	435296657	
100003	9/3/2004	4567	1333 Burr Ridge	2	4	333	435296657	
100004	9/4/2004	4567	1333 Burr Ridge	2	8	222	785934444	
100005	9/4/2004	5678	1222 Westminster	1	4	222	785934444	
100006	9/5/2004	1234	222 East Hampton	1	4	111	123456789	
100007	9/6/2004	2345	9 W. Palm Beach	2	5	333	785934444	
100008	9/6/2004	6789	4532 Lane Circle	1	8	222	785934444	
100009	9/7/2004	1234	987 Furlong	3	8	111	123456789	
100010	9/9/2004	6789	4532 Lane Circle	2	7	222	435296657	
100011	9/9/2004	4567	3500 Tomahawk	5	6	222	785934444	
0		0		0	0	0	0	

In most DBMSs, you'll find a variety of data manipulation tools, including views, report generators, query-by-example tools, and structured query language.

VIEWS   A *view* allows you to see the contents of a database file, make whatever changes you want, perform simple sorting, and query to find the location of specific information. Views essentially provide each file in the form of a spreadsheet workbook. The screen in Figure 3.5 shows a view in Microsoft Access for the *Order* file in Solomon's database. At this point, you can click on any specific field and change its contents. You could also point at an entire record and click on the Cut icon (the scissors) to remove a record. If you want to add a record, simply click in the *Order Number* field of the first blank record and begin typing. You can also perform a variety of other functions such as sorting, searching, spell checking, and hiding columns.

REPORT GENERATORS   *Report generators* help you quickly define formats of reports and what information you want to see in a report. Once you define a report, you can view it on the screen or print it. Figure 3.6 shows two intermediate screens in Microsoft Access. The first allows you to specify which fields of information are to appear in a report. We have chosen to include *Customer Number, Order Number, Order Date,* and *Amount* from the *Order* file. The second allows you to choose from a set of predefined report formats. Following a simple and easy-to-use set of screens (including the two in Figure 3.6), we went on to specify

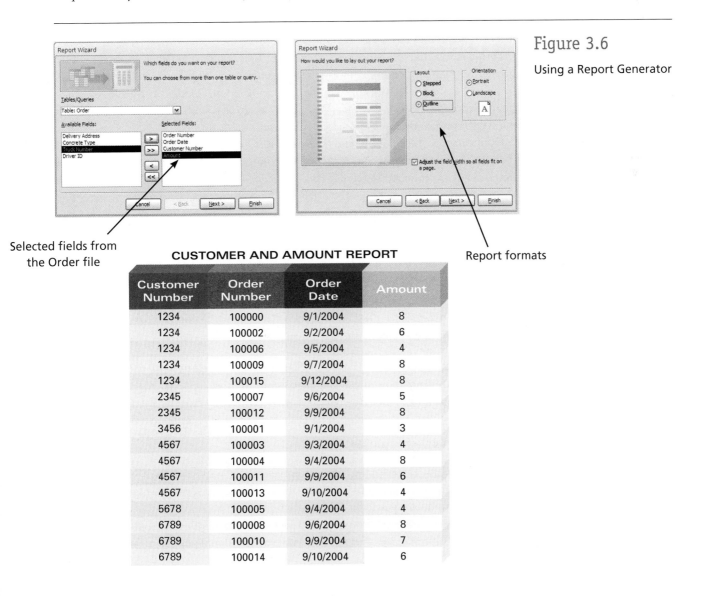

Figure 3.6

Using a Report Generator

Selected fields from the Order file

Report formats

CUSTOMER AND AMOUNT REPORT

Customer Number	Order Number	Order Date	Amount
1234	100000	9/1/2004	8
1234	100002	9/2/2004	6
1234	100006	9/5/2004	4
1234	100009	9/7/2004	8
1234	100015	9/12/2004	8
2345	100007	9/6/2004	5
2345	100012	9/9/2004	8
3456	100001	9/1/2004	3
4567	100003	9/3/2004	4
4567	100004	9/4/2004	8
4567	100011	9/9/2004	6
4567	100013	9/10/2004	4
5678	100005	9/4/2004	4
6789	100008	9/6/2004	8
6789	100010	9/9/2004	7
6789	100014	9/10/2004	6

that sorting should take place by *Customer Number* and that the name of the report should be "Customer and Amount Report." The completed report is also shown in Figure 3.6. Notice that it displays only those fields we requested, that it's sorted by *Customer Number,* and that the title is "Customer and Amount Report."

A nice feature about report generators is that you can save a report format that you use frequently. For example, if you think you'll use the report in Figure 3.6 often, you can save it by giving it a unique name. Later, you can request that report and your DBMS will generate it, using the most up-to-date information in the database. You can also choose from a variety of report formats (we chose a simple one for our illustration). And you can choose report formats that create intermediate subtotals and grand totals, which can include counts, sums, averages, and the like.

QUERY-BY-EXAMPLE TOOLS   *Query-by-example (QBE) tools* help you graphically design the answer to a question. Suppose for example that Janielle Smith from Triple A Homes (*Customer Number* 4567) has called and ordered a delivery of concrete. Although she can't remember the name of the driver, she would like to have the driver that comes out the most often to deliver concrete to Triple A Homes. Solomon's task, from a customer relationship management point of view, is to go through all the orders and determine which employee most often delivers concrete to Triple A Homes. The task may seem simple considering that Solomon currently has very few orders in its database. However, can you imagine trying to answer that question if there were thousands of orders in Solomon's database? It would not be fun.

Fortunately, QBE tools can help you answer this question and perform many other queries in a matter of seconds. In Figure 3.7, you can see a QBE screen that formulates the answer to the question. When you perform a QBE, you (1) identify the files in which the needed information is located, (2) drag any necessary fields from the identified files to the QBE grid, and (3) specify selection criteria.

For the names of employees who have delivered concrete to Triple A Homes, we identified the two files of *Order* and *Employee.* Second, we dragged *Customer Number* from the *Order* file to the QBE grid and dragged *Employee Last Name* and *Employee First Name* from the *Employee* file to the QBE grid. Finally, we specified in the Criteria box that we wanted to view only the orders for *Customer Number* 4567 (Triple A Homes). Access did the rest and provided the information in Figure 3.7.

QBEs rely heavily on the logical relationships within a database to find information. For example, *Order Number* 100004 has the *Customer Number* of 4567 (Triple A Homes). So, the QBE tool took the *Driver ID* from the *Order* file for that order and found a match in the *Employee* file. When it found a match, it presented the *Employee Last Name* and *Employee First Name* (John Robertson). Without the logical relationships being correctly defined, this QBE query would not have worked properly.

STRUCTURED QUERY LANGUAGE   *Structured query language (SQL)* is a standardized fourth-generation query language found in most DBMSs. SQL performs the same function as QBE, except that you perform the query by creating a statement instead of pointing, clicking, and dragging. The basic form of an SQL statement is

SELECT . . . FROM . . . WHERE . . .

After the SELECT, you list the fields of information you want; after the FROM, you specify what logical relationships to use; and after the WHERE, you specify any selection criteria. Thoroughly introducing you to the syntax of building SQL statements is outside the scope of this text and would easily require almost 100 pages of material. But you should be aware that SQL does exist. If you're majoring in IT or MIS, you'll undoubtedly take a course in SQL.

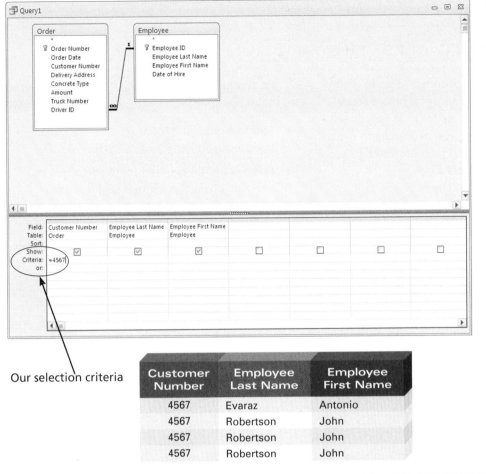

APPLICATION GENERATION SUBSYSTEM

The *application generation subsystem* of a DBMS contains facilities to help you develop transaction-intensive applications. These types of applications usually require that you perform a detailed series of tasks to process a transaction. Application generation subsystem facilities include tools for creating visually appealing and easy-to-use data entry screens, programming languages specific to a particular DBMS, and interfaces to commonly used programming languages that are independent of any DBMS.

As with SQL, application generation facilities are most often used by IT specialists. As a knowledge worker, we recommend that you leave application generation to IT specialists as much as you can. You need to focus on views, report generators, and QBE tools. These will help you find information in a database and perform queries so you can start to build and use business intelligence.

DATA ADMINISTRATION SUBSYSTEM

The *data administration subsystem* of a DBMS helps you manage the overall database environment by providing facilities for backup and recovery, security management, query optimization, concurrency control, and change management. The data administration subsystem is most often used by a data administrator or database administrator— someone responsible for

WHEN USERS BUILD APPS, THEY WILL VISIT

Cities are increasingly turning to social media to aid in economic development and make the city more accessible to vacationers. Such is the case for New York City. It recently made available to the app development community 350 public data sets and held a contest to see who could develop the most useful app.

The contest had two goals. The first was to make NYC's government agency data more accessible to the public. Data ranged from crime reports to building complaints to traffic statistics to public health. These are all open to the public but not very convenient to get to. In many instances, if you wanted this information, you had to visit city hall, complete a request form, pay some money, and then wait several weeks to receive a report by mail. The newly generated apps place the data only an app button away on your smartphone.

The second goal was to make New York City a more vibrant and desirable place to visit. That may seem a bit odd but consider some of the apps that were entered into the competition.

- **Sportaneous**—find pickup games like basketball in your surrounding area.

- **DontEat.at**—an app that sends you a text message when you check into a restaurant that has a risk of being closed because of a health violation.

- **Roadify**—an app that sends alerts about driving, bus, and subway conditions.

Each of these is useful not only to people visiting the city but also to New York City residents.

The cost of the contest? Not much actually. The team with the winning app won $10,000. But there were over 50 contest entries, so, effectively, New York City bought each app for $200.[8]

---

assuring that the database (and data warehouse) environment meets the entire information needs of an organization:

- *Backup and recovery facilities*—provide a way for you to (1) periodically back up information and (2) restart or recover a database and its information in case of a failure. A **backup** is simply a copy of the information stored on a computer. **Recovery** is the process of reinstalling the backup information in the event the information was lost. In Chapter 7, we talk specifically about how to develop plans and strategies in the event of some sort of failure. We call this business continuity planning or disaster recovery planning.

- *Security management facilities*—allow you to control who has access to what information and what type of access those people have. Always remember **CRUD**—**C**reate, **R**ead, **U**pdate, and **D**elete. Identifying who can perform those functions on various database information is vitally important.

- *Query optimization facilities*—often take queries from users (in the form of SQL statements of QBEs) and restructure them to minimize response times. Basically, these facilities find the "shortest route" to the information you want so you don't have to.

- *Reorganization facilities*—continually maintain statistics concerning how the DBMS engine physically accesses information and reorganizes how information is physically stored. For example, if you frequently access a file by a specific order, the reorganization facilities may maintain the file in that presorted order by creating an index that maintains the sorted order in that file.

- *Concurrency control facilities*—ensure the validity of database updates when multiple users attempt to access and change the same information. Consider your school's online registration system. What if you and another student try to register for a class with only one seat remaining at exactly the same time? Who gets enrolled in the class? What happens to the person who does not get his or her desired class schedule?

- *Change management facilities*—allow you to assess the impact of proposed structural changes to a database. For example, if you decide to add a character identifier to a numeric truck number, you can use the change management facilities to see how many files would be affected.

All these—backup and recovery, security management, query optimization, reorganization, concurrency control, and change management—are vitally important facilities in any DBMS and thus any database environment. As a user and knowledge worker, you probably won't deal with these facilities specifically as far as setting them up and maintaining them is concerned. But how they're set up and maintained will affect what you can do. So knowing that they exist and understanding their purpose are important.

Data Warehouses and Data Mining

Suppose as a manager at Victoria's Secret, you wanted to know the total revenues generated from the sale of shoes last month. That's a simple query, which you could easily implement using either SQL or a QBE tool. But what if you wanted to know, "By actual versus budgeted, how many size 8 shoes in black did we sell last month in the southeast and southwest regions, compared with the same month over the last five years?" That task seems almost impossible, even with the aid of technology. If you were actually able to build a QBE query for it, you would probably bring the organization's operational database environment to its knees.

This example illustrates the two primary reasons so many organizations are opting to build data warehouses in support of their analytics initiatives. First, while operational databases may have the needed information, the information is not organized in a way that lends itself to building business intelligence within the database or using various data manipulation tools. Second, if you could build such a query, your operational databases, which are probably already supporting the processing of hundreds of transactions per second, would seriously suffer in performance when you hit the Start button to perform the query.

To support such intriguing, necessary, and complex queries to create business intelligence, many organizations are building data warehouses and providing data-mining tools. A data warehouse is simply the next step (beyond databases) in the progression of building business intelligence. And data-mining tools are the tools you use to mine a data warehouse and extrapolate the business intelligence you need to make a decision, solve a problem, or capitalize on an opportunity to create a competitive advantage.

WHAT IS A DATA WAREHOUSE?

LEARNING OUTCOME 3

A *data warehouse* is a logical collection of information—gathered from many different operational databases—used to create business intelligence that supports business analysis activities and decision-making tasks. Sounds simple enough on the surface, but data warehouses represent a fundamentally different way of thinking about organizing and managing information in an organization. Consider these key features of a data warehouse, detailed in the sections that follow.

DATA WAREHOUSES ARE MULTIDIMENSIONAL   In the relational database model, information is represented in a series of two-dimensional files or tables. Not so in a data warehouse—most data warehouses are multidimensional, meaning that they contain layers of columns and rows. For this reason, most data warehouses are really *multidimensional databases.* The layers in a data warehouse represent information according to different dimensions. This multidimensional representation of information is referred to as a *hypercube.*

In Figure 3.8 you can see a hypercube that represents product information by product line and region (columns and rows), by year (the first layer), by customer segment (the second layer), and by the timing of advertising media (the third layer). Using this hypercube, you can easily ask, According to customer segment A, what percentage of total sales for product line 1 in the southwest territory occurred immediately after a radio advertising blitz? The information you would receive from that query constitutes business intelligence.

Any specific subcube within the larger hypercube can contain a variety of summarized information gathered from the various operational databases. For example, the forwardmost and top-left subcube contains information for the North territory, by year, for product line 1. So, it could contain totals, average, counts, and distributions summarizing in some way that information. Of course, what it contains is really up to you and your needs.

DATA WAREHOUSES SUPPORT DECISION MAKING, NOT TRANSACTION PROCESSING   In an organization, most databases are transaction-oriented. That is, most databases support online transaction processing (OLTP) and, therefore, are operational databases. Data warehouses are not transaction-oriented: They exist to support decision-making tasks in your organization. Therefore, data warehouses support only online analytical processing (OLAP).

Figure 3.8

A Multidimensional Data Warehouse with Information from Multiple Operational Databases

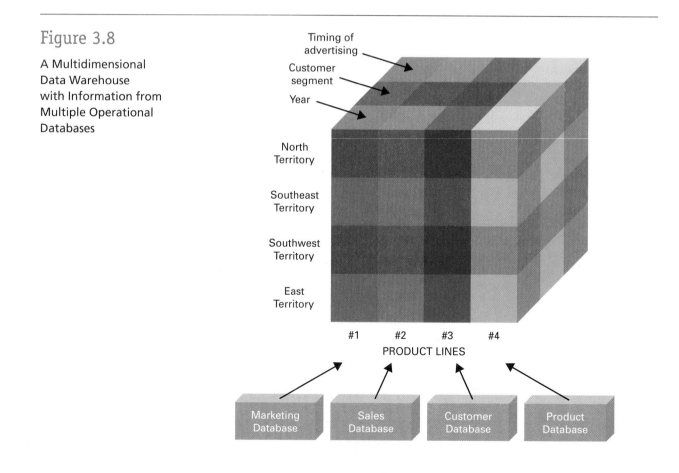

As we just stated, the subcubes within a data warehouse contain summarized information. So, while a data warehouse may contain the total sales for a year by product line, it does not contain a list of each individual sale to each individual customer for a given product line. Therefore, you simply cannot process transactions with a data warehouse. Instead, you process transactions with your operational databases and then use the information contained within the operational databases to build the summary information in a data warehouse.

THE TOOL SET OF THE ANALYTICS PROFESSIONAL

Data-mining tools are the software tools you use to query information in a data warehouse. These data-mining tools support the concept of OLAP—the manipulation of information to support decision-making tasks. Data-mining tools include query-and-reporting tools, artificial intelligence multidimensional analysis tools, digital dashboards, and statistical tools (see Figure 3.9). Essentially, data-mining tools are to data warehouse users what data manipulation subsystem tools are to database users.

QUERY-AND-REPORTING TOOLS   *Query-and-reporting tools* are similar to QBE tools, SQL, and report generators in the typical database environment. In fact, most data warehousing environments support simple and easy-to-use data manipulation subsystem tools such as QBE, SQL, and report generators. Most often, data warehouse users use these types of tools to generate simple queries and reports.

ARTIFICIAL INTELLIGENCE   Artificial intelligence includes tools such as neural networks and fuzzy logic to form the basis of "information discovery" and build business intelligence in OLAP. For example, Wall Street analyst Murray Riggiero uses OLAP software called Data/Logic, which incorporates neural networks to generate rules for his highly successful stock and bond trading system.[9] Other OLAP tools, such as Data Engine, incorporate fuzzy logic to analyze real-time technical processes.

AI represents the growing convergence of various IT tools for working with information. Today, you can find AI being used not only for OLAP in a data warehouse environment but also for searching for information on the Web. In Chapter 4, we'll explore artificial intelligence techniques such as intelligent agents and neural networks.

Figure 3.9

The Analytics Professional's Tool Set

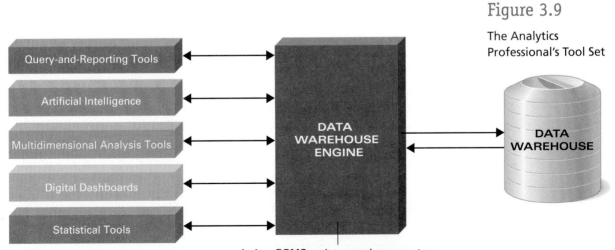

As in a DBMS, a data warehouse system has an engine responsible for converting your logical requests into their physical equivalent.

MULTIDIMENSIONAL ANALYSIS TOOLS *Multidimensional analysis (MDA) tools* are slice-and-dice techniques that allow you to view multidimensional information from different perspectives. For example, if you completed any of the recommended group projects for Chapter 1, you were using spreadsheet software to literally slice and dice the provided information. Within the context of a data warehouse, we refer to this process as "turning the cube." That is, you're essentially turning the cube to view information from different perspectives.

This turning of the cube allows you to quickly see information in different sub-cubes. If you refer back to the data warehouse in Figure 3.8, you'll notice that information by customer segment and timing of advertising is actually hidden. Using MDA tools, you can easily bring this to the front of the data warehouse for viewing. What you've essentially done is to slice the cube vertically by layer and bring some of the background layers to the front. As you do this, the values of the information are not affected.

DIGITAL DASHBOARDS A *digital dashboard* displays key information gathered from several sources on a computer screen in a format tailored to the needs and wants of an individual knowledge worker (see Figure 3.10). The key items of information are called *key performance indicators (KPIs)*, the most essential and important quantifiable measures used in analytics initiatives to monitor success of a business activity. KPIs can obviously be different for different people in the same organization. The beauty of it is that the digital dashboard is designed uniquely for each individual user. For a sales manager, key performance indicators would include measures related to sales—new contacts per month, conversions, sell-through rates, upsell percentages, and so on. To a social media manager, key performance indicators could include average number of retweets, followers on Facebook, number of complaints by customers on blogs, and so on.

Digital dashboards can also work in real time, providing minute-by-minute changes to KPI data. You can set a digital dashboard to send you a text or e-mail message if a certain key performance indicator falls below a certain level. While digital dashboards certainly won't tell you what action to take, they can and do alert you to the presence of opportunities and problems.

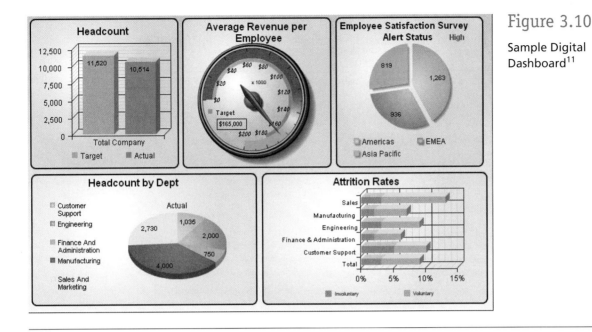

Figure 3.10

Sample Digital
Dashboard[11]

STATISTICAL TOOLS   Statistical tools help you apply various mathematical models to the information stored in a data warehouse to discover new information. For example, you can perform a time-series analysis to project future trends. You can also perform a regression analysis to determine the effect of one variable on another.

Sega of America, one of the largest publishers of video games, uses a data warehouse and statistical tools to effectively distribute its advertising budget of more than $50 million a year.[12,13] With its data warehouse, product line specialists and marketing strategists "drill" into trends of each retail store chain. Their goal is to find buying trends that will help them better determine which advertising strategies are working best (and at what time of the year) and how to reallocate advertising resources by media, territory, and time. Sega definitely benefits from its data warehouse, and so do retailers such as Toys "Я" Us, Walmart, and Sears—all good examples of customer relationship management through technology.

THE ANALYTICS LIFE CYCLE

Creating a culture of analytics in an organization doesn't happen overnight. Decision makers must buy into the fact that they need hard-core data to make the right decisions. But it doesn't end there. Now, an analytics professional must design and implement an analytics system that provides the decision maker with the information he/she needs.

Let's consider that you're the analytics professional and a key decision maker needs a series of analytics reports. To create this, you would follow the steps in Figure 3.11 on the next page. First, you would interview the decision maker to determine what key performance indicators need to be present in the reports. You would ask about preference of different types of graphs or tables and perhaps even the most suitable colors. Equipped with the analytics requirements, you would then set out to find the data needed to generate the KPIs. The data could be located internally in operational databases such as financial and manufacturing data. You may also need external data such as demographics and perhaps even economic data provided by the government.

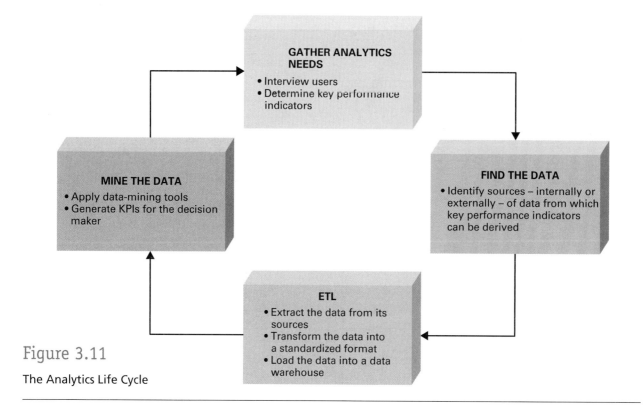

Figure 3.11

The Analytics Life Cycle

Third, you would have to execute a process known as ETL. ***ETL (extraction, transformation, and loading)*** is a three-step process that includes:

1. Extracting needed data from its sources.
2. Transforming the data into a standardized format.
3. Loading the transformed data into a data warehouse.

Finally, you would apply whatever data-mining tools are necessary to generate the analytics reports. You would want to write some basic software to generate the analytics reports, so that the software could be run by the decision maker any time he/she wanted an updated report with new KPI data.

DATA MARTS: SMALLER DATA WAREHOUSES

Data warehouses are often perceived as organizationwide, containing summaries of all the information that an organization tracks. However, some people need access to only a portion of that data warehouse information as opposed to all of it. In this case, an organization can create one or more data marts. A ***data mart*** is a subset of a data warehouse in which only a focused portion of the data warehouse information is kept (see Figure 3.12).

Lands' End first created an organizationwide data warehouse for everyone to use, but soon found out that there can be "too much of a good thing."[14] In fact, many Lands' End employees wouldn't use the data warehouse because it was simply too big, too complicated, and included information they didn't need access to. So, Lands' End created several smaller data marts. For example, Lands' End created a data mart just for the merchandising department. That data mart contains only merchandising-specific information and not any information, for instance, that would be unique to the finance department.

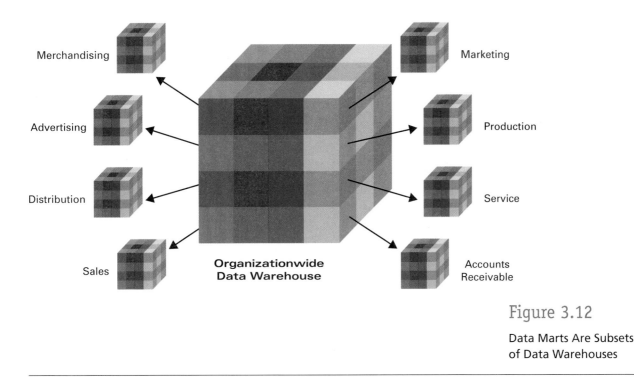

Figure 3.12

Data Marts Are Subsets
of Data Warehouses

Because of the smaller, more manageable data marts, knowledge workers at Lands'
End are making better use of information. If some of your employees don't need access
to organizationwide data warehouse information, consider building a smaller data mart
for their particular needs.

If you do choose to build smaller data marts for your employees, the data-mining
tools are the same. That is, data marts support the use of query-and-reporting tools,
AI, multidimensional analysis tools, digital dashboards, and statistical tools. This yields
efficiency in an organization with respect to training. Once you've trained your employees to use any or all data-mining tools, they can apply them to an organizationwide data
warehouse or smaller data marts.

IMPORTANT CONSIDERATIONS IN USING A DATA WAREHOUSE

As is true with all types of technology, you can't simply implement a data warehouse and
use data-mining tools just because they're a "hot" set of technologies and expect automatically to increase your efficiency and effectiveness. Always let your business needs
drive your technology decisions. You have to need the technology and the technology
has to fit your needs. With respect to data warehouse and data-mining tools, consider
your answers to the following questions.

1. **Do you need a data warehouse?** Although great IT tools, they are not
   necessarily the best technologies for all businesses because (1) they are
   expensive, (2) they may not be necessary since some businesses can easily extract
   all the business intelligence they need from databases, and (3) they require
   extensive and often expensive support.

2. **Do all your employees need an entire data warehouse?** If not, consider
   building data marts.

3. **How up-to-date must the information be?** To create a data warehouse, you take "snapshots" of database information and load it into a data warehouse. If crucial information changes every second, this may not be possible.

4. **What data-mining tools do you need?** User needs should always drive the answer to this question. Whichever you choose, training will be key. If your users can fully exploit all the features of their chosen data-mining tools, your entire organization will reap the benefits.

Information Ownership

Your organization will be successful, in part, because of your ability to organize and manage information in a way that best moves the organization toward its goals. As we close this chapter, let's look at the notion of *information ownership* and what it means.

LEARNING OUTCOME 5

STRATEGIC MANAGEMENT SUPPORT

Technology and information are valuable organizational resources, just like all other resources in an organization. And just as an organization typically has a CFO (chief financial officer) to oversee the financial well-being of the organization, there are several C-level positions associated with technology and information. Some of these include:

- *CIO (chief information officer)*—responsible for overseeing every aspect of an organization's information resource.
- *CTO (chief technology officer)*—responsible for overseeing both the underlying IT infrastructure within an organization and the user-facing technologies (such as CRM systems).
- *CSO (chief security officer)*—responsible for the technical aspects of ensuring the security of information such as the development and use of firewalls, intranets, extranets, and anti-virus software.
- *CPO (chief privacy officer)*—responsible for ensuring that information is used in an ethical way and that only the right people have access to certain types of information such as financial records, payroll, and health care.

All these C-level positions are strategic in nature. At the tactical level, you will find an additional two important functions or positions that oversee technology and information: data administration and database administration.

Data administration is the function in an organization that plans for, oversees the development of, and monitors the information resource. This function must be completely in tune with the strategic direction of the organization to assure that all information requirements can be and are being met. *Database administration* is the function in an organization that is responsible for the more technical and operational aspects of managing the information contained in organizational information repositories (databases, data warehouses, and data marts). Database administration functions include defining and organizing database structures and contents, developing security procedures (in concert with the CSO), and approving and monitoring the development of database and database applications.

In large organizations, both of these administrative functions are usually handled by steering committees rather than by a single individual. These steering committees are responsible for their respective functions and for reporting to the CIO.

DR PEPPER SNAPPLE GROUP RELIES ON INFORMATION AND ANALYTICS TO BE COMPETITIVE

In the highly competitive beverage industry, you can't afford to make a bad decision, run at less than peak efficiency, or miss a production mark by even a single percent. Dr Pepper Snapple Group knows that very well but is also challenged by it on a daily basis. The company manufactures and distributes over 50 brands of soft drinks, juices, teas, mixes, and other beverages. The company employs some 20,000 employees spread throughout 24 manufacturing centers and more than 200 distribution centers in North America. Annual revenues are in excess $6 billion.

To organize all its information and create and disseminate business intelligence throughout the company for decision making, Dr Pepper Snapple uses IBM Cognos software, some of the best analytics software on the market today. With it, Dr Pepper Snapple has been able to:

- Provide better insight in to production and operations.

- Make information easily accessible.
- Identify manufacturing inefficiencies.
- Generate richer business intelligence to support all decision-making activities.
- Prioritize investments.
- Foster a culture of continuous improvement.

With its readily available information and BI, plant managers can monitor production volumes and inefficiencies and make corrective decisions in near real-time. According to Craig Sindorf, BI Manager of Supply Chain at Dr Pepper Snapple, "When it comes to manufacturing, it all comes down to cost. For us, the main goal is to reduce cost per case. So you've got to find every feature, everything that goes into what it costs to make your product, and then start being able to nail down where you're losing money, because waste just doesn't work."[15]

SHARING INFORMATION WITH RESPONSIBILITY

Information sharing in your organization means that anyone—regardless of title or department—can access and use whatever information he or she needs. But information sharing brings to light an important question: Does anyone in your organization *own* the information? In other words, if everyone shares the information, who is ultimately responsible for providing the information and assuring the quality of the information? Information ownership is a key consideration in today's information-based business environment. Someone must accept full responsibility for providing specific pieces of information and ensuring the quality of that information. If you find the wrong information is stored in the organization's data warehouse, you must be able to determine the source of the problem and whose responsibility it is.

INFORMATION CLEANLINESS

Information "cleanliness" (an aspect of information ownership) is an important topic today and will be for many years. Have you ever received the same piece of advertising mail (snail mail, that is) multiple times from the same company on the same day? Many people have, and it's an example of "unclean" information. The reason may be your name may appear twice in a database, once with your middle initial and once without it. Or your name may appear twice in a database with two different spellings of your last name.

In all popular business-oriented DBMSs, such as Oracle, you can find utilities to help you "clean" your information. In the case of having your information twice in a database with two different spellings of your last name, the utility would probably determine that the two records actually belong to the same person (you) because of the identical nature of other associated information such as your address and phone number. Always remember GIGO—garbage in, garbage out (from Chapter 1). If bad information—such as duplicate records for the same customer—goes into the decision-making process, you can rest assured that the decision outcome will not be optimal.

■ SUMMARY: STUDENT LEARNING OUTCOMES REVISITED

1. **List and describe the key characteristics of a relational database.** The *relational database* model uses a series of logically related two-dimensional tables or files to store information in the form of a database. Key characteristics include

   - A collection of information—Composed of many files or tables of information that are related to each other
   - Contain logical structures—You care only about the logical information and not about how it's physically stored or where it's physically located
   - Have logical ties among the information—All the files in a database are related in that some *primary keys* of certain files appear as *foreign keys* in others
   - Possess built-in *integrity constraints*—When creating the data dictionary for a database, you can specify rules by which the information must be entered (e.g., not blank, etc.)

2. **Define the five software components of a database management system.** The five software components of a database management system include

   - *DBMS engine*—Accepts logical requests from the various other DBMS subsystems, converts them into their physical equivalent, and actually accesses the database and data dictionary as they exist on a storage device
   - *Data definition subsystem*—Helps you create and maintain the data dictionary and define the structure of the files in a database
   - *Data manipulation subsystem*—Helps you add, change, and delete information in a database and query it for valuable information
   - *Application generation subsystem*—Contains facilities to help you develop transaction-intensive applications
   - *Data administration subsystem*—Helps you manage the overall database environment by providing facilities for backup and recovery, security management, query optimization, concurrency control, and change management

3. **List and describe the key characteristics of a data warehouse.** The key characteristics of a data warehouse include

   - Multidimensional—While databases store information in two-dimensional tables, data warehouses include layers to represent information according to different dimensions

- Support decision making—Data warehouses, because they contain summarized information, support business activities and decision-making tasks, not transaction processing

4. **Define the five major types of data-mining tools in a data warehouse environment.** The four major types of data-mining tools in a data warehouse environment include

- *Query-and-reporting tools*—Similar to QBE tools, SQL, and report generators in the typical database environment
- **Artificial intelligence**—Tools such as neural networks and fuzzy logic to form the basis of "information discovery" and building business intelligence in OLAP
- *Multidimensional analysis (MDA) tools*—Slice-and-dice techniques that allow you to view multidimensional information from different perspectives
- *Digital dashboard*—Displays key information gathered from several sources on a computer screen
- **Statistical tools**—Help you apply various mathematical models to the information stored in a data warehouse to discover new information

5. **List key considerations in information ownership in an organization.** Key considerations in information ownership in an organization include:

- Strategic management support
- The sharing of information with responsibility
- Information cleanliness

CLOSING CASE STUDY ONE

When Making a Database of Public Information Available to the Public Can Be Bad

You can find an app for just about anything you want. Many of them are focused on helping drivers on the road—directions, reviews of local entertainment venues, and so on. But in early 2011 a wave of apps aimed at helping drivers avoid law enforcement checkpoints were made available in the iPhone, Blackberry, and Android markets. Some were free, some cost the standard 99 cents, and a few even cost upwards of $100 for a lifetime subscription. A few of the more popular ones included:

- Cobra's iRadar, which connects to an iPhone.
- Trapster, which relies on a database of information supplied by other drivers.
- Fuzz Alert, which works with iPhones and iPads.
- PhantomAlert, an online database that drivers download to their GPS devices and smartphones.

What had many people concerned was that most of these apps included information for DUI checkpoints. When nearing a DUI checkpoint contained in the database, the device (smartphone, GPS device, or iPad) would provide an audible alert so the driver could find an alternate route. According to Capt. Paul Starks of the Montgomery County Police Department, "If people are going to use those, what other purpose are they going to use them for except to drink and drive? They're only thinking of one consequence, and that's not being arrested. They're not thinking of ending the lives of other motorists, pedestrians, other passengers in their cars or themselves."

Several lawmakers jumped on the checkpoint-app-bashing bandwagon as well. In a letter to Apple, Research In Motion, and Google, Senators Harry Reid, Charles Schumer, Frank Lautenberg, and Tom Udall wrote, "We know that your companies share our desire to end the scourge of drunk driving, and we therefore ask you to remove these applications from your store unless they are altered to remove the DUI/DWI checkpoint functionality." The senators went on to explain, "One application contains a database of DUI checkpoints updated in real-time. Another application, with more than 10 million users, also allows users to alert each other to DUI checkpoints in real-time. We appreciate the technology that has allowed millions of Americans to have information at their fingertips, but giving drunk drivers a free tool to evade checkpoints, putting families and children at risk, is a matter of public concern."

These checkpoint apps use huge databases of information (supplied by both users and law enforcement agencies) to inform drivers of DUI checkpoints, speed traps, and red-light camera programs. Most people agree that the DUI checkpoint feature should be disabled, but there are mixed feelings regarding information on speed traps and red-light camera programs. According to Officer Brian Walters, who operates a red-light camera program in Virginia Beach, "I'm all for them. A couple of GPS companies have sent me requests to verify and validate where our cameras are. I helped them. If that's what gets them to comply, that's fine."

In early summer 2011, Research In Motion pulled all the checkpoint apps from its market for the Blackberry smartphone. Apple and Google, however, did not. Instead, Apple released a new policy stating: "Apps which contain DUI checkpoints that are not published by law enforcement agencies, or encourage and enable drunk driving, will be rejected." But the policy only restricts future checkpoint apps; checkpoint apps

currently in Apple's market will remain. In response, Senator Charles Schumer explained, "This victory will remain only half-won until the existing apps are removed from the store."[16, 17, 18]

Questions

1. Let's separate the two issues. First, law enforcement agencies frequently publish the location of red-light camera programs and speed traps. Should that published information be made available through an app to help drivers avoid getting a ticket? Why or why not?
2. Second, let's consider location information for DUI checkpoints. If law enforcement agencies publish this information, is it okay to have an app for drivers? Why or why not? If law enforcement agencies do not publish DUI checkpoint information, is it okay to have an app that alerts drivers to those locations? Why or why not?
3. Many people believe that drivers should not use a smartphone at all, even for making phone calls, while operating a vehicle. What kind of potential danger does this added distraction create? How often do you drive and use your phone? For what purpose do you use your phone?
4. Isn't the sharing of information, such as the location of a DUI checkpoint, protected freedom of speech by the Constitution? Can the government really create laws to prohibit this? On the other hand, is it ethical for drivers to share this type of information so that a drunk driver can avoid being caught?

CLOSING CASE STUDY TWO

When Making a Database of Private and Company-Strategic Information Available to the Public Can Be Good

In the previous case study, we considered the publishing of publicly available information and how it might potentially be "bad" for society. Let's now consider the extreme opposite, that of an organization opening its private database of its most strategic and sensitive

information and intellectual property and how such an act can be "good" for society.

In operational databases and other data repositories, an organization guards its most sensitive and strategic information. Most organizations don't even want other organizations to see the detailed list of transactions stored in a sales database. In other types of data repositories, organizations store intellectual capital such as best practices, patents, and trademarks. These are certainly considered proprietary. Such is the case in the pharmaceutical industry in which "knowledge" regarding chemical compounds, how to combine them, and the interaction effects of the combinations can create billions of dollars of revenue streams for a pharmaceutical company.

It may take years to find the right chemical compound to treat or cure a disease. Further, pharmaceutical companies spend even more years thoroughly testing the compound before the Food and Drug Administration (FDA) will approve its release to the public. And, unfortunately, the cures for some diseases simply aren't profitable, like malaria. Malaria is called a *neglected disease* because it exists primarily only in third-world countries where people can't pay enough for the cure to create a return on investment for the pharmaceutical company. So, pharmaceutical companies focus their efforts on cures for other diseases and have neglected malaria, for instance.

GlaxoSmithKline knows that the cure for malaria won't generate billions of dollars in return on investment, but it does believe that it probably has the cure for malaria buried somewhere within its vast intellectual property. It simply doesn't have the human capacity to sift through all its compounds, use a trial-and-error process to see what yields favorable results, and then spend the years in testing.

So, Glaxo has decided to make publicly available its intellectual capital on 13,500 compounds that may be capable of inhibiting the parasite that causes malaria. Researchers from all over the world can use Glaxo's intellectual property to move through the tedious and long trial-and-error process in search of the cure for malaria. Glaxo has even created a way for researchers to upload their own information on chemical compounds to share with other researchers. Further, Glaxo has stated that it won't seek any patent rights on chemical compounds that may produce the cure.

This is a form of *crowdsourcing*, which you read about in previous chapters. Glaxo realizes that thousands of volunteers working with its data will most likely find a cure before its own in-house researchers could. According to Nick Cammack, head of Glaxo's Medicines Development Campus in Spain, other researchers ". . . may look at these structures in a quite different way and see something that we don't." Glaxo also has an obligation to its shareholders; it can't afford to spend potentially hundreds of millions of dollars to find a cure, knowing all along that the cure will never provide the necessary return on investment, but perhaps opening its database fulfills an ethical obligation.[19]

Questions

1. What is your first reaction to Glaxo's approach to finding a cure for malaria? Is it a legitimate initiative or simply a smoke-and-mirrors marketing ploy to get the public to believe that it cares about so-called neglected diseases in third-world countries?
2. What role could a social media tool like Facebook play in supporting this initiative? What information could Glaxo and the volunteer researchers share on Facebook to speed up the process of finding a cure for malaria?
3. Search the Web and find at least two sites at which you can participate in "saving the world" through some sort of crowdsourcing initiative. What sites did you find? Who sponsors the sites? What is the "save the world" focus?
4. What role can analytics play in facilitating this type of research? What "intelligence" would be important to capture and share with everyone? What sort of information regarding the 13,500 available compounds could be displayed in a digital dashboard?

■ KEY TERMS AND CONCEPTS

Analytics, 66
Application generation subsystem, 77
Backup, 78
Business intelligence (BI), 66
Chief information officer (CIO), 86
Chief privacy officer (CPO), 86

■ SHORT-ANSWER QUESTIONS

1. What is business intelligence? Why is it more than just information?
2. What is online transaction processing (OLTP)?
3. What is online analytical processing (OLAP)?
4. What is the most popular database model?
5. How are primary and foreign keys different?
6. What are the five important software components of a database management system?
7. How are QBE tools and SQL similar? How are they different?
8. What is a data warehouse? How does it differ from a database?
9. What are the five major types of data-mining tools?
10. What is a data mart? How is it similar to a data warehouse?

■ ASSIGNMENTS AND EXERCISES

1. **FINDING "HACKED" DATABASES** *The Happy Hacker* (www.happyhacker.org/) is a Web site devoted to "hacking"—breaking into computer systems. When people hack into a system, they often go after information in databases. There, they can find credit card information and other private and sensitive information. Sometimes, they can even find designs of yet-to-be-released products and other strategic information about a company. Connect to *The Happy Hacker* Web site and find an article that discusses a database that was hacked. Prepare a short report for your class detailing the incident.

2. **DEFINING QUERIES FOR A VIDEO RENTAL STORE** Consider your local video rental store. It certainly has an operational database to support its online transaction processing

   (OLTP). The operational database supports such things as adding new customers, renting videos (obviously), ordering videos, and a host of other activities. Now, assume that the video rental store also uses that same database for online analytical processing (OLAP) in the form of creating queries to extract meaningful information. If you were the manager of the video rental store, what kinds of queries would you build? What answers are you hoping to find?

3. **CREATING A QUERY** On the Web site that supports this text (www.mhhe.com/haag, choose Chapter 3 and then Solomon Enterprises), we've provided the database (in Microsoft Access) we illustrated in this chapter. Connect to the text's Web site and download that database. Now, create three queries using

the QBE tool. The first one should extract information from only one file (your choice). The second one should extract information found in at least two files. The third should include some sort of selection criteria. How easy or difficult was it to perform these three queries? Would you say that a DBMS is just as easy to use as something like word processing or spreadsheet software? Why or why not? (By the way, *Extended Learning Module J* takes you through the step-by-step process of creating a query in Access.)

4. **CAREER OPPORTUNITIES IN YOUR MAJOR**
Knowledge workers throughout the business world are building their own desktop databases (often called end-user databases or knowledge worker databases). To do so, they must understand both how to design a database and how to use a desktop DBMS such as Microsoft Access or FileMaker (made by FileMaker). The ability to design a database and use a desktop DBMS offers you a great career advantage. Research your chosen major by looking at job postings (the Web is the best place to start). How many of those jobs want you to have some database knowledge? Do they list a specific DBMS package? What's your take—should you expand your education and learn more about databases and DBMSs? Why or why not?

5. **SALARIES FOR DATABASE ADMINISTRATORS**
Database administrators (DBAs) are among the highest paid professionals in the information technology field. Many people work for 10 to 20 years to get a promotion to DBA. Connect to Monster.com (www.monster.com) or another job database of your choice and search for DBA job openings. As you do, select all locations and job categories and then use "dba" as the keyword search criteria. How many DBA job postings did you find? In what industries were some of the DBA job openings? Read through a couple of the job postings. What was the listed salary range (if any)? What sort of qualifications were listed?

6. **HOW UP-TO-DATE SHOULD DATA WAREHOUSE INFORMATION BE?**
Information timeliness is a must in a data warehouse—old and obsolete information leads to poor decision making. Below is a list of decision-making processes that people go through for different business environments. For each, specify whether the information in the data warehouse should be updated monthly, weekly, daily, or by the minute. Be prepared to justify your decision.
   a. To adjust classes sizes in a university registration environment.
   b. To alert people to changes in weather conditions.
   c. To predict scores of professional football games.
   d. To adjust radio advertisements in light of demographic changes.
   e. To monitor the success of a new product line in the clothing retail industry.
   f. To adjust production levels of food in a cafeteria.
   g. To switch jobs to various printers in a network.
   h. To adjust CD rates in a bank.
   i. To adjust forecasted demands for tires in an auto parts store.

■ DISCUSSION QUESTIONS

1. Databases and data warehouses clearly make it easier for people to access all kinds of information. This will lead to great debates in the area of privacy. Should organizations be left to police themselves with respect to providing access to information or should the government impose privacy legislation? Answer this question with respect to (1) customer information shared by organizations, (2) employee information shared within a specific organization, and (3) business information available to customers.

2. Business intelligence sounds like a fancy term with a lot of competitive advantage potentially rolled into it. What sort of business intelligence does your school need? Specifically, what business intelligence would it need to predict enrollments in the coming years? What business intelligence would it need to determine what curriculums to offer? Do you

think your school gathers and uses this kind of business intelligence? Why or why not?

3. Consider your school's registration database that enforces the following integrity constraint: to enroll in a given class, the student must have completed or currently be enrolled in the listed prerequisite (if any). Your school, in fact, probably does have that integrity constraint in place. How can you get around that integrity constraint and enroll in a class for which you are not taking nor have completed the prerequisite? Is this an instance of when you should be able to override an integrity constraint? What are the downsides to being able to do so?

4. In this chapter, we listed the five important software components of a DBMS: the DBMS engine, the data definition, data manipulation, application generation, and data administration subsystems. Which of those are most and least important to users of a database? Which of those are most and least important to technology specialists who develop data applications? Which of those are most and least important to the chief information officer (CIO)? For each of your responses, provide justification.

5. Some people used to believe that data warehouses would quickly replace databases for both online transaction processing (OLTP) and online analytical processing (OLAP). Of course, they were wrong. Why can data warehouses not replace databases and become

"operational data warehouses"? How radically would data warehouses (and their data-mining tools) have to change to become a viable replacement for databases? Would they then essentially become databases that simply supported OLAP? Why or why not?

6. Consider that you work in the human resources management department of a local business and that many of your friends work there. Although you don't personally generate payroll checks, you still have the ability to look up anyone's pay. Would you check on your friends to see if they're earning more money than you? For that matter, would you look up their pay just out of simple curiosity, knowing that you would never do anything with the information or share it with anyone else? Why or why not? People working at the Internal Revenue Service (IRS) were caught just curiously looking up the reported incomes of movie stars and other high-profile public figures. Is this acceptable? Why or why not?

7. In spite of the need for "clean" information, many organizations have databases with duplicate records for you. You've probably experienced the consequences of this by receiving two identical pieces of junk mail from the same company. One record in the database may have your middle initial while the other doesn't, or there is some other type of minor discrepancy. Why would some organizations intentionally *not* go through a process of cleaning their database information?

■ CHAPTER PROJECTS

GROUP PROJECTS

E-COMMERCE PROJECTS

CHAPTER FOUR OUTLINE

STUDENT LEARNING OUTCOMES

1. Compare and contrast decision support systems and geographic information systems.
2. Describe the decision support role of specialized analytics like predictive analytics and text analytics.
3. Describe the role and function of an expert system in analytics.
4. Explain why neural networks are effective decision support tools.
5. Define genetic algorithms and the types of problems they help solve.
6. Describe data-mining agents and multi-agent systems as subsets of intelligent agents and agent-based technologies.

PERSPECTIVES

WEB SUPPORT

www.mhhe.com/haag

- Best in computer statistics and resources
- Consumer information
- Meta data
- Bureau of Labor and Statistics
- Demographics
- Exploring Google Earth
- Gold, silver, interest rates, and money
- Learning about investing
- Stock quotes

SUPPORTING MODULES

XLM/D Decision Analysis with Spreadsheet Software
Extended Learning Module D provides hands-on instructions concerning how to use many of the powerful decision support features of Excel including Basic Filter, Custom Filter, conditional formatting, and pivot tables (in both two and three dimensions). Each of these takes only minutes to learn and requires just a few clicks.

XLM/M Programming in Excel with VBA
Extended Learning Module M covers the basics of learning how to write macros (short programs) in Excel using VBA, Visual Basic for Applications. It covers how to use the Visual Basic Editor (VBE), how to use the macro recorder, and how to write procedures, functions, if-then structures, and loops.

CHAPTER FOUR

Analytics, Decision Support, and Artificial Intelligence
Brainpower for Your Business

OUTRAGEOUS INDUSTRY TRANSFORMATION: ONLINE LEARNING

You may very well be an active participant in this outrageous industry transformation. It's going on in the education industry, specifically higher or post-secondary education. There are actually quite a few transformations occurring in this industry, like textbooks going digital, but our focus right now is on those of you who are taking courses online.

It goes by numerous different terms—distance learning, online learning, virtual learning, etc. If you are taking a course partially face-to-face and partially online, then it's probably called hybrid or blended learning. Regardless, more and more students every year are opting to take online courses. Review the accompanying graph. Notice that overall total enrollment has been growing at a rate of somewhere between 1.2 and 2 percent per year.

Online enrollment has been growing at a rapid annual rate, somewhere between approximately 10 percent (from 2005 to 2006) to almost 37 percent (from 2004 to 2005). You can't say the same for non-online enrollment. It had a positive annual growth in only one year, about 0.01 percent from 2003 to 2004. Other than that, it's been declining every year, with the largest decline of 4.25 percent occurring from 2004 to 2005.

So, what does this mean for today's traditional (i.e., non-online) higher education institution? A couple of thoughts come to mind. The first is that many traditional institutions are beginning to offer online courses, perhaps not full programs online but certainly some courses and certainly many blended or hybrid courses. The second thought is in regard to physical building space. Higher education institutions have huge investments in infrastructure, that is, classroom space. As more students opt for online courses, what will happen to that very expensive space? Will much of it be needed anymore? How will colleges and universities attempt to use their space for other revenue-generating activities to offset their costs? Will the lessening need for classroom space encourage even more online competitors to enter the education market?[1]

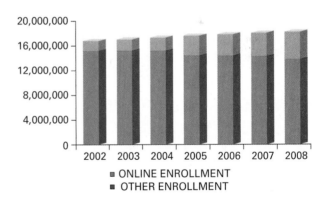

- ONLINE ENROLLMENT
- OTHER ENROLLMENT

Questions

1. Have you taken or are you currently taking an online course? Was it, or is it, fully online, or a hybrid course?

2. What are the major reasons why students opt to take online courses over traditional classroom courses?

3. To what extent do you believe this transformation is occurring at the K–12 level?

Introduction

Decision making is crucial to business. Using all forms of intellectual assets—basic data, information, business intelligence, knowledge—decision makers in the business world ponder "make-or-break" decisions. Some are responding to changes in customer demographics (customer relationship management); others are considering the trade-offs of using low-cost suppliers as compared to higher-cost suppliers that deliver fewer defective products in faster time (supply chain management); still others are attempting to determine the best overall strategy for the organization. Does the organization position itself for overall cost leadership, differentiation, or focus? How does the organization combat an abundance of e-commerce businesses on the Web offering the same products and services (i.e., buyer power)? The stream of decisions to be faced is endless. According to *Management Review,* the big winners in tomorrow's business race will be those organizations that are "big of brain and small of mass."[2]

That's why the field of analytics is becoming so important in the business world. In this chapter, we want to build upon the learning from Chapter 3. That chapter started with your developing a basic understanding of databases and how organizations manage the information asset. We then moved into data warehouses and data-mining tools, your first real introduction to the world of analytics. And there's much more analytics to cover. Of course, we certainly can't cover the remainder of the entire analytics field in a single chapter, but we will touch on some of the more important and high-profile analytics tools (see Figure 4.1).

Decisions and Decision Support

To develop a true appreciation for and understanding of the role of analytics, it's helpful to first understand how we go about making decisions.

DECISIONS

In business, decision making has four distinct phases, as proposed by Herbert Simon (see Figure 4.2).[3] These four phases are:

1. ***Intelligence*** (find what to fix): Find or recognize a problem, need, or opportunity (also called the *diagnostic phase* of decision making). The intelligence phase involves detecting and interpreting signs that indicate a situation which needs

---

Figure 4.1

Our Focus in This Chapter

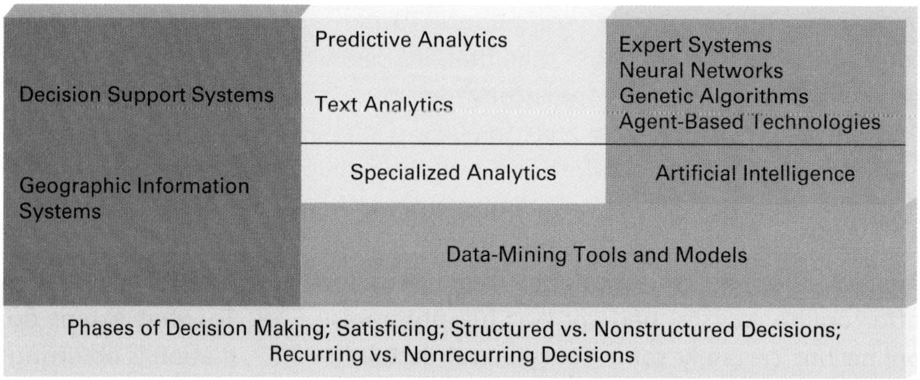

Decision Support Systems	Predictive Analytics	Expert Systems
	Text Analytics	Neural Networks
		Genetic Algorithms
		Agent-Based Technologies
Geographic Information Systems	Specialized Analytics	Artificial Intelligence
Data-Mining Tools and Models
Phases of Decision Making; Satisficing; Structured vs. Nonstructured Decisions; Recurring vs. Nonrecurring Decisions

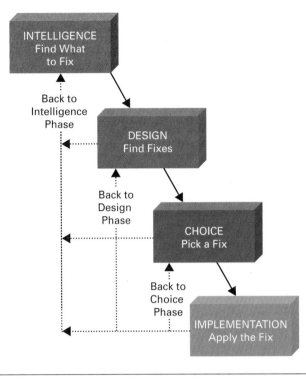

Figure 4.2

Four Phases of Decision Making

your attention. These "signs" come in many forms: consistent customer requests for new product features, the threat of new competition, declining sales, rising costs, an offer from a company to handle your distribution needs, and so on. "Detecting and interpreting signs" is achieved primarily by using various analytics tools to gather information and then convert it into business intelligence, perhaps by combining multiple sets of information or slicing and dicing your way through a data warehouse.

2. **Design** (find fixes): Consider possible ways of solving the problem, filling the need, or taking advantage of the opportunity. In this phase, you develop all the possible solutions you can. Here again, you can use analytics tools to build models of numerous proposed solutions. These models—like break-even analysis which we covered in Chapter 1—allow you to create many solutions "on paper." In this way, you can review the outcomes of proposed solutions without having to implement them.

3. **Choice** (pick a fix): Examine and weigh the merits of each solution, estimate the consequences of each, and choose the best one (which may be to do nothing at all). The "best" solution may depend on such factors as cost, ease of implementation, staffing requirements, and timing. This is the *prescriptive phase* of decision making—it's the stage at which a course of action is prescribed. Analytics still plays a role here, by allowing you to perhaps build a spreadsheet that shows the outcomes of each solution and rank orders them according to whatever criteria you choose.

4. **Implementation** (apply the fix): Carry out the chosen solution, monitor the results, and make adjustments as necessary. Simply implementing a solution is seldom enough. Your chosen solution will always need fine-tuning, especially for complex problems or changing environments. Here, analytics takes on the role of quality control, allowing you to gather information regarding your solution to ensure that it's staying on target.

This four-phase process is not necessarily linear: You'll often find it useful or necessary to cycle back to an earlier phase. When choosing an alternative in the choice phase, for example, you might become aware of another possible solution. Then you would go back to the design phase, include the newly found solution, return to the choice phase, and compare the new solution to the others you generated.

A second model of decision making, also proposed by Simon, is *satisficing*, which differs from the four-phase process. **Satisficing** is making a choice that meets your needs and is satisfactory without necessarily being the best possible choice available. Organizations in the private and public sectors are "satisficing" all the time in setting goals such as "fair price" or "reasonable profit." There's a fundamental difference between setting a goal of "high growth" and one of "maximum growth." "Maximum growth" is an optimizing strategy while "high growth" is a satisficing strategy. Usually a term like "high growth" is precisely defined. It may be 3 percent or 30 percent, but the idea is that when you reach that level, you can declare success.

In both business and your personal life, you'll face decisions that are some combination of four main types of decisions (see Figure 4.3). The first type is a **structured decision,** which involves processing a certain kind of information in a specified way so that you will always get the right answer. No "feel" or intuition is necessary. These are the kinds of decisions you can program. If you use a certain set of inputs and process them in a precise way, you'll arrive at the correct result. Calculating gross pay for hourly workers is an example. You can easily automate these types of structured decisions with IT.

On the other hand, a **nonstructured decision** is one for which there may be several "right" answers, and there is no precise way to get a right answer. No rules or criteria exist that guarantee you a good solution. Deciding whether to introduce a new product line, employ a new marketing campaign, or change the corporate image are all examples of decisions with nonstructured elements. In reality, most decisions fall somewhere between structured and unstructured, for example, choosing a job. Structured elements of choosing a job include consideration of such things as salary and signing bonus. Nonstructured elements of such a decision include things like the potential for

Figure 4.3

Categorizing Decisions
by Type

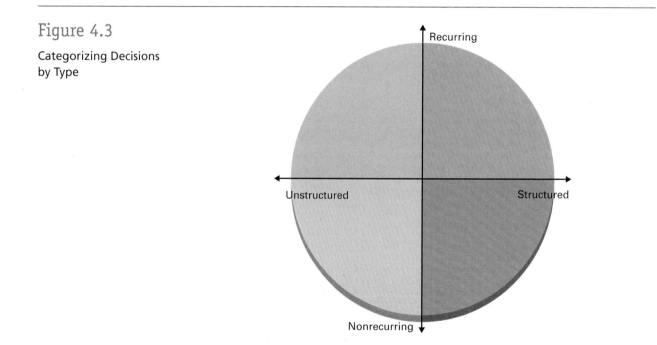

advancement. Regardless of the decision at hand, analytics is most useful for decisions that have nonstructured elements. Good analytics tools allow you to model several different scenarios by adjusting the nonstructured elements. This gives you greater insight to make the right decision.

Another type of decision regards frequency with which the decision is made. A *recurring decision* is one that happens repeatedly, and often periodically, whether weekly, monthly, quarterly, or yearly. Deciding how much inventory to carry and deciding at what price to sell the inventory are recurring decisions. A *nonrecurring,* or *ad hoc, decision* is one that you make infrequently (perhaps only once), and you may even have different criteria for determining the best solution each time. Deciding where to build a distribution center or company mergers are examples of nonrecurring or ad hoc decisions (although, the general trend in business today is for companies to consider mergers on a more consistent basis).

DECISION SUPPORT SYSTEMS

In reality, any technology-based system that helps you make decisions could be classified as a decision support system; even something as simple as an inventory report that highlights inventory with low stock would qualify. But in the IT field there is a long-standing definition of what constitutes a decision support system. A *decision support system (DSS)* is a highly flexible and interactive IT system that is designed to support decision making when the situation includes nonstructured elements. Thus, a DSS is definitely a part of the analytics professional's tool set. The primary objectives of a DSS include providing you with:

LEARNING OUTCOME 1

- A simple and easy-to-use graphical user interface (GUI)
- Access to large amounts of information
- Models and tools (statistical and analytical) that you can use to massage the information

So, a DSS typically has three components, with each focusing on one of the three objectives above (see Figure 4.4 on the next page). As we discuss them, think in terms of Excel, perhaps the quintessential decision support system. Excel is perhaps the most powerful and easy-to-use analytics tool you will have in your arsenal.

USER INTERFACE MANAGEMENT COMPONENT   The *user interface management component* allows you to communicate with the DSS. The user interface is the part of the system you see; through it you enter information, commands, and models. For Excel, the user interface management component includes things like buttons, menu options, formulas and functions, your ability to enter information into cells, and even your ability to manipulate a graph or table, for example, by switching the row and column orientations. In a digital dashboard, a type of decision support system, you can easily click on a graph of sales by year and see further detail that might include a graphical depiction of sales by month. Whatever the case, the user interface component of a DSS should be intuitive and easy-to-use.

DATA MANAGEMENT COMPONENT   The *data management component* of a DSS performs the functions of storing and maintaining information and also that of giving you access to information you want your DSS to use. Again, think about Excel. You can build, store, and retrieve workbooks, and each workbook can contain numerous worksheets. As well, you can import data from a variety of other sources like a database or perhaps external information in an XML format, common to what you might find on the Web. Information

Figure 4.4

Components of a
Decision Support System

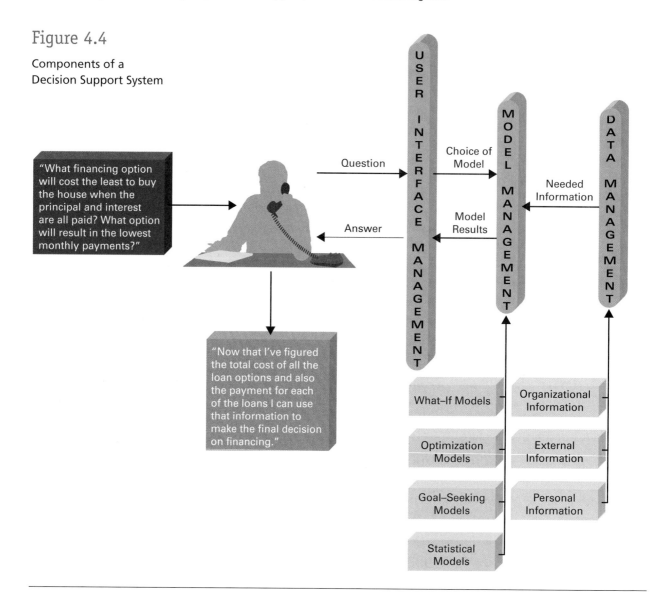

is key in the world of analytics, as it is the basis from which you will generate business intelligence. The information you use in your DSS comes from one or more of three sources:

1. *Organizational information:* You can design your DSS to access information directly from your company's databases, data warehouses, and a host of specialized systems such as CRM and SCM.

2. *External information:* Some decisions require input from external sources of information. Various branches of the federal government, Dow Jones, and the Internet, to mention just a few, can provide additional information for use with a DSS.

3. *Personal information:* You can incorporate your own insights and experience—your personal information—into your DSS.

MODEL MANAGEMENT COMPONENT   The *model management component* consists of a wide variety of statistical and analytical tools, techniques, and models. The tools, techniques, and models you choose to use will vary greatly depending on the decision-making task at hand. Again, think about Excel. It contains basic descriptive statistics tools, goal-seek, solver, financial functions, math and trigonometry functions, engineering functions, and a host of others too numerous to mention. You can even create your own models by writing macros in Visual Basic. In an upcoming section on data-mining tools and models, we'll delve more deeply into many tools and models including some highly specialized and powerful analytics tools.

Geographic Information Systems

On February 1, 2003, after 16 days of intensive research conducted while orbiting the earth, the space shuttle Columbia headed home. But something went terribly wrong and the shuttle exploded over East Texas and arrived on earth in small pieces. To figure out what had happened, it was necessary to gather the pieces and try to reconstruct the sequence of events that led to the disaster. The exact locations of the pieces of debris were key, as scientists and researchers worked backward from that information to determine how and why the space shuttle exploded. Teams of people used global positioning system (GPS) gear to mark the exact location of each piece of debris as they came across it. All of that information was fed into a geographic information system that helped scientists and researchers better understand the situation by visually representing the fallen debris and its backward trajectory.[4]

A *geographic information system (GIS)* is a decision support system designed specifically to analyze spatial information. Spatial information is any information that can be shown in map form, such as roads, the distribution of bald eagle population, sewer systems, the path of a hurricane, and even the shortest driving route from beginning location to destination.

GISs are an important addition to the analytics tool set. When businesses use GIS software to generate maps showing information of interest, we call it *business geography*. Business geography has many dimensions or layers called themes. With themes, you can show any combination of layers you need according to the decision at hand. For example, the U.S. Census Bureau has a vast GIS database of demographic information and the Bureau of Labor Statistics has employment information, both of which you can use in numerical form or see in map form.

In Figure 4.5 you can see a GIS with which you are probably familiar, Google Earth showing the Eiffel Tower. In the bottom left corner, you can see various options (like

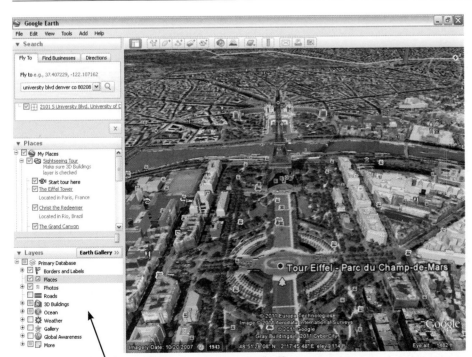

Layers (or themes) you can turn on and off.

Figure 4.5

Google Earth as a GIS and the Eiffel Tower

Geographic information systems (GISs) have broad application across a wide variety of industries and also in your personal life. You probably use a GIS/GPS system, like a Garmin or embedded car system, to help you drive from one place to another. You can use something like Google Places to find businesses in your general vicinity.

Another interesting personal application you might want to check out is Historypin at www.historypin.com. You can use the service for free. At Historypin, you pin photos to locations on a worldwide map. And while specifying the location (i.e., pinning) of a photo, you also provide an approximate date, and a short description, like "The 1906 San Francisco earthquake." The location, date, and description (categorized into what Historypin calls *Collections*) become themes or layers

on the map. So, you adjust the map to look at the San Francisco area. Then, you can specify a date range such as 1900–1910. Historypin will respond by showing you only photos of the San Francisco area from 1900 to 1910. You can also search Collections and select our previous example of the 1906 San Francisco earthquake. That will show you only photos relating to that event. The date feature provides an interesting timeline of a specific location. As you adjust the date, Historypin reveals different photos, allowing you see how a location has changed over time.

You can even join *Communities* like schools and projects. If you're in a project Community, for example, the building of a bridge, you can use the timeline feature to see photos of the bridge in various stages of development.

Places), all of which represent themes. By selecting or unselecting the various options, information will appear or disappear on the screen.

GIS information is becoming increasingly interesting to the business world, especially for those companies that have individual consumers like you and me. Recall our discussion about social locationing and location-based services in Chapter 2. Social locationing systems are in fact GIS systems that use GPS technology to gather information regarding people's location. Knowing where you are because you've checked in with a service like Foursquare, companies can offer you discounts and special deals in your surrounding area. As services like Foursquare become more popular, you can be sure that companies will employ sophisticated analytics to predict consumer movement, identify the best places for new stores, and a host of other GIS-related activities.

Data-Mining Tools and Models

In Chapter 3, we briefly introduced you to several of the many data-mining tools commonly associated with data warehouses. Those data-mining tools come with a data warehouse tool, just like a database management system comes with a database tool. In short, you can't have one without the other. However, the complete and broad spectrum of data-mining tools and models are not just limited to their application in a data warehouse environment. To categorize all data-mining tools and models, we offer the following:

1. *Databases and DBMSs*—the heart of every organization and any analytics initiative. These help gather, store, and organize a wealth of information from which business intelligence can be derived.

2. *Query-and-reporting tools*—similar to QBE tools, SQL, and report generators in the typical database environment (Chapter 3).

3. *Multidimensional analysis (MDA) tools*—slice-and-dice techniques that allow you to view multidimensional information from different perspectives (Chapter 3).

4. *Digital dashboards*—display key information gathered from several sources on a computer screen in a format tailored to the needs and wants of an individual knowledge worker (Chapter 3).

5. *Statistical tools*—help you apply various mathematical models to information to discover new information.

6. *Geographic information systems*—decision support systems designed specifically to analyze spatial information. We discussed these in the previous section.

7. *Specialized analytics like predictive analytics and text analytics*—these have broad application to all industries and a variety of business domains.

8. *Artificial intelligence*—the science of making machines imitate human thinking and behavior.

You're already familiar with the first five, as we covered them in Chapter 3. Also, you've probably already completed one or more courses in statistics which included things like descriptive statistics, probability, hypothesis testing, ANOVA, regression, and chi-square tests. As well, we introduced you to geographic information systems and their role in analytics in the previous section.

In the remainder of this section we'll cover predictive analytics and text analytics, two highly specialized analytics tools that the business world is quickly embracing. In the two sections to follow, we'll talk about some artificial intelligence models and their role in analytics.

In terms of decision making, each and all of the data-mining tools and models in the list above are designed to help you with intelligence-related tasks such as:

1. **Association or Dependency Modeling**—for example, a grocery store may find that one purchase, say, peanut butter, is mostly done in conjunction with another product, like jelly. Think of how powerful this type of business intelligence is in terms of coupon offerings and cross-selling opportunities, not to mention recommendation engine effectiveness.

2. **Clustering**—discovering groups of entities (like customers) that are in some way or another "similar," without using any a priori and known structures. The book *Freakonomics* was the best at this, asking questions like, "What do school teachers and sumo wrestlers have in common?" (You have to read *Freakonomics*; it is the best example of the repeated use of analytics without ever using the term "analytics.")

3. **Classification**—also known as prediction (although the two are not the same). Here, you attempt to evaluate historical, known data to derive structures and inferences that can be applied to newly gathered or perhaps future data.

4. **Regression**—although this is a statistical term, it is not solely executed using regression analysis. The goal here is to find corollary and often causal relationships between sets of data.

5. **Summarization**—this is the most basic, yet often the most powerful, form of data mining. Sums, averages, standard deviations, histograms, frequency distributions, and many other forms of descriptive statistics can be very revealing, often eliminating the need to perform any further data mining.

PREDICTIVE ANALYTICS

Predictive analytics is a highly computational data-mining technology that uses information and business intelligence to build a predictive model for a given business application. So, predictive analytics is all about using historical information to predict future

LEARNING OUTCOME 2

events and outcomes. Predictive analytics has application in a wide variety of industries including insurance, retail, healthcare, travel, and financial services. Within each of those, the business applications will obviously vary but include applications like customer relationship management, supply chain management, and credit scoring (a very popular predictive analytics application within financial services for determining the likelihood a credit applicant will be able to make future payments).

Predictive analytics includes a prediction goal and numerous prediction indicators. A *prediction goal* is the question you want addressed by the predictive analytics model. Prediction goals might include:

- Which suppliers are most likely to deliver raw materials in the next six months with a defective rate higher than 0.001%?

- What customers are mostly likely to respond to a social-media campaign within 30 days by purchasing at least two products in the advertised product line?

Defining the right prediction goal is key. If you build a predictive analytics model for a prediction goal that is in some way wrong, you can expect your subsequent activities to be erroneous (i.e., a failure) as well.

A *prediction indicator* is a specific measurable value based on an attribute of the entity under consideration. The best way to understand prediction goals and prediction indicators is by example, so let's focus on the second prediction goal listed above. This is a CRM application which will use customer profile information, customer history information, and campaign history information (see Figure 4.6). The predictive analytics engine will use many pieces of information from which it will develop a set of prediction indicators that produce the best model for predicting the customer behavior you seek.

Figure 4.6

Analytics Process of Customer Prediction[5]

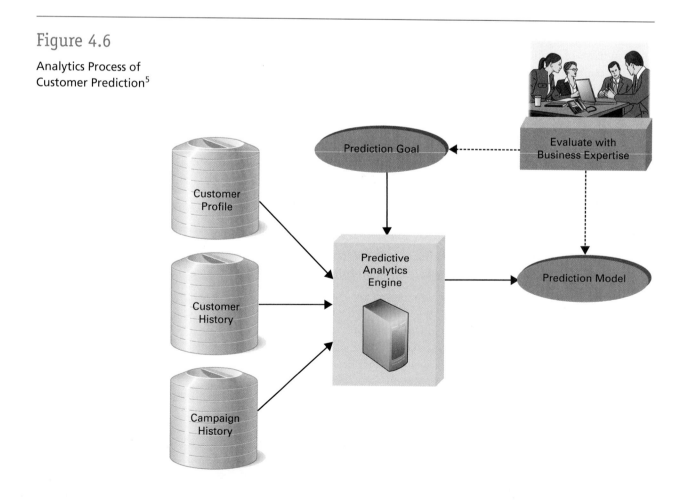

USING PREDICTIVE ANALYTICS TO REDUCE LOAN DEFAULT RATES

Dealer Services is a nationwide company that lends money to dealerships acquiring used cars. Dealer Services was founded in 2005 and grew so fast that it had reached its three-year goals for revenue, number of loans, and number of customers in just six months. But then tough times hit, the economy tanked, and the nation fell into recession. When times were good, making "guesses" for good and bad loans was effective. But in a time when many car dealerships are not only having difficulty in making loan payments but often defaulting on those loans, Dealer Services needed predictive analytics to better understand its data and make better decisions.

According to Chris Brady, CIO at Dealer Services, "There was underlying data from dealers that indicated something was brewing." Some of that data included where the dealership had previously obtained loans. If a dealership applied to be a Dealer Services customer because it had lost its line of credit at a bank, that was definitely a warning sign.

So, Brady had Dealer Services purchase Information Builders predictive analytics tools (http://www .informationbuilders.com/). Those tools give managers the ability to analyze information in real-time and create business intelligence. For example, Dealer Services noticed that many dealerships hadn't slowed their pace of buying used vehicles, even as the economy worsened. But it did notice that those vehicles were beginning to sell more slowly, which indicated that loan defaults were more probable. According to Chris, "The number of loans can be big for good reasons or bad. If you don't know the difference, you're in trouble."[6]

In the end, the predictive analytics engine produces a predictive model as a formula for each customer that provides a single predictive value by which customers can be ranked from most to least likely to respond to a social-media campaign within 30 days by purchasing at least two products in the advertised product line.

As we stated earlier, a prediction indicator is a measurable value based on an attribute of the entity under consideration. Regarding the entity *customer*, the predictive analytics engine may determine that the following attributes are important for making the right prediction:

- Frequency of purchases
- Proximity of date of last purchase (called recency)
- Presence on Facebook (Yes = 1; No = 0)
- Presence on Twitter (Yes = 1; No = 0)
- Number of purchases with multiple products

Then, the predictive analytics engine will assign weights to each prediction indicator that represent the relative significance of each indicator as compared to the other indicators. This is the "highly computational" aspect of predictive analytics and something certainly beyond the scope of this text. Computational models and algorithms used here by the predictive analytics engine include things like linear programming, regression, association rules, market basket analysis, cluster analysis, and so on. The predictive model final formula might look like this:

```
Customer# = (Frequency of Purchases in Last 30 Days)*.2 +
(Recency)*.1 + (Presence on Facebook)*.3 + (Presence on
Twitter)*.1 + (Number of Multiple Product Purchases)*.3
```

As you can see, the predictive analytics engine determined that the indicators of *Presence on Facebook* and *Number of Multiple Product Purchases* were most important, with each receiving a weight of 0.3. (All of the weights sum to 1.)

Once the formula is applied to all customers, each customer receives an overall predictive indicator score, allowing you to rank order them. Then, it's up to you to determine where to draw the line (i.e., the cutoff point in the list) and identify the subset of customers on whom you will focus your social-media campaign.

That in a nutshell is predictive analytics, using historical information to predict the outcome of future events. If you choose analytics as a business career, you'll most likely take classes in building a predictive analytics engine as well as many of the highly computational processes we mentioned such as regression and cluster analysis. If you choose a career that is focused on a business domain such as marketing or perhaps supply chain management, you'll most likely encounter the use of predictive analytics in the business world. So, while you won't be responsible for building a predictive analytics engine, you will need to be able to build quality, highly relevant prediction goals and evaluate the predictive models produced by the predictive analytics engine.

To read customer success stories in predictive analytics and learn more about predictive analytics vendors, we suggest you visit the following resources.

- Angoss Software – www.angoss.com
- KXEN – www.kxen.com
- Oracle – www.oracle.com
- Portrait Software – www.portraitsoftware.com
- SAS – www.sas.com
- SPSS (IBM) http://www-01.ibm.com/software/analytics/spss/
- TIBCO Software – www.tibco.com

TEXT ANALYTICS

Text analytics is a process of using statistical, artificial intelligence, and linguistic techniques to convert information content in textual sources—like surveys, e-mails, blogs, and social media—into structured information. Text analytics most definitely falls within the categories of analytics in general and more specifically decision support systems because it works primarily with nonstructured elements, that is, natural language. Let's consider an example to see text analytics in action.

Gaylord Hotels is using text analytics to better understand the thousands of customer satisfaction surveys it receives every day.[7] The surveys are digitized and fed into a text analytics engine, analogous to the predictive analytics engine we discussed earlier. The text analytics engine can identify negative and positive comments, which are then quickly correlated to structured information such as the specific hotel, facilities, amenity services, the room, and employee shifts. With that correlation, employees of Gaylord Hotels can follow up with customers by phone or perhaps letter to acknowledge the problem and to offer an apology and even discounts for a return stay. Using text analytics to create business intelligence, Gaylord Hotels found that noisy rooms weren't the biggest of its problems, but the analysis did yield that noisy rooms were among the most serious because of their correlation with survey responses of "wouldn't return" or "wouldn't recommend."

Gaylord is a good example because it demonstrates that organizations find text analytics most useful when the text analytics-generated business intelligence is analyzed in conjunction with structured information. Gaylord correlated the text analytics business intelligence with structured information such as the specific hotel and employees on shift during the customer's stay.

Text analytics is even more complicated and technical than predictive analytics. While predictive analytics relies mainly on statistical models to build predictive models, text analytics makes use of statistical models and also linguistic models. Some of these include:

- Lexical analysis—the study of word frequency distributions.
- Named entity recognition—the identification of names for people, places, and things.
- Disambiguation—the process of determining the specific meaning of a named entity recognition. For example, "Ford" may refer to a previous U.S. president, the Ford Motor Company, or perhaps a notable person like Harrison Ford.
- Coreference—the handling of differing noun phrases that refer to the same object.
- Sentiment analysis—discerning subjective business intelligence such as mood, opinion, and emotion.

All of the above fall within the category of linguistic processing or what is often referred to as *natural language processing*. Professionals in the field of natural language processing have expertise in both linguistics and computer science (a very interesting mix of two disparate fields).

The text analytics field is small but growing at an accelerating rate. According to one study, text analytics revenue was almost $1 billion in 2010.[8] That's roughly 10 percent of Gartner's estimate that revenue for the entire analytics fields in 2010 was a little over $10 billion. However, as companies focus more and more of their efforts on engaging customers via social media, which is largely nonstructured, textual data, they will also focus more of their efforts and budgets on incorporating the use of text analytics.

ENDLESS ANALYTICS

Beyond specialized "analytics" like predictive analytics and text analytics, you'll come across many other analytics applications focused on specific areas of business. While these may use sophisticated data-mining and statistical tools, they are considered broadly within the field of analytics because they focus on fact-based decision making. Analytics here include:

- *Web analytics*—the analysis of data related to the Internet, often focusing on optimizing Web page usage. An important subset of Web analytics is *search engine optimization (SEO)*, improving the visibility of a Web site through the use of tags and key terms found by search engines.
- *HR analytics*—the analysis of human resource or talent management data for such purposes as work-force capacity planning, training and development, and performance appraisal.
- *Marketing analytics*—the analysis of marketing-related data to improve the efficiency and effectiveness of marketing efforts including product placement, marketing mix, and customer identification and classification.
- *CRM analytics*—the analysis of CRM data to improve functions such as sales force automation and customer service and support. (Refer back to Chapter 2 for more on CRM, its functions, and its analytics.)
- *Social media analytics*—the analysis of data related to social media use, mainly by customers or competitors, to help an organization better understand the interaction dynamics of itself with its customers and also to help an organization scan social media for competitive intelligence.

- *Mobile analytics*—the analysis of data related to the use of mobile devices by customers and employees. Mobile computing and mobile e-commerce are exploding, and you'll read more about them in Chapter 5.

There are, no doubt, many more such applications of analytics. In Chapter 7, we'll revisit some of these and the specific measures they use.

Artificial Intelligence

IT can further expand business brainpower and use analytics by means of *artificial intelligence (AI)*—the science of making machines imitate human thinking and behavior. Financial analysts use a variety of artificial intelligence systems to manage assets, invest in the stock market, and perform other financial operations. Hospitals use artificial intelligence in many capacities, from scheduling staff, to assigning beds to patients, to diagnosing and treating illness. Many government agencies, including the IRS and the armed forces, use artificial intelligence. Credit card companies use artificial intelligence to detect credit card fraud, and insurance companies use artificial intelligence to spot fraudulent claims. Artificial intelligence lends itself to tasks as diverse as airline ticket pricing, food preparation, oil exploration, and child protection. It is widely used in the insurance, meteorology, engineering, and aerospace industries. Whatever the case, artificial intelligence is an important tool in the field of analytics. AI systems can be independent, stand-alone decision-making systems, or they can be embedded into a larger analytics system, carrying out and executing specific functions. The AI systems that businesses use most can be classified into the following major categories:

1. Expert systems
2. Neural networks (and fuzzy logic)
3. Genetic algorithms
4. Agent-based technologies

LEARNING OUTCOME 3

EXPERT SYSTEMS

An *expert system,* also called a *knowledge-based system,* is an artificial intelligence system that applies reasoning capabilities to reach a conclusion. Expert systems are excellent for diagnostic and prescriptive problems. Diagnostic problems are those requiring an answer to the question, "What's wrong?" and correspond to the intelligence phase of decision making. Prescriptive problems are those that require an answer to the question, "What to do?" and correspond to the choice phase of decision making.

An expert system is usually built for a specific application area called a *domain.* You can find expert systems in the following domains, among others: in accounting for tax planning, auditing, and the like; in medicine to prescribe antibiotics and diagnose diseases; in HR to determine whether a company is in compliance with an array of federal employment laws; and in forestry management to help with harvesting timber on forest lands.

An example of a very simple expert system that would tell a driver what to do when approaching a traffic light is illustrated in Figure 4.7. Dealing with traffic lights is an example of the type of problem to which an expert system is well-suited. It is a recurring problem, and to solve it you follow a well-defined set of steps. You've probably gone through the following mental question-and-answer set hundreds of times without even realizing it. When you approach a green traffic light, you proceed on through. If the light is red, you know you need to stop. If you're unable to stop, and if traffic is approaching from either side, you'll surely be in trouble if the light is red. If the light is yellow, you

Rule	Symptom or Fact	Yes	No	Explanation
1	Is the light green?	Go through the intersection.	Go to Rule 2.	Should be safe if light is green. If not, need more information.
2	Is the light red?	Go to Rule 4.	Go to Rule 3.	Should stop, may not be able to.
3	Is the light likely to change to red before you get through the intersection?	Go to Rule 4.	Go through the intersection.	Will only reach this point if light is yellow, then you'll have two choices.
4	Can you stop before entering the intersection?	Stop.	Go to Rule 5.	Should stop, but there may be a problem if you can't.
5	Is traffic approaching from either side?	Prepare to crash.	Go through the intersection.	Unless the intersection is clear of traffic, you're likely to crash.

Is the light green (Yes/No)?   No.

Is the light red (Yes/No)?   No.

Is the light likely to change to red before you get through the intersection (Yes/No)?   Why?

Will only reach this point if light is yellow, and then you'll have two choices.

Is the light likely to change to red before you get through the intersection (Yes/No)?   No.

Conclusion: Go through the intersection.

Figure 4.7

Traffic Light Expert System Rules

may be able to make it through the intersection before the light turns red. If not, you will again be faced with the problem of approaching traffic. You must decide.

As you can see, expert systems use rules, very similar to the association rule or dependency modeling concept we discussed earlier. For example, if a grocery store customer always buys peanut butter and jelly in the same purchase, then it makes no sense to offer coupons for both to that customer. In this case, the "rule" would be to offer a coupon for peanut butter or jelly but not both, knowing that it would encourage a customer to buy two goods. So, an expert system can be a stand-alone application like the one a doctor would use to aid in the diagnosis of a problem, or it may be embedded into an analytics system that helps determine what coupons to offer customers.

NEURAL NETWORKS AND FUZZY LOGIC

LEARNING OUTCOME 4

Suppose you see a breed of dog you've never encountered before. Would you know it's a dog? For that matter, would you know it's an animal? Probably so. You would know, because you've learned by example. You've seen lots of living things, have learned to classify them, and so can recognize a dog when you see one. A neural network simulates this human ability to classify things without taking prescribed steps leading to the solution. A *neural network* (often called an *artificial neural network* or *ANN*) is an artificial intelligence system that is capable of finding and differentiating patterns. Your brain has learned to consider many factors in combination to recognize and differentiate objects.

NEURAL NETWORK ART EXPERT

Vincent Van Gogh's paintings can fetch somewhere in the neighborhood of $100 million dollars each. Much of his work is thought to remain undiscovered to this day. When he died, his mother sent dozens of his paintings and drawings to a local flea market. Many were not signed. During his brief seven years of creative activity, he painted in several styles. He had a Dutch period, a French period, an Impressionist period, an Arles period, a Saint Remy period, and an Auvers period. He also copied portions of other artists' work, for example, Pissarro's and Suerat's styles and Millet's and Daumier's paintings. With all these variations in his work, authenticating a Van Gogh is not simple.

At Maastricht University in the Netherlands researchers have designed a neural network that can do just that though. In an ambitious move, they set out to devise a computer-based system that could determine whether a painting attributed to Van Gogh actually is his work.

The software literally analyzes a painting's style by examining the painting's canvas, brush strokes, and colors to determine whether the painting is an original Van Gogh. By digitizing 145 paintings and examining the pixels the system developed the ability to recognize patterns unique to the painter.

The software is called "Authentic." In early tests it performed as well as a team of 15 art experts who were each given a small part of a painting to examine.

The researchers used the brain's method of processing images to find and measure patterns and compare them to samples from other paintings. The software they designed uses high-resolution transparencies of X-rayed paintings and "learns" to recognize the style of the painter. Each painter has unique brushstrokes, techniques, and color combinations, that is, each painter has a subconscious signature. The characteristics that the software analyzes include the curvature of the brushstrokes, the angle of the brushstrokes, and the separation, thickness, and repetition of the brushstrokes. In this manner the software can determine the likelihood that a sample is or is not a fake.

The "Authentic" software not only can identify a Van Gogh, but can even specify what period of the artist's career the painting is from.[13, 14, 15]

This is also the case with a neural network. A neural network can learn by example and can adapt to new concepts and knowledge. Neural networks are widely used for visual pattern and speech recognition systems. If you've used a tablet PC that deciphered your handwriting, it was probably a neural network that analyzed the characters you wrote.[9]

Neural networks are useful in a variety of situations. For example, bomb detection systems in U.S. airports use neural networks that sense trace elements in the air that may indicate the presence of explosives. The Chicago Police Department uses neural networks to identify corruption within its ranks. In medicine, neural networks check 50 million electrocardiograms per year, check for drug interactions, and detect anomalies in tissue samples that may signify the onset of cancer and other diseases. Neural networks can detect heart attacks and even differentiate between the subtly different symptoms of heart attacks in men and women.[10, 11, 12] In business, neural networks are very popular for securities trading, fraud detection, real estate appraisal, evaluating loan applications, and target marketing, to mention a few. Neural networks are used to control machinery, adjust temperature settings, and identify malfunctioning machinery.

Neural networks are most useful for identification, classification, and prediction when a vast amount of information is available. By examining hundreds, or even thousands of examples, a neural network detects important relationships and patterns in the information. For example, if you provide a neural network with the details of numerous credit card transactions and tell it which ones are fraudulent, eventually it will learn to identify suspicious transaction patterns.

Because neural networks are good at identification, classification, and prediction, you will often find them used within a predictive analytics application. Our earlier example of attempting to identify customers most likely to respond to a social-media campaign by purchasing multiple products from the advertised product line is a good one. In this application, a neural network would aid in identifying the critical predictive indicators for the predictive analytics engine to use.

Fuzzy logic is a mathematical method of handling imprecise or subjective information. The basic approach is to assign values between 0 and 1 to vague or ambiguous information. The higher the value, the closer it is to 1. For example, you might assign the value of 0.8 to the value "hot." Then you would construct rules and processes, called *algorithms,* to describe the interdependence among variables. A fuzzy logic algorithm is a set of steps that relate variables representing inexact information or personal perceptions.

Thus, fuzzy logic is an important part of most text analytics systems. If you recall, text analytics converts textual information into structured information. Here, fuzzy logic is often employed to assign numerical values to comment data on a survey form. Fuzzy logic is also very good at disambiguation, the ability to specifically identify a named entity recognition based on surrounding text.

GENETIC ALGORITHMS

LEARNING OUTCOME 5

Today significant research in AI is devoted to creating software capable of following a trial-and-error process, leading to the evolution of a good result. Such a software system is called a genetic algorithm. A ***genetic algorithm*** is an artificial intelligence system that mimics the evolutionary, survival-of-the-fittest process to generate increasingly better solutions to a problem. In other words, a genetic algorithm is an optimizing system: It finds the combination of inputs that gives the best outputs. Here are a few examples of genetic algorithms in action.

- Staples used a genetic algorithm to evaluate consumer responses to over 22,000 package designs to determine the optimal set of package design characteristics.[16]
- Boeing uses genetic algorithms in its design of aircraft parts such as the fan blades on its 777 jet. Rolls Royce and Honda also use genetic algorithms in their design processes.[17]
- Retailers such as Marks and Spencer, a British chain that has 320 stores, use genetic algorithm technology to better manage inventory and to optimize display areas.[18]

Suppose you were trying to decide what to put into your stock portfolio. You have countless stocks to choose from but a limited amount of money to invest. You might decide that you'd like to start with 20 stocks and you want a portfolio growth rate of 7.5 percent.

Probably you'd start by examining historic information on the stocks. You would take some number of stocks and combine them, 20 at a time, to see what happens with each grouping. If you wanted to choose from a pool of 30 stocks, you would have to examine 30,045,015 different combinations. For a 40-stock pool, the number of combinations rises to 137,846,500,000. It would be an impossibly time-consuming, not to mention numbingly tedious, task to look at this many combinations and evaluate your overall return for each one. This is just the sort of repetitive number-crunching task at which computers and genetic algorithms excel, however.

This particular decision uses a clustering framework for optimization analysis by attempting to find groups of stocks that have similar characteristics. This makes genetic algorithms an important part of the analytics professional's tool set. And because genetic algorithms are best suited for problems with millions and millions of possible outcomes, they facilitate the evaluation of all those outcomes with great speed and efficiency.

Agent-Based Technologies

An *agent-based technology*, or a *software agent*, is a small piece of software that acts on your behalf (or on behalf of another piece of software) performing tasks assigned to it. Essentially, an agent-based technology is an "agent," much like an agent that represents a movie star or athlete, performing assigned tasks like negotiating contract terms and setting up media blitzes.

There are five main types of agent-based technologies (see Figure 4.8). These include:

1. *Autonomous agent*—software agent that can adapt and alter the manner in which it attempts to achieve its assigned task.
2. *Distributed agent*—software agent that works on multiple distinct computer systems.
3. *Mobile agent*—software agent that can relocate itself onto different computer systems.
4. *Intelligent agent*—software agent that incorporates artificial intelligence capabilities such as learning and reasoning.
5. *Multi-agent system*—group of intelligent agents that have the ability to work independently but must also work with each other in order to achieve their assigned task.

Our focus in this chapter is on the latter two categories—intelligent agents and multi-agent systems, both of which incorporate some form of artificial intelligence.

INTELLIGENT AGENTS

LEARNING OUTCOME 6

Intelligent agents incorporate some form of AI—like reasoning and learning—to assist you, or act on your behalf, in performing repetitive computer-related tasks. As you can see in Figure 4.8, there are four types of intelligent agents. We'll focus here on data-mining agents because of their use in the field of analytics. However, it is worth defining the other three so you'll be familiar with them.

Figure 4.8

Categories of Agent-Based Technologies

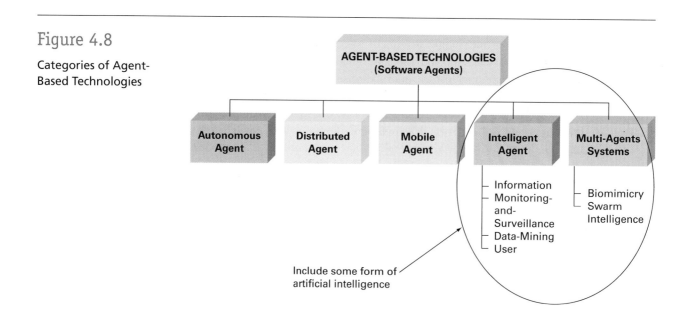

- *Information agents*—intelligent agents that search for information of some kind and bring it back. The best known of these are **buyer agents** (also known as **shopping agents**), agents on a Web site that help you, the customer, find products and services you need.

- *Monitoring-and-surveillance agents*—intelligent agents that constantly observe and report on some entity of interest, a network, or manufacturing equipment.

- *User agents (personal agents)*—intelligent agents that take action on your behalf, such as sorting your e-mail by priority, dumping unsolicited e-mail into your spam folder, and playing computer games as your opponent.

DATA-MINING AGENTS   A *data-mining agent* operates in a data warehouse discovering information. As you learned in Chapter 3, database queries answer questions like "How much did we spend on transportation in March of this year?" Multidimensional analysis is the next step in complexity and answers questions like "How much did we spend on transportation in the southeast during March of the last five years?" Data mining goes deeper and may suggest questions you may not even have thought to ask like the retail manager we mentioned in Chapter 1 who thought "What else do young men buy on Friday afternoons when they come in to buy diapers?"[19]

One of the most common types of data mining is classification, which finds patterns in information and categorizes items into those classes. You may remember that this is just what neural networks do best. So, not surprisingly, neural networks are part of many data-mining tools. And data-mining agents are another integral part, since these intelligent agents search for information in a data warehouse.

A data-mining agent may detect a major shift in a trend or a key indicator. It can also detect the presence of new information and alert you. Volkswagen uses an intelligent agent system that acts as an early-warning system about market conditions. If conditions become such that the assumptions underlying the company's strategy are no longer true, the intelligent agent alerts managers.[20] For example, the intelligent agent might see a problem in some part of the country that is about to or will shortly cause payments to slow down. Having that information early lets managers formulate a plan to protect themselves.

MULTI-AGENT SYSTEMS

What do cargo transport systems, book distribution centers, the video game market, a flu epidemic, and an ant colony have in common? They are all complex adaptive systems and thus share some common characteristics. By observing parts of the ecosystem, like ant or bee colonies, artificial intelligence scientists can use hardware and software models that incorporate insect characteristics and behavior to (1) learn how people-based systems behave; (2) predict how they will behave under a given set of circumstances; and (3) improve human systems to make them more efficient and effective. This concept of learning from ecosystems and adapting their characteristics to human and organizational situations is called **biomimicry.**

In the last few years, AI research has made much progress in modeling complex organizations as a whole with the help of multi-agent systems, which we defined a moment ago as a group of intelligent agents that have the ability to work independently but must also work with each other in order to achieve their assigned task. Again, think about ants. Each has a specific task and works throughout the day on that task without any management oversight. But no ant alone can build a colony of canals, an ant hill structure, and so on. That takes all the ants working together.

Figure 4.9

Companies that Use
Multi-Agent Systems[21]

- Southwest Airlines—to optimize cargo routing.

- Procter & Gamble—to overhaul its handling of what the company calls its "supply network" of 5 billion consumers in 140 countries.

- Air Liquide America—to reduce production and distribution costs of liquefied industrial gases.

- Merck & Co.—to find more efficient ways of distributing anti-AIDS drugs in Africa.

- Ford Motor Co.—to build a model of consumer preferences and find the best balance between production costs and customers' demands.

- Edison Chouest Offshore LLC—to find the best way to deploy its service and supply vessels in the Gulf of Mexico.

Multi-agent systems are being used to model stock market fluctuations, predict the escape routes that people seek in a burning building, estimate the effects of interest rates on consumers with different types of debt, and anticipate how changes in conditions will affect the supply chain, to name just a few. See Figure 4.9 for examples of companies that have used multi-agent systems to their advantage.

SWARM (COLLECTIVE) INTELLIGENCE   The ant ecosystem is one of the most widely used types of simulations in business problems. If you've ever tried to remove ants from your home, you know how determined and effective ant colonies are. Individual ants are autonomous, acting and reacting independently. (If you drop a crumb into the middle of a group of ants, they'll all scatter in different directions.) However, ants are unusual insects in that they are social. (Less than 2 percent of insects are social, with termites being the only other entirely social species, although some types of bees and wasps are, too.) The term "social" implies that all the members of a colony work together to establish and maintain a global system that's efficient and stable. So, even though the ants are autonomous, each ant contributes to the system as a whole. Ants have been on Earth for 40 million years, compared to the relatively short human occupation of 100 thousand years, and their extraordinary evolutionary success is the result of ants' collective behavior, known as *swarm intelligence*.

Swarm (collective) intelligence is the collective behavior of groups of simple agents that are capable of devising solutions to problems as they arise, eventually leading to coherent global patterns.[22] So, how are the workings of ant colonies related to information technology in modern business? Swarm intelligence gives us a way to examine collective systems where groups of individuals have certain goals, solve problems, and make decisions without centralized control or a common plan.

A comparison of the activities of forager ants and those of the cargo-handling arm of Southwest Airlines affords a striking example of the similarities between ecosystems and human organizations, which we will consider shortly. There are some uncanny parallels that surprised Southwest's management. First, though, let's ponder the ants some more.

Forager ants have the sole responsibility of providing food to the colony. They don't form committees and discuss strategies or look to a central authority for direction; they just find food and bring it back to the nest, and in doing so they follow a simple procedure.

Say two ants (A and B) leave the same point to search for food. Ant A finds food first because ant B has to go around several rocks before finding food (i.e., Ant A found a shorter route to the food). Having found a food source, Ant A returns to the nest by

DON'T TELL SANTA; TELL GOOGLE

Sometimes, you don't need complex data or sophisticated data-mining techniques. You don't always need artificial intelligence or elaborate text analytics engines that convert comment data into a structured form. Often, all you need to know is what people are searching for, and Google is more than happy to share that with you. Google Insights for Search is a free analytics tool at http://www.google.com/insights/search/. There, you can search by date, by country, and by major category (about 30 or so). Or, you can simply request to see the most popular search terms within the last 30 days. We did so when we wrote this section (it was late July 2011), and the most popular terms included Amy Winehouse, Tour de France, Casey Anthony, Harry Potter, and Google +.

In October 2010, *CNN Money* produced a report of the hottest toys for the upcoming 2010 holiday season according to the popularity of their searches on Google. That list included:

- Hasbro's Nerf Stampede
- Mattel's Sing-a-Ma-Jigs
- Silly Bandz
- Japanese Iwako erasers

Guess what? Each went on to have blockbuster sales for the year. Was that because of the report? Probably not. If you top Google's list of search terms, it's because millions of people are very interested.

Then again, if you're a clueless retailer and have no idea what to put on your shelves during the Christmas holiday season, we'd recommend checking out Google Insights for Search. Of course, if you really are that clueless, chances are you're not in business.[23]

---

the same route, leaving behind a trail of pheromones (a biological breadcrumb trail) so that it will know what path to take next time and so will the other ants. The first ant that returns "lays the trail" first so that's the one that other ants take. Then the other ants strengthen the pheromone trail on their return journey by leaving their own pheromone tracks along the path Ant A found.

Meanwhile, Ant B arrives back at the nest after the shorter path has already been established. The other ants that are already on the move don't change their route. The pheromone trail on the unused path (that left by ant B) evaporates after a certain length of time so that it's effectively deleted from the system as a desirable route to food. The approach is straightforward but effective, and can be expressed in the following rules:

- Rule 1: Follow the trail if one exists, otherwise create one.
- Rule 2: Find food.
- Rule 3: Return to the nest, making a pheromone trail.

If changes occur (say, for example, that the food source is removed), the ants cease returning to the place where the food used to be, and the trail disappears. Then the process begins again, and proceeds relentlessly, with forager ants finding a new food source and creating pheromone corridors that lead the way.

The problem that the ants have just solved is one of the oldest problems that humans (as well as ants) have faced. It's known as "the shortest path problem" or the "traveling salesman problem." Anyone who schedules drop-off and pick-up routes for delivery trucks, or schedules jobs on the factory floor, or even colors maps, making sure that no two adjacent components have the same color, has had to find a solution to the same type of problem.

Taking their cue from nature, AI researchers built sets of small robots and incorporated software that allowed the robots to follow rules and interact with each other in the same basic ways as the ants. They also dispensed with the physical forms altogether, creating virtual ants in the form of small autonomous blocks of code that we call intelligent agents. And each code block could follow certain rules, interact, and adapt. These virtual ants were then arranged into multi-agent systems that were further refined into agent-based models.

Now let's look at Southwest Airlines as a case in point. Even though cargo is a small part of Southwest's business, it was causing management headaches and bottlenecks at busy airports. Southwest consulted with swarm intelligence experts, who used a virtual model of foraging ants to simulate the cargo-handling process. And that was how Southwest managers discovered, to their surprise, that there were actually better ways to handle cargo than to put it on the first plane flying in the right direction. Surprisingly, the computer's swarm intelligence model showed that it might actually be better to leave cargo on a plane heading in the wrong direction. For example, cargo headed from Chicago to Boston would be better left on a plane going from Chicago to Atlanta and then reloaded onto a flight to Boston, requiring less unloading and reloading. Following the ant model, Southwest decreased its cargo transfer rates by 80 percent, reduced the workload of cargo employees by 20 percent, and also found that there was spare cargo space on flights that were previously full, enabling the company to accept more business. The overall gain to Southwest was in excess of $10 million per year.[24]

The future will see many more uses of intelligent agents. It's a pretty safe bet that these applications will include swarm intelligence and agent-based modeling. Already, swarm intelligence is being implemented widely for scheduling, resource allocation, and routing. Other applications in the early stages include networks that have self-organizing components and robots that assemble themselves. There must be many, many more that have not yet been dreamt of. Some people believe that intelligent agents will replace many of the other types of simulations in the future since swarm intelligence supports individuality, flexibility, and entities that can adapt quickly and effectively in a fast-changing business environment.

■ SUMMARY: STUDENT LEARNING OUTCOMES REVISITED

1. **Compare and contrast decision support systems and geographic information systems.** A *decision support system (DSS)* is a highly flexible and interactive IT system that is designed to support decision making when the situation includes nonstructured elements. A *geographic information system (GIS)* is a decision support system designed specifically to analyze spatial information. So, they both are designed to support decision-making efforts. While traditional DSSs mainly use text and numeric data, GISs represent many types of information in spatial or map form.

2. **Describe the decision support role of specialized analytics like predictive analytics and text analytics.** *Predictive analytics* is a highly computational data-mining technology that uses information and business intelligence to build a predictive model for a given business application. Predictive analytics focuses on using historical information to predict future events and outcomes. *Text analytics* is a process of using statistical, artificial intelligence, and linguistic

techniques to convert information content in textual sources—like surveys, e-mails, blogs, and social media—into structured information. Text analytics focuses on natural language processing, that is, understanding what is being said (or written) and converting that language into a structured data format more suitable for processing by a computer.

3. **Describe the role and function of an expert system in analytics.** An *expert system,* also called a *knowledge-based system,* is an artificial intelligence system that applies reasoning capabilities to reach a conclusion. Expert systems are good for diagnostic (what's wrong) and prescriptive problems (what to do). So, they can aid in identifying problems or opportunities in the intelligence phase of decision making and also in choosing an approach to the problem or opportunity in the choice phase of decision making.

4. **Explain why neural networks are effective decision support tools.** A *neural network* (also called an *artificial neural network* or *ANN*) is an artificial intelligence system that is capable of finding and differentiating patterns. Neural networks are most useful for identification, classification, and prediction when a vast amount of information is available. They are often used in conjunction with a predictive analytics application to identify the most important predictive indicators.

5. **Define genetic algorithms and the types of problems they help solve.** A *genetic algorithm* is an artificial intelligence system that mimics the evolutionary, survival-of-the-fittest process to generate increasingly better solutions to a problem. These systems are best suited to problems where thousands or millions of solutions are possible and you need an optimal solution.

6. **Describe data-mining agents and multi-agent systems as subsets of intelligent agents and agent-based technologies.** A *data-mining agent* operates in a data warehouse discovering new information. A data-mining agent is considered to be an intelligent agent because it incorporates the use of various artificial intelligence techniques. *Multi-agent systems* are groups of intelligent agents that have the ability to work independently but must also work with each other in order to achieve their assigned task. They too incorporate the use of various artificial intelligence techniques.

CLOSING CASE STUDY ONE

Crystal Ball, Clairvoyant, Fortune Telling . . . Can Predictive Analytics Deliver the Future?

In the Tom Cruise movie *Minority Report*, police are able to accurately predict a crime, its location, and the criminal in advance of the event in time to send police to prevent the crime from occurring. Science fiction at its best, huh? Actually, that's somewhat of a reality now through predictive analytics.

As we discussed in the chapter, *predictive analytics* or *analytics* uses a variety of decision tools and techniques to analyze current and historical data and make predictions about the likelihood of the occurrence of future events. Along the lines of *Minority Report*, police in Richmond, Virginia, are using predictive analytics to determine the likelihood (probability) that a particular type of crime will occur in a specific neighborhood at a specific time.

Using the system, the mobile task force of 30 officers is deployed to the areas with the greatest likelihood of crimes occurring. According to Richmond Police Chief, Rodney Moore, "Based on the predictive models, we deploy them [the mobile task force] almost every three or four hours." Sixteen fugitives have been arrested directly as a result of the system's prediction of the next time and location of a crime. Moreover, in the first week of May in 2006, no homicides occurred, compared to three in the same week of the previous year.

The predictive analytics system uses large databases that contain information on past calls to police, arrests, crime logs, current weather data, and local festivals and sporting and other events. From an IT point of view, the system is a combination of software—SPSS's Clementine predictive analysis software and reporting and visualization tools from Information Builder—and decision support and predictive models developed by RTI International.

The Richmond police afford just one of many examples of the use predictive analytics. Some others include the following:

- *Blue Cross Blue Shield of Tennessee*—uses a neural network predictive model to predict which health care resources will be needed by which postoperative patients months and even years into the future. According to Soyal Momin, manager of research and development at Blue Cross Blue Shield, "If we're seeing a pattern that predicts heart failure, kidney failure, or diabetes, we want to know that as soon as possible."

- *FedEx*—uses a predictive analytics system that is delivering real and true results 65 to 90 percent of the time. The system predicts how customers will respond to new services and price changes. It also predicts which customers will no longer use FedEx as a result of a price increase and how much additional revenue the company will generate from proposed drop-box locations.

- *University of Utah*—uses a predictive analytics system to generate alumni donations. The system determines which of its 300,000 alumni are most likely to respond to an annual donation appeal. This is particularly appealing to most higher-education institutions as they have limited resources to devote to the all-important task of fund raising. Donations

increased 73 percent in 2005 for the University of Utah's David Eccles School of Business as a result of the system.

The future of predictive analytics is very bright. Businesses are beginning to build predictive analytics into mainstream, operational applications—such as CRM, SCM, and inventory management—which will further increase their use. According to Scott Burk, senior statistician and technical lead for marketing analytics at Overstock.com, "Predictive analytics is going to become more operational. We're definitely doing things a lot smarter than we were six months ago." Overstock.com uses its predictive analytics system to predict demand levels for products at various price points.[25]

Questions

1. Many predictive analytic models are based on neural network technologies. What is the role of neural networks in predictive analytics? How can neural networks help predict the likelihood of future events. In answering these questions, specifically reference Blue Cross Blue Shield of Tennessee.

2. What if the Richmond police began to add demographic data to its predictive analytics system to further attempt to determine the type of person (by demographic) who would in all likelihood commit a crime. Is predicting the type of person who would commit a crime by demographic data (ethnicity, gender, income level, and so on) good or bad?

3. In the movie *Gattaca*, predictive analytics were used to determine the most successful career for a person. Based on DNA information, the system determined whether or not an individual was able to advance through an educational track to become something like an engineer or if the person should complete only a lower level of education and become a janitor. The government then acted on the system's recommendations and placed people in various career tracks. Is this a good or bad use of technology? How is this different from the variety of personal tests you can take that inform you of your aptitude for different careers?

4. What role can geographic information systems (GISs) play in the use of predictive analytics? As you answer this question, specifically

reference FedEx's use of predictive analytics to (1) determine which customers will respond negatively to a price increase and (2) project additional revenues from proposed drop-box locations.

5. The Department of Defense (DoD) and the Pacific Northwest National Laboratory are combining predictive analytics with visualization technologies to predict the probability that a terrorist attack will occur. For example, suspected terrorists caught on security cameras who loiter too long in a given place might signal their intent to carry out a terrorist attack. How can this type of predictive analytics be used in an airport? At what other buildings and structures might this be used?

CLOSING CASE STUDY TWO

Decision Support Is Good for Your Health

The New York City Health and Hospitals Corporation (HHC) has proved that, using information technology, it's possible to give high-quality health care to low income, mostly uninsured, patients.

The company serves 1.3 million people, about 60 percent of whom are on Medicaid and 450,000 of whom are uninsured. HHC employs 39,000 people in a range of facilities including 4 long-term care facilities, 6 diagnostic and treatment centers, 11 acute-care hospitals, and 80 neighborhood clinics. HHC is the biggest municipal hospital system in the country treating about one-fifth of all general hospital admissions and more than a third of emergency room and hospital-based clinic visits in New York City.

The company prides itself on being a medical innovator by investing in advanced, integrated technology throughout its facilities. HHC has high standards and is often cited as a model of excellent hospital care based on widely accepted performance measures such as hospital-acquired infection rates and mortality rates. A fundamental factor in HHC's success is its $100 million investment in its IT infrastructure. The primary feature of this system is a diagnosis decision support system called Isabel.

Isabel has a database with tens of thousands of diseases and thousands of drugs that can be accessed using natural language—no keyboard involved. The database also contains information from medical textbooks, journals, and other sources.

This is how Isabel works: The health care professional enters the patient's symptoms and instantly gets back a list of possible illnesses. Along with each possible diagnosis comes a list of tests to be performed and treatment options. Isabel also provides histories of previous cases and recent advances in treatment. The Isabel decision support system has computerized physician order entry, along with medication management and digital patient imaging.

Part of the problem in providing health care is the fragmentation of information. One patient may be seen in different departments for different ailments. So that those caring for the patient can get a clear, comprehensive view of each patient, HHC uses electronic medical records that are collated across departments.

Isabel is not the only decision tool available to professionals in HHC. In its home health care division, HHC uses telemonitoring that allows personnel to track patients with chronic illnesses, like diabetes. Diabetes is a disease afflicting about 50,000 of HHC's patients, and it requires careful monitoring. Not only that, but patients need help and support in managing their own illness, and telemonitoring helps.

Using telemonitoring, health care professionals can monitor blood sugar levels and blood pressure as well as other health indicators. Telemonitoring is a way of keeping track of the vital signs of people while allowing them to remain in their own homes. On a regular basis, perhaps every day, a recorded voice tells a patient to take readings for blood pressure, pulse, oxygen level, and so on. The system also asks relevant questions about swelling or bleeding or wound condition. The patient answers using the phone's touchpad. Telemonitoring is a cost-effective way to tell when something is wrong before the problem requires an emergency room visit or worse. When the data are collected and combined with all the other relevant information, health care professionals can build a clear picture of the patient and the outcomes of various treatments.

The HHC system addresses a very worrying problem in medicine—misdiagnosis. We have all heard the horror stories of people who woke up after surgery to find that the wrong leg had been amputated or that a healthy kidney had been removed instead of the diseased one. Such cases may be very rare, but they are the most dramatic examples of the much larger problem of misdiagnosis. Costing millions in malpractice lawsuits, it's one of the causes of increasing insurance premiums and, consequently, the overall cost of medical care.

According to the May 2008 issue of the *American Journal of Medicine* 10 to 30 percent of cases are misdiagnosed. Apart from the human cost in pain and suffering the financial cost is staggering. Kaiser Permanente's medical and legal costs of misdiagnosis were about $380 million for the period 2000 to 2004.

How is this possible? A VA study showed that 65 percent of system-related factors contribute to diagnostic error. Such system factors include protocol, policies and procedures, inefficient processes, and communication problems. Seventy-four percent of misdiagnosis cases involved premature closure, i.e., the failure to continue considering reasonable alternatives after an initial diagnosis was reached.

Doctors carry very, very large data sets in their heads. The medical industry is a truly knowledge-intensive sector. It's almost impossible for one person to keep track of all the symptoms of, treatments for, research about, and case histories of such a huge range of diseases. This is where a decision support system can be invaluable.[26, 27]

Questions

1. The system discussed in this case was a decision support system. However, other types of computer-aided support are utilized in medicine. Can you think of ways that the medical profession could use AI systems? For example, how about pattern recognition? Could that help in diagnosing illness?

2. A big worry in the collating and aggregation of medical information across departments and even medical institutions is that the more access there is to a person's medical information, the more exposed that personal information becomes. HIPAA (Health Insurance Portability and Accountability Act), signed into law in 1996, addresses the security and privacy of your health data. The law was enacted to try to ensure that medical records, electronically stored and transferred, would be protected. Do you think that making your medical records available to the various branches of the medical industry (doctors, therapists, insurance companies, hospital billing, etc.) is, on the whole, good or bad? Why? Can you think of any instances where disclosure of medical information could cause problems for a patient?

3. Could predictive analytics be a part of the HHC decision support system? If so, what sort of data would it analyze? What might it tell medical staff? Would it be useful only to those who are already ill or could it help healthy people? How?

4. A clinical study has shown that telemonitoring, discussed briefly in this case, helps in keeping down medical costs. In fact, monitored patients were hospitalized about half as often as those with the same illnesses who were not monitored. Emergency room visits were five times more likely among those who were unmonitored. What types of illnesses could be monitored this way (think chronic diseases like high blood pressure)? Would it make sense to use the system as follow-up care? How could the data be utilized to help those who might become sick in the future? Into what part of Isabel would the data fit?

5. Could an automated medical diagnosis system ever replace live doctors? Why or why not? Would you trust an experienced doctor over a database that you could query yourself? Why or Why not?

◼ KEY TERMS AND CONCEPTS

SHORT-ANSWER QUESTIONS

1. What are the four steps in making a decision?
2. What are the four types of decisions discussed in this chapter?
3. What are the three components of a decision support system?
4. What type of information is a geographic information system designed specifically to work with?
5. What are the five intelligence-related tasks that data-mining tool and models help you address?
6. What is predictive analytics?
7. What are the roles of a predictive goal and predictive indicators in predictive analytics?
8. What is text analytics?
9. What sort of problems is an expert system used for?
10. What sort of problems does a neural network solve?
11. Why is fuzzy logic important to text analytics?
12. What is an agent-based technology?
13. How are biomimicry and swarm intelligence related?

ASSIGNMENTS AND EXERCISES

1. **MAKE A GIS** Make a GIS-type map using transparencies. Draw a map of your campus on one plastic transparency sheet. You can use software or felt-tip pens to do the actual drawing of the map. Next, use a second sheet as an overlay and mark on it what classes you have taken in what buildings. Take a third sheet and enter the type of classroom you had the course in (i.e., auditorium, lab, small, medium, large room). Make a fourth layer with special facilities, like a computer lab or a biology lab, and so on. What problems did you encounter while designing your GIS? What other information would you like to see in a real GIS of this type? Would this handmade GIS be helpful for new students? What layers would you keep for general use? What layers would you keep for sentimental value when your college days are over?

2. **CHOOSE A FINANCING OPTION** Using a spreadsheet (like Excel, for example) evaluate your options for a $12,000 car. Compare the payments (use the = pmt function in Excel), the total amount of interest, and the total you'll pay for the car under the following four options:
   a. 3 years at 0 percent interest
   b. 2 years at 1.99 percent annual percent rate (APR)
   c. 4 years at 5 percent APR
   d. 6 years at 6 percent APR

What other considerations would you take into account if you were going to buy a new car? Are there considerations other than the interest rate and the other parts that can be calculated? What are they? How is a car different from other purchases, such as CDs or TV sets or computers?

3. **WHICH SOFTWARE WOULD YOU USE?** Which type or types of computer-aided decision support software would you use for each of the situations in the table below? Note why you think each of your choices is appropriate. The decision support alternatives are

- Decision support system
- Geographic information system
- Expert system
- Neural network
- Genetic algorithm
- Intelligent agent

Problem	Type of Decision Support
You and another marketing executive on a different continent want to develop a new pricing structure for products	
You want to predict when customers are about to take their business elsewhere	
You want to fill out a short tax form	
You want to determine the fastest route for package delivery to 23 different addresses in a city	
You want to decide where to spend advertising dollars (TV, radio, newspaper, direct mail, e-mail)	
You want to keep track of competitors' prices for comparable goods and services	

4. **IDENTIFYING PREDICTIVE INDICATORS** Think about your school and its building of a predictive analytics model. What do you believe would be the 10 most important predictive indicators for determining whether or not an applicant to your school will attend if accepted? Think very broadly here in terms of all the factors a potential student might use in making his or her choice.

DISCUSSION QUESTIONS

1. Some experts claim that if a business gets 52 percent of its decisions right, it will be successful. Would using a decision support system guarantee better results? Why or why not? What does the quality of any decision depend on? Do you think it matters what type of decisions are included in this 52 percent? For example, would getting the right type of paper clips be as influential a decision as deciding where to locate the business? Can you think of a situation where the type of paper clip matters a great deal?

2. Consider the topic of data warehouses in Chapter 3. In the future, AI systems will be increasingly applied to data warehouse processing. Which AI systems do you think might be helpful? For which tasks, or situations, might they best be applied? Do you think that AI systems will someday play a greater role in the design of databases and data warehouses? Why or why not?

3. Consider the differences and similarities among the four AI techniques discussed in this chapter. Name some problems that might be amenable to more than one type of AI system. Say you sell baseballs from your Web site. What types of AI systems could you use to generate information that would be useful to you in deciding what direction to take your company in the future? If you were pretty

successful at selling baseballs, would you expect to have the amount of information on customers that, say, Walmart has? Why or why not?

4. AI systems are relatively new approaches to solving business problems. What are the difficulties with new IT approaches in general? For each of the systems we discussed, identify some advantages and disadvantages of AI systems over traditional business processes. Say you were selling specialty teas and had both brick and click stores. Would you use the same type of AI systems for each part of your business? In what way would you use them or why would you not? Is there a place for decision support and artificial intelligence techniques in small specialty businesses? In what way would decision support add value? Can you think of how a DSS or an AI system would be value reducing (in terms of the value chain concept we discussed in Chapter 1)? What do you see as the major differences between running a mammoth concern and a small specialty business?

5. Neural networks recognize and categorize patterns. If someone were to have a neural network that could scan information on all aspects of your life, where would that neural network potentially be able to find information about you? Consider confidential (doctor's office) as well as publicly available (department of motor vehicles) information.

6. What type of AI systems could your school use to help with registration? Intelligent agents find vast amounts of information very quickly. Neural networks can classify patterns instantaneously. What sorts of information might your school administration be able to generate using these (or other AI systems) with all of its student data?

7. For which activities that are part of college life could you use agent-based modeling to simulate what happens? Describe three such scenarios.

CHAPTER PROJECTS

GROUP PROJECTS

- Assessing the Value of Customer Relationship Management: Trevor Toy Auto Mechanics (p. 286)
- Analyzing the Value of Information: Affordable Homes Real Estate (p. 287)
- Executive Information System Reporting Political Campaign Finance (p. 288)
- Building a Decision Support System: Creating an Investment Portfolio (p. 292)
- Creating a Decision Support System: Buy versus Lease (p. 298)
- Building a Decision Support System: Break-Even Analysis (p. 304)
- Building a Scheduling Decision Support System: Airline Crew Scheduling (p. 306)

E-COMMERCE PROJECTS

- Best in Computer Statistics and Resources (p. 310)
- Consumer Information (p. 310)
- Meta Data (p. 311)
- Bureau of Labor Statistics (p. 312)
- Demographics (p. 312)
- Exploring Google Earth (p. 314)
- Gold, Silver, Interest Rates, and Money (p. 316)
- Learning about Investing (p. 318)
- Stock Quotes (p. 319)

CHAPTER FIVE OUTLINE

STUDENT LEARNING OUTCOMES

1. Define and describe the nine major e-commerce business models.

2. Identify the differences and similarities among customers and their perceived value of products and services in the B2B and B2C e-commerce business models.

3. Compare and contrast the development of a marketing mix for customers in the B2B and B2C e-commerce business models.

4. Summarize the various ways of moving money in the world of e-commerce and related issues.

5. Discuss some major trends that are impacting both the e-commerce business world and society in general.

PERSPECTIVES

WEB SUPPORT

www.mhhe.com/haag

- Exploring Google Earth
- Learning about investing
- Gathering competitive intelligence
- Researching storefront software
- Finding hosting services
- Gold, silver, interest rates, and money
- Free and rentable storage space
- Small Business Administration
- Global statistics and resources

SUPPORTING MODULES

XLM/B The World Wide Web and the Internet
Extended Learning Module B is a fast-paced tour of the Web and the Internet. The first focus is on learning just enough about the Web to be an effective surfer. Then, explore the technology infrastructure behind the Web that makes it all possible. Finally, conclude with an overview of the options for connecting to the Web and the emerging life of Web 2.0.

XLM/E Network Basics
Extended Learning Module E provides an introduction to the vast, exciting, and dynamic field of information technology networks. The module includes discussions of what is needed to set up a small network at home, the components used to build large business networks, Internet connection possibilities, types of communications media, and network security.

CHAPTER FIVE

Electronic Commerce
Strategies for the New Economy

OUTRAGEOUS INDUSTRY TRANSFORMATION: ADVERTISING DOLLARS GO WHERE THE EYES ARE

In the world of commerce, which is now to a great extent electronic commerce or e-commerce, you need to spend your advertising dollars well. That means developing effective campaigns, creating memorable advertising assets, using the appropriate media mix, and placing your ads where the eyes are. "Eyes" in this case refers to viewership, where people will see your advertising.

In the past, most advertising dollars were spent on paper-based-media such as newspapers and magazines and on TV and radio advertising. Take a look at the accompanying graph. Where are people now spending a large portion of their time? Right, on the Internet. Adults spend 29 percent of their time on the Internet. If you add in young adults and teenagers, that number increases to 38 percent.

So, where are advertisers spending their dollars today? Interestingly enough, not always where people spend a lot of their time. Adults spend 37 percent of their time on TV. Nearly one-third (32 percent) of all advertising dollars are spent on TV, so the correlation there is fairly good. But look at newspapers. Adults spend only 8 percent of their time with their eyes on a newspaper, but advertisers spend 20 percent of their advertising dollars there. You have to question the effectiveness of that decision.

Adults spend 29 percent of their time on the Internet, but advertisers spend only 8 percent of their advertising dollars there. That's a significant ad-dollar-to-viewership ratio. The ratio for TV is almost 1-to-1 (1 percent of viewership time

is reached by 1 percent of advertising dollars). For the Internet, on the other hand, the ratio is 3.5-to-1. That is, 3.5 percent of viewership time is reached by only 1 percent of advertising dollars.

So, where do you think this outrageous industry transformation is going? In the advertising industry, you can expect to see an increasing shift of advertising dollars from TV and newspaper to the Internet. This certainly makes sense. If people are spending more time on the Internet, then businesses will focus more of their advertising dollars there.[1]

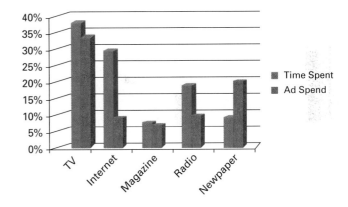

Questions

1. In a typical week, what is the ratio of the time you spend watching TV as compared to the time you spend on the Internet?

2. When watching TV, what do you do when a commercial comes on? Do you channel surf? Get up and get something to eat or drink? Something else?

3. When advertisers start spending fewer dollars in newspapers, what will happen to the cost of a newspaper? Will newspapers be able to survive?

Introduction

The past 15 years of the new economy introduced by the World Wide Web have certainly been interesting. There has been an entrepreneurial frenzy unlike anything the world has ever seen. Fortunes have been made and lost. Dot-com millionaires and billionaires were literally created overnight—many became dot-bomb paupers in about the same amount of time.

What fueled this frenzy and is still doing so today? It's electronic commerce enabled by information technology. *Electronic commerce (e-commerce)* is commerce, but it is commerce accelerated and enhanced by IT, in particular the Internet. E-commerce enables customers, consumers, and companies to form powerful new relationships that would not be possible without the enabling technologies. E-commerce breaks down business barriers such as time, geography, language, currency, and culture. In a few short hours, you can set up shop on the Internet and be instantly accessible to millions of consumers worldwide.

Is there a catch? The answer is both no and yes. It's "no" because it doesn't take much effort to create your own e-commerce Web site. It's "yes" because you still have to follow sound business fundamentals and principles to be successful. Let's not forget that fundamentally it's still all about commerce, businesses and people buying and selling products and services. E-commerce is no "silver bullet," as some entrepreneurs have found out to their chagrin.

In short, you must have a clear path-to-profitability. A *path-to-profitability (P2P)* is a formal business plan that outlines key business issues such as customer targets (by demographic, industry, etc.), marketing strategies, operations strategies (e.g., production, transportation, and logistics), and projected targets for income statement and balance sheet items. That is to say, running an e-commerce operation is no different from running a traditional brick-and-mortar business. You must identify your customers, determine how to reach them with a compelling story, and so on. The major error that most dot-com businesses made in the late 1990s—and they are no longer in existence today—is that they never developed a clear *path-to-profitability*.

E-Commerce Business Models

As illustrated in Figure 5.1, there are nine major e-commerce business models. We'll start by defining and briefly describing some of lesser known and used e-commerce models and then move on to the more prominent e-commerce models.

LEARNING OUTCOME 1

- *Business to Government (B2G) e-commerce*—occurs when a business sells products and services to a government entity. Lockheed Martin, for example, generates almost 80 percent of its revenue by providing products and services to the U.S. Department of Defense (DoD).[2]
- *Consumer to Government (C2G) e-commerce*—occurs when an individual sells products and services to a government entity. To sell products and services to the U.S. federal government, you must register yourself as a formal business, so you're not really an individual anymore but rather an individual "doing business as" (DBA) some organization or business.
- *Government to Business (G2B) e-commerce*—occurs when a government entity sells products and services to businesses. The Small Business Administration (SBA), for example, offers services such as loans, surety guarantees, disaster assistance, ombudsman, and so on.

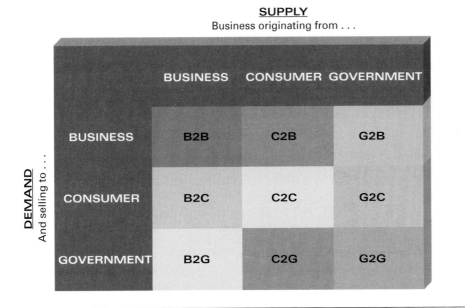

Figure 5.1

Nine Major E-Commerce
Business Models

- *Government to Consumer (G2C) e-commerce*—refers to the electronic commerce activities performed between a government and its citizens or consumers including paying taxes, registering vehicles, providing information and services, and so on.
- *Government to Government (G2G) e-commerce*—refers to the electronic commerce activities performed within a nation's government or between two more nations' governments including providing foreign aid and the sharing of border patrol activities.

BUSINESS TO BUSINESS (B2B) E-COMMERCE

Business to Business (B2B) e-commerce occurs when a business sells products and services to customers who are primarily other businesses. So, for example, when Gates Rubber Company sells belts, hoses, and other rubber and synthetic products to Ford Motor Company or any other manufacturer that needs those parts, this is B2B e-commerce. B2B e-commerce is where all the money is right now in the e-commerce world. It's not the flashy consumer-oriented businesses you read about and see everyday such as eBay, Facebook, and so on. It's the many behind-the-scenes interactions that businesses engage in ultimately to support interacting with you as a customer, such as Gates selling a hose to Ford for a car that you eventually buy. Another example is First Data Corporation. First Data Corporation is a payments infrastructure provider that many businesses use. When you pay with a credit card at most major stores, your credit card authorization and verification is handled by First Data for the store. You may not have even heard of First Data, but it is one of America's top-250 largest corporations.

As you can see in Figure 5.2 on the next page, businesses are taking full advantage of e-commerce by creating and using B2B e-marketplaces. *B2B e-marketplaces* are virtual marketplaces in which businesses buy from and sell products to each other, share information (as in information partnerships from Chapter 2), and perform other important activities. B2B e-marketplaces represent one of the fastest growing trends in the B2B e-commerce model. Businesses are increasingly aware that they must create supply chain management systems, drive out costs, create information partnerships with other businesses, and even collaborate with other businesses on new product and service offerings. B2B e-marketplaces offer tremendous efficiencies to businesses for performing all of these tasks.

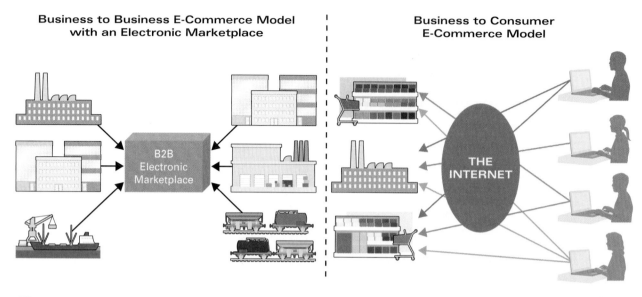

Figure 5.2

Business to Business and
Business to Consumer
E-Commerce Business
Models

BUSINESS TO CONSUMER (B2C) E-COMMERCE

Business to Consumer (B2C) e-commerce occurs when a business sell products and
services to customers who are primarily individuals. You are no doubt familiar with this
model of e-commerce. If you've ever ordered a book on Amazon (www.amazon.com),
purchased a CD from Circuit City online (www.circuitcity.com), or ordered a movie
from Netflix (www.netflix.com), you've participated in B2C e-commerce.

B2C e-commerce garners most of the attention these days in the popular media.
B2C e-commerce is the model that fueled the early growth of e-commerce in the
1990s. B2C e-commerce is very much a cutthroat environment, no matter what the
product and service. Amazon, one of the most well-known B2C businesses, daily faces
stiff competition from hundreds of other e-commerce businesses selling books, movies, music, clothing, computers, consumer electronics, health and beauty products,
and home and garden products.

As you can see in Figure 5.2, the B2C e-commerce business model is very different from the B2B e-commerce business model. Consumers interact directly with businesses via the Web. Consumers surf around the Web evaluating products and services at
numerous separate e-commerce sites until they eventually choose one site from which to
make a purchase. And while businesses prefer to enter into long-term partnerships with
other businesses in B2B e-commerce, consumers are fickle and purchase the same types
of products and services from many different sites.

CONSUMER TO BUSINESS (C2B) E-COMMERCE

Consumer to Business (C2B) e-commerce occurs when an individual sells products and
services to a business. The C2B e-commerce business model is a true inversion of the
B2C e-commerce business model. In the B2C e-commerce business model, demand is

driven by the consumer and supply is driven by the business. In C2B it is inverted; the consumer drives supply and the business drives demand.[3] Many people have mistakenly lumped such sites as Priceline.com (www.priceline.com) into the C2B category. At Priceline.com you, as a consumer, can set your price for items such as airlines tickets and hotel rooms, but you (as a consumer) still provide the demand and the airline or hotel still provides the supply.

A good example of a true C2B e-commerce business model is offered by Fotolia (www.fotolia.com). There, as an individual, you can post your photos and videos for sale to businesses. Businesses search through the photo and video archives, and, if they choose yours, will pay you a royalty fee to use the photo or video.

Affiliate programs are another good example of the C2B e-commerce business model. Through an affiliate program relationship with Amazon, for example, you can post links on your personal Web site to Amazon for products and services it sells. If a visitor to your site clicks on one of those links and eventually buys the product or service from Amazon, Amazon will pay you a commission fee, which is usually some small percentage of the sale. With this arrangement, you are selling advertising space to Amazon on your Web site; hence, it is an example of the C2B e-commerce business model.

Currently, the C2B e-commerce business model represents only a fraction of the total revenues in the e-commerce space, but it is expected to grow as businesses realize that individuals are more than just consumers of products and services. Blogging, for example, can easily become a C2B e-commerce business model, if you know what you're doing.

CONSUMER TO CONSUMER (C2C) E-COMMERCE

Consumer to Consumer (C2C) e-commerce occurs when an individual sells products and services to another individual. C2C e-commerce usually takes place through an intermediary organization, such as eBay. eBay is a hybrid of both a B2C e-commerce site and a C2C e-commerce site. It is a B2C e-commerce site because it sells a service to you, that of giving you the ability to interact in the auctioning of items. (You pay eBay only if you're the seller, not the buyer.) And it is really an intermediary supporting your engagement in a C2C e-commerce business model. That is, you use eBay to sell products and services to other consumers, and you use eBay to buy products and services from other consumers.

Many C2C Web sites don't really support any sort of e-commerce (i.e., money exchanging hands for products and services). Rather, they facilitate the gathering of people with common interests and something to share. Kazaa (www.kazaa.com) is an example of such a site because it brings together people who want to share mainly MP3 music files. Blogs might also fall into the category of C2C, as they support people sharing and discussing common interests. Many of these types of sites are **ad-supported**, meaning that they derive their revenue by selling advertising space, much like the concept of an affiliate program.

That ends our overview of the nine e-commerce business models. Although conceptually distinct, in practice each overlaps with one or more of the other models. The question for you now is how to execute on the e-commerce model in which your business operates. We'll focus specifically on B2B and B2C e-commerce, since that is where you'll most likely be working. We will explore three e-commerce *critical success factors:* (1) Understand your business and your customers; (2) Find and establish relationships with customers; (3) Move money easily and securely.

Understand Your Business, Products, Services, and Customers

To gain a competitive advantage and be successful in any business, you must clearly define the nature of your products and services, know who your target customers are, and understand how your customers perceive the use of your products and services in their business activities (for the B2B model) or in their personal lives (for the B2C model). To create sound business strategies you have to understand the value that your customers place on your products and services.

There are many worthwhile business activities. But as important as writing a mission statement and producing glitzy marketing brochures may be, what must come first is an objective, very down-to-earth understanding of what your business does. The reality is you can't be all things to all customers. You must answer two questions: (1) Who are your target customers? and (2) What is the value of your products and services as perceived by your customers? Let's look at each in turn.

WHO ARE YOUR CUSTOMERS?

Just as in a brick-and-mortar business, in the e-commerce world you focus your efforts on selling to other businesses, to individual end consumers, or to some combination of the two. If you were in a business like Gates Rubber Company, which produces mostly rubber and synthetic products primarily for sale to the automotive industry and manufacturers of such products as boats and bicycles, you would focus almost exclusively on the B2B e-commerce model, with other businesses as your target customers. If, however, you were selling resumé writing and job placement services to individuals looking for careers, your customers would be B2C individual end consumers. Finally, you might be like Monster.com (www.monster.com), which provides an electronic marketplace catering to both individuals looking for careers and businesses looking for employees. If you were in a business like Monster's, your customer mix would include both end consumers and businesses and you'd need to carefully consider both groups of customers, their needs, and the value to them of the products and services you sell.

Many businesses in the travel industry, American Express, for example, cater to both businesses and end consumers. As an individual consumer, you might work with American Express to plan and pay for a vacation. At the same time, many businesses use the services of American Express to handle all their business travel needs.

Whatever the nature of your business, you must know who your customers are. In the world of e-commerce, that means clearly distinguishing between end consumers (B2C) and other businesses (B2B), even if you target both. As you will see throughout this chapter, individual end consumers and other businesses have dramatically different needs.

WHAT IS THE VALUE OF YOUR PRODUCTS AND SERVICES AS PERCEIVED BY YOUR CUSTOMERS?

If a customer orders a product or service from your organization, it is because that customer perceives some value in what you provide—the customer either *wants* or *needs* your product or service. When we examine wants and needs, the distinctions between end consumers and businesses as customers become increasingly important and clearly evident. Let's look at product/service categories needed by each customer group in turn. (See Figure 5.3.)

Business to Consumer (B2C)	Business to Business (B2B)
• **Convenience**—low-priced but something needed on a frequent basis	• **Maintenance, repair, and operations (MRO) materials**—necessary items that do not relate directly to the company's primary business activities
• **Specialty**—higher-priced, ordered on a less frequent basis, and often requiring customization	• **Direct materials**—materials used in production in a manufacturing company or placed on the shelf for sale in a retail environment
• **Commoditylike**—the same no matter where you buy it	
• **Digital**—the best of all because of low cost of inventory and shipping	

Figure 5.3

B2C and B2B Products and Services

B2C: CONVENIENCE VERSUS SPECIALTY   In many respects, you can differentiate between convenience and specialty merchandise (or services) on the basis of price and consumers' frequency of purchase. To end consumers, *convenience* merchandise is typically lower priced but something they often need, usually frequently. Nonperishable food items such as breakfast cereals are a good example. From organizations such as Peapod (www.peapod.com), you can easily order food items and have them delivered to your home within 24 hours of making the order or at predetermined time intervals such as weekly. Consumers might pay more for these low-priced items in order to have them "conveniently."

Specialty merchandise might be such things as home stereo systems, computers, name-brand clothing, furniture, and the like. For consumers, these are higher-priced (than convenience merchandise) items, are typically ordered on a less-frequent basis, and often require some sort of customization or feature specification. For specialty merchandise, consumers will spend more time "shopping around," not only to find the best deal in terms of price but also because value for these items is perceived in terms of customization, warranty, service, and other after-sales features.

B2C: COMMODITYLIKE AND DIGITAL   In B2C e-commerce, as a general rule, the best merchandise to sell is either commoditylike, digital, or a combination of the two. This enables you to minimize your internal costs, but requires that you be innovative in how you offer your merchandise and attract consumers to your site.

Commoditylike merchandise, to your customers, is the same regardless of where they purchase it, and it is similar to convenience items in that respect. Books are a good example. No matter where you buy a particular book, it is the same. As a business, you compete in a commoditylike environment on the basis of:

- Price
- Ease and speed of delivery
- Ease of ordering
- Your return policy

Of course, commoditylike business environments are typically easy to enter (i.e., they have low barriers to entry) and thus buyer power is high (from Porter's Five Forces

Model in Chapter 1). Your organization's goals in this type of environment would have to include (1) minimizing price to the end consumer and (2) minimizing your internal costs by creating a tight supply chain management system (from Chapter 2). You also want to create a "sticky" Web site that not only attracts consumers but also encourages them to return to your site again and again.

Digital merchandise offerings are also important in the B2C e-commerce model. The goal here is to eliminate shipping costs by delivering the digital product over the Internet once a consumer has made a purchase. Music is a good example. Apple's iTunes Web site (www.apple.com/itunes/store/) allows you to select exactly the song you want, pay for it, and then download it from the Internet. Apple can offer each song for just 99 cents (or a little more or a little less depending on the song) because it has no physical delivery costs and no physical inventory. As this example illustrates, digital products are also advantageous (to the business and to the consumer) because they are customizable. That is, customers don't have to purchase an entire music CD—they can pick only the song or songs they want.

B2C: MASS CUSTOMIZATION   End consumers are often interested in customizing their purchases. In the B2C e-commerce model this need gives rise to the concept of *mass customization*—the ability of an organization to give its customers the opportunity to tailor its product or service to the customer's specifications. Customization can be appropriate and is a key competitive advantage regardless of other customer value perceptions. For example, Dell Computer (www.dell.com) is well regarded in its market especially for being the best at allowing consumers to customize a computer purchase. Music sites, such as Apple, now allow you to pick the songs you want instead of an entire CD. Clothing sites allow you to select from among various styles, colors, and sizes of clothing to fit your needs.

In a B2C environment, you're potentially dealing with millions of different consumers, each with unique tastes and needs. You must support the concept of mass customization.

B2B: MRO VERSUS DIRECT   *Maintenance, repair, and operations (MRO) materials* (also called *indirect materials*) are materials that are necessary for running a modern corporation, but do not relate to the company's primary business activities. MRO materials include everything from ballpoint pens to three-ring binders, repair parts for equipment, and lubricating oils. Thus, B2B MRO materials are similar to convenience and commoditylike items in the B2C e-commerce model.

In their purchases of these materials, however, business customers (B2B) are very different from end consumers (B2C) in many ways. For example, a business because of its volume of MRO materials purchases can bargain with suppliers for a discount (end consumers in the B2C e-commerce model usually don't have this ability). Many businesses may band together to create even more volume and thus demand an even higher discount from a supplier. This practice is known as *demand aggregation*—the combining of purchase requests from multiple buyers into a single large order, which justifies a discount from the business. If your organization is a supplier of MRO materials in the B2B e-commerce model, you will compete mostly on price (including discounts), delivery, and ease of ordering.

Direct materials are materials that are used in production in a manufacturing company or are placed on the shelf for sale in a retail environment. So, as opposed to MRO materials, direct materials relate to a company's primary business activities. It is critically important that the customer business receives exactly what is needed in terms of quality, quantity, and the timing of delivery of direct materials.

For direct materials acquisition, some businesses participate in a reverse auction (through an electronic marketplace). A *reverse auction* is the process in which a buyer posts its interest in buying a certain quantity of items with notations concerning quality, specification, and delivery timing, and sellers compete for the business by submitting successively lower bids until there is only one seller left. Reverse auctions create tremendous "power" for the buyer because multiple sellers are competing for the same business.

B2B: HORIZONTAL VERSUS VERTICAL   As a supplier to other businesses, you also need to understand whether you are selling in a horizontal or vertical e-marketplace (see Figure 5.4). An *electronic marketplace (e-marketplace)* is an interactive business providing a central market space where multiple buyers and suppliers can engage in e-commerce and/or other e-commerce business activities. E-marketplaces feature a variety of implementations including value-added network providers (which we'll discuss later in the chapter), horizontal e-marketplaces, and vertical e-marketplaces. A *horizontal e-marketplace* is an electronic marketplace that connects buyers and sellers across many industries, primarily for MRO materials commerce. Again, MRO materials include a broad of range of both products and services including office supplies, travel, shipping, and some financial services. Because horizontal e-marketplaces

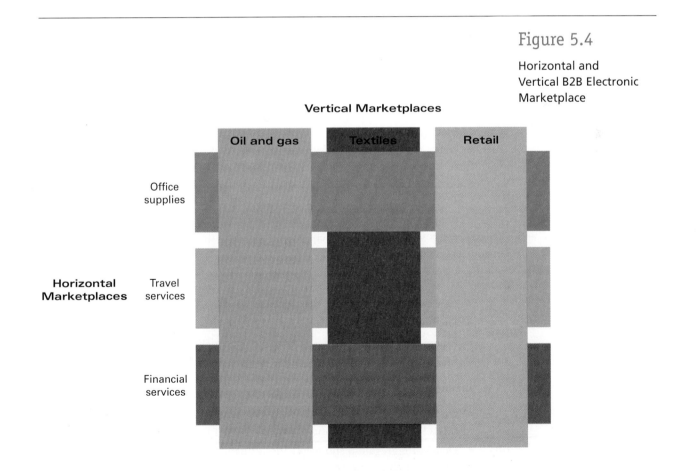

Figure 5.4

Horizontal and Vertical B2B Electronic Marketplace

support MRO materials commerce, much of our previous discussion on B2B e-commerce for MRO materials holds true here.

A *vertical e-marketplace* is an electronic marketplace that connects buyers and sellers in a given industry (e.g., oil and gas, textiles, and retail). Covisint (www.covisint.com) is a good example. Covisint provides a B2B e-marketplace in the automotive industry where buyers and sellers specific to that industry conduct commerce in products and services, share mission-critical information for the development of products and parts, collaborate on new ideas, and deploy infrastructure applications that enable the seamless communication of each other's proprietary IT systems.

To summarize, we have offered you some ideas to think about regarding the following aspects of e-commerce that will help you in understanding the nature of your business, products, services, and customers.

- **Business to Consumer**

  - Greatly varying customer demographics, lifestyles, wants, and needs
  - Distinctions of products and services by convenience versus specialty
  - E-commerce works best for commoditylike and digital products and services
  - Mass customization adds value in some instances

- **Business to Business**

  - Distinctions of products and services by maintenance, repair, and operations (MRO) materials versus direct materials
  - Demand aggregation and negotiation capabilities enhanced for businesses as customers (buyer power)
  - E-marketplaces connect buyers and sellers—horizontal e-marketplaces (primarily for MRO materials) and vertical e-marketplaces (specific to a given industry)

Find Customers and Establish Relationships

You can't make a sale until you find and reach customers and establish a relationship with them. This is *marketing.* There are special features of and technical considerations about marketing and creating customer relationships in e-commerce to keep in mind that can create a competitive advantage for you.

BUSINESS TO CONSUMER

With well over 1 billion people on the Internet, you'd think it would be easy to find and attract customers to your B2C e-commerce site. But that's not necessarily true because all your competition is trying to do the same thing—drive customers to their Web site and encourage them to make a purchase.

First, you need to determine your appropriate ***marketing mix***—the set of marketing tools that your organization will use to pursue its marketing objectives in reaching and attracting potential customers. In B2C e-commerce, your marketing mix will probably include some or all of the following: registering with search engines, online ads, viral marketing, and affiliate programs (and most definitely social media, which we've discussed at great length).

Many Web surfers use *search engines* to find information and products and services. While some search engines will include your site for free (FreeSearch.com at www .freesearch.com is an example), almost all the popular search engines such as Yahoo! and Google require you to pay a fee. Most of these sites will guarantee that your site appears in the top portion of a search list for an additional fee.

Online ads (often called ***banner ads***) are small advertisements that appear on other sites (see Figure 5.5). Variations of online ads include pop-up and pop-under ads. A

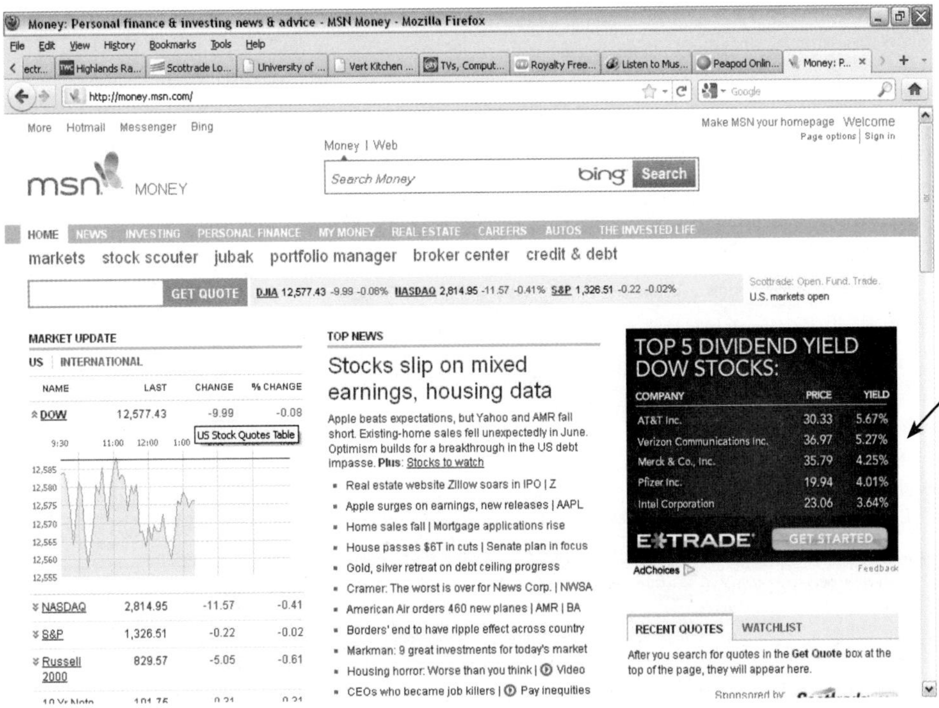

Figure 5.5

Banner ads at MSN Money.com

Banner ad for a stock brokerage firm

pop-up ad is a small Web page containing an advertisement that appears on your screen outside the current Web site loaded into your browser. A *pop-under ad* is a form of a pop-up ad that you do not see until you close your current browser window. A word of caution here: Most people don't mind banner ads because they appear as a part of the site they're visiting. However, most people consider pop-up and pop-under ads to be very annoying.

Viral marketing encourages users of a product or service supplied by a B2C e-commerce business to encourage friends to join in as well. Blue Mountain Arts (www.bluemountain.com) is a good example. When you use Blue Mountain to send an e-birthday card (or some other type of card), the intended recipient will receive an e-mail directing him or her to Blue Mountain's site. Once the recipient views the card, Blue Mountain provides a link so that person can send you a card in return. Of course, Blue Mountain charges for each card sent, so it makes money both ways.

An *affiliate program* is an arrangement made between two e-commerce sites that directs viewers from one site to the other. Amazon.com is the most well-known creator of an affiliate program. If you become an Amazon associate, your e-commerce Web site directs viewers to Amazon's site for certain purchases. If a sale results, Amazon pays you a fee, which is usually a percentage of the sale (see Figure 5.6). Likewise, you can pay another site to direct traffic to yours, which may be through an online ad. In some instances, affiliate programs create relationships such that a payment is made for each click-through. A *click-through* is a count of the number of people who visit one site, click on an ad, and are taken to the site of the advertiser.

In general, you want your marketing mix to drive as many potential customers as possible to have a look at your B2C e-commerce offerings. From there, however, you need to focus on your conversion rate. A *conversion rate* is the percentage of potential customers who visit your site who actually buy something. So, while total views or "hits" to your e-commerce Web site are important, obviously even more so is your conversion rate.

Figure 5.6

Amazon.com's Affiliate Program Is Called *Associates*

THE WORLD OF FACEBOOK NOW INCLUDES A FULL ECONOMY

There is no doubt that Facebook, which started out as a seemingly simple project for sharing information at one school, has had a significant and profound effect on our society. All you have to do is visit Facebook's statistics page at http://www.facebook.com/press/info.php?statistics and read about the depth and breadth of Facebook and you will quickly come to understand the extent to which Facebook has permeated our lives.

And like any good innovative company, Facebook wants more. It wants you to spend more time there; it wants you to be connected to more communities; it wants you to have more friends. And now, it wants your money. No, Facebook has no plans to charges users. Facebook is creating a virtual economy with its own currency, called Facebook credits.

Facebook began testing its currency in mid-2009 and fully rolled it out in 2010. Facebook now requires all game developers to accept payment using Facebook credits. However, that won't be the only way gamers can pay; they can still use the likes of PayPal. But Facebook is offering incentives for game developers who focus solely on accepting Facebook credits.

Facebook has also begun competing with Groupon and Living Social. Through its daily deal offerings, Facebook users can instantly purchase real goods with Facebook credits. Users will get the daily deals in their news feeds and are just a few clicks away from spending money. How does Facebook make money? Several ways actually. First, when a user buys merchandise—a daily deal, a game, whatever—Facebook keeps 30 percent of the revenue and passes 70 percent along to the merchant or developer.

Second, Facebook makes money from money. When you buy Facebook credits, there's a good chance that some of those credits will remain in your account, that is, you will always have some sort of balance. All the while, Facebook will be making interest from a bank on your money. Social Times Pro, a research firm, estimated that $600 million would be moving through Facebook's virtual economy in a 12-month period. If 10 percent stays in users' accounts, then Facebook will be accruing interest on $60 million.

And there's a future revenue stream that Facebook is eyeing. As we move increasingly toward mobile commerce and thus mobile payments, Facebook is positioning itself as a mobile payments provider. So someday soon (or perhaps even now), you'll be able to make a purchase on your mobile device using Facebook credits. And that purchase could be for a Starbucks coffee, an app in Apple's store, or perhaps even a computer from Dell.[5]

BUSINESS TO BUSINESS

Finding and attracting customers to your B2B e-commerce site is much different. Businesses—customers in the B2B model—don't usually find products and services by surfing the Web or using search engines. Instead, business customers prefer to actively participate in e-marketplaces to find suppliers. Within an e-marketplace, an organization can participate in a reverse auction to find a supplier, as we discussed earlier.

Moreover, an organization can search an e-marketplace for suitable suppliers and then enter into negotiations outside the e-marketplace. This happens for organizations needing to purchase millions of dollars in inventory, parts, or raw materials, and it occurs for organizations wanting to establish a long-term relationship with just one supplier.

Relationships among businesses in B2B are very important. These relationships, characterized by trust and continuity, extend into the IT realm. In the B2B e-commerce business model, you must provide a level of integration of your IT systems with those of your business partners. Once a formal business relationship has been established, the goal is to use IT to streamline the ordering and procurement processes to create tight supply chain management systems and drive out cost, so your IT systems have to work closely together.

To summarize, some ideas about marketing, or finding customers and creating relationships with them, in e-commerce are:

- **Business to Consumer**
  - Design marketing mix to drive potential customers to a Web site
  - Register with a search engine; use online ads, viral marketing, and affiliate programs
  - Conversion rates measure success
- **Business to Business**
  - Businesses participate in e-marketplaces—business customers don't surf the Web, so e-marketplaces need your attention, not a broad and generic marketing mix
  - Formal establishment of business relationships based on trust and continuity required
  - Some level of IT system integration between you and your customer required
  - Online negotiations for pricing, quality, specifications, and delivery timing

Move Money Easily and Securely

In the world of e-commerce, you must create IT systems that enable your customers (other businesses or end consumers) to pay electronically, easily, and securely for their purchases. Of course, you can still accept credit cards as the form of payment just like in the brick-and-mortar world, but credit card payments are really an electronic form of payment.

BUSINESS TO CONSUMER PAYMENT SYSTEMS

Your customers in the Business to Consumer e-commerce model will most often pay for products and services using credit cards, financial cybermediaries, electronic checks, Electronic Bill Presentment and Payment (EBPP), or smart cards.

- *Financial cybermediary*—an Internet-based company that makes it easy for one person to pay another person or organization over the Internet. PayPal (www.paypal.com) is the best-known example of a financial cybermediary (see Figure 5.7). You create a PayPal account by logging on to the PayPal Web site and providing it with personal, credit card, and banking information. When you want to send money, you go to the PayPal site and enter the amount of money you want to send and provide information for either the person or organization you want to send the money to. You can also accumulate money in your personal PayPal account by accepting money from other people. You can transfer the money to one of your banking accounts, use it for other purposes, send the funds to someone else, or just leave it there for awhile.
- *Electronic check*—a mechanism for sending money from your checking or savings account to another person or organization. There are many implementations of electronic checks, with the most prominent being online banking.
- *Electronic Bill Presentment and Payment (EBPP)*—a system that sends bills (usually to end consumers) over the Internet and provides an easy-to-use mechanism (such as clicking on a button) to pay for them if the amount looks correct. EBPP systems are available through local banks or online services such as Checkfree (www .checkfree.com) and Quicken (www.quicken.com/banking_and_credit/).

GOOGLE UPS THE ANTE IN THE MOBILE PAYMENTS MARKET

According to Stephanie Tilenius, Google's Vice President of Commerce, "We're about to embark on a new era of commerce where we bring online and offline together. We believe the shopping experience has not yet been transformed by technology or by magical experience. Now, your phone can be your wallet—you just tap, pay, and save." Those are profound words which were accompanied by the announcement of Google Wallet, a mobile app that lets you pay for goods via your smartphone.

Inside Google Wallet, you'll be able to store credit card information and also information relating to a Google debit card. When you buy merchandise at a physical store, you wave your Android phone in front of a reader to make payment. Once you do, you can select on your screen which credit or debit card (stored in your Google Wallet) you wish to use. It's based on a technology called **Near Field Communication,** or **NFC,** a wireless transmission technology developed primarily for mobile phones to support mobile commerce (m-commerce) and other phone activities.

Unlike most credit card companies like MasterCard, Google won't be taking a cut of the transaction if you use your Google debit card. Instead, Google will help companies to target their advertising by providing customer information, including their purchase history. That program, called Google Offers, will allow retailers to direct offers and discounts to specific people.

Is security a consideration? It most definitely is. According to Osama Bedier, Google's Vice President of Payments, "It [security] was a fundamental consideration from day 1." Google also went on to point out that consumers are becoming more comfortable with digital transactions, even those involving credit cards. According to Google, a decade ago 70 percent of consumers were reluctant to pay for merchandise online. Today, over 70 percent of consumers access their credit card information over the Internet.[6, 7]

Figure 5.7

PayPal Is the Most Well-Known Financial Cybermediary

- *Smart card*—plastic card the size of a credit card that contains an embedded chip on which digital information can be stored and updated. The chip, in this case, can contain information about how much money you have. When you swipe your card to pay for a purchase, the swiping device deducts the purchase amount from the amount you have stored on the chip. Some debit cards are implementations of the smart card concept.

The entire payment process encompasses more than accepting a form of payment. It also includes determining the shipping address for your customer. You can create a competitive advantage by having a way of asking each customer only once for his or her delivery information and storing it, thus creating a switching cost because when your customer makes another purchase, you can simply ask him or her to verify the delivery information and not have to provide it all over again. One implementation of this is called a digital wallet. A *digital wallet* is both software and information—the software provides security for the transaction and the information includes payment information (for example, the credit card number and expiration date) and delivery information. Digital wallets can be stored either on the client side or the server side. A *client-side digital wallet* is one that you create and keep on your computer; you can then use it at a variety of e-commerce Web sites. Most browsers such as Internet Explorer support your ability to create this type of digital wallet. A *server-side digital wallet* (sometimes referred to as a *thin wallet*) is one that an organization creates for and about you and maintains on its server. Many credit card issuers use this type of digital wallet to verify your credit card transactions.

All of this is significant because your customers in the B2C e-commerce model exhibit some common characteristics when paying for your products and services.

- They tend to make numerous purchases for small amounts.
- They pay for each transaction individually.
- You must validate each transaction.

BUSINESS TO BUSINESS PAYMENT SYSTEMS

Payments for products and services in the Business to Business e-commerce model are usually much different from those in the Business to Consumer e-commerce model. In B2B e-commerce, your customers tend to make very large purchases and will not pay using a credit card or a financial cybermediary such as PayPal. Instead, other businesses will want to pay (1) through financial EDI and (2) often in large, aggregated amounts encompassing many purchases.

ELECTRONIC DATA INTERCHANGE   In the B2B model, another business wants to order products and services from your organization via electronic data interchange. *Electronic data interchange (EDI)* is the direct computer-to-computer transfer of transaction information contained in standard business documents, such as invoices and purchase orders, in a standard format. Your organization can implement EDI-facilitated transactions in many ways; one of the more prominent is a B2B e-marketplace that supports EDI through a value-added network. A *value-added network (VAN)* is a B2B service that offers information-sharing intermediary services between organizations based on various standards regarding the format of the information and how it will be sent and received. Using a VAN, businesses can easily, for example, order products and send invoices electronically.

FINANCIAL ELECTRONIC DATA INTERCHANGE   After the ordering of products and the sending of invoices, money needs to exchange hands. This occurs via financial electronic data interchange. *Financial electronic data interchange (financial EDI)* is the electronic process used primarily within the B2B e-commerce model for the payment for purchases. The actual reconciliation of the funds may occur through a bank or an automated clearing house (ACH) support site such as National Cash Management Systems (www.ach-eft-ncms.com).

SECURITY: THE PERVADING CONCERN

Regardless of whether your customers are other businesses or end consumers, they are all greatly concerned about the security of their transactions. This includes all aspects of electronic information, but focuses mainly on the information associated with payments (e.g., a credit card number) and the payments themselves, that is, the "electronic money." Here, you need to consider such issues as encryption, Secure Sockets Layers, and Secure Electronic Transactions. This is by no means an exhaustive list but rather representative of the broad field of security relating to electronic commerce.

ENCRYPTION   *Encryption* scrambles the contents of a file so that you can't read it without having the right decryption key. Encryption can be achieved in many ways: by scrambling letters in a known way, replacing letters with other letters or perhaps numbers, and other ways.

Some encryption technologies use multiple keys. In this instance, you would be using *public key encryption (PKE)*—an encryption system that uses two keys: a public key that everyone can have and a private key for only the recipient (see Figure 5.8). When implementing security using multiple keys, your organization provides the public key to all its customers (end consumers and other businesses). The customers use the public key to encrypt their information and send it along the Internet. When it arrives at its destination, your organization would use the private key to unscramble the encrypted information.

SECURE SOCKETS LAYERS   A *Secure Sockets Layer (SSL)* (1) creates a secure and private connection between a Web client computer and a Web server computer, (2) encrypts the information, and (3) then sends the information over the Internet. SSLs do provide good security for transferring information and are used widely by B2C e-commerce Web sites. As an end consumer, you can tell your information is being transferred via SSL if you see either (1) the Web site address starts with https:// (notice the inclusion of the "s") as opposed to just http:// or (2) the presence of a lock icon in the bottom portion of your Web browser window (see Figure 5.9 on the next page).

SECURE ELECTRONIC TRANSACTIONS   A *Secure Electronic Transaction (SET)* is a transmission security method that ensures transactions are *legitimate* as well as secure.

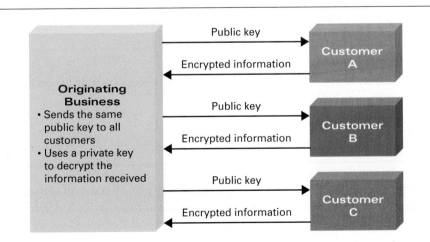

Figure 5.8

Public Key Encryption (PKE) System

Figure 5.9

Secure Sockets Layer (SSL) on a Web Site

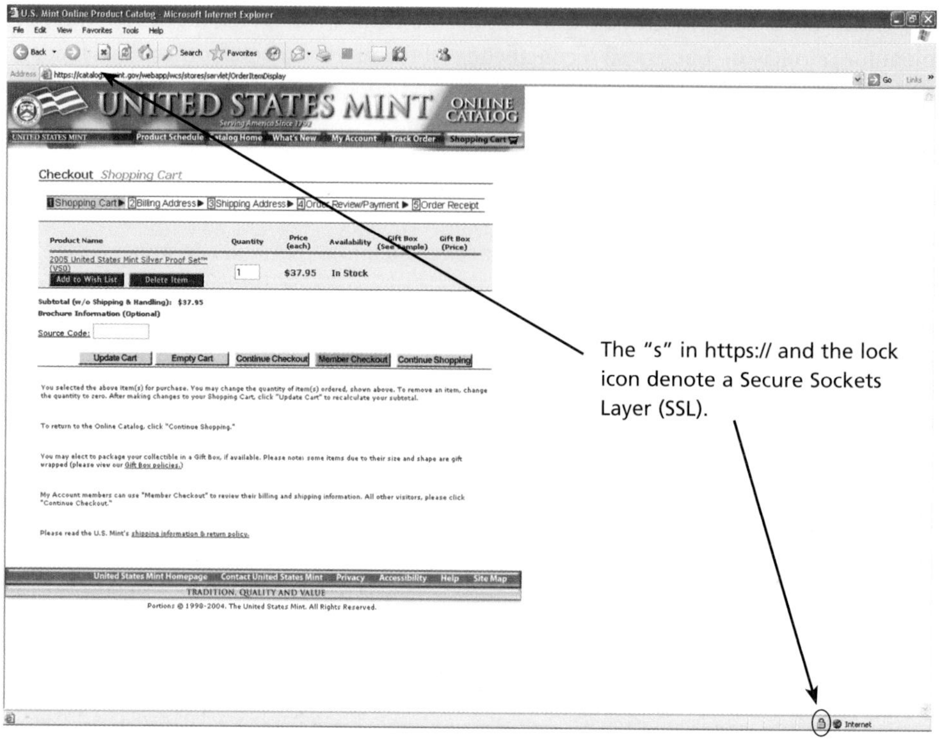

The "s" in https:// and the lock icon denote a Secure Sockets Layer (SSL).

Much like an SSL, an SET encrypts information before sending it over the Internet. Taking it one step further, an SET enables you, as a merchant, to verify a customer's identity by securely transmitting credit card information to the business that issued the credit card for verification. SETs are endorsed by major e-commerce players including MasterCard, American Express, Visa, Netscape, and Microsoft.

To summarize:

- **Business to Consumer**
  - Methods include credit cards, financial cybermediaries, electronic checks, Electronic Bill Presentment and Payment (EBPP), smart cards, and digital wallets.
  - Consumers make numerous individual purchases for small amounts that must each be validated.
- **Business to Business**
  - The use of electronic data interchange (EDI) facilitates the ordering process.
  - Value-added network providers used for EDI and financial EDI.
  - Financial EDI used for payment of purchases.
- **Both Business to Consumer and Business to Business**
  - Security is an overriding concern.
  - Security is provided by the use of encryption, Secure Sockets Layers (SSLs), and Secure Electronic Transactions (SETs).

E-Business Trends

LEARNING OUTCOME 5

If you look out over the e-business horizon, you can see many trends. All of the chapter-opening cases (the Outrageous Industry Transformations that start each chapter) in this book are about e-business trends that are changing entire industries. Here, we focus on four trends destined to radically transform *all* industries.

LONG-TAIL ECONOMICS

Think about Amazon, Netflix, and Rhapsody (a competitor to iTunes). In purely financial terms, how would you describe their paths-to-profitability? For Rhapsody, you might say that it has no physical store, no unsold inventory that must be eventually dumped at a loss, and so on. You would, in fact, be partially correct. And you might similarly describe Amazon and Netflix—no stores to manage, fewer employees, etc. Again, you would be partially correct. But the real key to their success lies in the Long Tail.

The **Long Tail**—a notion first offered by Chris Anderson, Editor-in-Chief of *Wired* magazine, as a way of explaining e-commerce profitability—actually refers to the tail of a sales curve (see Figure 5.10).[8, 9] Figure 5.10 shows music song titles, ranked by popularity, for Walmart and Rhapsody (www.rhapsody.com). What you see is that a typical Walmart store stocks about 25,000 songs. Because of the cost of shelf placement in a retailing environment, that's about all Walmart can carry and make a profit. Rhapsody, however, because everything is digital and retail shelf placement costs are irrelevant, carries 1.5 million tracks. Moreover, a full 40 percent of Rhapsody's total sales come from songs in the Long Tail of the sales distribution. Hence, the importance of the notion of the Long Tail.

E-commerce businesses that can reach the audience in the Long Tail can do so without the typical brick-and-mortar retail costs and expenses (representing both fixed and variable costs in break-even analysis). This is real *mass customization,* of which we spoke earlier, and also goes by the terms *slivercasting* (as opposed to *broadcasting*) and *massclusivity* (a combination of *mass production* and *exclusivity*). In Figure 5.11 on the next page, we've provided inventory and sales data for Rhapsody, Netflix, and Amazon. Notice that Netflix generates 21 percent of its total sales from the Long Tail, and Amazon generates 25 percent of its total sales from the Long Tail.

Long Tail represents an entirely new business model and requires new business thinking. Traditional business thinking looks at sales in terms of economies of scale, seeking to sell as many of one item as possible to offset fixed costs (such as shelf placement costs). The Long Tail model is quite different. Because fixed costs are so minimal, Rhapsody and iTunes can afford to sell only one or two downloads of a given song and still make a profit. Walmart can't do that. In fact, Walmart will only carry music CDs

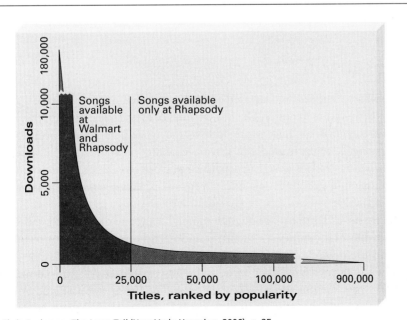

Figure 5.10

The Long Tail

Source: Chris Anderson, *The Long Tail* (New York: Hyperion, 2006), p. 25.

Figure 5.11

The Long Tail Economics for Rhapsody, Netflix, and Amazon

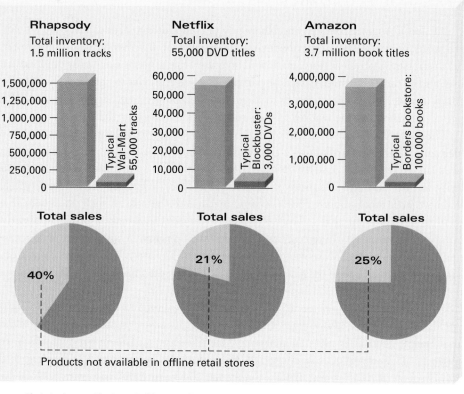

Source: Chris Anderson, *The Long Tail* (New York: Hyperion, 2006), p. 23.

for which it believes sales will be at least several thousand (worldwide). So, it doesn't carry niche products, whereas Rhapsody and iTunes do. The same is true for Netflix. While a typical Blockbuster rental store carries only 3,000 movie DVDs, Netflix carries over 55,000. Likewise, while a typical Borders bookstore carries only 100,000 books, Amazon has over 3.7 million book titles in inventory.

This is a significant trend in the world of e-business. Some older, more traditional brick-and-mortar financial and inventory models no longer apply. It requires a new way of thinking. It is this sort of thinking that a younger generation like you can embrace and act on.

CROWDSOURCING

In the first three chapters, we provided examples of crowdsourcing including New York City's app development contest, Glaxo's opening of its database of 13,500 compounds that might cure malaria, and social "saving the world" contests. Formally defined, *crowdsourcing* is when businesses provide enabling technologies that allow people (i.e., crowds)—instead of designated paid employees—to create, modify, and oversee the development of a product or service. Let's look at a couple of high-powered crowdsourcing examples.

Goldcorp is a Toronto-based gold mining company in Canada. Shortly after the turn of the 21st century, Goldcorp found itself literally going out of business.[10] Uncontrollable debt, labor strikes, increasing production costs, and poor gold market conditions seemed they would doom the 50-year-old company. Internal employees (geologists) were unable to accurately determine the location of gold deposits on Goldcorp's 55,000 acres, and without the gold Goldcorp would fold.

So, Goldcorp held a crowdsourcing contest. On the Web, it published all of its geological data for the 55,000-acre property. It invited everyone around the world to massage the data and make recommendations regarding the best place to find gold and the appropriate extraction methods. Goldcorp put up $575,000 in prize money for the person(s) with the best recommendations. Thousands of people submitted ideas, everyone from graduate students in geology to retired government workers to rock-hound hobbyists.

Were the ideas any good? Yes, over 8 million ounces of gold were extracted using the ideas of nonpaid nonemployees. That equates to a return of $3 billion on a $575,000 investment. That is a true demonstration of the power of crowdsourcing.

Netflix held a similar contest, focusing on its lucrative recommendation engine.[11] You're familiar with a recommendation engine; for Netflix it offers additional movies you may want to watch based on your searches and selections. On the Web, Netflix published its recommendation engine algorithm plus a full year of transaction data. It also offered an amazing $1 million in prize money to the team who could improve Netflix's recommendation engine by at least 10 percent.

Teams from all over the world competed in the contest. Every few months, Netflix required all teams to upload their current work. That ensured that each team got to see and use the best algorithm so far. In the end, the winning team improved Netflix's recommendation engine technology by 14 percent. For a multibillion-dollar company, the $1 million in prize money was small compared to the return.

What you need to realize is that crowdsourcing signals a whole new approach to doing business. Think about the following examples. Each provides customers with enabling technologies and allows them to create value. Because the value exists, other customers become a part of the community as well.

- eBay
- Facebook
- Twitter
- YouTube
- Flickr
- Craigslist
- Monster.com

Consider eBay. Its employees are not paid to post items for sale and bid on other items. Instead, eBay has created a marketplace for people like you and me. You find value there because, perhaps, you can buy the books you need for school or get a good deal on an MP3 player. The sellers of those items find value on eBay because people like you buy their products.

Crowdsourcing isn't limited to only the Internet. Think about the show *American Idol*. It uses a variant of crowdsourcing called *contribution-defined*. Millions of viewers cast their votes for the best musician. Think carefully here. If millions of people vote for the top musician, don't you think that an album by that musician will sell really well? Of course, and that's exactly what recording studios are hoping to find. And better yet, they're getting market data (i.e., the millions of votes) for free.

VIRTUAL GOODS

Broadly defined, a ***virtual good*** is a nonphysical object. There are examples all around you—the music in your iTunes account, digital seeds in e-mails that bloom into flowers when you click on them (sent around Valentine's Day of course), and a whole host of toys, weapons, clothes, accessories, and so forth that you buy for use in online communities and games like Farmville, World of Warcraft, and the like. Think about apps for your smartphone. Technically each app is a virtual good.

Virtual goods is definitely an emerging e-business trend that you cannot ignore. According to market research firm In-Stat, consumers in 2007 purchased $2.1 billion worth of virtual goods. In-Stat predicted that the dollar value of virtual goods purchases would rise by 245 percent in 2010 to $7.3 billion. Further, the market research firm predicted growth of another 100 percent by 2014 to more than $14 billion.[12] ($14 billion is larger than the GDP of roughly 80 individual countries in the world.)

In Figure 5.12, you can see an unusual set of data, very much related to virtual goods. A large portion of virtual goods purchases occur in online games like World of Warcraft and those offered by Zynga. In Figure 5.12 you will notice that total worldwide gaming revenues are expected to grow by about $3 billion per year. As the online gaming market grows, so will the purchases of virtual goods.

Is virtual goods really a big business on a personal level? We would have to answer yes. Just ask Jon Jacobs. Jon is a long-time player of Entropia Universe. And Jon is quite well-known in that online community as an avid entrepreneur. In 2005, he paid $100,000 for an Entropia Universe asteroid. But a couple of years later he topped that by selling a bio dome, a mall, a stadium, and a club to John Foma Kalun. The value of the transaction was an amazing $335,000.[13]

MOBILE COMMERCE

Mobile computing is a broad general term describing your ability to use technology to wirelessly connect to and use centrally located information and/or application software. Mobile computing is all about wireless connectivity—just think about how important your smartphone is to you in your daily life and you'll quickly grasp the significance of this e-business trend.

Mobile commerce (m-commerce or wireless e-commerce) describes electronic commerce conducted over a wireless device such as a smartphone, laptop, or tablet PC. In Figure 5.13, you can see the mobile commerce numbers for the United States. Mobile

Figure 5.12

The Global Online Game Market (in $ Millions)[14]

YEAR	China	Korea	N. America	Europe	Japan	Developing Countries	TOTAL
2007	$2,200	$1,700	$1,500	$1,600	$700	$800	$8,500
2008	$2,400	$2,600	$1,700	$2,000	$800	$900	$10,400
2009	$2,900	$4,000	$1,800	$2,000	$900	$1,000	$12,600
2010 (Forecast)	$3,700	$5,000	$2,200	$2,500	$900	$1,100	$15,400
2011 (Forecast)	$4,500	$6,000	$2,500	$2,900	$1,000	$1,000	$18,000
2012 (Forecast)	$5,600	$7,200	$2,900	$3,300	$1,000	$1,200	$21,200

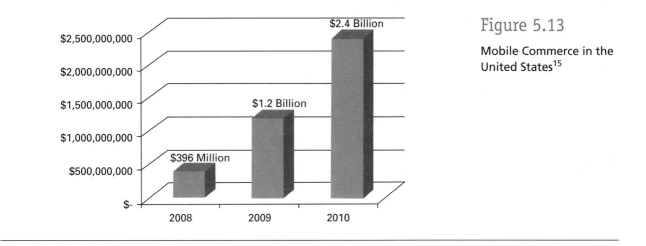

Figure 5.13

Mobile Commerce in the United States[15]

commerce revenues rose by some 600 percent in just two years, from $396 million in 2008 to $2.4 billion in 2010. By 2015, it is predicted that worldwide mobile commerce will exceed $119 billion.

■ SUMMARY: STUDENT LEARNING OUTCOMES REVISITED

1. **Define and describe the nine major e-commerce business models.** The nine major e-commerce business models are:

   - *Business to Business (B2B) e-commerce*—businesses selling products and services to other businesses.
   - *Business to Consumer (B2C) e-commerce*—businesses selling products and services to individual consumers.
   - *Consumer to Business (C2B) e-commerce*—individuals selling products and services to businesses.
   - *Consumer to Consumer (C2C) e-commerce*—individuals selling products and services to other individuals.
   - *Business to Government (B2G) e-commerce*—businesses selling products and services to a government entity.
   - *Consumer to Government (C2G) e-commerce*—individuals selling products and services to a government entity.
   - *Government to Business (G2B) e-commerce*—the government selling products and services to businesses.
   - *Government to Consumer (G2C) e-commerce*—the government selling products and services to individuals.
   - *Government to Government (G2G) e-commerce*—e-commerce activities within a single government or among two or more governments.

2. **Identify the differences and similarities among customers and their perceived value of products and services in the B2B and B2C e-commerce business models.** Customers in the B2C e-commerce business model are

CROWDS CREATE "VALUE" THROUGH FUNDING

Crowdsourcing can be a powerful tool for most organizations. On a personal level, you should think about taking advantage of crowdsourcing as well. How? By letting the crowd fund your business idea. Let's face it, as an entrepreneur with a great idea but very little cash, it's hard for you to find funding for your new business venture. It can be as difficult to find $25,000 in venture capital as it can be to find $2.5 million. If this is your first foray into a small business entrepreneurial effort, lending institutions are even more reluctant to lend money, no matter how small the amount.

So, many entrepreneurs are turning to crowdfunding, peer-to-peer loans, and microloans. On a crowdfunding site, you provide all the details of your idea. Lenders, usually individuals with small amounts of money, review all ideas and pledge an amount to the most promising one(s). The ideas that get fully funded by numerous small pledges then move forward with the funding. Peer-to-peer loan sites are similar except they focus on helping you find one lender to completely fund your idea. Finally, microloans are, in fact,

"micro," often in the range of $25 to $1,000. Lenders don't get interest on their money. Often, lenders agree to never receive their money back, even if the project is successful. If they do get their money back, they typically re-invest it in another entrepreneurial effort.

If any of these sound appealing to you, consider researching the following funding opportunities.

- Samuel Adams Brewing American Dream Project—microloans to food-, beverage-, and hospitality-related ventures (http://www.samueladams.com/btad/index.aspx)
- Lending Club—peer-to-peer site connecting lenders and borrowers (http://www.lendingclub.com/home.action)
- Kickstarter.com—microloan site where lenders agree to not get their money back (http://www.kickstarter.com/)
- Kiva.com—a combination of crowdfunding and microloans (http://www.kiva.org/)[16]

end consumers. They (1) exhibit greatly varying demographics, lifestyles, wants, and needs, (2) distinguish products and services by convenience versus specialty, (3) often shop for commoditylike and digital products, and (4) sometimes require a level of *mass customization* to get exactly what they want. Customers in the B2B e-commerce business model are other businesses. They (1) distinguish products and services by *maintenance, repair, and operations (MRO) materials* versus *direct materials,* (2) aggregate demand to create negotiations for volume discounts on large purchases, and (3) most often perform e-commerce activities within an e-marketplace.

3. **Compare and contrast the development of a marketing mix for customers in the B2B and B2C e-commerce business models.** A *marketing mix* is the set of marketing tools that your organization will use to pursue its marketing objectives in reaching and attracting potential customers. In B2B e-commerce, marketing mixes do not usually include broad and generic strategies that reach all potential businesses. Instead, marketing often occurs in the context of an e-marketplace. Once a contact has been made between businesses, the development of the relationship is still formal and often includes negotiations for pricing, quality, specifications, and delivery timing.

In B2C e-commerce, a marketing mix will include some or all of the following:

- Registering your site with a search engine.
- *Online ads* (small advertisements that appear on other sites), including *pop-up ads* (small Web pages containing an advertisement that appear on your screen outside the current Web site loaded into your browser) and *pop-under ads* (a form of a pop-up ad that you do not see until you close your current browser session).
- *Viral marketing*—encourages users of a product or service supplied by a B2C e-commerce business to encourage friends to join in as well.
- *Affiliate program*—arrangement made between two e-commerce sites that directs viewers from one site to the other.

4. **Summarize the various ways of moving money in the world of e-commerce and related issues.** B2C e-commerce payment systems most commonly include credit cards, *financial cybermediaries* (such as PayPal), *electronic checks* (with online banking being an implementation), *Electronic Bill Presentment and Payment (EBPP)*, *smart cards* (credit card with an embedded computer chip on which digital information can be stored and updated), and *digital wallets* (software and instructions for completing a transaction). In the B2B e-commerce business model, financial EDI is the norm. *Financial EDI* is an electronic process used primarily in the Business to Business e-commerce business model for the payment of purchases. Security for the electronic transfer of funds is an overriding concern. Techniques such as *encryption, public key encryption (PKE), Secure Sockets Layers (SSLs),* and *Secure Electronic Transactions (SETs)* all address this issue of security.

5. **Discuss some major trends that are impacting both the e-commerce business world and society in general.** Major trends include:

- *Long Tail model*—the tail of a sales curve which traditional businesses ignore but e-commerce businesses profit from
- *Crowdsourcing*—when businesses provide enabling technologies that allow people (i.e., crowds)—instead of designated paid employees—to create, modify, and oversee the development of a product or service
- *Virtual goods*—nonphysical objects
- *Mobile commerce (m-commerce or wireless e-commerce)*—electronic commerce conducted over a wireless device such as a smartphone, laptop, or tablet PC

CLOSING CASE STUDY ONE

When You're Big, You Can Be Your Own B2B E-Marketplace

Business to Business (B2B) e-marketplaces are the growing trend in the B2B e-commerce business model. Businesses from all industries and countries can gather, perform commerce functions, share mission-critical information, and deploy infrastructure applications that allow those organizations to tie their internal systems to each other.

But some companies—the largest ones—don't have to play in the generic B2B e-marketplaces. Instead, they can build their own and literally require that their suppliers participate. Once such company is Volkswagen AG. Its B2B e-marketplace is called VWgroupsupply.com (www.vwgroupsupply.com).

Volkswagen AG offers eight brands of automobiles—Volkswagen (passenger), Volkswagen Commercial Vehicles, Audi, Bentley, Bugatti, Lamborghini, Seat, and Skoda. In 2003, Volkswagen spent almost 60 billion euros, or approximately $77 billion, on components, automotive parts, and MRO materials for its manufacturing operations. When you spend that much money with your suppliers, you can open and run your own B2B e-marketplace.

VWgroupsupply.com handles 90 percent of Volkswagen global purchases. Almost all requests for quotes, contract negotiations, catalog updating and buying, purchase-order management, vehicle program management, and payments are handled electronically and online through VWgroupsupply.com.

Gains in efficiency and productivity coupled with material costs reductions have been tremendous. The cost savings alone generated over the last three years were more than 100 million euros, or approximately $127 million.

Volkswagen requires that each of its 5,500 suppliers use VWgroupsupply.com for any interactions. Suppliers place product and pricing catalogs on the system, respond to requests for quotes, and collaborate with Volkswagen engineers on new product designs, all in the safe and secure environment of Volkswagen's proprietary B2B e-marketplace.

By requiring its suppliers to interact with Volkswagen in the e-marketplace, purchasing agents no longer have to spend valuable time searching for information and pricing. Volkswagen has, in essence, created a system that brings the necessary information to the purchasing agents. This new system within VWgroupsupply.com is called iPAD, or Internal Purchasing Agent Desk.

Prior to the implementation of iPAD, purchasing agents entering a purchase order for a vehicle front module had to use numerous separate systems to complete the process. They had to retrieve information from a supplier system and its database, query information in Volkswagen's internal parts information system, obtain information from a request-for-quotes database, enter information into a contract-negotiation transcript system, and interact with several other systems and databases. In all, the purchasing agent had to log into and use seven separate systems. Analysis revealed that Volkswagen purchasing agents were spending 70 percent of their time finding, retrieving, analyzing, validating, and moving information. This took away valuable time from such tasks as negotiating better prices with suppliers.

Using a form of an integrated collaboration environment, purchasing agents now participate in a simple three-step process. First, iPAD captures and sends a business event to the purchasing agent, such as the need to order vehicle front modules. Second, iPAD attaches to that communication other necessary information such as information about potential suppliers, their costs, and other forms of analysis and descriptive information. Finally, iPAD sends the corresponding business processes and work flows to be completed electronically.

It works much like a digital dashboard, which we introduced you to in Chapter 3. When purchasing agents log onto the iPAD portal in the morning, they receive a customized Web page with announcements, business alerts, analyses, and digital workflows to be completed. The purchasing agents can set out immediately to complete the tasks for the day, without having to spend 70 percent of their time finding, retrieving, and analyzing information. iPAD even customizes the Web page according to the purchasing agent's native language, something very necessary for a global manufacturer of automobiles with more than 2,000 purchasing agents worldwide.[17,18]

Questions

1. Volkswagen operates its own proprietary B2B e-marketplace in which its suppliers participate. What are the disadvantages to Volkswagen of not using a generic B2B e-marketplace with even more suppliers? What are the advantages to Volkswagen of developing and using its own proprietary B2B e-marketplace?

2. When Volkswagen needs a new part design, it uses VWsupplygroup.com to get its suppliers involved in the design process early. This creates a tremendous amount of interorganizational collaboration. What are the advantages to the suppliers and to Volkswagen in doing so?

3. How is Volkswagen's VWgroupsupply.com B2B e-marketplace an example of a vertical e-marketplace implementation? How is it an example of a horizontal e-marketplace implementation? Why is it necessary that Volkswagen combine both of these e-marketplaces into one e-marketplace? What would be the drawbacks to creating two different e-marketplaces—one for suppliers of direct materials and one for suppliers of MRO materials?

4. To make effective purchasing decisions, Volkswagen's purchasing agents need business intelligence. What kind of business intelligence does iPAD provide to purchasing agents for carrying out their tasks? What additional kinds of business intelligence not discussed in this case could Volkswagen's purchasing agents take advantage of to make more effective decisions?

5. IPAD manages the workflow for purchasing agents. Describe how iPAD manages this process including information provided, steps to be executed, and the presentation of information.

CLOSING CASE STUDY TWO

The Mobile Commerce Explosion

It's happening right now all around you. Although the "outrageous transformation" has yet to occur, more and more people every day are turning to their smartphones for shopping convenience and comparison. For a Christmas gift for his girlfriend in 2010, Tri Tang went shopping for a Garmin global positioning system (GPS). He found exactly what he wanted at a Best Buy store for $184.85. But instead of dropping it into his cart and proceeding to the cashier, Tri pulled out his smartphone and typed in the model number. He found the exact same Garmin GPS on Amazon's Web site for $106.75, with no shipping and no tax.

Tri is part of a growing number of consumers using their smartphones to find the best deals, even when in a store with the product in hand. According to Mike Duke, CEO of Walmart, smartphone-enhanced shopping has ushered in a whole "new era of price transparency." The "old" traditional model of using advertising to get a consumer in the store no longer works. In that old model, if a retailer got a consumer in the store, it could reasonably assume that the consumer would make the purchase there. Not so anymore. Once consumers find what they want in a store, they're turning to their smartphones to compare prices and read product reviews.

According to a Nielsen survey, 38 percent of all U.S. consumers now own a smartphone. In a 90-day period from March through May of 2011, 55 percent of consumers who bought a "wireless" phone purchased a smartphone with all the apps (most of them free) necessary to scan bar codes and compare prices.

According to another survey conducted by IDC Retail Insights, 45 percent of smartphone owners had used them to compare prices while in a retail store. As IDC's Greg Girard explains it, "The retailer's advantage has eroded. The four walls of the store have become porous." To fully comprehend how quickly this transformation is generating speed, consider the findings of IBM. According to Coremetrics, a division of IBM, on Black Friday (the day after Thanksgiving) in 2009, mobile devices accounted for only 0.1 percent of all visits to retailers' Web sites. In 2010's Black Friday, that number increased to 5.6 percent, a 50-fold increase.

And it's not just limited to smartphone-enabled price comparisons. Many smartphone owners are turning to their smartphones for service. According to an Accenture study in 2010, 73 percent of smartphone owners preferred to use their smartphones for basic assistance over talking to a retail clerk. So, the very notion of "personalized" service is on shaky ground. This used to be a stronghold for brick-and-mortar retailers, claiming that the shopping experience was more meaningful because shoppers were engaged by sales people instead of technology. Now it seems that smartphone-wielding savvy shoppers prefer technology over the personal touch.

Matt Binder was hoping to save some money, just like Tri Tang at the beginning of this case study. But Matt was more than willing to save just a couple of dollars, whereas Tri saved almost $80. Armed with his smartphone and Amazon's Price Check App, Matt found a 2Gb USB drive at a Best Buy store for $11.99. When he snapped a photo of it, his Price Check App alerted him that Amazon had the same USB drive for $9.99. Matt opted for the cheaper price. Now, $2 may not seem like a lot but Matt didn't have to go anywhere else to make his cheaper purchase. He did it right there on his phone in the Best Buy store. As Matt explained it, "I wouldn't drive somewhere else to save $2." And he didn't have to, thanks to the mobile commerce explosion.[19, 20, 21]

Questions

1. Take a survey in one of your classes. What percentage of students own smartphones? Gather some data regarding how they use their smartphones for shopping. Do they use a smartphone to compare prices? Do they use a smartphone to read product reviews? For what other shopping-related activities do they use their smartphones?

2. How do you think large brick-and-mortar retailers like Best Buy and Walmart can compete in a world quickly moving to smartphone-enhanced shopping? Do you think smartphone-enhanced shopping will outrageously transform brick-and-mortar retail, perhaps putting many retail chains out of business? Why or why not?

3. Many retailers are creating proprietary in-store apps for shoppers. Some of these apps help shoppers find the location of products in the store, while others recommend complementary products based on product searches. For an in-store app, say, for a Best Buy store, identify and describe three additional features that you believe shoppers would benefit from and encourage them to make purchases in the store.

4. Esurance (www.esurance.com) has a slogan that states, "People when you want them, technology when you don't." This speaks very much to the increasing role of technology in customer service. What do you think about this? Can (and should) technology take over the primary customer-facing role for an organization, especially a retail store? Will stores like Nordstrom lose their competitive advantage based on superior customer service?

5. What about people who can't afford a smartphone? Will they be disadvantaged while shopping? When do you think smartphones will become affordable to all, say in the price range of $40 to $50?

■ KEY TERMS AND CONCEPTS

Ad-supported, 131
Affiliate program, 138
Business to Business (B2B) e-commerce, 129
Business to Consumer (B2C) e-commerce, 130
Business to Government (B2G) e-commerce, 128
Click-through, 138
Consumer to Business (C2B) e-commerce, 130
Consumer to Consumer (C2C) e-commerce, 131
Consumer to Government (C2G) e-commerce, 128
Conversion rate, 138
Crowdsourcing, 146
Demand aggregation, 134
Digital wallet, 142
Direct materials, 134
Electronic Bill Presentment and Payment (EBPP), 140

Electronic check, 140
Electronic commerce (e-commerce), 128
Electronic data interchange (EDI), 142
Electronic marketplace (e-marketplace), 135
Encryption, 143
Financial cybermediary, 140
Financial EDI (financial electronic data interchange), 142
Government to Business (G2B) e-commerce, 128
Government to Consumer, (G2C) e-commerce, 129
Government to Government (G2G) e-commerce, 129
Horizontal e-marketplace, 135
Long Tail, 145
Maintenance, repair, and operations (MRO) materials (indirect materials), 134

Marketing mix, 137
Mass customization, 134
Mobile commerce (m-commerce or wireless commerce), 148
Mobile computing, 148
Near field communication (NFC), 141
Online ad (banner ad), 137
Path-to-profitability (P2P), 128
Pop-under ad, 138
Pop-up ad, 138
Public key encryption (PKE), 143
Reverse auction, 135
Secure Electronic Transaction (SET), 143
Secure Sockets Layer (SSL), 143
Smart card, 142
Value-added network (VAN), 142
Vertical e-marketplace, 135
Viral marketing, 138
Virtual good, 147

SHORT-ANSWER QUESTIONS

1. What is electronic commerce?
2. How can you use a B2B e-marketplace to reduce your dependence on a particular supplier?
3. How do convenience and specialty items differ in the B2C e-commerce business model?
4. Why do commoditylike and digital items sell well in the B2C e-commerce business model?
5. What is mass customization?
6. How does a reverse auction work?
7. How are vertical and horizontal e-marketplaces different?
8. What can a marketing mix include for a B2C e-commerce business?
9. What are the major types of B2C e-commerce payment systems?
10. What is the difference between a client-side digital wallet and a server-side digital wallet?
11. How are Secure Sockets Layers (SSLs) and Secure Electronic Transactions (SETs) different? How are they the same?

ASSIGNMENTS AND EXERCISES

1. **YOUR STATE AND LOCAL GOVERNMENT E-COMMERCE ACTIVITIES** Visit the Web sites for your state and local governments. Do some looking around and make a list of what services, information deliveries, and transaction processing they offer that you previously could handle only by visiting a physical building. How are these different from and similar to comparable e-government activities now offered by the U.S. federal government?

2. **DEALING WITH THE GREAT DIGITAL DIVIDE** The "great digital divide" is a term coined to address the concerns of many people that the world is becoming one marked by "have's" and "have not's" with respect to technology—that is, the traditional notion of a "third world" is now also being defined by the extent to which a country has access to and uses technology. Find out what, if anything, the United Nations is doing about this issue and express an opinion on whether or not you believe its efforts will be successful. Determine if there are organizations such as private companies or foundations that have the digital divide high on their agendas. For any such organizations you find, evaluate their efforts and express an opinion as to whether or not they will be successful. Finally, search for a less developed country that is making significant local efforts to deal with the digital divide. If you can't find one, prepare a list of the countries you reviewed and briefly describe the conditions in one of them with respect to technology.

3. **RESEARCHING A BUSINESS TO BUSINESS E-MARKETPLACE** Biz2Biz (www.biz2biz .com/Marketplace/) is a B2B e-marketplace. Connect to its site and do some looking around. What sort of marketing services does it provide through its Biz2BizCommunication program? What sort of services does it provide for creating and maintaining an electronic catalog? If you owned a business and wanted to join, what process would you have to go through? How much does it cost your organization to join Biz2Biz? What buyer tools does Biz2Biz provide its membership?

4. **LONG-TAIL EXAMPLES** The Long Tail is all around you, not just in electronic commerce. Consider the Long Tail graph of students and their participation in class. Some students talk a great deal and then there are students who say nothing at all. (The latter are in the tail.) Consider people's first names. Some are very common (the fat part of the tail) and some are unique (i.e., in the tail) like Moon and Dweezil, both children of Frank Zappa. Think of three other noncommerce Long Tail examples. For each, build a Long Tail graph.

5. **FINDING THE MOST POPULAR B2C E-COMMERCE SITES** Connect to the Web and do some research to find the most popular B2C e-commerce Web sites in terms of number of hits or views per month. What are the sites? Which of the sites in some way or another support the concept of an e-marketplace where end consumers can gather?

■ DISCUSSION QUESTIONS

1. In what ways can shopping over the Internet be more convenient for consumers? In what ways can it be less convenient? List at least five products you would have no hesitation buying over the Internet, five products you might want to think about a bit before buying, and five products you would never consider buying over the Internet. Justify your reasons in each case.

2. In your opinion, according to Porter's Five Forces Model (refer to Chapter 1), has competition increased or decreased overall as a result of the Internet and e-commerce? Specifically address each of the five forces in Porter's model.

3. Under what circumstances would it be appropriate to consider using viral marketing? See if you can think of an organization with an online presence that could benefit from viral marketing but is not currently using it. It could be your school, for example, or it could be an organization you are involved with. How would you suggest the organization go about using viral marketing in order for it to achieve the desired results? What are some of the other marketing techniques available for an e-commerce Web site to use? Why is it important to consider a mix of techniques rather than just relying on a single one?

4. In this chapter, we've identified differences between end consumers and businesses as customers. Review those differences and then write down the three you consider most significant. Discuss those three. For the differences that you did not choose as the three most important, be prepared to justify your decision.

5. In this chapter, we discussed using such technologies as B2B e-marketplaces to create tighter supply chain managements, thereby driving out costs. If you refer back to Chapter 2, you'll recall that another major business initiative is customer relationship management (CRM). How can B2C e-commerce businesses use the Internet to further enhance their CRM initiatives? How can B2B e-commerce businesses use the Internet to further enhance their CRM initiatives? Does it become easier or harder to maintain relationships with customers as businesses move toward more electronic commerce? Why?

■ CHAPTER PROJECTS

GROUP PROJECTS

- Building Value Chains: Helping Customers Define Value (p. 289)

- Advertising with Banner Ads: HighwaysAndByways.com (p. 293)

- Building a Web Database System: Web-Based Classified System (p. 297)

- Assessing a Wireless Future: Emerging Trends and Technology (p. 300)

- Evaluating the Next Generation: Dot-Com ASPs (p. 301)

E-COMMERCE PROJECTS

- Free and Rentable Storage Space (p. 313)

- Gathering Competitive Intelligence (p. 313)

- Exploring Google Earth (p. 314)

- Finding Hosting Services (p. 315)

- Global Statistics and Resources (p. 316)

- Gold, Silver, Interest Rates, and Money (p. 316)

- Learning about Investing (p. 318)

- Small Business Administration (p. 319)

- Researching Storefront Software (p. 320)

CHAPTER SIX OUTLINE

STUDENT LEARNING OUTCOMES

1. Define the traditional systems development life cycle (SDLC) and describe the seven major phases within it.

2. Compare and contrast the various component-based development methodologies.

3. Describe the selfsourcing process as an alternative to the traditional systems development life cycle.

4. Discuss the importance of prototypes and prototyping within any systems development methodology.

5. Describe the outsourcing environment and how outsourcing works.

WEB SUPPORT

www.mhhe.com/haag

- Best in computer resources and statistics
- Meta data
- Finding hosting services
- Searching for freeware and shareware
- Researching storefront software

SUPPORTING MODULES

XLM/F Building a Web Page with HTML
Extended Learning Module F provides hands-on instructions for building a Web page by writing the HTML (hypertext markup language) code. You'll learn how to work with headings; adjust text sizes, fonts, and colors; manipulate background colors and images; insert links to documents, other Web pages, and e-mail addresses; manipulate images; and insert both bulleted and numbered lists.

XLM/L Building Web Sites with FrontPage
Extended Learning Module L provides hands-on instructions for building a Web site using Microsoft's Web authoring software FrontPage. Like Extended Learning Module F, you'll learn how to incorporate such things as list, images, and links. You'll also learn much more in this module as FrontPage truly enhances your ability to create a Web page that takes advantage of many of today's exciting Web features.

XLM/M Programming in Excel with VBA
Extended Learning Module M covers the basics of learning how to write macros (short programs) in Excel using VBA, Visual Basic for Applications. It covers how to use the Visual Basic Editor (VBE), how to use the macro recorder, and how to write procedures, functions, if-then structures, and loops.

CHAPTER SIX

Systems Development
Phases, Tools, and Techniques

OUTRAGEOUS INDUSTRY TRANSFORMATION: CAMERAS USE FILM?

As little as 10 years ago, before vacationers hit the road, hikers and hobbyists like bird watchers took to nature trails, and people took off for wherever in search of family fun, they checked their cameras to make sure they had plenty of film. That has certainly changed.

First came the digital camera, with "good enough" quality for most people and storage for thousands of digital images. Interestingly enough, that transformation was quickly followed by another, the phone with camera capabilities. Again, the new handhelds were good enough in terms of photo quality and could store thousands of images. And why carry a digital camera and a digital phone if you could have both in one device?

So, this outrageous industry correction was felt far and wide. Sales of 35mm cameras declined rapidly. Kodak, the largest and most well-known organization in the camera and film industry, saw its film sales slashed from $7 billion in 2004 to an estimated $1.9 billion in 2010 (see the accompanying graph). The same for film processing. According to Robert Keane, a spokesperson for Stop & Shop, "With the prevalence of digital cameras, to continue to do film processing where demand has continued to decline just wasn't feasible." Robert made that statement when Stop & Shop announced it would cease film processing services at all of its 300 stores.

You learned about long-tail economics in the previous chapter. In long-tail economics you have the hits which account for most revenue and then the non-hits (i.e., the long tail) that still exhibit possible revenue. Ten years ago, film

cameras and their associated activities were the hits, accounting for most revenue in the industry. Today, digital cameras and smartphones account for most of the revenue, while film-based cameras are in the long tail.

When transformations such as these take place in an industry, the industry must change its order-processing systems. Where the industry once invested heavily in the development of film-processing order systems, we now see the dominance of Web-based systems that enable you to upload your photos, create photo albums, and print the ones you want paper copies of. Popular sites for this include SnapFish, Photo Bucket, Flickr, and many others.[1,2,3]

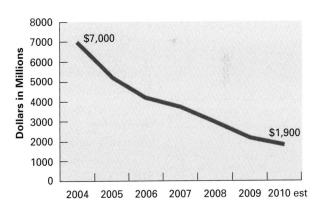

Questions

1. Do you own a camera that uses traditional 35mm film? When was the last time you had a roll of 35mm film processed the "old" way?

2. Do you believe that smartphones with embedded cameras will eventually spell the end for digital cameras? Why or why not?

3. Do you know someone who still owns and uses a 35mm camera? For what purpose(s) does that person use the camera?

Introduction

Billions of dollars are spent each year on the acquisition, design, development, implementation, and maintenance of information systems. The ongoing need for safe, secure, and reliable systems solutions is a consequence of companies' increasing dependence on information technology to provide services and develop products, administer daily activities, and perform short- and long-term management functions.

Systems developers must ensure that all the business's needs and requirements are met when developing information systems, establish uniform privacy and security practices for system users, and develop acceptable implementation strategies for the new systems. This chapter focuses on the many factors that must come together to develop a successful information system.

You have three primary choices as to who will build your system (see Figure 6.1). First, you can choose *insourcing,* which involves in-house IT specialists within your organization to develop the system. Second, you can choose *selfsourcing* (also called *end-user development*), which is the development and support of IT systems by end users (knowledge workers) with little or no help from IT specialists. Third, you can choose *outsourcing,* which is the delegation of specific work to a third party for a specified length of time, at a specified cost, and at a specified level of service.

As we introduce you to the systems development life cycle in the next section, we'll focus on insourcing and how the overall process works, key activities within each phase, roles you may play as an end user or knowledge worker, and opportunities you can capitalize on to ensure that your systems development effort is a success.

Insourcing and the Systems Development Life Cycle

LEARNING OUTCOME 1

The *systems development life cycle (SDLC)* is a structured step-by-step approach for developing information systems. It includes seven key phases and numerous activities within each (see Figure 6.2). This version of the SDLC is also referred to as a *waterfall methodology*—a sequential, activity-based process in which one phase of the SDLC is followed by another, from planning through implementation (see Figure 6.2).

There are literally hundreds of different activities associated with each phase of the SDLC. Typical activities include determining budgets, gathering business requirements, designing models, writing detailed user documentation, and project management. The

Figure 6.1

Insourcing, Selfsourcing, and Outsourcing

Insourcing

IT Specialists Within Your Organization

Selfsourcing

Knowledge Workers

Outsourcing

Another Organization

SDLC Phase	Activities
1. Planning	• Define the system to be developed • Set the project scope • Develop the project plan including tasks, resources, and timeframes
2. Analysis	• Gather the business requirements for the system
3. Design	• Design the technical architecture required to support the system • Design system models
4. Development	• Build the technical architecture • Build the database and programs
5. Testing	• Write the test conditions • Perform the testing of the system
6. Implementation	• Write detailed user documentation • Provide training for the system users
7. Maintenance	• Build a help desk to support the system users • Provide an environment to support system changes

Figure 6.2

The Systems Development Life Cycle (SDLC), Phases and Activities, and the Waterfall Methodology

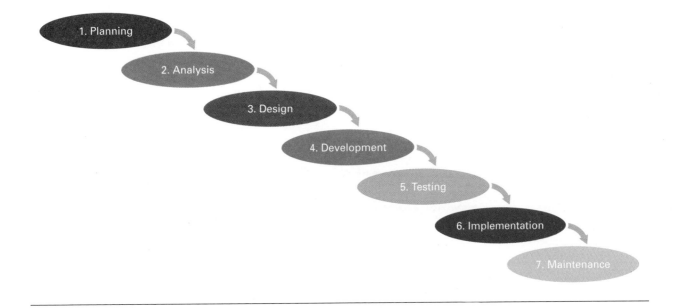

activities you, as an end user, perform during each systems development project will vary depending on the type of system you're building and the tools you use to build it. Since we can't possibly cover them all in this brief introduction, we have chosen a few of the more important SDLC activities that you might perform on a systems development project as an end user.

PHASE 1: PLANNING

During the ***planning phase*** of the SDLC you create a solid plan for developing your information system. The following are the three primary activities performed during the planning phase.

1. *Define the system to be developed:* You must identify and select the system for development or determine which system is required to support the strategic goals of your organization. Organizations typically track all the proposed systems and prioritize them based on business impact or critical success factors. A ***critical success factor (CSF)*** is simply a factor critical to your organization's success. This process allows your organization to strategically decide which systems to build.

2. *Set the project scope:* You must define the project's scope and create a project scope document for your systems development effort. The project scope clearly defines the high-level requirements. Scope is often referred to as the 10,000-foot view of the system or the most basic definition of the system. A ***project scope document*** is a written document of the project scope and is usually no longer than a paragraph. Project scoping is important for many reasons; most important it helps you avoid *scope creep* and *feature creep*. ***Scope creep*** occurs when the scope of the project increases beyond its original intentions. ***Feature creep*** occurs when developers (and end users) add extra features that were not part of the initial requirements.

3. *Develop the project plan:* You must develop a detailed project plan for your entire systems development effort. The ***project plan*** defines the *what, when,* and *who* questions of systems development including all activities to be performed, the individuals, or resources, who will perform the activities, and the time required to complete each activity. The project plan is the guiding force behind ensuring the on-time delivery of a complete and successful information system. Figure 6.3 provides a sample project plan. A ***project manager*** is an individual who is an expert in project planning and management, defines and develops the project plan, and tracks the plan to ensure that all key project milestones are completed on time. ***Project milestones*** represent key dates by which you need a certain group of activities performed. Either of the two *creeps* alluded to above can throw off a project plan.

Figure 6.3

A Sample Project Plan

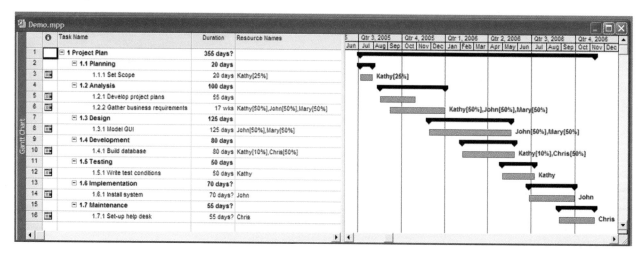

PHASE 2: ANALYSIS

Once your organization has decided which system to develop, you can move into the analysis phase. The *analysis phase* of the SDLC involves end users and IT specialists working together to gather, understand, and document the business requirements for the proposed system. The following are the two primary activities you'll perform during the analysis phase.

1. *Gathering the business requirements:* **Business requirements** are the detailed set of end-user requests that the system must meet to be successful. The business requirements drive the entire system. A sample business requirement might state, "The CRM system must track all customer inquiries by product, region, and sales representative." The business requirement states what the system must do from the business perspective. Gathering business requirements is similar to performing an investigation. You must talk to everyone who has a claim in using the new system to find out what is required. An extremely useful way to gather business requirements is to perform a joint application development session. During a *joint application development (JAD)* session users and IT specialists meet, sometimes for several days, to define and review the business requirements for the system.

2. *Prioritize the requirements:* Once you define all the business requirements, you prioritize them in order of business importance and place them in a formal comprehensive document, the *requirements definition document.* The users receive the requirements definition document for their sign-off. *Sign-off* is the users' actual signatures indicating they approve all the business requirements. Typically, one of the first major milestones in the project plan is the users' sign-off on business requirements.

One of the key things to think about when you are reviewing business requirements is the cost to the company of fixing errors if the business requirements are unclear or inaccurate. An error found during the analysis phase is relatively inexpensive to fix; all you typically have to do is change a Word document. An error found during later phases, however, is incredibly expensive to fix because you have to change the actual system. Figure 6.4 displays how the cost to fix an error grows exponentially the later the error is found in the SDLC.

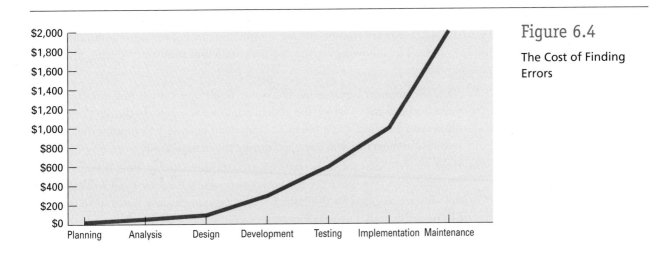

Figure 6.4

The Cost of Finding Errors

PHASE 3: DESIGN

The primary goal of the *design phase* of the SDLC is to build a technical blueprint of how the proposed system will work. During the analysis phase, end users and IT specialists work together to develop the business requirements for the proposed system from a logical point of view. That is, during analysis you document business requirements without respect to technology or the technical infrastructure that will support the system. As you move into design, the project team turns its attention to the system from a physical or technical point of view. You take the business requirements generated during the analysis phase and define the supporting technical architecture in the design phase. The following are the primary activities you'll perform during the design phase.

1. *Design the technical architecture:* The **technical architecture** defines the hardware, software, and telecommunications equipment required to run the system. Most systems run on a computer network with each employee having a workstation and the application software running on a server. The telecommunications requirements encompass access to the Internet and the ability for end users to connect remotely to the server. You typically explore several different technical architectures before choosing the final technical architecture.

2. *Design the system model:* Modeling is the activity of drawing a graphical representation of a design. You model everything you build including screens, reports, software, and databases (with E-R diagrams as we described in *Extended Learning Module C*). There are many different types of modeling activities performed during the design phase including a graphical user interface screen design.

It is at the point of the design phase in the SDLC that you, as an end user, begin to take a less active role in performing the various activities and divert your attention to "quality control." That is, IT specialists perform most of the functions in the design through maintenance phases. It is your responsibility to review their work, for example, verifying that the models of the screens, reports, software, and databases encapsulate all of the business requirements.

PHASE 4: DEVELOPMENT

During the **development phase** of the SDLC, you take all your detailed design documents from the design phase and transform them into an actual system. This phase marks the point at which you go from physical design to physical implementation. Again, IT specialists are responsible for completing most of the activities in the development phase. The following are the two main activities performed during the development phase.

1. *Build the technical architecture:* For you to build your system, you must first build the platform on which the system is going to operate. In the development phase, you purchase and implement equipment necessary to support the technical architecture you designed during the design phase.

2. *Build the database and programs:* Once the technical architecture is built, you initiate and complete the creation of supporting databases and writing the software required for the system. These tasks are usually undertaken by IT specialists, and it may take months or even years to design and create the databases and write all the software.

PHASE 5: TESTING

The *testing phase* of the SDLC verifies that the system works and meets all the business requirements defined in the analysis phase. Testing is critical. The following are the primary activities you'll perform during the testing phase.

1. *Write the test conditions:* You must have detailed test conditions to perform an exhaustive test. **Test conditions** are the detailed steps the system must perform along with the expected results of each step. The tester will execute each test condition and compare the expected results with the actual results to verify that the system functions correctly. Each time the actual result is different from the expected result, a "bug" is generated, and the system goes back to development for a "bug fix." A typical systems development effort has hundreds or thousands of test conditions. You must execute and verify all of these test conditions to ensure the entire system functions correctly.

2. *Perform the testing of the system:* You must perform many different types of tests when you begin testing your new system. A few of the more common tests include:
    -   **Unit testing**—tests individual units or pieces of code for a system.
    -   **System testing**—verifies that the units or pieces of code written for a system function correctly when integrated into the total system.
    -   **Integration testing**—verifies that separate systems can work together.
    -   **User acceptance testing (UAT)**—determines if the system satisfies the business requirements and enables users to perform their jobs correctly.

PHASE 6: IMPLEMENTATION

During the *implementation phase* of the SDLC you distribute the system to all the users and they begin using the system to perform their everyday jobs. The following are the two primary activities you'll perform during the implementation phase.

1. *Write detailed user documentation:* When you install the system, you must also provide employees with **user documentation** that highlights how to use the system. Users find it extremely frustrating to have a new system without documentation.

2. *Provide training for the system users:* You must also provide training for the users who are going to use the new system. You can provide several different types of training, and two of the most popular are online training and workshop training. **Online training** runs over the Internet or off a CD or DVD. Employees perform the training at any time, on their own computers, at their own pace. This type of training is convenient because they can set their own schedule to undergo the training. **Workshop training** is held in a classroom environment and is led by an instructor. Workshop training is most suitable for difficult systems for which employees need one-on-one time with an individual instructor.

You also need to choose the implementation method that best suits your organization, project, and employees to ensure a successful implementation. When you implement the new system, you have four implementation methods you can choose from:

1. **Parallel implementation** uses both the old and new systems until you're sure that the new system performs correctly.

2. **Plunge implementation** discards the old system completely and immediately uses the new system.

3. **Pilot implementation** has only a small group of people using the new system until you know it works correctly and then the remaining people are added to the system.

GREEN SYSTEMS DEVELOPMENT

Much of our discussion in the past few pages has focused on the development of software. Rightfully so, software development efforts easily account for 80 percent or more of all effort within the SDLC. But there are other "development" issues you need to consider; one of them is building a green IT center.

In March 2008, Honda opened its green IT center, a 61,000-square-foot facility, in Longmont, Colorado. It is one of only a handful of U.S. data centers certified by the Leadership in Energy and Environmental Design rating system for green building construction. What does it really mean to "go green"? Here are a few interesting things about Honda's environmentally friendly building.

- Floors made of recycled concrete
- Office furniture made of recycled steel and newsprint
- Low-flow automatic faucets
- Motion-sensor lights
- 73 percent of construction waste recycled
- Surrounding grounds left undeveloped
- Surrounding grounds that were disturbed by construction replanted with indigenous trees and shrubs
- Use of videoconferencing to avoid air travel
- Recycling almost everything from old computers to batteries to slide projectors (employees brought in 9 tons of old equipment from their home offices)
- Eliminating screen savers in favor of monitors that turn off

The list goes on and on. Even printing the right way saves Honda money. By defaulting to black-and-white and double-sided printing, Honda expects to save tens of thousands of dollars per year.[4]

---

4. *Phased implementation* installs the new system in phases (e.g., accounts receivable, then accounts payable) until you're sure it works correctly and then the remaining phases of the new system are implemented.

PHASE 7: MAINTENANCE

Maintaining the system is the final phase of any systems development effort. During the *maintenance phase* of the SDLC, you monitor and support the new system to ensure it continues to meet the business goals. Once a system is in place, it must change as your business changes. Constantly monitoring and supporting the new system involves making minor changes (for example, new reports or information retrieval) and reviewing the system to be sure that it continues to move your organization toward its strategic goals. The following are the two primary activities you'll perform during the maintenance phase.

1. *Build a help desk to support the system users:* One of the best ways to support users is to create a help desk. A *help desk* is a group of people who respond to users' questions. Typically, users have a phone number for the help desk they call whenever they have issues or questions about the system. Providing a help desk that answers user questions is a terrific way to provide comprehensive support for users using new systems.

2. *Provide an environment to support system changes:* As changes arise in the business environment, you must react to those changes by assessing their impact on the system. It might well be that the system needs to be adapted or updated to meet the ever-changing needs of the business environment. If so, you must modify the system to support the new business environment.

Component-Based Development

The systems development life cycle you just read about is one of the oldest software development methodologies. In design and development (as well as the other phases), the SDLC takes a very singular view of the system under consideration and focuses solely on its development. That is, the SDLC does not really allow the development team to look around a software library and find existing code that can be reused for the new system under consideration. This has some tremendous disadvantages. Most notably, all software is written from scratch each time it is needed for each application. For example, there are probably many applications in the typical organization that have some sort of customer view screen and the ability to update a customer's information. However, within the traditional SDLC, the software that supports the customer view screen and the ability to update the information would be written each time for each application.

This has given rise to the notion of component-based development. ***Component-based development (CBD)*** is a general approach to systems development that focuses on building small self-contained blocks of code (components) that can be reused across a variety of applications within an organization. The goal here, for example, is to write the customer view screen and updating software only once, place it in a library of software components, and then allow software development teams to plug in that component (rather like the notion of *plug-and-play*) into whatever system needs to be developed.

Component-based development dramatically changes the systems development life cycle. It requires teams to (1) look through the software library for reusable code that already exists and (2) build new software in the form of components that can be reused later in other software development projects. In this approach, you can find new systems development methodologies being used including *rapid application development, extreme programming,* and *agile.*

RAPID APPLICATION DEVELOPMENT METHODOLOGY

The ***rapid application development (RAD)*** (also called ***rapid prototyping) methodology*** emphasizes extensive user involvement in the rapid and evolutionary construction of working prototypes of a system to accelerate the systems development process (see Figure 6.5).

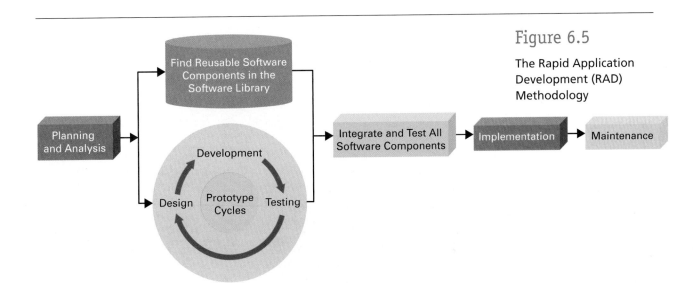

Figure 6.5

The Rapid Application Development (RAD) Methodology

The fundamentals of RAD include:

1. Perform the planning and analysis phases in a similar manner as if you were using the traditional systems development life cycle.
2. Review the software library to determine if components already exist that can be used as part of the new system.
3. Create prototypes (i.e., working models of software components) that look and act like aspects of the desired system. Design, develop, and test the prototypes until they become fully functional software components.
4. Integrate the software components from the previous two steps and test them as a complete system.
5. Implement the new system, following many of the guidelines found in the traditional SDLC.
6. Provide ongoing support and maintenance.

Overall, you want to actively involve end users in the analysis phase and in the iterative approach to the design, development, and testing of new software components. This end-user involvement and the use of prototyping tend to greatly accelerate the collecting of business requirements and the development of the software (i.e., software components). Moreover, if you can find reusable software components in the software library, the acceleration of the overall process is even greater. Prototyping is an essential part of the RAD methodology and we'll discuss it in more detail in a later section.

EXTREME PROGRAMMING METHODOLOGY

The *extreme programming (XP) methodology* breaks a project into tiny phases and developers cannot continue on to the next phase until the current phase is complete. XP is a lot like a jigsaw puzzle; there are many small pieces (i.e., software components). Individually, the pieces make no sense, but when they are combined together an organization can gain visibility into the entire system. The primary difference between the traditional SDLC and XP methodologies is that XP divides its phases into iterations. For example, the traditional SDLC approach develops the entire system, whereas XP develops the system in iterations (see Figure 6.6). Although not shown in Figure 6.6, the XP methodology, much like the RAD methodology, does rely heavily on reusing existing software components contained in a software library.

Figure 6.6

The Extreme Programming Methodology

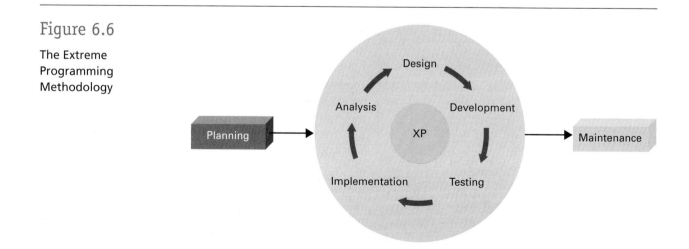

MERCEDES-BENZ: BUILT-TO-ORDER TRUCKS FROM BUILT-TO-ORDER SOFTWARE

"Which driver's cabs and radios are available for a 24-ton rig?" In the past, such a question would have cost Mercedes-Benz dealers a lot of time leafing through big manuals. Today, the Mercedes-Benz Web site offers orientation to the multitude of equipment variations with the Mercedes-Benz customer advisory system (MBKS), developed by CAS Software AG.

The online program, called Truck Online Configurator (TOC), required much more development time than simply displaying the finished online systems for the automobile and transporter divisions with other data and image material. The TOC was given a completely new user guide that orients itself on the different demands of the Web site visitors in three ways: through technical features, trade solution, and transport task. For example, interested customers are able to compile their own vehicle preference by entering the required technical details, such as the type of drive, wheelbase, or engine performance needed. Or an interested customer can select by trade solution or transport task (where he or she simply tells the TOC that a truck is required for the transportation of frozen foods, for example) and a list of suitable models is offered.

CAS had only five months in which to realize this complex and extensive application, from the definition of the specialist requirements, to the technical specifications, right up to the development, testing, and installation of the software. This tight deadline required a risk-driven project management, which meant that individual phases of the project would overlap. While a few developers, together with the project managers of Mercedes-Benz, were clarifying the technical requirements of the individual functions, other parts of the TOC were already being implemented.

The CAS solution was virtually tailor-made for this project. The finished programs run in an extremely fast and stable manner. These were the central, technical requirements of Mercedes-Benz for the TOC: The company wanted an application which boasts maximum availability but with minimum response times.

Thanks to using the rapid application development (RAD) process, CAS was capable of creating very fast a high-quality application.[5]

Microsoft Corporation developed Internet Explorer and Netscape Communications Corporation developed Communicator using extreme programming. Both companies did a nightly compilation (called a *build*) of the entire project, bringing together all the current components. They established release dates and expended considerable effort to involve customers in each release. The extreme programming approach allowed both Microsoft and Netscape to manage millions of lines of code as specifications changed and evolved over time. Most important, both companies frequently held user design reviews and strategy sessions to solicit and incorporate user feedback.[6]

XP is a significant departure from traditional software development methodologies, and many organizations in different industries have developed successful software using it. One of the reasons for XP's success is that it stresses customer satisfaction. XP empowers developers to respond to changing customer and business requirements, even late in the systems development life cycle, and emphasizes teamwork. Managers, customers, and developers are all part of a team dedicated to delivering quality software. XP implements a simple, yet effective, way to enable group style development. The XP methodology supports quickly being able to respond to changing requirements and technology.

AGILE METHODOLOGY

The *agile methodology,* a form of XP, aims for customer satisfaction through early and continuous delivery of useful software components. Agile is similar to XP but with less focus on team coding and more on limiting project scope. An agile project sets a minimum number of requirements and turns them into a deliverable product. Agile means what it sounds like: fast and efficient; small and nimble; lower cost; fewer features; shorter projects.

The Agile Alliance, a group of software developers, has made its mission to improve software development processes. Its manifesto includes the following tenets:

- Satisfy the customer through early and continuous delivery of valuable software.
- Welcome changing requirements, even late in development.
- Business people and developers must work together daily throughout the project.
- Build projects around motivated individuals. Give them the environment and support they need, and trust them to get the job done.
- The best architectures, requirements, and designs emerge from self-organizing teams.
- At regular intervals, the team reflects on how to become more effective, then tunes and adjusts its behavior accordingly.[7]

SERVICE-ORIENTED ARCHITECTURE—AN ARCHITECTURE PERSPECTIVE

Regardless of which component-based methodology your organization chooses to use as its software development approach, it will most likely be employing a software architecture perspective called a *service-oriented architecture.* A *service-oriented architecture (SOA or SoA)* is a software architecture perspective that focuses on the development, use, and reuse of small self-contained blocks of code (called *services*) to meet all the application software needs of an organization. These *services* within the SoA architecture perspective are exactly the same as *components* in any of the component-based development methodologies.

An SoA is a high-level, holistic organizational approach to how your organization views and acts on all its software needs. If adopted, your organization would, in essence, be saying that all software will be developed and managed as a series of reusable services (blocks of code). From within your SoA perspective, you would then choose from among the different component-based development methodologies that support the concept of reusable services (i.e., components) for the development of specific systems. Those development methodologies would not include the traditional SDLC, but rather the approaches we just covered—RAD, XP, and agile.

SoA is growing rapidly in business importance and we'll cover this topic further in Chapter 7.

Selfsourcing (End-User Development)

LEARNING OUTCOME 3

What we want to look at now is how you, as a knowledge worker and end user, can go about developing your own systems, which we call *selfsourcing* or *end-user development.* Recall that *selfsourcing (end-user development)* is the development and support of IT systems by end users (knowledge workers) with little or no help from IT specialists. End users are individuals who will use a system, who, although skilled in their own domain, are not IT or computer experts, and yet they know very well what they want from a system and are capable of developing such systems. Applications developed by end users support a wide range of decision-making activities and contribute to business processing in a wide range of tasks. Although certainly not on the level of enterprisewide enterprise resource planning systems, applications developed by end users are an important source for the organization's portfolio of information systems. The major tools for selfsourcing have been, and still continue to be, spreadsheets and database management systems and Web development.

Rapidly gaining in acceptance is the idea that selfsourcing can be a potent source of stress *relief* rather than a cause of stress. Rather than combating the trend toward end-user application development, IT staff should leverage it to offload solution building to end users. IT then frees its own scarce resources for complex, visible, infrastructure management tasks. A successful strategy for selfsourcing relies on two keys: (1) knowing which applications are good candidates and (2) providing end users with the right tools. After working through the selfsourcing process, we'll revisit the two keys.

THE SELFSOURCING PROCESS

You can probably create many of the small end-user computing systems in a matter of hours, such as customizing reports, creating macros, building queries, and interfacing a letter in a word processing package with a customer database to create individualized mailings. More complicated systems, such as a student registration system or an employee payroll system, require that you follow the formal SDLC process during development.

In Figure 6.7, we've illustrated the selfsourcing process. As you can see, the selfsourcing process is similar to the phases in the SDLC. However, you should notice that the selfsourcing process encompasses prototyping (model building, steps 3 through 6), which we'll cover thoroughly in the next section. This is key—when you develop a system for yourself, you will most often go through the process of prototyping, continually building on and refining your model or prototype until the system is complete. As you consider the key tasks in selfsourcing in Figure 6.8, we would alert you to several important issues.

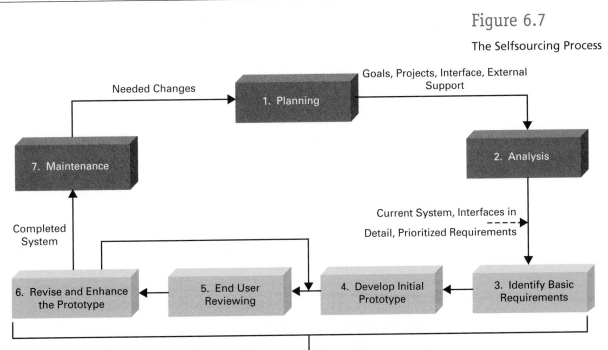

Figure 6.7

The Selfsourcing Process

The Prototyping Process

Figure 6.8

Key Tasks in Selfsourcing

KEY TASKS IN SELFSOURCING

Planning
- Define system goals in light of organizational goals
- Create a project plan
- Identify any systems that require an interface
- Determine what type of external support you will require

Analysis
- Study and model the current system
- Understand the interfaces in detail
- Define and prioritize your requirements

Support
- Completely document the system
- Provide ongoing support

ALIGNING YOUR SELFSOURCING EFFORTS WITH ORGANIZATIONAL GOALS

When you first begin planning a system that you want to develop, you must consider it in light of your organization's goals. If you're considering developing a system for yourself that is counterintuitive to your organization's goals, then you should abandon it immediately. You also have to consider how you spend your time building systems carefully, since you are busy and your time is extremely valuable. It's important to remember that building a system takes time—your time.

DETERMINING WHAT EXTERNAL SUPPORT YOU WILL REQUIRE Some selfsourcing projects may involve support from IT specialists within your organization. These may be located within the IT department, as is the case when the IT function is located within its own area (i.e., top-down silo or matrix structure). They may also be located within your department, as is the case when the IT function is fully integrated across all units. Your in-house IT specialists are a valuable resource during the selfsourcing process. Don't forget about them and be sure to include them in the planning phase. The chances of building a successful system increase greatly when you have both end users and IT specialists working together.

DOCUMENTING THE SYSTEM ONCE COMPLETE Even if you're developing a system just for yourself, you still need to document how it works. When you get promoted, other people will come in behind you and probably use the system you developed and might even make changes to it. For this reason, you must document how your system works from a technical point of view as well as create an easy-to-read user's manual.

PROVIDE ONGOING SUPPORT When you develop a system through selfsourcing, you must be prepared to provide your own support and maintenance. Since you are the primary owner and developer of the system, you're solely responsible for ensuring the system continues to function properly and continues to meet all the changing business requirements. You must also be prepared to support other end users who use your system, as they will be counting on you to help them learn and understand the system you developed. The systems development process doesn't end with implementation: It continues on a daily basis with support and maintenance.

THE ADVANTAGES OF SELFSOURCING

- *Improves requirements determination*—During insourcing, end users tell IT specialists what they want. In selfsourcing, end users essentially tell themselves what they want. Potentially, this greatly improves the chances of thoroughly understanding and capturing all the business requirements and thus the prospect of success for the new system.

- *Increases end user participation and sense of ownership*—No matter what you do, if you do it yourself, you always take more pride in the result. The same is true when developing an IT system through selfsourcing. If end users know that they own the system because they developed it and now support it, they are more apt to participate actively in its development and have a greater sense of ownership.

- *Increases speed of systems development*—Many small systems do not lend themselves well to insourcing and the traditional SDLC. These smaller systems may suffer from "analysis paralysis" because they don't require a structured step-by-step approach to their development. In fact, insourcing may be slower than selfsourcing for smaller projects.

- *Reduces the invisible backlog*—Literally no organization has all the resources to develop every system that end users need. If end users can take on the development of some of the smaller systems, the end result is the reduction of the backlog of systems that the organization needs to develop. The ***invisible backlog*** is the list of all systems that an organization needs to develop but—because of the prioritization of systems development needs—never get funded because of the lack of organizational resources.

POTENTIAL PITFALLS AND RISKS OF SELFSOURCING

- *Inadequate end user expertise leads to inadequately developed systems*—Many selfsourcing systems are never completed because end users lack the real expertise with IT tools to develop a complete and fully working system. This might seem like no big deal, since the system couldn't have been that important if the people who needed it never finished developing it. But that's not true. If end users devote time to the selfsourcing process and never complete the system, that time is wasted time.

- *Lack of organizational focus creates "privatized" IT systems*—Many selfsourcing projects are done outside the IT systems plan for an organization, meaning there may be many private IT systems that do not interface with other systems and that contained uncontrolled and duplicated information. Such systems serve no meaningful purpose in an organization and can only lead to more problems.

- *Insufficient analysis of design alternatives leads to subpar IT systems*—Some end users jump to immediate conclusions about the hardware and software they should use without carefully analyzing all the possible alternatives. If this happens, end users may develop systems whose components are inefficient.

- *Lack of documentation and external support leads to short-lived systems*—When end users develop a system, they often forgo documentation of how the system works and fail to realize that they can expect little or no support from IT specialists. All systems—no matter who develops them—must change over time. End users must realize that anticipating those changes is their responsibility and making those changes will be easier if they document their system well.

WHICH APPLICATIONS FOR IT TO OFFLOAD

The following checklist helps IT staff to determine which applications are in IT's domain and which are good candidates for selfsourcing. IT delivers maximum value to the enterprise by focusing on high-cost, high-return applications with the following characteristics:

- Infrastructure-related
- Mission-critical ERP, CRM, SCM, business intelligence and e-business
- Support large numbers of concurrent users, for example, call center applications

Other applications may be good candidates for selfsourcing.

THE RIGHT TOOL FOR THE JOB

Requirements for selfsourcing tools and enterprise development tools (for IT specialists) are quite different. Ease of use is paramount for selfsourcing development tools. That's because end users are not skilled programmers and might use the development tools so infrequently that they can forget commands that aren't intuitive. Therefore, end users must have development tools that:

- *Are easy to use:* This is essential for rapid, low-cost development. For application programs, specific characteristics of ease-of-use include: simple data entry, error checking for values in lists and ranges, easy report generation (e.g., drag and drop), and ease of Web publishing.
- *Support multiple platforms:* To minimize support requirements, end users should select one or two development tools that run on the range of hardware platforms and operating systems within the organization.
- *Offer low cost of ownership:* Cost factors include not only the tool's purchase price, but also training time, speed of application development, and required skill level.
- *Support a wide range of data types:* By its very nature, data is dynamic. Therefore, the toolset should support all the features normally found in database management system products.

Prototyping

LEARNING OUTCOME 4

Prototyping is the process of building a model that demonstrates the features of a proposed product, service, or system. A ***prototype,*** then, is simply a model of a proposed product, service, or system. If you think about it, people prototype all the time. Automobile manufacturers build prototypes of cars to demonstrate and test safety features, aerodynamics, and comfort. Building contractors construct models of homes and other structures to show layouts and fire exits.

In systems development, prototyping can be an invaluable tool for you. Prototyping is an iterative process in which you build a model from basic business requirements, have users review the prototype and suggest changes, and further refine and enhance the prototype to include suggestions. Especially, prototyping is a dynamic process that allows end users to see, work with, and evaluate a model and suggest changes to that model to increase the likelihood of success of the proposed system. Prototyping is an invaluable tool in the component-based development methodologies (RAD, XP, and agile), selfsourcing, and insourcing.

You can use prototyping to perform a variety of functions in the systems development process:

- *Gathering requirements:* Prototyping is a great requirements gathering tool. You start by simply prototyping the basic system requirements. Then you allow end users to add more requirements (information and processes) as you revise the prototype.

- *Helping determine requirements:* In many systems development projects, end users aren't sure what they really want. They simply know that the current system doesn't meet their needs. In this instance, you can use prototyping to help end users determine their exact requirements.

- *Proving that a system is technically feasible:* Let's face it, there are some things to which you cannot apply technology. And knowing whether you can is often unclear when defining the scope of the proposed system. If you're uncertain about whether something can be done, prototype it first. A prototype you use to prove the technical feasibility of a proposed system is a ***proof-of-concept prototype.***

- *Selling the idea of a proposed system:* Many people resist changes in IT. The current system seems to work fine, and they see no reason to go through the process of developing and learning to use a new system. In this case, you have to convince them that the proposed system will be better than the current one. Because prototyping is relatively fast, you won't have to invest a lot of time to develop a prototype that can convince people of the worth of the proposed system. A prototype you use to convince people of the worth of a proposed system is a ***selling prototype.***

THE PROTOTYPING PROCESS

Prototyping is an excellent tool in systems development. Most often, IT specialists (insourcing) use prototyping in the SDLC to form a technical system blueprint. In self-sourcing, however, you can often continue to refine the prototype until it becomes the final system. The prototyping process for either case is almost the same up to a point; only the result differs. Figure 6.9 (on the next page) illustrates the difference between insourcing and selfsourcing prototyping. Regardless of who does the prototyping, the prototyping process involves four steps:

1. *Identify basic requirements:* During the first step, you gather the basic requirements for a proposed system. These basic requirements include input and output information desired and, perhaps, some simple processes. At this point, you're typically unconcerned with editing rules, security issues, or end-of-period processing (for example, producing W-2s for a payroll system at the end of the year).

2. *Develop initial prototype:* Having identified the basic requirements, you then set out to develop an initial prototype. Most often, your initial prototype will include only user interfaces, such as data entry screens and reports.

3. *End user reviewing:* Step 3 starts the truly iterative process of prototyping. When end users first initiate this step, they evaluate the prototype and suggest changes or additions. In subsequent returns to step 3 (after step 4), they evaluate new versions of the prototype. It's important to involve as many end users as possible during this iterative process. This will help resolve any discrepancies in such areas as terminology and operational processes.

4. *Revise and enhance the prototype:* The final sequential step in the prototyping process is to revise and enhance the prototype according to any end user suggestions. In this step, you make changes to the current prototype and add any new requirements. Next, you return to step 3 and have the end users review the new prototype; then step 4 again, and so on.

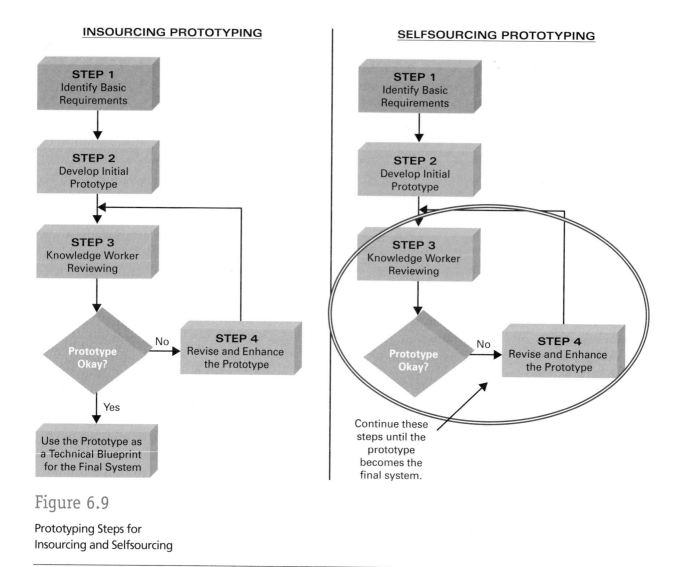

Figure 6.9

Prototyping Steps for
Insourcing and Selfsourcing

For either insourcing or selfsourcing, you continue the iterative processes of steps 3 and 4 until end users are happy with the prototype. What happens to the prototype after that, however, differs.

During selfsourcing, you're most likely to use the targeted application software package or application development tool to develop the prototype. This simply means that you can continually refine the prototype until it becomes the final working system. For example, if you choose to develop a simple CRM application using Microsoft Access, you can prototype many of the operational features using Microsoft Access development tools. Because you develop these prototypes using the targeted application development environment, your prototype can eventually become the final system. This also holds true for component-based development methodologies.

That process is not necessarily the same when insourcing and using the traditional SDLC. Most often, IT specialists develop prototypes using special prototyping development tools. Many of these tools don't support the creation of a final system—you simply use them to build prototypes. Therefore, the finished prototype becomes a blueprint or technical design for the final system. In the appropriate stages of the SDLC, IT specialists will implement the prototype in another application development environment better suited to the development of production systems.

THE ADVANTAGES OF PROTOTYPING

- *Encourages active end user participation*—First and foremost, prototyping encourages end users to actively participate in the development process. As opposed to interviewing and reviewing documentation, prototyping allows end users to see and work with models of a proposed system.

- *Helps resolve discrepancies among end users*—During the prototyping process, many end users participate in defining the requirements for and reviewing the prototype. The word *many* is key. If several end users participate in prototyping, you'll find it's much easier to resolve any discrepancies the end users may encounter.

- *Gives end users a feel for the final system*—Prototyping, especially for user interfaces, provides a feel for how the final system will look and work. When end users understand the look and feel of the final system, they are more likely to see its potential for success.

- *Helps determine technical feasibility*—Proof-of-concept prototypes are great for determining the technical feasibility of a proposed system.

- *Helps sell the idea of a proposed system*—Finally, selling prototypes can help break down resistance barriers. Many people don't want new systems because the old ones seem to work just fine, and they're afraid the new system won't meet their expectations and work properly. If you provide them with a working prototype that proves the new system will be successful, they will be more inclined to buy into it.

THE DISADVANTAGES OF PROTOTYPING

- *Leads people to believe the final system will follow shortly*—When a prototype is complete, many people believe that the final system will follow shortly. After all, they've seen the system at work in the form of a prototype—how long can it take to bring the system into production? Unfortunately, it may take months or even years. You need to understand that the prototype is only a model, not the final system missing only a few simple bells and whistles.

- *Gives no indication of performance under operational conditions*—Prototypes seldom take all operational conditions into consideration. This problem surfaced at the Department of Motor Vehicles in a state on the East Coast. During prototyping, the system, which handled motor vehicle and driver registration for the entire state, worked fine for 20 workstations at two locations. When the system was finally installed for all locations (which included more than 1,200 workstations), the system spent all its time just managing communication traffic; it had absolutely no time to complete any transaction. This is potentially the most significant drawback to prototyping. You must prototype operational conditions as well as interfaces and processes.

- *Leads the project team to forgo proper testing and documentation*—You must thoroughly test and document all new systems. Unfortunately, many people believe they can forgo testing and documentation when using prototyping. After all, they've tested the prototype; why not use the prototype as the documentation for the system? Don't make that mistake.

CROWDSOURCING SYSTEMS DEVELOPMENT TO CHANGE THE WORLD

Throughout this text, we've discussed the notion of crowdsourcing, getting nonpaid, nonemployees to participate in the development of value. Crowdsourcing can be applied to any "value creation" process including systems development. In this way, it becomes an interesting variation of selfsourcing.

Organizations of all sizes and in all industries are spinning up crowdsourcing competitions to encourage nonemployees to create IT-based systems. Some of these are profit-motivated, such as NetFlix's contest to see who could develop a better recommendation engine. Others, however, are not solely focused on making money but rather are more about changing the world. Below are numerous examples.

- **Qualcomm and the X Prize Foundation**—$10 million crowdsourced contest for a smartphone app that can diagnose health problems as accurately as an in-person attending physician.
- **Heritage Provider Network (California-based medical provider)**—$3 million contest for an

algorithm that accurately predicts which of its patients are most likely to be admitted to a hospital within the next 12 months.

- **Recyclebank**—business plan competition to grow from 2 million users to 10 million users in six months by expanding its offerings beyond curbside recycling to encourage good behavior by all people.

Perhaps the most extensive example is that of the U.S. federal government, which in 2010 passed legislation creating the America Competes Act. It annually sets aside $50 million for government agencies to use for holding crowdsourcing competitions to create applications that, in a sense, "save the world." Anyone, including you, can easily enter these government-sponsored contests, which range from defense to energy and environment to international affairs to education. To learn more, visit Challenge.gov at http://challenge.gov.[8, 9]

Outsourcing

The third choice as to who will build your IT systems—beyond insourcing (in-house IT specialists) and selfsourcing (end users)—is outsourcing. ***Outsourcing*** is the delegation of specific work to a third party for a specified length of time, at a specified cost, and at a specified level of service. With competitive pressures to cut costs and reduce time-to-market, many organizations are looking to outsource their IT systems development (not to mention ongoing operation, maintenance, and support). The Outsourcing Research Council recently completed a study indicating that human resources (HR) is the top outsourcing area for many companies. Fifty percent of the companies surveyed said they were already outsourcing some or all of their payroll processing and another 38 percent said they were considering it.[10]

Energizer, the world's largest manufacturer of batteries and flashlights, outsourced its HR operations to ADP, one of the top HR outsourcing companies. Energizer currently has more than 3,500 employees and 2,000 retired employees who all require multiple HR IT-related services. ADP provides Energizer with centralized call centers, transaction-processing services, and Web-based employee self-service systems. Energizer's vice president of Human Resources, Peter Conrad, stated, "ADP was clearly the most capable, and offered the kind of one-stop shopping our company was looking for." For several of the systems provided by ADP employee usage topped over 80 percent in the first six months the systems were active.[11]

The main reasons behind the rapid growth of the outsourcing industry include the following:

- **Globalization:** As markets open worldwide, competition heats up. Companies may engage outsourcing service providers to deliver international services. And outsourcing service providers may be located throughout the globe.
- **The Internet:** Barriers to entry, such as the lack of capital, are dramatically reduced in the world of e-business. New competitors enter the market daily.
- **Growing economy and low unemployment rate:** Building a competitive workforce domestically is much harder and more expensive.
- **Technology:** Technology is advancing at such an accelerated rate that companies often lack the resources, workforce, or expertise to keep up.
- **Deregulation:** As private industries such as telecommunications and energy deregulate, markets open and competition increases.

IT outsourcing today represents a significant opportunity for your organization to capitalize on the intellectual resources of other organizations by having them take over and perform certain business functions in which they have more expertise than IT specialists in your company. Information technology outsourcing enables organizations to keep up with market and technology advances with less strain on human and financial resources and more assurance that the IT infrastructure will keep pace with evolving business practices. IT outsourcing for software development can take one of four forms (see Figure 6.10):

1. Purchasing existing software.
2. Purchasing existing software and paying the publisher to make certain modifications.
3. Purchasing existing software and paying the publisher for the right to make modifications yourself.
4. Outsourcing the development of an entirely new and unique system for which no software exists.

In these instances, we're not talking about personal productivity software you can buy at a local computer store. We're talking about large software packages that may cost millions of dollars. For example, every organization has to track financial information, and

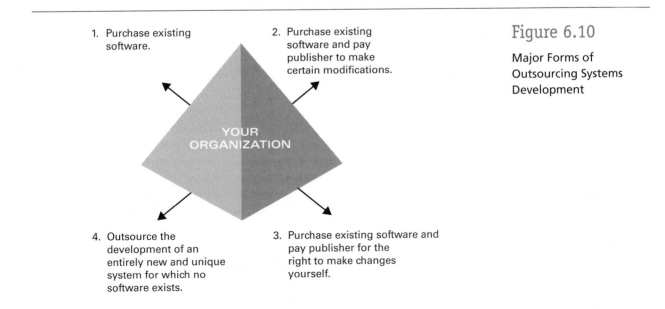

1. Purchase existing software.

2. Purchase existing software and pay publisher to make certain modifications.

YOUR ORGANIZATION

4. Outsource the development of an entirely new and unique system for which no software exists.

3. Purchase existing software and pay publisher for the right to make changes yourself.

Figure 6.10

Major Forms of Outsourcing Systems Development

there are several different systems they can purchase that help them perform this activity. Have you ever heard of Oracle Financials? This is a great system your organization can buy that tracks all the organizational financial information. If Oracle Financials is exactly what you need (i.e., it meets all your business requirements), then you act on option 1. If it meets most of your needs, you can act on either option 2 or 3. However, if you have a need for a unique suite of software that doesn't exist in the commercial market, you need to act on option 4. Let's explore that process.

THE OUTSOURCING PROCESS

The outsourcing process is both similar to and quite different from the systems development life cycle. It's different in that you turn over much of the design, development, testing, implementation, and maintenance steps to another organization. It's similar in that your organization begins with planning and defining the project scope (see Figure 6.11). It's during one of these first two phases of the process that your organization may come to understand that it needs a particular system but cannot develop it in-house. If so, that proposed system can be outsourced. That is step 3 of the process in Figure 6.11, the selection of a target system for outsourcing. Below, we briefly describe the remaining steps in the outsourcing process, starting with step 4.

ESTABLISH LOGICAL REQUIREMENTS   Regardless of your choice of insourcing or outsourcing, you must still perform the analysis phase—especially the primary activity of gathering the business requirements for the proposed system. Remember that identification of the business requirements drives the entire systems development effort; if the business requirements are not accurate or complete, there is no way the system will be successful. If you choose to outsource, part of gathering the business requirements becomes step 5, your *request for proposal.*

Figure 6.11

The Outsourcing Process

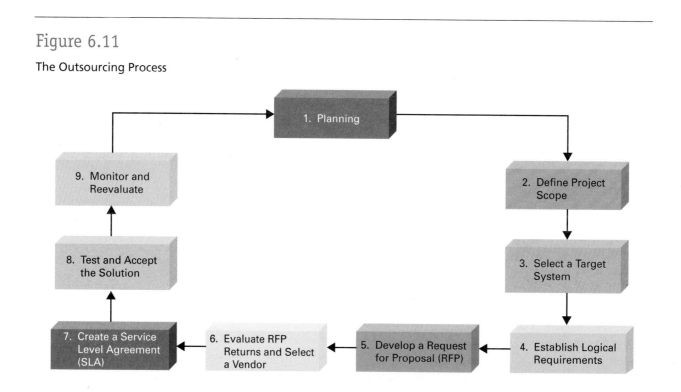

DEVELOP A REQUEST FOR PROPOSAL (RFP)   Outsourcing involves telling another organization what you want. What you want is essentially the logical requirements for a proposed system, and you convey that information by developing a request for proposal. A *request for proposal (RFP)* is a formal document that describes in excruciating detail your logical requirements for a proposed system and invites outsourcing organizations (which we'll refer to as *vendors*) to submit bids for its development. An RFP is one of the two most important documents in the outsourcing process. (The other is a service level agreement and we'll not debate which is the most important.) For systems of great size, your organization may create an RFP that's hundreds of pages long and requires months of work to complete.

It's vitally important that you take all the time you need to create a complete and thorough RFP. Eventually, your RFP will become the foundation for a legal and binding contract into which your organization and the vendor will enter. At a minimum, an RFP includes key information such as an overview of your organization, underlying business processes that the proposed system will support, a request for a detailed development time frame, and a request for a statement of detailed outsourcing costs.

All this information is vitally important to both your organization and the vendors. For your organization, the ability to develop a complete and thorough RFP means that you completely understand what you have and what you want. For the vendors, a complete and thorough RFP makes it easier to propose a system that will meet most, if not all, your needs.

EVALUATE RFP RETURNS AND SELECT A VENDOR   Your next activity in outsourcing (step 6 in Figure 6.11) is to evaluate the RFP returns and choose a vendor. You perform this evaluation of the RFP returns according to a scoring mechanism you identified in the RFP. This is not a simple process. No two vendors will ever provide RFP returns in the same format, and the RFP returns you receive are usually longer than the RFP itself.

CREATE A SERVICE LEVEL AGREEMENT (SLA)   Once you've chosen a vendor, a lengthy legal process follows. Outsourcing is serious business, and serious business between two organizations almost always requires a lot of negotiating and the use of lawyers. Eventually, your organization has to enter into a legal and binding contract that very explicitly states the features of the proposed system, the exact system costs, the time frame for development, acceptance criteria, criteria for breaking the contract for nonperformance or noncompliance, and postdevelopment metrics for activities such as maintenance, support, operational performances, and so on. This legal and binding contract is often called a *service level agreement,* which we'll discuss in more detail after explaining the remaining steps in the outsourcing process.

TEST AND ACCEPT THE SOLUTION   As with all systems, testing and accepting the solution are crucial. Once a vendor installs the new system, it's up to you and your organization to test the entire system before accepting it. You'll need to develop detailed test plans and test conditions that test the entire system. This alone may involve months of running and testing the new system while continuing to operate the old one (the parallel method).

When you "accept" a solution, you're saying that the system performs to your expectations and that the vendor has met its contractual obligations thus far according to the service level agreement. Accepting a solution involves granting your sign-off on the system, which releases the vendor from any further development efforts or modifications to the system.

MONITOR AND REEVALUATE   Just like the systems you develop using the SDLC, systems you obtain through outsourcing need constant monitoring and reevaluation. In outsourcing, you also have to reassess your working relationship with the vendor. Is the vendor providing maintenance when you need it and according to the service level agreement? Does the system really perform the stated functions? Do month-end and year-end processes work according to your desires? Does the vendor provide acceptable support if something goes wrong? These are all important questions that affect the ultimate success of your outsourcing efforts.

THE SERVICE LEVEL AGREEMENT

When you contract the services of an outsourcing organization (i.e., vendor), you will most likely do so using a service level agreement. Broadly, a *service level agreement (SLA)* is a formal contractually obligated agreement between two parties. Within different environments, an SLA takes on different meanings. In the context of systems development, an SLA defines the work to be done, the time frame, the metrics that will be used to measure the success of the systems development effort, and the costs. Most SLAs are business oriented and void of detailed technical specifications. Technical specifications are included in a supporting document (similar to a contract addendum) called a *service level specification (SLS)* or *service level objective (SLO)*.

If the vendor further agrees to provide postdevelopment maintenance and support, then the SLA would outline in detail the terms of the maintenance and support activities, their costs, and—again—key metrics by which the success of those activities will be measured. The metrics you include in an SLA are the real key, and we'll describe and define such metrics in Chapter 7 when discussing how to create quantifiable measures of the value of an IT system.

GEOPOLITICAL OUTSOURCING OPTIONS

In a geopolitical sense, furthermore, there are three types of outsourcing:

1. *Onshore outsourcing* is the process of engaging another company in the same country for services. Much of the current jargon relating to outsourcing is based on the United States as the reference point. Thus, "onshore" outsourcing typically means contracting a U.S. company to provide business services.
2. *Nearshore outsourcing* is contracting an outsourcing arrangement with a company in a nearby country. Often, this country will share a border with the native country. Again, this term is often used with the United States as the frame of reference. In this case, nearshore outsourcing will take place in either Canada or in Mexico, usually.
3. *Offshore outsourcing* is contracting with a company that is geographically far away. For many companies, certain IT services, such as application development, maintenance, and help desk support, fall within the category of functions that are ideal for offshore outsourcing.

Although onshore and nearshore outsourcing are important forms in the outsourcing industry, when outsourcing is spoken about nowadays, it is usually *offshore* outsourcing that is being referenced.

OFFSHORE OUTSOURCING   From a humble beginning as a mere cost-cutting concept, offshore outsourcing has gradually moved ahead and established itself as a successful business model by rendering not only cost-effective but also sophisticated and highly efficient quality services. According to International Data Corporation (IDC), U.S.-based companies tripled their offshore outsourcing spending from $5.5 billion in 2000 to more than $17.6 billion in 2005. The offshore outsourcing trend has overcome all barriers of political turmoil, language problems, and culture differences, and has proved that no matter in which part of the world your outsourcer resides, what really matters is industry-standard, high-quality service together with decisive cost advantage.[12]

WEIGHING THE PROS AND CONS OF OUTSOURCING

The Neat Company, based in Philadelphia, Pennsylvania, is a manufacturer of cutting-edge optical character recognition (OCR) technology. In 2007, the company experienced worldwide growth, a good kind of growth that is always accompanied by problems. Neat had a difficult time filling key open positions with the right talent. Product development cycles were short and meeting them was critical to continued success.

So, the management at Neat considered the idea of outsourcing, focusing on China. Many people believe the question of outsourcing is easily answered by looking at costs, but not Neat. It knew that several factors had to be considered to make the right decision. In the end, Neat did decide to outsource to the China-based firm Symphony Services. Below is a list of a few of the factors Neat considered.

- *Labor market:* Definitely less expensive in China (as compared to the U.S.) but language and culture barriers create challenges for the development teams that must work together from each organization.
- *Project development:* Faster in China but the 12-hour time difference always plays havoc with communications.
- *Big market (China):* Very much a positive because Neat could create a presence in a potentially huge market but the potential is high for theft or loss of intellectual property or customer data in China.[13]

Since the mid-1990s, major U.S. companies have been sending significant portions of their software development work offshore—primarily to vendors in India, but also to vendors in China, Eastern Europe (including Russia), Ireland, Israel, and the Philippines. The big selling point for offshore outsourcing to these countries is "good work done cheap." A programmer who earns $63,000 per year in the United States is paid as little as $5,000 per year overseas (see Figure 6.12). Companies can easily realize cost savings of 30 to 50 percent through offshore outsourcing and still get the same, if not better, quality of service.

Stories about U.S. companies outsourcing work offshore to India have been reported for years; however, it is becoming increasingly apparent that Romania, Bulgaria, Russia, China, Ghana, the Philippines, and dozens of other countries are also clamoring for and getting business from the United States. The reality is that offshore outsourcing is a growing trend. According to a recent study from Meta Group, the worldwide offshore outsourcing market will grow 20 percent annually through 2008. Meta also claims

Figure 6.12

Typical Salary Ranges for Computer Programmers

Country	Salary Range per Year
China	$5,000–9,000
India	$6,000–10,000
Philippines	$6,500–11,000
Russia	$7,000–13,000
Ireland	$21,000–28,000
Canada	$25,000–50,000
United States	$60,000–90,000

that offshoring growth will outpace outsourcing in general and predicts that the average enterprise will offshore 60 percent of application development by 2008 or 2009.[14]

What types of functions or projects make good candidates for offshore outsourcing? Data conversions and system migrations with well-defined requirements and specifications and minimal end-user interaction with the development team are typical projects taken offshore. Naturally, the company must be willing to allow its application code to be located offsite during development. Application development projects are also good offshore candidates. From a SDLC perspective, offshore work is most beneficial in the development and testing phases where end-user interaction is limited, and the task is well defined. For stable applications, most maintenance activities can be performed remotely so application maintenance is also a good candidate for offshore outsourcing. With the right communication infrastructure and a clear understanding of your company's business language requirements, call center or help desk functions can also be moved offshore.

THE ADVANTAGES AND DISADVANTAGES OF OUTSOURCING

Making the decision to outsource may be critical one way or the other to your organization's success. Thus far in our discussion of outsourcing, we've alluded to some advantages and disadvantages of outsourcing. Following is a summary of the major advantages and disadvantages of outsourcing the systems development process, in order to help you make the important outsourcing decision.

ADVANTAGES   Your organization may benefit from outsourcing because outsourcing allows you to:

- *Focus on unique core competencies:* By outsourcing systems development efforts that support noncritical business functions, your organization can focus on developing systems that support important, unique core competencies.
- *Exploit the intellect of another organization:* Outsourcing allows your organization to obtain intellectual capital by purchasing it from another organization. Often you won't be able to find individuals with all the expertise required to develop a system. Outsourcing allows you to find those individuals with the expertise you need to get your system developed and implemented.
- *Better predict future costs:* When you outsource a function, whether systems development or some other business function, you know the exact costs.
- *Acquire leading-edge technology:* Outsourcing allows your organization to acquire leading-edge technology without having to acquire technical expertise and bear the inherent risks of choosing the wrong technology.
- *Reduce costs:* Outsourcing is often seen as a money saver for organizations. Reducing costs is one of the important reasons organizations outsource.
- *Improve performance accountability:* Outsourcing involves delegating work to another organization at a specified level of service. Your organization can use this specified level of service to guarantee that it gets exactly what it wants from the vendor.

DISADVANTAGES   Outsourcing may *not* be a beneficial option for you because it:

- *Reduces technical know-how for future innovation:* Outsourcing is a way of exploiting the intellect of another organization, so it can also mean that your organization will no longer possess that expertise internally. If you outsource because you don't have the necessary technical expertise today, you'll probably have to outsource for the same reason tomorrow.

- *Reduces degree of control:* Outsourcing means giving up control. No matter what you choose to outsource, you are in some way giving up control over that function.
- *Increases vulnerability of your strategic information:* Outsourcing systems development involves telling another organization what information you use and how you use that information. In doing so, you could be giving away strategic information and secrets.
- *Increases dependency on other organizations:* As soon as you start outsourcing, you immediately begin depending on another organization to perform many of your business functions.

SUMMARY: STUDENT LEARNING OUTCOMES REVISITED

1. **Define the traditional systems development life cycle (SDLC) and describe the seven major phases within it.** The *systems development life cycle (SDLC)* is a structure d step-by-step approach for developing information systems. The seven major phases within it include:

   - *Planning*—creating a solid plan for developing your information system
   - *Analysis*—gathering, understanding, and documenting the business requirements
   - *Design*—building a technical blueprint of how the proposed system will work
   - *Development*—taking all the design documents and transforming them into an actual system
   - *Testing*—verifying that the system works and meets all the business requirements
   - *Implementation*—distributing and using the new system
   - *Maintenance*—monitoring and supporting the new system

2. **Compare and contrast the various component-based development methodologies.**

   Component-based methodologies (CBD) include:

   - *Rapid application development (RAD or rapid prototyping)*—extensive user involvement in the rapid and evolutionary construction of working prototypes of a system to accelerate the systems development process
   - *Extreme programming (XP)*—breaks a project into tiny phases, with each phase focusing on a small aspect of the system that eventually becomes a component or small software module
   - *Agile*—aims for customer satisfaction through early and continuous delivery of useful software components

3. **Describe the selfsourcing process as an alternative to the traditional systems development life cycle.** *Selfsourcing (end-user development)* is the development and support of IT systems by end users with little or no help from IT specialists. While the traditional SDLC uses in-house IT specialists to develop a system, selfsourcing has the user developing his or her own system. The user typically prototypes the system using the targeted application software

environment and can thus continually refine and enhance the prototype until it becomes the final working system.

4. **Discuss the importance of prototypes and prototyping within any systems development methodology.**   *Prototyping* is the process of building a model (i.e., *prototype*) that demonstrates the features of a proposed product, service, or system. Prototyping can be used effectively to gather requirements, help determine requirements when they are unknown, prove that a system is technically feasible (*proof-of-concept prototype*), and sell the idea of a proposed system (*selling prototype*).

5. **Describe the outsourcing environment and how outsourcing works.**   *Outsourcing* is the delegation of specific work to a third party for a specified length of time, at a specified cost, and at a specified level of service. Outsourcing is growing today because of globalization, the Internet, a growing economy and low unemployment rate, technology, and deregulation. Everything from food service to payroll services to call centers is being outsourced. In the outsourcing process, you target a system for outsourcing and build a *request for proposal (RFP)* that invites vendors to bid for its development. You choose a vendor and enter into an agreement called a *service level agreement (SLA)* that states exactly what the vendor is going to do. In the end, you test and accept the solution from the vendor and begin using the system.

CLOSING CASE STUDY ONE

The Good-Enough Technology Economy

In the opening vignette of this chapter, we described how digital cameras and phones with embedded cameras are outrageously correcting the camera and film industries. We noted that these new technologies are "good enough." What did we mean? What does it mean to be *good enough?* While the answer probably won't surprise you, the fact that *good enough* has become an important characteristic of today's new economy may.

The *good-enough technology economy* is one marked by the lack of seeking perfection, focusing rather on getting "good enough" products out the door, often allowing them to evolve and improve over time through user feedback. It may sound rather nebulous, so let's consider some examples.

- **Skype**—If you use Skype's service, you know that it's definitely *not* perfect. But it works most of the time. And for pennies per minute, you can make international calls. See how that price compares to using traditional telephone service providers.
- **Cell phones**—They aren't perfect either. Sometimes the voice on the other end cuts in

and out. Sometimes, calls are even dropped. But the technology is good enough because it makes you mobile.

- **Cameras in phones**—Remember our opening discussion on the death of film-based cameras? Film-based cameras actually produce much better quality photos. But the phone in your camera is with you always and takes "good enough" quality photos.
- **Wireless connectivity**—It's good enough, again, because it makes you mobile. A hard-wired Internet line is always much faster and less susceptible to interruption but wireless is good enough.

Let's consider another example with which you are probably very familiar, *Angry Birds.* Rovio Mobile first released Angry Birds in December 2009. At the time we wrote this case study (July 2011), Rovio had released its sixth version, less than two years after the initial release. This is true for most smartphone apps. New releases are constantly coming out, each better than the previous version which was "good enough" to get out the door and in the hands of consumers.

If you explore the many examples of good-enough technologies, you can begin to extrapolate many of the nontraditional rules of this new economy.

- **Throw-away society**—The average owner of a cell phone keeps his/her cell phone for slightly over 20 months before upgrading to a new one. The simple fact is that most people today don't mind "throwing away" a perfectly good (or good-enough) product in favor of a new one. So, there's no reason to seek product perfection (from a provider point of view) when most of your customers will upgrade to the next version without hesitation.

- **Focus on technology innovation failure**—Innovation failure is not a characteristic of traditional business. "Old" business models focused on gathering data, holding numerous focus groups, launching repeated product betas, and seeking the golden moment of product perfection before market release. Today's new business model focuses on getting something out the door, gathering data regarding its use, and then determining how to make it better with each new release. Because of this, many product releases fail. But they were cheap and time to market was short.

- **Speed of competitive innovation forces "good-enough" positions**—The speed of innovation and change is unbelievable. In most industries, entry barriers no longer exist, making it possible for entrepreneurial efforts to penetrate markets overnight. Organizations today simply cannot afford to be in product development for years before releasing a perfect product. Amazon didn't seek perfection for its Kindle. It got something out the door, and that something turned out to be "good enough" to transform the entire book publishing industry.

- **Perfection isn't worth it**—With the market moving so quickly and consumers being so willing to throw away existing versions in favor of new ones, it's not worth it to seek perfection. In fact, you can probably make more money in the long haul by releasing an upgrade every year (that consumers can purchase) as opposed to releasing one really great version every five years.[15, 16, 17, 18, 19, 20]

Questions

1. As we alluded to, the outrageous transformation taking place in the camera and film industries is being caused by good-enough products, specifically digital cameras and phone-embedded cameras. Read the Outrageous Industry Transformation cases at the beginning of Chapters 2 through 8. Which corrections are being caused by good-enough technology products?

2. What does all this mean for systems development? In the good-enough technology economy, which will organizations come to rely on more heavily: insourcing, selfsourcing, or outsourcing? Can organizations afford to use the traditional SDLC and completely gather requirements before proceeding with development? For what systems can organizations still use the traditional SDLC?

3. How is this notion of getting things out the door quickly and then using market feedback for product improvement similar to the concept of prototyping? What are the disadvantages of using such an approach to the release of products that aren't perfect?

4. Can manufacturers of automobiles use the concepts of the good-enough technology economy to produce automobiles? What features of an automobile must be perfect (or very close to it)? What features of an automobile can simple be "good enough"?

CLOSING CASE STUDY TWO

Tablets Take Their Place in the PC Market

The PC revolution changed the technology world beginning in the early 1980s. That was soon followed by the very bulky "luggables," the first portable personal computers. Then, luggables became lightweight, ushering in the laptop era. In early 2000, Microsoft introduced the first tablet PC. Our society fully embraced the tablet PC concept when Apple introduced the iPad in 2010. Since then, the "personal computer" market has changed dramatically.

- In March 2011, The Gartner Group downgraded its forecasted growth for worldwide PC shipments from 15.9 percent to just 10.5 percent.
- Tablet and smartphone sales (in units) are expected to exceed PC sales by 2012.
- By 2014, tablet and smartphones combined are predicted to represent 64 percent of all computers.
- By 2017, approximately two tablet PCs will be sold for every three laptop computers worldwide.
- Apple sold almost 15 million iPads in 2010, generating $9.5 billion in revenue. It is forecasted to sell 43.7 million iPads in 2011 and 63.3 million in 2012.
- In August 2010, year-on-year growth of laptop unit sales went negative to [–]4%.

The tablet PC is no "flash in the pan." It's here and here to stay. With an ever-increasing focus on mobility and battery life, more and more consumers are choosing tablet PCs over their bigger, bulkier, and power-hungry desktop and laptop predecessors. Of course, Apple's iPad is leading the charge, but others are sure to follow, creating a highly competitive market. Tablets are not just for personal use. All types of organizations are finding unique and innovative ways to incorporate tablet PCs into their operations.

RESTAURANTS

The tablet PC is not much larger than the typical paper menu in a restaurant, but it offers much more functionality.

- **Flagstaff House** (Boulder, Colorado's best known restaurant) places iPads on each table to display its 2,500+ wine list. According to Scott Monette, General Manager and Partner of Flagstaff, "When I saw the iPads come out, I thought it would be great to have our wine list on them. I was a little concerned that we should keep some paper lists around if people don't want the iPad. But we haven't had that happen yet."
- **Food Well Built's** (a Southern California restaurant chain) tables come standard with an iPad so patrons can design and order meals, all without ever talking to the wait staff.
- **BJs Restaurants** patrons can view menu options, including designing their own burgers

and pizzas. Patrons can even pay for meals using the tablet PC.
- **Restaurants by Delta Airlines** at JFK and LaGuardia airports provide tablets so patrons can order meals.

SCHOOLS

In Auburn, Maine, all kindergarteners now receive the Apple iPad2 as a part of their school supplies. The children use their tablet PCs to learn their ABCs, 1-2-3s, art, and music. According to Angus King, the former Maine Governor who championed the use of tablet PCs in the classroom, "If your students are engaged, you can teach them anything. If they're bored and looking out the window, you can be Socrates and you're not going to teach them anything. These devices are engaging."

Not everyone shares Angus's enthusiastic views. According to Larry Cuban, Stanford University professor emeritus and author of "Oversold and Underused: Computers in Schools," there is no proof that children learn better in a technology-rich environment as opposed to by more traditional methods. He states, "There's no evidence in research literature that giving iPads to 5-year-olds will improve their reading scores."

AIRLINES

The Federal Aviation Administration (FAA) recently approved the use of tablet PCs by pilots instead of paper charts and manuals. Many airlines, such as Delta, American, and Alaska Airlines, quickly made the transition to tablet PCs. Alaska Airlines is transitioning all of its 1,400 pilots to iPads. According to Randy Kleiger, a 15-year pilot for Alaska Airlines, "Now we have all the information in the iPad. And that makes it more efficient and safer."

But again, some people believe that there may be downsides to the pilot-use of technology in the cockpit. For example, in November 2009 pilots of a Northwest Airlines flight flew past their destination while using a laptop and not talking to air traffic controllers. It's rather like driving a car. The GPS system can be very useful, but something like texting can be a distraction.[21, 22, 23, 24, 25, 26]

Questions

1. Computers, using some AI techniques like those we discussed in Chapter 4, can learn. In the classroom while a child is using a tablet PC to learn the basics of addition, how can software

be developed to aid in the learning process? Does this mean that teachers are no longer needed for some subjects? Are teachers needed in earlier grades while computer-based training can take over in later grades? Why or why not?

2. End-user systems, like those that allow patrons to order meals on an iPad, must be "idiot proof." (We apologize for the crudeness of that term.) That is, systems must be usable without training and created in such a way, for example, that a patron at one table can't accidentally change the order of a patron at another table. What does this mean for systems development? Can complex and complicated end-user systems be developed and deployed on tablet PCs so that people can use the systems without training and without intervention by a knowledgeable person such as a waiter or waitress?

3. What security issues are involved in allowing people to pay with tablet PCs? Does this payment process make it easier for someone to steal your credit card information? Are you comfortable using a restaurant-supplied technology to enter your credit card information? Why or why not?

4. What will happen to offshore outsourcing for software development? Can outsourcing firms in India and China, for example, be expected to develop software systems for use in U.S. schools? Can those same firms be expected to develop systems that meet FAA rules and restrictions?

KEY TERMS AND CONCEPTS

Agile methodology, 170
Analysis phase, 163
Business requirement, 163
Component-based development (CBD), 167
Critical success factor (CSF), 162
Design phase, 164
Development phase, 164
Extreme programming (XP) methodology, 168
Feature creep, 162
Good-enough technology economy, 186
Help desk, 166
Implementation phase, 165
Insourcing, 160
Integration testing, 165
Invisible backlog, 173
Joint application development (JAD), 163
Maintenance phase, 166
Nearshore outsourcing, 182
Offshore outsourcing, 182

Online training, 165
Onshore outsourcing, 182
Outsourcing, 160, 178
Parallel implementation, 165
Phased implementation, 166
Pilot implementation, 165
Planning phase, 162
Plunge implementation, 165
Project manager, 162
Project milestone, 162
Project plan, 162
Project scope document, 162
Proof-of-concept prototype, 175, 186
Prototype, 174
Prototyping, 174
Rapid application development (RAD) (rapid prototyping) methodology, 167
Request for proposal (RFP), 181
Requirements definition document, 163
Scope creep, 162

Selfsourcing (end-user development), 160, 170
Selling prototype, 175
Service level agreement (SLA), 182
Service level objective (SLO), 182
Service level specification (SLS), 182
Service-oriented architecture (SOA or SoA), 170
Sign-off, 163
Systems development life cycle (SDLC), 160
System testing, 165
Technical architecture, 164
Test condition, 165
Testing phase, 165
Unit testing, 165
User acceptance testing (UAT), 165
User documentation, 165
Waterfall methodology, 160
Workshop training, 165

SHORT-ANSWER QUESTIONS

1. What are the three primary groups of people who undertake the systems development process?
2. What is the systems development life cycle?
3. What are scope creep and feature creep?

4. How do the four implementation methods differ?
5. What is component-based development?
6. How are component-based development and a service-oriented architecture related?
7. Why do organizations prototype?
8. What are the advantages of selfsourcing?

9. What is the difference between a selling prototype and a proof-of-concept prototype?
10. What is the role of a service level agreement (SLA) in outsourcing?
11. What are the three geopolitical forms of outsourcing?

■ ASSIGNMENTS AND EXERCISES

1. **REQUEST FOR PROPOSAL** A request for proposal (RFP) is a formal document that describes in detail your logical requirements for a proposed system and invites outsourcing organizations to submit bids for its development. Research the Web and find three RFP examples. Briefly explain in a one-page document what each RFP has in common and how each RFP is different.

2. **MAKING THE WHO DECISION** Complete the table below by answering yes, no, or maybe in the columns of insource, selfsource, and outsource for each systems development condition listed on the left.

	INSOURCE	SELFSOURCE	OUTSOURCE
The system will support a unique core competency			
Cost is an overriding consideration			
Time-to-market is critical			
You possess the necessary expertise			
Organizational control of the system is critical			
The system will support a common business function			
Gaining and having technical expertise is part of your strategic plan			
The system will support only a very few users			

3. **YOUR RESPONSIBILITIES DURING EACH STEP IN THE SDLC** During insourcing, you have many responsibilities because you're a business process expert, liaison to the customer, quality control analyst, and manager of other people. According to which step of the SDLC you're in, your responsibilities may increase or decrease.

In the table below, determine the extent to which you participate in each SDLC step according to your four responsibilities. For each row you should number the SDLC steps 1 through 7, with a 1 indentifying the step in which your responsibility is the greatest and a 7 identifying the step in which your responsibility is the least.

	SDLC STEP						
	PLANNING	ANALYSIS	DESIGN	DEVELOPMENT	TESTING	IMPLEMENTATION	MAINTENANCE
Business process expert							
Liaison to the customer							
Quality control analyst							
Manager of other people							

4. **CONSTRUCTION AND THE SDLC** The systems development life cycle is often compared to the activities in the construction industry. Fill in the following chart listing some of the activities performed in building a house and how they relate to the different SDLC steps.

SDLC	Activities for Building a Home
Planning	
Analysis	
Design	
Development	
Testing	
Implementation	
Maintenance	

■ DISCUSSION QUESTIONS

1. Why is it important to develop a logical model of a proposed system before generating a technical architecture? What potential problems would arise if you didn't develop a logical model and went straight to developing the technical design?

2. If you view systems development as a question-and-answer session, another question you could ask is, "Why do organizations develop IT systems?" Consider what you believe to be the five most important reasons organizations develop IT systems. How do these reasons relate to topics in the first five chapters of this book?

3. Your company has just decided to implement a new financial system. Your company's financial needs are almost the same as those of all the other companies in your industry. Would you recommend that your company purchase an

existing system or build a custom system? Would you recommend your company use end-user development or outsource the new system?

4. There are seven phases in the systems development life cycle. Which one do you think is the hardest? Which one do you think is the easiest? Which one do you think is the most important? Which one do you think is the least important? If you had to skip one of the phases, which one would it be and why?

5. You are talking with another student who is complaining about having to learn about the systems development life cycle, because he is not going to work in an IT department. Would you agree with this student? What would you say to him to convince him that learning about the systems development life cycle is important no matter where he works?

6. A company typically has many systems it wants to build, but unfortunately it usually doesn't have the resources to build all the systems. How does a company decide which systems to build?

7. People often think that a system is complete once it is implemented. Is this true? What happens after a system is implemented? What can you do to ensure the system continues to meet the knowledge workers' needs?

■ CHAPTER PROJECTS

GROUP PROJECTS

- Executive Information System Reporting: Political Campaign Finance (p. 288)
- Using Relational Technology to Track Projects: Foothills Construction (p. 291)
- Assessing the Value of Outsourcing Information Technology: Creating Forecasts (p. 294)
- Creating a Decision Support System: Buy versus Lease (p. 298)

E-COMMERCE PROJECTS

- Best in Computer Statistics and Resources (p. 310)
- Meta Data (p. 311)
- Finding Hosting Services (p. 315)
- Researching Storefront Software (p. 320)
- Searching for Shareware and Freeware (p. 320)

CHAPTER SEVEN OUTLINE

STUDENT LEARNING OUTCOMES

1. Describe how a service-oriented architecture can be used as a philosophical approach to help the organization of the future meet all its IT-related needs.

2. Define and describe the various hardware and software infrastructure considerations in an organization.

3. Describe cloud computing, its various implementations, and its advantages.

4. Compare and contrast commonly used metrics for assessing the success of IT systems and IT-related initiatives.

5. Describe business continuity planning (BCP) and its phases.

PERSPECTIVES

WEB SUPPORT

www.mhhe.com/haag

- Best in computer statistics and resources
- Meta data
- Finding hosting services
- Searching for shareware and freeware

SUPPORTING MODULES

XLM/E NETWORK BASICS
Extended Learning Module E provides an introduction to the vast, exciting, and dynamic field of information technology networks. The module includes discussions of what is needed to set up a small network at home, the components used to build large business networks, Internet connection possibilities, types of communications media, and network security.

XLM/G Object-Oriented Technologies
Extended Learning Module G provides an introduction to the world of object-oriented technologies and concepts. Specifically, you will learn about the five primary object-oriented concepts, how classes and objects are related, and the three fundamental principles of object-oriented technologies.

CHAPTER SEVEN

Infrastructure, Cloud Computing, Metrics, and Business Continuity Planning
Building and Sustaining the Dynamic Enterprise

OUTRAGEOUS INDUSTRY TRANSFORMATION: MONEY WILL ALWAYS BE MONEY

Money is a representation of value, no matter what form money takes. One hundred pennies has the same value as a dollar bill. In the 1700s and 1800s in this country, people used "odd-sized" coins such as half-cent pieces, two-cent pieces, three-cent pieces, and even 20-cent pieces. Today, we are witnessing an outrageous industry transformation with regard to a new form of money, that of electronic or digital money.

Take a look at the accompanying graph. Paper money as a form of payment is expected to decline in use from 58 percent in 2003 to 36 percent in 2013. For the same time frame, the use of credit cards as a form of payment is expected to grow from 35 percent to 50 percent. And, again for the same time frame, the use of digital or electronic money is expected to grow from 7 percent to 14 percent.

The projected use of electronic money may seem small, but consider the growth projections carefully. From 2003 to 2013, the use of credit cards is expected to have grown by approximately 43 percent—that is, 15 percent (50 percent minus 35 percent) divided by 35 percent. During the same time frame, the use of electronic money is expected to grow by 100 percent, or double from 7 percent to 14 percent. In other words:

- The use of paper money is on the decline.
- The use of credit cards is increasing but at a decreasing rate.
- The use of electronic money is increasing at an increasing rate.

Now, please understand that "paper" in this instance includes both folding currency and coins. The latter is long overdue for a transformation. For years, it has cost the U.S. federal government more than a penny to mint a penny and more than a nickel to mint a nickel. Given the problems the United States has in dealing with its increasing debt, it doesn't make sense to mint money when the costs of minting the money costs more than the money itself.[1]

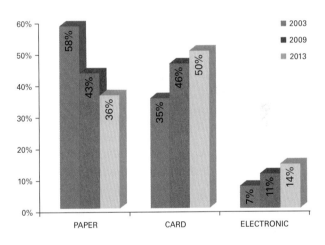

Questions

1. Do you use an electronic form of money such as Google wallet or a smartphone app? If so, which one?

2. Which do you think is easier—the counterfeiting of paper money or the counterfeiting of electronic money? Why?

3. Why does the government continue to mint pennies when the process costs more than a penny?

Introduction

In Chapter 6, we introduced you to the concept of a service-oriented architecture within the context of systems development. A **service-oriented architecture (SOA or SoA)** is a software architecture perspective that focuses on the development, use, and reuse of small self-contained blocks of code (called *services*) to meet all the application software needs of an organization. Thus new applications build on past solutions organically using established building blocks. If SoA is adopted, the organization is saying that instead of bringing in brand new systems all its software will be developed from reusable units of code. SoA is a high-level, holistic organizational approach to how an organization views and acts on all its software needs.

By way of illustration, let's move away from software development—and IT in general—for just a moment and consider the concept of your organization adopting a service-oriented architecture perspective for *everything* it does, such that those self-contained building-blocks of code (services) apply not just to software but also to people, processes, departments and units, operations, and best practices. What would that look like? Your organization with a service-oriented architecture philosophy would:

- Be a lean, agile organization that takes advantage of every resource in the most efficient and effective way.
- React quickly in a proactive way to perceived changes in the market, competition, and customer demographics, wants, and desires.
- Respond quickly to and adapt to new advances in technology.
- Transform its processes, structure, and HR initiatives to match a changing and dynamic workforce.

In short, SoA would enable your organization to become the organization of the future . . . bound by very few structural constraints, able to change on a moment's notice, always looking for and capitalizing on the next great competitive advantage.

Of course this is a book about how organizations use technology, and exploring a service-oriented architecture approach to things like HR or changing customer demographics is beyond our scope. So, let's refocus on IT, referring to Figure 7.1, which outlines how an SoA perspective enables your organization to respond more adeptly to customers, end users, software development, information needs, and hardware requirements.

CUSTOMERS

An IT-enabled SoA philosophy allows your organization to provide customers with multi-channel service delivery options and customizable products and services. Customers should be able to *plug-and-play* into any communications channel with your organization, such as fax, the Web, face-to-face contact, social media, phone call, and so on. Regardless of the communications channel, the experience should be the same—a consistent and high-quality interaction with your organization.

Customers should also be able to interact with IT systems that allow them to customize and personalize products and services. By simply "plugging in" their desires and wants, your organization should respond with unique and individually tailored offerings that satisfy and delight the customer. We spoke about the concept of mass customization (*slivercasting* and *exclusivity*) in Chapter 5.

Figure 7.1

A Service-Oriented
Architecture (SoA)
Philosophy

THE FOCUS	NOTES
CUSTOMERS	• Multi-channel service delivery • Consistent, high-quality interactions regardless of the venue • Customizable product and service capabilities
END USERS	• Fully integrated ERP system • Interoperability among vendors • Interoperability of modules by the same vendor • Mobile computing (access to information and software regardless of location and device)
SOFTWARE DEVELOPMENT	• SoA as a framework • RAD, XP, and agile as development methodologies • Exciting new deployments like Web 2.0
INFORMATION NEEDS	• End users with access to all types of information • Integrated information, business intelligence, and knowledge • Data warehouses • Standard information formats • Integrity controls • No duplicate information
HARDWARE REQUIREMENTS	• Integration of different technologies and technology platforms • Large storage capacity • Your focus on logical, not physical • Safe and secure telecommunications platform

END USERS

An SoA philosophy requires that your organization view its end users of IT (i.e., employees within the organization) just as it does external customers. This is mainly achieved through a fully integrated enterprise resource planning (ERP) system that meets every application software and information need of each and every employee. The ERP system should support transparent interoperability across multiple vendors and within ERP modules provided by the same vendor. Although we covered ERP in Chapter 2, we'll revisit it here because it is so vitally important to today's integrated and agile organization.

End users should be able to take advantage of multi-channel service delivery as well. In this case, end users (employees) should be able to access computing and information resources regardless of where they are (the notion of *mobile computing* from Chapter 5). And regardless of the IT device in hand (laptop, desktop, smartphone), employees should enjoy access to a full range of application software services and information.

SOFTWARE DEVELOPMENT

Organizations today can choose among numerous software development methodologies that focus on the production and reuse of blocks of code to speed the process of software development—rapid application development (RAD), extreme programming (XP), and agile methodology are among them.

If you delve into the nitty-gritty of software development, you'll find infrastructure platforms that support a service-oriented architecture approach. Some of these include Ajax (**A**synchronous **J**avaScript **a**nd **X**ML), SOAP (**S**ervice **O**riented **A**rchitecture **P**rotocol), WSDL (**W**eb **S**ervices **D**escription **L**anguage), UDDI (**U**niversal **D**escription, **D**iscovery, and **I**ntegration), and CORBA (**C**ommon **O**bject **R**equest **B**roker Architecture). Many of these platforms support the Web 2.0 applications—such as wikis, blogs, and mashups—that we discussed in *Extended Learning Module B* and Chapters 2 and 4.

INFORMATION NEEDS

A service-oriented architecture philosophy leverages the most vitally important organizational resource—information. End users need access to all types of information on a moment's notice, regardless of where that information is located (or where the end user is located). People throughout your organization need access to information, business intelligence, and knowledge that supports their decision-making efforts (analytics). Recall from Chapter 3 that data warehouses are built by combining information from multiple sources. These data warehouses are of paramount importance to good decision making.

For those reasons and many more, an SoA approach to information requires that:

- Information be in a standard format no matter where it exists.
- Strict and rigorous integrity control mechanisms are in place to ensure the completeness, accuracy, and validity of the information.
- No duplicate information exists in disparate silos anywhere in your organization.
- Any kind of information from any source (even external) can be quickly and easily coupled with other information.

HARDWARE REQUIREMENTS

Finally, a service-oriented architecture philosophy must pervade all choices in the realm of hardware. Organizations should be free to choose different technologies and different technology platforms and integrate them seamlessly (i.e., plug-and-play). Powerful storage area networks should have the capacity to store all your information needs. And you should not have to care where within these networks information is stored; your access to the information should be simple and easy.

Your telecommunications platform should be safe and secure and, at the same time, enable you to access a network either wired or wirelessly using the same steps or procedures. You should never have to look at the back of your computer to determine if you need to log on using a wired protocol or a wireless protocol.

That is what a service-oriented architecture philosophy is all about. Of course, the question now becomes how you implement such a philosophy. That's what the remainder of this chapter is about, specifically:

1. Hardware and software infrastructure
2. Metrics for determining success
3. Measures to ensure consistent, uninterrupted success

Hardware and Software Infrastructure

Generally, *infrastructure* is a relative term meaning "the structure beneath a structure." This definition implies different layers of structure, which provide support or services. An IT infrastructure is the implementation of an architecture—in our discussion here a service-oriented architecture. In a city, the infrastructure includes its streets and street lighting, hospitals, schools, utility lines running above and below the ground, and so on. We all depend on this public infrastructure to make lives of communities, cities, and people safe and prosperous. In a corporation, the IT infrastructure includes the hardware, software (such as ERP software), and information that (1) ensure the components work together and (2) enable people, business processes, and customers to interact and perform their tasks (see Figure 7.2).

ENTERPRISE RESOURCE PLANNING (ERP) REVISITED

Two of the primary goals of an ERP system within a service-oriented architecture are:

1. Provide interoperability within an ERP vendor and for modules among different ERP vendors.
2. Hide the underlying IT infrastructure of information and hardware from end users and customers.

In the first instance, *interoperability* refers to the capability of two or more computing components to share information and other resources, even if they are made by

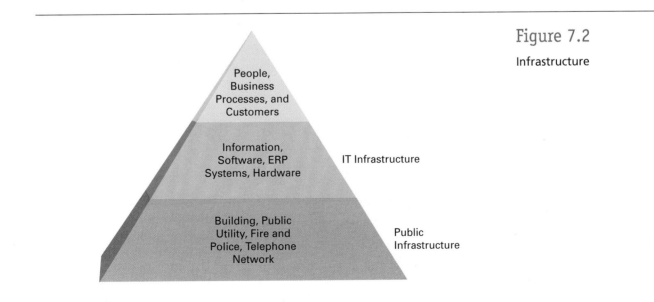

Figure 7.2

Infrastructure

different manufacturers. In the top layer of Figure 7.3, you can see the software infra-structure of an ERP system. Let's assume it's provided by Infor, a leading publisher of ERP software. Notice that you see all the typical software modules present—accounting, distribution, supply chain, and the like.

However, two modules have been replaced in Figure 7.3—the HR component by in-house developed software and data analytics by BI and reporting software from Cognos. This is the concept of interoperability. Your organization chooses the best ERP solu-tion on that market that meets most of its needs. Within the chosen ERP suite, you can replace software modules with in-house developed software and software modules from

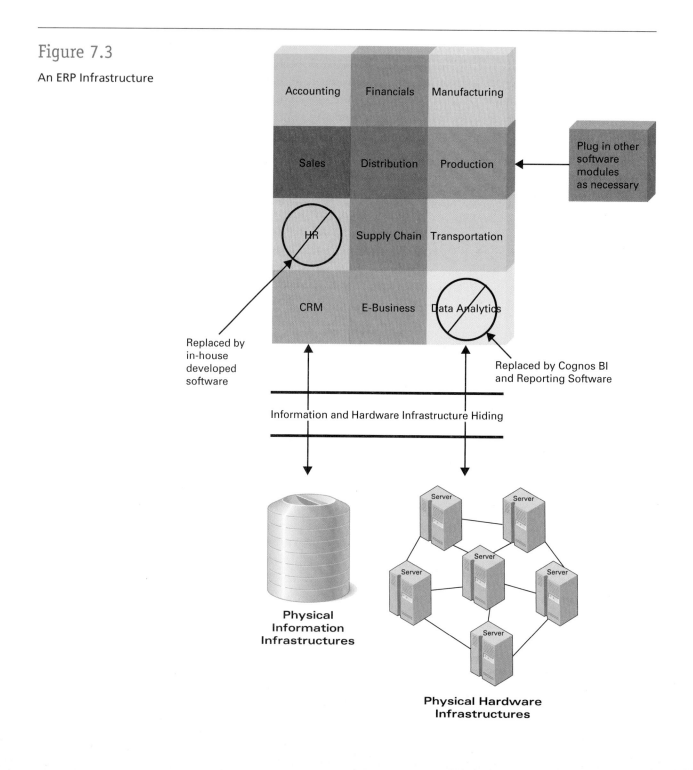

Figure 7.3

An ERP Infrastructure

other vendors (and software developed through outsourcing for that matter). Long after implementation, you can add other modules and plug them directly into your ERP solution, as well. This is the concept of *sustainable interoperability*.

In the lower portion of Figure 7.3, you can see the implementation of the second goal of an ERP system, that is, to hide the underlying IT infrastructure of information and hardware from end users and customers. The ERP system—specifically screens, reports, and the like—are the *customer-facing* aspect of the system. The physical structure and location of information should not be of concern to you, nor should the physical hardware infrastructure matter.

SUPPORTING NETWORK INFRASTRUCTURES

The fundamental underlying infrastructure for any IT environment is a network, two or more computers sharing information, software, peripheral devices, and processing power. Network infrastructure is such a wide and vast field that volumes have been written on the subject and many schools (primarily within the computer science department) offer entire programs and majors in IT networks. Our discussion here focuses on only the most common types of network infrastructures.

DISTRIBUTED INFRASTRUCTURE   A *distributed infrastructure* involves distributing the information and processing power of IT systems via a network. (This is the first true *network* infrastructure.) By connecting all the information systems via a distributed infrastructure, all locations can share information and applications (see Figure 7.4). The major benefit of this is that processing activity can be allocated to the locations(s) where it can most efficiently be done. To improve performance and reduce network traffic, a distributed infrastructure will often store the same application and/or information in two or more locations.

CLIENT/SERVER INFRASTRUCTURE (CLIENT/SERVER NETWORK) A *client/ server infrastructure* (or *client/server network*) has one or more computers that are

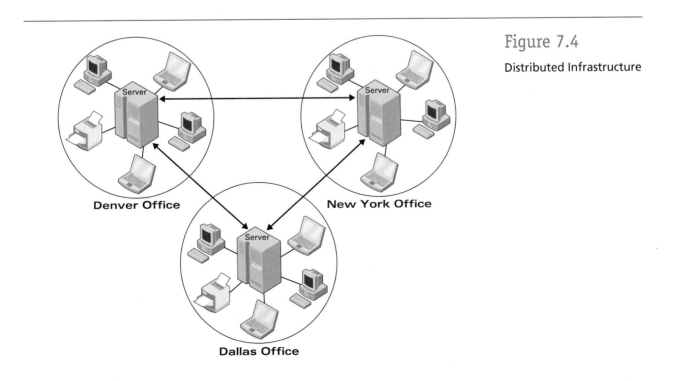

Figure 7.4

Distributed Infrastructure

ONE VIEW FOR DEL MONTE FOODS

From its roots in the California Gold Rush era, San Francisco–headquartered Del Monte Foods has grown to become the nation's largest producer and distributor of premium quality processed fruits, vegetables, and tomato products. With annual sales of over $3 billion, Del Monte is also one of the country's largest producers, distributors, and marketers of private-label food and pet products with a powerful portfolio of brands including Del Monte, StarKist, Nature's Goodness, 9Lives, and Kibbles 'n Bits.

Del Monte's acquisition of certain businesses (such as StarKist, Nature's Goodness, 9Lives, and Kibbles 'n Bits) from the H. J. Heinz Company required an integration between Del Monte's and H. J. Heinz's business processes. Del Monte needed to overhaul its IT infrastructure, migrating from multiple platforms including UNIX and mainframe systems and consolidating applications centrally on a single system. The work required integration of business processes across manufacturing, financial, supply chain, decision support, and transactional reporting areas.

The revamp of Del Monte's architecture stemmed from a strategic decision. Del Monte decided to implement an ERP system to support its entire U.S. operations, headquarters in San Francisco, operations in Pittsburgh, and distribution centers and manufacturing facilities across the country. The company concluded that the only way it could unite its global operations and open its system to its customers, which are mainly large retailers, was through the use of an ERP system.

Among other key factors was the need to embrace an e-business strategy. The challenge facing Del Monte was to select an ERP system to merge multiple systems quickly and cost effectively. If financial and customer service targets were to be achieved, Del Monte needed to integrate new businesses that more than doubled the size of the company. Since implementing the ERP system, customers and trading partners are now provided with a single, consistent, and integrated view of the company.[2,3]

Figure 7.5

Client/Server
Infrastructure

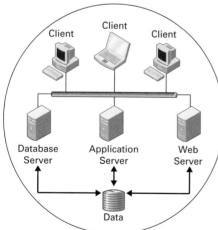

servers which provide services to other computers, called *clients.* The client/server infrastructure is a form of distributed infrastructure. The basic notion of a client/server infrastructure is that application processing is divided between the client and the server. The functions of an information system are divided among connected computers (or clients) on a network while centralizing processing and storage for all information on a server. For instance, when you are surfing on the Internet, this is an example of a client/server infrastructure. Typical components of this type of infrastructure include an Internet browser, a personal computer (e.g., the client), and a Web server.

The primary advantage of the client/server infrastructure is that it offloads the application programs and information from the server. However, because processing occurs at many client locations, and the client and server interact frequently and extensively, information must flow rapidly between server and clients for adequate performance (see Figure 7.5). The client/server infrastructure thereby places a heavy load on the network capacity, which can sometimes be a disadvantage.

TIERED INFRASTRUCTURE Most enterprise applications are now developed using a tiered infrastructure. In a ***tiered infrastructure*** (sometimes referred to as a ***layer infrastructure***), the IT system is partitioned into tiers (or layers) where each tier (or layer) performs a specific type of functionality. The concept of a tiered infrastructure has evolved from 1-tier to n-tiers. A "tier" can be defined as "one of two or more rows, levels, or ranks arranged one above another." Figure 7.6 illustrates the concept of a tiered infrastructure.

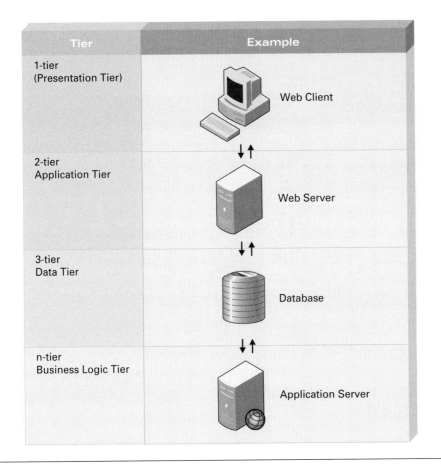

Figure 7.6

n-Tier Infrastructure Model

- A *1-tier infrastructure* is the most basic setup because it involves a single tier on a single machine. Think of an application that runs on your PC—everything you need to run the application (data storage, business logic, user interface, and so forth) is wrapped up together. An example of a 1-tiered application is a basic word processor or a desktop file utility program.

- A *2-tier infrastructure* is the basic client/server relationship. In essence, the client handles the display, the server handles the request (e.g., database query), and the application tier is contained on one or both of the two tiers.

- A *3-tier infrastructure* is the most common approach used for Web applications today. A typical example of this model is the Web browser that acts as the client, an application server that handles the business logic, and a separate tier (such as a DBMS) that handles database functions.

- An *n-tier infrastructure* balances the work of the network over several different servers. The letter "n" stands for any number of tiers. Traditionally, an n-tier infrastructure starts with a basic 3-tier model and expands on it to allow for greater performance, scalability, and a host of other benefits.

CLOUD COMPUTING: NO INFRASTRUCTURE AT ALL

Perhaps the hottest topic right now in all of technology is cloud computing. *Cloud computing* is a technology model in which any and all resources—application software, processing power, data storage, backup facilities, development tools . . . literally everything—are delivered as a set of services via the Internet (see Figure 7.7 on the next page). Think of cloud computing as you would utilizing the services of a taxi cab:

LEARNING OUTCOME 3

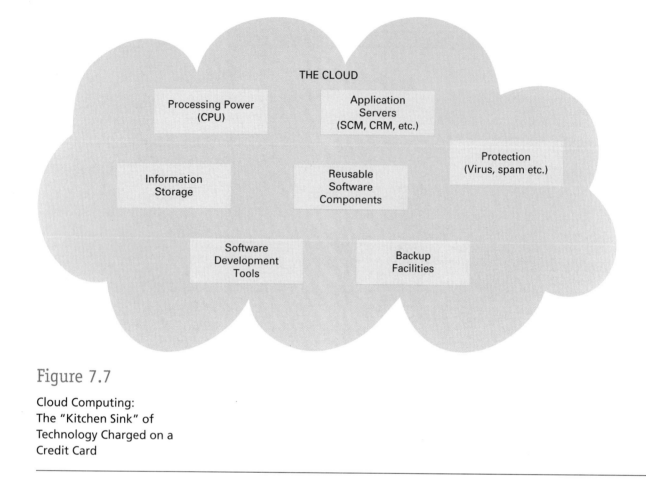

Figure 7.7

Cloud Computing:
The "Kitchen Sink" of
Technology Charged on a
Credit Card

- **Utility, pay-as-you-go, metered model**—You pay for only what you use when you use it; the taxi cab ride across town costs $40; 10 Gb of storage in the cloud for a month costs $1.50 (really . . . just 150 pennies).

- **Enables near real-time scalability (growing or shrinking)**—Get how much or how little you need; if you have 6 people in your group on a certain trip, hail two taxis for only that trip; pay on a monthly basis for what you rent in the cloud and easily adjust your monthly requirements up or down.

The goal of taking advantage of cloud computing is to have your computing costs (for example, infrastructure like ERP and SCM software and associated hardware) align with the activity level of your organization. As sales grow and you add more employees, perhaps sales representatives, customers, and the like, you pay for more computing resources in the cloud. If your business slows and so does your business activity, then the cost of cloud-based resources would decline.

Now, before we dive into the details of the cloud, we need to provide a disclaimer of sorts. Cloud computing is very new, growing rapidly, and changing every day. So, while many experts agree on the concepts associated with the cloud, definitions and even terminologies are in a state of flux. What we present here is the "status quo" for mid-2011; things will have undoubtedly changed by the time you read this book.

SOFTWARE-AS-A-SERVICE (SaaS)   In Chapter 2, we introduced you to software-as-a-service. *Software-as-a-service (SaaS)* is a delivery model for software in which you pay for software on a pay-per-use basis instead of buying the software outright. SaaS is among the first implementations of cloud computing and probably the most well-known.

The concept is quite simple. Instead of buying a site license for software, say CRM software from NetSuite, you rent it by the month based on the number of users you have.

NetSuite stores the software and your organization's information on its servers in the cloud. Your employees log onto NetSuite and use the CRM software and access your organization's information. As your organization does so, many other organizations are doing the same (see Figure 7.8). It's like using Facebook's software to view your wall, leave messages, and perform other tasks. While using Facebook's software, you aren't using a single instance of the software just for you; instead you're sharing one instance of the software with millions of other people (in the case of Facebook). This is the concept of **multi-tenancy**—when multiple people can simultaneously use a single instance of a piece of software. Notice in Figure 7.8, however, that your organization's data is securely partitioned away from the data of other organizations.

All vendors of popular application software for all types of software—ERP, CRM, SCM, financials, etc.—offer their software through a SaaS model—which raises an interesting question: Are these software vendors financially better off by renting their software on a monthly basis as opposed to selling expensive site licenses? The answer is yes. The SaaS model has opened the very large market of small- to medium-sized businesses (SMBs) to software vendors. Previously, most SMBs couldn't afford expensive software site licenses. With SaaS, software vendors have two outlets for their software: (1) selling site licenses to large organizations for which it makes sense economically to buy a site license instead of renting, and (2) charging a per-user, per-month fee to SMBs.

PLATFORM-AS-A-SERVICE (PAAS) *Platform-as-a-service (PaaS)* is a delivery model for software identical to SaaS with the additional features of (1) the ability to customize data entry forms, screens, reports, and the like and (2) access to software development tools to alter the way in which the software works by adding new modules (services) and/or making modifications to existing modules (see Figure 7.9 on the next page). The first additional feature of PaaS beyond SaaS is fairly straightforward. Using the SaaS model, you have access to a broad range of reports, for example, that have been pre-built for you, but you don't have the ability to change them. In PaaS, you can change the look, feel, and structure of reports in a variety of ways including adding your organization's logo, changing the sort option, generating different types of page and report

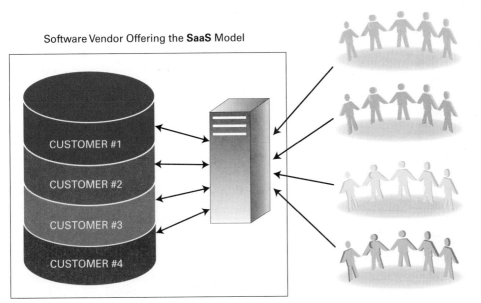

Software Vendor Offering the **SaaS** Model

CUSTOMER #1

CUSTOMER #2

CUSTOMER #3

CUSTOMER #4

Figure 7.8

SaaS and Multi-Tenancy

Figure 7.9

Platform-as-a-Service
(PaaS)

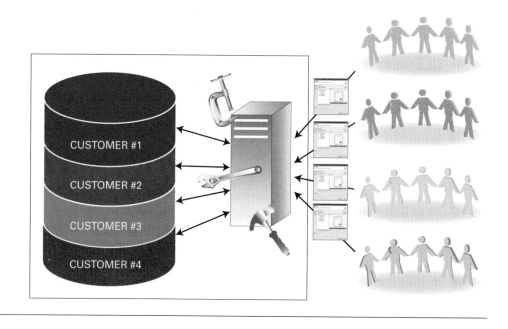

titles, and so on. The same is true for data entry forms and screens; you can change their design and structure as well. But with this first additional feature you are not changing the way the software works; you are only changing the interfaces.

The second feature is much more robust. Using software development tools (programming languages, testing facilities, and the like), your organization can, for example, add a new feature to the software such as a unique billing structure that might be required by several doctors sharing the lab. This feature is very appealing to many organizations, but also makes PaaS more expensive than SaaS. With PaaS, you are paying for the right to change the way the software works and you are paying for the use of the development tools to do so.

NetSuite offers the PaaS model. And once you've created a new module that you may need, you have the option of placing it in NetSuite's library of software of modules. If another organization likes the module you created and rents it from NetSuite, NetSuite will pay you a royalty.

INFRASTRUCTURE-AS-A-SERVICE (IAAS) *Infrastructure-as-a-service (IaaS)* is the cloud computing model in which you acquire all your technology needs—storage hardware and data, network equipment, application software, operating system software, data backups, CPU processing capabilities, anti-you-name-it software—in the cloud. Your only investment, literally, is something like a smartphone or tablet PC and a few peripheral devices like a printer. Using the IaaS model, you attempt to minimize your capital investment in technology. And if you recall our discussions of breakeven from Chapter 1, this is advantageous because investments in technology represent fixed costs.

So, on one end of the cloud spectrum is SaaS and renting application software and using it "as is," while on the other end is using the cloud for the vast majority of all your computing needs (IaaS).

SERVICE LEVEL AGREEMENTS REVISITED   An important consideration in moving to the cloud is that of the service level agreement (SLA) offered by your cloud service provider. From an organizational point of view, we cannot overstate the significance of a well-written and thoughtful SLA with your cloud service provider. Especially if you move important application software and information to the cloud, you need an SLA that will guarantee both security and uptime.

Suppose, for example, that you choose to use Amazon Web Services (AWS) to store information in the cloud. As you can see in Figure 7.10, AWS charges anywhere from 14 cents per gigabyte (Gb) per month to 5.5 cents per Gb per month, with the more you use resulting in lower costs. In the second screen in Figure 7.10 you can see that Amazon guarantees 99.99 percent availability to your information and backs it with the Amazon S3 Service Level Agreement. In the last screen in Figure 7.10, Amazon provides its S3 SLA policy for the credit you will receive if you do not have access to your data.

PUBLIC VERSUS PRIVATE CLOUDS   The *public cloud,* as its name suggests, comprises cloud services that exist on the Internet offered to anyone and any business. Just a few of the popular public cloud service providers include:

- Amazon Web Services (AWS)—http://aws.amazon.com
- Windows Azure—http://www.microsoft.com/windowsazure/
- Rackspace Cloud—http://www.rackspace.com/cloud/
- Google Cloud Connect—http://www.google.com/apps/intl/en/business/officeconnect.html
- ElasticHosts—http://www.elastichosts.com/

Figure 7.10

Storage Pricing and an SLA for Amazon Web Services (AWS)

Storage Pricing

Region: US Standard

	Standard Storage	Reduced Redundancy Storage
First 1 TB / month	$0.140 per GB	$0.093 per GB
Next 49 TB / month	$0.125 per GB	$0.083 per GB
Next 450 TB / month	$0.110 per GB	$0.073 per GB
Next 500 TB / month	$0.095 per GB	$0.063 per GB
Next 4000 TB / month	$0.080 per GB	$0.053 per GB
Over 5000 TB / month	$0.055 per GB	$0.037 per GB

Amazon S3's standard storage is:

- Backed with the Amazon S3 Service Level Agreement.
- Designed to provide 99.999999999% durability and 99.99% availability of objects over a given year.
- Designed to sustain the concurrent loss of data in two facilities.

Amazon S3 provides further protection via Versioning. You can use Versioning to preserve, retrieve, and restore every version of every object stored in your Amazon S3 bucket. This allows you to easily recover from both unintended user actions and application failures. By default, requests will retrieve the most recently written version. Older versions of an object can be retrieved by specifying a version in the request. Storage rates apply for every version stored.

Service Credits
Service Credits are calculated as a percentage of the total charges paid by you for Amazon S3 for the billing cycle in which the error occurred in accordance with the schedule below.

Monthly Uptime Percentage	Service Credit Percentage
Equal to or greater than 99% but less than 99.9%	10%
less than 99%	25%

TAKING THE CLOUD PRIVATE AT GE

Cloud computing is a valuable tool for small businesses and start-ups in need of computing technology at an affordable price. By taking advantage of the pay-per-use utility model associated with cloud computing, an organization (or person) can gain access to valuable technologies at a fraction of their total price.

What we've discussed so far in this chapter is the "public" cloud, kind of like the Internet, only with a whole lot more technologies, applications, and the like. But many organizations are also exploring the notion of a *private* cloud, kind of like an intranet of sorts. Such is the case with General Electric (GE). If you consider a large organization, it will probably have thousands (and thousands) of personal technologies such as PCs and laptop computers. It will also have hundreds and hundreds of server computers like those discussed in the n-tier infrastructure model.

The question really becomes, "How much time are those technologies idle?" An organization like GE employs numerous servers to handle peak capacities of information and process requests. What do those servers do during nonpeak times? Further, GE has multiple server farms—one for sales and marketing, one for manufacturing, and so on.

Those are the questions GE is wrestling with. Can it (GE) create a private cloud and minimize the number of servers while still supporting peak capacity times? The logic is simple: Not all units (sales and marketing, manufacturing, etc.) have the same peak capacity times. So, can they share one virtual server farm, with that server farm still getting the job done when capacity requirements are at their highest? [4]

These public cloud service providers (as well as many, many others) will sell their services to anyone.

A *private cloud,* on the other hand, is cloud computing services established and hosted by an organization on its internal network and available only to employees and departments within that organization. So, a private cloud doesn't exist on the Internet but rather within a specific organization. In the case of a private cloud, for example, an organization wouldn't set up a separate server for each of its various departments including sales, distribution, accounting, HR, and the like. Instead, the organization would establish perhaps only one server and allow all departments to share it. This is typically done to save money. Most departments don't utilize the full capacity of a server, so many departments can share a server, which reduces costs.

THE BENEFITS OF CLOUD COMPUTING As you can see, cloud computing holds great promise for both established organizations and also start-up businesses. For the latter, cloud computing enables a start-up business to minimize investments in technology while still being able to take advantage of large-scale, fully-robust application software such as CRM and SCM. In summary, some of the many advantages of cloud computing include:

- **Lower capital expenditures**—You don't buy what you need in terms of hardware and software, which can be very expensive. Instead, you take advantage of the pay-as-you-go cloud computing model and pay for only what you need and use.

- **Lower barriers to entry**—Cloud computing lowers barriers to entry in markets that require a significant investment in technology. Since you don't have to buy the technology, you can enter a market without the expense of the technology. In doing so, you can spend your money in other areas like customer relationship management initiatives.

- **Immediate access to a broad range of application software**—On a moment's notice, you can begin to use almost any application software you need—ERP, SCM, CRM, BI and analytics tools, etc. Again, you pay only for how much you use them.
- **Real-time scalability**— This goes either way, up or down. You can scale down and your costs move in like manner. You can scale up just as easily also.

IT Success Metrics

As with any organizational initiative, you must build a case for the acquisition, development, and use of technology. Technology costs money, not only for the hardware, software, and other IT-related components but also for the people involved, the changes to business processes, and the foregone opportunity to pursue other initiatives.

To justify the costs of technology, you need to be able to measure the success of technology. *Benchmarking* is the process of continuously measuring system results and comparing those results to *benchmarks*—baseline values a system seeks to attain. Benchmarks are most often industry-specific, process-specific, generated internal to your organization, or some combination of the three. With these metrics in hand you can make a cost/benefit judgment about technology. Benchmarking can lead to identifying steps and procedures to improve system performance.

EFFICIENCY AND EFFECTIVENESS METRICS

One way to categorize *metrics* (or ways to measure something) is by *efficiency* versus *effectiveness*. **Efficiency** means doing something right (e.g., in the least time, at the lowest cost, with the fewest errors, etc.), while **effectiveness** is doing the right thing. While the difference may seem subtle or purely semantic, it is not—the concepts are quite distinct. Let's consider a Web development project. A success metric would be Web traffic, perhaps as measured by the number of unique visitors. We refer to that as an *efficiency* metric because it simply means your organization is really good at driving customers to its Web site (i.e., creating traffic volume). But if those customers don't buy anything, it doesn't matter how many customers come to your site. So, while you may be very efficient in driving customers to your Web site, your Web site is not *effective* at getting those customers to make a purchase.

Most infrastructure-centric metrics today in the IT world are *efficiency metrics*. An **infrastructure-centric metric** is typically a measure of the efficiency, speed, and/or capacity of technology. Infrastructure-centric metrics include:

- *Throughput*—the amount of information that can pass through a system in a given amount of time. This is often associated with telecommunications capabilities (bandwidth) such as transmission speeds (kilobits per second, Kbps, and megabits per second, Mbps).
- *Transaction speed*—the speed at which a system can process a transaction.
- *System availability*—usually measured inversely as *downtime,* or the average amount of time a system is down and unavailable to end users and customers. This does not include regularly scheduled maintenance.
- *Accuracy*—also usually measured inversely as *error rate,* or the number of errors per thousand (or million) that a system generates. This is analogous to defects per thousand or million in manufacturing.
- *Response time*—average time to respond to a user-generated event, such as a request for a report, a mouse click, and so on.

- *Scalability*—how well a system can adapt to increased demands. This is more of a conceptual metric that assesses your ability to upgrade the implemented infrastructure at minimal cost and service interruption.

Effectiveness metrics, on the other hand, measure results of the technology or application in some environment. For example, call centers have numerous effectiveness (success) metrics as do Web e-business applications. We'll explore several metrics for both of those in a moment. Customer relationship management and supply chain management systems have numerous associated metrics, as well, including (but certainly not limited to):

- Customer relationship management (CRM)
  - Number of cross-selling successes
  - Cost-per-thousand (CPM)—sales dollars generated per dollar of advertising
  - Number of new customers generated
  - Average length of time a customer stays active (i.e., continues to buy products and services from you)
- Supply chain management (SCM)
  - Number of stockouts
  - Excess inventory
  - Distribution and warehousing costs

It's interesting to note in the above lists that you want to increase the value of all of the CRM metrics (e.g., the more cross-selling successes you have the better). This is a common characteristics of metrics that measure growth (from the RGT framework) initiatives. Conversely, you want to reduce the value of all the SCM metrics (e.g., have as little excess inventory as possible). This is a common characteristic of metrics that measure run initiatives.

If you consider the graph in Figure 7.11, you can begin to understand the relationship between efficiency and effectiveness metrics. Run initiatives, such as supply chain management, seek to optimize efficiency metrics while not negatively affecting effectiveness metrics, and growth initiatives, such as customer relationship management, seek to optimize effectiveness metrics while not negatively affecting efficiency metrics. (It might appear in Figure 7.11 that the optimal area of operation is the upper-right area, but that's simply not true and seldom achievable except when undertaking extraordinary transformational activities. An excellent example here is that of Apple iTunes, which created both tremendous efficiency and effectiveness.)

Figure 7.11

Efficiency and Effectiveness Metrics

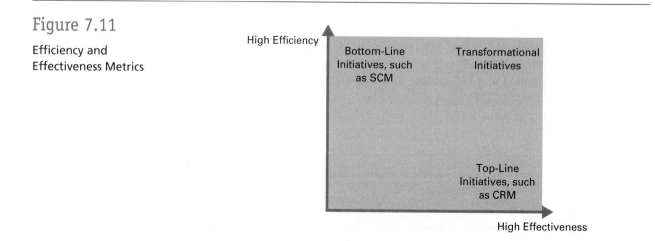

According to Facebook's latest self-published statistics, its content is available in more than 70 languages. Furthermore, about 70 percent of its users are outside the United States. With some 750 million users, that means over 500 million of those users are outside the U.S. That's a substantial worldwide presence.

But for Facebook, "international" goes beyond its customer base. Facebook recently announced its "Open Compute Project," which is focused on sharing with the world how it designs its data centers. This is an innovative, unusual, and industry-questioned notion. Large tech companies like Google believe data center design to be a key source of competitive advantage. But not Facebook. Its hope is that the rest of the world will benefit by learning how Facebook designs and builds data centers.

And "world" has two meanings. First, the project opens data center details to every organization in the world. Second, and equally important if not more important, is that Facebook hopes other companies will learn how to build more efficient and environmentally friendly data centers. For example, at its new data center in Prineville, Oregon, operations are 38 percent more energy-efficient and 24 percent more cost-effective than what Facebook had previously been using.

This "open" initiative is similar in many respects to other open initiatives such as open-source software and open-source information. The former allows the community to collaborate and use innovative techniques to build software such as Linux. The latter allows communities of people to build quality information repositories such as Wikipedia. With regard to Facebook's open initiative for data center design, Rich Fichera, Forrester Research analyst, explains, "At the bottom of this, the motivation is to try to foster a commercial competitive marketplace for the technology that they [Facebook] need going forward."[5, 6]

WEB-CENTRIC METRICS

A *Web-centric metric* is a measure of the success of your Web and e-business initiatives. There are literally hundreds of Web-centric metrics you can use, with some being general to almost any Web or e-business initiative and others being very dependent on the particular initiative. Common Web-centric metrics include:

- *Unique visitors*—the number of unique visitors to your sites in a given time. This is commonly used by Nielsen/Net ratings to rank the most popular Web sites.
- *Total hits*—number of visits to your Web site, many of which may be by the same visitor.
- *Page exposures*—average number of page exposures to an individual visitor.
- *Conversion rate*—percentage of potential customers who visit your site who actually buy something.
- *Click-through*—count of the number of people who visit a site, click on an ad, and are taken to the site of the advertiser.
- *Cost-per-thousand (CPM)*—sales dollars generated per dollar of advertising. This is commonly used to make the case for spending money to appear on a search engine.
- *Abandoned registrations*—number of visitors who start the process of completing a registration page and then abandon the activity.
- *Abandoned shopping carts*—the number of visitors who create a shopping cart and start shopping and then abandon the activity before paying for the merchandise.

CALL CENTER METRICS

Call center metrics measure the success of call center efforts. Typical call center metrics include:

- *Abandon rate*—the percentage number of callers who hang up while waiting for their call to be answered.
- *Average speed to answer (ASA)*—the average time, usually in seconds, that it takes for a call to be answered by an actual person.
- *Time service factor (TSF)*—the percentage of calls answered within a specific time frame, such as 30 or 90 seconds.
- *First call resolution (FCR)*—the percentage of calls that can be resolved without having to call back.

If your call center operations are partly automated in the hope of helping people with common questions, then you have additional metrics such as the percentage of people who use the automated system and then request also to speak to a service representative.

Business Continuity Planning

Business continuity planning (BCP) is a rigorous and well-informed organizational methodology for developing a *business continuity plan,* a step-by-step guideline defining how the organization will recover from a disaster or extended disruption of its business processes. In past years, with respect to IT systems and information, the business continuity plan went by other names, *disaster recovery plan* and *contingency plan.* Given the number of natural disasters and terrorist attacks worldwide, along with businesses' increasing dependency on all their processes and resources (not just IT and information), however, the general trend has been to develop a more all-encompassing *business continuity plan* that includes all aspects of the organization.

The BCP methodology looks very similar to the systems development life cycle (see Figure 7.12). It starts with the organization's strategic plan and moves through various phases including analysis, design, implementation, testing, and maintenance. We'll focus our discussion of BCP on information technology and IT-related issues.

Figure 7.12

Business Continuity Planning (BCP)

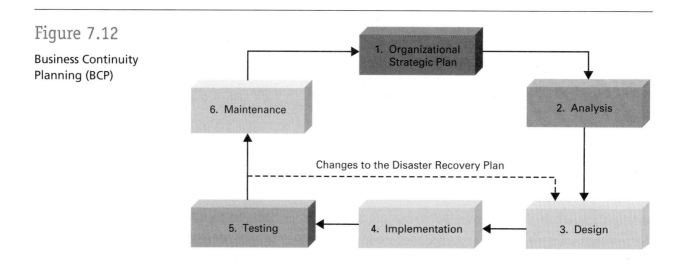

PHASE 1: ORGANIZATIONAL STRATEGIC PLAN

Business continuity planning starts with your organization's strategic plan, which informs you of the relative importance of resources, processes, systems, and other organizational assets. It's important to understand and develop a ranking of the importance of these assets because you cannot (and should not) develop a business continuity plan that enables you to recover every asset within minutes of some sort of disaster. That would be prohibitively expensive and unnecessary. Your organization can afford to live without some assets (i.e., systems and information) for several days or even weeks. Payroll software may be an example here. For other assets, such as customer ordering and supply chain applications, it may critical that your organization gets those up and running with minimal interruption. Data centers are also typically identified as high priorities for most organizations. According to CPM Research, "improved business continuity" was cited 70 percent of the time by respondents as being a key data center issue.[7]

PHASE 2: ANALYSIS

In the BCP analysis phase, you perform impact analysis, threat analysis, and impact scenario analysis, and then build a requirement recovery document.

- (1) *Impact analysis*—Here you seek to truly differentiate between critical, core IT applications and information and those that are noncritical. Key factors supporting your analysis include: the financial impact to the organization for the loss of IT applications and information over time, implications for stakeholders (e.g., customer loss of power if you provide utilities), and cost estimates of recovery. Impact analysis is often called ***risk assessment,*** the process of evaluating IT assets, their importance of the organization, and their susceptibility to threats.

- (2) *Threat analysis*—In step 2 of BCP analysis, you document the possible threats to your organization and its assets. These can and often do include disease, earthquakes (depending on the geographical location of your organization), fire, flood, cyber attack, terrorism, and utility outages. An assessment of these helps you develop an understanding of the magnitude of threats and how you should choose to recover from them. Note that in the case of e-business activities threats can include greatly increased shopping traffic. For example, on the day after Thanksgiving in 2006 Walmart's Web site went down because so many people visited its site in the hope of buying the hard-to-find T.M.X. Elmo.[8]

- (3) *Impact scenario analysis*—In step 3, you consider each threat (from step 2) and build a worst-case scenario for each (as opposed to smaller impact scenarios such as 10 percent of the workforce out due to a flu outbreak). An impact scenario analysis provides further definition and detail concerning the scope and magnitude of each possible disaster.

- (4) *Requirement recovery document*—Armed with the information from steps 1 through 3, you finally build a ***requirement recovery document,*** a detailed document which describes (a) the distinction between critical and noncritical IT systems and information, (b) each possible threat, and (c) the possible worst-case scenarios that can result from each disaster. This document becomes the basis for the design phase which follows.

PHASE 3: DESIGN

Using the requirement recovery document, in the design phase, you design a formal, technical, and detailed plan for recovering from a disaster—a **disaster recovery plan.** A good disaster recovery plan takes into consideration the location of the backup information. Many organizations choose to store backup information in an off-site storage facility, or a place that is located separate from the company and often owned by another company, such as a collocation facility. A **collocation facility** is available to a company that rents space and telecommunications equipment from another company. One such company is StorageTek, which specializes in providing off-site data storage and disaster recovery solutions.

A good disaster recovery plan also considers the actual facility where employees will work. A **hot site** is a separate and fully equipped facility where the company can move immediately after a disaster and resume business. A **cold site** is a separate facility that does not have any computer equipment but is a place where employees can move after the disaster.

A disaster recovery plan should be based on a *disaster recovery cost curve* (Figure 7.13). A **disaster recovery cost curve** charts (1) the cost to your organization of the unavailability of information and technology and (2) the cost to your organization of recovering from a disaster over time. Where the two curves intersect is the best recovery plan in terms of cost and time. Being able to restore information and IT systems quickly in the event of a disaster is obviously a crucial aspect of an IT infrastructure.

PHASE 4: IMPLEMENTATION

At this point, business continuity planning diverges somewhat from the SDLC. In the SDLC, you would develop and test the solution before implementing it. In business continuity planning, you must begin to implement your disaster recovery plan before testing it. That is, you need to engage any businesses that will be providing collocation facilities, hot sites, and/or cold sites, and implement the necessary procedures for recovering from a disaster. You train your employees concerning what to do in case of any of the disasters. You also evaluate each IT system and ensure that it is configured optimally for recovering from a disaster. You can now test the disaster recovery plan.

Figure 7.13

Deciding How Much to Spend on Disaster Recovery

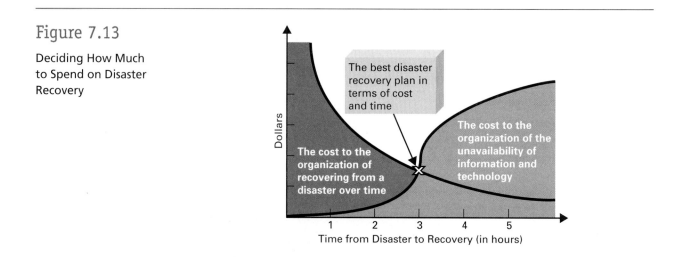

BUSINESS CONTINUITY PLANNING: WHY NOT AND WHAT

According to an *InformationWeek Analytics* survey of mid-size companies, 79 percent stated that they have a business continuity plan in place. Interestingly, those companies varied widely in response to an equally important question: How long will it take you to recover from a disaster? Thirty-five percent stated they would be up and running in a few days while 28 percent stated it would be several weeks.

The ability to recover from a disaster is critical to any business, and having a good business continuity plan in place makes it possible to plan for and recover from a disaster. According to the same survey, here are the top reasons why companies find it difficult to undertake the process of business continuity planning.

- Cost—89 percent
- Complexity—57 percent
- Other projects are higher priority—56 percent
- Lack of C-level/senior management buy-in—42 percent
- Lack of internal skills—21 percent
- Don't know where to start—2 percent

Two somewhat disturbing numbers above relate to lack of C-level support and "don't know where to start." It's hard to believe that 42 percent of companies surveyed stated that senior management (C-level like chief executive officer and chief operating officer) was a barrier to developing an effective business continuity plan. The fact that one in every 50 companies don't even know where to start in developing a business continuity plan is equally startling.

Of those companies that do have a business continuity plan in place, responses once again vary greatly concerning what parts of the IT infrastructure are covered by their business continuity plan. The most popular are below.

- Mission-critical servers—99 percent
- Messaging systems—70 percent
- Telephone call redirection—59 percent
- Remote user access—53 percent
- Tier-2 servers—53 percent
- Other servers—39 percent
- Desktops—30 percent
- User laptops—26 percent

These all make sense. Servers handle processing and information access. Messaging systems and telephone systems enable communication. Desktops and laptops act as the primary conduit to the organization's IT infrastructure for all employees.[9]

PHASE 5: TESTING

Testing in business continuity planning involves executing simulated scenarios of disasters and having employees execute on the disaster recovery plan to ensure that the solution satisfies your organization's recovery requirements. If noticeable deficiencies are identified, your organization should return to steps 3 and 4 (design and implementation) and reconfigure and reimplement the disaster recovery plan accordingly.

This sort of testing does not stop once you believe you have developed an optimal plan. The environment in which your organization operates changes almost daily. You should test your disaster recovery plan on at least an annual basis, and more realistically several times a year.

PHASE 6: MAINTENANCE

Finally, you need to continually assess new threats and reevaluate your IT systems and related assets to determine their changing importance to the organization. As with the SDLC, no "system" is ever complete; it needs constant monitoring, support, and maintenance.

▪ SUMMARY: STUDENT LEARNING OUTCOMES REVISITED

1. **Describe how a service-oriented architecture can be used as a philosophical approach to help the organization of the future meet all its IT-related needs.** A service-oriented architecture can be applied to help your organization respond to:

   - *Customers*—through multichannel service delivery and the provision of customizable products and services.
   - *End users*—through fully integrated ERP systems supporting interoperability and mobile computing.
   - *Software development*—as a framework for supporting development methodologies such as RAD, XP, and agile that lead to exciting new deployments such as Web 2.0.
   - *Information needs*—including access to all types of integrated information (and business intelligence and knowledge), standard information formats, integrity controls, and the elimination of redundant information.
   - *Hardware requirements*—through the integration of different technologies, providing large storage capacities, and maintaining safe and secure telecommunications platforms.

2. **Define and describe the various hardware and software infrastructure considerations in an organization.** Hardware and software infrastructure considerations include:

   - Enterprise resource planning (ERP) systems provide interoperability within an ERP vendor and among modules of different ERP vendors and also hide the underlying IT infrastructure of information and hardware from end users and customers.
   - Common network infrastructures include:

     Distributed—distributing the information and processing power of IT systems via a network;

     Client/server—one or more computers that are servers which provide services to other computers, called clients; ***Tiered (layer)***—the IT system is partitioned into tiers where each tier performs a specific type of functionality.

3. **Describe cloud computing, its various implementations, and its advantages.** ***Cloud computing*** is a technology model in which any and all resources—application software, processing power, data storage, backup facilities, development tools, literally everything—are delivered as a set of services via the Internet. Implementations include:

   - ***Software-as-a-service (SaaS)***—delivery model for software in which you pay for software on a pay-per-use basis instead of buying the software outright.
   - ***Platform-as-a-service (PaaS)***—delivery model for software identical to SaaS with the additional features of (1) the ability to customize data entry forms, screens, reports, and the like, and (2) access to software development tools to alter the way in which the software works by adding new modules and/or making modifications to existing modules.

- *Infrastructure-as-a-service (IaaS)*—model in which you acquire all your technology needs in the cloud.

Advantages of cloud computing include:

- Lower capital expenditures
- Lower barriers to entry
- Immediate access to a broad range of application software
- Real-time scalability

4. **Compare and contrast commonly used metrics for assessing the success of IT systems and IT-related initiatives.** Metrics are simply ways to measure something. Common IT metrics can be categorized as:

- *Infrastructure-centric metrics*—Measures of efficiency, speed, and/or capacity of technology, including ***throughput, transaction speed, system availability, accuracy, response time,*** and ***scalability.***
- *Web-centric metrics*—Measures of the success of your Web and e-business initiatives, including ***unique visitors, total hits, page exposures, conversion rate, click-through, cost-per-thousand (CPM), abandoned registrations,*** and ***abandoned shopping carts.***
- *Call center metrics*—Measures of the success of call center efforts, including ***abandon rate, average speed to answer (ASA), time service factor (TSF),*** and ***first call resolution (FCR).***

5. **Describe business continuity planning (BCP) and its phases.** *Business continuity planning (BCP)* is a rigorous and well-informed organizational methodology for developing a ***business continuity plan,*** a step-by-step guideline defining how the organization will recover from a disaster or extended disruption of its business processes. The phases of business continuity planning include:

- *Phase 1: Organizational strategic plan*—it all starts here with understanding the relative importance of resources, systems, processes, and other organizational assets.
- *Phase 2: Analysis*—perform impact analysis, threat analysis, and impact scenario analysis and build a ***requirement recovery document,*** a detailed document that describes (1) the distinction between critical and noncritical IT systems and information, (2) each possible threat, and (3) the possible worst-case scenarios that can result from each disaster.
- *Phase 3: Design*—using the requirement recovery document, create a ***disaster recovery plan,*** which identifies collocation facilities, hot sites, and cold sites and illustrates a disaster recovery cost curve (the cost to your organization of the unavailability of information and technology as compared to the cost to your organization of recovering from a disaster over time).
- *Phase 4: Implementation*—engage businesses that will provide collocation facilities, hot sites, and cold sites; implement necessary procedures for recovering from a disaster; train employees; evaluate each IT system to ensure its configuration is optimal for recovering from a disaster.
- *Phase 5: Testing*—executing simulated scenarios of disasters and having employees execute on the disaster recovery plan.
- *Phase 6: Maintenance*—continually assess new threats and reevaluate your IT systems and related assets to determine their changing importance to the organization.

CLOSING CASE STUDY ONE

Public "Personal" Clouds

Cloud computing is not solely focused on helping organizations better manage their investments in IT infrastructure and have access to scalable IT resources in real-time. The cloud has gone "personal," and there are now a wide range of cloud services for just you as an individual. Three companies offering personal cloud services are Amazon, Apple, and Microsoft.

AMAZON

Amazon is definitely the retail giant of the Web, but even it concedes that its market share in the digital services space is "insignificant" compared to that of Apple. So, Amazon has launched a series of personal cloud services in the hope of stealing away many of Apple's customers. One such cloud service is *Amazon Cloud Drive*. Cloud Drive is an external hard disk for your computer (or tablet PC or smartphone) in the cloud. On it, you can store music, photos, videos, and documents. With any Web browser, you can access all your digital assets on Cloud Drive.

You can load your music onto Cloud Drive in one of two ways. First, when you buy digital music at Amazon's MP3 store, you can have that music automatically loaded into your Cloud Drive space. Second, if you currently have music on your laptop or desktop (even if that music comes from iTunes), you can upload that with a few clicks. It's also similarly easy to upload any of your other digital assets—photos, videos, or documents.

Amazon provides you with a limited amount of free space on your Cloud Drive, somewhere in the range of 5 to 10Gb. Even better, if you buy music from Amazon's MP3 store, it doesn't count against your free limit. If you exceed your limit with other content—photos, videos, or documents or perhaps music from some organization other than Amazon—you can buy additional storage space, which will cost approximately $1 per year per Gb. (A Gb of storage typically holds about 200 to 250 songs, depending on their length and quality.)

APPLE

Partly in response to Amazon's move, Apple also announced a personal cloud service called *iCloud*. iCloud is completely free, no matter how much content you store in it. iCloud is different from Amazon's Cloud Drive in that it is built into the normal workings of Apple computers and mobile devices. When you take a photo using your iPhone, for example, that photo will be available on your Mac or iPad within a few seconds. So, whenever you create and store a document on your Mac, you are also automatically storing it in iCloud. That means you can then view and change the document on your iPad without first having to transfer the file from your Mac to your iPad.

The iCloud constantly synchronizes all your Apple digital assets, including music, photos, videos, documents, calendar, contacts, and mail across all your Apple devices. The goal is to encourage you to buy only Apple devices (a Mac, an iPad, and an iPhone) because they all remain synchronized without your ever having to do anything. And what happens when you buy a new iPhone? Just enter your ID and password and you will be instantly connected to your *iCloud* space, giving you access to everything you have.

MICROSOFT

It makes obvious sense that Microsoft would also be in this space. Microsoft is still the dominant provider of personal productivity software (Microsoft Office) and personal operating system software (Windows XP and Windows 7, mainly). To maintain its dominance, not lose market share, and hopefully gain market share, Microsoft offers *Windows Live,* personal cloud space for its users. Windows Live offers free storage space in SkyDrive, where you can upload any of your digital assets. If you own multiple Windows-based machines, SkyDrive can help you keep your digital assets on those machines always in sync. And like iCLoud, Windows Live will also synchronize your calendar, contacts, and e-mail across your Windows devices.

Windows Live allows you to create groups in your cloud space, so you can collaborate with other people on documents and projects. That feature is much easier to use while collaborating as opposed to e-mailing documents to other people, trying to keep track of changes and versions, and attempting to determine who made what changes and the order in which the changes were made.[10, 11, 12]

Questions

1. Do some research on Amazon's Cloud Drive. What is the amount of free storage space? What is the annual cost for additional storage? What about Apple's iCLoud? Is it still free? Does Microsoft charge anything for use of its SkyDrive cloud service?

2. Putting all your personal information in the cloud means letting go of some control over information like your tax files, personal photos that you might not want anyone else to see, term papers you're currently writing, and so on. What is your level of concern for the security of these personal digital assets in the cloud? Explain why your level of concern is high or low.

3. As we move more of our personal storage needs to the cloud, will computers really need disk storage space? Is it possible that we're in the early stages of an outrageous industry transformation? Who are the major manufacturers of disk storage for personal computers and laptops?

4. If you choose to store all your personal information in the cloud, you'll need a *personal continuity plan,* much like organizations have business continuity plans in case of some sort of disaster. Suppose that right now you begin storing all your personal information only in the cloud. Of that information, what will you also back up onto a flash drive? How often would you perform the back up process? How often do you currently back up information on your computer's hard drive?

5. Do some research on personal cloud providers. What sort of service level agreement (SLA) do they offer? Are you willing to store your information with a personal cloud provider that offers no SLA? Why or why not?

CLOSING CASE STUDY TWO

Denver Health Operates with a Private Cloud and Thin Clients

Along with its main hospital, Denver Health operates the 911 emergency medical services response system for Denver, 12 clinics based in the Denver Public Schools, the Rocky Mountain Poison Drug Center, and eight family health centers. That's a big organization with substantial technology needs.

Denver Health faced a problem of lost time incurred by physicians and nurses upon entering a patient's room and having to log on to a computer. Even though Gregg Veltri, Denver Health's CIO, had procedures and processes in place to keep patient-room computers as new as possible and to refresh those computers often to rid them of spyware, adware, and other inhibitors of performance, log-on time was still about two minutes. If you multiply those two minutes throughout the day by the number of doctor visits to rooms, Denver Health calculated that it was losing almost $4 million annually in physician lost time.

So, Gregg turned to a solution called *ThinIdentity.* ThinIdentity utilizes a thin client—basically a high-quality monitor, mouse, and keyboard—in each patient room. All processing and information storage are maintained in Denver Health's private cloud. These thin clients (Sun Rays) need to be upgraded only every eight years, instead of the typical two to three years for a PC. Further, each Sun Ray costs only $600, a fraction of the price for a full-blown PC.

Equally important is the sign-on procedure doctors and nurses use now. Upon arriving at work each day, a doctor or nurse signs onto a single station (Sun Ray terminal or a PC in an office), which takes about one minute, by inserting a smart card and then providing a log-on name and password. The doctor or nurse then removes the smart card, which logs off the session at that station, but leaves the session active in the cloud for the doctor or nurse. When entering a patient's room during the day, the doctor or nurse needs only to insert the smart card and provide the log-on name and password to reactivate the session that is still active in the cloud. This process takes only 5 or 10 seconds.

ThinIdentity takes advantage of a concept called *virtual location awareness (VLA).* VLA maps each room to each patient according to Denver Health's transaction processing system. When a nurse or doctor enters a specific room and reactivates his/her session in the cloud, VLA recognizes the room and immediately pulls up that patient's information within that doctor's or nurse's session. This saves even more time. In total, the ThinIdentity-based system has saved Denver Health an estimated $5.7 million. The savings are presented below.

- One-Time Savings
  - $1.2 million reduction of desktop replacements
  - $300,000 reduction of desktop resource needs
- Annual Savings
  - $135,000 reduction of energy needs (Sun Rays use much less energy than traditional desktop computers)
  - $56,000 reduction in help desk calls
  - $250,000 reduction in full-time employees operating the help desk
  - $3.7 million reduction in physician log-on time[13]

Questions

1. Privacy laws and regulations require medical facilities to take measurable steps to ensure the confidentiality of patient information. From this case study, can you tell what Denver Health has done to ensure the confidentiality of its patient information?

2. Think about your school. How could it use the ThinIdentity solution to support the technology needs of (1) faculty and (2) students such as yourself?

3. In thinking about cloud computing (focusing on the public cloud), what role could it play in business continuity planning for Denver Health? That is, how could the public cloud act as a backup for Denver Health's private cloud?

4. If Denver Health were to give each patient a smart card, log-on name, and password, which functions, features, and information could benefit patients? What security would have to be in place to ensure that patients have access to only their own information?

5. How could Denver Health extend the ThinIdentity solution beyond its brick-and-mortar walls? How would it work (i.e., need to change) to have doctors and nurses log on from home or use a mobile device such as a Blackberry or iPhone?

6. The reduction in physician log-on time is an efficiency metric. What are some effectiveness metrics that could justify Denver Health's use of ThinIdentity?

■ KEY TERMS AND CONCEPTS

SHORT-ANSWER QUESTIONS

1. How can a service-oriented architecture (SoA) be used to guide the organization of the future?
2. Why is ERP interoperability important?
3. How does a client/server infrastructure work?
4. What are the four types of a tiered infrastructure?
5. What additional features does platform-as-a-service (PaaS) offer beyond software-as-a-service (SaaS)?
6. What is the difference between a public cloud and a private cloud?
7. What are the benefits of cloud computing?
8. How do efficiency and effectiveness metrics differ?
9. What are some commonly used infrastructure-centric metrics?
10. What are some commonly used Web-centric metrics?
11. What is a business continuity plan?
12. Why do organizations implement a disaster recovery plan before testing it?

ASSIGNMENTS AND EXERCISES

1. **SECURITY METRICS** In this chapter, we focused on metrics for measuring the success of your IT systems including infrastructure-centric metrics, Web-centric metrics, and call center metrics. Another important area of metrics is security metrics, or how well you are doing at stopping viruses from coming in, protecting against identify theft, and the like. Do some research on the Web and develop a list of commonly used metrics in the area of security. Be sure to define each metric.

2. **CREATING A CAMPUS IT INFRASTRUCTURE** You have been assigned the role of student IT infrastructure manager. Your first assignment is to approve the designs for the new on-campus Internet infrastructure. You're having a meeting at 9:00 a.m. tomorrow morning to review the designs with the student IT employees. To prepare for the meeting, you must understand the student requirements and their current use of the Internet, along with future requirements. The following is a list of questions you must answer before attending the meeting. Provide an answer to each question.

   - Do you need to have a disaster recovery plan? If so what might it include?
   - Does the system require backup equipment?
   - When will the system need to be available to the students?
   - What types of access levels will the students need?
   - How will you ensure the system is reliable?
   - How will you build scalability into the system?
   - What are the minimum performance requirements for the system?
   - How will the system handle future growth?

3. **EFFICIENCY AND EFFECTIVENESS METRICS** Choose any of the Perspective boxes in this chapter or one of the closing cases and identify and describe at least seven metrics that could be used to measure the success of the IT systems in your chosen example. For each metric, categorize it as either an efficiency or effectiveness metric. Justify your categorizations.

4. **SAAS PROVIDERS** There are numerous SaaS providers that enable organizations to access

and use Web-based application software. In the chapter we identified Salesforce.com as one such SaaS provider. Search the Web and find at least five other ASPs. What are the names of the companies? What application software do they provide over the Web? What additional services do they provide, if any?

5. **PERSONAL BENCHMARKS AND BENCHMARKING** How do you use benchmarks and benchmarking in your personal life? Think about grades, making money, supporting charities, and the like. Choose one significant way in which you use benchmarks and benchmarking in your personal life and describe it. What are your benchmark values? How were you able to derive your benchmark values? Where did they come from?

■ DISCUSSION QUESTIONS

1. On page 211, we listed and defined numerous Web-centric metrics. Which of those are efficiency metrics and which of those are effectiveness metrics? For each, provide justification for your answer and an illustration using a real-life or hypothetical Web business example.

2. What type of IT infrastructure does your school have? If it uses a client/server infrastructure how does your school's client/server network increase student productivity? What recommendations, based on the contents of this chapter, could you recommend to the IT people who manage the infrastructure?

3. How is the concept of interoperability an important aspect that you rely on in your daily life? Think about the many devices, appliances, modes of transportation, and so on that you use every day. Which of these support the concept of interoperability? How would your life change if they didn't support interoperability?

4. Many people say that efficiency and effectiveness metrics are interrelated and that you can't really have one without the other or that no organization can truly be successful without both. How are efficiency and effectiveness metrics interrelated? Must you succeed in one set before addressing the other? If so, which is first and why?

5. Consider an e-business like Amazon.com. Which Web-centric metrics on page 211 would be most important to it? Justify your answers. Now consider a content provider like CNN (www .cnn.com). Which Web-centric metrics would be most important to it? Justify your answers. Why would two e-businesses have such a different focus on Web-centric metrics?

■ CHAPTER PROJECTS

GROUP PROJECTS

- Assessing the Value of Outsourcing Information Technology: Creating Forecasts (p. 294)

- Creating a Decision Support System: Buy versus Lease (p. 298)

- Developing an Enterprise Resource Planning System: Planning, Reporting, and Data Processing (p. 299)

- Evaluating the Next Generation: Dot-Com ASPs (p. 301)

- Evaluating the Security of Information: Wireless Network Vulnerability (p. 308)

E-COMMERCE PROJECTS

- Best in computer statistics and resources (p. 310)

- Meta data (p. 311)

- Finding hosting services (p. 315)

- Searching for shareware and freeware (p. 320)

CHAPTER EIGHT OUTLINE

STUDENT LEARNING OUTCOMES

1. Define ethics and describe the two factors that affect how you make a decision concerning an ethical issue.

2. Define and describe intellectual property, copyright, Fair Use Doctrine, and pirated software.

3. Define privacy and describe ways in which it can be threatened.

4. Describe the ways in which information on your computer or network is vulnerable and list measures you can take to protect it.

PERSPECTIVES

WEB SUPPORT

www.mhhe.com/haag

- Exploring Google Earth
- Protecting your computer against viruses
- Searching for shareware and freeware
- Ethical computing guidelines
- Privacy laws and legislation

SUPPORTING MODULES

XLM/E Network Basics
Extended Learning Module E provides an introduction to the vast, exciting, and dynamic field of information technology networks. The module includes discussions of what is needed to set up a small network at home, the components used to build large business networks, Internet connection possibilities, types of communications media, and network security.

XLM/H Computer Crime and Digital Forensics
Extended Learning Module H provides an overview of computer and computer-aided crime and its investigation. First, you'll read about the various types of computer crime, malware, and hackers. Next, you'll explore digital forensics starting with the investigation process. You'll learn about the digital forensics software and hardware that experts use along with the anti-forensics measures that the bad guys employ.

CHAPTER EIGHT

Protecting People and Information
Threats and Safeguards

OUTRAGEOUS INDUSTRY TRANSFORMATION: TRANSFORMATIONS IN MEDICINE MEAN BETTER LIVES

Our outrageous industry transformations to this point have focused on how innovations in technology are changing the landscape of entire industries, in many instances putting many traditional and old-style businesses out of business. But the field of medicine tends to be a bit different. In medicine, technological innovations are more quickly and uniformly embraced by the entire industry. Importantly, these innovations often lead to saving lives, reducing health care costs, and helping people lead longer, healthier lives.

One such innovation is that of robotics surgery for prostate cancer. In the accompanying graph, you can see that from 2005 to 2008, the percentage of prostate cancer surgeries using the da Vinci Prostatectomy, a type of robotics surgery, increased from 20 percent to 71 percent. During the same period, the percentage of open surgeries for prostate cancer decreased from almost 80 percent to less than 30 percent. The advantages of robotics surgery include:

- Less pain and faster recovery
- Reduced need for blood transfusion
- Lower infection risk
- Better cancer control
- Reduction in urinary incontinence and erectile dysfunction

These types of technological innovations meet the criteria of triple-bottom-line processes. The profit motive is still met; they are kind to the environment (fewer gauzes, fewer plastic blood bags, etc.); and they are better for people.[1]

2005 USA Radical Prostatectomy Rations

20%	da Vinci Prostatectomy
0.7%	Laparoscopic
79.3%	Open Surgery

2006 USA Radical Prostatectomy Rations

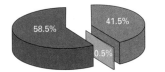

41%	da Vinci Prostatectomy
0.5%	Laparoscopic
58.5%	Open Surgery

2007 USA Radical Prostatectomy Rations

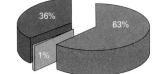

63%	da Vinci Prostatectomy
1%	Laparoscopic
36%	Open Surgery

2008 USA Radical Prostatectomy Rations

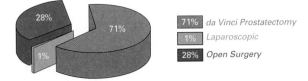

71%	da Vinci Prostatectomy
1%	Laparoscopic
28%	Open Surgery

Questions

1. Search robotics in surgery on YouTube. For what kinds of robotics surgeries did you find demonstrations?

2. Will taking robotics-type surgical procedures into third-world countries be easier and cheaper than traditional "open" surgical procedures? Why or why not?

3. Why does the medicine industry more quickly and uniformly embrace innovations than other industries?

Introduction

As you know, the three components of an IT system are people, information, and information technology. Most of what you've seen in previous chapters has dealt with IT and how it stores and processes information. In this chapter we're going to concentrate on information—its use, ownership, and protection. The best environment for handling information is one that has stability without stagnation and change without chaos.

To handle information in a responsible way you must understand

- The importance of ethics in the ownership and use of information.
- The importance to people of personal privacy and the ways in which it can be compromised.
- Threats to information and how to protect against them (security).

The most important part of any IT system consists of the people who use it and are affected by it. How people treat each other has always been important, but in this information-based and digital age, with huge computing power at our fingertips, we can affect more people's lives in more ways than ever before. How we act toward each other, and this includes how we view and handle information, is largely determined by our ethics.

You don't have to look far to see examples of computer use that is questionable from an ethical viewpoint. For example,

- People copy, use, and distribute software they have no right to.
- Employees search organizational databases for information on celebrities and friends.
- Organizations collect, buy, and use information and don't check the validity or accuracy of that information.
- Misguided people create and spread viruses that cause trouble for those using and maintaining IT systems.
- Information system developers put systems on the market before they're completely tested. A few years ago, the developers of an incubator thermostat control program didn't test it fully, and two infants died as a result.[2]
- Unethical people break into computer systems and steal passwords, information, and proprietary information.
- Employees destroy or steal proprietary schematics, sketches, customer lists, and reports from their employers.
- People snoop on each other and read each other's e-mail and other private files.

Ethics

LEARNING OUTCOME 1

Ethical people have integrity. They are people who are as careful to attend to their responsibilities toward others as they are to look after their own legitimate interests. They desire to do what is fair and good and not what merely seems fair and good. At a minimum, being an ethical person means that one takes seriously the *rights* of others, the *consequences* that one's actions will have for others, and the habits of mind and behavior that make for *virtuous living*. But even the most ethical people must face the nearly inevitable dilemmas involving choices between incompatible good outcomes and conflicting loyalties. An ethical dilemma is not the choice of whether or not to be ethical; rather, an ethical dilemma is when one's responsibilities seem to lead in opposite directions.

LACK OF ETHICS IN THE WORKPLACE CAN LEAD TO LOST PRODUCTIVITY

It's now almost commonplace for people to perform personal tasks on their computers while at work. They shop for and buy merchandise. They send personal e-mails. They bid on auction items on eBay. The list goes on and on.

But there is a particular time of the year when the most productivity is lost on account of nonwork activities on the Web. Think for a minute. Can you guess when it is? It's not associated with a holiday or selling season. It's March Madness, the spring of each year when 68 college basketball teams from around the country battle it out in a single-elimination format. During the 2008 NCAA tournament, for example, $1.7 billion was lost in productivity according to Challenger, Gray, & Christmas, a Chicago-based outplacement firm.

That $1.7 billion most probably pales by comparison to the lost productivity during the most recent NCAA tournament. No organization has attempted to estimate March Madness lost productivity again, but it has most assuredly increased since 2008. As a surrogate measure, consider this. During the NCAA tournament in 2010, almost 12 million hours of live games were streamed on the Internet. (Most of those hours were during typical business hours.)

It won't take you long to put two and two together to come up with the fact that social media has a lot to do with lost productivity in the workplace. In 2011, Coca-Cola spent 20 percent of its tournament advertising budget on social media. That compares to just 2 percent spent on social media in the previous year by Coke.

Hershey's Reece's Peanut Butter Cups brand went social media–wild as well. That brand sponsored the halftime festivity of allowing one fan to attempt to make a shot from half-court for a cool $1 million. The more times you visited the brand's Facebook page, the more times you could enter your name into the drawing. And it wasn't just a couple of thousand or so people hoping to win the chance at fan immortality. The brand has more than 6.6 million followers on Facebook.[3, 4]

In Plato's *Republic,* written in the fourth century B.C., Socrates tells his interlocutors that they are discussing "how we ought to live." That is a good characterization of ethics. *Ethics* can be defined as the principles and standards that guide our behavior toward other people. One might add that ethics is also about the *reasons* we give for thinking we ought to live one way rather than another, make one decision rather than another, or opt for one policy over another. We generally think of ethical people as those who give equal weight to the interests of the individuals who will be affected by what they do. Acting ethically means behaving in a principled fashion and treating other people with dignity and respect. This is simple to say but not always so simple to do since some situations are complex or ambiguous.

As the quote from Plato makes clear, the important role of ethics in our lives has long been recognized. In 44 B.C., Cicero said that ethics is indispensible to anyone who wants to have a good career. "Good," however, must mean more than "successful," for being ethical involves measuring oneself by standards that transcend one's career goals. One might be a successful embezzler, but one would have failed to live morally. That being said, Cicero, along with some of the greatest minds over the centuries, struggled with questions such as "What rules are ethically binding?" "What are 'rights' and who or what has them?" "What consequences can be considered good?" and "What is it that makes a person virtuous?"

Our sense of what is right and wrong or what is better or worse is rooted in our history, culture, and religion. Despite the variety of societies that exist, ethical norms are surprisingly stable. The values, for example, of truthfulness, care for the young, or respect for one's neighbor's life and property don't go out of style. But if it is true that ethics remain relatively stable, it is equally true that society changes and this creates new challenges for us to expand our ethical horizons and to think in novel and creative ways about "how we ought to live." Ethical dilemmas abound, not less so in this electronic age, when there is a new dimension in ethical debates related to the amount of personal information that we can collect and store and the speed with which we can access and process that information. New information technology raises new ethical questions. It raises questions about how values that we cherish are to be preserved and applied in an information rich world.

TWO FACTORS THAT DETERMINE HOW YOU DECIDE ETHICAL ISSUES

How you collect, store, access, and use information depends to a large extent on your ethics—what you perceive as right and wrong. Two factors affect how you make your decision when you're faced with an ethical dilemma. The first is your basic ethical structure, which you developed as you grew up. The second is the set of practical circumstances inevitably involved in the decision that you're trying to make, that is, all the shades of gray in what are rarely black or white decisions.

Your ethical structure and the ethical challenges you'll face exist at several levels (see Figure 8.1).[5] At the outside level are things that most people wouldn't consider bad, such as taking a couple of paper clips or sending an occasional personal e-mail on company time. Do these things really matter? At the middle level are more significant ethical challenges. One example might be accessing personnel records for personal reasons. Could there ever be a personal reason so compelling that you would not feel ethical discomfort doing this? Reading someone else's e-mail might be another middle-level example. At the innermost ethical level are ethical violations that you'd surely consider very serious, such as embezzling funds or selling company records to a competitor. And yet, over time, your ethical structure can change so that even such acts as these could seem more or less acceptable. For example, if everyone around you is accessing confidential records for their own purposes, in time you might come to think such an act is no big deal. And this might spell big trouble for you.

Figure 8.1

Your Ethical Structure

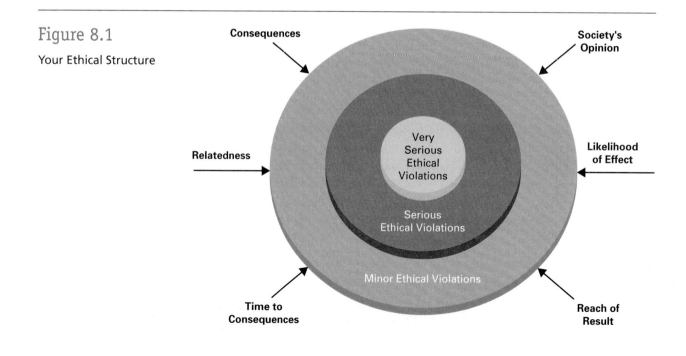

One of the elementary lessons of ethics, too often forgotten, is that something is not made morally acceptable merely because most people do it.

It would be nice if every ethical decision were crystal clear, such as in the innermost circle in Figure 8.1, but ethical decisions are not always so easy. Ideally, your sense of what is ethical should tell you what to do. But practically speaking, any assessment of what is right or wrong can rarely be divorced from a variety of considerations:[6]

1. *Consequences.* How much or how little benefit or harm will come from a particular decision?

2. *Society's opinion.* What is your perception of what society really thinks of your intended action?

3. *Likelihood of effect.* What is the probability of the harm or benefit that will occur if you take the action?

4. *Time to consequences.* How long will it take for the benefit or harm to take effect?

5. *Relatedness.* How much do you identify with the person or persons who will receive the benefit or suffer the harm?

6. *Reach of result.* How many people will be affected by your action?

No matter how strong your sense of ethics is, these practical aspects of the situation may affect you as you make your decision—perhaps unduly, perhaps quite justifiably. Thus, ethical dilemmas usually arise not out of simple situations but from a clash between competing goals, responsibilities, and loyalties. Ethical decisions are complex judgments that balance rewards for yourself and others against responsibilities to yourself and others. Inevitably, your decision process is influenced by uncertainty about the magnitude of the outcome, by your estimate of the importance of the situation, sometimes by your perception of conflicting "right reactions," and more than one socially acceptable "correct" decision. You are the one who has to live with yourself afterward.

INTELLECTUAL PROPERTY

LEARNING OUTCOME 2

An ethical issue you will almost certainly encounter is one related to the use or copying of proprietary software. Software is a type of intellectual property. ***Intellectual property*** is intangible creative work that is embodied in physical form.[7] Music, novels, paintings, and sculptures are all examples of intellectual property. So also are your company's product sketches and schematics and other proprietary documents. These documents along with music, novels, and so on are worth much more than the physical form in which they are delivered. For example, a single Lady Gaga song is worth far more than the CD on which it's purchased. The song is also an example of intellectual property that is covered by copyright law.

Copyright law protects the authorship of literary and dramatic works, musical and theatrical compositions, and works of art. ***Copyright*** is the legal protection afforded an expression of an idea, such as a song, video game, and some types of proprietary documents. Having a copyright means that no one can use your song or video game without your permission. As a form of intellectual property, software is usually protected by copyright law, although sometimes it falls under patent law, which protects an idea, such as the design of a sewing machine or an industrial pump valve.

Copyright law doesn't forbid the use of intellectual property completely. It has some notable exceptions. For example, a TV program could show a video game you created without your permission. This would be an example of the use of copyrighted material for the creation of new material, i.e., the TV program. And that's legal; it falls under the Fair Use Doctrine. The ***Fair Use Doctrine*** says that you may use copyrighted material in certain situations, for example, in the creation of new work or, within certain limits, for teaching purposes. One of those limits is on the amount of the copyrighted material you may use.

Generally, the determining factor in legal decisions on copyright disputes is whether the copyright holder has been or is likely to be denied income because of the infringement. Courts will consider factors such as how much of the work was used and how, and when and on what basis the decision was made to use it.

Remember that copyright infringement is *illegal*. That means it's against the law, outside of a fair use situation, to simply copy a copyrighted picture, text, or anything else without permission, whether the copyrighted material is on the Internet or not.

Even without knowing of or thinking about it, you may have committed copyright infringement during your education. Have you ever created a slide presentation and inserted an image you found on the Web? Did you provide a citation for the image? Unfortunately, most students don't. And, truth be told, it's only a minor ethical violation (although still illegal) according to Figure 8.1. That is, it didn't really hurt anyone and you most likely didn't deny the owner an opportunity to make money. But if it's not your original work, you have to provide a citation. At a minimum, you may have violated your school's code of ethical conduct. In preparing material (term papers and the like) for your classes, keep one simple rule in mind: If it isn't your original work, then provide a citation.

It's also illegal to copy copyrighted software. But there's one exception to that rule: In the United States, you may always make one copy of copyrighted software to keep for backup purposes. When you buy copyrighted software, what you're paying for is the right to use it—and that's all. How many more copies you may make depends on the copyright agreement that comes with the software package. Some software companies state emphatically that you may not even put the software on a second computer, even if they're both yours and no one else uses either one. Other companies are less restrictive, and agree to let you put a copy of software on multiple machines—as long as only one person is using that software package at any given time. In this instance, the company considers software to be like a book in that you can have it in different places and you can loan it out, but only one person at a time may use it. Music companies often allow three copies of a CD or individual music track to be played on different platforms, like your computer, your stereo system, and your MP3 player.

If you copy copyrighted software and give it to another person or persons, you're pirating the software. **Pirated software** is the unauthorized use, duplication, distribution, or sale of copyrighted software.[8] Software piracy costs businesses billions of dollars a year in lost revenue. Microsoft gets more than 25,000 reports of software piracy every year, and the company reportedly follows up on all of them. Countries with the highest software piracy rates are Georgia (93%), Zimbabwe (91%), Bangladesh (90%), Moldova (90%), Yemen (90%), Armenia (89%), Venezuela (88%), Belarus (88%), Libya (88%), and Azerbaijan (88%).[9] Countries with the lowest software piracy rates include the United States, Japan, Luxembourg, New Zealand, Australia, Austria, Sweden, Belgium, and Finland (all 25 percent or less). According to a BSA-IDC Piracy Impact Study in 2010, reducing the overall global piracy rate by 10 percentage points over four years would create:

- $142 billion in new economic global activity
- 500,000 new high-tech jobs
- $32 billion in new tax revenues for governments

Interestingly enough, the study concluded that more than 80 percent of the above benefits would be realized by local governments and economies where the software piracy is taking place.

Privacy

Privacy is the right to be left alone when you want to be, to have control over your own personal possessions, and not to be observed without your consent. It's the right to be free of unwanted intrusion into your private life. Privacy has several dimensions. Psychologically, it's a need for personal space. All of us, to a greater or lesser extent, need to feel in control of our most personal possessions, and personal information belongs on that list. Legally, privacy is necessary for self-protection.[10] If you put the key to your house in a special hiding place in your yard, you want to keep that information private. This information could be abused and cause you grief. In this section, we'll examine some specific areas of privacy: individuals snooping on each other; employers' collection of information about employees; businesses' collection of information about consumers; government collection of personal information; and the issue of privacy in international trade.

PRIVACY AND OTHER INDIVIDUALS

Other individuals, like family members, associates, fellow employees, or unknown hackers, could be electronically invading your privacy. Their motives might be simple curiosity, an attempt to get your password, or a wish to access something they have no right to. Obviously, there are situations in which they'd be well within their rights, and would be well advised, to see what's going on. You would be too. Examples might be if you suspect that your child is in electronic contact with someone or something undesirable, or if you think that someone is using your computer without permission. Many Web sites offer programs, collectively referred to as snoopware, to help people monitor what's happening on a computer.

For general snooping you can get key logger software and install it on the computer you want to monitor. ***Key logger,*** or ***key trapper, software,*** is a program that, when installed on a computer, records every keystroke and mouse click. It records all e-mail, instant messages, chat room exchanges, Web sites you visit, applications you run, and passwords you type in on that computer.

Also available for monitoring computer use are screen capture programs that periodically record what's on the screen. (They get the information straight from the video card.) These programs don't trap every single screen, just whatever is on the screen when the capturing program activates. But they still give whoever is doing the monitoring a pretty good idea of what the computer user is up to. Other tools for monitoring include packet sniffers (that examine the information passing by) on switches, hubs, or routers (the devices on networks that connect computers to each other), and log analysis tools that keep track of logons, deletions, and so forth.

As you're probably already aware, e-mail is completely insecure. E-mail content might as well be written on a postcard for all the privacy it has. Not only that, but each e-mail you send results in at least three or four copies being stored on different computers (see Figure 8.2 on the next page). It's stored first in the computer you're using. Second, it's stored by the e-mail server, the computer through which it gets onto the Internet. Third, it's stored on the recipient's computer, and may also be archived on the recipient's e-mail server.

While you probably realize that your e-mail is not totally private, do you realize that other electronic output leaves its mark too? For example, if you use a color laser printer, your printouts have patterns of yellow dots on the back that are not visible unless you have a blue light and a microscope. These dots identify the model and serial number of your printer and the time the printout was made. Printer manufacturers introduced this feature at the request of the Secret Service, which is the agency responsible for investigating counterfeit currency.

Figure 8.2

The E-Mail You Send
Is Stored on Many
Computers

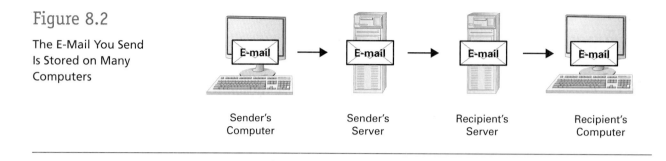

Sender's   Sender's   Recipient's   Recipient's
Computer   Server   Server   Computer

Another example is those photos you take with your digital camera. With the right software you can load the photo and see a whole block of information like the date the photo was taken, the camera type and serial number, whether the owner of the camera signed up for a warranty, and various other details. Your CD burner leaves a distinct signature on the CDs you burn. That is, any CD that your computer burns can be traced back to your CD drive. Of course, it stands to reason that your cell phone, when it's on, can tell people where you are by virtue of the fact that it registers itself with the towers it uses to send and receive calls.

EDRs or Event Data Recorders are now becoming a standard feature on new vehicles. The EDR is part of the airbag control module and was originally included to improve the performance of airbags. When the airbag is deployed, data for the five seconds prior to impact is transferred to a computer chip. About seven pages of information can be downloaded from the chip. This information includes the car's speed at the time of impact, the engine's RPMs, the percent throttle, whether the brakes were applied, and whether the driver's seat belt was buckled. The system is even designed to record a second impact which is frequently what happens in a collision. This is invaluable information to have about an accident and many reckless and inebriated drivers have been taken off the roads because of it.

IDENTITY THEFT

Identity theft is the forging of someone's identity for the purpose of fraud. The fraud is often for financial gain, and the stolen identity is used to apply for and use credit cards in the victim's name or to apply for loans. But it can also be simply to disguise a real identity, particularly if the thief is hiding from law enforcement or is running some sort of scam. Below are some statistics related to identity theft.[11, 12]

- 10%—Americans who have had their identities stolen
- $54 billion—estimated loss to businesses and consumers in the United States in 2009
- $4,841—average amount taken from an identity theft victim
- 15%—victims who don't learn about their identity being stolen for four or more years
- $631—average out-of-pocket expense for victims
- 43%—victims who knew the person who stole their identity (this is called ***friendly fraud***)
- 330 hours—average number of hours it takes to repair damage done by identity theft

Worldwide it is estimated that the cost of identity theft to business and consumers in 2010 was a staggering $221 billion. If "identity theft costs" was a country, it would be the 38th largest country in the world in terms of GDP, or gross domestic product.

Figure 8.3 provides three very revealing graphs regarding identity theft in the United States from 2005 to 2010. Notice the general upward trend in the number of data breaches, from 157 in 2005 to 662 in 2010. 2009 showed a decline, but the general upward trend is very prominent. The revelation: The hackers are winning. Notice also that there were some 223 million records exposed due to data breaches in 2009. That may have been an anomaly but, then again, perhaps not. In that year, there were two big data breaches: The U.S. Military reported a breach that exposed 76 million records; and Heartland Payment Systems reported a breach that exposed 130 million records.

Social networking sites can be 10 times more effective in hooking phishing victims than other sites since people are more likely to click on a link sent by a trusted friend. Facebook is a frequent target. A ploy that has been effective for phishers is to send you a short message that directs you to a Web site that looks very like the social networking site. When you then type in your ID and password the phishers get it.

To avoid this sort of problem, type in the Web address of your social networking site or bookmark it and never follow the suggested link. This is good advice to take if you're at all unsure about where you're being sent. For example, look at this link: www.micosoft.com. Does that look OK to you? Look more closely and you'll see that the company name is misspelled. This is the sort of trick that phishers use.

Following are three examples of what happened when people became the victims of identity theft.

- An 82-year-old woman in Fort Worth, Texas, discovered that her identity had been stolen when the woman using her name was involved in a four-car collision. For 18 months, she kept getting notices of lawsuits and overdue medical bills that were really meant for someone else. It took seven years for her to get her financial good name restored after the identity thief charged over $100,000 on her 12 fraudulently acquired credit cards.

- A 42-year-old retired Army captain in Rocky Hill, Connecticut, found that an identity thief had spent $260,000 buying goods and services that included two trucks, a Harley-Davidson motorcycle, and a time-share vacation home in South Carolina. The victim discovered his problem only when his retirement pay was garnished to pay the outstanding bills.

- In New York, members of a pickpocket ring forged the driver's licenses of their victims within hours of snatching the women's purses. If you steal someone's cash only, your haul usually won't be more than $200, probably much less. On the other hand, if you steal the person's identity, you can net on average between $4,000 and $10,000.

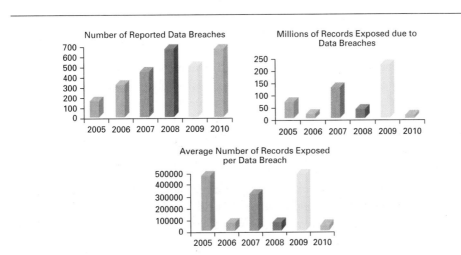

Figure 8.3

2005–2010 U.S. Identity Theft Information[13]

INDUSTRY PERSPECTIVE

PERSONALLY IDENTIFIABLE INFORMATION NOT NEEDED

Cybercriminals need very little information to pull off a very sophisticated spear-phishing e-mail campaign. In fact, they don't even need social security numbers, date of births, or any payment card information. All they need is to be able to correlate consumer names and e-mail addresses to where those people bank, shop, and purchase services. Then, they can build fraudulent e-mails from the legitimate merchant or bank and send them to legitimate customers of those businesses.

And that has a lot of people scared, especially considering the data breach that occurred at Epsilon. Epsilon is a Dallas-based e-mail marketing service provider for 2,500 very large clients including Citigroup, JP Morgan Chase, U.S. Bank, Barclays, Best Buy, Hilton Worldwide, Marriott International, Disney Destinations, and The College Board (which administers the SATs), just to name a few. In early 2011, Epsilon reported that a data breach had occurred, with only names and e-mail addresses of customer's customers being stolen. But that's all the data a good spear-phishing e-mail campaign needs. It was estimated that information was stolen on 60 million individual consumers.

According to CyberFactors, a cyber-risk analytics and intelligence firm, the worst-case scenario would put total losses at $4 billion by Epsilon, its customers like Citigroup, and customers of all Epsilon's customers. That includes millions of dollars in lost business for Epsilon, $225 million in Epsilon liabilities, and the $5 million each of its customers will spend just to notify all their customers that a breach occurred.

Older data breaches focused exclusively on gaining access to personally identifiable information (PII) like your social security numbers and to payment card data. Now, all that's needed is a name and an e-mail address and a correlation to a place of business.[14, 15, 16]

A common way to steal identities online is called phishing. **Phishing** (also called **carding** or **brand spoofing**) is a technique to gain personal information for the purpose of identity theft, usually by means of fraudulent e-mail. One way this is done is to send out e-mail messages that look as though they came from legitimate businesses like AOL, MSN, eBay, PayPal, insurance companies, or online retailers like Amazon.com. The messages look genuine with official-looking formats and logos. These e-mails typically ask for verification of important information like passwords and account numbers. The reason given is often that this personal information is needed for accounting or auditing purposes.

Legitimate businesses don't send out such e-mails. If you get such an e-mail, DON'T provide any information without checking further. For example, you could call the company and ask about it. Another clue is bad grammar and misspellings. Even one typo in an official communication is a warning sign.

A second kind of phishing is to persuade people by e-mail to click on a Web site included in the message and provide personal information. Favorite targets of this type of scheme are eBay and PayPal. You get an e-mail that purports to come from eBay and tells you that your account has been compromised or one pretending to come from PayPal saying that your PayPal account is about to pay out on merchandise worth hundreds of dollars that you didn't order. The idea is to get you to "bite" and go to a site that will steal information like your eBay or PayPal password and then ask for other information, like credit card numbers.

There are now numerous variations of phishing. As we have described it thus far, phishing sends out thousands and perhaps even millions of e-mails, attempting to find anyone to reply. You may not even have a PayPal account and still receive a phishing e-mail claiming to be from PayPal regarding your (nonexistent) account. On the other hand, *spear phishing* is phishing that is targeted to specific individuals. In this case, the creator of the fraudulent e-mail already has some of your personal information and wants more. Finally, there is *whaling,* the use of phishing targeted at senior business executives, government leaders, and other types of high-profile individuals.

A more sophisticated variation on this is *pharming,* which is the rerouting of your request for a legitimate Web site. You may type in the correct address for your bank and be redirected to a fake site that collects information from you. You may even get to the legitimate site and then be linked to the fake site after you have put in identifying information. You don't notice this because the fake site address is very slightly different from the real one, perhaps just one letter off or different. Make sure to look for the padlock—in the browser, not the site—to let you know that you are at a secure site before entering data (see Chapter 5 on Web e-commerce security).

Pharming is accomplished by getting access to the giant databases that Internet providers use to route Web traffic. Once they have access, they can make little changes so that you are diverted to the fake site either before or after you access the real one. It works so well because it's very hard to spot the fake site.

One of the most worrying types of identity theft is medical record theft. Someone who steals your medical records to get medical care will most likely add to or change your records so that when you need care your records are not accurate. This could lead to your getting medication that you're allergic to or not getting a procedure that you need. According to the World Privacy Forum (WPF) almost 20,000 people filed complaints about theft of their medical records between January 1992 and April 2006. Again, according to the WPF, about $100 billion dollars of health care costs are the result of health care fraud. More than 600 health identity theft cases were tried in 2005 and 516 of those people were convicted.

Figure 8.4 on the next page shows some ways to protect yourself.

PRIVACY AND EMPLOYEES

Employers need to know about their employees to operate effectively. If you're applying for a job, you may fill out an application. However, that's not the only source of information to which your prospective employer has access. For a fee, and sometimes for free, an employer can find out your driving record, your eviction records, your credit standing, your telephone usage, your insurance coverage, and so on. Another good source of information is what you put on the Internet from photos to videos to text communications. Once you have put something on the Internet, whether it's in instant messaging or Facebook, you lose control of that information. Data collection companies gather up such information, organize it, and sell it.

After you're hired, your employer can monitor where you go, what you do, what you say, and what you write in e-mails—at least during working hours. The American Management Association says as many as 60 percent of employers monitored employee e-mails, both incoming and outgoing. One reason that companies monitor employees' e-mail is that they can be sued for what their employees send to each other and to people outside the company.

About 70 percent of Web traffic occurs during work hours, and this is reason enough for companies to monitor what, and for how long, employees are surfing the Web. The FBI reports that 78 percent of surveyed companies indicated that employees had abused Internet privileges by downloading pornography, pirating software, or some other activity that wasn't work related. Also, 60 percent of employees said that they visit Web sites or surf for personal use at work. Again, various software packages are available to keep track of people's Web surfing. Some software actually blocks access to certain sites.

Figure 8.4

Protecting Yourself from
Identity Theft[17]

- Use strong passwords with a combination of upper and lower case letters, and a mixture of letters, numbers, and special symbols

- Use different passwords for every application (that may be many)

- Change all your passwords every 60 days

- Shred personal documents you are throwing away

- Store personal documents you keep at the house in a secure, nonpublic place (a safe would be best)

- Check your credit report at least once a year at all three credit reporting agencies (Experian, Transunion, and Equifax)

- Do not carry your social security number around with you

- Do not leave outgoing mail in an unsecured area (such as clipped to the exterior of your mailbox)

- Do not have your social security number or driver's license number printed on your checks

- Do not have your personal checks (i.e., the box of checks you order from the bank) sent to your home address; have them sent to the bank and then pick them up

- Never give out personal information in a communication (email, phone call, etc.) unless you have initiated the communication

- Never respond to suspect email

- Never unsubscribe to emails you don't recognize and don't know are legitimate

- You can't win a lottery you haven't entered

- Always check for the https or lock icon on Web sites you use to enter personal and/or financial information (see Chapter 5)

- Consider putting a "freeze" on your credit. Many states allow you to do this. If you do freeze your account, you must first unfreeze your credit before performing such tasks as opening a new account. Unfreezing your account is a very difficult task for an identity thief to perform.

Businesses have good reasons for seeking and storing personal information on employees. They

- Want to hire the best people possible and to avoid being sued for failing to adequately investigate the backgrounds of employees.

- Want to ensure that staff members are conducting themselves appropriately and not wasting or misusing company resources. Financial institutions are even required by law to monitor all communications including e-mail and telephone conversations.

- Can be held liable for the actions of employees.

MONITORING TECHNOLOGY   Numerous vendors sell software products that scan e-mail, both incoming and outgoing. The software can look for specific words or phrases

CYBERATTACKS NOW CONSIDERED AN ACT OF WAR

In mid-2011, both the United States and the United Kingdom publicly acknowledged that nation-sponsored cyberattacks can be considered an act of war. The very next day, Google reported that a cyberattack originating in Jinan, China, had breached the Gmail accounts of senior U.S. government officials, Chinese political activists, officials in several Asian countries (predominantly South Korea), military personnel, and journalists.

About the same time, Chinese Premier Wen Jiabao and German Chancellor Angela Merkel were holding their first joint cabinet meeting to finalize the details on more than $15 billion in business deals between the two countries. It was during that meeting that the Cologne-based Bundesverfassungsschutz intelligence agency reported a dramatic increase in the number of China-originated cyberattacks on German officials and businesses. According to the report, "Most of the attacks aimed at federal officials and German businesses, because of their characteristics, can be assigned an origin of China. Influential people (e.g., ministers, state secretaries, department heads) as well as positions that deal intensively with issues to do with China were commonly attacked."

China, along with Russia, has long been known as a country whose government sponsors cyberattacks against other countries, specifically Western governments, and large corporations with home offices in that country. According to Harry Sverdlove, Chief Technology Officer at security firm Bit9, "It's a lot easier to hack into a system than it is to tap a phone line or break into an office and take pictures."

As an "act of war," cyberattacks can now be responded to by the United States using military force. That is, if a cyberattack is as bad as a traditional military attack (in terms of death, destruction, and disruption), the United States may respond with a use of force.[18, 19]

in the subject lines or in the body of the text. An e-mail-scanning program can sneak into your computer in Trojan-horse software. That is, it can hide in an innocent-looking e-mail or some other file or software.

An employer can track your keyboard and mouse activity with the type of key logger software that you read about in the previous section. An alternative that's sometimes harder to detect is a hardware key logger. A **_hardware key logger_** is a hardware device that captures keystrokes on their journey from the keyboard to the motherboard. These devices can be in the form of a connector on the system-unit end of the cable between the keyboard and the system unit. There's another type of hardware key logger that you can install into the keyboard. Both have enough memory to store about a year's worth of typing. These devices can't capture anything that's not typed, but they do capture every keystroke, including backspace, delete, insert, and all the others. To defeat them you'd have to copy the password (or whatever you want kept secret) and paste it into its new location. The key logger keeps a record of the keystrokes you use, if any, in your copy-and-paste operation, but not what you copied and pasted.

There is little sympathy in the legal system for the estimated 27 million employees whom the American Management Association says are under surveillance. Employers have the legal right to monitor the use of their resources and that includes the time they're paying you for. In contrast to your home, you have no expectation of privacy when using the company's resources.

The most recent federal bill that addressed electronic monitoring of employees is the Electronic Communications Privacy Act of 1986. Although, in general, it forbids the interception of wired or electronic communications, it has exceptions for both prior consent and business use.

Some state laws have addressed the issue of how far employers can go and what they can do to monitor employees. Connecticut has a law that took effect in 1999 that requires employers in the private sector to notify employees in writing of electronic monitoring. And Pennsylvania, a year earlier, permitted telephone marketers to listen in on calls for quality control purposes as long as at least one of the parties is aware of the action.[20]

PRIVACY AND CONSUMERS

Businesses face a dilemma.

- Customers want businesses to know who they are, but, at the same time, they want them to leave them alone.
- Customers want businesses to provide what they want, but, at the same time, they don't want businesses knowing too much about their habits and preferences.
- Customers want businesses to tell them about products and services they might like to have, but they don't want to be inundated with ads.

Like it or not, massive amounts of personal information are available to businesses from various sources. A relatively large Web site may get about 100 million hits per day, which means that the site gets about 200 bytes of information for each hit. That's about 20 gigabytes of information per day.[21] This level of information load has helped to make customer relationship management (CRM) systems one of the fastest growing areas of software development. Part of managing customer relationships is personalization. Web sites that greet you by name and Amazon.com's famous recommendations that "People who bought this product also bought . . ." are examples of personalization, which is made possible by the Web site's knowledge about you.[22]

Apart from being able to collect its own information about you, a company can readily access consumer information elsewhere. Credit card companies sell information, as do the Census Bureau and mailing list companies. Web traffic tracking companies such as DoubleClick follow you (and other surfers) around the Web and then sell the information about where you went and for how long. DoubleClick can collect information about you over time and provide its customers with a highly refined profile on you. DoubleClick is also an intermediary for companies that want to advertise to Web surfers. When hired by a company wanting to sell something, DoubleClick identifies people who might be receptive and sends the ad to them as a banner or pop-up ad. Proponents of this practice claim that it's good for the surfers because they get targeted advertising and less unwanted advertising.

COOKIES   The basic tool of consumer Web monitoring is the cookie. A *cookie* is a small file that contains information about you and your Web activities, which a Web site you visit places on your computer. A cookie has many uses. For example, it's used to keep ID and password information so that you don't have to go through the whole verification process every time you log onto a Web site. It's also used to store the contents of electronic shopping carts, so that the next time you log on, the Web site will be able to see your wish list (which is stored on your computer in a cookie).

A cookie can also be used to track your Web activity. It can monitor and record what sites you visit, how long you stay there, what Web pages you visited, what site you came from and the next site you went to. This type of cookie is called a *unique cookie*. Some cookies are temporary and some stay on your computer indefinitely.

Third-party or *common cookies* are the ones that have many privacy advocates disturbed. These are different from the unique cookies that a Web site you visit puts onto your hard disk. A common cookie is one that started out as a unique cookie, but the original site sold access to it to a third party, like DoubleClick, that can then change the cookie so that the third party can track the surfer's activity across many sites. The third party collects information about surfers without names or other identifiable personal information. They usually collect an IP address, which they then link to a random identifying ID so that the surfer can be identified at other sites. Surveys have shown that the vast majority of people (91 percent) don't like the idea of unknown companies gathering information about them that they have provided to sites with whom they chose to interact.[23]

You have two options if you want to block cookies. First, you can set your browser to accept or reject all cookies. Or you can get it to warn you when a site wants to put a cookie on your computer. Second, you can get cookie management software with additional options that are not available on your browser. For example, CookieCop 3, from *PC Magazine,* will let you accept or reject cookies on a per-site basis. It also allows you to replace banner ads with the image of your choice and to block ads for sites you find offensive. With this or other cookie-stopper software, you can disable pop-up windows, and stipulate that certain cookies can stay on your hard drive for the duration of one session only.

SPAM   *Spam* is unsolicited e-mail (electronic junk mail) from businesses that advertise goods and services. Often spam mass mailings advertise pornography, get-rich-quick schemes, and miracle cures. Experts at Commtouch.com, a computer security company, estimate that about 80 percent of all e-mails in 2007 were spam, with levels peaking at 96 percent, during the last quarter of the year. The spam level rose higher during certain periods in 2008 and the first half of 2009.[24, 25] If you haven't been inundated with spam, you're either very lucky or you don't use the Internet much. Spam has become a severe irritant to consumers and a costly matter for businesses, who must sort through hundreds of e-mail messages every day deleting spam and hoping that they don't delete e-mail messages that are actually legitimate customer orders.

You can get spam filters to block out spam, but spammers are clever about including nonprinting characters in their subject lines and addresses that fool the filters into letting them pass. For example, say a spammer wanted to send out a message about a new weight loss drug called *Off.* The spammer would alter the spelling of the word or add invisible HTML tags so that the subject line would be: O*F*F or O<i></i>F<u></u>F. The HTML tags <i> and <u> would normally italicize and underline text, respectively, and the </i> and </u> would undo the italicizing and bolding, but since there's no text in between the tags do nothing except evade the filter.

Many states have passed laws to regulate spam and the Federal Government passed an anti-spam law in 2003 called the CAN-Spam Act (see Figure 8.6 on page 243), which was widely criticized by anti-spam activists as legitimizing spam, since it set down rules for spamming rather than banning it altogether.

Most experts doubt that the CAN-Spam Act hurts the spammers who are the source of most of the spam. They say that it just costs legitimate businesses time and money since they have to maintain do-not-spam lists and follow the legal guidelines when sending out e-mails to customers. Since the bulk of spam comes from spammers who spoof (disguise) the origin of the e-mail, they can usually operate for a long time in defiance of the law. Irate spam trackers, some of whom have become cyber vigilantes, have gone so far as to "out" spammers and publicize information about them on the Web in an effort to stop them.

One trick that spammers use to collect addresses for spamming is to send out e-mail purporting to add you to a general do-not-spam list if you reply. In fact, what it does is add your e-mail address to the list of "live" ones.

ADWARE AND SPYWARE   If you've downloaded a game or other software from the Web for free, you may have noticed that it came with banner ads. These ads are collectively known as adware. *Adware* is software to generate ads that installs itself on your computer when you download some other (usually free) program from the Web (see Figure 8.5). Adware is a type of *Trojan horse software*, meaning that it's software you don't want hidden inside software you do want. There's usually a disclaimer, buried somewhere in the multiple "I agree" screens, saying that the software includes this adware. At the bottom of several small-print screens you're asked to agree to the terms. Very few people read the whole agreement, and advertisers count on that. This sort of product is sometimes called *click-wrap* because it's like commercial software that has an agreement that you agree to by breaking the shrink-wrap.

Most people don't get upset about pure adware, since they feel it's worth having to view ads to get software for free. (Many apps for your smartphone come with adware.) However, there's a more insidious extra that's often bundled with free downloadable software called spyware. *Spyware* (also called *sneakware* or *stealthware*) is malicious software that collects information about you and your computer and reports it to someone without your permission. It usually comes hidden in downloadable software and tracks your online movements and/or mines the information stored on your computer. The first release of RealNetworks' RealJukebox sent information back to the company about what CDs the people who downloaded the software were playing on that computer. This information collection was going on when the customer wasn't even on the Web.[26]

Spyware is fast becoming the hidden cost of free software. Software such as Kazaa Media Desktop and Audiogalaxy, the successors to Napster for sharing music and other files online, includes spyware. If you download free software and it has banner ads, it's quite possible that it has spyware, too. There's usually something in the "I agree" screens telling you about spyware, but it can be hard to find. Spyware can stay on your computer long after you've uninstalled the original software.

Figure 8.5

Adware in a Free Version of Eudora, an E-Mail Application from Qualcomm

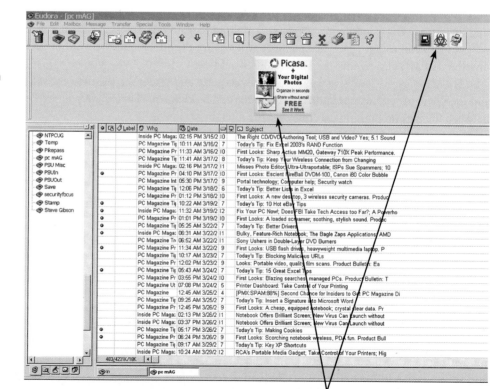

Adware

You can detect various kinds of Trojan horse software with The Cleaner from www.moosoft.com. Also check out www.wilderssecurity.com for Trojan First Aid Kit (TFAK). The best-known spyware detection programs, also called stealthware blockers, are Ad-Aware (free from www.lavasoft.com) and PestPatrol. The software scans your whole computer, identifies spyware programs, and offers to delete them. If you want to check out free software for spyware before you download it, go online to www.spychecker.com, a site that will tell you if particular free software includes adware or spyware.

Even without spyware, a Web site can tell a lot about its Web visitors from its Web log. A *Web log* consists of one line of information for every visitor to a Web site and is usually stored on a Web server. At the very least, a Web log can provide a Web site company with a record of your clickstream.

A *clickstream* records information about you during a Web surfing session such as what Web sites you visited, how long you were there, what ads you looked at, and what you bought. If, as a consumer, you want to protect information about your surfing habits, you can use various software packages to do so. Apart from cookie management software you can avail yourself of *anonymous Web browsing (AWB)* services, which, in effect, hide your identity from the Web sites you visit. An example is Anonymizer at www.anonymizer.com. This site, and others like it, sends your Web browsing through its server and removes all identifying information. Some of the ABW services that are available include disabling pop-up promotions, defeating tracking programs, and erasing browsing history files. If you don't want to go through an outside server, you can download software to do the job. SurfSecret is a shareware antitracking package available from www.surfsecret.com.

As a final note on the subject, remember that even if a company promises, and fully intends, to keep its customer information protected, it may not be possible. When faced with a subpoena, the company will have to relinquish customer records. Furthermore, courts have ruled in bankruptcy cases that customer files are assets that may be sold to pay debts.

PRIVACY AND GOVERNMENT AGENCIES

Government agencies have about 2,000 databases containing personal information on individuals.[27] The various branches of government need information to administer entitlement programs, such as social security, welfare, student loans, law enforcement, and so on.

LAW ENFORCEMENT   You've often heard about someone being apprehended for a grievous crime after a routine traffic stop for something like a broken taillight. The arrest most likely ensued because the arresting officer ran a check on the license plate and driver's license. The officer probably checked the National Crime Information Center (NCIC) database and found the outstanding warrant there. Timothy McVeigh and others responsible for the bombing of the Federal building in Oklahoma City were caught in this way.

The NCIC database contains information on the criminal records of more than 20 million people. It also stores information on outstanding warrants, missing children, gang members, juvenile delinquents, stolen guns and cars, and so on. The NCIC has links to other government and private databases, and guardians of the law all over the country can access NCIC information. Sometimes they do so in response to something suspicious, and other times it's just routine. For example, Americans returning from outside the country are routinely checked through the NCIC when they come through customs.

Given its wealth of information and accessibility, it's not surprising that the NCIC system has been abused. Several police departments have found that a significant number of employees illegally snooped for criminal records on people they knew or wanted to know.

The Federal Bureau of Investigation (FBI) has caused a stir because of its electronic surveillance methods. First there was Carnivore, a rather unfortunate name, which has since been changed to DCS-1000. DCS-1000 connects hardware to an ISP to trap all e-mail sent to or received by the target of the investigation. It takes a court order to use DCS-1000, and, of course, the target is typically unaware of the surveillance. Intercepting communications is not new: The FBI put the first tap on a phone in 1885, just four years after the invention of the telephone.[28] DCS-1000, with a court order, traps all communications involving the individual named in the court order.

Because it can be hard to identify the data packets of one individual's e-mail amongst all the other Internet traffic, it's entirely possible that other people's e-mail might be scooped up in the net. And this is what happened in March 2000 when FBI agents were legally intercepting messages of a suspect, but someone else was caught in the trap. The information on the innocent party was obtained under the Freedom of Information Act. The FBI said the incident was an honest mistake and a result of miscommunication between it and the ISP.[29] But this is the sort of mistake that scares people. Most people want law enforcement to be able to watch the bad guys—that's necessary for our collective safety. But the prospect of information being collected on law-abiding citizens who are minding their own business worries a lot of people.

In 2001, the FBI acknowledged an enhancement to DCS-1000 called Magic Lantern, which is key logger software. The FBI installs it by sending the target an innocent-looking Trojan-horse e-mail, which contains the key logger software. The hidden software then sends information back to the FBI periodically.[30]

Another federal agency, the National Security Agency (NSA), uses a system called Echelon that uses a global network of satellites and surveillance stations to trap phone, e-mail, and fax transmissions. The system then screens all this information looking for certain keywords and phrases and analyzes the messages that fit the search criteria.

At the local level, the actions of the Tampa Police Department at the 2001 Super Bowl caused an outcry from privacy advocates. Police, with the agreement of the NFL, focused video cameras on the faces of tens of thousands of spectators as they entered the stadium. The images were sent to computers which, using facial recognition software, compared the images to a database of pictures of suspected criminals and terrorists. The police spokesperson said that the action was legal since it's permissible to take pictures of people in public places. That's true in so far as you have no expectation of privacy in a public place. Indeed surveillance of people has been going on for years without much protest in gambling casinos, Walmart stores, and other businesses in the private sector. But the American Civil Liberties Union (ACLU) protested the surveillance of Super Bowl spectators on the grounds that it was surveillance by a government agency without court-ordered authorization. The fact that the state was involved made it unacceptable to the ACLU.

OTHER FEDERAL AGENCIES   The Internal Revenue Service (IRS) gets income information from taxpayers. But the agency has access to other databases, too. For example, the IRS keeps track of vehicle registration information so that it can check up on people buying expensive cars and boats to make sure they're reporting an income level that corresponds to their purchases. The IRS can go to outside government databases as well. Verizon says that it gets 22,000 requests for phone records from the IRS, FBI, and other government agencies per year. It seldom informs the customer of the request. America Online (AOL) has a special fax number reserved just for subpoenas.

The Census Bureau collects information on all the U.S. inhabitants it can find every 10 years. All citizens are requested to fill out a census form, and some people get a very long and detailed form requiring them to disclose a lot of personal information. The information that the Census Bureau collects is available to other government agencies and even to commercial enterprises. The bureau doesn't link the information to respondents' names but sells summarized information about geographic regions. Some of these regions are relatively small, however, consisting of fewer than 100 city blocks.

It's fairly safe to assume that anytime you have contact with any branch of government, information about you will be subsequently stored somewhere. For example, if you get a government-backed student loan, you provide personal information such as your name, address, income, parents' income, and so on. Some of the information nuggets attached to the loan would be the school you're attending, the bank dispersing the loan, your repayment schedule, and later, your repayment pattern.

LAWS ON PRIVACY

The United States doesn't have a comprehensive or consistent set of laws governing the use of information. However, some laws are in place. Recent legislation includes the

Figure 8.6

Recent Information-Related Laws

- **Identity Theft and Assumption Deterrence Act,** 1998, strengthened the criminal laws governing identity theft, making it a federal crime to use or transfer identification belonging to another. It also established a central federal service for victims.

- **USA Patriot Act,** 2001 and 2003, allows law enforcement to get access to almost any information, including library records, video rentals, bookstore purchases, and business records when investigating any act of terrorism or hostile intelligence activities. In 2003 Patriot II broadened the original law.

- **Homeland Security Act,** 2002, provided new authority to government agencies to mine data on individuals and groups including e-mails and Web site visits; put limits on the information available under the Freedom of Information Act; and gave new powers to government agencies to declare national heath emergencies.

- **Sarbanes-Oxley Act,** 2002, sought to protect investors by improving the accuracy and reliability of corporate disclosures and requires companies to (1) implement extensive and detailed policies to prevent illegal activity within the company and (2) respond in a timely manner to investigate illegal activity. (You'll find more about the business implications of Sarbanes-Oxley in *Extended Learning Module H: Computer Crime and Digital Forensics.*)

- **Fair and Accurate Credit Transactions Act,** 2003, included provisions for the prevention of identity theft including consumers' right to get a credit report free each year, requiring merchants to leave all but the last five digits of a credit card number off a receipt, and requiring lenders and credit agencies to take action even before a victim knows a crime has occurred when they notice any circumstances that might indicate identity theft.

- **CAN-Spam Act,** 2003, sought to regulate interstate commerce by imposing limitations and penalties on businesses sending unsolicited e-mail to consumers. The law forbids deceptive subject lines, headers, return addresses, etc., as well as harvesting e-mail addresses from Web sites. It requires businesses that send spam to maintain a do-not-spam list and to include a postal mailing address in the message.

Health Insurance Portability and Accountability Act (HIPAA) and the Financial Service Modernization Act. HIPAA, enacted in 1996, requires that the health care industry formulate and implement the first regulations to keep patient information confidential. The act seeks to

- Limit the release and use of your health information without your consent.
- Give you the right to access your medical records and find out who else has accessed them.
- Overhaul the circumstances under which researchers and others can review medical records.
- Release health information on a need-to-know basis only.
- Allow the disclosure of protected health information for business reasons as long as the recipient undertakes, in writing, to protect the information.

The Financial Services Modernization Act requires that financial institutions protect personal customer information and that they have customer permission before sharing such information with other businesses. However, the act contains a clause that allows the sharing of information for "legitimate business purposes." See Figure 8.6 for recent information-related laws.

Security

LEARNING OUTCOME 4

So, what can put your important information resource in jeopardy? Well, countless things. Hard disks can crash, computer parts can fail, hackers and crackers can gain access and do mischief, thieves engaged in industrial espionage can steal your information, and disgruntled employees or associates can cause damage. The FBI estimates that computer sabotage costs businesses somewhere close to $10 billion every year. Companies are increasing their spending on Internet security software, a fact that Symantec Corp. can attest to. Symantec is the largest exclusive developer of computer security software and has a market value of $14 billion, making it one of the most valuable software companies in the world.

SECURITY AND EMPLOYEES

Most of the press reports are about outside attacks on computer systems, but actually, companies are in far more danger of losing money from employee misconduct than they are from outsiders. It's estimated that 75 percent of computer crime is perpetrated by insiders, although this is not a problem that's restricted to computer misuse. A 300-restaurant chain with 30 employees in each location loses, on average, $218 per employee.

But white-collar crime is where the big bucks are lost (see Figure 8.7). White-collar crime in general, from Fortune 100 firms to video stores to construction companies, accounts for about $400 billion in losses every year—$400 billion is $108 billion more than the whole federal defense budget—and information technology makes it much easier to accomplish and conceal the crime. Of all white collar fraud, the biggest losses are those incurred by management misconduct. Manager theft of various kinds is about four times that of other employees. Take embezzlement, for example. The average cost of a nonmanagerial employee's theft is $60,000, while that for managerial employees is $250,000. The most astonishing aspect of this is that most insider fraud (up to two-thirds) is never reported to the legal authorities, according to the Association of Certified Fraud Examiners (ACFE).

Figure 8.7

Figures on Fraud[31]

FIGURE	COMMENT
$2.9 trillion	2009 Potential total worldwide loss due to fraud
$160,000	Median loss caused by fraud
85%	First-time fraudsters
42%	Fraud committed by employees
41%	Fraud committed by managers
17%	Fraud committed by owners/executives
24 months	Months to detect fraud by owners/executives
67%	Fraud committed by males

Computer-aided fraud includes the old standby crimes like vendor fraud (sending payment to a nonexistent vendor or payment for goods not delivered), writing payroll checks to fictitious employees, claiming expense reimbursements for costs never incurred, and so on. In addition, there are newer crimes such as stealing security codes, credit card numbers, and proprietary files. Intellectual property is one of the favorite targets of theft by insiders. In fact, the companies that make surveillance software say that employers are buying and installing the software not so much to monitor employees as to track how intellectual property, like product design sketches, schematics, and so on, is moving around the network.

Fraud examiners have a rule of thumb that in any group of employees, about 10 percent are completely honest, 10 percent will steal, and, for the remaining 80 percent, it will depend on circumstances. Most theft is committed by people who are strapped for cash, have access to funds that are poorly protected, and perceive a low risk of getting caught.

SECURITY AND OUTSIDE THREATS

In 2010, companies spent, on average, $7.2 million each to recover corporate data that was lost or stolen. That's 6 percent more than in 2009. The losses are the result of many problems such as someone breaking into their systems, malicious insider activity, malware like spyware and viruses, and the theft of USB devices, notebook computers, and flash memory cards. The average cost per record that was compromised was $214.[32]

The threats from outside are many and varied. Competitors could try to get your customer lists or the prototype for your new project. Cyber vandals could be joyriding in cyberspace looking for something interesting to see, steal, or destroy. You could become the victim of a generalized attack from a virus or worm, or could suffer a targeted attack like a denial-of-service attack. If you have something worth stealing or manipulating on your system, there could be people after that, too. For example, the online gambling industry is plagued by attacks where hackers have illicitly gained access to the servers that control the gambling, corrupting games to win millions of dollars. Exploiting well-known system weaknesses accounts for a large part of hacker damage, while only 5 percent results from breaking into systems in new ways.[33]

The people who break into the computer systems of others are "hackers" (see Figure 8.8). *Hackers* are generally knowledgeable computer users who use their knowledge to invade other people's computers. They have varying motives. Some just do it for the fun of it. Others (called hacktivists) have a philosophical or political message they want to share, and still others (called crackers) are hired guns who illegally break in, usually to steal information, for a fee. The latter can be a very lucrative undertaking. Some highly skilled crackers charge up to $1 million per job. There are also "good guys," called white-hat hackers, who test the vulnerability of systems so that protective measures may be taken.

TYPES OF CYBER CRIME   Cyber crimes range from electronically breaking and entering to cyberstalking and murder. In October 1999, a 21-year-old woman was shot and killed outside the building where she worked. Her killer had been electronically stalking her for two years. He became obsessed with the young lady and had even posted a Web site dedicated to her on which he announced his intention to kill her. He got her Social Security number online, found out where she worked, tracked her down, and shot her, after which he shot himself.

Most cyber crimes are not as bad as murder, but they can be serious nonetheless. Computer viruses and denial-of-service attacks are the two most common types of cyber crime against which companies need to protect themselves.

A *computer virus* (or simply a *virus*) is software that is written with malicious intent to cause annoyance or damage. A virus can be benign or malicious. The benign ones just display a message on the screen or slow the computer down, but don't do any damage. The malicious kind targets a specific application or set of file types and corrupts or destroys them.

Today, worms are the most prevalent type of virus. Worms are viruses that spread themselves; they don't need your help, just your carelessness.

A *worm* is a type of virus that spreads itself, not just from file to file, but from computer to computer via e-mail and other Internet traffic. It finds your e-mail address book and helps itself to the addresses and sends itself to your contacts, using your e-mail address as the return address. The Love Bug worm was one of the early worms that did a lot of

Figure 8.8

Hacker Types

- White-hat hackers find vulnerabilities in systems and plug the holes. They work at the request of the owners of the computer systems.

- Black-hat hackers break into other people's computer systems and may just look around, or they may steal credit card numbers or destroy information, or otherwise do damage.

- Hacktivists have philosophical and political reasons for breaking into systems. They often deface a Web site as a protest.

- Script kiddies, or script bunnies, find hacking code on the Internet and click-and-point their way into systems, to cause damage or spread viruses.

- Crackers are hackers for hire and are the hackers who engage in corporate espionage.

- Cyberterrorists are those who seek to cause harm to people or to destroy critical systems or information. They try to use the Internet as a weapon of mass destruction.

MOBILE DEVICES: THE NEW BIG CORPORATE SECURITY HEADACHE

"As mobile devices become a replacement for the desktop computer, the problem of malware (malicious software) will grow significantly on the mobile platform," explains Anup Gosh, founder of Web browser security firm Invincea. "Unfortunately, the security industry has not developed products suitable for battery-constrained mobile devices, which makes it ripe ground for malware writers."

Those are some pretty alarming statements, but they're true. Employees are bringing more personal mobile devices to work than ever before. The employees are not only performing work-related tasks on their mobile devices, they're also mixing in personal and social activities. Companies are having a difficult time in developing policies to deal with the plethora of personal devices in the workplace. According to one survey, 21 percent of companies have no restrictions on the use of personal mobile devices. Some 58 percent have "lightweight" policies, and only 20 percent have very strict guidelines in place.

In 2010, white-hat hackers and researchers found 163 security holes in various mobile operating systems. That's up from 115 in 2009. These mobile OS security holes present some real problems. In 2010, 40 percent of surveyed organizations stated that mobile devices had been lost or stolen, many of which held critical business information. Theft is certainly a problem but so is downloading infected apps, which can allow a cybercriminal to steal information. One attack on legitimate game and entertainment apps corrupted 50 of the apps, all of which totaled more than 250,000 downloads.

On a personal level the lesson learned here is that you need to treat your mobile device like your laptop (or equivalent) computer. Don't leave it lying around; don't download content from a provider you can't verify; and keep your protection software up-to-date.[34, 35]

---

damage and got major press coverage. It's estimated that the Love Bug and its variants affected 300,000 Internet host computers and millions of individual PC users causing file damage, lost time, and high-cost emergency repairs costing about $8.7 billion.[36,37] Ford Motor Company, H. J. Heinz, Merrill Lynch, AT&T, Capitol Hill, and the British Parliament all fell victim to the Love Bug worm. Newer versions of worms include Klez, a very rapidly spreading worm, Nimda, and Sircam.

A *denial-of-service attack (DoS)* floods a server or network with so many requests for service that it slows down or crashes. The objective is to prevent legitimate customers from accessing the target site. E*Trade, Yahoo!, and Amazon.com have all been victims of this type of attack. For more information about viruses and hackers and DoSs see *Extended Learning Module H.*

As well as knowing what viruses can do, you need to know what they can't do. Computer viruses can't

- Hurt your hardware, such as your monitor, or processor.
- Hurt any files they weren't designed to attack. A virus designed for Microsoft's Outlook, for example, generally doesn't infect Qualcomm's Eudora, or any other e-mail application.

SECURITY PRECAUTIONS

In Chapter 7, Infrastructure, Cloud Computing Metrics, and Business Continuity Planning, you learned about business contigency plans and in *Extended Learning Module E: Network Basics* you read about intrusion detection. These are both very important components of any company's computer system security. There are also standard precautions that a company, and any individual who wants protection from the computer-based attacks, should take.

The most basic protection is to have anti-virus software running on your computer. ***Anti-virus software*** detects and removes or quarantines computer viruses. New viruses are created every day and each new generation is more deadly (or potentially more deadly) than the previous one. You should update your anti-virus software regularly and make sure it's running all the time so that it kicks in when you download e-mail and other files.

Many of the anti-virus software packages on the market also protect you against other cyber evils, like spyware and adware. They will also block cookies, pop-up ads, and embedded objects and scripts such as you get if you download a Flash file, for instance.

Spam protection is good to have, although it may let some spam through and may mark as spam something that isn't. You can usually choose to have the spam deleted, quarantined (in its own folder), or marked so that it stands out when you look in your Inbox. *Anti-phishing software* is also available to protect you from identity theft. The MyVault feature of ZoneAlarm, for example, will block data such as Social Security Number, credit card numbers, and passwords from leaving your computer. Anti-phishing toolbars warn you when you arrive at a known phishing site. Symantec's anti-phishing software places a toolbar beneath the Address Bar which turns red if you land at a phishing site.

ZoneAlarm, which is a firewall program with additional features, will let you know if a program is trying to access the Internet for whatever reason, as spyware on your computer may be attempting to do ZoneAlarm from www.zonealarm.com is a very popular software firewall. ZoneAlarm also offers protection from ads and cookies. A ***firewall*** is hardware and/or software that protects a computer or network from intruders. The firewall examines each message as it seeks entrance to the network, like a border guard checking passports. Unless the message has the "right" markings, the firewall will block it from entering. You can set your firewall so that it identifies certain programs that are always allowed to visit a Web site. Your e-mail program would be an example. Any competent network administrator will have at least one firewall on the network to keep out unwelcome guests.

There are also programs that will block certain sites, which is useful if you have underage children. Some people suggest using FireFox or Opera as your default browser since Microsoft's Internet Explorer has long been a favorite target of hackers.

ACCESS AUTHENTICATION   While firewalls keep outsiders out, they don't necessarily keep insiders out. In other words, unauthorized employees may try to access computers or files. One of the ways that companies try to protect computer systems is with authentication systems that check who you are before they let you have access.

There are three basic ways of proving your access rights: (1) what you know, like a password; (2) what you have, like an ATM card; (3) what you look like (more specifically what your fingerprint or some other physical characteristic looks like).

Passwords are very popular and have been used since there were computers. You can password-protect the whole network, a single computer, a folder, or a file. But passwords are not by any means a perfect way to protect a computer system. People forget their passwords, so someone may have to get them new passwords or find the old one. Banks spend $15 per call to help customers who forget their passwords. Then if a hacker breaks into the system and steals a password list, everyone has to get a new password. One bank had to change 5,000 passwords in the course of a single month at a cost of $12.50 each.[38]

Which brings us to biometrics, or what you look like. ***Biometrics*** is the use of physiological characteristics—such as your fingerprint, the blood vessels in the iris of your eye, the sound of your voice, or perhaps even your breath—to provide identification. Roughly a dozen different types of biometric devices are available at the moment, with fingerprint readers being the most popular. About 44 percent of the biometric systems sold are fingerprint systems. They work just like the law enforcement system where your fingerprint is stored in the database, and when you come along, your finger is scanned, and the scan is compared to the entry in the database. If they match, you're in. See Chapter 9 for more information on biometrics.

ENCRYPTION   If you want to protect your messages and files and hide them from prying eyes, you can encrypt them. ***Encryption*** scrambles the contents of a file so that you can't read it without having the right decryption key. There are various ways of encrypting messages. You can switch the order of the characters, replace characters with other characters, or insert or remove characters. All of these methods alter the look of the message, but used alone, each one is fairly simple to figure out. So most encryption methods use a combination.

Companies that get sensitive information from customers, such as credit card numbers, need some way of allowing all their customers to use encryption to send the information. But they don't want everyone to be able to decrypt the message, so they might use public key encryption. ***Public key encryption (PKE)*** is an encryption system that uses two keys: a public key that everyone can have and a private key for only the recipient. So if you do online banking, the bank will give you the public key to encrypt the information you send them, but only the bank has the key to decrypt your information. It works rather like a wall safe, where anyone can lock it (just shut the door and twirl the knob), but only the person with the right combination can open it again.

SUMMARY: STUDENT LEARNING OUTCOMES REVISITED

1. **Define ethics and describe the two factors that affect how you make a decision concerning an ethical issue.** ***Ethics*** are the principles and standards that guide our behavior toward other people. How you decide ethical issues must depend especially on your basic ethical structure but also for better or worse on the practical circumstances. Your basic ethics you probably acquired growing up. The practical circumstances that you might allow to affect you include

   - *Consequences.* How much or how little benefit or harm will come from a particular decision?
   - *Society's opinion.* What do you perceive society thinks of your intended action?
   - *Likelihood of effect.* What is the probability of the harm or benefit if you take the action?
   - *Time to consequences.* How long will it take for the benefit or harm to take effect?
   - *Relatedness.* How much do you identify with the person or persons who will receive the benefit or suffer the harm?
   - *Reach of result.* How many people will be affected by your action?

2. **Define and describe intellectual property, copyright, Fair Use Doctrine, and pirated software.** *Intellectual property* is intangible creative work that is embodied in physical form. *Copyright* is the legal protection afforded an expression of an idea, such as a song or a video game and some types of proprietary documents. The *Fair Use Doctrine* says that you may use copyrighted material in certain situations. *Pirated software* is the unauthorized use, duplication, distribution or sale of copyrighted software.

3. **Define privacy and describe ways in which it can be threatened.** *Privacy* is the right to be left alone when you want to be, to have control over your own personal possessions, and not to be observed without your consent. Your privacy can be compromised by other individuals snooping on you; by employers monitoring your actions; by businesses that collect information on your needs, preferences, and surfing practices; and by the various government agencies that collect information on citizens.

4. **Describe the ways in which information on your computer or network is vulnerable and list measures you can take to protect it.**

   - Employees can embezzle and perpetrate fraud of other types. Most of the financial losses due to computer fraud that is suffered by companies is caused by employees.
   - Hackers and crackers try to break into computers and steal, destroy, or compromise information.
   - Hackers can spread *computer viruses* or launch *denial-of-service attacks (DoS)* that can cost millions in prevention and cleanup.

   Measures you can take include

   - Anti-virus software to find and delete or quarantine viruses
   - Anti-spyware and anti-adware software
   - Spam protection software
   - Anti-phishing toolbar
   - Firewalls
   - Encryption
   - Biometrics

CLOSING CASE STUDY ONE

Sexting Now Almost Commonplace

Sexting is the sending of sexually explicit messages and/or photos, primarily between mobile phones. *Adult sexting* is sexting between two consenting adults. In short, you take a suggestive (and perhaps sexually explicit) photo of yourself with your phone, attach a message to it, and send it to someone else's phone. The message itself is called a *sext*. Sexting first caught the public's attention in 2007 or so when numerous reports

and stories began to surface about teen sexting. In a few instances, a teen took a sexually explicit photo of friends while in the school's shower facility and then texted it to numerous friends. Some teens have even been charged with child pornography for participating in sexting.

Adult sexting really grabbed the public's attention in mid-2011 when U.S. Congressman Anthony Weiner of New York sent sexually explicit photos of himself via

Twitter to a 21-year-old woman in Washington. At first, Weiner denied the allegations, stating that his Twitter account had been hacked and someone was attempting to slur his good name. Later, it came out that Weiner had sexted six women over a three-year period, both before and during his marriage. Not long after, Weiner admitted that the sexting was his own and he resigned from Congress.

Earlier that year, U.S. Representative (also of New York) Chris Lee had performed a similar type of sexting. He had used Craigslist to solicit a relationship. Eventually he used his Gmail account to send a shirtless photo of himself to a woman. When the *Gawker* broke the story, Lee resigned from his political position.

Below are some statistics related to teen and young adult sexting.

- Teens who have sent sexually suggestive messages:
  - 39 percent overall
  - 37 percent of teen girls
  - 40 percent of teen boys
  - 48 percent—teens reporting having received sexts
- Teens who have posted/sent sexually explicit photos/videos of themselves:
  - 20 percent overall
  - 22 percent of teen girls
  - 18 percent of teen boys
  - 11 percent of young teen girls ages 13–16
- 71 percent of teen girls and 67 percent of teen boys who have sexted have done so to a boyfriend/girlfriend.
- 21 percent of teen girls and 39 percent of teen boys who have sexted have done so to someone they wanted to date or to hook up with.

Sexting statistics among adults have been much harder to gather and have not yet been published. However, psychologist Susan Lipkins performed an online survey of people ages 13 to 72. She found that 66 percent had sent sexually explicit messages. Her published study went on to identify that individuals in a position of power or those who thirsted for power were more likely to sext than those who were not in a position of power or did not crave power. According to Gary Lewandowski, both men and women in power are more likely to cheat, flirt, and participate in sexting. As Lewandowski explains, "I am this great, powerful person. Who's going to question me?" (He was of course paraphrasing what a powerful person might say.) To many people, the statistics are absolutely alarming. Further, consider that many teens—for fear of reprisal—probably did not answer the survey honestly.

However, some people see the use of technology to support sexting as just another communication medium. If you have a phone conversation with your partner and say something suggestive regarding sex, have you committed sexting by telephone? What about a face-to-face communication? If you bare part of your body (something sexual obviously), have you committed a form of sexting without using technology?[39, 40, 41]

Questions

1. Adult sexting is perfectly legal, as it is the sharing of sexually explicit content between two consenting adults. But what about teen sexting—should that be legal? If a 16-year-old boy sends a sext to his 16-year-old partner, should that be considered child pornography? Why or why not?
2. If you refer back to Figure 8.1 on page 228, where would you place adult sexting—a minor ethical violation, a serious ethical violation, or a very serious ethical violation? What circumstances—consequences, society's opinion, likelihood of effect, time to consequences, relatedness, and reach of result—might move adult sexting from a minor ethical violation to a serious ethical violation and then finally on to a very serious ethical violation?
3. Consider the whole notion of power being tied to sexting, flirting, and cheating. From a psychological point of view why might this be true? Do some research into Tiger Woods's troubles with extra-marital affairs. Could his cheating be tied to his position of power? Is "power" and the temptations that go with it an excuse for such behavior?
4. What role can and should employers play in limiting (perhaps eliminating) sexting in the workplace? What about employee-to-employee sexting? What about employee-to-customer sexting? Regarding the latter, what sort of legal liability does an organization have if an employee sends an unwanted and unwelcome sext to another employee or to a customer?
5. These are purely for you to answer to yourself. Have you ever participated in sexting? Have you received a sext? Has learning more about ethics and the nonprivacy of technology-enabled communications reshaped your thinking about participating in questionable activities like sexting?

CLOSING CASE STUDY TWO

Sony Reels from Multiple Hacker Attacks

This may very well be a story with which you are personally familiar. Between April 17, 2011, and April 19, 2011, the Sony PlayStation Network (PSN) was hacked. Personally identifiable information (PII) on some 77 million users was compromised. On April 20, Sony announced that it was taking down the PSN site, preventing owners of PlayStation 3 and PlayStation Portable consoles from participating in any online activities on the PSN network. What followed is a story you cannot make up.

The outage lasted for approximately 23 days, until May 15, when Sony began bringing some gaming services back online on a country-by-country basis starting with North America. During the 23-day outage, Sony postured, hoping to downplay the significance of the breach. At first, Sony understated the number of user records compromised. Periodically, Sony stated that it had the situation under control, that it had developed a clear and concise strategy for bringing services back online, and that things would be up and running within a few days.

In the end, Sony admitted that its PlayStation Network had been the target of one of the largest data breaches ever. It offered free game time for returning customers and other perks. It even announced that it was paying for $1 million in identity theft insurance for each of its compromised users. The insurance was to last for 12 months and include Internet surveillance and complete identity repair in the event of identity theft and fraudulent use. Sony estimated that the cost of the PSN outage would be $177 million.

Lawsuits quickly followed. On April 27, 2011, Kristopher Johns filed a class-action lawsuit on behalf of all PlayStation users. His lawsuit alleged many things including: (1) Sony failed to encrypt data, (2) Sony failed to provide prompt and adequate warnings of a security breach to users, and (3) Sony created unreasonable delays in bringing PSN services back online. A similar lawsuit was filed in Canada by Natasha Maksimovic. She sought $1 billion (Canadian dollars) in damages which included free credit monitoring and identity theft insurance. The lawsuit con-

tained the following quote: "If you can't trust a huge multinational corporation like Sony to protect your private information, who can you trust? It appears to me that Sony focuses more on protecting its games than its PlayStation users."

But Sony's hacker troubles didn't end there. On May 3, 2011, in the middle of attempting to bring its PSN services back online, Sony Online Entertainment was hacked. With this breach, another 24.6 million user records were compromised. Sony stated that it believed the two hacks were related. Then, on June 2, 2011, the SonyPictures.com Web site was hacked, further compromising unencrypted password and personally identifiable information.[42, 43, 44, 45, 46, 47]

Questions

1. Do some research on the Sony PSN debacle. What are the new cost estimates for the incident? How many customers have left Sony because of the incident? Have there been any reports of fraudulent use of identities obtained from the hack? Has Sony's PlayStation Network been hacked again?

2. Gaming and virtual services on the Internet, like Sony's PSN, World of Warcraft, and Second Life, boast millions of users. For each user, the service must store credit card information and personally identifiable information. What must these organizations do to protect the private information of their customers? Is it even reasonable to assume that any organization can have protection measures in place to stop the world's best hackers?

3. If an extremely intelligent hacker is caught by a law enforcement agency, should that hacker be prosecuted and sent to jail? Is there perhaps a way that the hacker might be "turned" for the good of the digital world? What would that be?

4. Every survey taken of businesses regarding data breaches has found that many businesses are reluctant to publicly announce a data breach. Further, most businesses will

downplay the significance of the breach. Why do organizations behave like this? What is there to gain by not operating in a transparent fashion? Is this an ethical issue, a legal issue, or both?

5. What's your personal identity theft story? Has someone used your credit card fraudulently? How many phishing e-mails have you received in the last year? How often do you check your credit report?

■ KEY TERMS AND CONCEPTS

Adult sexting, 250
Adware, 240
Anonymous Web browsing
   (AWB), 241
Anti-virus software, 248
Biometrics, 249
Clickstream, 241
Computer virus (virus), 246
Cookie, 238
Copyright, 229
Denial-of-service attack
   (DoS), 247
Encryption, 249

Ethics, 227
Fair Use Doctrine, 229
Firewall, 248
Friendly fraud, 232
Hacker, 246
Hardware key logger, 237
Identity theft, 232
Intellectual property, 229
Key logger software (key trapper
   software), 231
Pharming, 235
Phishing (carding or brand
   spoofing), 234

Pirated software, 230
Privacy, 231
Public key encryption
   (PKE), 249
Sexting, 250
Spam, 239
Spear phishing, 235
Spyware (sneakware or
   stealthware), 240
Trojan horse software, 240
Web log, 241
Whaling, 235
Worm, 246

■ SHORT-ANSWER QUESTIONS

1. What are ethics, and how do ethics apply to business?
2. What situation would qualify as an exception to the copyright law?
3. What is privacy?
4. What is pirated software?

5. What is identity theft?
6. What does a key logger do?
7. What is spyware?
8. What is a denial-of-service attack?
9. What is public key encryption?

■ ASSIGNMENTS AND EXERCISES

1. **HELPING A FRIEND** Suppose you fully intend to spend the evening working on an Excel assignment that's due the next day. Then a friend calls. Your friend is stranded miles from home and desperately needs your help. It will take most of the evening to pick up your friend, bring him home, and return to your studying. Not only that, but you're very tired when you get home and just fall into bed. The next day your friend, who completed his assignment earlier, suggests you just make a copy, put your own name on the cover, and hand it in as your own work. Should you do it? Isn't it only fair that since you helped your friend, the friend should do something about making sure you don't lose points because of your generosity? What if your friend promises not to hand in his or her own work so that you can't be accused of copying? Your friend wrote the assignment and gave it to you, so there's no question of copyright infringement.

2. **FIND OUT WHAT HAPPENED** In December 2001, British Telecom (BT) filed a lawsuit against Prodigy in New York federal court, claiming it owns the hyperlinking process. If BT wins this lawsuit then the company will be able to collect licensing revenue from the 100 billion or so links on the Web. BT has a patent that it says amounts to ownership of the hyperlinking process. Prodigy (and everyone else in the world) stores Web pages with a displayed part, which the browser shows, and a hidden part that the viewer doesn't see, and which contains hidden information including the addresses that are used by the displayed portion. This, BT said, is the essence of its U.S. patent No. 4873662. In reference to this case, answer the following questions:
   A. Has a ruling been handed down on this matter yet? If so, what was the result?
   B. If any kind of hyperlinking is, in fact, the essence of the patent held by BT, what about library card catalogs; are they infringements, too? Why or why not? What else could be?

3. **INVESTIGATE MONITORING SYSTEMS** The text listed several monitoring systems, other systems that defeat them, and an e-mail encryption program. Find two more of the following:
   A. Programs that monitor keyboard activity
   B. Programs that find keyboard monitoring programs
   C. E-mail encryption programs

4. **CHECK OUT THE COMPUTER ETHICS INSTITUTE'S ADVICE** The Computer Ethics Institute's Web site at www.cspr.org/program/ethics.htm offers the "Ten Commandments of Computer Ethics" to guide you in ethical computer use. The first two are
   - *Thou shalt not use a computer to harm other people.* This one is the bedrock for all the others.
   - *Thou shalt not interfere with other people's computer work.* This one stems from the first and includes small sins like sending frivolous e-mail and crimes like spreading viruses and electronic stalking.

   Look up the other eight and give at least two examples of acts that would be in violation of these guidelines.

■ DISCUSSION QUESTIONS

1. When selling antiques, you can usually obtain a higher price for those that have a *provenance,* which is information detailing the origin and history of the object. For example, property owned by Jacqueline Kennedy Onassis and Princess Diana sold for much more than face value. What kinds of products have value over and above a comparable product because of such information? What kind of information makes products valuable? Consider both tangible (resale value) and intangible value (sentimental appeal).

2. Personal checks that you use to buy merchandise have a standard format. Checks have very few different sizes, and almost no variation in format. Consider what would happen if everyone could create his or her own size, shape, and layout of personal check. What would the costs and benefits be to business and the consumer in terms of buying checks, exchanging them for merchandise, and bank check processing?

3. Consider society as a business that takes steps to protect itself from the harm of illegal acts. Discuss the mechanisms and costs that are involved. Examine ways in which our society would be different if no one ever broke a law. Are there ever benefits to our society when people break the law, for example, when they claim that the law itself is unethical or unjust?

4. Can you access all the IT systems at your college or university? What about payroll or grade information on yourself or others? What kinds of controls has your college or university implemented to prevent the misuse of information?

5. You know that you generally can't use a PC to access the information stored on a Macintosh-formatted storage medium. What other instances of difficulty in accessing information have you experienced personally or heard of? For example, have you used different versions of MS PowerPoint or MS Access that won't work on all the PCs that you have access to?

6. Have you, or someone you know, experienced computer problems caused by a virus? What did the virus do? Where do you think you got it? How did you fix the problem? What was the cost to you in time, trouble, and stress?

7. What laws do you think the United States should pass to protect personal information? Or none? Why? Should some personal information be more protected than other information? Why or why not?

8. The issue of pirated software is one that the software industry fights on a daily basis. The major centers of software piracy are in places like Russia and China where salaries and disposable income are comparatively low. Given that people in developing and economically depressed countries will fall behind the industrialized world technologically if they can't afford access to new generations of software, is it reasonable to blame someone for using pirated software when it costs two months' salary to buy a legal copy of MS Office? If you answered no, specify at what income level it's okay to make or buy illegal copies of software. What approach could software companies use to combat the problem apart from punitive measures, like pressuring the government to impose sanctions on transgressors?

CHAPTER PROJECTS

GROUP PROJECTS

- Assessing the Value of Outsourcing Information Technology: Creating Forecasts (p. 294)
- Making the Case with Presentation Software: Information Technology Ethics (p. 296)
- Assessing a Wireless Future: Emerging Trends and Technology (p. 300)
- Evaluating the Next Generation: Dot-Com ASPs (p. 301)
- Evaluating the Security of Information: Wireless Network Vulnerability (p. 308)

E-COMMERCE PROJECTS

- Ethical Computing Guidelines (p. 314)
- Exploring Google Earth (p. 314)
- Privacy Laws and Legislation (p. 317)
- Protecting Your Computer (p. 317)
- Searching for Shareware and Freeware (p. 320)

CHAPTER NINE OUTLINE

STUDENT LEARNING OUTCOMES

1. Describe the emerging trends and technologies that will have an impact on the changing Internet.

2. Define the various types of technologies that are emerging as we move toward physiological interaction with technology.

3. Describe the emerging trends of Near Field Communication, Bluetooth, WiFi, smartphones, and RFID, as they relate to the wireless environment.

4. Define and describe emerging technologies that, while purely technology, can and will impact the future.

PERSPECTIVES

WEB SUPPORT

www.mhhe.com/haag

- Searching job databases
- Interviewing and negotiating tips
- Financial aid resources
- Searching for MBA programs
- Free and rentable storage space
- Global statistics and resources

SUPPORTING MODULES

XLM/I Building an E-Portfolio
Extended Learning Module I provides you with hands-on instructions for the most appropriate way to build an e-portfolio, an electronic resume that you publish on the Web in the hope of attracting potential employers. Important issues also cover aspects of building a strong objective statement and using strong action verbs to describe yourself and your accomplishments.

XLM/K Careers in Business
Extended Learning Module K provides an overview of job titles and descriptions in the fields of accounting, finance, hospitality and tourism management, information technology, management, marketing, productions and operations management, and real estate and construction management including what IT skills you should acquire to be successful in each field.

CHAPTER NINE

Emerging Trends and Technologies
Business, People, and Technology Tomorrow

OUTRAGEOUS INDUSTRY TRANSFORMATION: THERE IS NO LONGER ONE IN EVERY TOWN

It's one of the oldest institutions in this country. Established in 1775, Ben Franklin became its first leader. What organization are we talking about? Of course, the United States Post Office. (Ben Franklin's official appointment was as Postmaster General.) The U.S. Post Office has been an integral part of this country since its inception.

But that certainly seems to be changing. And it makes sense. The likes of UPS and FedEx have taken away a lot of business, forcing the Post Office to move toward innovative mailing programs such flat-rate shipping, home pickup of packages using online-produced postage, and the like.

But the greater impact has been felt from a technology, and that technology is e-mail. In 2009, the Post Office delivered 84 billion pieces of first-class mail. That number is expected to decline by 34 percent to 53 billion in 2020. According to the Boston Consulting Group, the Post Office delivered 177 billion pieces of all types of mail in 2009. Best-case scenario puts that number at 150 billion pieces in 2020, a 15 percent decline. Worst-case scenario, and what a lot of people believe is more realistic, puts that number at 118 billion pieces in 2020, a 34 percent decline.

In mid-2011 the Post Office operated an estimated 31,000 individual post offices in the country. It published a list of some 3,700 post offices it was considering closing because of sharp declines in revenue associated with dwindling mail volume. According to Postmaster General Patrick Donahoe, most under review were generating less than $27,500 in revenue and had only enough customers and mail volume to keep them open two hours a day.

This transformation—that of the Post office losing out to electronic communications—follows many of the transformations we've discussed in this book. Music and books being produced more digitally than in physical form are a couple of the examples we have noted. Indeed, as we move further into the digital age, you can expect more businesses and industries to suffer from our using less paper, fewer CDs, DVDs, etc.[1,2]

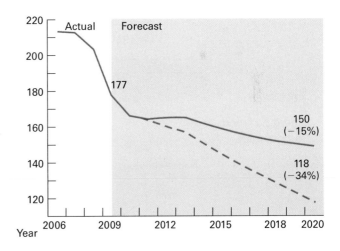

Questions

1. When was the list time you bought postage stamps?

2. What is the cost of a first-class postage stamp? (If you don't know, answer this question with "I don't know.")

3. Should we subsidize postal operations with government funding? Why or why not?

Introduction

Technology is changing every day. But even more important than simply staying up with the changes in technology, you need to think about how those changes will affect your life. It's fun to read and learn about "leading- and bleeding-edge" technologies. It is something we encourage you to do. The consequences of those technology changes, however, may have an impact on all our lives more far reaching than you can imagine.

In this final chapter, we will take a look at several leading- and bleeding-edge technologies. These new technologies can and will impact your personal and business life. (Many of them probably already are.) Technology for the sake of technology (though fun) is never necessarily a good thing, and can even be counterproductive. Using technology appropriately to enhance your personal life and to move your organization toward its strategic initiatives, on the other hand, is always a good thing.

This has been both an exciting and a challenging chapter for us to write. The excitement is in the opportunity to talk with you about some emerging technological innovations. The challenge has been to not spotlight the technologies themselves overmuch, so as to help you focus on how those technologies will affect your life.

So, as you read this chapter, have fun but don't get caught up exclusively in the technology advances themselves that are on the horizon. Try to envision how those new technologies will change the things that you do and the way you do them, both from a personal and organizational perspective.

Figure 9.1 presents many of the emerging technologies we'll discuss in this final chapter. At the time we wrote this text, they were, in fact, "emerging." As you read this, however, they may already be an integral part of society and the business world. We close this chapter with 13 predications regarding our future with technology. You should develop your own list of crystal-ball predictions as well.

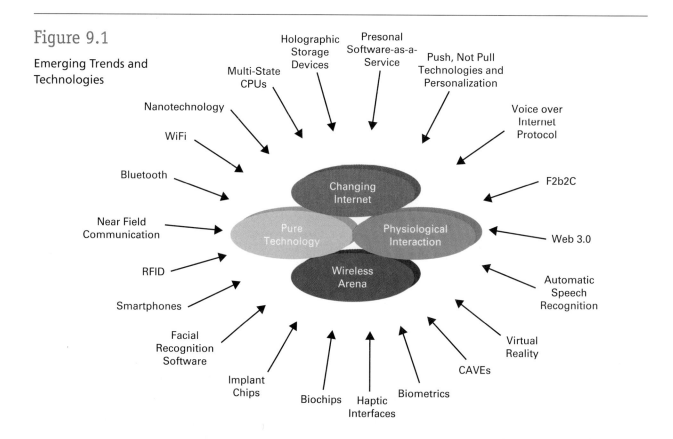

Figure 9.1

Emerging Trends and Technologies

The Changing Internet

Few technologies have grown to widespread use and changed as fast as the Internet. Over the next several years, you will witness many new Internet-based trends and technologies. Among those will be personal software-as-a-service; push (not pull) technologies and personalization; F2b2C (which also enables personalization); Internet telephony (i.e., Voice over Internet Protocol, VoIP); and Web 3.0. All of these trends and technologies are fostering the concept of an e-society.

PERSONAL SOFTWARE-AS-A-SERVICE

In one of the closing case studies in Chapter 7 we discussed personal clouds and the growing movement of cloud providers offering their services not only to businesses but also to individuals. Some of those providers included Amazon and its *Cloud Drive,* Apple and its *iCloud,* and Microsoft and its *SkyDrive.* Those mainly focused on two things: (1) your ability to store information in the cloud, and (2) your ability to do so while working with primarily nontextual information like personal photos and videos.

We certainly expect that to change and may have already changed with the ushering in of ***personal software-as-a-service (personal SaaS)***, a delivery model for personal productivity software such as Microsoft Office in which you pay for personal productivity software on a pay-per-use basis instead of buying the software outright (see Figure 9.2). As more technology choices become available to you (smartphones, tablet PCs, and the like) and your need to be mobile while using them increases, these devices may not have the capacity necessary to store all your personal productivity software needs. For that matter, you may need a given piece of software—photo and video editing software, for instance—perhaps only a couple of times a year. It makes sense then that renting software would be a good alternative for a lot of individuals. That is what the personal SaaS model aims to deliver.

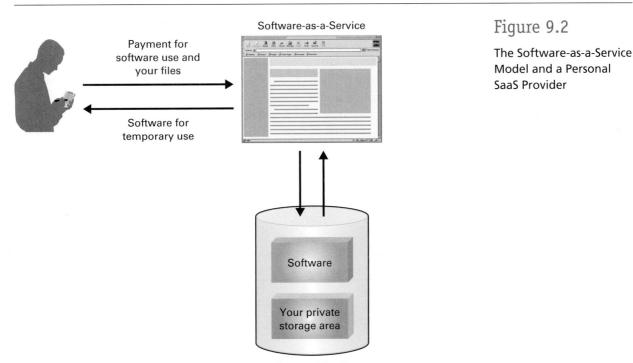

Figure 9.2

The Software-as-a-Service Model and a Personal SaaS Provider

We've discussed the SaaS model throughout this text. Many businesses are using that model to rent CRM, SCM, ERP, and a host of other types of organizationally focused software instead of buying a license. On a personal level, the personal SaaS model recognizes that it will be more cost beneficial for some people to rent personal productivity software than to pay for the license.

Let's focus for a moment on your personal use of a personal SaaS provider (see Figure 9.2). In the future, personal SaaS providers will provide personal productivity software for you to use (for a pay-per-use fee or monthly subscription fee using the SaaS model) and storage so you can store your files on their Web servers as opposed to on your own personal devices.

For example, you might be in an airport and need to build a workbook with your smartphone, which might not have a complete version of Excel. So, you would use your smartphone to connect to the Internet and a personal SaaS provider. With your smartphone, you would use the personal SaaS provider's Excel software to create your workbook and save it on the personal SaaS provider's Web server. When you finally got back to the office, you would use your computer there, connect to the same personal SaaS provider, and retrieve your workbook and save it on your computer.

There are many issues you'll have to consider when determining whether or not to use a personal SaaS provider, with privacy and reliability definitely being important ones. If all your information is on a Web-based server, it will be easier for someone to gain access to it (for the wrong reasons) than if you stored all your information on your home or office computer. When considering reliability, you need to think about what happens if the personal SaaS provider's Web site goes down. How will you perform your work? These are important facets of your personal service level agreement into which you would enter with your personal SaaS provider. In spite of potential drawbacks, we believe personal SaaSs providers and the SaaS model will become a part of your everyday life in the future.

PUSH, NOT PULL, TECHNOLOGIES AND PERSONALIZATION

Future emphasis will be on *push* technologies as we discussed in Chapter 2 when we introduced you to Web 2.0. In a ***push technology*** environment, businesses and organizations come to you via technology with information, services, and product offerings based on your profile. This isn't spam or mass e-mailings.

For example, in some parts of the country you can subscribe to a cell service that pushes information to you in the form of video rental information. Whenever you pass near a video store, your smartphone (which is GPS-enabled) triggers a computer within the video store that evaluates your rental history to see if any new videos have arrived that you might be interested in viewing. In this case, the system generates a personal data warehouse of rental history—including dimensions for the day of the week, the time of the day, and video categories—concerning you and then evaluates information in the smaller cubes (see Figure 9.3). The evaluation seeks to affirm that (1) you usually rent videos on that particular day, (2) you usually rent videos during that time of that day, and (3) there is a distinct video category from which you rent videos during that time of the day. If so, the system then checks to see if there are any movies in that category that you haven't rented and that it hasn't previously contacted you about.

If so, the video store computer will call your smartphone with a message concerning a new release. It will also give you street-by-street directions to the video store and hold the video for you. If the video store doesn't have any new releases that might interest you, you won't receive a phone call.

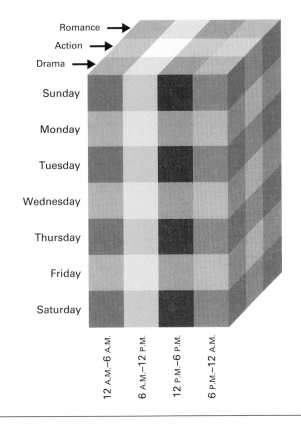

Figure 9.3

Tracking What You Want
and When You Want It
with a Data Warehouse

You might also someday receive a personalized pizza delivery message on your television as you start to watch a ball game. The message might say, "We'll deliver your favorite sausage and mushroom pizza to your doorstep before the game begins. On your remote control, press the ORDER NOW button."

Of course, situations such as these rely on IT's ability to store vast amounts of information about you. Technologies such as databases, data warehouses, and predictive analytics will definitely play an important role in the development of push technologies that do more than just push spam and mass e-mail. In the instance of the pizza delivery message on your television, a local pizza store would have determined that you like sausage and mushroom pizza and that you order it most often while watching a ball game.

F2b2C: A NEW E-COMMERCE BUSINESS MODEL

In the e-commerce world, business models are identified by the players such as B2B (Business-to-Business) and G2C (Government-to-Consumer). We now have the notion of introducing a third player to create an entirely new e-commerce business model. The first of these new business models to surface is *F2b2C (Factory-to-business-to-Consumer),* an e-commerce business model in which a consumer communicates through a business on the Internet and directly provides product specifications to a factory that makes the customized and personalized product to the consumer's specifications and then ships it directly to the consumer.

You should notice in F2b2C that the "F" and "C" are capitalized while the "b" (for business) is not. In this model, the business is simply an Internet intermediary that provides a communication conduit between the factory and the consumer. When this happens, a form of disintermediation occurs. Broadly defined, *disintermediation* is the use of the Internet as a delivery vehicle, whereby intermediate players in a distribution channel can be bypassed. The travel agent industry is a good example of where disintermediation has occurred. Now, you can connect directly to an airline and purchase tickets, often receiving bonus mileage if you do. The Internet has disintermediated travel agents, since you need them less.

Think about connecting to a site on the Internet and custom-ordering something like a pair of pants. You would specify your exact size, inseam, waist, hip, and thigh measurements, and so on, and other information such as color, style of pockets, how many belt loops (if any) . . . the list could grow quite long. The Web site would immediately pass along your information to a factory that would create a customized and personalized pair of pants for you and ship them to your door. Is this possible? Well, it already exists to some extent. Later in the chapter, you'll read about how companies are using biometrics to create custom-fitting clothing and shoes.

VOICE OVER INTERNET PROTOCOL (VOIP)

VoIP, or *Voice over Internet Protocol,* allows you to send voice communications over the Internet and avoid the toll charges that you would normally receive from your long distance carrier. Simply put, VoIP allows you to use your Internet connection (which must be broadband such as DSL or cable) to make phone calls. This is different from today's DSL model which splits your phone line so that you can make phone calls and surf the Web at the same time. In today's model, your telephone calls are still routed through your traditional telephone service provider to whom you must pay charges for long distance phone calls. Using VoIP, your telephone calls are routed through a VoIP provider (which may be your ISP) and you pay only a flat monthly fee—usually in the neighborhood of $20 to $25 per month—to make unlimited long distance calls.

For home use, you can already use the VoIP services offered by the likes of Vonage, Lingo, Quintum, and AT&T. You can keep your existing phone number and you do have access to a number of value-added features such as call-waiting, caller ID, and so on. Most VoIP providers offer you free unlimited long distance calling only within your country; international long distance calls may still incur an additional fee.

This certainly speaks to the growing importance of the Internet. Most of you probably cannot imagine life without the Internet already. That will be even more true once the Internet becomes the technological infrastructure that also supports all your phone calls. You can read more about VoIP in *Extended Learning Module E.*

WEB 3.0 (IS WEB 2.0 ALREADY OLD?)

As discussed in *Extended Learning Module B (The World Wide Web and the Internet),* the *Web 2.0* is the so-called second generation of the Web and focuses on online collaboration, users as both creators and modifiers of content, dynamic and customized information feeds, and many other engaging Web-based services. To be sure, "2.0" has caught on as a hot buzz term, for example, the Family 2.0 (family members living on and communicating through the Internet), Company 2.0 (the complete Web-enabled company), and TV 2.0 (TV-type broadcast shows delivered via the Web).

Many people believe we are poised for another evolution of the Web called Web 3.0. In its most extreme vision, *Web 3.0* is the third generation of the Web focused on semantics. In this case, *semantics* refers to ability of Web technologies to interpret and understand human-generated content. On a purely semantic Web, for example, search engines would be able to better return more usable search results based on the Word document that you have open at the time. So, if you were writing a term paper on ancient life in

DRIVING GIRL SCOUT COOKIE SALES WITH SMARTPHONES

It started out in 1917 in Muskogee, Oklahoma, with a group of Girl Scouts baking cookies in their homes and selling them around town as a fundraiser. The sale of the popular Girl Scout cookies went commercial and nationwide in 1935. Today, the Girl Scouts generate about $714 million in revenue annually from the sale of cookies.

But hauling around a wagon-load of Thin Mints and Samoas or setting up a stand at the local grocery store wasn't the best way to ensure the most sales. Many people simply didn't have cash-in-hand to make a purchase. According to Marianne Love, Director of Business Services for the Girl Scouts of Northeast Ohio, "Normally, I think a lot of customers would love to buy cookies, but they have to walk by the booth because they're not carrying cash. I know I never carry cash when I'm out shopping."

So, Girl Scouts have begun testing taking credits using GoPayment, a free credit-card reader that clips onto smartphones. Intuit, the maker of the GoPayment device and processor of the credit card transactions, charges the Girl Scouts 1.7 percent of the transaction plus 15 cents per transaction. According to Todd Ablowitz, President of Double Diamond Group, a consulting company that focuses on the mobile payments industry, "Everyone from delivery drivers to Girl Scouts to babysitters are swiping cards on their phones to take a payment. I mean, this barely existed before 2010. The numbers are staggering."

And, indeed, the numbers are staggering for the mobile payments industry. But the Girl Scouts are seeing dramatic changes as well. While testing the idea in Ohio, one Girl Scout troop reported a 20 percent increase in sales in the same location over what they were able to do the previous year. According to Marianne, "And we had a customer earlier today say he was taking out cash to buy two boxes, and he ended up buying seven because he was able to use his credit card."[3]

Greece and searched for "daily work habits in Greece," your search engine would only return results related to life in ancient Greece and not life in modern-day Greece.

In this case, the Web will become much more personable by using technologies such as intelligent agents (from Chapter 4). For instance, based on your personal attributes such as your age, marital status, and income level (which will be knowledge embedded into your computer system), the Web may bring to you recommendations regarding the best deals for car insurance, suitable schools for continuing your education, and the like. It will do so without your ever having to ask for such information.

Some people believe Web 3.0 may never get to this point. Nonetheless, they do see technology advances in Web 3.0 for things like:

- TV-quality video
- 3D simulations
- Augmented reality

Augmented reality is definitely one of those technologies already finding its way into your life. *Augmented reality* is the viewing of the physical world with computer-generated layers of information added to it. For example, when you're watching a football game on TV, you've probably noticed it is very common now for a computer to generate lines across the field showing the first-down yardage. You can also take photos of a street with your smartphone and a computer utility will overlay onto the image something like menu options of restaurants in the photo.

Whatever the case, expect the Web in the coming years to get better in many respects. You'll receive more personalized information through intelligent push technologies. Non-2-dimensional technologies like 3D simulations and augmented reality will enhance your viewing of and interacting with information.

E-SOCIETY

In so many ways we have come to live in an e-society. Intuitively you know this. You daily confront our e-society. You grasp that it is all about living life in, on, and through technology, with the Internet being at the epicenter. People are finding life-long soul mates on Match.com and numerous other dating-related sites; others (especially young people) are flocking to, spending a great deal of time on, and developing friendships on sites such as Facebook and YouTube; we receive breaking world news via YouTube and Twitter; people are building very successful home-based e-businesses on eBay; children are receiving tutoring via the Web.

Just consider one seemingly simple example that has brought us closer to becoming an e-society, YouTube. In July 2011, YouTube reported the following statistics:[4]

- More than 2 billion views per day.
- 35 hours of video uploaded every minute.
- More video uploaded to YouTube in 60 days than the three major U.S. networks created in 60 years.
- YouTube mobile gets over 320 million views a day (up 3x year/year), representing 10 percent of all daily views.
- The YouTube player is embedded across tens of millions of Web sites.

If you are a younger person you take all this mostly for granted perhaps. You shouldn't. You will see many more changes, and you need to make them work for you. We live in a digital world. Technology is enabling business and pervading our personal lives so much so that we cannot imagine a world without technology. The new technology-based dimensions of our world are creating an e-society.

Physiological Interaction

LEARNING OUTCOME 2

Right now, your primary interfaces to your computer are physical. They include a keyboard, mouse, monitor, and printer (that is, your input and output devices). These are physical devices, not physiological. *Physiological* interfaces capture and utilize your body characteristics, such as your breath, your voice, your height and weight, and even the iris in your eye. Physiological innovations include automatic speech recognition, virtual reality, cave automatic virtual environments, haptic interfaces, and biometrics, along with many others.

AUTOMATIC SPEECH RECOGNITION

An *automatic speech recognition (ASR)* system not only captures spoken words but also distinguishes word groupings to form sentences. To perform this, an ASR system follows three steps.

1. *Feature analysis*—The system captures your words as you speak into a microphone, eliminates any background noise, and converts the digital signals of your speech into phonemes (syllables).
2. *Pattern classification*—The system matches your spoken phonemes to a phoneme sequence stored in an acoustic model database. For example, if your phoneme was "dü," the system would match it to the words do and due.
3. *Language processing*—The system attempts to make sense of what you're saying by comparing the word phonemes generated in step 2 with a language model database. For example, if you were asking a question and started with the phoneme "dü," the system would determine that the appropriate word is do and not due.

ASR is certainly now taking its place in computing environments. The important point is that ASR allows you to speak in a normal voice; thus it supports physiological interaction.

VIRTUAL REALITY

On the immediate horizon (and in some instances here today) is a new technology that will virtually place you in any experience you desire. That technology is *virtual reality,* a three-dimensional computer simulation in which you actively and physically participate. In a virtual reality system, you make use of special input and output devices that capture your physiological movements and send physiological responses back to you. These devices include:

- *Glove*—An input device that captures and records the shape and movement of your hand and fingers and the strength of your hand and finger movements.
- *Headset (head-mounted display)*—A combined input and output device that (1) captures and records the movement of your head and (2) contains a screen that covers your entire field of vision and displays various views of an environment based on your movements.
- *Walker*—An input device that captures and records the movement of your feet as you walk or turn in different directions.

APPLICATIONS OF VIRTUAL REALITY   Virtual reality applications are popping up everywhere, sometimes in odd places. The most common applications are found in the entertainment industry. There are a number of virtual reality games on the market, including downhill Olympic skiing, race-car driving, golf, air combat, and marksmanship. Other applications include

- Matsushita Electric Works—You design your kitchen in virtual reality and then choose the appliances you want and even request color changes.
- Volvo—For demonstrating the safety features of its cars.
- Airlines—To train pilots how to handle adverse weather conditions.
- Motorola—To train assembly-line workers in the steps of manufacturing a new product.[5]
- Health care—To train doctors how to perform surgery using virtual cadavers.[6]

Let's consider the potential ramifications of virtual reality and how you might someday interact with your computer. New virtual reality systems include aroma-producing devices and devices that secrete fluid through a mouthpiece that you have in your mouth. So, you could virtually experience a Hawaiian luau. The aroma-producing device would generate various smells and the mouthpiece would secrete a fluid that tastes like pineapple or roasted pig. If you were using virtual reality to surf big waves, the mouthpiece would secrete a fluid that tastes like salt water.

CAVE AUTOMATIC VIRTUAL ENVIRONMENTS

A *CAVE (cave automatic virtual environment)* is a special 3-D virtual reality room that can display images of other people and objects located in other CAVEs all over the world. CAVEs are *holographic devices,* that create, capture, and/or display images in true three-dimensional form. If you watch any of the *Star Trek* movies, you'll see an example of a holographic device called the holodeck.

Figure 9.4

CAVEs (Cave Automatic
Virtual Environments)

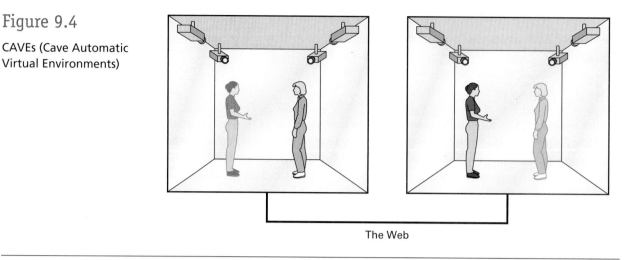

The Web

In working form, you would enter a CAVE room. At the same time, someone else would enter another CAVE room in another location (see Figure 9.4). Numerous digital video cameras would capture the likenesses of both participants and re-create and send those images to the other CAVEs. Then, you and the other person could see and carry on a normal conversation with each other, and you would feel as if that other person were in the same room with you.

Current CAVE research is also working on the challenges of having other physical objects in the room. For example, if you sat on a couch in your CAVE, the couch would capture the indentation you made in it and pass it to the couch in the other CAVE. That couch would respond by constricting a mesh of rubber inside it so that your indentation would also appear there. And what about playing catch? Which person would have the virtual ball and which person would have the real ball? The answer is that both would have a virtual ball. When throwing it, the CAVE would capture your arm movement to determine the speed, arc, and direction of the ball. That information would be transmitted to the other CAVE, and it would use that information to make the virtual ball fly through the air accordingly.

Unlike virtual reality, in some CAVEs you don't need any special gear. Let your imagination run wild and think about the potential applications of CAVEs. An unhappy customer could call a business to complain. Within seconds, a customer service representative would not answer the phone but rather appear in the room with the unhappy customer. That would be an example of great customer service. Your teacher might never attend your class. Instead the teacher would enter a CAVE and have his or her image broadcast into the classroom. You might not really be in class either but rather a holographic likeness of you. Are CAVEs a realistic possibility? The answer is definitely yes. We believe that CAVEs are the successor to virtual reality. So, virtual reality may not be a long-term technological innovation but rather a stepping-stone to the more advanced CAVE. Whatever the case, CAVEs will not only significantly alter how you interact with your computer (can you imagine the thrill of video games in a CAVE?), they will even more significantly alter how you interact with other people. With CAVE technologies, you can visit your friends and relatives on a daily basis no matter where they live. You may even have television shows and movies piped into your home CAVE.

HAPTIC INTERFACES

A *haptic interface* uses technology to add the sense of touch to an environment that previously only had visual and textual elements. Applications of virtual reality we discussed previously that incorporate the use of gloves and walkers use implementations of haptic interfaces.

Many arcade games include haptic interfaces. For example, when you get on a stationary jet ski and control its movement (on screen) by adjusting your weight side-to-side and leaning backward and forward, you are interfacing with the arcade game via a haptic interface. Many joysticks and game controllers provide feedback to the user through vibrations, which is another form of a haptic interface.

Interacting with an arcade game via a haptic interface is a "fun" application of the technology and one that is making companies a lot of money. But consider this: With a haptic interface, sight-challenged people can feel and read text with their fingers while interacting with a computer. The fact is anyone can use technology to make money. Perhaps the most exciting thing about new technologies is the potential benefits for people. Can you envision ways to use technology to help people less fortunate than yourself?

BIOMETRICS

Biometrics is the use of physiological characteristics—such as your fingerprint, the blood vessels in the iris of your eye, the sound of your voice, or perhaps even your breath—to provide identification. That's the strict and narrow definition, but biometrics is beginning to encompass more than just identification. Consider these real-world applications in place today (see Figure 9.5):

- *Custom shoes*—Several shoe stores, especially those that offer fine Italian leather shoes, no longer carry any inventory. When you select a shoe style you like, you place your bare feet into a box that scans the shape of your feet. That information is then used to make a custom pair of shoes for you. It works extremely well if your feet are slightly different from each other in size or shape (as is the case with most people). To see this, visit www.digitoe.com.
- *Custom wedding gowns*—Following the custom-fit shoe idea, many bridal boutiques now do the same thing for wedding dresses. Once the bride chooses the style she likes, she steps into a small room that scans her entire body. That information is used to create a wedding dress that fits perfectly. Both custom shoes and custom wedding dresses are examples of the future implementation of F2b2C.

Figure 9.5

Custom-Fit Clothes through Biometrics

- *Custom bathrobes*—Some high-end spa resorts now actually have patrons walk through a body-scanning device upon check-in. The scanning device measures the patron's body characteristics and then sends that information to a sewing and fabricating facility that automatically creates a custom-fit bathrobe.

BIOMETRIC SECURITY   The best form of security for personal identification encompasses three aspects:

1. What you know
2. What you have
3. Who you are

The first—*what you know*—is something like a password, something that everyone can create and has. The second—*what you have*—is something like a card such as an ATM card you use at an ATM (in conjunction with your password, what you know). Unfortunately, most personal identification security systems stop there. That is, they do not include *who you are*, which is some form of a biometric.

It's no wonder crimes like identity theft are spiraling out of control. Without much effort, a thief can steal your password (often through social engineering) and steal what you have. For the latter, the thief doesn't actually have to steal your physical card; he or she simply has to copy the information on it. However, stealing a biometric—such as your fingerprint or iris scan—is much more difficult.

Many banks are currently converting ATMs to the use of biometrics, specifically an iris scan, as the third level of personal identification security. When you open an account and request ATM use, the bank will issue you an ATM card (you pick the password). The bank will also scan your iris and create a unique 512-byte representation of the scan. To use an ATM, you must insert your card, type in your password, and allow the machine to scan your iris. The ATM uses all three forms of identification to match you to your account. You can then perform whatever transaction you wish.

Some private schools for young children now require parents and guardians to submit to iris scans. Once the scan is captured and the person is verified as a parent or guardian, the information is entered into a security database. Then, when the parent or guardian comes to the school to pick up a child, his or her iris scan is compared to the one stored in the database. Parents and guardians cannot, under any circumstances, take a child from the school without first going through verification via an iris scan.

INTEGRATING BIOMETRIC PROCESSING AND TRANSACTION PROCESSING
Once society accepts the use of biometrics for security and identification purposes, organizations of all types will be able to add another dimension of business intelligence to their data warehouses—that dimension will capture and record changes in physiological characteristics (see Figure 9.6).

Figure 9.6

Integrating Biometric and Transaction Processing to Create Business Intelligence

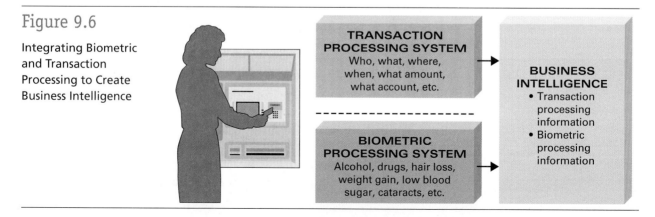

THE GLASSES-FREE 3D SMARTPHONE

Two-dimensional viewing was a long-standing standard for screens—in the movie theater, on your home TV, for your tablet PC and smartphone. Things changed shortly after the turn of the century. Movie theaters and producers rolled out 3D movies. Of course, these required special glasses but consumers didn't care. Manufacturers of home TVs quickly followed, requiring the use of the same sort of special glasses. Personal technology manufacturers, however, for devices like PCs and smartphones didn't follow, because it didn't make sense for a user to continually have to put on special glasses to view limited 3D content and then take them off for traditional 2D content.

Then, things changed again. TV manufacturers learned how to produce and deliver 3D television programming without the need of special 3D glasses. And smartphone providers followed shortly thereafter. Sprint was one of the first to do so with its HTC EVO 3D model. Not only did that model deliver glasses-free 3D content, it also enabled users to capture 3D content up to the then-standard 720p high definition.

No doubt, this has probably changed again since the time we wrote this Industry Perspective. Glasses-free 3D smartphones were just being rolled out with no known applications. Surely the real estate market has latched onto this technology so that potential home buyers can view a home in 3D on their phones. Perhaps sports games can now be viewed in 3D on a smartphone. Do a little research. What applications can you find using glasses-free 3D viewing on a smartphone?[7]

Consider, as a hypothetical example, a woman using an ATM—equipped with iris scanning capabilities—to withdraw cash. Current research suggests that it might be possible to use an iris scan to determine not only that a woman is pregnant but also the sex of the unborn child. (That is a very true statement.) When the woman has her iris scanned, the bank might be able to tell that she is pregnant and expecting a boy. When the woman receives her cash and receipt, the receipt would have a coupon printed on the back for 10 percent off any purchase at Babies "Я" Us. Furthermore, the ATM would generate another receipt that says "buy blue."

The key here is for you to consider that transaction processing systems (TPSs) of the future will be integrated with biometric processing systems (BPSs). The TPS will capture and process the "events" of the transaction—when, by whom, where, and so on. The BPS will capture and process the physiological characteristics of the person performing the transaction. Those physiological characteristics may include the presence of alcohol or illegal drugs, hair loss, weight gain, low blood sugar, vitamin deficiencies, cataracts, and yes—even pregnancy.

When businesses start to gather this type of intelligence, you can leave it to your imagination to envision what will happen. For example, because of the noted pregnancy in our previous example of the woman using an ATM, the bank might offer financing for a mini-van, evaluate the size of the family's home and perhaps offer special financing for a second mortgage so another room can be added, or establish a tuition account for the child and place $25 in it. These possibilities will further intensify competition in almost all industries.

OTHER BIOMETRICS AND BIOMETRIC DEVICES Biometrics is a "hot topic" in research circles right now. Although we haven't the space to discuss them all, you might want to watch for these:

- *Biochip*—a technology chip that can perform a variety of physiological functions when inserted into the human body. Biochips have been proven in some cases to block pain for people who suffer severe spinal injuries, help paralyzed people regain some portion of their motor skills, and help partially blind people see better.

- *Implant chip*—a technology-enabled microchip implanted into the human body that stores important information about you (such as your identification and medical history) and that may be GPS-enabled to offer a method of tracking.
- *Facial recognition software*—software that provides identification by evaluating facial characteristics.

Whatever becomes a reality in the field of biometrics promises to forever change your life and how you interact with technology.

The Wireless Arena

LEARNING OUTCOME 3

Throughout this text, we've discussed the technologies that make wireless communications possible and applications of wireless technologies in which companies have gained a significant competitive advantage. We've discussed such wireless technologies as Bluetooth, WiFi, and Near Field Communication (NFC) all of which were designed to activate wireless communication via technology devices such as smartphone, printers, network hubs, and of course computers.

- *Bluetooth* is a standard for transmitting information in the form of short-range radio waves over distances of up to 30 feet.
- *WiFi (wireless fidelity)* is a standard for transmitting information in the form of radio waves over distances up to about several miles.
- *Near Field Communication (NFC)* is a wireless transmission technology developed primarily for mobile phones to support mobile commerce (m-commere) and other phone activities.

Bluetooth has become very popular for the wireless headsets (actually more like ear pieces) for smartphones. You may own one of these for your smartphone, and you've undoubtedly seen people using them. WiFi is usually the type of wireless communication used in a network environment. Verizon, for example, offers the BroadbandAccess PC Card, which you can use to wirelessly connect your computer or laptop to Verizon's wireless broadband network. Many businesses have private, firewalled wireless networks that use WiFi for their employees. NFC is a widely adopted standard for wirelessly processing credit card transactions.

Let's now turn our attention to (1) smartphones and (2) RFID (radio frequency identification). Smartphones are a significant "disruptive technology" now and will be more so in the future. RFID, while still emerging as a technology, will definitely be around for many years and dramatically change your personal life and the way the business world works.

THE NEXT GENERATION OF SMARTPHONE TECHNOLOGY

For most people, a smartphone is a necessary part of life. Even today's most basic smartphones support phone calls (that's obvious) and also real-time text messaging, photos (taking, sending, and receiving), games, and many other features. Tomorrow's smartphones may very well become the only technology you need.

Among the many innovations you'll see in smartphones over the next couple of years will be storage (in the form of a hard disk), processor capability, music enhancements, and video support. Already, new smartphones are being demonstrated that have 2 gigabytes of storage and processor speeds up to 500 Mhz. As these capacities and speeds increase, you may be able to wirelessly connect a keyboard, monitor, mouse, and printer to your smartphone. Your smartphone will essentially become your notebook computer.

Tomorrow's smartphones may spell the end for dedicated MP3 players like Apple's iPod. With enough battery life and storage capacity, many people will opt to use their smartphones for music and eliminate the other piece of equipment they have to carry around to listen to music. Video on demand will also become a reality through your smartphone. Apple's iPhone, for example, combines three technologies: (1) smartphone, (2) iPod, and (3) wireless Internet communication.

But there is a downside. smartphones are the next great and uncharted space for hackers and viruses. The even worse news is that the development of antivirus smartphone software is very much in its infancy, far behind the capabilities of the people wanting to hack into your smartphone and unleash deadly smartphone viruses. Think about your ISP. It has antivirus software (and many more types of "anti" software such as spam blocker software and anti-spyware software) on its servers to stop a lot of malware from making it to your computer via e-mail. But that doesn't stop all malware from getting to you. You still need all types of "anti" software loaded onto and running on your computer at all times.

When was the last time your smartphone service provider contacted you about new types of "anti" software you can download onto your smartphone for added protection? That has probably never happened, and it should raise a red flag for you. Do you download ring tones from the Internet? If so, your smartphone is susceptible to getting a virus. Some smartphone viruses, created in a laboratory environment, can make international calls and run your battery dead and your bill into the thousands of dollars.

As your smartphone becomes increasingly more important to you—and it will—and becomes increasingly more supportive of complex computer tasks, your challenge will continue to be: Be protected.

RFID (RADIO FREQUENCY IDENTIFICATION)

RFID (radio frequency identification) uses a microchip (chip) in a tag or label to store information, and information is transmitted from, or written to, the tag or label when the microchip is exposed to the correct frequency of radio waves. You're probably already familiar with some implementations of RFID. For example, toll roads have lanes through which drivers can move if they have an RFID device that automatically charges to an account as they drive down the road. Exxon/Mobil provides an RFID-enabled key ring (called Speedpass) to its customers. The Speedpass key ring contains customer account information. A customer, when making a purchase, simply waves the key ring at a reader (as opposed to swiping a credit card). The reader communicates with the RFID chip on the key ring, reads the customer's account information, and proceeds with the account charge.

The most common implementation of RFID is the passive RFID chip (see Figure 9.7 on the next page). A passive RFID chip has no power source itself and sits idle until passed near a reader that emits radio waves. The antenna surrounding the RFID chip picks up the radio waves and the RFID chip stores those waves as a form of energy until it has enough to literally "jolt" itself to life. The RFID chip then sends its information to the reader, which is connected to some sort of computer system containing account information and the like. After sending its information, the RFID chip goes back into passive mode. This is exactly how Exxon/Mobil's Speedpass RFID key ring works.

Figure 9.7

How Passive RFID Works

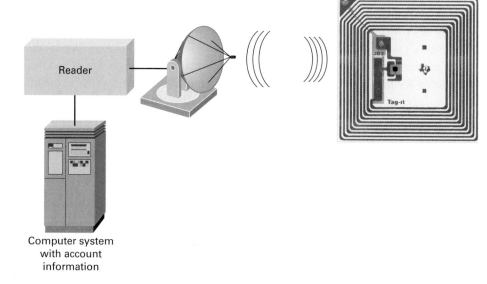

RFID IN USE TODAY   The current applications of RFID technologies are many, including:

- **Anti-theft car keys**—inside the casing of the car key is an RFID chip. When you insert the key into the ignition, the RFID chip must communicate with the reader in your ignition system (and pass the equivalent of a password) for the car to start. So, it does criminals no good to make a copy of your car key. Of course, if you lose your car keys, it often costs in excess of $300 to get them replaced.

- **Library book tracking**—instead of a bar code on which the ISBN is stored, the RFID chip contains that information. Books are much easier to check in and check out. Even the Vatican library now uses RFID chips in its books. The old inventory process took over 30 days. Using wireless handheld RFID readers, the new inventory process takes only a day.

- **Livestock tracking**—livestock of all kinds is now tagged with RFID chips upon entering the country. The system can then track where the livestock has been on its journey throughout the United States. In the case of a biological outbreak, the system can easily identify which livestock were at the location where the outbreak is believed to have occurred.

- **Supply chain**—almost every major participant in the supply chain process is now mandating that the other participants tag merchandise, trays of merchandise, boxes and skids of merchandise, and so on with RFID chips. These major participants include Walmart, the Department of Defense (DOD), the Food and Drug Administration (FDA), Target, Albertson's, TESCO (United Kingdom retailer), and Carrefour (France retailer).

- **Passports**—implemented in the United States in 2007, all newly issued U.S. passports now contain an RFID chip in the cover of the passport. The RFID chip contains all your passport information.

The above list is just a few of the thousands of implementations of RFID in the business world.

EDIBLE RFID TAGS IN YOUR FOOD

RFID tags are finding their way into every aspect of your life. Given that certain types of RFID tags cost only a couple of pennies to manufacture, the added cost of an RFID tag is most certainly outweighed by the many benefits tagging and tracking support.

Hannes Harms, a student at the Royal College of Art in London, has envisioned a new use of RFID tags, that of placing them in food. This "invention" has numerous applications:

- The tags could be embedded into food at the origin and then tracked throughout its entire supply chain management trip.
- Tags in food in a refrigerator could notify the owner when the food is nearing its expiration date.
- Tags in food at the dinner table could notify the consumer of foods that are on food allergy lists or perhaps bad for diabetics.

- Tags could simply send nutritional information to your smartphone so you could more easily manage what you eat.

Hannes has even shared his plans for a technology-based plate on which your food with edible RFID tags will be presented to you. The plate could provide a digital readout of all the nutritional content in the food.

This particular invention may take a while to come to pass. The U.S. Food and Drug Administration will certainly weigh in on the health issues related to the consumption of RFID tags. (The whole notion of eating an RFID tag makes many people cringe.) And, as always, there is the cost. Sometimes, adding even a couple of pennies to the cost of food makes the food not profitable for grocers to carry.[8,9]

THE FUTURE OF RFID   Today, almost every product is identified uniquely by a UPC (universal product code). However, every like product has the same UPC. So, two cans of diet Coke with lime, for example, have identical UPCs. This makes them indistinguishable. With RFID technologies, each individual piece of merchandise will have a unique EPC (electronic product code). The EPC will include the UPC designation but then also provide a unique number for each different can of diet Coke with lime that can be tied to expiration dates, supply chain movements, and just about anything else you can imagine.

Once again, use your imagination here. If every product in a grocery store can wirelessly communicate with the checkout system, there will be no need to go through that process. While you shop, you'll bag your items when placing them in your cart. When you walk out the front door, an RFID system will wirelessly communicate with your credit card in your wallet, wirelessly communicate with every product in your grocery cart, tally up your bill, and charge your credit card account appropriately.

And think about washing clothes. Suppose you load your washer full of "whites" like socks and towels. Accidentally, you throw in a red shirt but don't see it. Fortunately, each piece of clothing will have an RFID chip that will include washing instructions. Your washing machine will wirelessly communicate with each piece of clothing and determine that one piece does not belong. The washing machine will not work and will notify you that you are mixing clothes.

Are these all realities destined for the future? We believe so. What the future holds for RFID is limited only by your imagination.

Let's face it, most of us have imagined ourselves as a famous movie star on the big screen. With the help of technology, you can now be in the movies and share your acting with the world. The technology is called *Yoostar 2: In the Movies.*

Yoostar is a home video game that you can play on your Kinect for Xbox 360 or Sony PlayStation 3 (or newer models). Yoostar comes with 80 different movie and television show scenes. All you need is a camera to place you into them. It's rather like an acting version of karaoke.

Popular movie scenes include *Casablanca, 300, Tropic Thunder, The Godfather,* and *The Wizard of Oz.* Popular TV shows include *Mad Men* and *CSI: Miami.*

Once in the scene, you read words off your TV screen, basically your teleprompter, or you can adlib your lines. As you act out your movie-star fantasy, the system provides you with a score and star rating for your performance. Then, you can upload your performance to the Yoostar Playground community. There your friends on Facebook, Twitter, or within the YooStar Playground community can watch, rate, and even edit your movie clips.

Future features of Yoostar include the ability of the system to manipulate the other actors and actresses in the scene. So, when you adlib your lines, the actor/actress will respond with a different set of lines accordingly.[12]

Pure Technology

LEARNING OUTCOME 4

Let's close our look at emerging technologies with a few that have broad applicability in numerous ways. These include nanotechnology, multistate CPUs, and holographic storage devices.

NANOTECHNOLOGY

One of the single greatest drawbacks to technological advances is size. The best chip manufacturers can do is to make circuit elements with a width of 130 nanometers. A nanometer is one-hundred-thousandth the width of a human hair. That may seem very, very small, but current manufacturing technologies are beginning to limit the size of computer chips, and thus their speed and capacity.

Nanotechnologies aim to change all that. As a greatly simplified definition, we would say that *nanotechnology* is a discipline that seeks to control matter at the atomic and sub-atomic levels for the purpose of building devices on the same small scale. So, nanotechnology is the exact opposite of traditional manufacturing. In the latter, for example, you would cut down a tree and whittle it down until it becomes a toothpick. That is, traditional manufacturing starts with something large and continually compresses and slices it until it becomes the desired small size. In nanotechnology, you start with the smallest unit and build up. That is, you start working with atoms and build what you want.

In nanotechnology, everything is simply atoms. Nanotechnology researchers are attempting to move atoms and encourage them to "self-assemble" into new forms. Nanotechnology is a bleeding-edge technology worth watching. The changes it will bring about will be unbelievable. Consider these:

Change the molecular structure of the materials used to make computer chips, for instance, and electronics could become as cheap and plentiful as bar codes on

Figure 9.8

3-D Crystal-Like Objects in a Holographic Storage Device

packaging. Lightweight vests enmeshed with sensors could measure a person's vital signs. Analysis of a patient's DNA could be done so quickly and precisely that designer drugs would be fabricated on the fly. A computer the size of your library card could store everything you ever saw or read.[10,11]

MULTI-STATE CPUS

Right now, CPUs are binary-state, capable of working only with information represented by a 1 or a 0. That greatly slows processing. What we really need to increase speed are CPUs that are multi-state. *Multi-state CPUs* work with information represented in more than just two states, probably 10 states with each state representing a digit between 0 and 9. When multi-state CPUs do become a reality, your computer will no longer have to go through many of the processes associated with translating characters into binary and then reversing the translation process later. (We covered this process in *Extended Learning Module A*.) This will make them much faster. Of course, the true goal is to create multi-state CPUs that can also handle letters and special characters without converting them to their binary equivalents.

HOLOGRAPHIC STORAGE DEVICES

Again, right now, storage devices store information on a two-dimensional surface, but research in the holographic realm will change that, creating *holographic storage devices* with many sides or faces (see Figure 9.8). This is similar in concept to small cards that you may have seen which change the picture or image as you view the cards from different angles.

If and when holographic storage devices do become a reality, you may be able to store an entire set of encyclopedias on a single crystal that may have as many as several hundred faces. Think how small technology will become then.

Most Important Considerations

Throughout this chapter, we've discussed some key emerging trends and technologies. They certainly are exciting and promise that the future will be different and dynamic, to say the least. We have suggested that you anticipate these changes and take charge of how they will affect you personally and in your career.

Let's take a final look at some implications of the material you've learned in this course. The following are five areas to think about to help you reflect on what you've learned and to place that knowledge within the bigger picture. Technology is a human invention and it presents us with some human, social, and personal challenges.

THE NECESSITY OF TECHNOLOGY

Like it or not, technology is a necessity today. It's hard to imagine a world without it. Just as we need electricity to function on an everyday basis, we need technology as well.

Of course, that doesn't mean you should adopt technology just for the sake of the technology or only because it sounds fun. Rather, you need to carefully evaluate each technology and determine if it will make you more productive, enhance your personal life, enrich your learning, or move your organization in the direction of its strategic goals and initiatives.

Technology is not a panacea. If you throw technology at a business process that doesn't work correctly, the result will be that you'll perform that process incorrectly millions of times faster per second. At the same time, you can ill afford to ignore technology when it really will help you and your organization become more efficient, effective, and innovative.

CLOSING THE GREAT DIGITAL DIVIDE

We must, as a human race, completely eliminate the great digital divide. The *great digital divide* means the world is becoming marked by "have's" and "have not's" with respect to technology. That is, the traditional notion of "third world" and "fourth world" countries is now being defined by the extent to which countries have only limited access to and use of technology.

The power of technology needs to be realized on a worldwide scale. We cannot afford to have any technology-challenged nation or culture (within reason). The great digital divide only adds to global instability. If you live and work in a technology-rich country, don't keep it to yourself. When possible, take technology to other countries by creating international business partnerships and strategic alliances. Join in a nonprofit program to spread computer literacy and access in a third world country, or in this country. This may afford you great satisfaction, and the world will benefit greatly from your efforts.

TECHNOLOGY FOR THE BETTERMENT OF SOCIETY

Life isn't just about making money. As you approach the development and use of technological innovations (or even standard technologies), think in terms of the betterment of people and society in general. Making money and helping people aren't mutually exclusive either. They often go hand in hand, in fact. But you'll learn a rich life isn't just measured in money.

Medical research is creating marvelous uses of technology to treat ailments and cure diseases. But if these efforts are purely profit-driven, we may never wholly realize the fruits of them. For example, therapists are using virtual reality to teach autistic people to cope with increasingly complex situations. We know for a fact that this use of technology isn't making anyone a lot of money. But it isn't always about making money. It's about helping people who face daily challenges far greater than ours. You're fortunate to be in an environment of learning. Give back when you have the chance.

EXCHANGING PRIVACY FOR CONVENIENCE

On a personal level, you need to consider how much of your personal privacy you're giving up in exchange for convenience. The extreme example is GPS-enabled implant chips. The convenience is knowing where you are and being able to get directions to your destination. But you're obviously giving up some privacy. Is this okay? Convenience takes on many forms. When you use a discount card at a grocery store to take advantage of sales, that grocery store then tracks your purchasing history in great detail. You can bet that the grocery store will use that information to sell you more tailored products.

It really is a trade-off. In today's technology-based world, you give up privacy when you register for sweepstakes on certain Web sites. You give up privacy just surfing the Web because tracking software monitors your activities. Even when you click on a banner ad, the Web site you go to knows where you came from. Although such trade-offs may seem insignificant, small trade-offs can add up to a big trade-off over time.

Because you are very much a part of this trend, it's often hard to see the big picture and understand that every day you're giving up just a little more privacy in exchange for a little more convenience. Don't ever think that organizations won't use the information they're capturing about you. They're capturing it so they can use it. Of course, much of it will be used to better serve you as a customer, but some of it may not.

ETHICS, ETHICS, ETHICS

As our final note to you, we cannot stress enough again the importance of ethics as they guide your behavior toward other people in your career. We realize that business is business and that businesses need to make money to survive. But the recent scandals involving Enron and others in the corporate world which sent people to prison and wiped out life savings should be a reminder of how important your personal ethical compass is to you. Personal success shouldn't come to the detriment of other people. It's quite possible to be very ethical and very successful. That's our challenge to you.

MAKING PREDICTIONS

There's nothing like closing a chapter titled "Emerging Trends and Technologies" with a few predictions, 13 to be exact. Before you read on, take a couple of minutes, consider everything you've learned about IT in this course and everything going on in life around you, and jot down a few predictions of your own. As you read this section, note which of your predictions are similar to ours. You'll no doubt find some similar ones, but we bet you come up with some we didn't think of. (After all, you're making your predictions at least two years after we penned the predictions in the coming pages. Things have certainly changed.)

Finally, keep both your list and ours; perhaps simply create a Word document containing both lists and store it on your computer. Make yourself a mental note to check the lists in a couple of years. We've done that for the many years we've made predictions while writing this text (in the neighborhood of 15 years now). Some have come true. For example, we predicted that smartphones might become the only computer you need; we see that happening today. We predicted personal cloud providers in 2008. In 2011, Microsoft, Google, and Apple announced personal cloud services. We predicted that smartphones would be the next great playground space for hackers; that's happening more each day.

Of course, we've made some predictions that have yet to come true. Ten years ago we were writing about how automatic speech recognition (and natural language processing) might end the need for input devices like keyboards and mice. That certainly hasn't come true (yet). Nonetheless, it's an interesting exercise to plot the future's course and then later look to determine how accurate the direction you perceived.

1. **3D and Holograms:** Our viewing interfaces with technology will be primarily 3D- and hologram-based. 3D will give the screen the third dimension of depth. Computers will generate holograms, free standing images, in the room with you.

2. **More Outrageous Industry Transformations:** This will continue for quite some time and will absolutely rock the business world. Big business based on

traditional business models will go out of business. The Fortune 500 of 2020 will look dramatically different from the Fortune 500 of 2010.

3. **And a Child Shall Lead Them:** Young people, and we mean teenagers and even pre-teenagers, will take over the app world and lead in the development and production of apps. Child entrepreneurs around the country will forego college because they don't need the money that an education can supposedly offer.

4. **The Overnight Million Dollar App:** As more people buy smartphones, some apps will have a million or more downloads within 24 hours of their being posted. Most of these apps will be developed by the "children" in #3 above.

5. **IPO Mania:** Social media, e-society, and digital economy start-ups will spring up overnight and shortly thereafter go public creating an onslaught of IPOs that the financial world has never seen. Many of these businesses will have a teenager as the CEO.

6. **Digital Money:** Retailers will start to charge a fee for accepting folding money and coins. Digital money will be mainstream.

7. **Web 3.0:** This will happen but be more evolutionary rather than revolutionary.

8. **It Won't Be _____ at the Top:** The likes of Facebook and Google may be at the top of the digital world right now but they'll be replaced by new start-ups in the coming years.

9. **Clouds:** Clouds will become the standard for software provision of all types and for information storage. This will happen at both the organizational and personal levels.

10. **The 140-Character Communication Standard:** The tweet format of 140 characters will become the standard length for most communications. Students will take classes in how to convey a single thought in 140 characters or less.

11. **Smartphones and Tablets:** Smartphones and tablets will overtake desktop computers and laptops as the preferred personal technology. Desktop computers, with standard keyboards and the like, will not be manufactured in 2020.

12. **Analytics:** Personalization will require that every business get in the game of analytics. Organizational strategy development will require the use of analytics. Business programs at colleges and universities will teach analytics (and call it that) as a business core discipline.

13. **Empire of One:** Individuals will start their own very successful businesses on the Web. Each will be the only employee in his/her business, opting to outsource everything to an outsourcing provider and the cloud. Each business will be worth millions of dollars.

What's on your list?

SUMMARY: STUDENT LEARNING OUTCOMES REVISITED

1. **Describe the emerging trends and technologies that will have an impact on the changing Internet.** Emerging trends and technologies that will have an impact on the changing Internet include:

   - *Personal software-as-a-service (SaaS)*—delivery model for personal productivity software such as Microsoft Office in which you pay for personal productivity software on a pay-per-use basis instead of buying the software outright.

- *Push*—technology environment in which businesses and organizations come to you via technology with information, services, and product offerings based on your profile.
- *F2b2C (Factory-to-business-to-Consumer)*—an e-commerce business model in which a consumer communicates through a business on the Internet and directly provides product specifications to a factory that makes the customized and personalized product to the consumer's specifications and then ships it directly to the consumer.
- *VoIP (Voice over Internet Protocol)*—allows you to send voice communications over the Internet and avoid the toll charges that you would normally receive from your long distance carrier.
- *Web 3.0*—the third generation of the Web focused on semantics.

2. **Define the various types of technologies that are emerging as we move toward physiological interaction with technology.** Emerging technologies in the area of physiological interaction include:

- *Automatic speech recognition (ASR)*—a system that not only captures spoken words but also distinguishes word groupings to form sentences.
- *Virtual reality*—three-dimensional computer simulation in which you actively and physically participate.
- *CAVE (cave automatic virtual environment)*—special 3-D virtual reality room that can display images of other people and objects located in other CAVEs all over the world.
- *Haptic interface*—uses technology to add the sense of touch to an environment that previously only had visual and textual elements.
- *Biometrics*—use of physiological characteristics—such as your fingerprint, the blood vessels in the iris of your eye, the sound of your voice, or perhaps even your breath—to provide identification.

3. **Describe the emerging trends of Near Field Communication, Bluetooth, WiFi, smartphones, and RFID, as they relate to the wireless environment.** Emerging trends related to the wireless environment include:

- *Near Field Communication (NFC)*—short-range wireless technology developed mainly for use in mobile phones.
- *Bluetooth*—standard for transmitting information in the form of short-range radio waves over distances of up to 30 feet.
- *Wifi*—standard for transmitting information in the form of radio waves over distances up to about several miles.
- Smartphones—advances in storage capacity, processor capability, music enhancements, and video support—and threats such as viruses and hackers.
- *RFID (radio frequency identification)*—the use of a chip or label to store information, by which information is transmitted from, or written to, the tag or label when the chip is exposed to the correct frequency of radio waves.

4. **Define and describe emerging technologies that, while purely technology, can and will impact the future.** These technologies include:

- *Nanotechnology*—a discipline that seeks to control matter at the atomic and sub-atomic levels for the purpose of building devices on the same small scale.
- *Multi-state CPU*—works with information represented in more than just two states, probably 10 states with each state representing a digit between 0 and 9.

- *Holographic storage device*—a device that stores information on a storage medium that is composed of 3-D crystal-like objects with many sides or faces.

CLOSING CASE STUDY ONE

Just How Big Is the Impact of Technology on Society?

To comprehend the impact of technology on today's society, you don't have to look very far. In fact, you can probably just look around you. Someone is talking on a smartphone or sending a text message. Someone is listening to music on an MP3 player. Someone else is surfing the Web.

A different perspective is to study how technology has impacted our language. And to do that, you can look to new words that have been added to the English language according to University Oxford Press and its annual list of newly recognized words for the English language. Let's start with the year 2005 and move forward through 2010. (In the lists below, we've provided the definitions for only technology-related new words.)

2005

New Word of the Year: Podcast—a digital recording of a radio broadcast or similar program, made available on the Internet for downloading to a personal audio player.
Runners-Up for 2005
- Bird flu
- ICE—an entry stored in one's cellular phone that provides emergency contact information
- IDP (internally displaced person)
- IED (improvised explosive device)
- Lifehack
- Persistent vegetative state
- Reggaeton
- Rootkit—software installed on a computer by someone other than the owner, intended to conceal other programs or processes, files, or system data
- Squick
- Sudoku
- Trans fat

2006

New Word of the Year: Carbon neutral—calculating your total climate-damaging carbon emissions, reducing

them where possible, and then balancing your remaining emissions, often by purchasing a carbon offset.
Runners-Up for 2006
- CSA (community-supported agriculture)
- DRM—digital rights management
- Dwarf planet
- Elbow bump
- Fishapod
- Funner
- Ghostriding
- Islamofascism
- Pregaming

2007

New Word of the Year: Locavore—a person who focuses on eating only locally grown food.
Runners-Up for 2007
- Aging in place
- Bacn—e-mail notifications, such as news alerts and social networking updates, that are considered more desirable than unwanted spam
- Cloudware—online applications, such as webmail, powered by massive data storage facilities, also called cloud servers
- Colony collapse disorder
- Cougar
- MRAP vehicle
- Mumblecore
- Previvor
- Social graph—the network of one's friends and connections on social Web sites such as Facebook and Myspace
- Tase
- Upcycling

2008

New Word of the Year: Hypermiling—an attempt to maximize gas mileage by making fuel-conserving adjustments to one's car and one's driving techniques.

Runners-Up for 2008

- Frugalista
- Moofer
- Topless meeting—a meeting in which the participants are barred from using their laptops, Blackberries, smartphones, etc.
- Toxic debt
- CarrotMob
- Ecohacking
- Hockey mom
- Link bait—content on a Web site that encourages (baits) a user to place links to it from other Web sites
- Luchador
- Rewilding
- Staycation
- Tweet—a short message sent via the Twitter service, using a smartphone or other mobile device
- Wardrobe

2009

New Word of the Year: Unfriend—to remove someone as a "friend" on a social networking site such as Facebook.
Runners-Up for 2009

- Hashtag—a # sign added to a word or phrase on Twitter
- Intexticated—distracted because of texting on a smartphone while driving a vehicle
- Netbook—a small, very portable laptop computer with limited memory
- Paywall—a way of blocking access to a part of a Web site which is only available to paying subscribers
- Sexting—the sending of sexually explicit texts and pictures by smartphone
- Freemium
- Funemployed
- Zombie bank
- Ardi
- Birther
- Choice mom
- Death panel
- Teabagger
- Brown state
- Green state
- Ecotown
- Deleb
- Tramp stamp

2010

New Word of the Year: Refudiate—used loosely to mean reject (a Sarah Palin faux paux).
Runners-Up for 2010

- Bankster
- Crowdsourcing—practice whereby an organization enlists a variety of freelancers, paid or unpaid, to work on a specific task or problem
- Double-dip
- Gleek
- Nom nom
- Retweet—repost or forward a message posted by another user on Twitter
- Tea Party
- Top kill
- Vuvuzela
- Webisode—an original episode derived from a television series, made for online viewing

You can perform some interesting analyses with the above information. For example, the new words of the year for the last six years have been in only three categories: political (2010), the environment with three; and technology with two—podcast (2005) and unfriend (2009). Furthermore, of the 72 runner-up words in the last six years, 17 or roughly 24 percent have been technology-related.

Questions

1. Visit University Oxford Press at http://global.oup.com/?cc=us. For all years after 2010, find the new word of the year and all the runner-up words. Perform the simple analysis we presented in the final paragraph above. How has technology impacted the English language in the years after 2010?

2. While technology has certainly impacted our language in the last several years, so has the environment, perhaps to an even greater extent than technology. Why have so many environment-related words inserted themselves into our language?

3. Create some new technology-related words. Think about the things you do with technology or have witnessed other people doing with technology. Create a list of at least five new technology-related words. For each, describe how you derived them and also provide their definition.

4. What about text message abbreviations, emoticons, and chat slang terms. Which have been formally recognized by University Oxford Press as a part of the English language? Is it good or bad that these are becoming a part of our formal language? Justify your answer.

CLOSING CASE STUDY TWO

Smartphones and the Great Digital Divide

Smartphones are rapidly becoming the technology of choice for a variety of functions beyond just making and receiving phone calls. Most notably, because of their relative inexpensiveness compared to desktop computers, laptops, and even tablets, many people are opting for a smartphone as their primary vehicle for accessing the Internet. In many cases, some people simply can't afford any kind of Internet-accessing device other than a smartphone. In Africa, for example, over 316 million people have become new mobile phone subscribers since 2000.

In the United States, smartphones offer a way for economically disadvantaged people to get connected to the Internet. In many respects, this may very well close the digital divide between the "haves" and "have-nots" with respect to technology. The following are some statistics from the Pew Research Center for you to consider.

- 83 percent of U.S. adults own a mobilephone. Of those, 42 percent own a smartphone. So, 35 percent of all adults in the United States own a smartphone.
- 59 percent of adults in households with earning income greater than $75,000 own a smartphone.
- 44 percent of African Americans and Latinos own a smartphone.
- 87 percent of smartphone owners access the Internet via their smartphones, while 68 percent do so on a daily basis.
- 25 percent of smartphone owners say they mostly go online using a smartphone instead of a computer.
- By Gender (for smartphone ownership):
  ○ Men—39 percent
  ○ Women—31 percent
- By Age (for smartphone ownership):
  ○ 18–24—49 percent

- 25–34—58 percent
- 35–44—44 percent
- 45–54—28 percent
- 55–64—22 percent
- 65 + —11 percent
- By Race/Ethnicity (for smartphone ownership):
  ○ White, non-Hispanic—30 percent
  ○ African American, non-Hispanic—44 percent
  ○ Hispanic—44 percent
- By Household Income (for smartphone ownership):
  ○ <$10,000—21 percent
  ○ $10,000–$20,000—20 percent
  ○ $20,000–$30,000—26 percent
  ○ $30,000–$40,000—36 percent
  ○ $40,000–$50,000—44 percent
  ○ $50,000–$75,000—38 percent
  ○ $75,000–$100,000—53 percent
  ○ $100,000–$150,000—57 percent
  ○ $150,000 + —73 percent
- By Education Level (for smartphone ownership):
  ○ No high school diploma—18 percent
  ○ High school graduate—27 percent
  ○ Some college—38 percent
  ○ College + —48 percent
- By Geographic Location (for smartphone ownership):
  ○ Urban—38 percent
  ○ Suburban—38 percent
  ○ Rural—21 percent
- Percentage of Smartphone Owners Who Also Own These Devices:
  ○ Laptop computer—79 percent
  ○ MP3 player—70 percent
  ○ Desktop computer—68 percent
  ○ E-book reader—20 percent
  ○ Tablet PC—18 percent

- By Race/Ethnicity (percentage of owners who use their smartphone as the dominant means to access the Internet):
  - White, non-Hispanic—17 percent
  - African American/Latino—38 percent[13,14,15]

Questions

1. Even though 44 percent of African Americans and Latinos own a smartphone while only 30 percent of white, non-Hispanics do, many people contend that this isn't really closing the great digital divide because African Americans and Latinos use their smartphones more for entertainment than empowerment. Build an argument to support the previous statement.

2. When accessing the Internet, what can you do on a desktop or laptop computer that you can't do on a smartphone? If smartphones have fewer Internet capabilities (than desktop and laptop computers), can you necessarily link an increase in smartphone ownership within a U.S.-based economically disadvantaged group of people to closing the great digital divide? Why or why not?

3. How does an increase in smartphone ownership in a third-world geographic region like Africa close the digital divide for countries in that region? If you owned a U.S. business and wanted to start doing business in Africa, what would be an essential part of your marketing strategy?

4. If you look at smartphone ownership by household income, you'll notice a fairly sizable dip for the category of $50,000–$75,000. To what do you attribute this? Justify your answer?

5. Finally, will greater access to the Internet cause a closing of the great digital divide? You can answer Yes, No, or Some. Whatever the case, build an argument for your answer.

◼ KEY TERMS AND CONCEPTS

Augmented reality,   263
Automatic speech recognition
    (ASR),   264
Biochip,   269
Biometrics,   267
Bluetooth,   270
Cave automatic virtual
    environment (CAVE),   265
Crowdsourcing,   281
Disintermediation,   261
Facial recognition software,   270
Factory-to-business-to-Consumer
    (F2b2C),   261

Feature analysis,   264
Glove,   265
Haptic interface,   266
Headset (head-mounted
    display),   265
Holographic device,   265
Holographic storage device,   275
Implant chip,   270
Language processing,   264
Multi-state CPU,   275
Nanotechnology,   274
Near Field Communication
    (NFC),   270

Pattern classification,   264
Personal software-as-a-service
    (Saas),   259
Push technology,   260
Radio frequency identification
    (RFID),   271
Virtual reality,   265
Voice over Internet Protocol
    (VoIP),   262
Walker,   265
Web 2.0,   262
Web 3.0,   262
WiFi (wireless fidelity),   270

◼ SHORT-ANSWER QUESTIONS

1. How does push technology differ from spam?
2. What is disintermediation? How does the F2b2C e-commerce model support disintermediation?
3. What exciting applications are associated with the Web 3.0?
4. How does automatic speech recognition work?
5. What are the devices commonly associated with virtual reality?

6. What role do haptic interfaces play?
7. What is the best form of personal identification?
8. How can you expect smartphones to change in the future?
9. What is RFID?
10. How does nanotechnology differ from traditional manufacturing?

■ ASSIGNMENTS AND EXERCISES

1. **SELLING THE IDEA OF IMPLANT CHIPS AT YOUR SCHOOL** Let's assume for a moment that your team is in favor of using implant chips that contain vitally important information such as identification and medical information. Your task is to put together a sales presentation to your school that would require all students to obtain implant chips. In your presentation, include the following:

   A. The school-related information that each implant chip would contain

   B. The nonschool-related information that each implant chip would contain

   C. The processes within your school that would use the information on the implant chips

   D. The benefits your school would realize by requiring implant chips

   E. The benefits students would realize by having implant chips

   Your presentation should be no more than five minutes, so it must be a powerful selling presentation.

2. **FINDING A GOOD AUTOMATIC SPEECH RECOGNITION SYSTEM** Research the Web for automatic speech recognition (ASR) systems. Make a list of the ones you find. What are the prices of each? Are they speaker-independent or speaker-dependent? Do they support continuous speech recognition or discrete speech recognition? What sort of add-on vocabularies can you purchase? How comfortable would you feel speaking the contents of a term paper as opposed to typing it? Would you have

to be more or less organized to use speech recognition as opposed to typing? Why?

3. **UNDERSTANDING THE RELATIONSHIPS BETWEEN TRENDS AND TECHNOLOGICAL INNOVATIONS** In this chapter, we presented you with numerous key technologies and how they relate to four important trends. (See Figure 9.1 on page 258 for the list of technologies and trends.) For each trend, identify all the technologies presented in this chapter that can have an impact. For each technology that you do identify, provide a short discussion of how it might have an impact.

4. **RESEARCHING APPLICATIONS OF RFID** Visit the Web and perform a search on RFID for applications that we didn't discuss in this chapter. Prepare a short PowerPoint presentation highlighting each. Also, search the Web for the leading providers of RFID technologies. What companies did you find? Does one seem to stand out above the rest? If so, which is it?

5. **RESEARCHING INTELLIGENT HOME APPLIANCES** Visit a local appliance store in your area and find three home appliances that contain some sort of intelligence (i.e., an embedded computer chip that takes over some of the functionality and decision making). For each appliance, prepare a short report that includes the following information:

   • A description and price for the intelligent home appliance

   • The "intelligent" features of the appliance

   • How those features make the appliance better than the nonintelligent version

■ DISCUSSION QUESTIONS

1. In a push technology environment, businesses and organizations will come to you with information, services, and product offerings based on your profile. How is a push technology environment different from mass mailings and spam? Is it an invasion of your privacy to have organizations calling you on your smartphone every time you come near a store? Why or why not? Should you be able to "opt in" or "opt out" of these offerings? Is

this really any different from someone leaving a flyer at your house or on your car while it's parked in a parking lot?

2. There are three steps in automatic speech recognition (ASR): feature analysis, pattern classification, and language processing. Which of those three steps is the most challenging for a computer to perform? Why? Which of those three steps is the least challenging for a computer to perform? Why? If ASR systems are

to become automatic speech understanding systems, which step must undergo the greatest improvement in its capabilities? Why?

3. Much debate surrounds the use of biometrics. Many people like it because biometrics can provide identification and increase security. Other people see it as a tremendous invasion of your privacy. Just as you read in this chapter, a bank—by using biometric identification—may be able to tell if a woman is pregnant. So, the greatest challenge to overcome is not technological but rather societal. What do you think needs to happen for society to accept the use of biometrics? How long do you think it will be before society accepts the use of biometrics? In what year do you believe the U.S. federal government will begin requiring a biometric of every newborn child?

4. What are the ethical dilemmas associated with using facial recognition software? Is the use of this type of software really any different from a store asking to see your driver's license when you use your credit card? Why or why not? Should the government be able to place digital video cameras on every street corner and use facial recognition software to monitor your movements? Why or why not?

5. When (and if) CAVEs become a common reality, you'll be able to visit your family and friends anytime you want no matter where they live. What sort of impact will this have on the travel industry? If you can see your relatives in a CAVE as often as you want, will you be more or less inclined to buy a plane ticket and visit them in person? Why or why not?

■ CHAPTER PROJECTS

GROUP PROJECTS

- Assessing the Value of Outsourcing Information Technology: Creating Forecasts (p. 294)
- Making the Case with Presentation Software: Information Technology Ethics (p. 296)
- Developing an Enterprise Resource Planning System: Planning, Reporting, and Data Processing (p. 299)
- Assessing a Wireless Future: Emerging Trends and Technology (p. 300)
- Evaluating the Next Generation: Dot-Com ASPs (p. 301)
- Evaluating the Security of Information: Wireless Network Vulnerability (p. 308)

E-COMMERCE PROJECTS

- Interviewing and Negotiating Tips (p. 311)
- Free and Rentable Storage Space (p. 313)
- Financial Aid Resources (p. 315)
- Global Statistics and Resources (p. 316)
- Searching for MBA Programs (p. 321)
- Searching Job Databases (p. 321)

PROJECTS

Group PROJECTS

CASE 1:
ASSESSING THE VALUE OF CUSTOMER RELATIONSHIP MANAGEMENT

TREVOR TOY AUTO MECHANICS

Trevor Toy Auto Mechanics is an automobile repair shop in Phoenix, Arizona. Over the past few years, Trevor has seen his business grow from a two-bay car repair shop with only one other employee to a 15-bay car repair shop with 21 employees.

Trevor wants to improve service and add a level of personalization to his customers. However, Trevor has no idea who his best customers are, the work that is being performed, or which mechanic is responsible for the repairs. Trevor is asking for your help. He has provided you with a spreadsheet file, **TREVOR.xls,** that contains a list of all the repairs his shop has completed over the past year including each client's name along with a unique identifier. The spreadsheet file contains the fields provided in the table below.

Column	Name	Description
A	CUSTOMER #	A unique number assigned to each customer
B	CUSTOMER NAME	The name of the customer
C	MECHANIC #	A unique number assigned to the mechanic who completed the work
D	CAR TYPE	The type of car on which the work was completed
E	WORK COMPLETED	What type of repair was performed on the car
F	NUM HOURS	How long in hours it took to complete the work
G	COST OF PARTS	The cost of the parts associated with completing the repair
H	TOTAL CHARGE	The amount charged to the customer for the repair

Your analysis should include (1) Trevor's best customers (top 10 in terms of volume and revenue); (2) Trevor's worst customers (bottom 10 in terms of lowest volume and lost revenue); and (3) the mechanics that perform the repairs for each customer.

SOME PARTICULARS YOU SHOULD KNOW

1. As you consider the information provided to you, think in terms of what information is important. You might need to use the existing information to create new information.
2. In your analysis, provide examples of the types of marketing campaigns Trevor should offer his most valuable customers.
3. Upon completing your analysis, please provide concise yet detailed and thorough documentation (in narrative, numeric, and graphic forms) that justifies your recommendations.
4. File: **TREVOR.xls** (Excel file).

CASE 2:
ANALYZING THE VALUE OF INFORMATION

AFFORDABLE HOMES REAL ESTATE

In late 1995, a national study announced that Eau Claire, Wisconsin, was the safest place to live. Since then, housing development projects have been springing up all around Eau Claire. Six housing development projects are currently dominating the Eau Claire market: Woodland Hills, Granite Mound, Creek Side Huntington, East River Community, Forest Green, and Eau Claire South. These six projects each started with 100 homes, have sold all of them, and are currently developing phase 2.

As one of the three partners and real estate agents of Affordable Homes Real Estate, it is your responsibility to analyze the information concerning the past 600 home sales and choose which development project to focus on for selling homes in phase 2. Because your real estate firm is so small, you and your partners have decided that the firm should focus on selling homes in only one of the development projects.

From the Wisconsin Real Estate Association you have obtained a spreadsheet file that contains information concerning each of the sales for the first 600 homes. It contains the following fields:

Column	Name	Description
A	LOT #	The number assigned to a specific home within each project
B	PROJECT #	A unique number assigned to each of the six housing development projects (see table to follow)
C	ASK PRICE	The initial posted asking price for the home
D	SELL PRICE	The actual price for which the home was sold
E	LIST DATE	The date the home was listed for sale
F	SALE DATE	The date on which the final contract closed and the home was sold
G	SQ. FT.	The total square footage for the home
H	# BATH.	The number of bathrooms in the home
I	# BDRMS	The number of bedrooms in the home

The following numbers have been assigned to each of the housing development projects:

Project Number	Project Name
23	Woodland Hills
47	Granite Mound
61	Creek Side Huntington
78	East River Community
92	Forest Green
97	Eau Claire South

It is your responsibility to analyze the sales list and prepare a report that details which housing development project your real estate firm should focus on. Your analysis should cover as many angles as possible.

SOME PARTICULARS YOU SHOULD KNOW

1. You don't know how many other real estate firms will also be competing for sales in each of the housing development projects.

2. Phase 2 for each housing development project will develop homes similar in style, price, and square footage to their respective first phases.

3. As you consider the information provided to you, think in terms of what information is important and what information is not important. Be prepared to justify how you approach your analysis.

4. Upon completing your analysis, please provide concise, yet detailed and thorough, documentation (in narrative, numeric, and graphic forms) that justifies your decision.

5. File: **REALEST.xls** (Excel file).

CASE 3:
EXECUTIVE INFORMATION SYSTEM REPORTING

POLITICAL CAMPAIGN FINANCE

When it comes to campaign finance, Americans want a system that minimizes the influence of "fat cats" and organized money, that keeps campaign spending at sensible levels, that fosters healthy electoral competition, that doesn't take advantage of wealthy candidates, and that doesn't require candidates to spend all of their waking hours raising money.

Indeed, the much maligned congressional campaign finance system we have now is itself a product of well-intended reform efforts, passed by Congress in 1974 to achieve these ideals. Dozens of new reform plans have emerged during the 1990s that also reach for these goals. Yet, no reform scheme, however well intended, is likely to produce a perfect congressional campaign finance system.

The city of Highlands Ranch, Colorado, wishes to organize its campaign contributions records in a more strategic format. The city council is considering various executive information system packages that can show them overall views of the contribution information as well as give them the ability to access more detailed information. You have been hired to make recommendations about what reports should be available through the soon-to-be-purchased executive information system.

The table below is a list of the information that will be the foundation for the reports in the proposed executive information system. To help you develop realistic reports, the city has provided you with a spreadsheet file that contains specific contributions over the last six months.

Column	Name	Description
A	DATE	The actual date that the contribution was made
B	CONTRIBUTOR	The name of the person or organization that made the contribution
C	DISTRICT	The district number that the councilperson belongs to
D	AMOUNT	The amount of the contribution
E	TYPE	The description type of where the contribution amount was given
F	COUNCILPERSON	The councilperson's name
G	PARTY	The councilperson's political party

What the city council is most interested in is viewing several overall reports and then being able to request more detailed reports. So, as a consultant, your goal is to develop different sets of reports that illustrate the concept of drilling down through the information provided. For example, you should develop a report that shows overall campaign contributions by district (each of the eight different districts) and then also develop more detailed reports that show contribution by political party and contribution by type.

SOME PARTICULARS YOU SHOULD KNOW

1. The council would much rather see information graphically than numerically. So, as you develop your reports, do so in terms of graphs that illustrate the desired relationships.

2. As you consider the information provided to you, think in terms of overall views first and then detailed views second. This will help you develop a logical series of reports.

3. If you wish, you can explore a variety of software tools or functions to help you create the reports. Then prepare your presentation using a presentation graphics package that lets you create a really great presentation of your recommendations.

4. Again, your goal is not to create reports that point toward a particular problem or opportunity. Rather, you are to design a series of logical reports that illustrate the concept of drilling down.

5. File: **CONTRIBUTE.xls** (Excel file).

CASE 4:
BUILDING VALUE CHAINS

HELPING CUSTOMERS DEFINE VALUE

StarLight is a Denver-based retailer of high-quality apparel, shoes, and accessories. In 1915, with money earned in the Colorado gold mines, Anne Logan invested in a small downtown Denver shoe store. A few years later, Anne expanded her business by adding fine apparel. Today, StarLight has 97 retail stores and discount outlets throughout the United States. Since the beginning, StarLight's business philosophy has reflected its founder's beliefs in exceptional service, value, selection, and quality. To maintain the level of service StarLight's customers have come to expect, the company empowers its employees to meet any customer demand, no matter how unreasonable it may seem. With so many stores, it's difficult for Cody Sherrod, StarLight's vice president for Business Information and Planning, to know the level of service customers receive, what customers value, and what they don't. These are important questions for a retailer striving to provide the finest customer experience and products while keeping costs to a minimum.

Cody decided a value chain analysis would be helpful in answering these questions. So, customer surveys were designed, distributed, completed, collected, and compiled into a database. Customers were asked to value their experience with various processes in the StarLight value chain. Specifically, for each value chain process, customers were asked whether this area added value to their experience or reduced the value of their experience. Customers were asked to quantify how much each process added or reduced the value of the services they received. Using a total of 100 points for the value chain, each customer distributed those points among StarLight's processes. The survey results in the database consist of the fields shown in the table on the next page.

Field Name	Description
Survey ID	An ID number uniquely identifying the survey
VA/VR	A field that identifies whether the current row of information reflects a value-added response or a value-reducing response
Date	Survey response date
Mgmt/Acctg/Finance/Legal	Customer value experience, if any, with management, accounting, finance, and the legal departments
HR Mgmt	Customer value of the attitude and general personnel environment
R&D/Tech Dev	Customer perceived value of the quality of research and technology support
Purchasing	Customer value placed on the quality and range of product selection
Receive and Greet Customers	Customer value placed on initial contact with employees
Provide Direction/Advice/Info	Customer value placed on initial information provided by employees
Store Location/Channel Availability & Convenience	Customer value placed on location, availability, and convenience
Product Display/Site or Catalog Layout	Customer value placed on aesthetic appeal of merchandise display and layout
Sales Service	Customer value placed on quality of service provided by sales associates
Marketing	Customer value placed on the effectiveness of marketing material
Customer Follow-up	Customer value placed on postsales service and follow-up

Cody has asked you to gather the raw survey material into two value chains, the value-added chain and the value-reducing chain. You'll create chains that summarize the survey information and size the process areas proportionately as described in Chapter 2. Specifically, your job is to perform the following:

1. Create queries or reports in the provided database to summarize the value-added amounts and the value-reducing amounts for each process.

2. Draw two value chains using that summary information to size the depicted area for each process. Use the value chains in Chapter 2 as reference.

3. Compare the value-added and value-reducing process percentages. Do they correlate in any way? If so, why do you think that is? If not, why not?

4. In the table description provided, a dashed line is drawn between the "purchasing" process and the "receive and greet customers" process. Processes above the line are considered support processes, while processes below are considered primary processes. Create a database query to compare how customers value the total of support processes versus primary processes. Do this for both value-added and value-reducing processes. Do the results make sense or are they surprising? Explain your answer.

SOME PARTICULARS YOU SHOULD KNOW

1. Remember that the total value-added/value-reducing amount for each process must equal 100 percent.
2. The survey values in the database are not percentages although the sum of all responses for a given survey equals 100.
3. File: **STARLIGHT.mdb** (Access file).

CASE 5:
USING RELATIONAL TECHNOLOGY TO TRACK PROJECTS

FOOTHILLS CONSTRUCTION

Foothills Construction Company is a Denver-based construction company that specializes in subcontracting the development of single family homes. In business since 1993, Foothills Construction Company has maintained a talented pool of certified staff and independent consultants allowing the flexibility and combined experience required to meet the needs of its nearly 300 completed projects in the Denver metropolitan area. The field of operation methods that Foothills Construction is responsible for as it relates to building include structural development, heating and cooling, plumbing, and electricity.

The company charges its clients by billing the hours spent on each contract. The hourly billing rate is dependent on the employee's position according to the field of operations (as noted below).

Figure GP.1 shows a basic report that Foothills Construction managers would like to see every week concerning what projects are being assigned as well as a summary of assignment hours and changes. Foothills Construction organizes its internal structure in four different operations: Structure (500), Plumbing (501), Electrical (502), and Heating and Ventilation (503). Each of these operational departments can and should have many subcontractors who specialize in that area.

Figure GP.1
Foothills Construction Project Detail

FOOTHILLS CONSTRUCTION PROJECT DETAIL

PROJECT NAME	ASSIGN DATE	EMP LAST NAME	EMP FIRST NAME	JOB DESCRIPTION	ASSIGN HOUR	CHARGE/HOUR
Chatfield						
	Thursday, February 10, 2005	Jones	Anne	Heating and Ventalation	3.4	$84.50
	Thursday, February 10, 2005	Sullivan	David	Electrical	1.8	$105.00
	Friday, February 11, 2005	Frommer	Matt	Plumbing	4.1	$96.75
	Saturday, February 12, 2005	Newman	John	Electrical	1.7	$105.00
	Saturday, February 12, 2005	Bavangi	Terry	Plumbing	4.1	$96.75
Summary of Assignment Hours and Charges					15.10	$1,448.15
Evergreen						
	Thursday, February 10, 2005	Smithfield	William	Structure	3.0	$35.75
	Thursday, February 10, 2005	Newman	John	Electrical	2.3	$105.00
	Thursday, February 10, 2005	Nenior	David	Plumbing	3.3	$96.75
	Friday, February 11, 2005	Marbough	Mike	Heating and Ventilation	2.6	$84.50
	Saturday, February 12, 2005	Johnson	Peter	Electrical	2.0	$105.00
	Saturday, February 12, 2005	Newman	John	Electrical	3.6	$105.00
	Saturday, February 12, 2005	Olenkoski	Glenn	Structure	1.9	$35.75
Summary of Assignment Hours and Charges					18.70	$1,543.65
Roxborough						

Page: 1

Because of the boom in home sales over the last several years, Foothills Construction has decided to implement a relational database model to track project details according to project name, hours assigned, and charges per hour for each job description. Originally, Foothills Construction decided to let one of its employees handle the construction of the database. However, that employee has not had the time to completely implement the project. Foothills Construction has asked you to take over and complete the development of the database.

The entity classes and primary keys for the database have been identified as the following:

Entity	Primary Key
Project	Project Number
Employee	Employee Number
Job	Job Number
Assign	Assign Number

The following business rules have also been identified:

1. A job can have many employees assigned but must have at least one.
2. An employee must be assigned to one and only one job number.
3. An employee can be assigned to work on one or more projects.
4. A project can be assigned to only one employee but need not be assigned to any employee.

Your job is to be completed in the following phases:

1. Develop and describe the entity-relationship diagram.
2. Use normalization to assure the correctness of the tables (relations).
3. Create the database using a personal DBMS package (preferably Microsoft Access).
4. Use the DBMS package to create the basic report in Figure GP.1.

SOME PARTICULARS YOU SHOULD KNOW

1. You may not be able to develop a report that looks exactly like the one in Figure GP.1. However, your report should include the same information.
2. Complete personnel information is tracked by another database. For this application, include only the minimum employee number, last name, and first name.
3. Information concerning all projects, employees, and jobs is not readily available. You should, however, create information for several fictitious systems to include in your database.
4. File: Not applicable.

CASE 6:
BUILDING A DECISION SUPPORT SYSTEM

CREATING AN INVESTMENT PORTFOLIO

Most experts recommend that if you're devising a long-term investment strategy you should make the stock market part of your plan. You can use a DSS to help you decide what stocks to put into your portfolio. You can use a spreadsheet to do the job. The information you need on 10 stocks is contained in a Word file called **STOCKS.doc.** This information consists of

1. Two years of weekly price data on 10 different stocks.
2. Stock market indices from
   - The Dow Jones Industrial Average
   - NASDAQ Composite
3. Dividends and cash flow per share over the last 10 years (Source: Yahoo Finance).

Using this information, build a DSS to perform stock analysis consisting of the following tasks:

1. Examine Diversification Benefits
   A. Calculate the average return and standard deviation(s) of each of the 10 stocks.
   B. Form six different portfolios: two with two stocks each; two with three stocks each; two with five stocks each.

   Answer the following questions using your DSS:

   - How does the standard deviation of each portfolio compare to the (average) standard deviation of each stock in the portfolio?
   - How does the average return of the portfolio compare to the average return of each stock in the portfolio?
   - Do the benefits of diversification seem to increase or diminish as the number of stocks in the portfolio gets larger?
   - In the two-stock and five-stock portfolios what happens if you group your stocks toward similar industries?

2. Value Each of the Stocks
   A. Estimate the dividend growth rate based on past dividends.
   B. Estimate next year's dividend using this year's dividend and the estimated growth rate.
   C. Generate two graphs, one for past dividends and one for estimated dividends for the next five years.

SOME PARTICULARS YOU SHOULD KNOW

1. When performing your calculations, use the weekly returns. That is, use the change in the price each week rather than the prices themselves. This gives you a better basis for calculation because the prices themselves don't usually change very much.
2. File: **STOCKS.doc** (Word file).

CASE 7:
ADVERTISING WITH BANNER ADS

HIGHWAYSANDBYWAYS.COM

Business is booming at HighwaysAndByways, a dot-com firm focusing on selling accessories for car enthusiasts (e.g., floor mats, grill guards, air fresheners, stereos, and so on). Throughout the past year, HighwaysAndByways has had Web site management software tracking what customers buy, the Web sites from which customers came, and the Web sites customers went to after visiting HighwaysAndByways. That information is stored in a spreadsheet file and contains the fields in the accompanying table. Each record in the spreadsheet file represents an individual visit by a customer that resulted in a purchase.

   HighwaysAndByways is interested in determining three items and has employed you as a consultant to help. First, HighwaysAndByways wants to know on which Web sites it should purchase banner ad space. Second, HighwaysAndByways wants to know which Web sites it should contact to determine if those Web sites would like to purchase banner ad space on the

Column	Name	Description
A	CUSTOMER ID	A unique identifier for a customer who made a purchase
B	TOTAL PURCHASE	The total amount of a purchase
C	PREVIOUS WEB SITE	The Web site from which the customer came to visit HighwaysAndByways
D	NEXT WEB SITE	The Web site the customer went to after making a purchase at HighwaysAndByways
E	TIME SPENT	The amount of time that the customer spent at the site

HighwaysAndByways Web site. Finally, HighwaysAndByways would like to know which Web sites it should develop reciprocal banner ad relationships with; that is, HighwaysAndByways would like a list of Web sites on which it would obtain banner ad space while providing banner ad space on its Web site for those Web sites.

SOME PARTICULARS YOU SHOULD KNOW

1. As you consider the information provided to you, think about the levels of information literacy. In other words, don't jump to conclusions before carefully evaluating the provided information.

2. You don't know if your customers made purchases at the Web site they visited upon leaving HighwaysAndByways.

3. Upon completing your analysis, please provide concise yet detailed and thorough documentation (in narrative, numeric, and graphic forms) that justifies your recommendations.

4. File: **CLICKSTREAMS.xls** (Excel file).

CASE 8:
ASSESSING THE VALUE OF OUTSOURCING INFORMATION TECHNOLOGY

CREATING FORECASTS

Founded in 1992, Innovative Software provides search software, Web site accessibility testing/repair software, and usability testing/repair software. All serve as part of its desktop and enterprise content management solutions for government, corporate, educational, and consumer markets. The company's solutions are used by Web site publishers, digital media publishers, content managers, document managers, business users, consumers, software companies, and consulting services companies. Innovative Software solutions help organizations develop long-term strategies to achieve Web content accessibility, enhance usability, and comply with U.S. and international accessibility and search standards.

Innovative Software has a 10-year history of approximately 1 percent in turnover a year and its focus has always been on customer service. With the informal motto of "Grow big, but stay small," it takes pride in 100 percent callbacks in customer care, knowing that its personal service has been one thing that makes it outstanding.

Innovative Software has experienced rapid growth to six times its original customer-base size and is forced to deal with difficult questions for the first time, such as, "How do we serve this many customers? How do we keep our soul—that part of us that honestly cares very much about our customers? How will we know that someone else will care as much and do as good a job as we have done?" In addition, you have just received an e-mail from the company CIO, Sue Downs, that the number of phone calls from customers having problems with one of your newer applications is on the increase.

As customer service manager for Innovative Software, your overriding goal is to maintain the company's reputation for excellent customer service, and outsourcing may offer an efficient means of keeping up with expanding call volume. Innovative Software is reviewing a similar scenario, that of e-BANK, which outsourced its customer service in order to handle a large projected number of customers through several customer interaction channels. Although e-BANK had excellent people, it felt that its competencies were primarily in finance, rather than in customer service and that it needed to have the expertise that a customer-service-focused company could offer. e-BANK also discovered that it was cost effective to outsource its customer service center.

Additionally, the outsourcing approach was relatively hassle-free, since e-BANK did not have to set up its own call center.

SOME PARTICULARS YOU SHOULD KNOW

1. Create a weekly analysis from the data provided in **FORECAST.xls.**

2. The price of the products, the actual product type, and any warranty information is irrelevant.

3. Develop a growth, trend, and forecast analysis. You should use a three-day moving average: a shorter moving average might not display the trend well and a much longer moving average would shorten the trend too much.

4. Upon completing your analysis, please provide concise yet detailed and thorough documentation (in narrative, numeric, and graphic forms) that justifies your recommendations.

5. File: **FORECAST.xls** (Excel file)

CASE 9:
DEMONSTRATING HOW TO BUILD WEB SITES

WITH HTML

Building a good Web site is simple in some respects and difficult in others. It's relatively easy to learn to write HTML code. Building an effective and eye-catching Web site is a horse of a different color. That is to say, there is a stretch between just using the technology and using the technology to your best advantage.

Your task in this project is to build a presentation (using presentation graphics software such as Microsoft PowerPoint) that achieves two goals. First, your presentation should show your audience how to write simple HTML code to create a Web site. Your presentation should include the HTML code for

- Text formatting (bold, italic, and the like)
- Font families and sizing
- Font colors
- Background colors and images
- Links
- Images
- Numbered and bulleted lists

Next, your presentation should provide the audience with a list of guidelines for creating an *effective* Web site. For this, you should definitely embed links into your presentation that go to Web sites that illustrate good Web site design, displaying examples of both effective and ineffective designs.

SOME PARTICULARS YOU SHOULD KNOW

1. In a file called **HTML.doc,** we've provided many links to Web sites that teach you how to write HTML code.
2. In a file called **DESIGN.doc,** we've provided many links to Web sites that teach you how to design Web sites effectively.
3. Files: **HTML.doc** and **DESIGN.doc** (Word files).

CASE 10:
MAKING THE CASE WITH PRESENTATION SOFTWARE

INFORMATION TECHNOLOGY ETHICS

Management at your company is concerned about the high cost of computer crime, from lawsuits over e-mail received to denial-of-service attacks and hackers breaking into the corporate network to steal information. You've been asked to make a presentation to inform your colleagues of these issues. Develop a presentation using a presentation package such as Microsoft's PowerPoint.

You can choose your presentation's emphasis from the following topics:

- Ethics as it relates to IT systems
- Types of crime aimed at IT systems (such as viruses)
- Types of crime that use IT systems as weapons (such as electronic theft of funds from one account to another)
- Security measures, how good they are, what they cost, how expensive they are to implement
- Electronic monitoring of employees (from employer and employee standpoints)
- Collection and use of personal information on consumers

SOURCES OF INFORMATION

- In the file **ETHICS.doc,** you'll find sources for the topics listed above.
- The Web is a great place to find lots of information.
- Most business publications, such as *BusinessWeek, InformationWeek, Fortune,* and *The Wall Street Journal,* frequently have good articles on ethics, cybercrime, and security. You can get some of these articles on the Web.
- General news publications such as *Newsweek* and *USA Today* print articles on these topics.

Your task is to weave the information you find into a coherent presentation using graphs and art where appropriate.

SOME PARTICULARS YOU SHOULD KNOW

1. Content Principles
   - Each slide should have a headline
   - Each slide should express one idea
   - Ideas should follow logically

2. Design Principles
   - Follow the "Rule of 7," which is no more than 7 lines per slide and 7 words per line
   - Keep it simple
   - Keep it organized
   - Create a path for the eye
   - Divide space in an interesting way
   - Use at least 30-point type
   - Use color and graphics carefully, consistently, and for a specific purpose
   - Use high-contrast colors (black/white, deep blue/white, etc.)
3. File: **ETHICS.doc** (Word file)

CASE 11:
BUILDING A WEB DATABASE SYSTEM

WEB-BASED CLASSIFIED SYSTEM

With the emergence of the Internet as a worldwide standard for communicating information, *Gabby's Gazetteer*, a medium-size community newspaper in central Colorado, is looking to enter the electronic commerce market.

In the listing of classified ads, advertisers place a small ad that lists items they wish to sell and provide a means (e.g., telephone number) by which prospective buyers can contact them.

The nature of a sale via a newspaper classified system goes as follows:

- During the course of the sale, the information flows in different directions at different stages.
- First, there is a downstream flow of information (from seller to buyer)—the listing in print on the newspaper. (Thus, the classified ad listing is just a way of bringing a buyer and seller together.)
- When a potential purchaser's interest has been raised, then that interest must be relayed upstream, usually by telephone or in person.
- Finally, a meeting should result that uses face-to-face negotiation to finalize the sale—if the sale can be agreed upon.

By placing the entire system on the Internet, the upstream and downstream communications are accomplished using a Web browser. The sale becomes more of an auction, because many potential buyers, all with equal status, can bid for the same item.

Any user who is trying to buy an item can

- View items for sale
- Bid on an item they wish to purchase

Any user who is trying to sell an item can

- Place a new item for sale
- Browse a list of the items that he or she is trying to sell, and examine the bids that have been made on each of those items
- Accept a bid on an item that he or she is selling

This system should also allow users to do some very basic administrative tasks, such as

- Browse the listings to see what is for sale
- Register with the system (users can browse without registering; but they must register if they want to sell an item or bid for an item)

Figure GP.2

Gabby's
Gazetteer
Classified
Registration
System

* Log on to the system
* Change their registration details

Your job will be to complete the following:

1. Develop and describe the entity-relationship diagram for the database that will support the above activities.
2. Use normalization to ensure the correctness of the tables.
3. Create the database using a personal DBMS package.

SOME PARTICULARS YOU SHOULD KNOW

1. Use Figure GP.2 as a baseline for your database design.
2. File: Not applicable.

CASE 12:
CREATING A DECISION SUPPORT SYSTEM

BUY VERSUS LEASE

A leading supplier of grapes to the wine-producing industry in California, On the Vine Grapes, wants to expand its delivery services and expand its reach to market by increasing its current fleet of delivery trucks. Some of the older vehicles were acquired through closed-end leases with required down payments, mileage restrictions, and hefty early termination penalties. Other vehicles were purchased using traditional purchase-to-own loans, which often resulted in high depreciation costs and large maintenance fees. All vehicles were acquired one at a time through local dealers.

On the Vine Grapes has asked you to assist in developing a lease/buy cost analysis worksheet in order to make the most cost-effective decision. Currently the director of operations, Bill Smith, has identified a 2005 Ford F-550 4x2 SD Super Cab 161.8 in. WB DRW HD XLT as the truck of choice for the business. This vehicle has a retail price of $34,997.00 or a lease price of $600/month through Ford Motor Credit Company.

Here are some basic fees and costs that you need to factor in:

1. **Lease Costs**

Refundable security deposit	$500
First month's payment at inception	$500
Other initial costs	$125
Monthly lease payment for remaining term	$600
Last month payment in advance	No
Allowable annual mileage	15,000
Estimated annual miles to be driven	20,000
Per mile charge for excess miles	0.10

2. **Purchase Costs**

Retail price including sales taxes, title	$34,997
Down payment	$4,000
Loan interest rate	8.75%
Will interest be deductible business or home equity interest?	Yes
Is the gross loaded weight of the vehicle over 6,000 lbs?	Yes

3. **Common Costs and Assumptions**

Total lease/loan term	36
Discount percent	8.75
Tax bracket—combined federal and state	33%
Business use percentage	100%

SOME PARTICULARS YOU SHOULD KNOW

1. In the file **BUYORLEASE.xls** is a template you can use to enter the information. There is also a sheet that has been developed to assist you with the annual depreciation for an automobile.
2. Create a detailed summary sheet of the lease/buy option for On the Vine Grapes.
3. File: **BUYORLEASE.xls** (Excel file).

CASE 13:
DEVELOPING AN ENTERPRISE RESOURCE PLANNING SYSTEM

PLANNING, REPORTING, AND DATA PROCESSING

The State Annual Report on Enterprise Resource Planning and Management was developed to provide a comprehensive view of the management and use of technology by the Higher Educational System of Colorado. This report shows the statewide issues surrounding information technology, priorities for the ensuing two years, initiatives and projects, performance management, and the information technology resources utilized to support the business processes of Higher Education during fiscal year 2004–2005. A comparison report is also generated to produce a percentage change in funds from fiscal year 2003–2004 to fiscal year 2004–2005.

Chief information officer (CIO) for the Department of Higher Education, David Paul, was required to report the estimated expenditures for technology across five appropriation categories: Employee Salaries/Benefits, Other Personal Services (OPS—noncareer service employees with no permanent status), Expenses (all hardware purchases under $1,000, travel, training, and general office expenses), Operating Capital Outlay (OCO), and Data Processing Services. Most of these performance management initiatives have been measured using manual processes. Several reporting units documented the need for automated measurement tools in the future to take advantage of the full opportunities for improvement. David Paul has asked you to assist him in organizing this information and calculating some of the requirements established by the State Board of Education. Along with the appropriation categories mentioned above, each institution is categorized according to status (2 Year, 4 Year Public, or 4 Year Private). This will aid in the overall analysis for current and future resource planning.

SOME PARTICULARS YOU SHOULD KNOW

1. You need to create a detailed report for:
   a. Summary of overall change from 2003–2004 fiscal year (FY) to 2004–2005 FY
   b. Percentage of budget allocated to data processing services
   c. Percentage of 2 year, 4 year public, and 4 year private institutions allocating resources to data processing services
2. Develop a graphical representation of the percentage of 2 year, 4 year public, and 4 year private institutions allocating resources to data processing services
3. File: **COLORADOHIGHERED.xls** (Excel file)

CASE 14:
ASSESSING A WIRELESS FUTURE

EMERGING TRENDS AND TECHNOLOGY

"Intelligent wireless handheld devices are going to explode, absolutely explode over the next several years."—Steve Ballmer, CEO, Microsoft.

Wireless, mobility, small form factor, pervasive computing, the anytime network—whatever name you choose—it's here. The price of easy-to-handle devices which provide access to a variety of applications and information is rapidly falling while the efficiencies of such devices are increasing. More and more, the business user is looking to use mobile devices to perform tasks that previously could be handled only by the desktop PC. End-user adoption is skyrocketing. The next 18 months will demonstrate a true growing period for mobile computing as the world changes to one characterized by the mobile user.

As this market sector grows, software and information companies are evolving their products and services. Wireless mobility and associated functionality provide new market opportunities for both established companies and new entrants to increase efficiency and take advantage of new revenue possibilities. The services to Internet-enabled mobile devices create a vast array of new business opportunities for companies as they develop products and services that utilize location, time, and immediate access to information in new and innovative ways.

Some of the lower profile topics that are currently being developed at this time include:

- Hard drives for wireless devices
- Global-roaming movement
- Mobile power supplies that run on next-generation fuel cells

All three could bring about significant changes in the wireless space.

You have been asked to prepare a presentation using a presentation package such as Microsoft's PowerPoint. Using the list of wireless solution providers and manufacturers provided in WIRELESS.htm, select at least two developers and create a presentation that will emphasize the following topics:

1. What are the current products or services under development?
2. What is the target market for that product or service?
3. What are the key features that product or service will bring to the wireless industry?
4. Which provider/manufacturer/developer seems to be the first to market with their product?
5. How is the wireless product or service content being delivered?
6. Are the products or services able to deploy interactive multimedia applications to any digital wireless device, on any carrier, or across any type of network?
7. Are there any new privacy concerns that are being discussed in relation to the new products or services? (These can include concerns from being able to track users' preferences, purchasing history or browsing preferences, or the capability to track a user's physical location while using a wireless device.)
8. How does this product or solution affect the global marketplace?
9. What is the current retail price for the wireless products or solutions?
10. Is current bandwidth available to the wireless industry a concern?

Your task is to weave the information you find into a coherent presentation using graphs and art where appropriate.

SOME PARTICULARS YOU SHOULD KNOW

1. Content Principles

   - Each slide should have a headline
   - Each slide should express one idea
   - Ideas should follow logically

2. Design Principles

   - Follow the "Rule of 7"—no more than 7 lines per slide and 7 words per line
   - Keep it simple
   - Keep it organized
   - Create a path for the eye
   - Divide space in an interesting way
   - Use at least 30-point type
   - Use color and graphics carefully, consistently, and for a specific purpose
   - Use high-contrast colors (black/white, deep blue/white, etc.)

3. File: **WIRELESS.htm** (html file)

CASE 15:
EVALUATING THE NEXT GENERATION

DOT-COM ASPS

E-business is creating a new set of challenges not only for dot-com start-ups but also for well-established brick-and-mortar companies. Driven by the need to capture increasing shares of business online, IT managers take the first step by deciding on a commerce application. Then they face the most important decision: whether to assign implementation, deployment, and application hosting to internal IT resources or to contract for these services with an ASP.

A few years ago, no one had even heard the term *application service provider (ASP)*. Now the ASP market is a certified phenomenon. In the short space of two years, the concept of leasing applications to businesses has grown to an interesting but unproven proposition in an ever-expanding industry.

You have been hired by Front Range Car Rental, a major car rental company in Colorado, to research ways to use technology to leverage more business. The company needs a Web service written which transacts reservations on its back-end mainframe system. This Web service will need to be made available to airline partners to integrate the travel booking process. When consumers book a flight, they are also given the option to reserve a car from the airline site. The rental details will need to be captured and transported to the car rental company's Web service, which processes the reservation. This new capability will help the car rental company to drive more bookings and achieve a competitive advantage in a highly commoditized market.

The major task that Front Range Car Rental needs you to research is what the cost benefits would be for in-house implementation and an ASP deployment. You have been given an analysis spreadsheet, **DOTCOMASP.xls,** with all the detailed information; however, you will need to use the Internet in order to find current price information. Another file, **DOTCOMASP_SEARCH. htm,** has been developed for you with a list of search engines that will provide you with a focal point for your research.

SOME PARTICULARS YOU SHOULD KNOW

1. All ASPs are not created equal. Here are some questions to help you identify their strengths, weaknesses, capabilities, and core competencies.

   - Does the ASP offer full life-cycle services, including proof-of-concept, installation, operations, training, support, and proactive evolution services?
   - What is the ASP's depth and breadth of technical expertise? What are the company's specialties?
   - Where and how did key technical staff obtain their expertise?
   - Does the ASP have actual customers online and if so, what results have they achieved?
   - Does the ASP offer service-level agreements and what are the penalties for SLA violations?
   - Specifically, how does the ASP's infrastructure deliver:

     High availability (uptime)?
     Assured data integrity?
     Scalability?
     Reliability?
     High performance?
     Security and access control?

   - Does the ASP offer 24 × 7 technical support to end users? Escalation procedures? High-priority problem resolution? Dedicated account managers?
   - Can the ASP provide development expertise to customize the applications?
   - How does the ASP handle updates? Adding product modules?
   - Is the ASP capable of assisting with add-on projects such as bringing a new factory online or adding a new supplier?
   - Can the ASP provide a comprehensive suite of integrated applications (versus a single application)?

2. File: **DOTCOMASP.xls** (Excel File) and **DOTCOMASP_SEARCH.htm** (html file).

CASE 16:
ANALYZING STRATEGIC AND COMPETITIVE ADVANTAGE

DETERMINING OPERATING LEVERAGE

Pony Espresso is a small business that sells specialty coffee drinks at office buildings. Each morning and afternoon, trucks arrive at offices' front entrances, and the office employees purchase various beverages with names such as Java du Jour and Café de Colombia. The business is profitable. But Pony Espresso offices are located to the north of town, where lease rates are less expensive, and the principal sales area is south of town. This means that the trucks must drive cross-town four times each day.

The cost of transportation to and from the sales area, plus the power demands of the trucks' coffee brewing equipment, is a significant portion of the variable costs. Pony Espresso could reduce the amount of driving—and, therefore, the variable costs—if it moves the offices much closer to the sales area.

Pony Espresso presently has fixed costs of $10,000 per month. The lease of a new office, closer to the sales area, would cost an additional $2,200 per month. This would increase the fixed costs to $12,200 per month.

Although the lease of new offices would increase the fixed costs, a careful estimate of the potential savings in gasoline and vehicle maintenance indicates that Pony Espresso could reduce the variable costs from $0.60 per unit to $0.35 per unit. Total sales are unlikely to increase as a result of the move, but the savings in variable costs should increase the annual profit.

You have been hired by Pony Espresso to assist in the cost analysis and new lease options to determine a growth in profit margin. You will also need to calculate a degree of operating leverage to better understand the company's profitability. Degree of operating leverage (DOL) will give the CEO of Pony Espresso, Darian Presley, a great deal of information for setting operating targets and planning profitability.

SOME PARTICULARS YOU SHOULD KNOW

1. Consider the information provided—especially look at the change in the variability of the profit from month to month. From November through January, when it is much more difficult to lure office workers out into the cold to purchase coffee, Pony Espresso barely breaks even. In fact, in December of 2005, the business lost money.

2. First, develop the cost analysis on the existing lease information using the monthly sales figures provided to you in the file **PONYESPRESSO.xls.** Second, develop the cost analysis from the new lease information provided above.

3. You need to calculate the variability that is reflected in the month-to-month standard deviation of earnings for the current cost structure and the projected cost structure.

4. Do not consider any association with downsizing such as overhead; simply focus on the information provided to you.

5. You will need to calculate the EBIT—earnings before interest and taxes.

6. Would the DOL and business risk increase or decrease if Pony Espresso moved its office? *Note:* Variability in profit levels, whether measured as EBIT, operating income, or net income, does not necessarily increase the level of business risk as the DOL increases.

7. File: **PONYESPRESSO.xls** (Excel file).

CASE 17:
BUILDING A DECISION SUPPORT SYSTEM

BREAK-EVEN ANALYSIS

Ski-YA! is a Colorado-based company that sells high-performance ski equipment. When it comes to the serious business of sliding downhill, the Ski-YA! dudes of Colorado don't trouble themselves with petty categories; to them, all alpine snow equipment is summed up in one word, AWESOME!

This season's offerings at Ski-YA! are no exception. Skis continue to grow wider for better flotation beyond the groomers, and the sidecuts, the stick's hourglass shape designed to help a skier turn, now reflect the needs of terrain skiers. Even bindings have been rejiggered: forget the drill and screwdriver; the latest fittings snap or slide into place, extending ski life and improving energy transfer.

The Ski-YA! company wants to begin selling a new pair of skis, labeled the Downhill Demons, in the upcoming ski season. It wants to know how many skis it will have to sell in order to break even on its investment in materials and equipment. The chief financial officer has provided the following information:

Fixed Costs

Metal molding machine:	$200,000
Milling machine:	$150,000
Sander and grinder:	$10,000
Presses:	$25,000
Silkscreen machine:	$50,000

Variable Costs (per Unit)

Packaging material	$5.00
Raw material	$100.00
Shipping	$20.00

The marketing department estimates that it can sell the new skis for $400.00 per unit. Further projections estimate that an average of 200 units will be sold per month. The goal is that the skis will break even and start to earn a profit within the first year. Ski-YA!'s target profit level for the end of the first fiscal year is $100,000.

SOME PARTICULARS YOU SHOULD KNOW

1. First, create a break-even analysis where your goal is to determine how many units you must sell to recover all of your fixed costs.

2. Then create a target profit analysis where your goal is to determine how many units you must sell to reach a predefined profit level. The difference between the two is that at breakeven your target profit is zero, whereas when you specify a target profit that is greater than zero, you are setting your goal above the break-even point.

3. You will want to create a table sheet that contains the data used to generate the break-even/target profit chart. This includes 10 data points on either side of the break-even/target profit point.

4. Finally create a chart where you can visually measure your break-even or target profit level along with total fixed and variable costs. If you choose to calculate the number of months before you reach a break-even or target profit, those numbers will be reported here.

5. File: **SkiYA.xls** (Excel file).

CASE 18:
CREATING A FINANCIAL ANALYSIS

QUALIFICATION AND AMORTIZATION WORKSHEETS

The Foothills Savings Bank (FSB) is a federally insured stock savings bank which was organized in 1982 as a privately insured savings and loan association in Denver, Colorado. It received federal insurance in 1985 and a federal savings bank charter in 1986. FSB is a member of the Federal Home Loan Bank (FHLB) system and its deposits are insured by the Federal Deposit Insurance Corporation (FDIC) to the maximum amount provided by law.

The Foothills Savings Bank offers loans for owner-occupied properties, second homes, and investment homes. FSB offers first trust residential conventional fixed rate and ARM (adjustable rate mortgage) loans. Conventional financing is any mortgage that is not insured or guaranteed by federal, state, or local governments. FSB is now offering an online prequalification worksheet for its customers or prospective customers to use. FSB requires a minimum of 10 percent down, which is generally required for conventional financing.

It is your responsibility to complete a mortgage qualification worksheet and then create a mortgage amortization analysis worksheet from the data in the mortgage qualification worksheet.

SOME PARTICULARS YOU SHOULD KNOW

1. A template for the mortgage qualification worksheet has been created; however, you need to complete the formulas.
2. The Qualifying Section:
   - The first qualifying number needs to calculate the maximum monthly payment, assuming there are no long-term debts. It is computed by multiplying the total income by the housing cost ratio and dividing the result by 12.
   - The second qualifying number takes into account the monthly debt payments, applying the total debt service ratio. It is calculated by multiplying the total debt by the debt service ratio and dividing the result by 12.
   - Mortgage companies usually qualify people for monthly payments that are no higher than the lesser of the two results.
   - By default, your worksheet should assume a housing cost ratio of 0.28 and a total debt service ratio of 0.36, which are standards often used for conventional mortgages.
3. The Loan Amount Section:

   The table created below the qualifying section calculates the amount of a loan you might qualify for with the monthly payment. Depending on the circumstances, some or all of the following will be true:

   In all cases, the monthly payment will include principal and interest payments.
   - In most cases, it will include a monthly escrow deposit to cover taxes and mortgage insurance, if any. In some cases, homeowner's insurance is also included in this calculation. Use your best guess estimates for these figures.
   - If the customer is buying a condominium or co-op unit, the monthly payment figure may also include the homeowner's dues and/or maintenance fees. You will need to estimate these monthly costs and type them into the appropriate cells.
4. Creating an amortization analysis worksheet:
   - Use the data from the mortgage qualification worksheet to create an amortization table. You will need to calculate beginning balance, principal paid, interest paid, total principal, total interest, and ending balance per payment period for the life of the loan.
5. File: **Mortgage.xls** (Excel file).

CASE 19:
BUILDING A SCHEDULING DECISION SUPPORT SYSTEM

AIRLINE CREW SCHEDULING

Rockies Airline is a new airline company that maintains a schedule of two daily flights between Salt Lake City, Denver, and Chicago. Rockies Airline took to the air on February 11, 2004, with the inauguration of service between Denver International Airport and Salt Lake City. Every Rockies Airline aircraft is outfitted with roomy all-leather seats, each equipped with 24 channels of DIRECTV programming.

Rockies Airline must strategically position itself as a low-cost provider in a very volatile industry. Therefore, it must work toward finding a minimum cost assignment of flight crews to a given flight schedule while satisfying restrictions dictated by the Federal Aviation Administration. Rockies Airline needs to solve the crew scheduling problem that is an involved and time-consuming process.

To begin, you will want to figure out all the possible crew rotations. You will want to find an approximate expected cost of each combination and then solve the traditional crew scheduling problem by using these costs. Second, you will want to calculate the crew constraints in order to determine the decision variables, constraints, and objectives.

You have been given Rockies Airline flight schedule as follows:

From	To	Departure	Arrival	Departure	Arrival
Salt Lake City	Denver	9:00 AM	12:00 PM	2:00 PM	5:00 PM
Salt Lake City	Chicago	10:00 AM	2:00 PM	3:00 PM	7:00 PM
Denver	Salt Lake City	8:00 AM	11:00 PM	2:00 PM	5:00 PM
Denver	Chicago	9:00 AM	11:00 PM	3:00 PM	5:00 PM
Chicago	Salt Lake City	8:00 AM	12:00 PM	2:00 PM	6:00 PM
Chicago	Denver	10:00 AM	12:00 PM	4:00 PM	6:00 PM

SOME PARTICULARS YOU SHOULD KNOW

1. A crew that leaves a city in the morning has to return there at night.
2. The crew can be brought back on another airline. This would always be on an 8 PM flight. There are 6 airplanes in use.
3. When a crew is flying, the cost is $200 per hour.
4. When a crew is waiting or being flown back, the cost is $75 per hour.
5. How should the company schedule its crews to minimize cost?
6. *Hint:* You will want to install the Solver Add-in to assist with this.
7. File: **CREWSCHEDULING.xls** (Excel file).

CASE 20:
CREATING A DATABASE MANAGEMENT SYSTEM

MOUNTAIN BIKE RENTALS

Vail Resort in Vail, Colorado, is internationally known as one of the best places in North America for mountain biking. Since 1973, Slopeside Bike Rentals has been a tradition in the area. At Slopeside Bike Rentals customers will find the largest selection of bikes, parts, accessories, books, maps, clothing, shocks, helmets, eyewear, shoes, car racks, and touring gear in the area with everything you need for on and off the road. Its state-of-the-art demo and rental program has everything from premium dual suspension to kids' bikes and trailers.

You have been employed for the past three summers by Slopeside Bike Rentals. Recently, there has been a surge in business and the owners need a more accurate way to manage the rental business. You have decided to create a database to help the owners keep track of the bike rentals, who the customers are, amount paid, and any damage to the bikes when they are rented. Currently Slopeside Bike Rentals owns 13 mountain bikes in its fleet of rentals. The bikes vary in type, size, and parts. When customers rent bikes, they are required to leave their driver's license number and to give you a home address, phone number, and credit card number.

You have designed the entity classes and primary keys for the database as the following:

Entity	Primary Key
Bike	Bike_ID
Customer	Customer_ID
Rental	Rental_ID

You have also identified the following business rules:

1. Rentals can have many customers assigned but must have at least one.
2. A bike must be assigned to one and only one rental type.
3. A customer can rent one or more bikes at one time.
4. A bike can be assigned to only one customer but need not be assigned to any customer.

Your job is to be completed in the following phases:

1. Develop and describe the entity-relationship diagram.
2. Use normalization to assure the correctness of the tables (relations).
3. Create the database using a personal DBMS package (preferably Microsoft Access).
4. Slopeside Bike Rentals has the following fee structures for its 13 bike rentals:
5. Use the DBMS package to create the basic report in Figure GP.3.

Description	Cost per Hour
Specialized Rockhopper	$12
Specialized Rockhopper	12
Trek Fuel 70	12
Trek Fuel 80	15
Trek Fuel 80	15
Trek Fuel 90	16
Marin Downhill FRS	16
Marin Downhill FRS	16
Marin Downhill FRS	16
Specialized Stumpjumper FSR	18
Specialized Stumpjumper FSR	18
Specialized Stumpjumper FSR	18
Specialized Stumpjumper Hardtail	20

Figure GP.3

Slopeside Bike
Rental Report

Slopeside Bike Rental Report

Description	Date	Last Name	First Name	Amount Paid
Specialized Rockhopper				
	5/30/2005	Smith	Sue	$24.00
	6/2/2005	Smith	Sue	$42.00
	7/5/2005	Dunn	David	$72.00
Summary for Specialized Rockhopper (3 detail records)				$138.00
Trek Fuel 70				
	6/29/2005	Myers	Mike	$24.00
	6/30/2005	Myers	Mike	$24.00
Summary for Trek Fuel 70 (2 detail records)				$48.00
Trek Fuel 80				
	7/5/2005	Elliott	Raymond	$30.00
	7/7/2005	Elliott	Raymond	$15.00
	7/11/2005	Lapierre	Lynne	$225.00
	7/12/2005	Lapierre	Lynne	$37.50
Summary for Trek Fuel 80 (4 detail records)				$307.50
Trek Fuel 90				
	7/1/2005	Smith	Sue	$48.00
	7/11/2005	Dunn	David	$32.00
Summary for Trek Fuel 90 (2 detail records)				$80.00
Grand Total				$573.50

SOME PARTICULARS YOU SHOULD KNOW

1. You may not be able to develop a report that looks exactly like the one in Figure GP.3. However, your report should include the same information.
2. One of your tables will need a composite primary key.
3. File: Not applicable.

CASE 21:
EVALUATING THE SECURITY OF INFORMATION

WIRELESS NETWORK VULNERABILITY

Empty cans of Pringles could be helping malicious hackers spot wireless networks that are open to attack. Security companies have demonstrated that a directional antenna made with a Pringles can most often significantly improves the chances of finding wirelessly networked computers. An informal survey carried out by i-sec (an Internet security research company) using the homemade antenna found that over two-thirds of the networks surveyed were doing nothing to protect themselves. Known as the "PringlesCantenna," these are rapidly becoming popular because they are cheap (under $10) and easy to set up.

Not surprisingly, wireless network security, particularly regarding wireless local area networks (WLANs), is the number one concern of network managers, and an entire industry has grown to serve the ever-changing demands of wireless-network-based information integrity. As companies and home users have gradually adopted wireless technology, special security precautions are required to deal with the unique nature of wireless communications. After all, wireless purposely puts information out on the airwaves, and anyone within range and equipped with an appropriate receiver (e.g., PringlesCantenna) would be able to grab this information and put it to all kinds of questionable use. Since this is the case, many wireless networks implement inherent authentication and encryption mechanisms to provide basic assurance to wireless users that their information will at least be difficult to decrypt and their networks at least challenging to crack.

SOME PARTICULARS YOU SHOULD KNOW

1. Create an analysis report based on a thorough Internet search that discusses the tips, techniques, and best practices to protect against this type of amateur hacking.

2. Include a summary of the types of detection and prevention technology available, specifically the use of firewalls and intrusion detection software.

3. In your analysis report, include the current statistics on identity theft, the number of times networks are hacked, and the total annual cost of online security breaches to corporations.

4. During your research, you might also consider finding statistics on the percentage of companies that have yet to implement adequate security measures and the percentage of companies that spend 5 percent or less of their IT budgets on security for their networks.

5. File: Not applicable.

CASE 22:
ASSESSING THE VALUE OF SUPPLY CHAIN MANAGEMENT

OPTIMIZING SHIPMENTS

One of the main products of the Fairway Woods Company is custom-made golf clubs. The clubs are manufactured at three plants (Denver, Colorado; Phoenix, Arizona; and Dallas, Texas) and are then shipped by truck to five distribution warehouses in Sacramento, California; Salt Lake City, Utah; Albuquerque, New Mexico; Chicago, Illinois; and New York City, New York. Because shipping costs are a major expense, management is investigating a way to reduce them. For the upcoming golf season, an estimate has been created as to the total output needed from each manufacturing plant and how much each warehouse will require to satisfy its customers. The CIO from Fairway Woods Company has created a spreadsheet for you, **FAIRWAYS.xls,** of the shipping costs from each manufacturing plant to each warehouse as a baseline analysis.

SOME PARTICULARS YOU SHOULD KNOW

1. The problem presented involves the shipment of goods from three plants to five regional warehouses.

2. Goods can be shipped from any plant to any warehouse, but it costs more to ship goods over long distances than over short distances.

3. The challenge presented is to determine the amounts to ship from each plant to each warehouse at a minimum total shipping cost in order to meet the regional demand, while not exceeding the plant supplies.

4. Specifically you need to focus on:

    a. Minimizing the total shipping cost.

    b. Total shipped must be less than or equal to supply at plant.

    c. Totals shipped to warehouses must be greater than or equal to demand at warehouses.

    d. Number to ship must be greater than or equal to 0.

5. File: **FAIRWAYS.xls** (Excel file).

Electronic Commerce PROJECTS

BEST IN COMPUTER STATISTICS AND RESOURCES

For both personal and professional reasons, you'll find it necessary to stay up with technology and technology changes throughout your life. Right now, knowing about technology—the latest trends, new innovations, processor speeds, wireless communications capabilities, and the like—can help you support technology infrastructure recommendations for a company in one of your term papers. That same kind of information can help you determine which personal technologies you need to buy and use.

As you progress through your career, you'll make numerous business presentations and recommendations, most of which will contain some sort of discussion of the best uses of technology from an organizational point of view. Indeed, if you plan to move up the corporate ladder to the C-level (CEO, CFO, CIO, etc.), a knowledge of the organizational uses of technology is essential. Connect to several Web sites that offer computer statistics and resources and answer the following questions for each.

A. What categories of personal technologies are covered?

B. What categories of organizational uses of technology are covered?

C. To what extent is time-based (e.g., year-by-year) numerical data provided?

D. Who supports the site? Is the site for-profit or not-for-profit?

E. Are the various types of research reports free or do you have to pay a fee?

F. How helpful is the site from a personal point of view?

G. How helpful is the site from an organizational point of view?

CONSUMER INFORMATION

Many consumer organizations provide databases of information on the Internet. At those sites you can read the latest product reviews, search for new pharmaceuticals that cure diseases (or alleviate symptoms of them), and access safety information for products such as automobiles and children's toys.

These types of sites are invaluable to you for a number of reasons. First, they can help you be better informed and make more intelligent decisions when making product and service purchases. Second, you'll also find these sites a good resource when writing term and research papers. Sites such as Better Business Bureau (www.bbb.org), Consumer Reports (www.consumerreports.org), Consumer World (www.consumerworld.org), and Consumer Information Publications (www.pueblo.gsa.gov) post a wealth of information you can use in your personal and academic life.

Pick a product you're interested in purchasing, do some looking around on the Internet at consumer information sites, and answer the following questions.

A. What sites did you review? Which were helpful and why?

B. Is the information opinion only, completely factual, or a combination of the two?

C. Who supports the sites you reviewed? The government? Not-for-profit organizations? For-profit organizations?

D. How important will this type of consumer information become as electronic commerce becomes more widespread on the Internet?

INTERVIEWING AND NEGOTIATING TIPS

During your job search process, the Internet can offer you very valuable specific information. In the area of interviewing and negotiating, for example, the Internet contains more than 5,000 sites devoted to interviewing skills, negotiating tips, and the like.

Interviewing and negotiating are just as important as searching for a job. Once you line up that first important interview, you may still not land the job if you're not properly prepared. If you do receive a job offer, you may be surprised to know that you can negotiate such things as moving expenses, signing bonuses, and allowances for technology in your home.

We've provided Web sites for you that address the interviewing and negotiating skills you need in today's marketplace. Review some of these sites (and any others that you may find). Then, develop a list of do's and don'ts for the interviewing process. Next, develop a list of tips that seem helpful to you that will increase your effectiveness during the negotiation process. Once you've developed these two lists, prepare a short class presentation. In your presentation, be sure to include the names of the Web sites you visited as well as their addresses. Distribute this presentation electronically to everyone in your class.

META DATA

Meta data means "data about the data." In the context of Web pages, it refers to the notations in the header (**<head>**) part of the Web page. Here's an example:

```
<html>
<head>
<title>Management Information Systems for the Information Age</title>
<META name = "description" content = "Everything you wanted to know about computer systems in business">
<Meta name = "keyword" content = "MIS, business IT, database, artificial intelligence, security, electronic commerce">
</head>
```

Although the **<title>** part of the header is not, strictly speaking, meta data, it is strongly related. That's the wording that describes the page when you add it to your Favorites list. It's also very important for search engines because it determines the placement of your Web site within the list of possible answers to a search term.

The wording within the **<META...>** tags is used by some search engines to classify your Web page. However, you can't depend on that since many do not. Find three of these sites and answer the following questions:

A. Does Google use the **<METAdata...>** tag to classify your Web page?

B. How can you ensure that a search engine will classify your Web site as being about the topic you intend? (Say, for instance, you have a site about robots.)

C. There are internationally recognized standards for meta data tags. What is the name of one of these?

D. Find a software package that generates meta data tags. What is it called and how much does it cost?

E. What was the best piece of advice you found on creating meta data on a Web page?

BUREAU OF LABOR STATISTICS

The Bureau of Labor Statistics (BLS, at www.bls.gov) of the U.S. Federal government states that its role is as the "principal fact-finding agency for the Federal Government in the broad field of labor economics and statistics." As you might well guess then, the BLS provides a wealth of information concerning employment and the economy. Connect to the BLS's Web site and answer the following questions.

    A. What type of information is contained on the *Kid's Page*? Did you find any of the information also suitable to you?

    B. What sort of information concerning workplace safety and illness is available? How is this information categorized? How would this type of information be helpful to a business manager?

    C. What type of demographic information is available? What "demographics" make up the key categories by which demographic information is provided?

    D. What is contained in the *Occupational Outlook Handbook*? How often is it updated? What parts of the handbook are particularly relevant to you as you prepare to enter the job market? Why?

    E. Within Inflation & Consumer Spending, the BLS provides a lot of information concerning consumer price indexes and producer price indexes. What is the consumer price index and what does it mean? What is the producer price index and what does it mean?

    F. What interesting statistics do you find when reviewing employment by state information? How is your state faring as compared to other states?

DEMOGRAPHICS

For organizations focusing on meeting wants or desires of end consumers, the demographic makeup of the target audience is key. The more you know about your target audience, the better equipped you are to develop and market products. Demographics is a broad general term that can include any characteristic such as zip code, annual income, gender, age, marital status, hobbies, and so on.

    And you can find all sorts of demographic information on the Internet. Connect to a couple of different demographic-related Web sites and see what they have to offer. As you do, answer the following questions for each.

    A. Who is the target audience of the site?

    B. Who is the provider of the site?

    C. Is the provider a private (for-profit) organization or a not-for-profit organization?

    D. How often is the demographic information updated?

    E. Does the site require that you pay a subscription fee to access its demographic information?

    F. How helpful would the information be if you wanted to start a new business or sell various types of products?

FREE AND RENTABLE STORAGE SPACE

Information is an essential resource in the information age. You must ensure its integrity, know that it's useful, and always know that you have a backup of your information just in case your primary storage is damaged or stolen. To help, you can use the services of a file hosting service on the Web. These sites offer you storage of your information that can be accessed from anywhere in the world. You can use the services of these sites to back up your information and also create an environment in which you can share your information with other people.

A few of these file hosting services include My Docs Online (www.mydocsonline.com), Box (www.box.net), and Yahoo! Briefcase (http://briefcase.yahoo.com). Visit any of these sites and a few others that you find through searches and answer the following questions for each.

- **A.** Does the site provide free storage? If so, what is the limit?
- **B.** What type of information can you store (video, text, photos, etc.)?
- **C.** Can you establish multiple users with different passwords who can access your storage area?
- **D.** Must you sign a contract for a certain duration (annual, etc.)?
- **E.** Are there different levels of services provided such as personal, enterprise, workgroup, and so on?
- **F.** To you, is using a file hosting service on the Web better than backing up your information to writable CDs or DVDs? Why or why not?

GATHERING COMPETITIVE INTELLIGENCE

When considering new business opportunities, you need knowledge about the competition. One of the things many new business owners fail to do is to see how many competitors there are and what differentiates them before launching their business. You may find there are too many and that they would be tough competition for you. Or, you may find that there are few competitors and the ones who are out there aren't doing a terrific job.

Generate a new business idea you could launch on the Internet. (Perform this task in less than 15 minutes focusing on the products or services you will sell.) Now, seek out and look at some of the Web sites of businesses in the competitive space you're thinking of entering. As you do, answer the following questions.

- **A.** How many sites did you find that are offering the same products or services you're planning to offer?
- **B.** How did you find those sites?
- **C.** How many are in your country and how many are in other countries?
- **D.** Did you come across a site from another country that has a unique approach that you did not see on any of the sites in your own country?
- **E.** In general, has competition intensified because of the Internet and the Web? Justify your answer.

ETHICAL COMPUTING GUIDELINES

Ethical computing encompasses many topics: privacy, intellectual property, abuse of resources, character defamation, to name just a few. Unethical behavior can be as mild as rudeness in an e-mail or as lethal as stalking and death threats. Some unethical behavior is illegal, but not all of it is.

The Computer Ethics Institute Web site at www.brook.edu/its/cei/cei_hp.htm has a list of 10 commandments to guide the use of information technology and the Association for Computer Machinery (ACM) specifies a code of ethical behavior as do many other organizations.

Find answers to the following questions on the Web:

A. Find a code of ethics from an organization of your choosing. What do you think are the best five guiding principles from all the tips that you found?

B. Are chain letters good or bad? Are they illegal? Summarize the opposing arguments you find.

C. How does anonymous e-mail work and why would you use it?

D. What are five ways that e-mail use can be unethical?

E. Why is the deliberate spreading of viruses unethical? Name at least five reasons.

EXPLORING GOOGLE EARTH

Google Earth is a free virtual globe program that uses satellite and aerial images combined with a geographic information system. It allows you to pick a place on the globe and zoom in to see all sorts of features like the locations of schools, sports venues, coffee shops, shopping malls, movie/DVD rental stores, etc. The list is very long.

You can even layer multiple searches and save your results. The site also hosts a large Google Earth Community that shares information and annotations.

The image resolution varies across regions, but most large cities around the world are depicted in high-resolution detail showing buildings and streets and trees and other features.

Download the Google Earth application from http://earth.google.com and answer the following questions:

A. In the area where you live, how is the resolution compared to the resolution for Washington, D.C.?

B. Can you see your own street? How about individual houses?

C. Zoom in to your home county and mark elementary schools. How many are there? Less than 10? More than 10? More than 50?

D. Choose a university location and zoom in. How clearly can you see the buildings? How about the cars in the parking lots?

E. Can you find the Eiffel Tower in Paris, France; the Brandenburg Gate (Brandenburger Tor) in Berlin, Germany; and Buckingham Palace in London, England?

FINANCIAL AID RESOURCES

On the Internet, you can find valuable databases that give you access to financial aid resources as you attend school. These resources can be in the form of scholarships—money you don't have to pay back—and standard student loans. And there are a variety of financial aid lenders, ranging from traditional banks, to the government, to private parties wanting to give something back to society. Find at least three Web sites that provide financial aid databases and answer the following questions for each.

A. Do you have to register as a user to access information?

B. Do you have to pay a fee to access information?

C. Can you build a profile of yourself and use it as you search?

D. Can you apply for aid while at the site or must you request paper applications that you need to complete and return by mail?

E. By what sort of categories of aid can you search?

F. What about your school? What sort of searchable database of financial aid does it offer? How does it compare to the other sites you visited? Does your school's financial aid site provide any links to other sources of information? If so, what are those sources?

FINDING HOSTING SERVICES

There are many options for hosting services for e-commerce Web sites. You can decide to acquire the necessary computer and communications hardware and software to manage your own technical infrastructure, or you can let a specialist firm do it for you. Unless you're really into the technical side of things, it's probably better to work with a firm that specializes in it. They are called *Web hosting services* and there are plenty of them around. Cost, reliability, security, and customer service are some of the criteria you might use in selecting a hosting service. If you're planning to have your business located in a country with poor telecommunications services, don't forget that you can choose a hosting service located in a country with a more reliable telecommunications infrastructure, anywhere in the world.

Some companies provide directories that make it easy for you to find and compare prices and features of Web hosting companies, sort of like shopping malls for Web hosting services. An example of such a company is FindYourHosting.com (www.findyourhosting.com). Take a look at its site to see some of the options available. As you consider Web hosting services, answer the following questions.

A. Compare the costs of the various hosting services. Were you able to find one that seems to be within a reasonable budget?

B. How can you evaluate the reliability of various Web hosting services?

C. How can you evaluate the quality of a Web hosting company's customer service? What do you have a right to expect in the way of customer service and also security?

GLOBAL STATISTICS AND RESOURCES

Thomas Friedman said it best: The world is flat. Simply put, we are one big group of people, no longer constrained by geographic borders, time zones, language, or even culture. To be successful in the business world, you must be willing to have international suppliers, international customers, and international business partners.

Therefore, knowing about specific regions and countries around the world is vitally important. Right now, regions such as the Pacific Rim are emerging as world economic powers. In 5 to 10 years that may be Central and South America or perhaps Russia. Beyond that, Africa may emerge. Within each of those regions, some countries are emerging more quickly than others.

Pick a country that interests you and also that you know little about. Connect to some of the global statistics and resources Web sites we've provided on the Web site for this book as well as any other sites you can find and answer the following questions for the country you chose.

A. What is the current population?

B. What are the primary industries and exports?

C. What is the primary language?

D. What are the country's natural resources?

E. What population demographics were you able to find (e.g., gender ratio, birth and death rates, education, income distribution, etc.)?

F. What is the country's government type?

GOLD, SILVER, INTEREST RATES, AND MONEY

Gold and silver have traditionally been kept as hedges against inflation and an uncertain future. Many people consider a rise in the price of gold and/or silver to be an early indicator of a slowing economy, perhaps leading to recession or even a depression.

During the first half of 2006, for the first time since 1981, when mortgage rates were 15 percent or more, the price of gold went above $600 per ounce. The reason is said to be the falling price of the dollar compared to other world currencies. The mounting national debt and uncertainty about U.S. foreign policy were also contributing to a sense of insecurity about the future.

Analysts were concerned that for the above reasons, inflation would start creeping up, although the Federal Reserve was working to try and keep inflation low, since high inflation rates damage the economy in many ways. Find answers to the following questions on the Web:

A. What is the current price of gold and silver? How does it compare to the price on January 1, 2006?

B. What is the Federal Reserve's current interest rate compared to the rate on January 1, 2006?

C. What is the current rate of inflation compared to what it was on January 1, 2006?

D. What is the current exchange rate for the dollar compared to the British pound (£), the Euro (€), and the Yen (¥) today? How do these compare to the rates on January 1, 2006?

E. What were all of the above values in the year that you were born?

PRIVACY LAWS AND LEGISLATION

Privacy laws in the United States tend to be aimed at specific industries, such as the video rental industry, or agencies of the federal government. There are also specific privacy laws that are passed on a state-by-state basis. For example, California has a law that requires companies that discover their databases have been breached to inform people whose personal information was included in that database. This law was passed to try to address the rising rate of identity theft.

Other industrialized countries have different approaches to privacy legislation. The European Union has issued a directive that all member nations enact laws to guarantee citizens specific privacy rights, but New Zealand has, perhaps, the most restrictive set of privacy laws.

Search the Web and find answers to the following questions:

A. How did Choice Point, the Bank of America, LexisNexis, and DSW Shoe Stores contribute to the heightened interest of legislators in privacy laws?

B. What are the major provisions of the European directive on the protection of personal information gathered by businesses?

C. What are the pro and con arguments on the topic of the U.S. Homeland Security Act as it applies to personal privacy? List at least three points on each side.

D. What are the main stipulations of the Family Educational Rights and Privacy Act (FERPA)?

E. What is the main stipulation of the Freedom of Information Act?

PROTECTING YOUR COMPUTER

As you've no doubt already learned, anti-virus software finds, and may eliminate, viruses that find their way onto your computer or are trying to get into your computer system.

One method that anti-virus software uses is to examine the files on your computer looking for virus signatures, that is, content embedded in the files that matches a virus definition in its virus dictionary. Another method is to recognize when your computer is "acting funny" in a way that might indicate the presence of a virus.

The key to successful virus detection is in keeping the virus dictionary and the definition of "acting funny" current so that new viruses can be detected. To do this you must update your anti-virus software regularly. Most anti-virus software lets you set it up so that it goes to the Internet and updates itself on a regular basis. Find three sites that offer anti-virus software and answer the following questions:

A. What does the software at each site cost?

B. Does the site have information on current and past viruses?

C. Does the site sell any other type of computer protection like a firewall or spyware protection? If so, list what's available.

D. Does the site sell different software for a network than it does for an individual user? What's the difference?

E. Does the software allow you to schedule automatic updating?

LEARNING ABOUT INVESTING

Investing can be as simple as finding a company that performs well financially and buying some of their stock. Or, if you want to spread your investment over a number of stocks and you don't want to select each stock personally, you can invest in a mutual fund. Of course, there are thousands of mutual funds with all types of investment objectives. So, any way you go you must pick your investment wisely. You can find many helpful Web sites on the Internet to get you up to speed quickly.

Choose three Web sites and answer the following questions:

A. Is the site designed for first-time investors or those that are more experienced? Who sponsors the site?

B. Can you search for a specific topic?

C. Are specific stocks or mutual funds reviewed or evaluated?

D. Does the site provide direct links to brokerage or stock quoting sites?

E. Is a forum for submitting questions available? If so, are frequently asked questions (FAQs) posted?

LOCATING INTERNSHIPS

Have you ever noticed that a large number of jobs require expertise or experience? That being the case, how does someone gain relevant experience through a job when job experience is required to get the job? As it turns out, that has always been a perplexing dilemma for many college students, and one way to solve it is by obtaining an internship. Internships provide you with valuable knowledge about your field, pay you for your work, and offer you that valuable experience you need to move up in your career.

On the Web site for this text (www.mhhe.com/haag), we have provided you with a number of Web sites that offer internship possibilities—visit a few of them. For each site you visit, answer the following questions.

A. Who owns and maintains the site? Is it a for-profit or not-for-profit organization?

B. Do you find any internships in line with your career?

C. What about pay? Do you find both paying and nonpaying internships?

D. How do these internship sites compare to the more traditional job database sites such as Monster.com?

E. What sort of internship resources does your school provide?

F. How does your school's internship site compare to the other sites you visited on the Web?

SMALL BUSINESS ADMINISTRATION

The Small Business Administration (SBA, at www.sba.gov) of the U.S. Federal government has a goal of assisting almost 1.2 million prospective and existing small businesses in the year 2008, an approximate 22 percent increase over the 980,000 small businesses it helped in 2002. You can be among those 1.2 million small businesses, if you have the entrepreneurial spirit, an innovative idea, and solid business skills.

For existing small businesses, the SBA provides consultative services and loans for business growth. For start-up businesses, the SBA aids in finding capital, refining business ideas, developing a pro forma income statement, and a host of other activities. Visit the SBA's Web site and answer the following questions.

A. What elements does the SBA require to appear in a business plan? What support does the SBA provide while you create your business plan?

B. What tools does the SBA provide to help you in estimating your costs and revenues?

C. While applying for a loan, what information does the SBA require that you provide?

D. What educational services does the SBA provide so you can learn the basics of incomes statements and balance sheets?

E. In what ways does the SBA support the creation of small businesses that are diversity-owned?

STOCK QUOTES

When you buy stock in a company, you're betting on its success. Although it's no guarantee of how the stock price will do in the future, most people look at the price of stock and how it has fared over previous months and years to get an indication of whether it's a strong buy or not.

Both stocks and mutual funds are offered by the share and you can buy as much or as little of the stock or mutual fund as you like. However, some stocks are priced at hundreds of thousands of dollars, and the price alone may take them off your list for consideration.

Choose three stock quoting services, examine what it takes to retrieve a stock or mutual fund quote and answer the following questions:

A. Are the quotes provided free of charge or for a fee?

B. Does the site require a ticker symbol (the abbreviation used by experienced investors) or can you type in a company name?

C. Are the quotes in real time or are they delayed (15 to 20 minutes old)? Can you get price charts?

D. Are prices charts available? How about historic prices?

E. Can you create and save a personal portfolio of stocks?

RESEARCHING STOREFRONT SOFTWARE

If you decide to sell products on the Internet, there is software that you can use to make it easy to create a Web site. This type of software is called *storefront software.* There are many software products for you to choose from. Some will cost you a lot of money, but others are free. FreeMerchant.com for example, has a Basic Store for $9.95 per month, a Bronze Package for $24.95 per month, a Silver Package for $49.95 per month, and a Gold Package for $99.95 per month. What you get in each of these packages is listed in detail on the FreeMerchant.com Web site (www.freemerchant.com).

Since there are many options to choose from, it would be worth your while to do a little research to see if you can find an article that compares current versions of storefront software. A site like ZDNet.com (www.zdnet.com) would be a good place to start your search. Build up a list of features that you will need for your e-commerce site, and then compare your needs with the features offered by the various software packages. They all sound good when you read about them on the vendor's Web sites so be sure you take a "test drive" of the software before you sign up.

Another possibility would be to sign up for a shopping mall. Find your way to Amazon.com's zShops or Yahoo!Store and see that you think of these alternatives. Finally, you'll need a way for your customers to pay you for what they buy. This involves getting a merchant account which permits you to accept credit cards. Most of the storefront sites will explain how merchant accounts work and will help you get a merchant account.

A. What features have you decided your storefront software must provide?

B. How have you evaluated the pros and cons of using a storefront software package versus the options offered by the likes of Amazon.com and Yahoo!?

C. See if you can track down users of software options you are considering. Send them an e-mail and ask them what they like and dislike. You may be surprised at their answers.

SEARCHING FOR SHAREWARE AND FREEWARE

Perhaps the notion of shareware/freeware appeals to you. You'd like to be able to try the software before you buy it. If you want software such as a screen saver or anti-virus software, you're in luck. But what if you want some shareware to help you compose music or keep track of your soccer team's schedule? Well, then you'll have to go searching for that software. You could use a general-purpose search engine such as Yahoo! and type in shareware and music or soccer. But suppose those few titles don't meet your needs.

Finding shareware/freeware titles can be daunting for two reasons. First, currently there are over 1 million shareware and freeware titles available to you. Second, most shareware/freeware developers don't have their own Web sites. As many don't develop their software as a business, they can't justify the cost of supporting their own Web sites. To address both of these challenges, Web sites have been created that maintain databases of thousands of shareware/freeware software titles. Find such a site and answer the following questions.

A. How does the site group the software?

B. Can you search by operating system or platform?

C. Does the site provide descriptions of the software?

D. Can you search by file size?

E. Are screen captures from the software provided?

F. Are reviews and/or ratings of the software provided?

G. When was the last update for the site?

SEARCHING JOB DATABASES

There are, quite literally, thousands of sites that provide you with databases of job postings. Some are better than others. Some focus on specific industries, others offer postings for only executive managers.

Think for a moment about the job you want. What would be its title? In which industry do you want to work? In what part of the country do you want to work? What exceptional skills can you offer an employer? Connect to a couple of different job search database sites, search for your job, and answer the following questions for each site.

A. What is the date of last update?

B. Are career opportunities abroad listed as a separate category or are they integrated with domestic jobs?

C. Can you search for a specific organization?

D. Can you search by geographic location? If so, how? By city? By zip code?

E. Can you apply for a position online? If so, how do you submit your résumé?

F. Do you have to register to build an online résumé (e-résumé)?

G. Once a potential employer performs a search that matches your résumé, how can that employer contact you?

H. Once you build your résumé, can you use it to perform a job search?

I. Are there valuable tips available for building a good résumé?

SEARCHING FOR MBA PROGRAMS

Many of you will undoubtedly choose to continue your education by obtaining an MBA. And you probably should. The market for the best business positions is extremely competitive, with hiring organizations seeking individuals who can speak more than one language, have job experience, and have extended their educational endeavors beyond just getting an undergraduate degree. Not too long ago, the key competitive advantage was in having that undergraduate degree, a true distinction over those with just a high school education. Now, the competitive advantage lies in having an MBA.

Each year, *U.S. News and World Report* ranks the top business schools in the nation. On the Web site that supports this text, you'll find a list of the Web sites for some of the top 50 business schools in the nation.

Choose a couple of different business schools from the list of 50, visit their Web sites, and answer the following questions for each.

A. What business school did you choose?

B. Does that school offer a graduate program in your area of interest?

C. Can you apply online?

D. Does the site list tuition and fee costs?

E. Does the site contain a list of the graduate courses offered in your area of interest?

F. Does the school offer some distance learning formats for some of the courses? Are you interested in taking courses via distance learning?

COMPUTER HARDWARE AND SOFTWARE

Student Learning Outcomes

1. Define information technology (IT) and its two basic categories: hardware and software.

2. Describe the categories of computers based on size.

3. Compare the roles of personal productivity, vertical market, and horizontal market software.

4. Describe the roles of operating system and utility software as components of system software.

5. Define the purpose of each of the six major categories of hardware.

A Quick Tour of Technology

Information technology (IT) is any computer-based tool that people use to work with information and support the information and information-processing needs of an organization. IT includes the Internet, spreadsheet software, a satellite, a gamepad for playing video games . . . the list of the technology you can find in your immediate life is almost endless (see Figure A.1). There are two basic categories of information technology: hardware and software. ***Hardware*** consists of the physical devices that make up a computer, for instance, keyboard, mouse, modem, flash memory drive (also called a

Figure A.1

Information Technology (IT) Includes Many Tools

thumb drive), printer. **Software** is the set of instructions your hardware executes to carry out a specific task for you such as creating a graph (spreadsheet software, for example) and surfing the Web (Internet Explorer, for example). All combined, hardware and software in aggregate are what people refer to as a *computer,* and even that term is becoming more blurred each day with digital media players, cell phones, and the like.

All hardware falls into one or another of six categories. Here's a quick summary.

1. Input: **Input devices** are tools you use to enter information and commands.
2. Output: **Output devices** are tools you use to see, hear, or otherwise recognize the results of your information-processing requests.
3. Storage: **Storage devices** are tools you use to store information for use at a later time.
4. Processing: The **central processing unit (CPU)** is the actual hardware that interprets and executes the software instructions and coordinates the operation of all other hardware. **RAM,** or **random access memory,** is a temporary holding area for the information you're working with, as well as the system and application software instructions that the CPU currently needs.
5. Telecommunications: A **telecommunications device** is a tool you use to send information to and receive it from another person or computer in a network. Telecommunications, as a field, and its associated devices is so broad that we've devoted an entire module to the topic. Please read *Extended Learning Module E* to learn about cable and DSL modems, home networks, fiber optics, and much more.
6. Connecting: *Connecting devices* include such things as USB ports into which you would connect a printer and connector cords to connect your printer to the port.

The two main types of software are application and system software. **Application software** is the software that enables you to solve specific problems or perform specific tasks. Microsoft PowerPoint, for example, can help you create slides for a presentation, so it's application software. Dream Weaver is an example of application software because it helps you create and publish a Web page or Web site. A business would use payroll software, collaborative software such as videoconferencing, and inventory management software.

System software handles tasks specific to technology management and coordinates the interaction of all technology devices. System software includes both operating system software and utility software. **Operating system software** is system software that controls your application software and manages how your hardware devices work together. Popular personal operating system software includes Microsoft Windows, Mac OS (for Apple computers), and Linux (an open-source operating system). There are also operating systems for networks (Microsoft Windows Server is an example), operating systems for phones (the Android Operating System is an example), and operating systems for just about every other type of technology configuration, even for refrigerators.

Utility software is software that provides additional functionality to your operating system software. Utility software includes anti-virus software, screen savers, spam blocker software, uninstaller software (for properly removing unwanted software), and a host of other types. Some types of utility software are nice to have, like screen savers, while others are essential. For example, anti-virus software protects you from computer viruses that can be deadly for your computer. You definitely need anti-virus software.

This ends our quick tour of technology. In the remainder of this module we'll explore categories of computers by size, software in more detail, and hardware in more detail.

Categories of Computers by Size

Computers come in different shapes, sizes, and colors. Some, like smart phones, are small enough that you can carry them around with you, while others are larger than family refrigerators. Size is usually related to power and speed, and thus price.

SMARTPHONES

A *smartphone* is a cell phone with additional features such as a camera; Internet connectivity; note taking capabilities; GPS capabilities; and digital music and video players. A smartphone is really a mobile phone integrated into a handheld computer (see Figure A.2). It usually has a touchscreen interface and may have a physical keyboard. The price of smartphones varies greatly and usually the best deals are available in conjunction with phone service contracts. A current issue with smartphones and tablet PCs (see next section) is that of speed. *3G* stands for third generation standard for mobile devices and its download speed usually varies from just under 1 Mbps (megabits, or millions of bits, per second) to just over 2 Mbps. Speed is determined by the underlying technology and the level of traffic on the network. *4G* is fourth generation standard and can be up to 10 times faster than 3G. It's fast enough to watch movies, although you might want to do your viewing on a tablet rather than on a smartphone since the screen would be bigger. 4G will help you to reach your data usage limit much faster too.

TABLET PCS, SLATES, AND E-READERS

A *tablet pc* is a slim-line handheld computer that is about the size of a notebook or smaller with a touchscreen and that has the functional capabilities of notebook or desktop computer. Some tablet PCs allow you to use a writing pen or stylus to write notes on the screen. Most use a touch screen to perform functions such as clicking on a link while visiting a Web site. Tablet PCs may have handwriting recognition, customized dictionaries, GPS, and video conferencing capabilities. Tablet PCs, which can weigh less than a pound, cost upwards of $200.

A slate tablet PC has traditionally been a lighter, slimmed-down tablet without a dedicated physical keyboard. But recently slates have come onto the market that incorporate a keyboard and are essentially computers that are midway between tablet PCs and notebook computers. The terms tablet PC and slate are becoming interchangeable.

An *e-book reader* (*e-book device* or *e-reader*) is a portable computer designed specifically for reading digitized books and periodicals. It is similar to a tablet PC in that it has touchscreen capabilities but is designed to be more readable in bright light and have a longer battery life. E-book readers range in price from about $100 to $400. Examples are Amazon's Kindle and Barnes & Noble's Nook. E-readers often have multimedia capabilities for playing music and videos and accessing the Internet.

NOTEBOOK COMPUTERS

A *notebook* or *laptop* computer is a small, portable, fully functional, battery-powered computer. Notebook computers come equipped with all of the features of larger desktop computers and are a very good solution if you need a fully functional computer that you can take from one place to another. Notebook computers come in a variety of sizes, weights and price brackets. Some notebook computers have screens of about 10 inches and others have 20-inch or larger screens. Prices range from about $300 for small notebooks to more than $2,000 for larger, more rugged, and more powerful versions.

Figure A.2

Types of Computers:
Smartphones, Tablet PCs,
and Notebooks

Figure A.3

All-in-One Desktop
Computer

DESKTOP COMPUTERS

A *desktop computer* is the most popular choice for personal computing needs. You can choose a desktop computer with a horizontal system box (the box is where the CPU, RAM, and storage devices are held) or one with a vertical system box (called a tower) that you usually place on the floor near your work area. Desktop computers range in price from a little less than $500 to several thousand dollars. Dollar for dollar with comparable characteristics, a desktop computer is faster and more powerful than a notebook computer. Some desktops are built as all-in-one computers where the system unit is attached to, or is part of, the monitor (see Figure A.3).

Which one you need—smartphone, tablet PC, notebook, or desktop computer—is a function of your unique individual needs. Smartphones offer great portability and allow you to keep a calendar, send and receive e-mail, take short notes, and even access the Web. But they're not designed to help you write a term paper, build a Web site, or create a complex graph with statistical software. For these and more complex tasks, you would need a notebook, tablet PC, or a desktop computer.

So, the next question is, should you buy a notebook or a tablet PC? Most likely, you need a computer that supports full word processing, spreadsheet, presentation, Web site development, and some other capabilities. You need to decide where you'll need your computer. If you need to use your computer both at home and at school (or perhaps at work), then you should buy one of these because they are, in fact, portable. So, if you'd like to be able to surf the Web and get e-mail in your hotel room while on a business or vacation trip, a notebook computer or a tablet PC may be what you need. To learn more about some of today's best consumer electronics, connect to the Web site that supports this text at www.mhhe.com/haag.

MINICOMPUTERS, MAINFRAME COMPUTERS, AND SUPERCOMPUTERS

Smartphones, notebooks, and desktop computers are designed to meet your personal information-processing needs. In business, however, many people often need to access and use the same computer simultaneously. In this case, businesses need computing technologies that multiple people (perhaps hundreds or even thousands) can access and use at the same time. Computers of this type include minicomputers, mainframe computers, and supercomputers (see Figure A.4).

A *minicomputer* (sometimes called a *mid-range computer*) is designed to meet the computing needs of several people simultaneously in a small to medium-size business environment. Minicomputers are more powerful than desktop computers but also cost more, ranging in price from $5,000 to several hundred thousand dollars. Businesses often use minicomputers as servers, either for hosting a Web site or as an internal computer on which shared information and software is placed. For this reason, minicomputers are well suited for business environments in which people need to share common information, processing power, and/or certain peripheral devices such as high-quality, fast laser printers.

A *mainframe computer* (sometimes just called a *mainframe*) is a computer designed to meet the computing needs of hundreds of people in a large business environment. So mainframe computers are a step up in size, power, capability, and cost from minicomputers. Mainframes can easily cost in excess of $1 million. With processing speeds greater than 1 trillion instructions per second (compared to a typical desktop that can process approximately 3 billion instructions per second), mainframes can easily handle the processing requests of hundreds (or thousands) of people simultaneously.

Figure A.4

Minicomputers, Mainframes, and Supercomputers

A *supercomputer* is the fastest, most powerful, and most expensive type of computer. Organizations such as NASA and the National Weather Service that are heavily involved in research and "number crunching" employ supercomputers because of the speed with which they can process information. Super computers have hundreds of thousands of Processors that work in parallel. Very large, customer-oriented businesses such as General Motors and AT&T also employ supercomputers just to handle customer information and transaction processing. Their business needs require the high level of support and the powerful processing power provided by supercomputers.

How much do you really need to know about the technical specifics (CPU speed, storage disk capacity, and so on), prices, and capabilities of minicomputers, mainframe computers, and supercomputers? Probably not much, unless you plan to major in information technology. What you should concentrate on is the technical specifics, prices, and capabilities of PDAs, tablet PCs, notebooks, and desktop computers. These tools will be your companions for your entire business career. Learn about them and know them well—on an ongoing basis.

Software: Your Intellectual Interface

LEARNING OUTCOME 3

The most important tool in your technology tool set is software. Software contains the instructions that your hardware executes to perform an information-processing task for you. So, software is really your *intellectual interface,* designed to automate processing tasks. Without software, your computer is little more than a very expensive doorstop. As we've stated, there are two categories of software: application software and system software.

APPLICATION SOFTWARE

Application software is the software you use to meet your specific information-processing needs, including payroll, customer relationship management, project management, training, word processing, and many, many others. Application software can be categorized as either personal productivity software or vertical and horizontal market software.

PERSONAL PRODUCTIVITY SOFTWARE   *Personal productivity software* helps you perform personal tasks—such as writing a memo, creating a graph, and creating a slide presentation—that you can usually do even if you don't own a computer. You're probably already familiar with some personal productivity software tools including Microsoft Word, Microsoft Excel, Mozilla Firefox, and Quicken (personal finance software).

Three modules in this text help you learn how to use some of these tools—*Extended Learning Module D* (for Microsoft Excel, spreadsheet software), *Extended Learning Module J* (for Microsoft Access, database management system software), and *Extended Learning Module L* (for Microsoft FrontPage, Web authoring software). Figure A.5 describes the 10 major categories of personal productivity software and some of the more popular packages within each category.

VERTICAL AND HORIZONTAL MARKET SOFTWARE   While performing organizational processes in your career, you'll also frequently use two other categories of application software: vertical market software and horizontal market software.

Vertical market software is application software that is unique to a particular industry. For example, the health care industry has a variety of application software unique to that market segment, including radiology software, patient-scheduling software, nursing allocation software, and pharmaceutical software. Vertical market software is written specifically for an industry. Health care industry patient-scheduling software wouldn't work well for scheduling hair styling and manicure appointments in a beauty salon.

Category	Examples*
Word processing—Helps you create papers, letters, memos, and other basic documents	• Microsoft Word • Corel WordPerfect
Spreadsheet—Helps you work primarily with numbers, including performing calculations and creating graphs	• Microsoft Excel • Corel Quattro Pro
Presentation—Helps you create and edit information that will appear in electronic slides	• Microsoft PowerPoint • Corel Presentations
Desktop publishing—Extends word processing software by including design and formatting techniques to enhance the layout and appearance of a document	• Microsoft Publisher • Quark QuarkXPress
Personal information management (PIM)—Helps you create and maintain (1) to-do lists, (2) appointments and calendars, and (3) points of contact	• Microsoft Outlook • Corel Central
Personal finance—Helps you maintain your checkbook, prepare a budget, track investments, monitor your credit card balances, and pay bills electronically	• Quicken • Microsoft Money
Web authoring—Helps you design and develop Web sites and pages that you publish on the Web	• Expression Web Designer • Macromedia Dreamweaver
Graphics—Helps you create and edit photos and art	• Microsoft PhotoDraw • Adobe PhotoShop
Communications—Helps you communicate with other people	• Microsoft Outlook • Microsoft Internet Explorer
Database management system (DBMS)—Helps you specify the logical organization for a database and access and use the information within a database	• Microsoft Access

*Publisher name given first.

Figure A.5

Categories of Personal Productivity Software

Horizontal market software, on the other hand, is application software that is general enough to be suitable for use in a variety of industries. Examples of horizontal market software include

- Inventory management
- Payroll
- Accounts receivable
- Billing
- Invoice processing
- Human resource management

The preceding functions (and many others) are very similar, if not identical, across many different industries, enabling software publishers to develop one particular piece of software (e.g., accounts receivable) that can be used by many different industries.

Personal productivity software is actually a type of horizontal market software in that it is general enough to be suitable for use in a variety of industries. No matter what industry you work in, you need basic word processing software for creating memos, business plans, and other basic documents.

There are, however, some key differences between personal productivity software and horizontal (and vertical) market software. First is the issue of price. You can buy a full suite of personal productivity software for less than $400. In contrast, some individual horizontal and vertical market software packages may cost $500,000 or more. Second is the issue of customizability. When you purchase personal productivity software, you cannot change the way it works. That is, you're buying the right to use it but not to change how it operates. With horizontal and vertical market software you may be able to purchase the right to change the way the software works. So, if you find a payroll software package that fits most of your organizational needs, you can buy the software and the right to change the operation of the software so that it meets your needs precisely. This is a very common business practice when purchasing and using horizontal and vertical market software.

In Chapter 6 (Systems Development), we discuss how organizations go about the process of developing software for their particular needs, including how organizations can and do purchase vertical and horizontal market software and then customize that software.

SYSTEM SOFTWARE

System software supports your application software. System software controls how your various technology tools work together as you use your application software to perform specific information-processing tasks. System software includes two basic categories: operating system software and utility software.

OPERATING SYSTEM SOFTWARE   *Operating system software* is system software that controls your application software and manages how your hardware devices work together. For example, using Excel to create a graph, if you choose to print the graph, your operating system software takes over, ensures that you have a printer attached and that the printer has paper (and tells you if it doesn't), and sends your graph to the printer along with instructions on how to print it.

Your operating system software supports a variety of useful features, one of which is multitasking. *Multitasking* allows you to work with more than one piece of software at a time. Suppose you wanted to create a graph in Excel and insert it into a word processing document. With multitasking, you can have both pieces of application software open at the same time, and even see both on the screen. So, when you complete the creation of your graph, you can easily copy and paste it into your word processing document without having to exit the spreadsheet software and then start your word processing software.

There are different types of operating system software for personal environments and for organizational environments that support many users simultaneously. The latter, called *network operating systems* or *NOSs,* we explore in *Extended Learning Module E: Network Basics.* Popular *personal* operating systems include Microsoft Windows 7, and its successor Windows 8, Mac OS, and Linux. *Mac OS* is Apple's operating system. *Linux* is an open-source operating system that provides a rich operating environment for high-end workstations and network servers.

Open-source software is software for which the source code (how the software was actually written) is publicly available and free of charge. Unlike commercial software, open-source software is created and maintained by a distributed network of engineers, software developers, and users, each making contributions to the open-source software.

The advantages of open-source software are numerous. Because the source code is available, users of the software may modify the software to suit their needs and take comfort in the fact that changes they wish to make to the software are fully under their control. You can compare this with commercial, or closed-source, software, for which the customer must go to the vendor and pay for changes to be made and wait until the vendor has made those changes.

There are many examples of open-source software, including

- The Apache Web server
- Linux operating system
- MySQL, an open-source DBMS with commercial support

If you're considering purchasing a notebook computer that you'll use extensively at school connected to a network there, we recommend that you contact your school's technology support department to determine which operating system is best for you.

UTILITY SOFTWARE   *Utility software* adds functionality to your operating system software. Sometimes it is crucial. A simple example is screen saver software (which is probably also a part of your operating system). The most important utility software is anti-virus software. *Anti-virus software* is utility software that detects and removes or quarantines computer viruses. Viruses are everywhere today, with 200 to 300 new ones surfacing each month. Some viruses are benign: They do something annoying like causing your screen to go blank but do not corrupt your information. Other viruses are deadly, perhaps reformatting your hard disk or altering the contents of your files. You definitely need anti-virus software to protect your computer. We talk much more about this vitally important topic and guarding against possible attacks that can be launched against your computer from cyberspace in Chapter 8 and *Extended Learning Module H.*

Other types of utility software include

- *Crash-proof software*—Utility software that helps you save information if your system crashes and you're forced to turn it off and then back on again.
- *Uninstaller software*—Utility software that you can use to remove software from your hard disk that you no longer want.
- *Disk optimization software*—Utility software that organizes your information on your hard disk in the most efficient way.
- *Spam blocker software*—Utility software that filters unwanted e-mail from your inbox. Spam is roughly equivalent to unsolicited telephone marketing calls. The term spam is said to derive from a famous Monty Python sketch ("Well, we have Spam, tomato and Spam, egg and Spam, egg, bacon and Spam . . .") that was current when spam first began arriving on the Internet.
- *Anti-spyware software*—Utility software that detects and removes spyware and other unwanted software that can track every electronic move you make.

You definitely need utility software. Don't think of utility software as "optional" software just because it "adds" functionality to your computer. The above examples are just a few of the many types of utility software you'll find in a utility software suite. If you think about the above examples of utility software and what it does for you, especially anti-virus software, you can see how various and helpful it is.

Hardware: Your Physical Interface

To properly understand the significant role of your hardware (the physical components of your computer), it helps to know something about how your computer works. You work with information in the form of characters (A–Z, a–z, and special ones such as an asterisk, a question mark, etc.) and numbers (0–9). Computers, on the other hand, work only with 1s and 0s in terms of what we call bits and bytes. Computers, that is, use electricity to function, and electrical pulses have two states: on and off, which are assigned the values of 0 and 1, respectively.

What are bits and bytes? A ***binary digit (bit)*** is the smallest unit of information that your computer can process. A bit can either be a 1 (on) or a 0 (off). The technical challenge is to be able to represent all our natural language characters, special symbols, and numbers in binary form. ASCII is one agreed-upon standard to do this. ***ASCII (American Standard Code for Information Interchange)*** is the coding system that most personal computers use to represent, process, and store information. In ASCII, a group of eight bits represents one natural language character and is called a ***byte.***

For example, if you were to type the word *cool* on the keyboard, your keyboard (a hardware device) would change it into four bytes—one byte for each character—that would look like the following to be used by your computer (see Figure A.6):

01100011	01001111	01001111	01001100
c	o	o	l

This grouping of 1s and 0s would be used for "cool" as it moves around or is stored on your computer—as it travels from one device to another, is stored on a storage device, and is processed by your CPU.

There are three important conclusions that you should draw from this discussion so far. First, your hardware works with information in a different form (although with the same meaning) than you do. You work with characters, special symbols, and the numbers 0–9. Your computer, on the other hand, represents all these in a binary form, a unique collection of 1s and 0s. Second, the term *byte* is the bridge between people and a computer. A computer can store one character, special symbol, or number in a byte.

Third, the primary role of your input and output devices is to convert information from one form to another. Input devices convert information from human-readable form into bits and bytes, while output devices convert the 1s and 0s to something people can recognize. All other hardware works with bits and bytes.

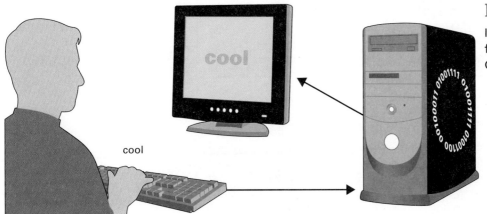

cool

Figure A.6

Information as It Moves from You through Your Computer

COMMON INPUT DEVICES

An *input device* is a tool you use to enter information and commands. You can use a keyboard to type in information, for example, and use a mouse to point and click on buttons and icons. As you saw in the previous section, input devices are responsible for converting information in human-readable form to the binary code that computers use. Below are the principal types of input devices being used today (see Figures A.7 and A.8).

- *Keyboards* are the most often used input devices for desktop and notebook computers. Keyboards and styluses allow you to input both information and commands and both are used in business and personal settings.
- *Pointing devices* are devices that are used to navigate and select objects on a display screen.
- *Mouse*—a pointing device that you use to click on icons or buttons.
- *Trackball*—is similar to a mechanical mouse, but it has the ball on the top.
- *Touchpad*—is the little dark rectangle that you use to move the cursor with your finger, often found on notebook computers.
- *Game controllers* are used for gaming to better control screen action.
  - *Gaming wheel*—is a steering wheel and foot pedals for virtual driving.

Figure A.7
Categories of Input Devices

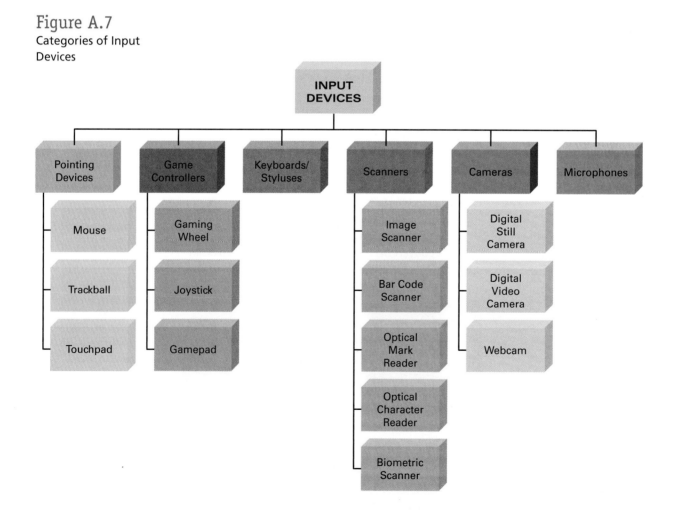

- *Joystick*—is a vertical handle with programmable buttons that control action.
- *Gamepad*—is a multifunctional input device with a directional pad and programmable buttons that you work with your thumbs.
- *Scanners* are used to convert information that exists in visible form into electronic form.
  - *Image scanner*—captures images, photos, text, and artwork that already exist on paper.
  - *Bar code scanner*—reads information that is in the form of vertical bars, where their width and spacing represent digits (often used in point-of-sale [POS] systems in retail environments).
  - *Optical mark reader*—detects the presence or absence of a mark in a predetermined spot on the page (often used for true/false and multiple choice exam answers).
  - *Optical character reader*—reads characters that appear on a page or sales tag (often used in point-of-sale [POS] systems in retail environments).
  - *Biometric scanner*—scans some human physical attribute like your fingerprint or iris for security purposes.
- *Digital cameras* capture still images or video as a series of 1s and 0s. You can use a still camera for short videos or a video camera for still photos.
  - *Digital still camera*—digitally captures still images in varying resolutions.
  - *Digital video camera*—captures video digitally.
  - *Webcam*—captures digital video to upload to the Web.
- *Microphones* capture audio for conversion into electronic form.

COMMON OUTPUT DEVICES

An *output device* is a tool you use to see, hear, or otherwise recognize the results of your information-processing requests. The most common output devices for both business and personal computing environments are monitors and printers, but speakers and plotters (printers that generate drawings) are also output devices (see Figure A.9). Any device that converts the digital form of information in a computer to something that you can see, read, or hear is an output device.

MONITORS   The screens we use today on which to view output are mostly *flat-panel LCD* (liquid crystal display). On desktop computers, the screen is separate from the computer and is usually referred to as a monitor. When the screen is part of the device, as on a smartphone or a notebook computer, it's called a display screen. (See Figure A.10.) A *liquid crystal display* (*LCD*) makes the screen image by sending electricity through crystalized liquid trapped between two layers of clear plastic or glass. Since liquid crystal displays do not emit light, such displays have to be lit from the back – called backlighting. A newer form of LCD display is lit with LEDs. An *LED* (*light-emitting diode*) is a very tiny bulb. Products such as alarm clocks and Christmas lights use LEDs. You may also have seen very large screens on buildings or at a football stadium or ballpark. These screens are very bright—you can see them in direct sunlight—and are made up of many LEDs. Using LEDs for backlighting improves the image on an LCD screen.

Some displays are now being developed that used OLED technology. *Organic light emitting diode* (*OLED*) displays use many layers of organic material emitting a visible light and therefore eliminating the need for backlighting. The advantage of an OLED technology is that it produces brighter, more efficient, and thinner displays than traditional LCDs.

When selecting a monitor, the important features to consider, besides price, are its image size and its resolution. The *viewable image size (VIS)* of a screen (4.3" on a cell

Figure A.9

Categories of Output Devices

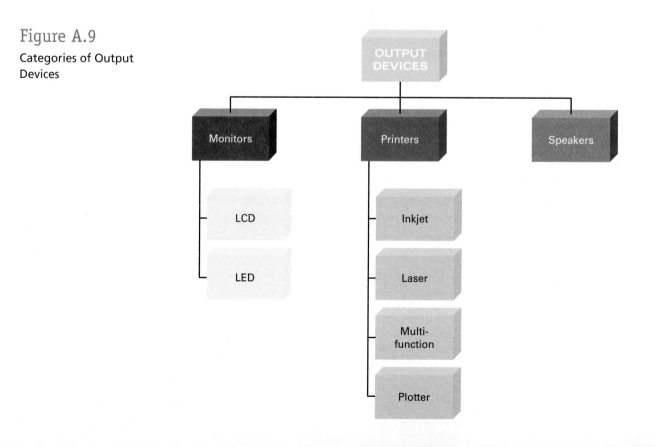

Display Screens Are
Common Output Devices

phone or 21" on a monitor) is measured diagonally from corner to corner. The ***resolution of a screen*** is the number of pixels it has. ***Pixels*** (picture elements) are the dots that make up the image on your screen. For example, a monitor with a resolution of 2560 × 1440 has 2560 pixels across and 1440 down the screen.

PRINTERS Printers are another common type of output device (see Figure A.11). The sharpness and clarity of a printer's output depend on the printer's resolution. The ***resolution of a printer*** is the number of dots per inch (dpi) it produces. This is the same principle as the resolution in monitors. As is the case with monitors, the more dots per inch, the better the image, and consequently, the more costly the printer. Some printers, especially those that advertise high-quality photo output, achieve higher resolutions by making multiple passes across the image to produce the clarity needed.

- ***Inkjet printers*** make images by forcing ink droplets through nozzles. Standard inkjet printers use four colors: black, cyan (blue), magenta (purplish pink), and yellow. Some inkjet printers produce high-quality images and are often advertised as photo printers. These have two shades each of magenta and cyan for a total of six colors. Others include colors such as orange and red.
- ***Laser printers*** form images using the same sort of electrostatic process that photocopiers use. Laser printers are usually more expensive than inkjets, but

Figure A.11
Printers Are Also
Common Output Devices

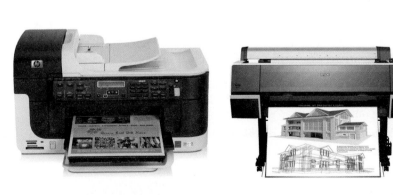

they have become dramatically cheaper lately. They usually provide better quality images than inkjets. They come in black and white and in color versions.

- *Multifunction printers* scan, copy, and fax, as well as print. These devices are very popular in homes and small offices since they offer so many features all in one unit. Multifunction printers can be either inkjet or laser.

- *Plotters* form their output by moving a pen across the surface of a piece of paper. Plotters were the first type of printer that could print with color and render graphics and full-size engineering drawings. As a rule, plotters are much more expensive than printers. They are most frequently used for CAE (computer-aided engineering) applications, such as CAD (computer-aided design) and CAM (computer-aided manufacturing).

- A *3D printer* is a printer that can produce solid, three-dimensional objects. One method involves first scanning the object and then sending the scan to the printer where a tray of powder is loaded. Then an inkjet-like arm solidifies a layer of the object. Successive layers of material are laid down until the object is completely formed. The process is great for prototypes, jewelry, art, machine parts and tools, medical equipment, etc. It's even being used to replicate body parts.

COMMON STORAGE DEVICES

As opposed to RAM, which is temporary memory, storage media don't lose their contents when you turn off your computer. The main issues to consider when choosing a storage medium are (1) whether you want portability, (2) how much storage space you need, and (3) whether you need to change the information on the medium.

Some storage devices, such as hard disks, offer you easy update capabilities and high storage capacity, but may not be portable. Others, like flash memory devices, while they are portable and updateable, have less storage space. Still others like DVD-ROMs are portable with high capacity, but the information that comes on them can't be changed (see Figure A.12).

Capacities of storage media are measured in megabytes, gigabytes, and terabytes. A *megabyte (MB or M or Meg)* is roughly 1 million bytes; a *gigabyte (GB or Gig)* is roughly 1 billion bytes; and a *terabyte (TB)* is roughly 1 trillion bytes. A consumer hard disk would have a capacity of 2 terabytes or more, while a hard disk for a large organization (also called a *hard disk pack*) can hold in excess of 100 TB of information. Common storage devices include

- Magnetic storage media:
  - *Hard disk*—magnetic storage device with one or more thin metal platters or disks that store information sealed inside the disk drive. You usually get one installed in your system unit (the computer box) when you buy a computer. If you need more hard disk space or want portability, you can get an external unit that you can plug into the USB ports. (We'll discuss USB ports in a later section.) A hard disk offers ease of updating and large storage capacity.

- *Optical storage media* are plastic discs on which information is stored, deleted, and/or changed using laser light and include CDs and DVDs, of which there are several types:
  - *CD-ROM (compact disc—read-only memory)*—an optical or laser disc whose information cannot be changed. A CD stores up to 800 Meg of information.
  - *CD-R (compact disc—recordable)*—an optical or laser disc that you can write to one time only.
  - *CD-RW (compact disc—rewritable)*—an optical or laser disc on which you can save, change, and delete files as often as you like.

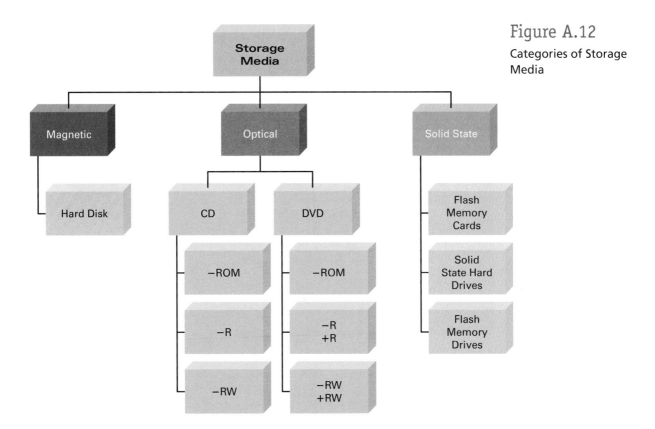

Figure A.12

Categories of Storage Media

- *DVD-ROM*—a high-capacity optical or laser disc whose information cannot be changed. The capacity of a DVD, unlike that of a CD, varies according to type.
- *DVD-R* or *DVD + R (DVD—recordable)*—a high-capacity optical or laser disc to which you can write one time only.
- *DVD-RW* or *DVD + RW* (depending on the manufacturer)—a high-capacity optical or laser disc on which you can save, change, and delete files.
- *Solid state media* are nonvolatile forms of storage where the data is stored on microchips. Nonvolatile means that the data remains after the power is switched off unlike the RAM or memory in a computer. One great advantage of solid state storage is that it has no moving parts, making it less susceptible to physical shock and mechanical problems. It operates silently and has faster access time for the data. Solid state media come in three varieties: solid state hard drives, flash memory drives, and flash memory cards. (See Figure A.13.)
  - A *solid state hard drive* is a hard drive that uses solid-state memory chips to store data long term. Solid state will most likely eventually replace magnetic hard drives because they are more robust and quiet.
  - A *flash memory drive* (also called a jump drive or thumb drive) is a solid state storage device that is small enough to fit on a key ring and plugs directly into the USB port on your computer.
  - A *flash memory card* consists of solid state memory chips laminated inside a small piece of plastic. You most likely have one for your digital camera. Flash memory cards differ from flash memory drives in that they need a reader. This reader device may be built into the computer or printer, otherwise you will need a separate device. *SD (Secure Digital)* cards are the most popular type of flash memory cards. Other examples are xD Picture Cards, Compact Flash (CF) Cards, and Memory Stick Media.

Figure A.13

Common Types of Flash Memory

CPU AND RAM

Together, your CPU and RAM make up the real brains of your computer (see Figure A.14). Your CPU largely determines the power (and also the price) of your computer. The ***central processing unit (CPU)*** is the hardware that interprets and executes the system and application software instructions and coordinates the operation of all other hardware. ***Random access memory (RAM)*** is a temporary holding area for the information you're working with as well as the system and application software instructions that the CPU currently needs.

A CPU used to have just one microprocessor, but nowadays CPUs can have two, four, six or more microprocessors. Such CPUs are called *multi-core processors.* You might expect that having six processors would speed up the processor by a factor of six, but that is not necessarily the case. The reason is that most software was written for a single processor. That means that it was built to do only one thing at a time. So, your spell-checker will not work six times faster if you have a 6-core CPU. However, some software,

Figure A.14

CPU and RAM

such as image processing software, can divide up the task into multiple smaller jobs that can be done simultaneously. Operating systems also sometimes separate out tasks so that they are running at the same time, such as loading a file while simultaneously playing music. In the future software will increasingly be written to take advantage of multi-core processing.

Today's CPU speed is usually quoted in gigahertz. ***Gigahertz (GHz)*** is the number of billions of CPU cycles per second that the CPU can handle. The more cycles per second, the faster the processing and the more powerful the computer. Gigahertz refers to how fast the CPU can carry out the steps it takes to execute software instructions—a process sometimes called the CPU cycle or machine cycle. A ***CPU cycle (machine cycle)*** consists of retrieving, decoding, and executing the instruction, then returning the result to RAM, if necessary (see Figure A.15). When you load (or open) a program, you're telling your computer to send a copy of the program from the storage device (hard disk or CD) into RAM. In carrying out the software instructions, the CPU repeatedly performs machine cycles as follows:

1. *Retrieve an instruction:* The ***control unit,*** which is the component of the CPU that directs what happens in your computer, sends to RAM for instructions and the information it needs. If the instruction says to add 4 and 6, for example, the two numbers travel as information with the *add* instruction. The instruction travels from RAM on the system bus. The ***system bus*** consists of electrical pathways that move information between basic components of the motherboard, including between RAM and the CPU. When the instruction reaches the CPU it waits temporarily in ***CPU cache,*** which is a type of memory on the CPU where instructions called up by the CPU wait until the CPU is ready to use them. It takes much less time to get the instruction from CPU cache to the control unit than from RAM, so CPU cache speeds up processing.

2. *Decode the instruction:* The CPU gets the instruction out of cache and examines it to see what needs to be done, in this case, add 4 and 6.

3. *Execute the instruction:* The CPU then does what the instruction says to do. In our example, it sends the two numbers to the arithmetic logic unit to be added. The ***arithmetic logic unit (ALU)*** is a component of the CPU that performs arithmetic, as well as comparison and logic operations.

Figure A.15
Your CPU and RAM at Work

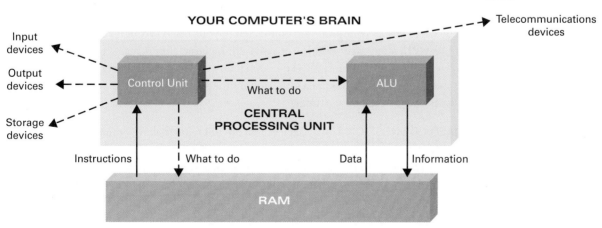

4. *Store the result in RAM:* The CPU then sends the result of the addition, 10, to RAM. There's not always a result to send back to RAM. Sometimes the CPU does intermediate calculations that don't get saved.

You'll sometimes hear the CPU speed referred to as the "clock speed." This refers to the CPU clock. Every CPU has its own *CPU clock,* which is simply a sliver of quartz that beats at regular intervals in response to an electrical charge. The beat of the CPU clock is like the drummer in a marching band. Just as the drummer keeps everyone marching in time, the CPU clock keeps all your computer's operations synchronized. Each beat or tick of the CPU clock is called a clock cycle and is equivalent to a CPU cycle (machine cycle). The CPU uses the CPU clock to keep instructions and information marching through your CPU at a fixed rate.

RAM is a sort of whiteboard that your CPU uses while it processes information and software instructions. When you turn off your computer, everything in RAM disappears—that's why we call it "temporary." When you first start your computer, system instructions that are necessary to keep your computer running get written into RAM. Then, as you open applications, like Microsoft Word or Excel, the instructions to make those programs run join the operating system in RAM. As you type in your document or enter information into your workbook, that too is stored in RAM. When you've finished your work and save it, a copy is transferred from RAM to your disk CD, or flash drive.

The most important thing you need to know about RAM is its capacity for storing instructions and information. RAM capacity is expressed in megabytes or gigabytes. You'll remember that a megabyte is roughly 1 million bytes. A byte is equivalent to a character. So RAM with a capacity of 2 gigabytes can hold 2 billion characters—that includes operating system instructions as well as the applications and information that you're currently using.

NOTEBOOK COMPUTER CPUS AND RAM   A notebook computer is to a desktop computer as a recreational vehicle is to a traditional home—everything is smaller, and power to run devices is limited since you have to carry the power sources with you. A *mobile CPU* is a special type of CPU for a notebook computer that changes speed, and therefore power consumption, in response to fluctuation in use. A desktop CPU, running at 2.6 GHz, uses between 75 and 1,090 watts of power whereas a mobile CPU might run at a much smaller 34 watts. RAM modules for notebook computers are smaller than those for desktop computers.

CONNECTING THE HARDWARE OUTSIDE TO THE HARDWARE INSIDE

Since the CPU controls all computer hardware, all hardware devices must be connected to the CPU, just as your limbs are connected to your brain through your spinal cord.

The CPU, along with RAM, is located on the large circuit board (called the *motherboard*) inside your system unit. The connector (or plug) on the end of the cable coming out of your printer connects it to the motherboard which then carries information between the CPU and the printer.

WIRED CONNECTIONS   All devices that are not wireless have connectors on the ends of cables that plug into ports on the computer. A *port* is the place on your system unit, monitor, or keyboard through which information and instructions flow to and from your computer system. For wired connections it's the opening or socket where you insert the connector, and for wireless devices a port is where the wave information goes in and out.

The ports are accessible on the outside of the system unit and that means that you don't have to open up the system unit to plug in your scanner. There are various types of connectors/ports (see Figure A.16) including:

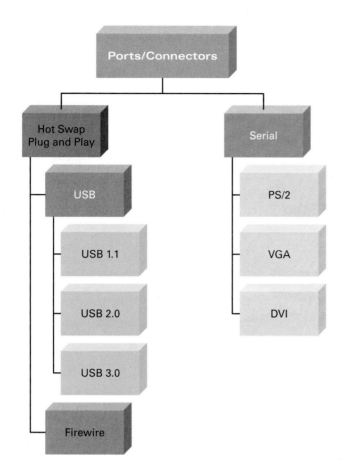

Categories of Connectors
and Ports

- *USB (universal serial bus) port*—fit small flat plug-and-play, hot-swap USB connectors, and, using USB hubs, you can connect up to 127 devices to a single USB port on your computer. The newest type is USB 3.0 which has faster transfer rates than its predocessors. *Hot swap* is an operating system feature that allows you—while your computer is running—to unplug a device and plug in a new one (without first shutting down your computer). *Plug and play* is an operating feature that finds and installs the device driver for a device that you plug into your computer. USB connectors come in two general physical shapes called Type A and Type B. Type A USB connectors/ports are all the same size and shape, but Type B USB connectors are smaller, more square, and come in several different sizes. Type B connectors are usually on the end of the cable that plugs into a device like a camera or a scanner.

- *Firewire ports*—(also called *IEEE 1394* or *I-Link*) fit hot-swap, plug-and-play Firewire connectors, and you can connect up to 63 Firewire devices to a single Firewire port by daisy-chaining the devices together.

- *PS/2 ports*—fit PS/2 connectors, which you often find on keyboards and mice. PS/2 is a special type of serial connector/port. Serial connectors/ports are gradually being replaced by USB and Firewire.

- *DVI* (Digital Visual Interface) and *VGA* (Video graphics Array) are two different types of ports for monitors. DVI Ports are the newer standard.

Figure A.17 provides photo illustrations of some of the connectors we've just described.

WIRELESS CONNECTIONS   Wireless devices transfer and receive information in the form of waves, either infrared or radio waves. Different types of waves have different

Figure A.17

Connectors Used to Connect Devices to the CPU on the Motherboard

USB connector

Firewire connector

DVI connector

VGA connector

frequencies. The three types most frequently used in personal and business computer environments are infrared, Bluetooth, and WiFi.

- **Infrared**—also called **IR** or **IrDA (infrared data association)** uses red light to send and receive information. Infrared light has a frequency that's below what the eye can see. It's used for TV remotes and other devices that operate over short distances (the effective distance is about one mile) that are free of obstacles.
- **Bluetooth**—is a standard for transmitting information in the form of short-range radio waves over distances of up to 30 feet and is used for purposes such as wirelessly connecting a cell phone or a PDA to a computer.
- **WiFi (wireless fidelity)**—is a standard for transmitting information in the form of radio waves over distances up to 400 feet. WiFi has several forms. For example, WiFi is also called **IEEE 802.11a, b, g,** or **n,** each of which is a unique type. WiFi is usually the type of wireless communication used in a network environment.

Figure A.18

Expansion Cards Add Functionality to a Computer

EXPANSION CARDS AND SLOTS Whether wired or wireless, ports are sometimes directly on the motherboard and sometimes on expansion cards. An ***expansion card*** (or ***board***) is a circuit board that you insert into the expansion slot on the motherboard and to which you connect a peripheral device. An ***expansion slot*** is a long skinny socket on the motherboard into which you insert an expansion card. Information coming from and going to expansion slots and ports moves along wires (called a "bus") to the CPU. The ***expansion bus*** is the set of pathways along which information moves between devices outside the motherboard and the CPU (see Figure A.18). We have already discussed the system bus that moves information between basic motherboard components, including RAM and the CPU.

To add devices to your notebook computer, you slide a PC Card into the PC Card slot on the notebook, and connect the device to the PC

Card. A **PC Card** is the expansion card you use to add devices to your notebook computer. PC Cards look like thick credit cards. **PC Card slots** are the openings, one on top of the other, on the side or front of a notebook, where you connect external devices with a PC Card (see Figure A.19). For example, if you wanted to add a CD-ROM drive, you'd slide a PC Card into the slot and then connect the CD-ROM drive to the connector on the PC Card. One of the great things about PC Cards is that you can hot-swap devices.

Figure A.19
PC Cards Connect External Devices to Your Notebook Computer

■ SUMMARY: STUDENT LEARNING OUTCOMES REVISITED

1. **Define information technology (IT) and its two basic categories: hardware and software.** *Information technology (IT)* is any computer-based tool that people use to work with information and support the information and information-processing needs of an organization. For example, IT includes cell phones, software such as spreadsheet software, and output devices such as printers. *Hardware* consists of the physical devices that make up a computer (often referred to as a computer system). *Software* is the set of instructions that your hardware executes to carry out a specific task for you.

2. **Describe the categories of computers based on size.** Categories of computers by size include Smartphones, tablet PCs, notebook computers, desktop computers, minicomputers, mainframe computers, and supercomputers. A *smartphone* is a cell phone with additional features such as a camera; Internet connectivity; note taking capabilities; GPS capabilities; and digital music and video players. A *tablet PC* is a slim-line handheld computer. An *e-book reader* is a portable computer designed specifically for reading digitized books and periodicals. A *notebook computer* is a small, portable, fully functional battery-powered computer designed for you to carry around with you. A *desktop computer* is the most popular choice for personal computing needs. These four are all computers designed for use by one person. A *minicomputer (mid-range computer)* is designed to meet the computing needs of several people simultaneously in a small to medium-size business environment. A *mainframe computer (mainframe)* is a computer designed to meet the computing needs of hundreds of people in a large business environment. A *supercomputer* is the fastest, most powerful, and most expensive type of computer. In the order given, PDAs are the smallest, least powerful, and least expensive while supercomputers are the largest, most powerful, and most expensive.

3. **Compare the roles of personal productivity, vertical market, and horizontal market software.** *Application software* executes your specific programs and tasks. *Personal productivity software* helps you perform personal tasks—such

as writing a memo, creating a graph, and creating a slide presentation—that you can usually do even if you don't own a computer. *Vertical market software* is application software that is unique to a particular industry. *Horizontal market software* is application software that is general enough to be suitable for use in a variety of industries. Personal productivity software is very inexpensive when compared to both vertical market and horizontal market software. With personal productivity software, you do not obtain the right to change the way the software works. If you buy vertical market or horizontal market software, you can often buy the right to change the way the software works.

4. **Describe the roles of operating system software and utility software as components of system software.** *System software* handles technology management tasks and coordinates the interaction of all your technology devices. *Operating system software* controls your application software and manages how your hardware devices work together. So, operating system software really enables you to run application software. *Utility software* adds additional functionality to your operating system, including such utilities as anti-virus software, screen savers, crash-proof software, uninstaller software, disk optimization, spam blocking, and anti-spyware software. Although these "add" functionality, you definitely need utility software, especially anti-virus software.

5. **Define the purpose of each of the six major categories of hardware.** The six major categories of hardware are

- *Input devices*—Convert information and commands from a form that you understand into a form your computer can understand.
- *Output devices*—Help you see, hear, or otherwise accept the results of your information-processing requests, that is, convert information from a form your computer understands into a form you can understand.
- *CPU and RAM*—The real brains of your computer that execute software instructions (CPU) and hold the information, application software, and operating system software you're working with (RAM).
- *Storage devices*—Store information for use at a later time.
- *Telecommunications devices*—Send information to and from persons and locations.
- Connecting devices—Connect all your hardware devices to the motherboard.

■ KEY TERMS AND CONCEPTS

■ SHORT-ANSWER QUESTIONS

1. What are the two categories of information technology (IT)?
2. What are the six categories of hardware?
3. What is the difference between application software and system software?
4. Dollar for dollar with comparable characteristics, which is faster and more powerful—a desktop computer or a notebook computer?
5. What is the difference between vertical and horizontal market software?
6. What do the terms *bit* and *byte* mean?
7. What is a gaming wheel and how does it differ from a gamepad?
8. What is the difference between a CRT and a flat-panel display?
9. How would you measure the size of a screen?
10. How is the resolution of a printer comparable to the resolution of a screen?
11. How does a CD differ from a flash drive?
12. What are three types of flash memory cards?
13. What is a mobile CPU?
14. Which wireless standard is used by networks?

■ ASSIGNMENTS AND EXERCISES

1. **COMPARING DIFFERENT TYPES OF COMPUTER SYSTEMS** Computers come in varying sizes and levels of power and performance. Use the Web to find out about computer system configurations. Do some comparison shopping for three types of computers: desktops, notebooks, and tablet PCs. Choose three Web sites that sell computer systems. From each of these sites, choose the most expensive and least expensive computer systems you can find for each of the three types of computers. Create a table for each of the three types of computers and compare them based on the following criteria:
   - Type and speed of CPU
   - Type and speed of RAM
   - Amount of CPU cache
   - System bus speed
   - Hard disk capacity and speed (revolutions per minute or rpm)
   - Number and type of ports

2. **CUSTOMIZING A COMPUTER PURCHASE** One of the great things about the Web is the number of e-tailers that are now online offering you a variety of products and services. One such e-tailer is Dell, which allows you to customize and buy a computer. Connect to Dell's site at www.dell.com. Go to the portion of Dell's site that allows you to customize either a notebook or desktop computer. First, choose an already-prepared system and note its price and capability in terms of CPU speed, RAM size, monitor quality, and storage capacity. Now, customize that system to increase CPU speed, add more RAM, increase monitor size and quality, and add more storage capacity. What's the difference in price between the two? Which system is more in your price range? Which system has the speed and capacity you need?

3. **UNDERSTANDING THE COMPLEXITY OF SOFTWARE** Software instructions on how to open Microsoft Word or send information to a printer must be provided to a computer in great detail and with excruciating accuracy. Writing code to make the computer execute these instructions properly and in the right order is not a simple task. To understand how detailed you must be, pick a partner for this project and envision that you are standing in a kitchen. The task for one of you is to write down all the instructions that are necessary to make a peanut butter and jelly sandwich. When the instructions are complete, have the other person follow those instructions exactly. How successful was the second person in making the sandwich? Did your instructions include every single step? What did you leave out?

4. **ADDING MEDIA TO A PRESENTATION** We certainly live in a "multimedia" society, in which it's often easy to present and receive

information using a variety (multi) of media. Presentation tools such as Microsoft's PowerPoint can help you easily build presentations that include audio, animation, and video. And this may help you get a better grade in school. Using your preferred presentation software, document the steps necessary to add a short audio or video clip to a presentation. How does the representation of the clip appear on a slide? How can you initiate it? Does your presentation software include any clips that you can insert or do you have to record your own? Now, try recording a short audio clip. What steps must you perform?

5. **COMPARE SMARTPHONES** People today use smartphones for calling, texting, checking e-mail, Web surfing, taking and storing photos, and many other tasks. Find four smartphones from different manufacturers and compare the following features.
- Speed (3G or 4G)
- Size
- Weight
- Screen size
- Screen resolution
- Resolution of camera
- GPS capability

Student Learning Outcomes

1. Define the relationships among Web site, Web site address, domain name, Web page, and uniform resource locator (URL).

2. Explain how to interpret the parts of an address on the Web.

3. Identify the major components and features of Web browser software.

4. Define Web 2.0 and its many technologies including wikis, social networking sites, blogs, RSS feeds, and podcasting.

5. Describe the various technologies that make up the Internet.

6. Identify key considerations in choosing an Internet service provider (ISP).

7. Describe the communications software and telecommunications hardware you need to connect to the Internet.

Introduction

The most visible and explosive information technology tool is the Internet, and with it the World Wide Web (Web). No matter where you look or what you read, someone always seems to be referring to one of the two. On television commercials, you find Web site addresses displayed (such as www.ibm.com for an IBM commercial or www.toyota.com for a Toyota commercial). In almost every magazine, you find articles about the Internet because of its growing significance in our society. Most major business publications, such as *Fortune, Forbes,* and *Bloomberg Businessweek,* devote entire issues each year to the Internet and how to use it for electronic commerce. Of course, many such publications have been carrying articles detailing how and why so many dot-coms failed in recent years (now affectionately referred to as *dot-bombs*).

The Internet really is everywhere—and it's here to stay. What's really great about the Internet is that it takes only a couple of hours to learn. Once you've read the text for this module, you should try your hand at the Internet scavenger hunts in the Assignments and Exercises at the end of this module. You'll be surprised to learn how easy it is to find information on the Internet.

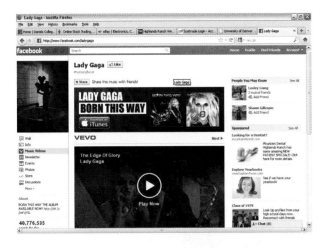

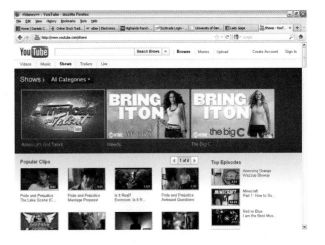

World Wide Web

The **World Wide Web,** or **Web,** as you probably know it, is a multimedia-based collection of information, services, and Web sites supported by the Internet. The **Internet** is a vast network of computers that connects millions of people all over the world. Schools, businesses, government agencies, and many others have all connected their internal networks to the Internet. The Internet and all its technological infrastructure are what make the Web possible. People tend to consider the Web and the Internet to be the same. (Although they are not.)

WEB SITES, ADDRESSES, AND PAGES

As you use the Web, you'll most often be accessing Web sites. A **Web site** is a specific location on the Web where you visit, gather information, and perhaps even order products. Each Web site has a specific Web site address. A **Web site address** is a unique name that identifies a specific site on the Web. Technically, this address is called a domain name. A **domain name** identifies a specific computer on the Web and the main page of the entire site. Most people use the term *Web site address* instead of the technical term *domain name.* For example, the Web site address for *USA Today* is www.usatoday.com (see Figure B.1).

Web site address or domain name

Figure B.1

The *USA Today* Web Site and Sports Web Page

Most Web sites include several and perhaps hundreds of Web pages. A ***Web page*** is a specific portion of a Web site that deals with a certain topic. The address for a specific Web page is called a URL. A ***URL (uniform resource locator)*** is an address for a specific Web page or document within a Web site. Most people opt for the common term of *Web page address* when referring to a URL. As you can see in Figure B.1, you can click on the link for **Sports** on the main page for *USA Today*. By clicking on that link, you will then be taken to a specific Web page within the *USA Today* Web site. The URL or Web page address for that page is www.usatoday.com/sports/default.htm. Links are important on the Web. A ***link*** (the technical name is ***hyperlink***) is clickable text or an image that takes you to another site or page on the Web.

UNDERSTANDING ADDRESSES

When you access a certain Web site or page, you do so with its unique address, such as www.usatoday.com (for our *USA Today* example). Addresses, because they are unique, tell you some important information about the site or page. Let's consider two different examples (see Figure B.2): Yahoo! (www.yahoo.com) and the University of Technology in Sydney, Australia (www.uts.edu.au).

Most addresses start with http://www, which stands for *hypertext transfer protocol* (http) and *World Wide Web* (www). The http:// part is so common now that you don't even have to use it in most cases. The remaining portion of the address is unique for each site or page. If you consider www.yahoo.com, you know that it's the address for Yahoo!. You can also tell it's a commercial organization by the last three letters: com. This extension can take on many forms and is referred to as the ***top-level domain (TLD).*** (See Figure B.3 on the following page for a complete list of TLDs.)

Some addresses have a two-character extension that follows the top-level domain. In this case, it's to identify the country location of the site. For example, the site address for the University of Technology in Sydney, Australia, is www.uts.edu.au. From that address, you can tell it's an educational institution (i.e., the TLD of edu) and that the site location is Australia (i.e., the country identifier of au).

The top-level domain ".com" identifies Yahoo! as a commercial or for-profit organization.

Figure B.2

Understanding Addresses

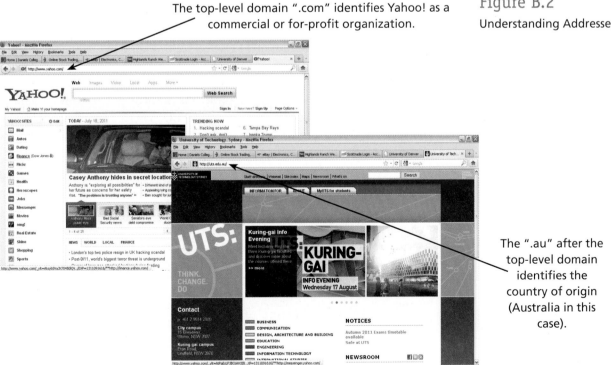

The ".au" after the top-level domain identifies the country of origin (Australia in this case).

Figure B.3

Top-Level Domains

Top-Level Domain	Description
.aero	Air-transport industry
.biz	Business
.catr	Catalan (language or related to Catalan culture)
.com	Commercial
.coop	Cooperative
.edu	Educational
.gov	Governmental
.info	Information
.int	International organization
.jobs	Companies with jobs to advertise
.mil	United States military
.mobi	Mobile device
.museum	Museum
.name	Individual, by name
.net	Network
.org	Organization
.pro	Profession
.travel	Travel or travel-agency related

The Internet Corporation for Assigned Names and Numbers (ICANN) is a nonprofit organization charged with numerous Internet-related responsibilities, one of which is the oversight of top-level domains. In mid-2011, ICANN announced a rather radical departure from the standardized set of TLDs you see in Figure B.3. Now, any organization (or person for that matter) can apply with ICANN for the use of any TLD. For example, the NBA may apply for .nba as a TLD and then have all its basketball teams use that TLD. The city of New York may apply for the use of .nyc. Then, any restaurant, sports league, etc. in New York City could use that TLD. There is a catch though. The application fee for a nonstandardized TLD is $185,000, which ICANN keeps regardless of whether or not the application is approved.

LEARNING OUTCOME 3

USING WEB BROWSER SOFTWARE

Web browser software enables you to surf the Web. When we viewed the sites for *USA Today,* Yahoo!, and University of Technology in Sydney, Australia, we were using Web browser software. The most popular Web browsers today are Internet Explorer (by Microsoft), Firefox (by Mozilla), and Chrome (by Google). All are free for you to use and you can download them at the following sites:

- Internet Explorer—www.microsoft.com/downloads
- Firefox—www.mozilla.com
- Chrome—www.google.com/chrome

To demonstrate how you use Web browser software, let's take a quick tour. In Figure B.4, you can see we have used all three Web browsers to access eBay (www.ebay.com). For Internet Explorer and Firefox, the menu bar appears across the top and includes such functions as **File, Edit, View, Tools,** and **Help.** Each has a few unique menu options,

Figure B.4

Internet Explorer, Firefox, and Chrome

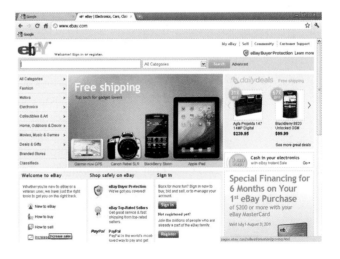

but both menu bars support the same basic functions. On Chrome, you can find those functions and many more by clicking on the tool icon (it looks like a wrench) in the upper right corner.

Near the top, you'll also find the **Address** field. If you know the address for where you want to go, click in the **Address** field, type in the address, and then hit **Enter.** If you're not precisely sure of a Web site address, you begin to search for it in one of two ways. The first is to use a search engine, which we'll discuss in the next section. The second is to type in a logical name in the **Address** field. For example, if you want to download tax forms from the IRS Web site but don't know the address of the IRS, you can simply type in "IRS" or "internal revenue service" in the **Address** field. Your Web browser will automatically begin a search for Web sites related to those terms and hopefully will find the right site for you. (In the instance of searching for the IRS, all three Web browsers do take you to the site you need.)

One of the most important features of any Web browser is that you can create, edit, and maintain a list of your most commonly visited addresses on the Web. In Internet Explorer, it's called a **Favorites list,** and in both Firefox and Chrome it's called a **Bookmarks list.** So, if you frequently visit eBay, you can save the address for eBay in one of these lists.

Another nice and often-used feature is tabs. Tabs appear near or at the top of the screen, depending on which Web browser you choose to use. Tabs allow you have multiple Web sites open at the same time. You can easily set the default on your browser software so that, upon launch, the browser will open a number of sites for you.

Search Engines

There will definitely be occasions when you want to find information and services on the Web, but you don't know exactly which site to visit. In this case, you can type in a logical name as we just demonstrated (with the Internal Revenue Service), or you can use a search engine. A *search engine* is a facility on the Web that helps you find sites with the information and/or services you want. There are many search engines on the Web, and although there are some subtle differences in using some of them, most will help you find what you're looking for.

Let's look at Ask (www.ask.com) and Google (www.google.com), two very popular search engines, and find information about the list of winners for the 2011 Academy Awards. In Figure B.5, you can see the results of our typing **2011 Academy Award Winners** in the **Search** field and clicking on the **Web Search** button in Ask. In that same figure, you can see the results of our typing **2011 Academy Award Winners** and clicking on the **Google Search** button in Google. The results are quite similar. In fact, if you were to peruse through the top 20 results from each search, about 15 or so are the same.

When you type in multiple terms for a search (such as **2011 Academy Award Winners**), most search engines will return sites that have all the terms appearing in them, although not necessarily in the order in which you typed them. If you want to further refine your search and exclude a certain term, then you would also type in the term to exclude preceded by a minus sign ($-$). For example, if you want information about the Miami Dolphins NFL football team, you could search on **Miami Dolphins.** That would probably yield a list of suitable sites, but it might also include sites that contain information about watching dolphins (the aquatic version) in the Miami area. To eliminate those sites, you could search using **Miami Dolphins** $-$ **aquatic** $-$ **mammal.** That search will eliminate any sites that contain either the term aquatic or mammal.

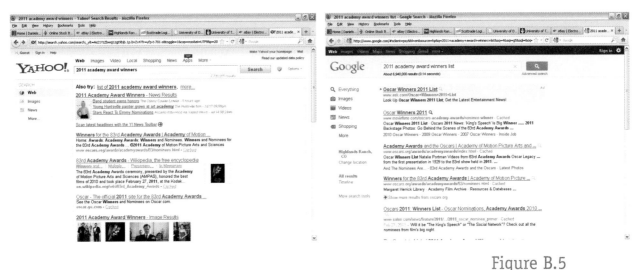

Figure B.5
Search Engines

The minus sign is referred to as a *Boolean operator* and can be used (along with other operators such as parenthetical marks, quote marks, and the plus sign) to help refine the list of Web sites you receive from a search. To learn more about using these, you should reference the searching options of the particular search engine you're using.

Web 2.0

LEARNING OUTCOME 4

In the past several years, the Web has evolved from a platform of pull technologies and static information to a more interactive one with constantly changing and dynamic information. The *Web 2.0* is this so-called second generation of the Web and focuses on online collaboration, users as both creators and modifiers of content, dynamic and customized information feeds, and many other engaging Web-based services.

From a purely technical perspective, there are a number of interesting and emerging technologies that make the Web 2.0 possible. If you dive into the technical side, you'll learn about technologies such as XML, Ajax, CSS, Webservice APIs, and SOAP. On the user side, everyone is interested in the dynamic applications of the Web 2.0 including:

- Wikis
- Social networking sites
- Blogs
- RSS feeds
- Podcasting
- Many, many others

WIKIS

A *Wiki* is a Web site that allows you—as a visitor—to create, edit, change, and often eliminate content. Wikipedia (www.wikipedia.org) is the most popular Wiki in existence today, boasting almost 4 million articles in English and couple of million more in other languages. Wikipedia is a free-content encyclopedia covering just about any topic you can think of, and any volunteer with access to the Web can create and edit content. Wiki, as a term, can refer either to the engine that makes Wiki sites possible or to a specific Wiki Web site such as Wikipedia, Wiktionary, Wikibooks, and Wikiquote.

SOCIAL NETWORKING SITES

A *social networking site* is a site on which you post information about yourself, create a network of friends, read about other people, share content such as photos and videos, and communicate with other people. "People" is a general term within social networking sites that includes actual people, music bands, organizations, and so on. The most popular social networking site is Facebook with almost 750 million users (see Figure B.6).

BLOGS

A *blog* is a Web site in the form of a journal in which you post entries in chronological order and often includes the capabilities for other viewers to add comments to your journal entries. Blogs cover a wide range of topics including news commentary, personal online diaries, travel, and so on. You can create your own blog at many different blogging Web sites including blog.com (www.blog.com).

A form of blogging with which you are probably familiar is *microblogging,* users exchanging small bursts of information that often include links to Web sites, videos, and the like. Within a social networking site like Facebook, you know microblogging as *status updates.* All social networking sites provide some sort of status update feature, and when you post a status update to your wall, you're participating in microblogging.

As a standalone application, microblogging is best known within the context of Twitter. Twitter, started in 2006, provides a platform on which people send tweets, text-based messages of 140 characters or less, to each other or to groups or circles of friends. These tweets are forms of microblogs.

Figure B.6

The Social Networking Site Facebook

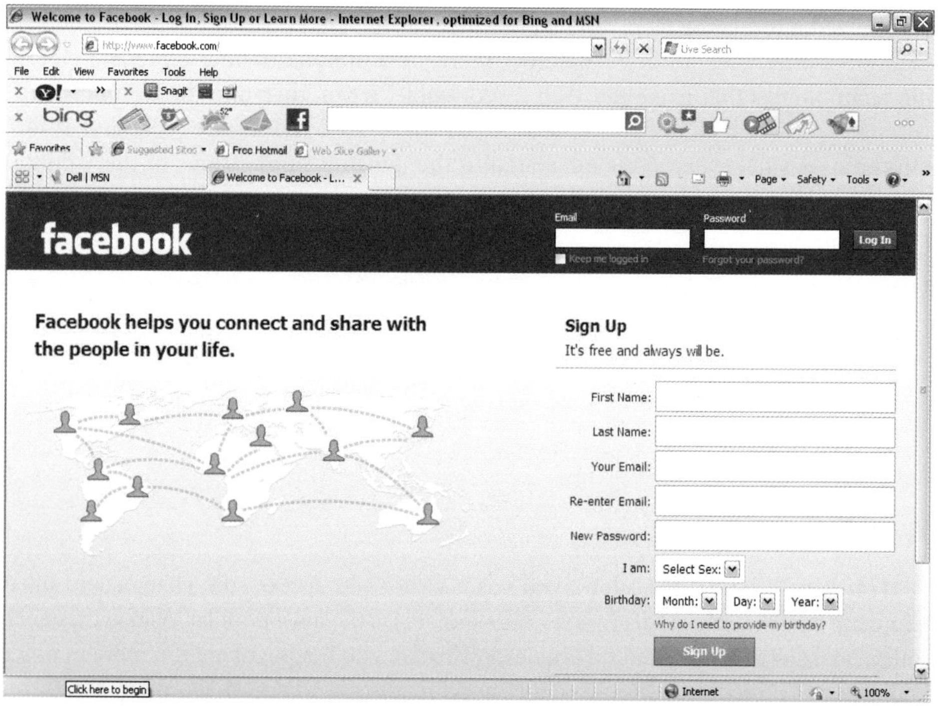

RSS FEEDS

An **RSS feed** is a technology that provides frequently published and updated digital content on the Web. You subscribe to an RSS feed and then provide what content you want in your RSS feed. With some RSS feeds, you click on a link to review updated content; with other RSS feeds, you can actually integrate them into your Web browser and have constantly updated information—such as stock quotes—stream across your Web browser interface.

PODCASTING

Podcasting is a term derived from **iPod** and broad**casting** and generally refers to your ability at any time to download audio and video files for viewing and listening using portable listening devices and personal computers. Podcasting is perhaps one of the most visible and widely used of all the Web 2.0 technologies. We performed a search of Google on July 18, 2011, and found 332 million hits for podcast and 25 million hits for podcasting. Apple's iTunes really gave birth to podcasting a few years ago, and many other digital content publishers have followed, such as syndicated TV shows which provide short videos of shows called *mobisodes.*

Internet Technologies

To best take advantage of everything the Web has to offer, it often helps to understand what's going on behind the Web, that is, the Internet. The Internet is really the enabling structure that makes the Web possible. Without the Web, the Internet still exists and you can still use it. But the reverse is not true. The Internet is the set of underlying technologies that makes the Web possible. The Web is somewhat of a graphical user interface (GUI) that sits on top of the Internet. The Web allows you to click on links to go to other sites, and it allows you to view information in multiple forms of media.

LEARNING OUTCOME 5

THE INTERNET BACKBONE

The **Internet backbone** is the major set of connections for computers on the Internet (see Figure B.7). A **network access point (NAP)** is a point on the Internet where several

Figure B.7

The Internet Backbone in the United States

connections converge. At each NAP is at least one computer that simply routes Internet traffic from one place to another (much like an airport where you switch planes to your final destination). These NAPs are owned and maintained by network service providers. A **network service provider (NSP),** such as MCI or AT&T, owns and maintains routing computers at NAPs and even the lines that connect the NAPs to each other. In Figure B.7, you can see that Dallas is a NAP, with lines converging from Atlanta, Phoenix, Kansas City, and Austin.

At any given NAP, an Internet service provider may connect its computer or computers to the Internet. An **Internet service provider (ISP)** is a company that provides -individuals, organizations, and businesses access to the Internet. ISPs include AOL, Juno, and perhaps even your school. In turn, you "dial up" or connect your computer to an ISP computer. So, your ISP provides you access to the Internet (and thus the Web) by allowing you to connect your computer to its computer (which is already connected to the Internet).

If you live in the San Francisco area and send an e-mail to someone living near Boston, your e-mail message might travel from San Francisco to Salt Lake City, then to Minneapolis, and finally to Boston. Of course, your e-mail message may very well travel the route of San Francisco, Phoenix, Dallas, Atlanta, Nashville, Pittsburgh, Orlando, New York, and then Boston. But, no matter—your message will get there. Can you imagine the route that your e-mail message would travel if you were in San Francisco sending it to someone in Venice, Italy? One time, it might go west around the world through Australia. The next time, it might go east around the world through New York and then on to London.

INTERNET SERVERS

There are many types of computers on the Internet, namely, router (which we've already discussed), client, and server computers (see Figure B.8). The computer that you use to access the Internet and surf the Web is called a *client computer.* Your client computer can be a traditional desktop or notebook computer, a Web or Internet appliance, a tablet PC, or your smartphone.

Internet server computers are computers that provide information and services on the Internet. There are four main types of server computers on the Internet: Web, mail, ftp, and IRC servers. A **Web server** provides information and services to Web surfers. So, when you access www.ebay.com, you're accessing a Web server (for eBay) with your client computer. Most often, you'll be accessing and using the services of a Web server.

A **mail server** provides e-mail services and accounts. Many times, mail servers are presented to you as a part of a Web server. For example, Hotmail is a free e-mail server and service provided by MSN. An **ftp (file transfer protocol) server** maintains a collection of files that you can download. These files can include software, screen savers, music files (many in MP3 format), and games. An **IRC (Internet Relay Chat) server** supports your use of discussion groups and chat rooms. IRC servers are popular hosting computers for sites such as www.epinions.com. There, you can share your opinions about various products and services, and you can also read the reviews written by other people.

COMMUNICATIONS PROTOCOLS

As information moves around the Internet, bouncing among network access points until it finally reaches you, it does so according to various communications protocols. A **communications protocol (protocol)** is a set of rules that every computer follows to

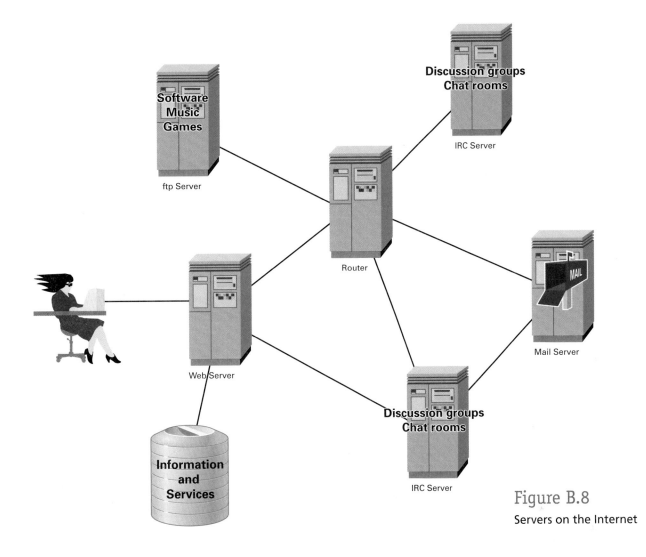

Figure B.8

Servers on the Internet

transfer information. The most widely used protocols on the Internet include TCP/IP, http, and ftp (and a few others such as PPP, Point-to-Point Protocol, and POP, Post Office Protocol).

TCP/IP, or *transport control protocol/Internet protocol,* is the primary protocol for transmitting information over the Internet. Whenever any type of information moves over the Internet, it does so according to TCP/IP. *Hypertext transfer protocol (http)* is the communications protocol that supports the movement of information over the Web, essentially from a Web server to you. That's why Web site addresses start with "http://." Most Web browser software today assumes that you want to access a Web site on the Internet. So you don't even have to type in the "http://" if you don't want to.

File transfer protocol (ftp) is the communications protocol that allows you to transfer files of information from one computer to another. When you download a file from an ftp server (using ftp), you're using both TCP/IP (the primary protocol for the Internet) and ftp (the protocol that allows you to download the file). Likewise, when you access a Web site, you're using both TCP/IP and http (because the information you want is Web based).

Connecting to the Internet

LEARNING OUTCOME 6

To access the Web (via the Internet), you need an Internet service provider (ISP), as we discussed earlier. ISPs can include your school, your place of work, commercial ISPs such as AT&T, and free ISPs such as NetZero. Which you choose is a function of many things.

One of the nice benefits of going to school or being employed is that you often get free Web access through school or your work. All you have to do is connect your home computer to your school's or work's computer (we'll talk about this process in a moment) and you're ready to surf. However, some schools and places of business may restrict where you can go on the Web. And they may even monitor your surfing.

Commercial ISPs charge you a monthly fee, just as your telephone company charges you a monthly fee for phone service. This fee usually ranges from a few dollars a month to about $50. Popular worldwide commercial ISPs include Microsoft (MSN), AOL, and AT&T just to name a few. Depending on your area, you may be able to get your cable TV programming, telephone, and Internet access all from one company. AT&T and Comcast offer this is many parts of the United States. By going with this "bundling" approach, you usually receive some sort of discount from the provider.

Free ISPs are absolutely free, as their names suggest—you don't pay a setup fee, you don't pay a monthly fee, and some offer unlimited access to the Web. But there are some catches. Many free ISPs do not offer you Web space, as opposed to most commercial ISPs which do. **Web space** is a storage area where you keep your Web site. So, if you want to create and maintain a Web site, you may have to choose a commercial ISP over a free ISP (your school probably also offers you Web space). Also when using a free ISP, you will often see banner ads that you can't get rid of. You can move them around and from side to side, but you can't remove them completely from your screen. Technical support is often limited with a free ISP. Some offer only e-mail support, while others do offer phone support but no toll-free number.

In spite of those drawbacks, many people do choose free ISPs over commercial ISPs, mainly because of cost (remember, $20 per month equals $240 per year). Popular free ISPs include NetZero (www.netzero.net, see Figure B.9). To decide which type of ISP is best for you, ask these questions:

- *Do you need Web space?* If yes, a free ISP may not be the right choice.
- *Is great technical support important?* If yes, then a commercial ISP may be the right choice.
- *Is money a serious consideration?* If yes, then a commercial ISP may not be the right choice.
- *Is privacy important to you?* If yes, then your school or work may not be the right choice.

LEARNING OUTCOME 7

COMMUNICATIONS SOFTWARE

To access and use the Web, you need communications software, namely,

- *Connectivity software*—Enables you to use your computer to dial up or connect to another computer.
- *Web browser software*—Enables you to surf the Web.
- *E-mail software* (short for *electronic mail software*)—Enables you to electronically communicate with other people by sending and receiving e-mail.

Figure B.9

NetZero Is a Popular Free ISP

NetZero free Internet access is for up to 10 hours per month.

Connectivity software is the first and most important. With connectivity software, while using a standard telephone modem, you essentially use your computer (and a phone line) to call up and connect to the server computer of your ISP. Connectivity software is standard on most personal computers today. To use connectivity software, you really only need to know the number to call. Then it's a relatively easy process: Within Microsoft Windows, click on **Start, All Programs, Accessories, Communications, Network Connections,** and then select **Create a new connection** (your exact sequence may vary slightly according to which version of Windows you're using).

Alternatively, if you're using connectivity software in conjunction with a high-speed modem connection such as a cable, DSL, or satellite modem (we'll discuss these further in a moment), you don't really "make a call" to connect to your ISP. Instead, you probably have an "always-on" high-speed Internet connection. So, when you turn on your computer, it goes through the process of connecting you to your ISP.

Web browser software and e-mail software are also standard software today. If your school or work is your ISP, then you'll most often be using commercially available Web browser software such as Internet Explorer, Netscape, or Firefox, and the e-mail software you use will vary according to your school's or work's preference. If you're using a commercial or free ISP, then your choice of Web browser software and e-mail software may depend on that particular organization.

TELECOMMUNICATIONS HARDWARE

In addition to communications software, you also need some telecommunications hardware to access the Web (again, via the Internet). If you're at school or work, you'll probably be able to connect your computer directly to a network that is then connected to the Internet. This often amounts to simply plugging a network line into your computer and starting your preferred Web browser or e-mail software. We discuss this type of connection to the Internet in more detail in *Extended Learning Module E.*

If you're connecting from home, you'll need some sort of modem. There are many types of modems, including

- A *telephone modem (modem)*—A device that connects your computer to your phone line so that you can access another computer or network.
- *Digital Subscriber Line (DSL)*—A high-speed Internet connection using phone lines, which allows you to use your phone line for voice communication at the same time.
- A *cable modem*—A device that uses your TV cable to deliver an Internet connection.
- A *satellite modem*—A modem that allows you to get Internet access from your satellite dish.

DSL, cable, and satellite modems are among the newest, most expensive, and fastest. They also don't tie up your phone line. If, for example, you're using a basic telephone modem, you can't use your telephone line for voice communications at the same time. A DSL modem on the other hand, for example, basically splits your telephone line so that you can use it simultaneously for voice communications and for connecting to the Internet (see Figure B.10). Even more so, DSL, cable, and satellite modems offer you an "always-on" Internet connection.

With these high-speed Internet connection options, you may also have the ability to connect wirelessly to the modem using a router or other piece of equipment. As you can see in Figure B.10, the DSL modem is wired directly to one computer and wirelessly connected to another computer. This gives you the ability to connect multiple computers to the DSL modem. Again, we'll cover both wired and wireless connections to the Internet in *Extended Learning Module E*.

The biggest factor in determining your choice of telecommunications hardware (beyond price) may be that of availability. In many areas of the country, phone companies and cable TV service providers do not yet support the use of DSL, cable, and satellite modems. So, you may be limited to just using a basic telephone modem. If some of the other options are available to you, we definitely recommend that you research them.

Figure B.10
DSL Modem Connection

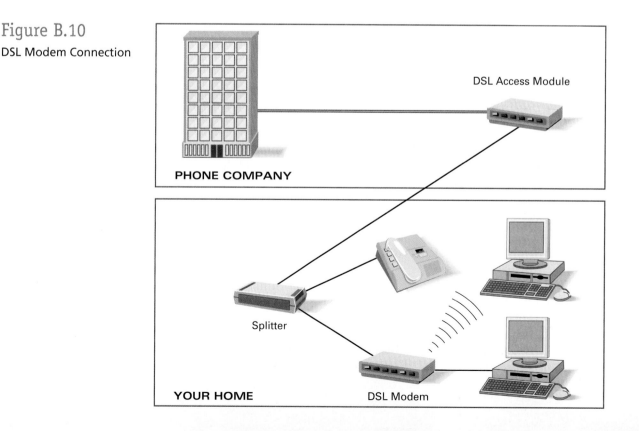

SUMMARY: STUDENT LEARNING OUTCOMES REVISITED

1. **Define the relationships among Web site, Web site address, domain name, Web page, and uniform resource locator (URL).** A *Web site* (such as www. usatoday.com for *USA Today*) is a specific location on the Web where you visit, gather information, order products and so on. A *Web site address* (www. usatoday.com) is a unique name that identifies a specific site on the Web. Technically, a Web site address is called a *domain name*. A *Web page* is a specific portion of a Web site that deals with a certain topic. Technically, the address for a specific Web page is called a *URL (uniform resource locator).*

2. **Explain how to interpret the parts of an address on the Web.** Most Web site addresses start with http://www. Beyond that, the address is unique. The first part (using www.uts.edu.au as an example) provides the name of the organization or Web site (UTS or University of Technology in Sydney). The next part tells the type of organization and is called the *top-level domain.* For UTS, it is "edu," describing it as an educational institution. If something follows after that, it usually provides a country of origin ("au" for UTS, which identifies its country of origin as Australia).

3. **Identify the major components and features of Web browser software.** The three most popular Web browsers are Internet Explorer, Netscape, and Firefox. Each includes a menu bar (with functions such as **File, Edit,** and **View**), a button bar (for commonly performed tasks such as printing), and an address or location field into which you can type a Web site address. Web browsers also include capabilities for maintaining a list of commonly visited sites. In Internet Explorer, this is called a **Favorites list,** while Firefox calls this a **Bookmarks list.**

4. **Define Web 2.0 and its many technologies including Wikis, social networking sites, blogs, RSS feeds, and podcasting.** The *Web 2.0* is the second generation of the Web and focuses on online collaboration, users as both creators and modifiers of content, dynamic and customized information feeds, and many other engaging Web-based services. The Web 2.0 includes:

   - *Wikis*—Web sites that allow you to create, edit, change, and often eliminate content
   - *Social networking sites*—sites on which you post information about yourself, create a network of friends, read about other people, share content such as photos and videos, and communicate with other people
   - *Blogs*—Web sites in the form of journals in which you post entries in chronological order and often include the capabilities for other viewers to add comments to your journal entries
   - *RSS feeds*—provide frequently published and updated digital content
   - *Podcasting*—your ability to download audio and video files to portable listening devices and personal computers

5. **Describe the various technologies that make up the Internet.** At the heart of the Internet is the *Internet backbone,* the major set of connections for computers on the Internet. A *network access point (NAP)* is a point on the Internet where several connections converge. *Network service providers (NSPs),* such as MCI or AT&T, own and maintain routing computers at NAPs and even the lines

that connect the NAPs to each other. Besides your computer (called a client computer) which you use to access the Internet, there are also four types of *Internet server computers* that provide information and services on the Internet. These include *Web servers* (providing information and services to Web surfers), *mail servers* (providing e-mail services and accounts), *ftp servers* (maintaining a collection of files that you can download), and *IRC servers* (supporting your use of discussion groups and chat rooms). As information travels from these servers to you, it follows a set of *communications protocols*—sets of rules that every computer follows to transfer information. The most common protocols include *TCP/IP* (the primary protocol for transmitting information), *http* (for supporting the movement of information over the Web), and *ftp* (for allowing you to transfer files of information from one computer to another).

6. **Identify key considerations in choosing an Internet service provider (ISP).** When choosing an ISP—whether it is a commercial ISP, a free ISP, your school, or your work—you need to consider the following:

- Web space—If you want to publish a Web site, then your ISP must provide you with Web space
- Technical support—Which can be in the form of e-mail, 24-hour toll-free assistance, or perhaps none at all
- Money—Commercial ISPs are the most expensive, while free ISPs, your school, and your work are free
- Privacy—Your school or work may monitor your surfing activities

7. **Describe the communications software and telecommunications hardware you need to connect to the Internet.** Communications software for connecting to the Internet includes *connectivity software* (for dialing up another computer), *Web browser software* (for actually surfing the Web), and *e-mail software* (for electronically communicating with other people). Telecommunications hardware includes the device that you use to physically connect your computer to a network, which may connect through a phone line or cable line. These devices are called modems and include *telephone modem, DSL, cable modem,* and *satellite modem.*

■ KEY TERMS AND CONCEPTS

■ SHORT-ANSWER QUESTIONS

1. How do the Web and Internet differ?
2. What is the relationship between a Web site and a Web page?
3. What are some of the technologies associated with the Web 2.0?
4. What is the relationship between the Internet backbone, a network access point, and a network service provider?
5. What is the role of an ISP?
6. What are the four major types of servers on the Internet?
7. What are the advantages and disadvantages of choosing a commercial ISP?
8. What communications software do you need to use the Web?
9. What are the four main types of modems you can use to access the Internet while at home?

■ ASSIGNMENTS AND EXERCISES

For each of the following Internet scavenger hunts, find the answer on the Web. When you do, write down the answer as well as the address where you found it. One restriction: You are not allowed to use sites such as *Encyclopedia Britannica, Wikipedia, and Fun Facts.*

1. What is the weight of the moon?
   Answer: _____
   Address: _____
2. Who was the first U.S billionaire?
   Answer: _____
   Address: _____
3. Who is Olive Oyl's brother?
   Answer: _____
   Address: _____
4. Who wrote "It was the worst of times . . ."?
   Answer: _____
   Address: _____
5. What does the Seine River empty into?
   Answer: _____
   Address: _____
6. What is a lacrosse ball made of?
   Answer: _____
   Address: _____
7. Who lives at 39 Stone Canyon Drive?
   Answer: _____
   Address: _____

8. What is the color of Mr. Spock's blood?
   Answer: _____
   Address: _____
9. At what number did the Nasdaq stock market close yesterday?
   Answer: _____
   Address: _____
10. Which is the most frequently broken bone in the human body?
    Answer: _____
    Address: _____
11. What is a pregnant goldfish called?
    Answer: _____
    Address: _____
12. Who was the first pope to visit Africa?
    Answer: _____
    Address: _____
13. How many tusks does an Indian rhinoceros have?
    Answer: _____
    Address: _____
14. What does a pluviometer measure?
    Answer: _____
    Address: _____
15. What is the fear of the number 13 called?
    Answer: _____
    Address: _____

16. Which ear can most people hear best with?

Answer: _____

Address: _____

17. Who is the patron saint of England?

Answer: _____

Address: _____

18. Which boxer's life story was told in the movie *Raging Bull?*

Answer: _____

Address: _____

19. Which was the first domesticated bird?

Answer: _____

Address: _____

20. What is the population of the United States right now?

Answer: _____

Address: _____

21. What is the capital of Bermuda?

Answer: _____

Address: _____

22. Who Wrote *The Ugly Duckling?*

Answer: _____

Address: _____

23. Which Hollywood actress was nicknamed *the legs?*

Answer: _____

Address: _____

24. What, translated literally, is the ninth month?

Answer: _____

Address: _____

25. What is the national airline of Australia?

Answer: _____

Address: _____

26. Who was Napoleon's first wife?

Answer: _____

Address: _____

27. What is another name for the Aurora Australis?

Answer: _____

Address: _____

28. How many pieces does each player start with in a game of checkers?

Answer: _____

Address: _____

29. Which writer was nicknamed "Papa"?

Answer: _____

Address: _____

30. What term does the computer word *bit* derive from?

Answer: _____

Address: _____

31. Which island was the jungle home of King Kong in the 1933 film?

Answer: _____

Address: _____

32. Which planet travels around the sun every 248 years?

Answer: _____

Address: _____

33. Who was the founder of Islam?

Answer: _____

Address: _____

34. How many sides does a nonagon have?

Answer: _____

Address: _____

35. What was Elvis Presley's middle name?

Answer: _____

Address: _____

36. What's the U.S. southern dish made from pigs' small intestines?

Answer: _____

Address: _____

37. Which French impressionist is famed for his paintings of ballet dancers?

Answer: _____

Address: _____

38. What did Clarence Birdseye perfect in 1924?

Answer: _____

Address: _____

39. What's a young female racehorse called?

Answer: _____

Address: _____

40. What is inside popcorn that makes it pop?

Answer: _____

EXTENDED LEARNING MODULE C

DESIGNING DATABASES AND ENTITY-RELATIONSHIP DIAGRAMMING

Student Learning Outcomes

1. Identify how databases and spreadsheets are both similar and different.

2. List and describe the four steps in designing and building a relational database.

3. Define the concepts of entity class, instance, primary key, and foreign key.

4. Given a small operating environment, build an entity-relationship (E-R) diagram.

5. List and describe the steps in normalization.

6. Describe the process of creating an intersection relation to remove a many-to-many relationship.

Introduction

As you learned in Chapter 3, databases are quite powerful and can aid your organization in both transaction and analytical processing. But you must carefully design and build a database for it to be effective. Relational databases are similar to spreadsheets in that you maintain information in two-dimensional files. In a spreadsheet, you place information in a cell (the intersection of a row and column). To use the information in a cell, you must know its row number and column character. For example, cell C4 is in column C and row 4.

Databases are similar and different. You still create rows and columns of information. However, you don't need to know the physical location of the information you want to see or use. For example, if cell C4 in your spreadsheet contained sales for Able Electronics (one of your customers), to use that information in a formula or function, you would reference its physical location (C4). In a database, you simply need to know you want *sales* for *Able Electronics.* Its physical location is irrelevant. That's why we say that a **database** is a collection of information that you organize and access according to the logical structure of that information.

LEARNING OUTCOME 1

So, you do need to design your databases carefully for effective use. In this module, we'll take you through the process of designing and building a relational database, the most popular of all database types. A **relational database** uses a series of logically related two-dimensional tables or files to store information in the form of a database. There are well-defined rules to follow, and you need to be aware of them.

As far as implementation is concerned, you then just choose the DBMS package of your choice, define the tables or files, determine the relationships among them, and start entering information. We won't deal with the actual implementation in this module. However, we do show you how to implement a database using Microsoft Access in *Extended Learning Module J.*

Once you've implemented your database, you can then change the information as you wish, add rows of information (and delete others), add new tables, and use simple but powerful reporting and querying tools to extract the exact information you need.

Designing and Building a Relational Database

LEARNING OUTCOME 2

Using a database amounts to more than just using various DBMS tools. You must also know *how* to actually design and build a database. So, let's take a look at how you would go about designing a database. The four primary steps include

1. Define entity classes and primary keys.
2. Define relationships among entity classes.
3. Define information (fields) for each relation (the term *relation* is often used to refer to a file while designing a database).
4. Use a data definition language to create your database.

Let's continue with the example database we introduced you to in Chapter 3, that of Solomon Enterprises. Solomon Enterprises specializes in providing concrete to commercial builders and individual home owners in the greater Chicago area. On page 68 (Figure 3.3) in Chapter 3, we provided a graphical depiction of some of the tables in Solomon's database, including *Customer, Concrete Type, Order, Truck,* and *Employee.* As you recall, an order is created when a customer calls in for the delivery of a certain concrete type. Once the concrete is mixed, Solomon has an employee drive the truck to the customer's location. That illustrates how you can use a database in support of your customer relationship management initiative and order-processing function.

In this module, we want to design and model the supply chain management side for Solomon Enterprises. Figure C.1 contains a supply chain management report that Solomon frequently generates. Let's make some observations.

Figure C.1

A Supply Chain Management Report for Solomon Enterprises

SOLOMON ENTERPRISES							
Supply Report Ending October 14, 2005							
CONCRETE		RAW MATERIAL				SUPPLIER	
Type	Name	ID	Name	Unit	QOH	ID	Name
1	Home	B	Cement paste	1	400	412	Wesley Enterprises
		C	Sand	2	1200	444	Juniper Sand & Gravel
		A	Water	1.5	9999	999	N/A
			TOTAL:	4.5			
2	Comm	B	Cement paste	1	400	412	Wesley Enterprises
		C	Sand	2	1200	444	Juniper Sand & Gravel
		A	Water	1	9999	999	N/A
			TOTAL:	4			
3	Speckled	B	Cement paste	1	400	412	Wesley Enterprises
		C	Sand	2	1200	444	Juniper Sand & Gravel
		A	Water	1.5	9999	999	N/A
		D	Gravel	3	200	444	Juniper Sand & Gravel
			TOTAL:	7.5			
4	Marble	B	Cement paste	1	400	412	Wesley Enterprises
		C	Sand	2	1200	444	Juniper Sand & Gravel
		A	Water	1.5	9999	999	N/A
		E	Marble	2	100	499	A&J Brothers
			TOTAL:	6.5			
5	Shell	B	Cement paste	1	400	412	Wesley Enterprises
		C	Sand	2	1200	444	Juniper Sand & Gravel
		A	Water	1.5	9999	999	N/A
		F	Shell	2.5	25	499	A&J Brothers
			TOTAL:	7			

- Solomon provides five concrete types: 1—home foundation and walkways; 2—commercial foundation and infrastructure; 3—premier speckled (with gravel); 4—premier marble; 5—premier shell.
- Solomon uses six raw materials: A—water; B—cement paste; C—sand; D—gravel; E—marble; F—shell.
- Mixing instructions are for a cubic yard. For example, one cubic yard of commercial concrete requires 1 part cement paste, 2 parts sand, and 1 part water. The terms "part" and "unit" are synonymous.
- Some raw materials are used in several concrete types. Any given concrete type requires several raw materials.
- QOH (quantity on hand) denotes the amount of inventory for a given raw material.
- Suppliers provide raw materials. For a given raw material, Solomon uses only one supplier. A given supplier can provide many different raw materials.
- QOH and supplier information are not tracked for water (for obvious reasons). However, Solomon places the value 9999 in the QOH for water and uses 999 for the ID of the supplier.

When you begin to think about designing a database application, you first need to capture your business rules. Business rules are statements concerning the information you need to work with and the relationships within the information. These business rules will help you define the correct structure of your database. From the report in Figure C.1 and the observations above, we derived the following business rules.

1. A given concrete type will have many raw materials in it.
2. A given raw material may appear in many types of concrete.
3. Each raw material has one and only one supplier.
4. A supplier may provide many raw materials. Although not displayed in Figure C.1, Solomon may have a supplier in its database that doesn't currently provide any raw materials.

Before you begin the process of designing a database, it's important that you first capture and understand the business rules. These business rules will help you define the correct structure of your database.

STEP 1: DEFINE ENTITY CLASSES AND PRIMARY KEYS

The first step in designing a relational database is to define the various entity classes and the primary keys that uniquely define each record or instance within each entity class. An *entity class* is a concept—typically people, places, or things—about which you wish to store information and that you can identify with a unique key (called a primary key). A *primary key* is a field (or group of fields in some cases) that uniquely describes each record. Within the context of database design, we often refer to a record as an instance. An *instance* is an occurrence of an entity class that can be uniquely described with a primary key.

From the supply chain management report in Figure C.1, you can easily identify the entity classes of *Concrete Type, Raw Material,* and *Supplier.* Now, you have to identify their primary keys. For most entity classes, you cannot use names as primary keys because duplicate names can exist. For example, your school provides you with a unique student ID and uses that ID as your primary key instead of your name (because other students may have the same name as you).

LEARNING OUTCOME 3

From the report on page 372, you can see that the entity class *Concrete Type* includes two pieces of information—*Concrete Type* and a name or *Type Description*. Although *Type Description* is unique, the logical choice for the primary key is *Concrete Type* (e.g., 1 for home, 2 for commercial, and so on). Notice that the primary key name is the same as the entity class name. This is perfectly acceptable; if it is a potential point of confusion for you, change the primary key name to something like *Concrete Type ID* or *Concrete Type Identifier*. For our purposes, we'll use *Concrete Type* as the primary key name.

If you consider *Raw Material* as an entity class, you'll find several pieces of information including *Raw Material ID*, *Raw Material Name*, and *QOH*. The logical choice for a primary key here is *Raw Material ID* (e.g., A for water, B for cement paste, and so on). Although *Raw Material Name* is unique, we still suggest that you not use names.

Likewise, if you consider *Supplier* as an entity class, you'll find two pieces of information: *Supplier ID* and *Supplier Name*. Again, we recommend that you use *Supplier ID* as the primary key.

To summarize, the goal in this first step is to define and identify entity classes and their primary keys for your database. An entity class is something like a student, a supplier, a book, and so on. The primary key for each entity class uniquely defines each record or instance within the entity class. For our example of Solomon Enterprises, the entity classes and their primary keys are:

Entity Class	Primary Key
Concrete Type	*Concrete Type*
Raw Material	*Raw Material ID*
Supplier	*Supplier ID*

Your success in completing this first step will, in part, determine your success in completing the remaining steps correctly. If you incorrectly define entity classes and primary keys in this first step, you are assured of being unable to successfully complete the remaining steps. Take all the time you need to complete this vitally important first step correctly.

STEP 2: DEFINE RELATIONSHIPS AMONG THE ENTITY CLASSES

LEARNING OUTCOME 4

The next step in designing a relational database is to define the relationships among the entity classes. To help you do this, we'll use an entity-relationship diagram. An **entity-relationship (E-R) diagram** is a graphic method of representing entity classes and their relationships. An E-R diagram includes five basic symbols:

1. A rectangle to denote an entity class
2. A dotted line connecting entity classes to denote a relationship
3. A | to denote a single relationship
4. A O to denote a zero or optional relationship
5. A crow's foot (shown as <) to denote a multiple relationship

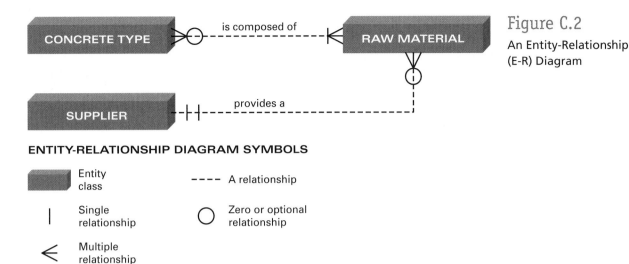

Figure C.2
An Entity-Relationship
(E-R) Diagram

ENTITY-RELATIONSHIP DIAGRAM SYMBOLS

	Entity class		A relationship
	Single relationship		Zero or optional relationship
	Multiple relationship		

To use these symbols, you must first decide among which entity classes relationships exist. If you determine that two particular entity classes have a relationship, you simply draw a dotted line to connect them and then write some sort of verb that describes the relationship.

In Figure C.2, you can see the E-R diagram for the supply chain management side of Solomon's database. To determine where the relationships exist, simply ask some questions and review your business rules. For example, is there a relationship between concrete type and raw material? The answer is yes because raw materials are used in mixing the various concrete types. Likewise, the raw materials are provided by suppliers (another relationship). However, there is no logical relationship between concrete type and supplier. So, we drew dotted lines between *Concrete Type* and *Raw Material* and between *Raw Material* and *Supplier*. We then added some verbs to describe the relationships. For example, a *Concrete Type* is composed of *Raw Material,* and a *Supplier* provides a *Raw Material.*

It should also make sense (both business and logical) when you read the relationships in reverse. To do this, simply flip the location of the nouns in the sentence and change the verb accordingly. For example,

- *Concrete Type–Raw Material:* A *Concrete Type* is composed of *Raw Material.*
- *Raw Material–Concrete Type:* A *Raw Material* is used to create a *Concrete Type.*
- *Supplier–Raw Material:* A *Supplier* provides a *Raw Material.*
- *Raw Material–Supplier:* A *Raw Material* is provided by a *Supplier.*

Each of the preceding statements makes logical sense, follows the relationships we identify in Figure C.2, and reflects the business rules listed on page 373. Again, we stress the importance of using business rules. Technology (databases, in this instance) is a set of tools that you use to process information. So, your implementations of technology should match the way your business works. If you always start by defining business rules and using those rules as guides, your technology implementations will most likely mirror how your business works. And that's the way it should be.

Figure C.3

Reading an Entity-
Relationship (E-R)
Diagram

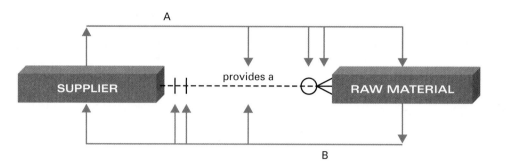

Once you determine that a relationship does exist, you must then determine the numerical nature of the relationship, what we refer to as "minimum and maximum cardinality." To describe this, you use a | to denote a single relationship, a O to denote a zero or optional relationship, and/or a crow's foot (<) to denote a multiple relationship. By way of illustration, let's consider the portion of your E-R diagram in Figure C.3 above. To help you read the symbols and diagram, we've added blue lines and arrows. Following the line marked A, you would read the E-R diagram as:

"A *Supplier* may not provide any *Raw Material* (denoted with the O) but may provide more than one *Raw Material* (denoted with the crow's foot)."

So, that part of the E-R diagram states that the logical relationship between *Supplier* and *Raw Material* is that a *Supplier* may provide no *Raw Material* currently in inventory but may provide more than one *Raw Material* currently in inventory. This is exactly what business rule 4 (on page 373) states.

Following the blue line marked B, you would read the E-R diagram as:

"A *Raw Material* must be provided by one *Supplier* (denoted with the first |) and can only be provided by one *Supplier* (denoted with the second |)."

That statement again reinforces business rule 4.

Similarly, you can also develop statements that describe the numerical relationships between *Concrete Type* and *Raw Material* based on that part of the E-R diagram in Figure C.2. Those numerical relationships would be as follows:

- A *Concrete Type* is composed of more than one *Raw Material* and must be composed of at least one *Raw Material*.

- A *Raw Material* can be used to create more than one *Concrete Type* but is not required to be used to create any *Concrete Type*.

Again, these statements reinforce business rules 1 and 2 on page 373.

To properly develop the numerical relationships (cardinality) among entity classes, you must clearly understand the business situation at hand. That's why it's so important to write down all the business rules.

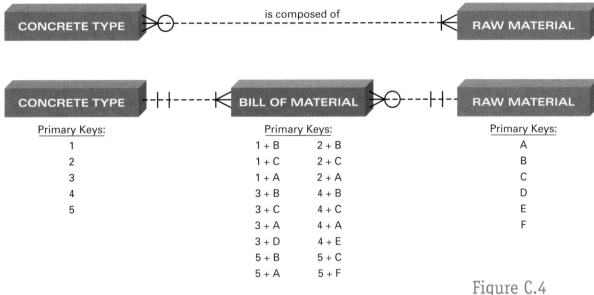

Figure C.4

Creating an Intersection Relation to Remove a Many-to-Many Relationship

After developing the initial E-R diagram, it's time to begin the process of normalization. ***Normalization*** is a process of assuring that a relational database structure can be implemented as a series of two-dimensional relations (remember: relations are the same as files or tables). The complete normalization process is extensive and quite necessary for developing organizationwide databases. For our purposes, we will focus on the following three rules of normalization:

LEARNING OUTCOME 5

1. Eliminate repeating groups or many-to-many relationships.
2. Assure that each field in a relation depends only on the primary key for that relation.
3. Remove all derived fields from the relations.

The first rule of normalization states that no repeating groups or many-to-many relationships can exist among the entity classes. You can find these many-to-many relationships by simply looking at your E-R diagram and note any relationships that have a crow's foot on each end. If you look back at Figure C.2 on page 375, you'll see that a crow's foot is on each end of the relationship between *Concrete Type* and *Raw Material*. Let's look at how to eliminate it.

In Figure C.4 above, we've developed the appropriate relationships between *Concrete Type* and *Raw Material* by removing the many-to-many relationship. Notice that we started with the original portion of the E-R diagram and created a new relation between *Concrete Type* and *Raw Material* called *Bill of Material*, which is an intersection relation. An ***intersection relation*** (sometimes called a ***composite relation***) is a relation you create to eliminate a many-to-many relationship. It's called an intersection relation because it represents an intersection of the primary keys between the first two relations. That is, an intersection relation will have a ***composite primary key*** that consists of the primary key fields from the two intersecting relations. The primary key fields from the two original relations now become foreign keys in the intersection relation. A ***foreign key*** is a primary key of one file (relation) that appears in another file (relation). When combined, these two foreign keys make up the composite primary key for the intersection relation.

For Solomon's supply chain management portion of its database, the intersection relation *Bill of Material* represents the combination of raw materials that go into each concrete type. Listed below is how you would read the relationships between *Concrete Type* and *Bill of Material* and *Raw Material* and *Bill of Material* (see Figure C.5).

- *Concrete Type–Bill of Material* From left to right: A *Concrete Type* can have multiple listings of *Raw Material* in *Bill of Material* and must have a listing of *Raw Material* in *Bill of Material*.
- From right to left: A *Concrete Type* found in *Bill of Material* must be found and can be found only one time in *Concrete Type*.
- *Raw Material–Bill of Material* From left to right: A *Raw Material* can be found in many *Bill of Material* listings but may not be found in any *Bill of Material* listing.
- From right to left: A *Raw Material* found in *Bill of Material* must be found and can be found only one time in *Raw Material*.

If you compare the E-R diagram in Figure C.5 to the E-R diagram in Figure C.2, you'll notice that they are very similar. The only difference is that the E-R diagram in Figure C.5 contains an intersection relation to eliminate the many-to-many relationship between *Concrete Type* and *Raw Material*.

Removing many-to-many relationships is the most difficult aspect when designing the appropriate structure of a relational database. If you do find a many-to-many relationship, here are some guidelines for creating an intersection relation:

1. Just as we did in Figure C.4, start by drawing the part of the E-R diagram that contains a many-to-many relationship at the top of a piece of paper.
2. Underneath each relation for which the many-to-many relationship exists, write down some of the primary keys.
3. Create a new E-R diagram (showing no cardinality) with the original two relations on each end and a new one (the intersection relation) in the middle.
4. Underneath the intersection relation, write down some of the composite primary keys (these will be composed of the primary keys from the other two relations).
5. Create a meaningful name (e.g., *Bill of Material*) for the intersection relation.
6. Move the minimum cardinality appearing next to the left relation just to the right of the intersection relation.
7. Move the minimum cardinality appearing next to the right relation just to the left of the intersection relation.

LEARNING OUTCOME 6

Figure C.5

The Completed E-R Diagram for the Supply Chain Management Side of Solomon's Database

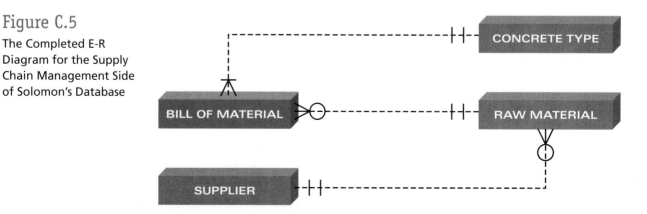

8. The maximum cardinality on both sides of the intersection relations will always be "many" (the crow's foot).

9. As a general rule, the new minimum and maximum cardinalities for the two original relations will be one and one.

We would stress again that removing many-to-many relationships is the most difficult aspect when designing the appropriate structure of a relational database.

The business world is full of many-to-many relationships that must be eliminated before an organization can correctly implement a relational database. Let's talk through another example of a many-to-many relationship to help you better understand how to eliminate them. Consider that Solomon sometimes has to use more than one truck to make a delivery of concrete to a customer. That is, what if—given that a truck can carry at most 8 cubic yards of concrete—Triple A Homes asks for 12 cubic yards of premier marble for a given delivery. In that case, Solomon would have two choices for modeling and storing multiple trucks for the order. First, it could create two separate orders, one for 8 cubic yards of premier marble concrete and the other for 4 cubic yards of premier marble concrete. That option doesn't make business sense—when a customer places an order, then the entire order should be contained in only *one* order, not two.

The second choice—which is the correct one—is to have the ability to specify multiple trucks on a single order. In that case, Solomon would have a many-to-many relationship between *Order* and *Truck*. That is, the revised business rule would be that an *Order* can have multiple *Trucks* assigned to make the delivery and a *Truck* can be assigned to make a delivery on multiple *Orders*.

But it doesn't stop there. Solomon may wish to sometimes send two employees in one truck to deliver one order of concrete. Then, Solomon would need the ability to specify more than one employee per delivery truck.

As you can see, the business world is complex and full of many-to-many relationships. If you can master the art and science of eliminating many-to-many relationships in a database environment, you have created a substantial career opportunity for yourself.

STEP 3: DEFINE INFORMATION (FIELDS)
FOR EACH RELATION

Once you've completed steps 1 and 2, you must define the various pieces of information that each relation will contain. Your goal in this step is to make sure that the information in each relation is indeed in the correct relation and that the information cannot be derived from other information—the second and third rules of normalization.

In Figure C.6 on the opposite page, we've developed a view of the relational database for Solomon based on the new E-R diagram with the intersection relation. To make sure that each piece of information is in the correct relation, look at each and ask, "Does this piece of information depend only on the primary key for this relation?" If the answer is yes, the information is in the correct relation. If the answer is no, the information is in the wrong relation.

Let's consider the *Raw Material* relation. The primary key is *Raw Material ID,* so each piece of information must depend only on *Raw Material ID.* Does *Raw Material Name* depend on *Raw Material ID?* Yes, because the name of a raw material depends on that particular raw material (as does *QOH* or quantity on hand). Does *Supplier ID* depend only on *Raw Material ID?* Yes, because the particular supplier providing a raw material depends on which raw material you're describing. In fact, *Supplier ID* in the *Raw Material* relation is a foreign key. That is, it is a primary key of one relation (*Supplier*) that appears in another relation (*Raw Material*).

What about *Supplier Name* in the *Raw Material* relation? Does it depend only on *Raw Material ID?* The answer here is no. *Supplier Name* depends only on *Supplier ID.* So, now the question becomes, "In which relation should *Supplier Name* appear?" The answer is in the *Supplier* relation, because *Supplier Name* depends on the primary key (*Supplier ID*) for that relation. Therefore, *Supplier Name* should appear in the *Supplier* relation (as it does) and not in the *Raw Material* relation.

Now, take a look at the intersection relation *Bill of Material.* Notice that it includes the field called *Unit. Unit* is located in this relation because it depends on two things: the concrete type you're describing and the raw material in it. So, *Unit* does depend completely on the composite primary key of *Concrete Type* + *Raw Material ID* in the *Bill of Material relation.*

If you follow this line of questioning for each relation, you'll find that all other fields are in their correct relations. Now you have to look at each field to see whether you can derive it from other information. If you can, the derived information should not be stored in your database. When we speak of "derived" in this instance, we're referring to information that you can mathematically derive: counts, totals, averages, and the like. Currently, you are storing the raw material total (*Raw Material Total*) in the *Concrete Type* relation. Can you derive that information from other information? The answer is yes—all you have to do is sum the *Units* in the *Bill of Material* relation for a given *Concrete Type.* So, you should not store *Raw Material Total* in your database (anywhere).

CONCRETE TYPE RELATION

Concrete Type	Type Description	Raw Material Total
1	Home foundation and walkways	5
2	Commercial foundation and infrastructure	4
3	Premier speckled (with smooth gravel aggregate)	8
4	Premier marble (with crushed marble aggregate)	7
5	Premier shell (with shell aggregate)	7

RAW MATERIAL RELATION

Raw Material ID	Raw Material Name	QOH	Supplier ID	Supplier Name
A	Water	9999	999	N/A
B	Cement paste	400	412	Wesley Enterprises
C	Sand	1200	499	A&J Brothers
D	Gravel	200	499	A&J Brothers
E	Marble	100	444	Juniper Sand & Gravel
F	Shell	25	444	Juniper Sand & Gravel

SUPPLIER RELATION

Supplier ID	Supplier Name
412	Wesley Enterprises
499	A&J Brothers
444	Juniper Sand & Gravel
999	N/A

BILL OF MATERIAL RELATION

Concrete Type	Raw Material ID	Unit
1	B	1
1	C	2
1	A	1.5
2	B	1
2	C	2
2	A	1
3	B	1
3	C	2
3	A	1.5
3	D	3
4	B	1
4	C	2
4	A	1.5
4	E	2
5	B	1
5	C	2
5	A	1.5
5	F	1.5

Unit belongs in this relation because it depends on a combination of how much of a given raw material *(Raw Material ID)* goes into each type of concrete type *(Concrete Type)*.

Figure C.6

A First Look at the Relations for the Supply Chain Management Side of Solomon's Database

Once you've completed step 3, you've completely and correctly defined the structure of your database and identified the information each relation should contain. Figure C.7 shows your database and the information in each relation. Notice that we have removed *Supplier Name* from the *Raw Material* relation and that we have removed *Raw Material Total* from the *Concrete Type* relation.

Figure C.7

The Correct Structure of the Supply Chain Management Side of Solomon's Database

CONCRETE TYPE RELATION

Concrete Type	Type Description
1	Home foundation and walkways
2	Commercial foundation and infrastructure
3	Premier speckled (with smooth gravel aggregate)
4	Premier marble (with crushed marble aggregate)
5	Premier shell (with shell aggregate)

RAW MATERIAL RELATION

Raw Material ID	Raw Material Name	QOH	Supplier ID
A	Water	9999	999
B	Cement paste	400	412
C	Sand	1200	444
D	Gravel	200	444
E	Marble	100	499
F	Shell	25	499

SUPPLIER RELATION

Supplier ID	Supplier Name
412	Wesley Enterprises
499	A&J Brothers
444	Juniper Sand & Gravel
999	N/A

BILL OF MATERIAL RELATION

Concrete Type	Raw Material ID	Unit
1	B	1
1	C	2
1	A	1.5
2	B	1
2	C	2
2	A	1
3	B	1
3	C	2
3	A	1.5
3	D	3
4	B	1
4	C	2
4	A	1.5
4	E	2
5	B	1
5	C	2
5	A	1.5
5	F	1.5

STEP 4: USE A DATA DEFINITION LANGUAGE TO CREATE YOUR DATABASE

The final step in developing a relational database is to take the structure you created in steps 1 through 3 and use a data definition language to actually create the relations. Data definition languages are found within a database management system. A ***database management system (DBMS)*** helps you specify the logical organization for a database and access and use the information within the database. To use a data definition language, you need the data dictionary for your complete database. Recall from Chapter 3 that the ***data dictionary*** contains the logical structure for the information in a database. Throughout this module and in the first part of Chapter 3, we provided you with the overall structure of Solomon's complete database including the relations of *Order, Truck, Customer, Employee, Concrete Type, Raw Material, Supplier,* and *Bill of Material.*

This is the point at which we'll end this extended learning module. But you shouldn't stop learning. We've written *Extended Learning Module J* to take you through the process of using a data definition language in Access to create the database for Solomon Enterprises.

■ SUMMARY: STUDENT LEARNING OUTCOMES REVISITED

1. **Identify how databases and spreadsheets are both similar and different.** Databases and spreadsheets are similar in that they both store information in two-dimensional files. They are different in one key aspect: physical versus logical. Spreadsheets require that you know the physical location of information, by row number and column character. Databases, on the other hand, require that you know logically what information you want. For example, in a database environment you could easily request total sales for Able Electronics, and you would receive that information. In a spreadsheet, you would have to know the physical location—by row number and column character—of that information.

2. **List and describe the four steps in designing and building a relational database.** The four steps in designing and building a relational database include

   1. Define entity classes and primary keys
   2. Define relationships among entity classes
   3. Define information (fields) for each relation
   4. Use a data definition language to create your database

3. **Define the concepts of entity class, instance, primary key, and foreign key.** An ***entity class*** is a concept—typically people, places, or things—about which you wish to store information and that you can identify with a unique key (called a primary key). A ***primary key*** is a field (or group of fields in some cases) that uniquely describes each record. Within the context of database design, we often refer to a record as an instance. An ***instance*** is an occurrence of an entity class that can be uniquely described. To provide logical relationships among various entity classes, you use ***foreign keys***—primary keys of one file (relation) that also appear in another file (relation).

4. **Given a small operating environment, build an entity-relationship (E-R) diagram.** Building an entity-relationship (E-R) diagram starts with knowing and understanding the business rules that govern the situation. These rules will help you identify entity classes, primary keys, and relationships. You then follow the process of normalization, eliminating many-to-many relationships, assuring that each field is in the correct relation, and removing any derived fields.

5. **List and describe the steps in normalization.** *Normalization* is the process of assuring that a relational database structure can be implemented as a series of two-dimensional tables. The normalization steps include

   1. Eliminate repeating groups or many-to-many relationships
   2. Assure that each field in a relation depends only on the primary key for that relation
   3. Remove all derived fields from the relations

6. **Describe the process of creating an intersection relation to remove a many-to-many relationship.** To create an intersection relation to remove a many-to-many relationship, follow these steps:

   1. Draw the part of the E-R diagram that contains a many-to-many relationship
   2. Create a new E-R diagram with the original two relations on each end and a new one (the intersection relation) in the middle
   3. Create a meaningful name for the intersection relation
   4. Move the minimum cardinality appearing next to the left relation just to the right of the intersection relation
   5. Move the minimum cardinality appearing next to the right relation just to the left of the intersection relation
   6. The maximum cardinality on both sides of the intersection relation will always be "many"
   7. As a general rule, the new minimum and maximum cardinalities for the two original relations will be one and one

KEY TERMS AND CONCEPTS

Composite primary key, 377
Database, 371
Database management system (DBMS), 383
Data dictionary, 383
Entity class, 373
Entity-relationship (E-R) diagram, 374

Foreign key, 377
Instance, 373
Intersection relation (composite relation), 377
Normalization, 377
Primary key, 373
Relational database, 371

SHORT-ANSWER QUESTIONS

1. How are relational databases and spreadsheets both similar and different?
2. What is a database?
3. What are the four steps in designing and building a relational database?
4. What are some examples of entity classes at your school?

5. What is the role of a primary key?
6. What is an entity-relationship (E-R) diagram?
7. How do business rules help you define minimum and maximum cardinality?
8. What is normalization?
9. What are the three major rules of normalization?

10. What is an intersection relation? Why is it important in designing a relational database?

11. Why must you remove derived information from a database?

12. What is a database management system (DBMS)?

■ ASSIGNMENTS AND EXERCISES

1. **DEFINING ENTITY CLASSES FOR THE MUSIC INDUSTRY** The music industry tracks and uses all sorts of information related to numerous entity classes. Find a music CD and carefully review the entire contents of the jacket. List as many entity classes as you can find (for just that CD). Now, go to a music store and pick out a CD for a completely different music genre and read its jacket. Did you find any new entity classes? If so, what are they?

2. **DEFINING BUSINESS RULES FOR A VIDEO RENTAL STORE** Think about how your local video rental store works. There are many customers, renting many videos, and many videos sit on the shelves unrented. Customers can rent many videos at one time. And some videos are so popular that the video rental store keeps many copies. Write down all the various business rules that define how a video rental store works with respect to entity classes and their relationships.

3. **CREATING AN E-R DIAGRAM FOR A VIDEO RENTAL STORE** After completing assignment 2, draw the initial E-R diagram based on the rules you defined. Don't worry about going through the process of normalization at this point. Simply identify the appropriate relationships among the entity classes and define the minimum and maximum cardinality of each relationship. By the way, how many many-to-many relationships did you define?

4. **ELIMINATING A MANY-TO-MANY RELATIONSHIP** Consider the following situation. At a small auto parts store, customers can buy many parts. And the same part can be bought by many different customers. That's an example of a many-to-many relationship. How would you eliminate it? What would you call the intersection relation? This one is particularly tough: You'll have to actually create two intersection relations to model this correctly.

5. **DEFINING THE CARDINALITY AMONG TWO ENTITY CLASSES** Consider the two entity classes of *Student* and *Advisor* at your school. How would you build an E-R diagram to show the relationship between these two entity classes? What is the minimum and maximum cardinality of the relationship?

6. **BUILDING A DATABASE OF STUDENTS, SEMINARS, AND TEACHERS** On the Web site for this text (www.mhhe.com/haag, select XLM/C), you'll find a robust running case study for this module. In Phase #1, you'll find a description of a school offering multiple sections of two different weekend seminars. You are charged with defining the entity classes and their primary keys for a supporting database. In Phase #2, you must define the relationships among the various entity classes. In Phase #3, you must define the cardinality for the relationships among the entity classes. In Phase #4, you'll have to create an intersection relation to take care of a many-to-many relationship. Finally, you must define all of the information (fields) for each relation. Tackle this case study to fully integrate everything you've learned in this module.

DECISION ANALYSIS WITH SPREADSHEET SOFTWARE

Student Learning Outcomes

1. Define a list and a list definition table within the context of spreadsheet software and describe the importance of each.

2. Compare and contrast the Filter function and Custom Filter function in spreadsheet software.

3. Describe the purpose of using conditional formatting.

4. Define a pivot table and describe how you can use it to view summarized information by dimension.

5. Describe the purpose of using Goal Seek.

Introduction

As you read in Chapter 4, technology can and does play a vitally important role in both supporting decision making and, in some instances, actually making decisions or recommendations. In this module, we'll focus on decision-making support by exploring many of the advanced and productive features of Microsoft Excel.

Microsoft Excel is spreadsheet software that allows you to work with any kind of information, with each individual piece of information located in a cell. A cell is the intersection of a row and column and is uniquely identified by its column character and row number. In Figure D.1 you can see two workbooks. The first (the one in the background) shows all the detailed information for a group of customers. The second shows the number of customers by region (North, South, East, and West) and by rent versus own.

There are a total of 487 customers (cell D9 in the workbook in the foreground), of which 262 own a home (cell B9) and 225 rent (cell C9). Within this workbook, you can easily see some interesting information. For example, there are 148 customers in the East region while only 98 live in the South region. By region and ownership status, 82 own a home in the East region while only 47 rent in the South region.

In this module, we'll be demonstrating decision-making support in Excel using Office 2010. If you use Office 2007 or an earlier version, you can find this same module in those versions of Office on the student CD that accompanies your text or on the Web at www.mhhe.com/haag.

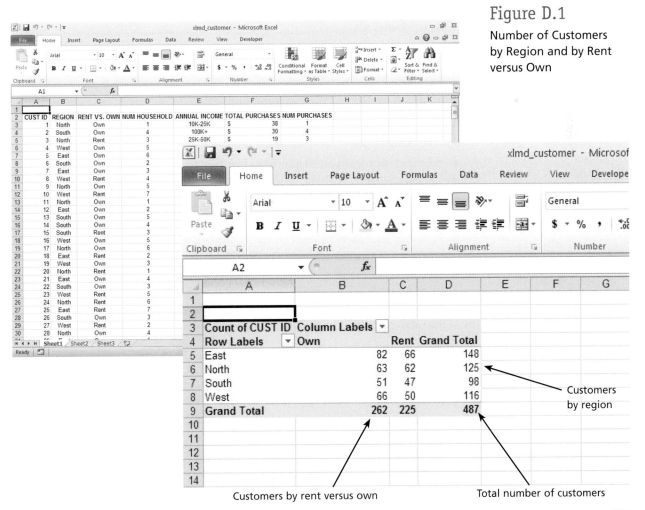

Figure D.1

Number of Customers by Region and by Rent versus Own

Customers by region

Customers by rent versus own

Total number of customers

Of course, now the question becomes, How is the information in Figure D.1 helpful? Well, it depends on the nature of your decision-making task. If you believe that home owners spend more money than those who rent and want to target advertising to the largest region, the information might be helpful. Then again, it might not be. It could very well be that home owners actually spend less than customers who rent. And perhaps you generate more sales in regions with a lower number of customers.

Let's see how spreadsheet software can help you make better decisions. As we do, we'll introduce you to some spreadsheet features for working with lists including Filter, conditional formatting, and pivot tables. In a later section, we'll demonstrate how to solve the break-even question from Chapter 1 using Goal Seek. Our goal here is not to provide in great detail how each of these work, but rather what's most important about each one of them in supporting your decision-making tasks. After completing this module, you'll definitely be able to use all features in their basic forms. We recommend that you continue to explore them in detail.

Lists

LEARNING OUTCOME 1

What we showed in Figure D.1 was a pivot table. A pivot table is a spreadsheet function that summarizes information by category. In our case, it summarized information by region (the rows) and rent versus own (the column). To create a pivot table (and use many of the other features we'll discuss in this module), you have to first build a list. You should work along with us on this. Connect to the Web site that supports this text (www.mhhe.com/haag and select XLM/D). There, you can download the file called **XLMD_Customer.xls.**

A *list* is a collection of information arranged in columns and rows in which each column displays one particular type of information. In spreadsheet software, a list possesses the following characteristics:

1. Each column has only one type of information.
2. The first row in the list contains the labels or column headings.
3. The list does not contain any blank rows.
4. The list is bordered on all four sides by blank rows and blank columns (it may not have a blank line above it, if it starts in the first row).

Take a look at the workbook in Figure D.2. It contains detailed information about our customers. In fact, we used this very list to generate the pivot table in Figure D.1.

First, notice that each column contains only one type of information: column A contains *CUST ID,* column B contains *REGION,* and so on. Second, notice that the first row (row 1) contains the labels or column headings. Third, if you scroll down completely through the list, you'll notice that there are 487 customers and there are no blank rows. Finally, notice that the list is bordered on all sides (except the top) by blank rows and columns. So, this is a list according to the four characteristics we listed.

We're going to be working extensively with this list throughout this module, so let's take a little time to explore the information in it. The columns of information include

A. *CUST ID*—A unique ID for each customer
B. *REGION*—The region in which the customer lives (North, South, East, or West)
C. *RENT VS. OWN*—Whether the customer rents or owns a home
D. *NUM HOUSEHOLD*—Number of family members in the household
E. *ANNUAL INCOME*—Total combined annual income of all family members

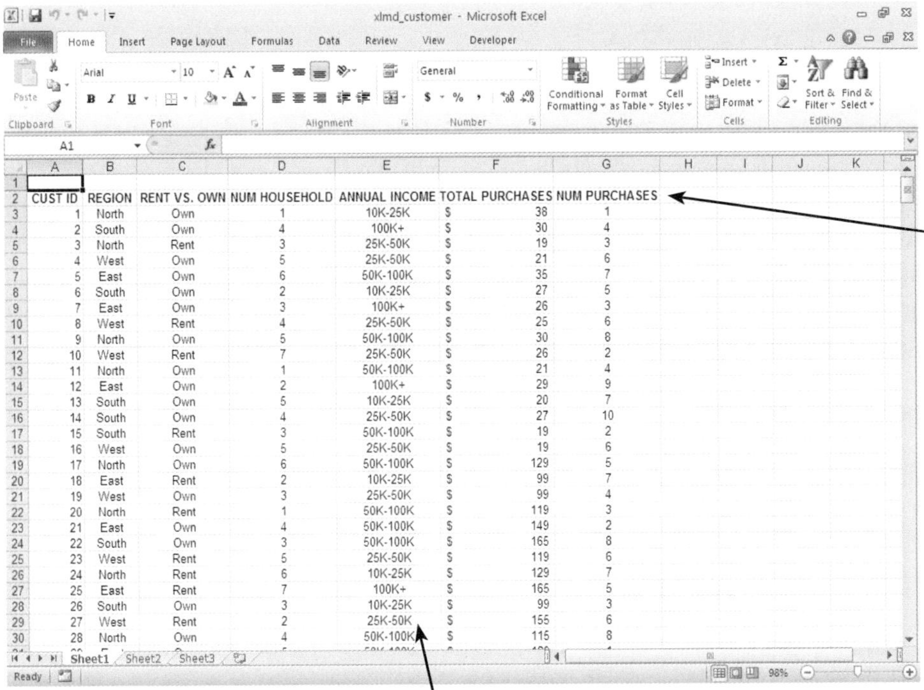

Figure D.2

The Complete List of Customers

CUST ID	REGION	RENT VS. OWN	NUM HOUSEHOLD	ANNUAL INCOME	TOTAL PURCHASES	NUM PURCHASES
1	North	Own	1	10K-25K	$ 38	1
2	South	Own	4	100K+	$ 30	4
3	North	Rent	3	25K-50K	$ 19	3
4	West	Own	5	25K-50K	$ 21	6
5	East	Own	6	50K-100K	$ 35	7
6	South	Own	2	10K-25K	$ 27	5
7	East	Own	3	100K+	$ 26	3
8	West	Rent	4	25K-50K	$ 25	6
9	North	Own	5	50K-100K	$ 30	8
10	West	Rent	7	25K-50K	$ 26	2
11	North	Own	1	50K-100K	$ 21	4
12	East	Own	2	100K+	$ 29	9
13	South	Own	5	10K-25K	$ 20	7
14	South	Own	4	25K-50K	$ 27	10
15	South	Rent	3	50K-100K	$ 19	2
16	West	Own	5	25K-50K	$ 19	6
17	North	Own	6	50K-100K	$ 129	5
18	East	Rent	2	10K-25K	$ 99	7
19	West	Own	3	25K-50K	$ 99	4
20	North	Rent	1	50K-100K	$ 119	3
21	East	Own	4	50K-100K	$ 149	2
22	South	Own	3	50K-100K	$ 165	8
23	West	Rent	5	25K-50K	$ 119	6
24	North	Rent	6	10K-25K	$ 129	7
25	East	Rent	7	100K+	$ 165	5
26	South	Own	3	10K-25K	$ 99	3
27	West	Rent	2	25K-50K	$ 155	6
28	North	Own	4	50K-100K	$ 115	8

Labels or column headings

Each column has only one type of information

F. *TOTAL PURCHASES*—Dollar total of all purchases made by the customer within the last six months

G. *NUM PURCHASES*—Count of all purchases made by the customer within the last six months

What we listed above is called a ***list definition table,*** a description of a list by column. List definition tables are important. If you can create one just as we did, then you can create a list in a workbook with the appropriate characteristics. If you can't, then you may not be able to use many of the features we're about to show you.

With the good solid list in place, you're now ready to start exploring many of the decision support features in Excel. Let's assume that you work for our hypothetical retail company and have been asked to perform the following tasks to aid in various decisions:

1. Show all information for only customers who live in the North region.

2. Show all information for only customers who (a) live in the North region, (b) own their homes, and (c) have only one household member.

3. Show all information for customers who have at least 4 household members.

4. Show all information for customers who (a) have spent less than $20 or (b) more than $100.

5. Show all information for all customers highlighting those customers who have spent more than $100.

6. Provide a two-dimensional table that counts the number of customers by the categories of *REGION* and *RENT VS. OWN.*

7. Provide a two-dimensional table that both (a) counts the number of customers and (b) sums the *TOTAL PURCHASES* of customers by the categories of *REGION* and *RENT VS. OWN.*

8. Provide a three-dimensional table that counts the number of customers by the categories of *REGION, RENT VS. OWN,* and *NUM HOUSEHOLD.*

We will use Excel to perform all of these tasks throughout the remainder of this module.

Basic Filter

LEARNING OUTCOME 2

Working with small lists that can be displayed in their entirety on a screen is seldom a problem. With a small list you can see the entire domain of information without scrolling up or down. But our list is much larger, containing 487 customers. So, you have to scroll through it to see all the information. If you were looking for specific information, such as all the customers in the North region (your first task in the list on the previous page), you could sort using the *REGION* column but you still get all the information (not to mention that customers in the North would come after the customers in the East region, alphabetically).

To quickly create smaller lists out of a much larger list, you can use the Filter function. The ***Filter function*** filters a list and allows you to hide all the rows in a list except those that match criteria you specify. To filter a list with the Filter function, perform the following steps (see Figure D.3):

1. Click in any cell within the list
2. From the menu bar, click on **Data** and then click on **Filter**

Figure D.3

Using Basic Filter to See Customers in the North Region

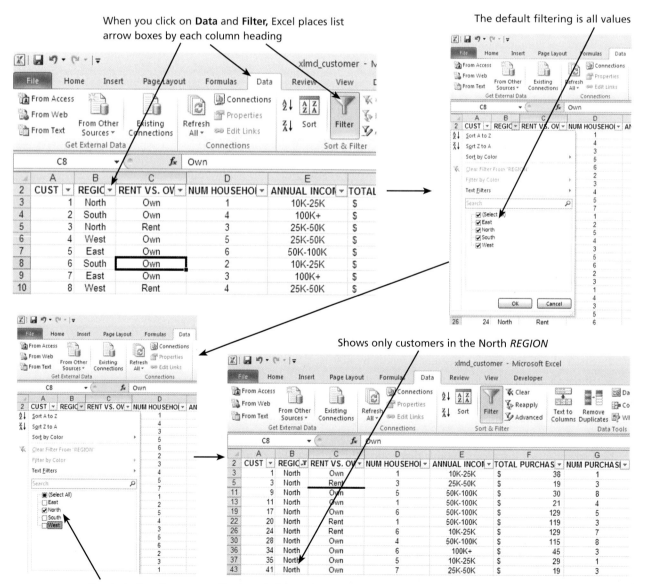

When you click on **Data** and **Filter,** Excel places list arrow boxes by each column heading

The default filtering is all values

Shows only customers in the North *REGION*

Deselect all regions except North and click on **OK**

Once you complete those two steps, Excel will place list box arrows next to each label or column heading. Now, all you have to do is click on the appropriate list box arrow and select the type of filtering you want. In Figure D.3, you can see that we clicked on the *REGION* list arrow box. Excel then presented us with a number of options for filtering within *REGION*. We deselected all regions except North and then clicked on the **OK** button. Excel then presented us with a filtered list of only those customers in the North region. Our list is still quite long, but it does show only customers in the North. To turn off the Filter function, from the menu bar, click on **Data,** then click on **Filter.**

When using the Filter function, you're not limited to working with just one column. In Figure D.3, we filtered using the *REGION* column. Now, what if you want a filtered list of those customers in the North who own a home and have only one household member (your second task in the list on page 389)? That's easy. Click in the *RENT VS. OWN* list arrow box and choose only **Own.** Then, click in the *NUM HOUSEHOLD* list arrow box and choose only **1.** That will show you the complete list (4 to be exact) of customers in the North who own a home and have only one household family member (see Figure D.4).

It's important to be clear what Excel is doing to your list when using the Filter function. No matter how you use the Filter function, Excel is simply hiding the rows you don't want to see. It is not eliminating or deleting them. You can see this in Figure D.4 by looking at the row numbers. Notice that they present the physical row number of each record of information according to where it is located in the original unfiltered list. To un-Filter a list, you can do either of the following:

1. Turn off the Filter function by clicking on **Data** in the menu bar and then clicking on **Filter.**

2. Turn off selected column filtering by clicking on the appropriate list arrow box and clicking on **Clear Filter from "columnname"** where *columnname* is the name of the column.

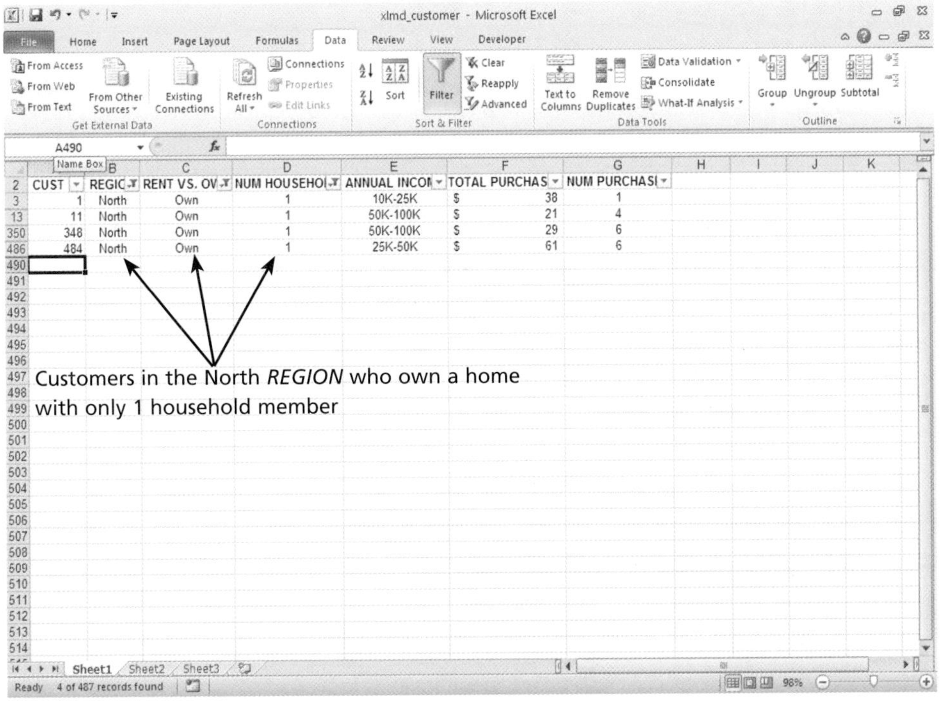

Figure D.4

A List Generated with Three Filters

Custom Filter

The basic Filter function allows you to create sublists using exact match criteria: *REGION* must be North, *NUM HOUSEHOLD* must be 1, and so forth. But what if you want to know all those customers who have at least four people in their households (your third task in the list on page 389)? In that case, you can't use the basic Filter function—you need to use the Custom Filter function. The ***Custom Filter function*** allows you to hide all the rows in a list except those that match criteria, besides "is equal to," you specify. Let's see how to use the Custom Filter function.

Given that you want to see a list of all customers who have at least four people in their households, perform the following steps:

1. Make sure you can see the entire list with the Filter function turned on
2. Click on the *NUM HOUSEHOLD* list arrow box
3. Select **Number Filters**
4. Click on **Greater Than** from the list of Boolean operations
5. Type the number **3** in the upper-right box of the Custom AutoFilter dialog box
6. Click on **OK**

Figure D.5

Using a Custom Filter

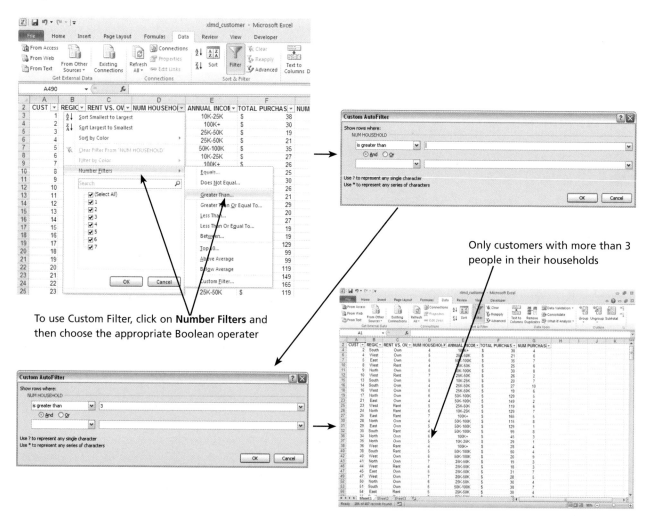

To use Custom Filter, click on **Number Filters** and then choose the appropriate Boolean operater

Only customers with more than 3 people in their households

Excel does the rest and shows you the appropriate list of customers with at least four people in their households.

You should notice in Figure D.5 that the Custom Filter box allows you to enter two criteria for creating a filtered list. So, you can easily create a Custom Filter that answers the following question: What customers have spent less than $20 or more than $100 in the past six months (your fourth task in the list on page 389)? In Figure D.6, we've shown you how to do that along with the result. To create this type of filtering, click on **Custom Filter** within **Number Filters** and then Select/enter the appropriate values and boolean operators.

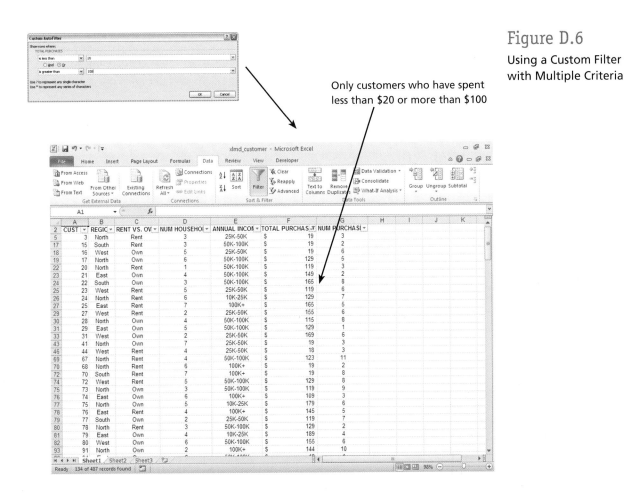

Figure D.6

Using a Custom Filter with Multiple Criteria

Only customers who have spent less than $20 or more than $100

Conditional Formatting

When you use Filter (either basic or custom), in a way you're highlighting information you want to see by basically hiding the other information you don't. As an alternative, you might want to highlight certain information while still being able to see all the other information. If so, you can use conditional formatting. ***Conditional formatting*** highlights the information in a cell that meets some criteria you specify.

For example, what if you still wanted to be able to scroll through the entire list of customers but also wanted to have all *TOTAL PURCHASES* greater than $100 highlighted (your fifth task in the list on page 389). This is a simple process in Excel. To do that, perform the following steps (see Figure D.7):

1. Select the entire *TOTAL PURCHASES* column (move the pointer over the F column identifier and click once)
2. From the menu bar, click on **Home** and then **Conditional Formatting** within **Styles**
3. Select **Highlight Cells Rules**
4. Click on **Greater Than**
5. Type the number **100** in the left box of the Greater Than dialog box
6. Click on **OK**

Figure D.7

The Steps in Applying Conditional Formatting to Highlight Information

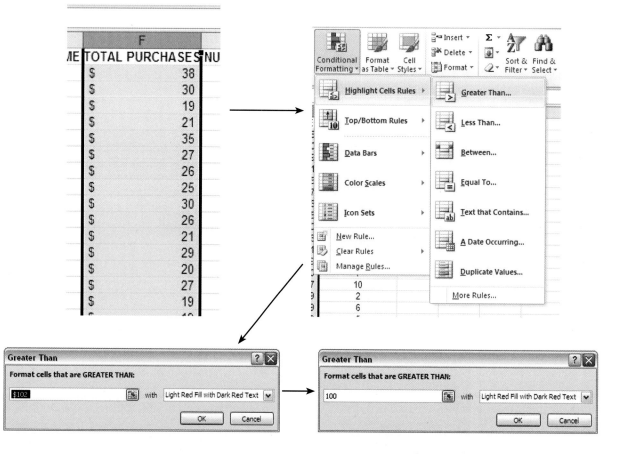

As you can see in Figure D.8, Excel left the list intact and highlighted all cells in the *TOTAL PURCHASES* column in which the value exceeded $100. The default "highlighting" is dark red text with a light red fill. You can change this in the Greater Than dialog box by clicking on the pull-down arrow for the right box.

You can remove conditional formatting in a couple of different ways:

- Option #1
  1. Click anywhere in the list
  2. Click on **Conditional Formatting**
  3. Select **Clear Rules**
  4. Click on **Clear Rules from Entire Sheet**
- Option #2
  1. Select the entire column in which conditional formatting appears
  2. Click on **Conditional Formatting**
  3. Select **Clear Rules**
  4. Click on **Clear Rules from Selected Cells**

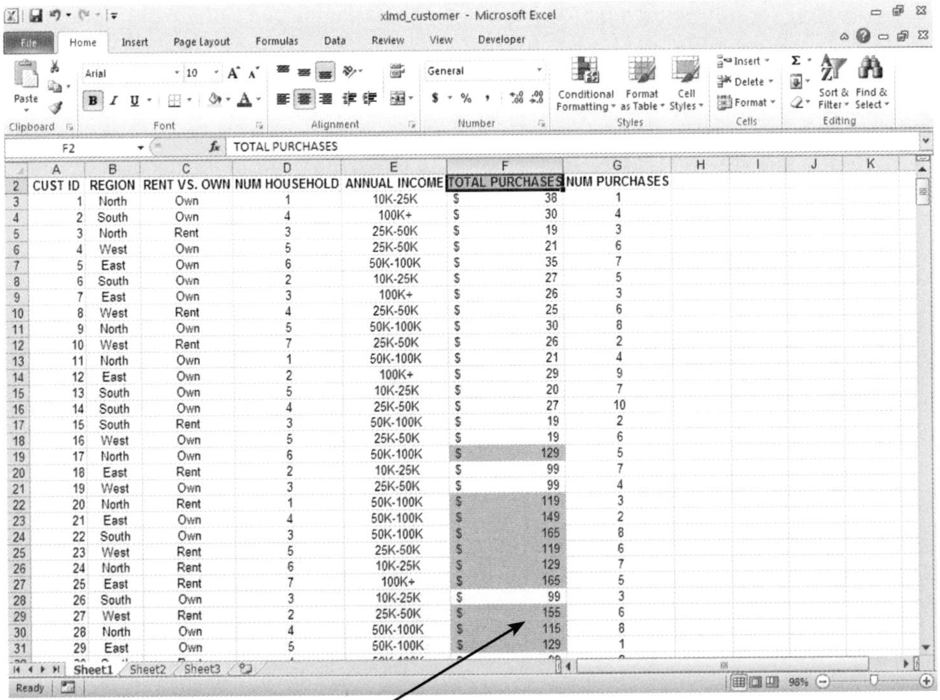

Figure D.8

The Result of Applying Conditional Formatting

CUST ID	REGION	RENT VS. OWN	NUM HOUSEHOLD	ANNUAL INCOME	TOTAL PURCHASES	NUM PURCHASES
1	North	Own	1	10K-25K	$ 38	1
2	South	Own	4	100K+	$ 30	4
3	North	Rent	3	25K-50K	$ 19	3
4	West	Own	5	25K-50K	$ 21	6
5	East	Own	6	50K-100K	$ 35	7
6	South	Own	2	10K-25K	$ 27	5
7	East	Own	3	100K+	$ 26	3
8	West	Rent	4	25K-50K	$ 25	6
9	North	Own	5	50K-100K	$ 30	8
10	West	Rent	7	25K-50K	$ 26	2
11	North	Own	1	50K-100K	$ 21	4
12	East	Own	2	100K+	$ 29	9
13	South	Own	5	10K-25K	$ 20	7
14	South	Own	4	25K-50K	$ 27	10
15	South	Rent	3	50K-100K	$ 19	2
16	West	Own	5	25K-50K	$ 19	6
17	North	Own	6	50K-100K	$ 129	5
18	East	Rent	2	10K-25K	$ 99	7
19	West	Own	3	25K-50K	$ 99	4
20	North	Rent	1	50K-100K	$ 119	3
21	East	Own	4	50K-100K	$ 149	2
22	South	Own	3	50K-100K	$ 165	8
23	West	Rent	5	25K-50K	$ 119	6
24	North	Rent	6	10K-25K	$ 129	7
25	East	Rent	7	100K+	$ 165	5
26	South	Own	3	10K-25K	$ 99	3
27	West	Rent	2	25K-50K	$ 155	6
28	North	Own	4	50K-100K	$ 115	8
29	East	Own	5	50K-100K	$ 129	1

Only customers whose *TOTAL PURCHASES* exceed $100 are highlighted in red

Pivot Tables

Now, let's return to our original pivot table in Figure D.1 on page 387. Formally defined, a *pivot table* enables you to group and summarize information. That's just what we did in Figure D.1. We created a two-dimensional pivot table that displayed a count of customers by *REGION* and by *RENT VS. OWN* (your sixth task in the list on page 389). Of all the Excel decision-support features we demonstrate in this module, pivot tables take the most steps to create, but they also tend to yield highly valuable information.

To create any two-dimensional pivot table, follow the two steps below (and see Figure D.9):

1. From the menu bar, click on **Insert** and then **PivotTable**
2. Click on **OK** in the Create PivotTable dialog box

The first step above simply specifies that you want to insert a pivot table. In the second step, we accepted the default pivot table settings by clicking on **OK.** While in the PivotTable dialog box, there are other options you should consider exploring on your own.

- *Selecting the information for the pivot table*—the default is the entire table. You can select another table or choose to highlight a subset of the current table.
- *Getting information from another source*—you can choose to use an external data source, such as a Word or Access table.
- *Location of the pivot table*—the default is to place the pivot table in a new worksheet. You can choose to place it in the current worksheet if you wish.

After you complete the two steps above, you will then see the skeletal structure of a pivot table as shown in Figure D.10.

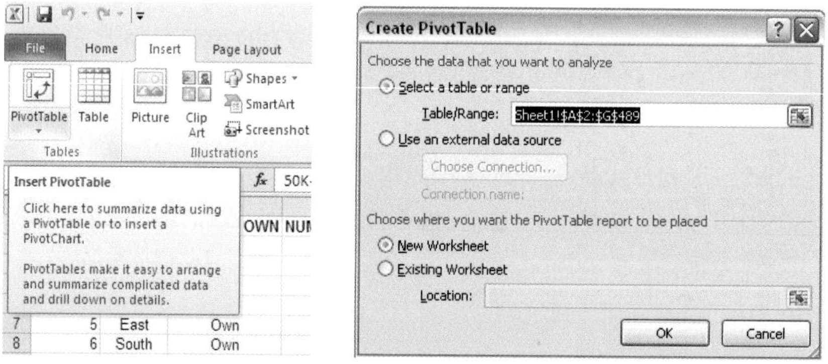

Figure D.9

The First Steps in Creating a Two-Dimensional Pivot Table

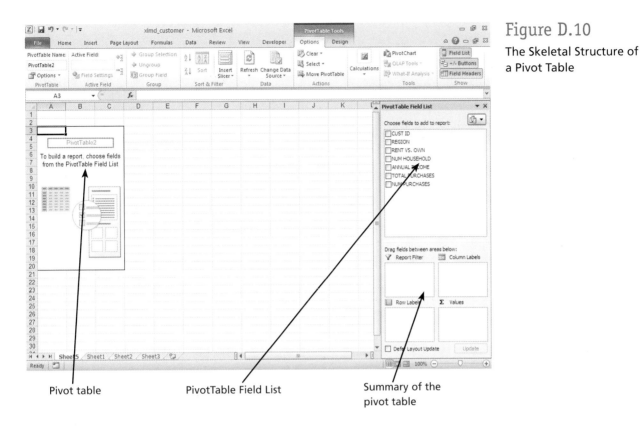

The screen in Figure D.10 has many elements to it. In the upper-left corner of the worksheet is where the pivot table will begin to appear as you identify fields of information. The upper-right area contains the PivotTable Field List, the list of fields in the original table that you can work with.

The lower-right area contains a summary of the pivot table as you build it and is also the place where you drag and drop fields of information. The Report Filter area is where you will drop a field of information to create pages or layers. This provides a three-dimensional aspect to the pivot table. In the Column Labels area, you drop the field of information that you want for the columns of information. In the Row Labels area, you drop the field of information that you want for the rows of information. Finally, in the Values area, you drop the fields of information that you want in the interior of the pivot table. This "interior" information is the information of focus, in our case in Figure D.1 a count of the number of customers.

Figure D.11

Creating a Pivot Table by Dragging and Dropping Information

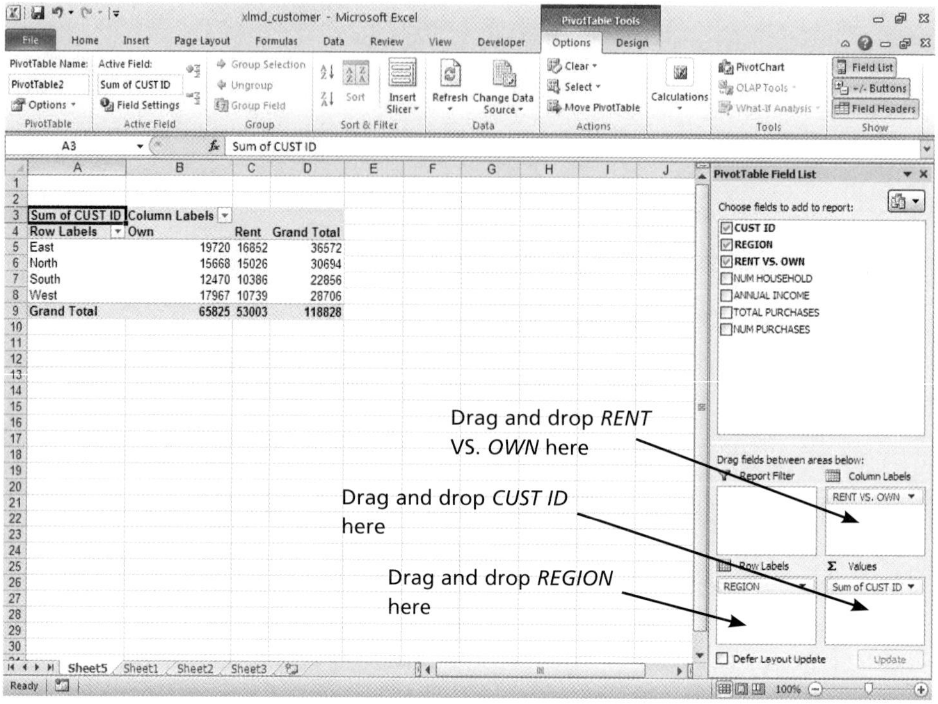

Recall that we are attempting to build a two-dimensional pivot table that looks like the one in Figure D.1 on page 387. So, you know that the row information is by *REGION*. To achieve this, drag the *REGION* field from the PivotTable Field List to the lower-right portion of the screen marked "Row Labels" (see Figure D.11). You also know that the column information is by *RENT VS. OWN*. So, drag that field name from the PivotTable Field List and drop it into the lower-right area marked "Column Labels."

Finally, you need to place something in the main area of the pivot table that will enable you to count customers by *REGION* and *RENT VS. OWN*. The simplest way to achieve this is to drag *CUST ID* from the PivotTable Field List and drop it into the lower-right area marked "Values." What you will have then is a pivot table that looks like the screen in Figure D.11, which is not at all what we want. Why?

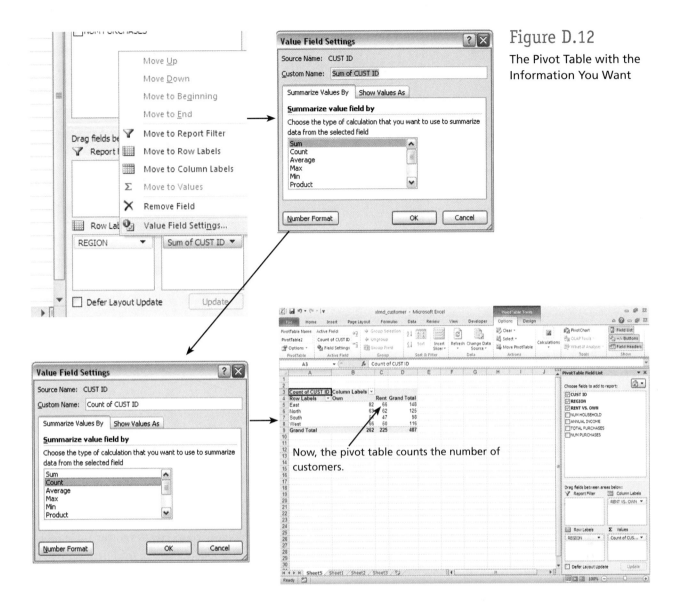

When you drop information into the "Values" area in the lower-right corner, the default aggregation or summarization is by summation. You don't want to sum customer IDs—that doesn't make any sense. What you want to do is count them. To change this, perform the following steps (see Figure D.12):

1. Click on the pull-down arrow next to Sum of *CUST ID* in the Values area in the lower-right portion of the screen.
2. Click on **Value Field Settings.**
3. Click on **Count** in the **Summarize Values by** tab of the Value Field Settings dialog box.
4. Click on **OK** in the same dialog box.

The final screen in Figure D.12 shows the correct information. Also, take a look at the lower-right portion of the screen which contains the summary of the pivot table. It now shows that aggregation of *CUST ID* is by Sum.

Figure D.13

An Added Field of Information to a Pivot Table

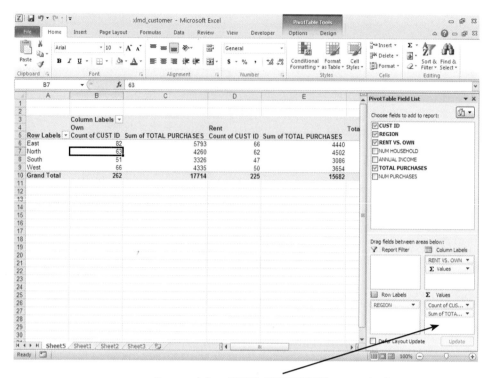

Drag and drop *TOTAL PURCHASES* here to obtain
a summary of another dimension of information

We now have a pivot table that shows a count of customers by *REGION* and *RENT VS. OWN*. But depending on what decision you're trying to make, that may not be enough information. What else might be helpful? Again, depending on the decision, it might be helpful to also know the total of all purchases by *REGION* and *RENT VS. OWN* (your seventh task in the list on page 389). If so, you don't need to create another pivot table. You simply add the field *TOTAL PURCHASES* to the Values area in the lower-right portion of the screen. To do so, drag that label from the PivotTable Field List and drop it into the Values area. Figure D.13 shows the result.

Is the information helpful? Again, it depends on the decision you're trying to make. But adding another piece of information to the main area of a pivot table is easy, and it does illustrate the true productivity of spreadsheet software.

Your final task in the list on page 389 is to create a three-dimensional pivot table that counts the number of customers by the categories of *REGION, RENT VS. OWN,* and *NUM HOUSEHOLD*. The result will look similar to the two-dimensional pivot table in Figure D.13 with two exceptions. First, you will not include the sum of *TOTAL PURCHASES* in the main area of the pivot table. Second, you will add depth to the pivot table, making it a three-dimensional pivot table. In short, you do this by dragging the *NUM HOUSEHOLD* label from the PivotTable Field List to the area in the lower-right portion of the screen marked "Report Filter."

In Figure D.14, you can see in the upper-left screen that we created a two-dimensional pivot table showing a count of customers by *REGION* and *RENT VS. OWN*. This is the same two-dimensional pivot table we created in Figure D.12 on page 399. To add depth to the pivot table, we dragged the *NUM HOUSEHOLD* label from the PivotTable Field List to the pivot table and dropped it into the area marked "Report Filter" in the lower-right portion of the screen. Notice that the new pivot table (the lower right screen in Figure D.14) still looks like a two-dimensional pivot table and provides the same information in the main area of the pivot table. That's because the default display for a three-dimensional pivot table is to show all summarized information for the depth. You can tell this because to the right of *NUM HOUSEHOLD* in cell A1 is the word "All."

To view the count of your customers by specific values for *NUM HOUSEHOLD*, simply click on the list box arrow immediately to the right of the word "All" as we did in the top screen in Figure D.15. You then click on the value you want in *NUM HOUSEHOLD* for displaying the count of customers for that value by *REGION* and *RENT VS. OWN*. We clicked on **4** and then **OK.** The bottom screen in Figure D.15 on the next page shows the result. It shows some interesting information that might help you make a decision. For example, in the West region there are 20 customers who own their homes and only 11 who rent their homes. Furthermore, across all regions there are 66 customers who own their homes and only 40 who rent. Again, is this helpful information? That depends on the decision you're trying to make.

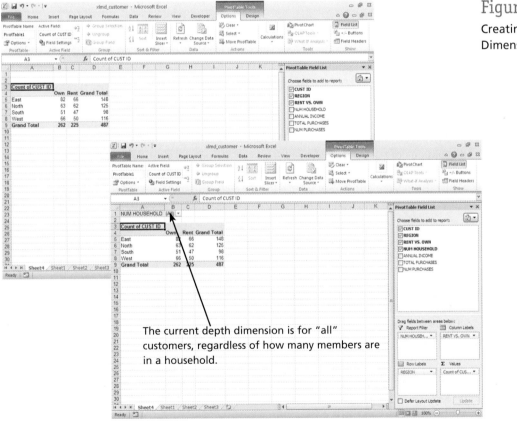

Figure D.14

Creating a Three-Dimensional Pivot Table

The current depth dimension is for "all" customers, regardless of how many members are in a household.

Figure D.15

Viewing Different Depths in a Three-Dimensional Pivot Table

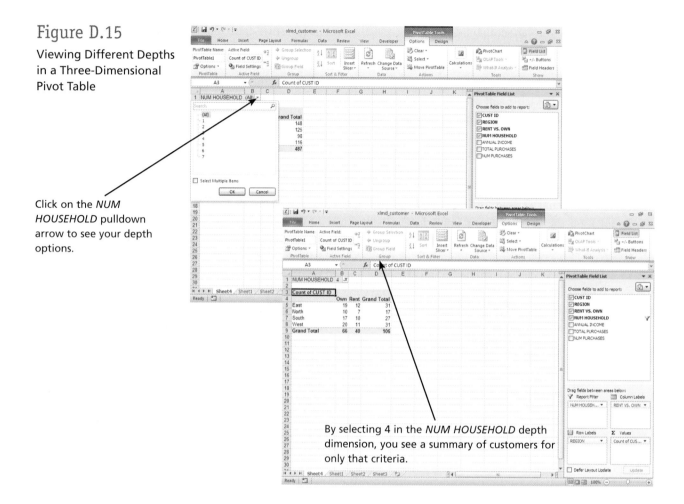

Click on the *NUM HOUSEHOLD* pulldown arrow to see your depth options.

By selecting 4 in the *NUM HOUSEHOLD* depth dimension, you see a summary of customers for only that criteria.

The three-dimensional pivot table feature in Excel is a powerful one. If you recall our discussions of data warehouses in Chapter 3, you can actually build a data warehouse with rows, columns, and layers by simply creating a three-dimensional pivot table in Excel. By selecting different values for the page (depth) field, you are actually bringing layers of information to the front.

Goal Seek

As you can easily see, Excel has numerous features beneficial for working with lists. But Excel offers much more than simply helping you work with lists. In fact, the majority of Excel's tools are designed to work with information in formats other than lists. Let's see how.

Consider our break-even example from Chapter 1 when we were discussing the financial impact of technology. You have worked out a deal with all the major movie studios to sell movie posters. You can buy each movie poster for $4 and sell it in your online store for $9. It costs you $2 to ship a movie poster to a customer. Your online store, product catalog, credit card processing, domain name registration, and search engine placement are all provided by GoDaddy (www.godaddy.com) at a cost of $1,500 per year. Recall that this $1,500 is a fixed cost, that is, no matter how many or how few posters you sell, this fixed cost never goes up or down.

In Figure D.16, we've created a workbook to reflect the information above. We've also entered some formulas into cells as follows:

$C14 = C13^*C7$; this is *Sales Price* $\times$ *Units Sold*

$C15 = C13^*C8$; this is *Cost* $\times$ *Units Sold*

$C16 = C13^*C9$; this is *Shipping* $\times$ *Units Sold*

$C18 = C14 - C15 - C16 - C17$; this is *Total Sales* less all costs

Feel free to work along with us through this example. Connect to the Web site that supports this text (www.mhhe.com/haag) and select XLM/D. There, you can download the file called **XLMD_BreakEven.xls.** The usefulness of setting up our workbook in this way is that we can now use Excel's Goal Seek tool and find an optimal Units Sold value (cell C13). *Goal Seek* works backward from an objective to compute an unknown value. In this case, the unknown value is *Units Sold.* All we have to do is tell Excel our objective; the objective is whatever net profit we want.

Let's go for $30,000 as a net profit in the first year. That is our objective. Now, we want Excel to determine the *Units Sold* value in C18 that will yield $30,000 in net profit in cell C18. Here are the steps (see Figure D.17 on the next page):

1. From the menu bar, click on **Data** and then **What-If Analysis.**
2. Select **Goal Seek.**
3. You will then see the Goal Seek dialog box.
4. For Set cell, enter **C18.**
5. For To value, enter **30000.**
6. For By changing cell, enter **C13.**
7. Click on **OK.**

Notice in the last screen in Figure D.17 Excel has computed that you must sell 10,500 posters in order to achieve a net profit of $30,000.

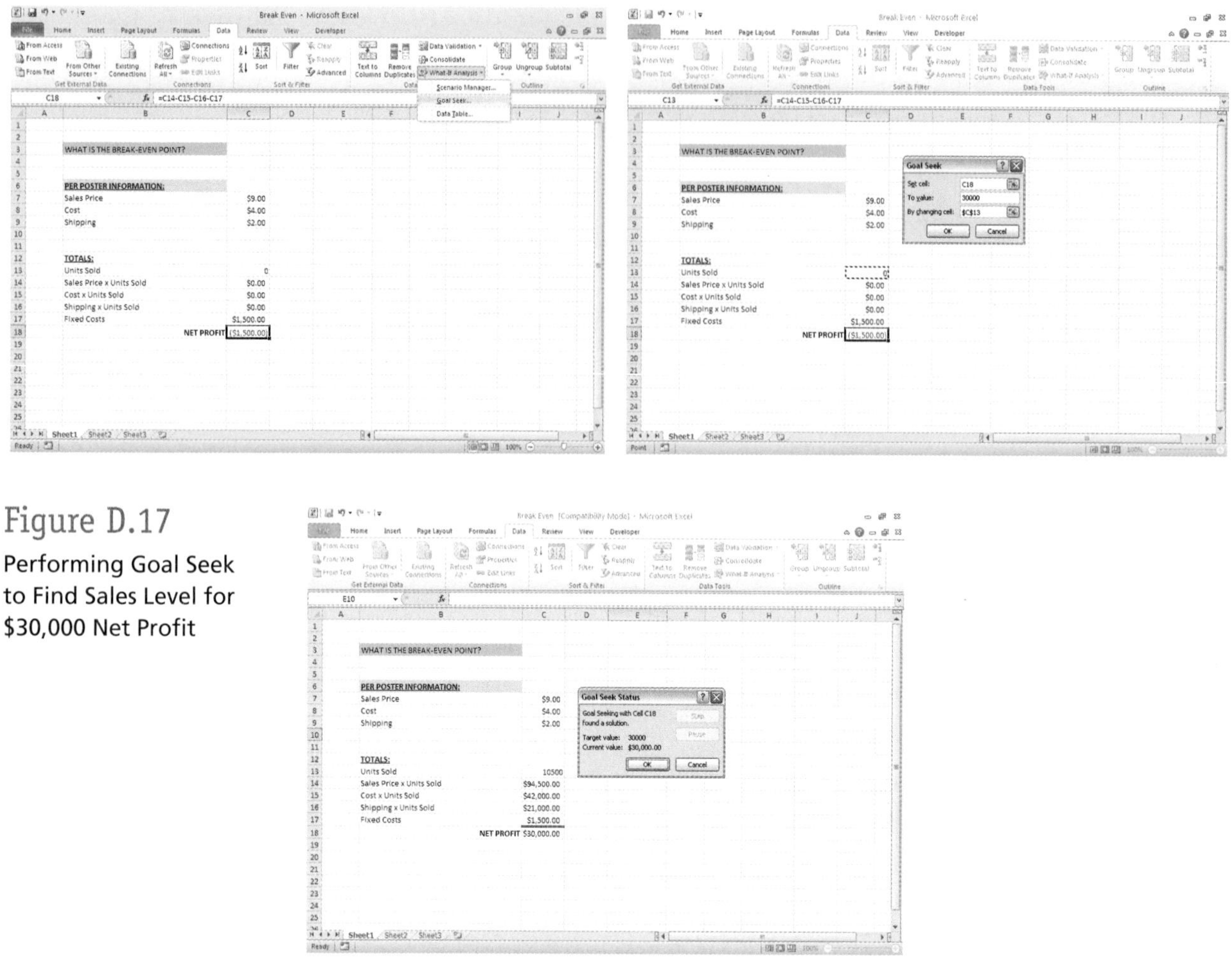

Figure D.17

Performing Goal Seek to Find Sales Level for $30,000 Net Profit

Let's review a few of the steps above. Steps 4 and 5 provide the objective, which in our case is to have $30,000 in net profit, cell C18. In step 6, we told Excel to get to $30,000 in net profit by adjusting *Units Sold,* C13.

Very powerful indeed. You can now use the workbook and start changing some values. For example, what happens if you can pass along the $2 in shipping charges to your customers without lowering your price? What is the new *Units Sold* value to achieve a $30,000 net profit? What if the movie studios start charging you more per poster?

SUMMARY: STUDENT LEARNING OUTCOMES REVISITED

1. **Define a list and a list definition table within the context of spreadsheet software and describe the importance of each.** A *list* is a collection of information arranged in columns and rows in which each column displays one particular type of information. A *list definition table* is a description of a list by column. Lists are important within the context of spreadsheet software because they enable you to use such spreadsheet features as AutoFilter, conditional

formatting, and pivot tables. Creating a list definition table is important because it requires you to adhere to the necessary rules for creating a list.

2. **Compare and contrast the Filter function and Custom Filter function in spreadsheet software.** The *Filter function* filters a list and allows you to hide all the rows in a list except those that match specific criteria you specify. The *Custom Filter function* allows you to hide all the rows in a list except those that match criteria, besides "is equal to," you specify. So, the basic Filter function makes use of "is equal to" as the criteria, while the Custom Filter function allows you to use other criteria such as greater than, less than, and so on.

3. **Describe the purpose of using conditional formatting.** *Conditional formatting* highlights the information in a cell that meets some criteria you specify. So, conditional formatting allows you to view the entire list while having certain information called to your attention.

4. **Define a pivot table and describe how you can use it to view summarized information by dimension.** A *pivot table* enables you to group and summarize information. When creating a pivot table, you create dimensions of information by specifying how information is to be summarized by dimension. You define the dimensions by dragging and dropping information labels or column headings into the row, column, and page areas of a pivot table.

5. **Describe the purpose of using Goal Seek.** *Goal Seek* works backward from an objective to compute an unknown value. So, you create your worksheet that includes an objective based on some unknown value in a cell. You can then direct Excel to use Goal Seek to obtain the desired objective by manipulating the unknown value.

KEY TERMS AND CONCEPTS

Conditional formatting, 394
Custom Filter function, 392
Filter function, 390
Goal Seek, 403

List, 388
List definition table, 389
Pivot table, 396

ASSIGNMENTS AND EXERCISES

1. **WHAT PRODUCTION PROBLEMS DO YOU HAVE?** For this assignment use **XLMD_ Production.xls.** Its list definition table is as follows:
   A. *BATCH*—A unique number that identifies each batch or group of products produced
   B. *PRODUCT*—A unique number that identifies each product
   C. *MACHINE*—A unique number that identifies each machine on which products are produced
   D. *EMPLOYEE*—A unique number that identifies each employee producing products
   E. *BATCH SIZE*—The number of products produced in a given batch

   F. *NUM DEFECTIVE*—The number of defective products produced in a given batch
   It seems you have some real problems. There are an unacceptable number of defective products being produced. Your task is to use some combination of Filter, conditional formatting, and pivot tables to illustrate where the problems seem to be concentrated, perhaps by product, by employee, by machine, or even by batch size. Based on your analysis, recommend how to correct the problems.

2. **EVALUATING TOTAL PURCHASES AND ANNUAL INCOME** Using **XLMD_Customer. xls,** create a pivot table that illustrates the relationship between *TOTAL PURCHASES* and

ANNUAL INCOME. What trends do you see in the information? Suppose your task is to concentrate marketing efforts and resources. On which annual income level would you concentrate? Why? If you were the marketing manager, what additional information would be helpful as you make your decision? Where would you be able to obtain such information?

3. **FINDING OUT INFORMATION ABOUT YOUR EMPLOYEES** Suppose you own a small business and have a workbook with the following list:

A. *ID*—Unique employee's identification number
B. *First Name*—Employee's first name
C. *Last Name*—Employee's last name
D. *Department*—Employee's department
E. *Title*—Employee's job title
F. *Salary*—Employee's annual salary
G. *Hire Date*—Date employee was hired
H. *Birth Date*—Employee's birthday
I. *Gender*—Female (F) or Male (M)
J. *Clearance*—N (none), C (confidential), S (secret), or TS (top secret)

You can obtain this workbook from the Web site that supports this text (www.mhhe.com/haag and select XLM/D). Its filename is **XLMD_Employee. xls.** Perform the following tasks:

a. Create a pivot table that shows average salary by gender within department.
b. Create a pivot table that shows the number of employees by clearance.
c. Use conditional formatting to highlight those employees in the Engineering department.
d. Use conditional formatting to highlight those employees who have no clearance (none).
e. Use basic Filter to show only those employees who have top secret clearance (TS).
f. Use Custom Filter to show only those employees who earn more than $50,000.

4. **EXPLORING INFORMATION AT B&B TRAVEL** Benjamin Travis and Brady Austin are co-owners of B&B Travel Consultants, a medium-size business in Seattle with several branch offices. B&B specializes in selling cruise packages. Ben and Brady maintain a workbook that contains the following list for each cruise package sale:

A. *LOCATION #*—A unique number that identifies which office location recorded the sale
B. *TRAVEL AGENT #*—A unique number that identifies which travel consultant recorded the sale

C. *CRUISE LINE*—The name of the cruise line for which the package was sold
D. *TOTAL PACKAGE PRICE*—The price charged to the customer for the package
E. *COMMISSION*—The amount of money B&B made from the sale of the package

Ben and Brady have decided to scale back their operations. So, they're looking to you for help. The workbook name is **XLMD_Travel.xls** and you can find it on the Web site that supports this text at www.mhhe.com/haag (select XLM/D). Using Filter, conditional formatting, and pivot tables, prepare a short report that answers each of the following questions and illustrates the justification for your answers.

a. Which, if any, location should be closed?
b. Which, if any, travel consultants should be downsized?
c. On which cruise lines should B&B focus its sales efforts?

5. **CREATE A LIST FOR A BOOKSTORE** Suppose that you're the manager for your school's bookstore. Your task is to create a list in a workbook that contains information about the textbooks it sells. In addition to tracking price, first author name, and publisher, identify five other pieces of information for each textbook. For this list, first provide a list definition table. Second, enter some information for 20 textbooks. Third, illustrate the use of the basic Filter function, the Custom Filter function, conditional formatting, and pivot tables. Finally, address how your bookstore might be able to use this information to support its decision-making tasks.

6. **GOAL SEEKING FOR NET PROFIT** Using **XLMD_ BreakEven.xls,** perform the task of computing the break-even when the following changes are made:

A. Shipping costs increase to $3
B. Fixed costs increase to $1,800
C. Shipping costs are passed on to your customers
D. Variable costs increase by 10% and sales price per poster increases by 10%

Assume each task is independent, so reset the break-even analysis to its original values after completing each task.

Student Learning Outcomes

1. Define a list and a list definition table within the context of spreadsheet software and describe the importance of each.

2. Compare and contrast the Filter function and Custom Filter function in spreadsheet software.

3. Describe the purpose of using conditional formatting.

4. Define a pivot table and describe how you can use it to view summarized information by dimension.

Extended Learning Module D provides hands-on instructions concerning how to use many of the powerful decision support features of Excel including Basic Filter, Custom Filter, conditional formatting, and pivot tables (in both two and three dimensions). Each of these takes only minutes to learn and requires just a few clicks.

The version of the module printed in the book demonstrates decision making support in Excel using Office 2010. If you have and use Office 2007 or an earlier version, you can find this same module in those versions of Office on the Web site that accompanies the text at www.mhhe.com/haag.

EXTENDED LEARNING MODULE E

NETWORK BASICS

Student Learning Outcomes

1. Identify and describe the four basic concepts on which networks are built and describe what is needed to set up a small peer-to-peer network at home.

2. Describe the components used to build large business networks and define and compare local area networks (LANs), wide area networks (WANs), and metropolitan area networks (MANs).

3. Compare and contrast the various Internet connection possibilities.

4. Compare and contrast the types of communications media.

5. State the four principles of computer security and describe how different network security devices reflect those principles.

Introduction

When you're surfing the Web, accessing software on your school's server, sending e-mail, or letting your roommate use his or her computer to access the files on your computer, your computer is part of a network. A **computer network** (which we simply refer to as a network) is two or more computers connected so that they can communicate with each other and share information, software, peripheral devices, and/or processing power. Many networks have dozens, hundreds, or even thousands of computers.

BASIC PRINCIPLES OF NETWORKS

LEARNING OUTCOME 1

Networks come in all sizes, from two computers connected to share a printer, to the Internet, which is the largest network on the planet, joining millions of computers of all kinds all over the world. In between are business networks, which vary in size from a dozen or fewer computers to many thousands.

Some basic principles apply to all networks, large or small.

1. Each computer on a network must have a network interface (either as an expansion card or integrated into the motherboard, or even through software for a modem) that provides the entrance or doorway in that computer for information traffic to and from other computers.

2. A network usually has at least one connecting device (like a hub, switch, or home/broadband router) that ties the computers on the network together and acts as a switchboard for passing information.

3. There must be communications media like cables or radio waves connecting network hardware devices. The communications media transport information around the network between computers and the connecting device(s).

4. Each computer must have software that supports the movement of information in and out of the computer. This could be modem software and/or a network operating system.

First, we'll examine the smallest networks—a few computers connected in a home or dorm room—and then move on to larger business networks. We'll discuss network devices, LANs, WANs, and MANs, communications media, and network security.

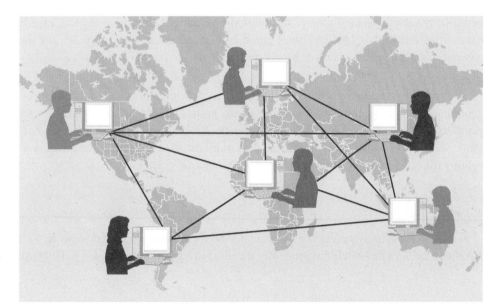

Home Networks

If you have a computer at home with cable or DSL Internet access, you may already be familiar with several network components. A typical home setup has

- An Ethernet network card in each computer, and/or a wireless Ethernet card in each laptop computer.
- Network cables to transmit signals, or no cables if you're using wireless.
- A DSL or cable line from your ISP, and a broadband or home router to pass messages and files back and forth.

NETWORK CARDS IN EACH COMPUTER

First, each computer needs a network interface. A ***network interface card (NIC)*** is an expansion card for a desktop computer or a PC card for a notebook computer that connects your computer to a network and provides the doorway for information to flow in and out. The network interface card has a jack (or port) for a network cable that connects your computer to a network. Most computers sold today have network interfaces built into their motherboards.

An ***Ethernet card*** is the most common type of network interface card. It has a jack, usually an RJ-45 that looks like a telephone jack, only a little larger. You run a network cable from your Ethernet card to a hub or switch, or you can use a cable with different wiring called a *crossover cable* to plug straight into another computer or printer if you have only two devices to connect.

WIRED AND WIRELESS TRANSMISSION MEDIA

The most common transmission medium for a home network is Cat 5 cable, which is similar to phone cable (ordinary twisted-pair cable). ***Cat 5,*** or ***Category 5,*** cable is a better-constructed version of the phone twisted-pair cable. Each end of the Cat 5 cable has an RJ-45 connector. One end plugs into the Ethernet card in your computer and the other end into a network switch or broadband router (which we'll discuss in a moment).

If you'd like to access your home network wirelessly with your computer, you'll need another device on the network. A ***wireless access point (WAP)*** is a device that allows a computer to use radio waves to access a network. A wireless access point has a transmitter and a receiver for the bidirectional flow of information. It also has an antenna to capture the radio waves out of the air.

If your wireless access point is a separate device, it connects to a wired network with a cable to the hub or switch the same way wired computers do (see Figure E.1). Many

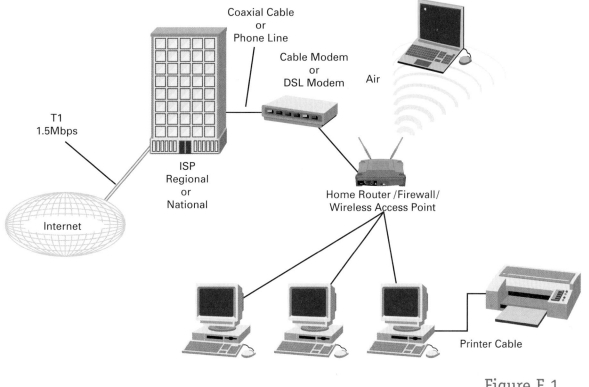

Figure E.1
Typical Home Network

broadband routers (described in the next section) come with a wireless access point built in, so you may not need any extra cables.

Your notebook and any other device that accesses the network wirelessly must have a wireless adapter. Wireless adapters are available as PC Cards for notebook computers, or are built into notebooks. The wireless adapter incorporates a transmitter, receiver, and antenna, just like the wireless access point. If all your devices have wireless adapters, you can create a completely wireless network, in which the only cable used is the one connecting to the cable or DSL service.

HOME INTERNET SERVICE AND BROADBAND ROUTERS

A home network with no outside connections can still be used to share files and printers. But in order to access any services or sites outside your home, you need Internet service and equipment to connect it to your home network. Two common types of home Internet service are DSL, available through your telephone company, and cable Internet connection, available from your cable company.

A DSL or cable modem connection is designed to support only one computer, so if you want to connect more computers, you need another device, commonly called a broadband router or home router. A ***broadband router*** or ***home router*** is a device to connect several computers together to share a DSL or cable Internet connection in a home or small office. It has one port to plug in your Internet connection, and usually has several ports to plug in home computers or printers. Most broadband routers today include a built-in wireless access point.

NETWORK SOFTWARE

As always, when you have hardware you need software to make it work. For a small network, Windows will do fine and must be installed on each network computer. To make the files on your computer available to the other computers on the network, you have to turn on the file-sharing option in Windows and indicate which drives, directories, or files to share. When you do this, the files on one computer will appear as additional folders on the other computer.

Network Components

Large networks are built in much the same way as small networks, using the same types of components. One difference is that home network devices often perform several different functions that are separated onto separate devices in large networks. Let's take a closer look at two of these network components.

SWITCHES

A *switch* is a network device that connects computers and passes messages by repeating each computer's transmissions only to the intended recipient, not to all the computers connected. Several computers can have different conversations at the same time through a switch, and such a network is called a *switched* network (see Figure E.2).

A switch works like a small business telephone system. When the marketing director needs to check on the status of a brochure, she calls the graphic artist to ask about it. At the same time, the shop supervisor can be giving a delivery date to the shipping manager. And the telephones all have speakers, so the operator can still get everyone's attention all at once if necessary.

Information transmitted over switches is generally private, unless it's specifically meant to be broadcast to all the computers on the network. Switches are the most commonly used components in networks today, and range in size from four- and eight-port models (connecting four or eight computers or printers) in home networks, to 24- and 48-port models (connecting 24 or 48 devices) common in business networks, to very large switches with hundreds of ports used to connect large call centers or run entire floors of office buildings.

Figure E.2
Switch

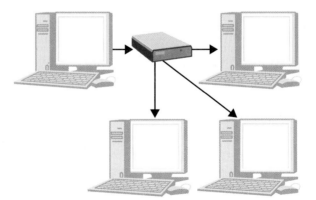

ROUTERS

Routers connect together separate networks of computers, unlike switches that connect individual computers. A ***router*** is a device that passes network traffic between smaller *subnetworks* (or *subnets*) of a larger network.

Think of a large business with a warehouse in one building, management offices in another, and manufacturing in yet another. Long ago, each building had its own telephone system with its own extensions—the warehouse has numbers 100–199; management has extensions 200–299; and manufacturing has numbers 400–699.

At first, the telephone systems weren't connected, and the telephones would call only within the same building. But then the business ran telephone cables from each building to a central phone system to tie them all together. Now the warehouse phone system "knows" that if it gets a call for any extension other than 100–199, it routes the call to the central system to direct to the proper building. And the central system knows to route any call starting with 1 to the warehouse phone system, any call starting with 2 to management, and any call starting with 4, 5, or 6 to manufacturing.

Routers work the same way. When a computer wants to send a message to another computer on a different subnet (like in a different building), it actually sends the message to the router on its subnet. The router then looks at the message's destination address—where the message is going—and figures out how to get it there. Medium-sized networks may have only one router at the center, in which case it can always deliver messages directly. Larger networks may have many routers connected together, in which case messages may pass through several routers on their way from one computer to another (see Figure E.3).

It's important to understand that even though you have a router, you still need a switch to plug the computers into. Because large routers are expensive, it's not practical to build them with enough ports to directly support all the computers on a network. Home routers that run your Internet connection usually have both a router and a switch

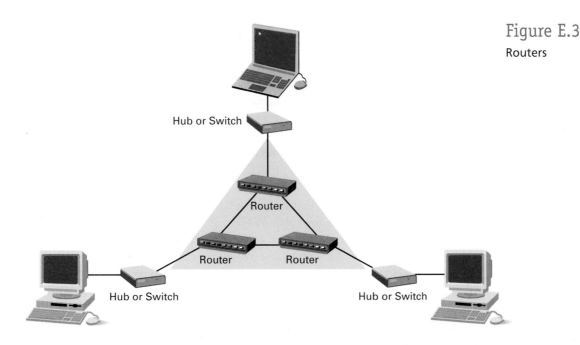

Figure E.3
Routers

built into the same box. But even though they may be labeled routers, remember that switching and routing are really two separate functions.

Switches can often be taken out of the box, hooked up to computers, and used without setting the configuration. But routers need to be programmed with information about which computer addresses are on which subnets, so installing a router generally requires someone with knowledge of network administration. Adding to or reconfiguring the network generally requires reconfiguring the router.

Classifying Networks by Distance

We've discussed the different devices used to build networks, and next we'll talk about ways networks are connected together. One way of describing large networks is in terms of the geographic area they cover. The size of a network can also impact whether an organization owns the communications lines or leases them from an independent provider.

LANS, WANS, AND MANS

A *local area network (LAN)* is a network that covers a building or buildings in close proximity, such as one campus of a university or corporation. The defining characteristic of a LAN isn't the actual size, but rather that the geographic area it serves is continuous. So the large network on a two-square mile campus of an aircraft manufacturer would be considered all one LAN, but the small networks of a daycare center with two buildings a city block apart would be considered separate LANs.

A *wide area network (WAN),* then, is a set of connected networks serving areas or buildings not in immediate proximity to each other. Another way to think of a WAN is as a network of networks. WANs generally use routers to connect LANs together, just as LANs can use routers to connect different subnets together.

Imagine a business that's large enough to have a production plant near a railroad and trucking depot, and separate corporate headquarters in a downtown office park. It has separate telephone systems on each site—in fact, the production plant has separate telephone systems in the warehouse, the manufacturing building, and the packing and shipping plant. But they also have telephone lines connecting the production plant and the headquarters, and the telephone systems know how to send calls from one to the other. In fact, except for using a different type of telephone line, sending calls from one site to the other is set up exactly the same as sending calls from one building to another.

WANs work the same way to connect networks (LANs) on different sites. WANs may connect networks at different locations around a city, or in different cities across a state, a country, or even the entire world.

Because WANs connect areas that are some distance apart, organizations don't usually own the communications lines that WANs run over. Instead, the lines are usually leased, often from a telephone or cable television company, or other commercial communications provider. Some types of WAN circuits are 56 kilobits per second (56 Kbps) leased lines; T1, running at 1.544 megabits per second (1.544 Mbps); and DS3, running at 44.736 Mbps. (T1 and DS3 are described in more detail in this module under Internet Connection Types.)

A metropolitan area network is a relatively recent term for a specific type of WAN. A *metropolitan area network* or *municipal area network (MAN)* is a set of connected networks all within the same city or metropolitan area, but not in immediate proximity to each other.

Internet

An internet, with a lowercase *i*, comes from the word internetworking, and is a network of networks, connecting networks managed by different organizations. The largest internet of all is the ***Internet*** (with a capital *I*) which is a vast network of computers that connects millions of people all over the world.

To understand how computers send network communications across the Internet, consider the business described earlier that has telephone systems in separate buildings and on separate sites. When employees place calls to other buildings, each building's phone system directs the calls through a central system that knows how to route the calls to their destinations.

Besides the connections to the different buildings, the company also has connections to the public telephone system, so employees can make phone calls to place materials orders, and receive calls to accept orders for products. The company's outside telephone lines don't run directly to each building, but rather to the central system that knows how to route calls among all the buildings.

When employees at this company want to make outside calls, they dial a code starting with 9 (a digit different from the first digit of any of their local extensions), and the central system knows to route their calls over the outside lines to the public telephone system. And when customers call, they dial one of the company's telephone numbers, and the public telephone system sends the calls over the company's outside phone lines to the central system, which routes the calls to the correct departments. If customers don't know the right phone numbers to call, they can look up the company's name in a telephone directory and find the numbers they need.

This is much the way the Internet works. When a computer needs to send a message to another computer somewhere else on the Internet, it sends the message to its local router. If the router doesn't recognize the recipient as being attached to one of its LAN, MAN, or WAN connections, it sends the message over the connection to its Internet Service Provider (ISP). The ISP has bigger routers that learn paths to get to even more networks. Even if they're not connected directly to the receiving network, the ISP's routers send the message to another router, which may send the message to still *another,* and so forth, until the message finally gets to the receiving network. There, the receiving router will at last deliver the message to the computer at the ultimate destination.

Computers and routers refer to each other using network addresses, commonly Internet Protocol (IP) addresses, like *192.168.1.1.* This is similar to the way telephone systems use telephone numbers, like *+ 1 (414) 555-1212,* to route calls. You probably remember the phone numbers of some of your friends and family, but no one knows all the different phone numbers in the world.

Similarly, you don't have to remember the low-level network address of every computer you send network messages to. Instead, you can use names for computers, like www.mhhe.com, and your computer looks up the receiving computer's address for you in a directory called the Domain Name System, or DNS. Without DNS, the Internet would be virtually impossible to use.

BANDWIDTH

The most common measurement used when comparing different types of communications media is bandwidth, which refers to capacity. ***Bandwidth,*** or capacity of the communications medium, is the amount of information that a communications medium can transfer in a given amount of time. You can think of bandwidth as the thickness of a drinking straw: the thicker the straw, the more quickly you can move the liquid from the cup into your mouth. In fact, in the communications industry, bandwidth is sometimes referenced informally as what size "pipe" you have between two locations.

Bandwidth is described as a quantity of data transferred in an amount of time, most commonly as a number of bits per second. A *bit* is the smallest possible amount of data, representing a single 1 or 0, and is abbreviated as the letter *b*. A *byte* is eight bits, and is used to store one letter or symbol of text, so the number of bits divided by eight gives you the approximate number of text characters. (See *Extended Learning Module A* for more information about bits, bytes, and characters.)

Bandwidth is sometimes represented in bits per second, abbreviated *bps*. Because a single bit is such a small quantity, and communications media speeds are constantly increasing, the bandwidth of different media is more likely to be represented in thousands of bits per second (kilobits per second—Kbps or kbps), millions of bits per second (megabits per second—Mbps), or billions of bits per second (gigabits per second—Gbps).

For example, if a particular communications medium has a bandwidth of 16 Mbps, then 16 millions bits can be transferred in a single second. This module has about 70,000 characters in it, which is approximately 560,000 bits, so it could be transferred in less than half a second across a 16 Mbps channel.

INTERNET CONNECTION TYPES

Like the circuits used to make wide-area connections, Internet circuits aren't usually owned by individual companies. Instead, the circuits are supplied by an Internet Service Provider. Types of Internet circuits include:

- Dial-up circuits, using an ordinary telephone line and a modem.
- Digital Subscriber Line (DSL), which runs a high-speed connection over a telephone line without interfering with the voice telephone service.
- Cable modem, which runs a high-speed connection over a cable television line without interfering with television reception.
- Satellite modem, which runs a high-speed connection through your cable TV satellite without interfering with television reception.
- Dedicated high-speed lines such as T1 and DS3, which run on separate circuits and are generally used for business connections.

DSL, cable modem, and dedicated lines are classified as broadband connections. A **broadband** connection is a high-bandwidth (high-capacity) telecommunications line capable of providing high-speed Internet service. The Federal Communications Commission defines broadband as a capacity of 200 kbps (200 kilobits, or thousands of bits, per second) both upstream (to the Internet) and downstream (from the Internet). Other industry experts feel that broadband implies a speed of at least 750 kbps.

Figure E.4

Digital and Analog Signals

Digital

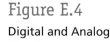

Analog

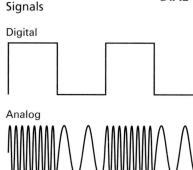

DIAL-UP CONNECTIONS   To make a telephone or dial-up connection, you need a computer, a phone line, a modem, and, of course, an Internet service provider. Just as people use telephones to talk over telephone lines, a *telephone modem (modem)* is a device that connects a computer to your phone line so that you can access another computer or network. And as is the case with people and telephones, the computer at the other end needs a modem too.

A modem converts the digital signals from your computer into an analog form (by modulating the signal) that can be transmitted over a phone line, and then converts the analog signal back to digital signals (by demodulating the signal) for the computer at the receiving end of the transmission (see Figures E.4 and E.5). The word modem is a contraction of the modem's function of **mo**dulating outgoing and **dem**odulating incoming transmissions.

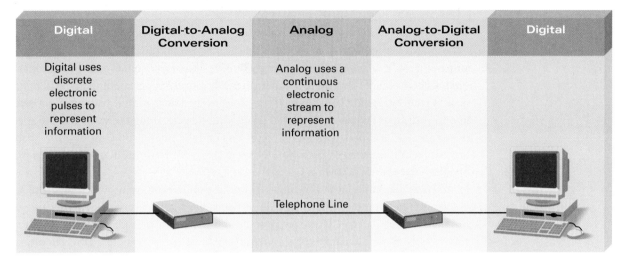

Figure E.5

The Role of a Telephone Modem

Modems are sometimes integrated into the motherboards of new computers, particularly laptops and notebook. If your computer doesn't have a built-in modem, you can buy a card to plug into an expansion slot of your desktop, or a PC card for your notebook. A modem is the slowest type of Internet connection you can get. The fastest possible transmission speed using a modem over a normal telephone line is 56 kbps, or about 56,000 bits per second.

DIGITAL SUBSCRIBER LINE A *Digital Subscriber Line (DSL)* is a high-speed Internet connection using phone lines, which allows you to use your telephone for voice communication at the same time. There are different kinds of DSL systems, including ADSL or asymmetric DSL, SDSL or symmetric DSL, and HDSL or high-bit-rate DSL, that offer different combinations of speeds from the Internet provider to the customer and from the customer to the provider.

DSL works similarly to a traditional modem, modulating and demodulating the computer's digital signal into an analog form for transmission over the telephone line. However, unlike traditional modems which modulate into audible sounds (the screech you hear if you pick up a telephone while your computer is connected to the Internet through its modem), DSL modems use frequencies too high for you to hear; this is how they can allow telephone conversations to happen at the same time. Even so, DSL modems sometimes cause clicks, pops, or buzzing on telephone lines, so most DSL connections use a splitter or filter to make sure that only voice calls go to the telephone and only DSL signals go to the DSL modem (see Figure E.6).

Figure E.6

DSL Internet Access

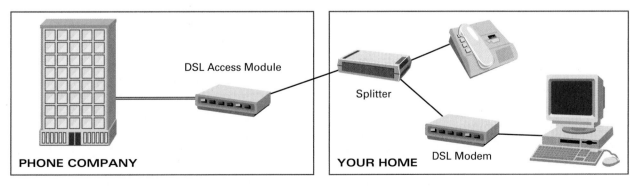

Because the high frequencies used by DSL are outside the range that telephone lines were originally designed to carry, only telephone lines that meet certain criteria can deliver DSL service. You need to live within about three miles of the phone company. (In larger cities, phone companies have branch offices that can connect you throughout the metropolitan area.) The phone company may have restrictions about the type of equipment it uses to provide your phone line—a relatively recent central system, and a direct line to your house without any signal processing devices along the way. And the speed of your connection may depend on the distance to the phone company and the quality of your line. Speeds may vary from 144 kbps to 1.5 Mbps, or even up to 6 Mbps for a business-class DSL connection.

DSL circuits—the physical cabling to your house—are always provided by the phone company. The phone company usually provides the Internet service that you use over the DSL connection, too. However, in some areas, you may be able to buy your Internet service from an independent service provider instead. To connect to a DSL circuit, you need the filter or splitter provided by the phone company (to keep noise out of your telephone conversations) and the DSL modem. The cable from the DSL modem connects to your computer in one of two ways: either to an Ethernet card, or to a USB port.

DSL service has three big advantages over dialup connections:

1. DSL is much faster—up to 30 times faster than a traditional modem.
2. You can use the line for voice calls at the same time.
3. DSL can be an always-on connection—because it doesn't interfere with voice calls, you can leave it connected all the time, instead of having to wait for your modem to connect each time you want to use the Internet.

CABLE MODEM   If you have wired cable television, you know it comes into your home on a coaxial cable that connects to your television set. This same cable can connect you to the Internet, too. Both cable TV signals and your Internet connection travel from the cable company on one wire.

A splitter at your home splits the signals on the incoming cable, sending one part to the TV and the other to your cable modem. A *cable modem* is a device that uses your TV cable to deliver an Internet connection (see Figure E.7). The cable from the cable modem attaches to either an Ethernet card (an expansion card that connects your

Figure E.7

Cable Internet Access

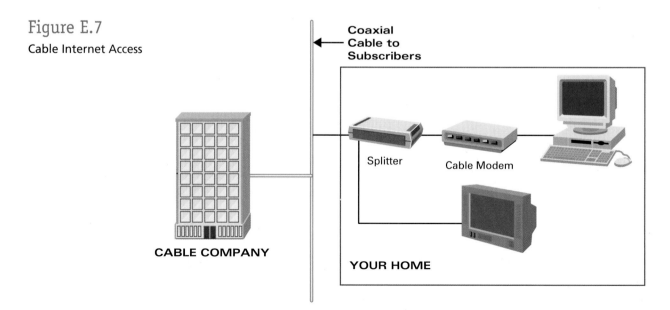

computer to a network) or to a port on the motherboard. Like DSL, cable modems provide an always-on connection. However, unlike DSL, cable modems don't use a phone line at all.

The speed of transmission with a cable modem is much faster than a phone modem, running at about 10 Mbps (10 million bits per second). While the speed of a DSL connection is guaranteed, though, the speed of a cable Internet connection depends on how many users are online, because the connection to the cable company is shared throughout a neighborhood. If all your neighbors are surfing the Web with a cable connection at the same time you are, you may notice a reduction in your access speed.

SATELLITE MODEM   If you have wireless cable television, that is, if you receive your cable programming via a satellite, you can often also obtain your Internet service through the same provider of your satellite cable. A *satellite modem* allows you to get Internet access from your satellite dish. In certain instances, you may not be receiving your cable programming via satellite, but you may be able to receive your Internet service via a dedicated satellite dish. It really all depends on where you live and what types of services are offered for cable programming and Internet service.

The concept and implementation of receiving your Internet service from your satellite cable programming provider are the same as for using a cable modem. You would have a splitter with wiring for your cable programming going to your television and wiring for your Internet service going to your computer or a connecting device such as a hub or router.

T1, DS3, FRAME RELAY, AND ATM   A *T1* is a high-speed circuit typically used for business connections, running at speeds up to 1.544 Mbps (1.544 million bits per second), and a *DS3* is a high-speed business network circuit running at 44.736 Mbps. T1s were originally designed to carry 24 telephone conversations on phone companies' long-distance lines between cities. Later, equipment was developed to connect computer networks over T1 and DS3 lines. A T1's speed of 1.544 Mbps is about 24 times the speed of an analog telephone modem. A DS3 line is equivalent to 28 T1 lines bundled together, and its total speed of 44.736 Mbps is about 672 times the speed of an analog modem.

With some providers, a portion of the price of T1 and DS3 lines depends on the distance they run. Because of this distance-based pricing and their overall higher cost than some other connection types, T1 and DS3 lines are most commonly used for metropolitan area network connections—between two branches of a business within the same city. One advantage of T1 lines is that, because of their origin in voice telephony, it's possible to split their 24 channels between voice and computer communications, using the same T1 circuit to connect both telephone systems and computer networks at two offices.

Frame Relay and Asynchronous Transfer Mode (ATM) are services that the phone company or other telecommunications providers can set up over high-speed lines like T1s and DS3s to create "virtual circuits" connecting multiple offices. These virtual circuits can provide network connections from each office to every other one without having to run physical lines directly between each pair.

For example, if a business had four offices that all needed to be connected to each other, it would take six T1 lines to hook them all up (see Figure E.8). With Frame Relay or ATM, each office has a single T1 line going to the communications provider (for a total of four), and the provider makes it work the same as it would if the six direct lines actually existed.

Remember that the price of T1 and DS3 lines can depend on the distance they run. With Frame Relay or ATM, the T1 or DS3 lines actually run from each office to the telecommunications provider, rather than from office to office, so the distance and price can both be lower than when T1 lines are run directly from office to office.

Figure E.8

Frame Relay/ATM Virtual
Circuits

T1 Lines without Frame Relay/ATM

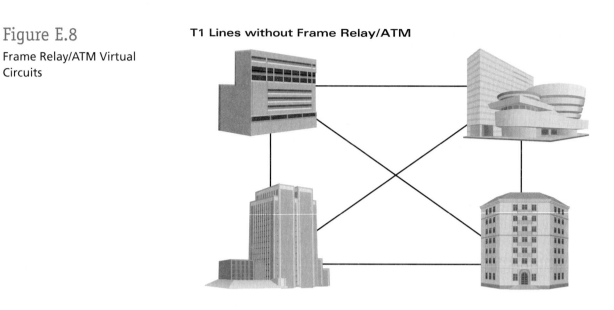

T1 Lines for Frame Relay/ATM

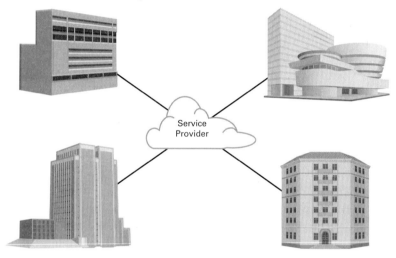

Virtual Circuits

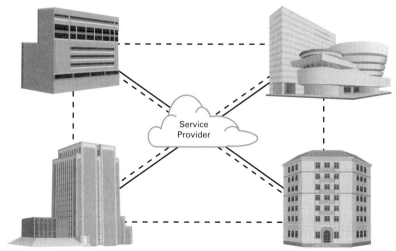

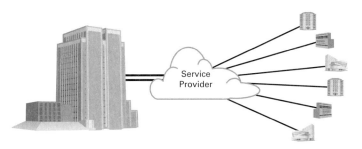

Branch Office Connections without Frame Relay/ATM

Branch Office Connections Using Frame Relay/ATM

Service Provider

Because of this, Frame Relay and ATM are also used to connect many branch offices to a single main office. If a business had six branch offices, it would take six T1 lines to connect all the branches back to the headquarters (see Figure E.9)—each potentially running a great distance. With Frame Relay or ATM, the business can instead install a DS3 from its headquarters to the communications provider and a T1 to each branch office. The provider makes it work as it would if the headquarters had a direct connection to each branch office, and the business potentially spends less money than if it ran all of the T1 lines directly between offices. And the company has a single DS3 connection at its headquarters instead of six separate T1 connections, simplifying circuit management and potentially increasing reliability.

VOICE OVER IP

We've just talked about different types of communications lines that can carry network information, but now it's time to turn that inside out. Several types of communications lines—telephone lines, T1s, and DS3s—were originally developed to transmit voice telephone calls, and later adapted to carry computer data. Voice over IP (VoIP) does the opposite—it's a means of transmitting a voice telephone call over a computer data network. ***Voice over IP (VoIP)*** allows you to send voice communications over the Internet and avoid the toll charges that you would normally receive from your long-distance carrier.

Why go to the trouble of sending voice calls over a computer network when they can already be sent directly through existing telephone systems and services? The answer has everything to do with overhead and with metered billing, meaning you pay an additional amount for each call and/or for each minute of the call.

Offices in most businesses and universities today have at least two different cables run to them—one that goes back to a telephone system, and one that goes back to a network switch. On many telephone systems, the telephone extension number is assigned to a particular port on the central equipment. So when an employee moves from one office to another, making his or her telephone extension work in the new office involves either changing wiring or reprogramming the phone system.

In contrast, network addresses are assigned directly to the computer or other device, regardless of which switch port it's connected to. So moving a VoIP extension from one office to another is as easy as unplugging the network phone from one location, carrying it to another, and plugging it back in. This reduction of maintenance effort can dramatically reduce the overhead of telephone system operation during office expansions and moves. Additionally, office technicians no longer have to maintain two sets of wiring to two different systems, which can also reduce overhead.

Both network companies like Cisco Systems and telephone companies like Nortel are producing VoIP telephones that look like any other business phone, except they plug into a network jack instead of a telephone jack. Many even have an extra network jack on them for your PC, so your phone and computer can share a single connection back to the building's hub or switch.

Voice over IP is gaining popularity with home users across the Internet. In most parts of the world, traditional telephone calls made from one local dialing area to another have metered billing, and some large U.S. cities even have metered billing for local calls.

Network access is often unmetered, though, particularly for broadband home access (cable modem and DSL). If you already have an Internet connection, you can use a network telephone or network phone software for your PC to make calls to other VoIP users anywhere in the world at no additional cost per call or per minute—for the moment, anyway. Most telephone billing rates in the United States are set by federal and state governments by regulations called tariffs, and it remains to be seen how long it will be before Voice over IP becomes tariffed as well.

Network Communications Media

LEARNING OUTCOME 4

The objective of networks and telecommunications is to move information from one place to another. This may be as simple as sending information to the office next door, or as far-reaching as sending a message to the other side of the world. Whatever the case, information must travel over some path from its source to its destination. *Communications media* are the paths, or physical channels, in a network over which information travels.

All communications are either wired or wireless. *Wired communications media* transmit information over a closed, connected path. *Wireless communications media* transmit information through the air. Forms of wired and wireless communications media include:

Wired	**Wireless**
• Twisted-Pair Cable	• Infrared
• Coaxial Cable	• Microwave
• Optical Fiber	• Satellite

WIRED COMMUNICATIONS MEDIA

Wired communications media are those which tie devices together using cables of some kind. Twisted-pair, coaxial cable, and optical fiber are the types of cabling you'd find in computer networks.

TWISTED-PAIR   *Twisted-pair cable* is a bundle of copper wires used for transmitting voice or data communications and comes in several varieties. The Cat 5 that you already read about in connection with home networks earlier in this module is one type. Most of the world's phone system is twisted-pair and since it's already in place, it's an obvious choice for networks.

The simplest type of twisted-pair phone cabling (Cat 1) provides a slow, fairly reliable path for information at up to 64 kilobits per second (Kbps), while a better type (Cat 3) provides up to 10 megabits per second (Mbps). However, distance, noise on the line, and interference tend to limit reliability for most types of twisted-pair cabling. For example, a crackle that changes a credit card number from 5244 0811 2643 741 to 5244 0810 2643 741 is more than a nuisance; in business it means retransmitting the information or applying a charge to the wrong person's credit card.

Cat 5 or Category 5 provides a much higher bandwidth than ordinary phone cable, meaning it carries more information in a given time period, at least for distances up to 100 meters. It's commonly used for connections at 100 megabits per second (Mbps), and an enhanced version called Category 5e is capable of carrying 1 gigabit per second (Gbps). Cat 5 is relatively inexpensive and is fairly easy to install and maintain. Because of these advantages, it's the most widely used cabling for data transfer in today's LANs. Note, however, that twisted-pair of any kind is relatively easy to tap into and so it's not very secure. It's even possible to access the information by simply detecting the signals that "leak" out.

COAXIAL CABLE   An alternative to twisted-pair cable is *coaxial cable (coax)*, which is one central wire surrounded by insulation, a metallic shield, and a final case of insulating material. (Coax is the kind of cable that delivers cable television transmissions and also carries satellite TV from the dish to your house.) While coaxial cable was once the cable of choice for internal LAN wiring, it has been almost completely replaced by twisted-pair cable. Coaxial cable is capable of carrying at least 500 Mbps, or the equivalent of 15,000 voice calls, simultaneously. Because of its shielded construction, coaxial cable is much less susceptible to outside interference and information damage than twisted-pair cable. However, coaxial cable is generally more expensive than twisted-pair and is more difficult to install and maintain. Security is about the same with coaxial cable as with twisted-pair, except that the radiation, or leaking, of information is much less. Coax is commonly used for leased line private networks.

OPTICAL FIBER   The fastest and most efficient medium for wired communication is *optical fiber,* which uses a very thin and flexible glass or plastic fiber through which pulses of light travel. Information transmission through optical fiber works rather like flashing code with a light through a hollow tube.

Optical fiber's advantages are size (one fiber has the diameter of a human hair); capacity (easily hundreds of gigabits per second, and getting faster every year); much greater security; no leakage of information. It's very hard to "tap" into optical fiber. Attempts are pretty easy to detect since installing a tap disrupts service on the line—and that's noticeable. Optical fiber is also used for nearly all connections between different buildings, as it doesn't conduct electricity and so is immune to damage from lightning strikes. Optical fiber is more expensive than twisted-pair cable, however, and requires highly skilled technicians to install and maintain.

WIRELESS COMMUNICATIONS MEDIA

For many networks, wired communications media are simply not feasible, especially for telecommunication across rugged terrain, great distances, or when one or more parties may be in motion. For whatever reason, if wired communications media don't fit your needs, wireless may be the answer. Wireless communications radiate information into the air, either very narrowly beamed or in many directions like ripples from a pebble tossed into a pond. Since they radiate through the air, they don't require direct cable connections of any kind. Obviously, security is a big problem since the information is available to anyone in the radiation's path. However, wireless encryption methods are good, and getting better.

INFRARED AND BLUETOOTH FOR VERY SHORT DISTANCES   Infrared is the oldest type of wireless communication. *Infrared* uses red light to send and receive information. The light is invisible to humans, but snakes and some other animals can see it. Your TV remote control uses infrared. You can use infrared to connect handheld devices, such as pocket PCs, to peripheral devices such as printers. Wireless keyboards and mice usually connect to your PC with an infrared link. Infrared communication is totally line-of-sight, meaning that you can't have anything blocking the path of the signal, or it won't work. Infrared transmission has very limited bandwidth (typically 1 Mbps).

A relatively new and competing wireless technology is called Bluetooth. Named for a Viking king, *Bluetooth* is a standard for transmitting information in the form of short-range radio waves over distances of up to 30 feet and is used for purposes such as wirelessly connecting a cell phone or PDA to a computer. Virtually all digital devices, like keyboards, joysticks, printers, and so on, can be part of a Bluetooth system. Bluetooth is also adaptable for home appliances like refrigerators and microwave ovens.

OMNIDIRECTIONAL MICROWAVE (WIFI) FOR SHORT DISTANCES   Another method of short-distance wireless communications is omnidirectional (all directions) microwave transmission. *Microwave transmission* is a type of radio transmission. Microwaves occupy a portion of the electromagnetic spectrum between television signals and visible light. Microwave ovens use high-powered microwaves to heat food and can interfere with some types of microwave wireless transmissions.

The most common types of wireless networking used today—802.11b and 802.11g (known to most people as Wi-Fi)—use microwave transmissions. *Wi-Fi (wireless fidelity)* is a standard for transmitting information in the form of radio waves over distances 100 feet or so. With the right equipment, the reach can be several miles. Wi-Fi is actually a wireless industry alliance that provides testing and certification that 802.11 devices communicate with each other properly. Several generations of Wi-Fi in common use are *IEEE 802.11b,* running at up to 11 Mbps; *802.11g,* running at up to 54 Mbps and compatible with 802.11b equipment at the slower rate; and *802.11a,* also running at up to 54 Mbps but not compatible with 802.11b equipment. The latest Wi-Fi version, *802.11n,* can operate in several different modes, but is typically used in a mode compatible with all previous versions at their slower rates and at up to 144.4 Mbps with other 802.11n devices.

Wi-Fi hotspots are sites that offer wireless Internet access for your laptop. Such places have a link through a wireless router to an Internet service provider that makes access available to the public. There may be a charge for this service or it may be free. You may have noticed signs offering Wi-Fi access at airports, restaurants like Starbucks, bowling alleys, and other public places. Be careful about using public networks that don't require a password and are not secure. Much of the data that moves around a network is clear text, meaning that it can be intercepted. Make sure that you use encrypted Web pages (the ones with https:// and a little padlock) and that you check your e-mail through a secure Web site rather than using an e-mail program like Thunderbird that doesn't encrypt incoming and outgoing data. Some Webmail sites encrypt only the ID and password but not the pages where you read and write e-mails messages, so watch for that. Others have the option of encrypting all Webmail pages. You can encrypt files that you are sending over a public network with programs such as Stuffit Deluxe. There are also encryption programs for specific systems such as Thunderbird.

DIRECTIONAL MICROWAVE FOR MEDIUM DISTANCES Microwaves may be transmitted very directionally with a parabolic dish antenna or can be radiated in a wide curved path for broader use. Microwave transmission is a line-of-sight medium. That is, the microwave signal cannot follow the curved surface of the earth. So to send the information over a distance of more than about 20 miles you'd have to use repeaters (see Figure E.10). A *repeater* is a device that receives a radio signal, strengthens it, and sends it on. (You've probably seen microwave towers—they're the tall towers with lots of little dishes on them that stand near an industrial complex.) Microwave signals have difficulty getting through walls or trees or other solid objects, so there must be a clear path from sender to receiver.

Figure E.10
Microwave

SATELLITES FOR LONG DISTANCES *Communications satellites* are microwave repeaters in space. They solve the problem of line-of-sight since the transmission shoots up into the sky in a straight line, bounces off, and shoots back down to earth again (see Figure E.11). Since satellites are so high, an array of them can cover essentially the whole earth (as the two dozen or so GPS satellites do). As with land-based repeaters, satellites receive information from one location and relay it to another. You'd usually use satellite communications to connect land-based networks in far-flung locations or to connect moving vehicles to each other or to the organizational network.

Satellite communications are cost effective for moving large amounts of information, especially given a large number of receiving sites. For example, K-Mart and other retailers place very small aperture terminal (VSAT) satellite dishes on the roofs of their stores. The VSATs allow individual stores to transmit information to the home office, and the

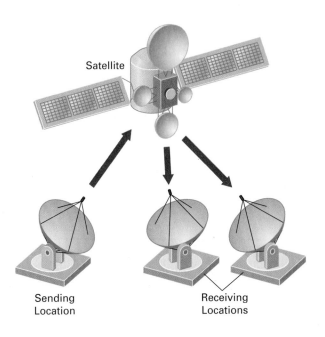

Satellite

Sending
Location

Receiving
Locations

Figure E.11
Satellite

home office, in turn, can transmit information to all the stores simultaneously. Satellite radio is another example of far-flung satellite transmission. If you have satellite radio in your car, you'll never be completely out of range of your favorite satellite radio station.

Network Security

LEARNING OUTCOME 5

Thinking about network security may call to mind images from movies of computer rooms criss-crossed by laser beams, voice and handprint recognition, security cameras, and CDs or DVDs full of top-secret blueprints. Or it may make you think of jumpsuit-wearing technicians clipping wires onto someone else's connection, greasy-haired teenagers illuminated only by the green glow of their computer monitors, or an investigator frantically trying to guess the criminal's password as the footsteps in the hallway get ever closer.

These images, although dramatic, don't give you much of an idea of the real threats to computer and network security and how to guard against them. In reality, connecting computers together can make it easier to take advantage of existing security weaknesses—attacks can be performed from any distance away instead of only from within the same room—and introduces some new weaknesses.

PRINCIPLES OF COMPUTER SECURITY

The best way to understand network security is to look at the components of computer security, evaluate different threats in terms of these components, and then figure out how to reduce the effectiveness or damage of those threats. The basic principles of computer and network security are confidentiality, authenticity, integrity, and availability. Within the context of computer and network security

- *Confidentiality* means that information can be obtained only by those authorized to access it. In even simpler terms, it means keeping secrets secret. Confidential information includes things like bank statements, business plans, credit card reports, and employee evaluations. Threats to confidentiality include network transmissions that can be captured or monitored by unauthorized individuals, passwords that are easily guessed, and even printouts left lying out in plain sight. In the world outside of computers, confidentiality is protected by sealing envelopes and locking doors and file cabinets.

- *Authenticity* means that information really comes from the source it claims to come from. It's important to be sure of the authenticity of things like military orders, medical diagnoses, and buy/sell directions to your stockbroker. Threats to authenticity include fraudulent e-mail messages claiming to be from your bank (probably spoofing), Web sites registered at names that are common misspellings of popular sites, and Web browsers that can be manipulated into making it look as though you're at a different site than you really are. Nonelectronic authenticity is provided by signatures (although they can be forged), or by trusting only people you know personally.

- *Integrity* means that information has not been altered. This is closely related to authenticity. You would be concerned about the integrity of your bank balance, contents of your corporate Web site, medical prescriptions, and credit card charges. Threats to integrity include network transmissions that can be forged or taken over by unauthorized individuals and Web servers with flaws that allow their content to be replaced. Integrity is hard to guarantee in the physical world—how can you *really* be sure that no one has changed even a single word of your mortgage contract?—and is generally dependent on a certain degree of trust that's much harder to apply to electronic communications.

- *Availability* means simply that a service or resource is available when it's supposed to be. If a mail-order Web site is unavailable during the Christmas season, a retailer could lose millions of dollars in sales. If a corporate e-mail server is frequently unavailable, the company may lose some of the trust of its business partners. Threats to availability include unintentional network failures, poorly written server software that stops working when presented with unusual inputs, and deliberate attempts to send so much traffic to a company's network that legitimate communications are unable to get through. Noncomputer-related availability is provided by designing buildings with multiple exits in case one is blocked by fire, making photocopies of important documents, and installing electrical generators in hospitals to keep life-critical equipment operating if the city power fails.

FIREWALLS AND INTRUSION DETECTION SYSTEMS

Networks are designed to connect computers together and move information between them. But what if attackers are trying to break into your computers through your network connection? Just as a company may install card readers or hire a guard to admit only staff wearing employee badges, a *firewall* is software and/or hardware that protects a computer or network from intruders (see Figure E.12). As hardware, a firewall is a device that permits or denies network traffic based on security policy. Firewalls provide protection against threats to *confidentiality, authenticity,* and *integrity* by blocking traffic that doesn't look like legitimate access to networked computers.

Some firewalls make their policy decisions based entirely on network addresses. For example, if you have caller ID on your telephone, you may choose to answer calls only if

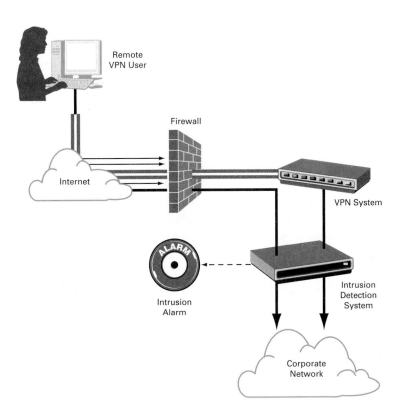

Figure E.12
Firewall, Intrusion Detection System, and Virtual Private Network

they come from your friends or family. Likewise, a simple firewall can examine network traffic and permit only the traffic coming from a known source.

Other firewalls may permit traffic from an unknown source if it appears to be a response to a request that was made by a computer on the protected network. For example, if you call a friend at the office but she's in a meeting, you might leave a message for her to call you back. When she does, you may recognize the phone number of her office as a number you just called and answer the call, even though the office number isn't on the list of phone numbers you'd normally answer.

Even more advanced firewalls make decisions based on the content of the network traffic. Thinking back to the company with a security guard in the lobby, the guard may allow a delivery person to enter the building if he's carrying envelopes or pizza, but not if he's carrying dynamite or bottles of acid. Of course, acid may be a regular delivery item in a chemical plant; not every company will want the same firewall policies.

While a firewall typically has a predefined policy about the network traffic it will allow, an *intrusion detection system (IDS)* is a device that watches network traffic for intrusion attempts and reports them. An *Intrusion prevention system (IPS)* is a type of IDS that also takes action against intrusion attempts, for example, by creating new policies in a firewall to block the source of the attack. Intrusion detection and prevention systems work by having information about many different types of network attacks and matching the current network traffic against their lists of attack characteristics. When they sense an attack in progress, they can e-mail or page network administrators about the attack, so they can take appropriate action.

Denial-of-service attacks simply interfere with network *availability*. A *denial-of-service (DoS)* attack floods a server or network with so many requests for service that it slows down or crashes. (See *Extended Learning Module H, Computer Crime and Forensics,* for more details about denial-of-service attacks.) Imagine if someone called every pizza delivery service in town and ordered 20 pizzas delivered to your office. Eventually you'd manage to sort out the confusion and you wouldn't have to pay for the pizzas, but meanwhile you'd be too busy dealing with the situation to get any work done.

Firewalls and intrusion detection and prevention systems can protect *availability* by preventing or reducing the effect of denial-of-service attacks. Some denial-of-service attacks use network capabilities that are technically permissible, but are almost never seen in legitimate network traffic; these attacks are easy to foil by denying those types of traffic. Other denial-of-service attacks send completely legitimate but useless traffic. Blocking those attacks involves recognizing an increase in network traffic beyond normal levels, determining the source or sources, and then blocking even legitimate-appearing traffic from those locations.

Most home broadband devices—for DSL and cable modem Internet connections—include a simple firewall. Home networking manufacturers have been packing more and more capabilities into their products, and even though the devices may be marketed as routers or firewalls, they generally contain a router, a firewall, and a switch or hub to connect multiple home computers. Some even include the DSL or cable modem, and some have a wireless access point, all in a device not much larger than a paperback book.

ENCRYPTED COMMUNICATIONS: SSL AND VIRTUAL PRIVATE NETWORKS

Earlier, we talked about types of network devices on which communications can be overheard, for example wireless access points. This is a threat to *confidentiality*—unauthorized individuals could be watching your communications. So if you're using wireless access or are somewhere that you don't know who has access to the communications lines and equipment between you and your network destination, what can you do to protect the privacy of your communications?

The solution is encrypted communication. ***Encryption*** scrambles the contents of a file so that you can't read it without having the right decryption key. It means scrambling your communication in such a way that only the intended recipient can unscramble it. If you wanted to send the message, "Reschedule the grand opening for April 10," the encrypted version might look like

V'9:P)9@A1,||>[D:J_sepnvlf.Xj2FAs_[Dhud+'.

One way of using encryption to protect network transmissions is called Secure Sockets Layer (SSL), or somewhat less commonly, by the name of its successor, *Transfer Layer Security (TLS)*. SSL is a security technology that encrypts each network conversation— between one network client and one server—individually. Web traffic using SSL is called https, instead of just http. When you browse to a secure Web site and see the padlock icon, it's telling you that your browser is using SSL/TLS to encrypt your communications with the Web server. We cover more on SSL and other types of security technologies with respect to electronic commerce in Chapter 5.

In contrast, a ***virtual private network (VPN)*** uses encryption to protect the confidentiality of *all* network transmissions between two endpoints. Typically, one endpoint is a large office or headquarters, and the other endpoint may be a single computer, or it may be another office. All network communications between the two locations are routed through the VPN to be encrypted. This makes it look as though they have a dedicated network connection between them, even though they may really be communicating over public network links, hence the name, *virtual private network*.

OTHER SECURITY THREATS: MALWARE

You've probably heard of computer worms, viruses, and spyware, collectively known as malware. ***Malware*** is a contraction of **mal**icious soft**ware**, and refers to software designed to harm your computer or computer security. Malware existed even before most computers were connected to networks, but increased connectivity between computers has made it dramatically easier for malware to transfer to new victims.

A ***virus*** is software that is written with malicious intent to cause annoyance or damage. The virus software is activated unintentionally by the computer user. A ***worm*** is a type of virus that replicates and spreads itself, not just from file to file, but from computer to computer via e-mail and other Internet traffic. Viruses spread by tricking users into running them, for instance, by pretending to be an interesting program or e-mail message; worms spread by taking advantage of errors or weaknesses in computer programs. Viruses and worms most commonly threaten *availability*, by damaging or removing files, or by tying up a computer doing so much unauthorized work that it can't get its real job done.

Viruses and worms can be countered by running anti-virus software. Anti-virus software works very similarly to the intrusion detection systems described earlier. It has a long list of characteristics of known worms and viruses, and when it sees files being transferred or software running on the computer that has those characteristics, it alerts the user and often "quarantines" the file to part of the hard drive where it can't do any harm. Some anti-virus software can even remove the malicious instructions from computer files so that they are still useful once they're disinfected.

Anti-virus software can be run at different places in the network. Some viruses are transferred from computer to computer in e-mail messages, and anti-virus software on the e-mail server will help protect against them. It's very important to run anti-virus software on every PC, to protect against worms and viruses trying to attack the computer directly. And some companies have servers where customers can upload purchase orders or problem reports; they may run anti-virus software on those servers to screen all incoming files.

Spyware is a more recent type of malware than viruses and worms. **Spyware** (also called **sneakware** or **stealthware**) is malicious software that collects information about you and your computer and reports it to someone else without your permission. Therefore, spyware is a threat to *confidentiality*. Spyware most often gets installed on your computer secretly along with a piece of software you knew you were getting; for example, some peer-to-peer file sharing programs are notorious for including spyware.

The best defense against spyware is to install software only from trustworthy sources, but that can be hard to determine. Anti-spyware software is available that works just like antivirus software, recognizing patterns of known spyware and removing them from your computer. Two popular anti-spyware programs are Ad-Aware (www.lavasoftusa.com) and Spybot Search & Destroy (www.safer-networking.org).

Another category of malware is servers and bots. Sometimes after breaking into a computer, attackers will set up *unauthorized servers.* These servers are often used to distribute illegal copies of movies, music, and software, or may even be used to distribute kits for breaking into other computers.

In the context of malware, *bots* are programs designed to be controlled by an attacker to perform unauthorized work over a period of time. Some bots are used to send spam, making it look like it's coming from the victim's computer instead of from the attacker's. Other bots try to break into computers or perform denial-of-service (DoS) attacks against other networks or systems.

Bots and unauthorized servers can sometimes be detected by anti-virus or anti-spyware software—but they may be indistinguishable from legitimate servers. They can also sometimes be discovered by network intrusion detection systems. Sometimes they're even discovered by network administrators, noticing an unusual amount of network traffic coming from a single computer.

■ SUMMARY: STUDENT LEARNING OUTCOMES REVISITED

1. **Identify and describe the four basic concepts on which networks are built and describe what is needed to set up a small peer-to-peer network at home.**
   There are four basic concepts on which almost all networks are built. They are

   - *Network interface cards (NICs)* in each computer
   - A connecting device like a **hub, switch,** or **home/broadband router**
   - At least one communications medium
   - Network operating system software

   To set up a peer-to-peer network at home, you'd need

   - *Ethernet cards* (as the NICs) in each computer
   - A home/broadband router
   - *Cat 5* cables
   - A network operating system, like Windows

2. **Describe the components used to build large business networks and define and compare local area networks (LANs), wide area networks (WANs), and metropolitan area networks (MANs).** Large business networks are built using

- Network interfaces in each computer
- *Switches* to connect the computers together into subnetworks
- *Routers* to connect the subnetworks together

  A *local area network (LAN)* covers a geographically contiguous area. A *wide area network (WAN)* is a set of connected networks serving areas not in immediate proximity. A *metropolitan area network (MAN)* is a set of connected networks all within the same city or metropolitan area, but not geographically continuous.

3. **Compare and contrast the various Internet connection possibilities.** There are five ways described in this book to connect a computer or network to the Internet. They are

- Phone line and *modem,* which uses a phone line and prevents your using the same line for voice communication at the same time. It's the slowest type of connection.
- Phone line and *Digital Subscriber Line (DSL),* which, although it uses the phone line, does not prevent simultaneous voice communication. A DSL connection is a *broadband* connection.
- Cable TV line and *cable modem,* which brings Internet access in with your cable modem and doesn't use the phone line at all. It's also broadband.
- Cable programming via a satellite and *satellite modem,* which supports both cable television programming and Internet access.
- *T1,* a high-speed business circuit running at 1.544Mbps, or *DS3,* a very-high-speed business circuit running at 44.736Mbps.

4. **Compare and contrast the types of communications media.** *Communications media* are the paths, or physical channels, over which information travels in a network. There are two options: wired and wireless. Wired communications media include *twisted-pair cable, coaxial cable,* and *optical fiber.* Of these, optical fiber is the fastest and the most secure. Wireless communications media include *infrared, Bluetooth, Wi-Fi, microwave,* and satellite. Infrared and Bluetooth are for very short distances only, Wi-Fi is for short distances, microwave has short and medium distance versions, and satellite is for long distance.

5. **State the four principles of computer security and describe how different network security devices reflect those principles.** The four principles of computer security are

- **Confidentiality,** meaning that information can only be obtained by those authorized to access it
- **Authenticity,** meaning that information really comes from the source it claims to come from
- **Integrity,** meaning that information hasn't been altered
- **Availability,** meaning that a service or resource is available when it's supposed to be

  Firewalls protect confidentiality, authenticity, and integrity by blocking traffic that doesn't look like legitimate access to networked computers. *Intrusion detection systems (IDSs)* protect all types of computer security by watching for network intrusion attempts and reporting them; intrusion prevention systems (IPSs) take action to block them. *Encryption methods,* including SSL and *virtual private networks (VPNs),* protect confidentiality by scrambling your communication in such a way that only the intended recipient can unscramble it.

■ KEY TERMS AND CONCEPTS

Bandwidth,   415
Bluetooth,   424
Broadband,   416
Broadband router (home
     router),   411
Cable modem,   418
Cat 5 (Category 5),   410
Coaxial cable (coax),   423
Communications media,   422
Communications satellite,   425
Computer network,   409
Denial-of-service (DoS)
     attack,   428
Digital Subscriber Line (DSL),   417
DS3,   419
Encryption,   429
Ethernet card,   410
Firewall,   427
Infrared,   424

Internet,   415
Intrusion detection system
     (IDS),   428
Intrusion prevention system
     (IPS),   428
Local area network (LAN),   414
Malware,   429
Metropolitan area network
     (municipal area network,
     MAN),   414
Microwave transmission,   424
Network interface card (NIC),   410
Optical fiber,   423
Repeater,   425
Router,   413
Satellite modem,   419
Spyware, (sneakware,
     stealthware),   430
Switch,   412

T1,   419
Telephone modem,   416
Twisted-pair cable,   423
Virtual private network
     (VPN),   429
Virus,   429
Voice over IP
     (VoIP),   421
Wide area network
     (WAN),   414
Wi-Fi (wireless fidelity),   424
Wi-Fi hotspot,   424
Wired communications
     media,   422
Wireless access point
     (WAP),   410
Wireless communications
     media,   422
Worm,   429

■ SHORT-ANSWER QUESTIONS

1. What are the four basic principles that apply to all networks?
2. What is an Ethernet card?
3. What does a network switch do?
4. What is bandwidth?
5. What do you need to have a dial-up connection to the Internet?
6. How is a DSL Internet connection different from a telephone modem connection?

7. What impact does Frame Relay have on a metropolitan area network?
8. What is Cat 5 cable used for?
9. What is Bluetooth?
10. What does Wi-Fi do?
11. How does a VPN protect confidentiality?
12. What are the four principles of computer security?

■— ASSIGNMENTS AND EXERCISES

1. **WHAT ARE THE INTERNET ACCESS OPTIONS IN YOUR AREA?** Write a report on what sort of Internet connections are available close to you. How many ISPs offer telephone modem access? Is DSL available to you? Is it available to anyone in your area? Does your cable company offer a cable modem? If your school has residence halls, does it offer network connections? Compare each available service on price, connection speed, and extras like a help line, list of supported computers and operating systems, and people who will come out to your home and help you if you're having difficulties. What type of Internet connection do you currently use? Do you plan to upgrade in the future? If so, to what type of connection? If not, why not?

2. **INVESTIGATE BUILDING YOUR OWN HOME NETWORK** Build your own home network on paper. Assume you have the computers already and just need to link them together. Find prices for switches and routers on the Web. Also research Ethernet cards and cables. If you were to get a high-speed Internet connection like DSL or cable modem, how much would it cost? Can you buy your own, or would you have to rent the modem from the phone or cable company?

3. **DEMONSTRATE THE IMPACT OF WIRELESS TECHNOLOGY** How many devices do you own or use that transmit signals (not just computer data) wirelessly? Think of as many as you can, and make a list showing the different types of signaling used by each device. Don't forget that some devices use multiple wireless technologies, like cell phones with both cellular signals for voice transmissions and Bluetooth for syncing their address books. Hint: Don't forget cordless phones, TV and stereo remotes, radios, and portable computers and smartphone with infrared capability (look for a small, glossy black window somewhere on the edge of the case). Can any of your devices communicate with each other?

4. **CONSIDER THE IMPORTANCE OF NETWORK SECURITY** Write a report about the importance of computer and network security in your daily life, in terms of the four principles of computer security. If you have a job in addition to being a student, write about computer security in your workplace. If you don't work outside the classroom, write about how computer security affects you at school and in your personal life. You may be surprised at how many things you do that depend on some aspect of secure computer records and communications, like banking, grades, e-mail, timesheets, library and movie rental records, and many more.

5. **FIND OUT ABOUT FIREWALLS** Go to the Web and find out about software and hardware that protect your computer and home network, respectively.

    If you have only one computer connected to the Internet, then a software firewall like Zone Alarm will most likely be enough protection from intruders. Find three different firewall software packages on the Web. A good place to start looking would be the sites that sell anti-virus software. Compare the firewall software on price and features. Some sites to try are

    - Symantec at www.symantec.com
    - Trend Micro at www.trendmicro.com
    - McAfee at www.mcafee.com

    If you have a home network, look into hardware firewall options. How many different hardware firewalls can you find on the Web site of your favorite electronics retailer? (Hint: Look in the feature lists of home routers and broadband routers, even if they don't have the word firewall in their name.)

EXTENDED LEARNING MODULE F

BUILDING A WEB PAGE WITH HTML

Student Learning Outcomes

1. Define an HTML document and describe its relationship to a Web site.

2. Describe the purpose of tags in hypertext markup language (HTML).

3. Identify the two major sections in an HTML document and describe the content within each.

4. Describe the use of basic formatting tags and heading tags.

5. Describe how to adjust text color and size in a Web site.

6. Describe how to change the background of a Web site.

7. List the three types of links in a Web site and describe their purposes.

8. Describe how to insert and manipulate images in a Web site.

9. Demonstrate how to insert lists in a Web site.

Extended Learning Module F provides hands-on instructions for building a Web page by writing the HTML (hypertext markup language) code. You'll learn how to work with headings; adjust text sizes, fonts, and colors; manipulate background colors and images; insert links to documents, other Web pages, and e-mail addresses; manipulate images, and insert both bulleted and numbered lists.

Extended Learning Module F can be found on the book's Web site at www.mhhe.com/haag.

EXTENDED LEARNING MODULE G

OBJECT-ORIENTED TECHNOLOGIES

Student Learning Outcomes

1. Explain the primary difference between the traditional technology approach and the object-oriented technology approach.

2. List and describe the five primary object-oriented concepts.

3. Explain how classes and objects are related.

4. Discuss the three fundamental principles of object-oriented technologies.

5. Describe two types of object-oriented technologies.

Extended Learning Module G provides an introduction to the world of object-oriented technologies and concepts. Specifically, you will learn about the five primary object-oriented concepts, how classes and objects are related, and the three fundamental principles of object-oriented technologies.

Extended Learning Module G can be found on the book's Web site at www.mhhe.com/haag.

EXTENDED LEARNING MODULE H

COMPUTER CRIME AND DIGITAL FORENSICS

Student Learning Outcomes

1. Define computer crime and list three types of computer crime that can be perpetrated from inside and three from outside the organization.

2. Identify the seven types of hackers and explain what motivates each group.

3. Define digital forensics and describe the two phases of a forensic investigation.

4. Describe what is meant by anti-forensics and give an example of each of the three types.

5. Describe two ways in which businesses use digital forensics.

Introduction

Computers play a big part in crime. They're used to commit crime, unfortunately. But they are also used to solve crimes. This should come as no surprise since computers are by now such an integral player in every part of our lives. Computers are involved in two ways in the commission of crime: as targets and as weapons or tools. A computer or network is a target when someone wants to bring it down or make it malfunction, as in a denial-of-service attack or a computer virus infection. Crimes that use a computer as a weapon or tool would include acts such as changing computer records to commit embezzlement, breaking into a computer system to damage information, and stealing information like customer lists. See Figure H.1 for examples of computer-related offenses in which computers are used as weapons/tools and targets of crime.

Some crimes are clearly what we call computer crimes, like Web defacing, denial-of-service attacks, e-mail scams, and so on. But as is the case in so many parts of our modern lives, computers are also so integrated into crime that it's hard to separate them out.

A member of a crime syndicate was sprayed with drive-by gunfire and was severely wounded. Believing that his services were no longer wanted by his crime gang, he switched sides, agreeing to become a witness for the state. The police secured an isolated intensive care unit room for him and guarded it heavily, allowing access only to medical staff and those on a very short list of visitors. Because the man was so badly wounded, there was a distinct danger of infection, and since he was allergic to penicillin, the doctor prescribed a synthetic alternative.

One evening, a nurse wheeling a medicine cart went through the police cordon and into the man's room. He injected the patient with penicillin, and the patient died shortly thereafter. An investigation started immediately and the nurse was potentially in big trouble. He insisted that when he looked at the patient's chart on the computer, there was an order there for penicillin. Subsequent examination of the computer records showed no such order. Eventually, it occurred to someone that perhaps a digital forensic expert should look at the computer angle more closely. Having retrieved the backup tapes (nightly backups are standard operating procedure in most places), the expert found evidence that exonerated the nurse. The patient chart had been changed in the computer to indicate penicillin and later changed back to its original form. Examination further revealed the point and time of access, and indicated that the medical record was

	Inside the Organization	Outside the Organization
Weapons/Tools	• Intellectual property theft • Accessing information on others for personal reasons • Acts of spite or revenge • Acts of extortion • Reading the e-mail of others	• Murder • Theft of information • Embezzlement • Harassment • Extortion • Credit card theft • Cargo theft by diverting shipments
Targets	• Information destruction • Planting destructive code • Stealing customer information • Altering information	• Virus attacks • Denial-of-service attacks • Web defacing • Rerouting network traffic • Crashing servers

Computers as

Figure H.1

Examples of Computer Crimes That Organizations Need to Defend Against changed by someone outside the hospital. A hacker had electronically slipped into the hospital's network unnoticed, made the change, and slipped out again—twice.

Most crimes involving a computer are not as lethal as murder, but that doesn't mean they're insignificant. Organizations want to make sure their networks' defenses are strong and can prevent their computers from being used for unlawful or unethical acts. That's why so much time, money, and effort goes into security. We discussed security in Chapter 8.

This module focuses on the sort of threats that computer systems are susceptible to and the examination of electronic evidence. The latter is called *digital (or computer) forensics.*

Computer Crime

LEARNING OUTCOME 1

For our purposes, a **computer crime** is a crime in which a computer or computers play a significant part. See Figure H.2 for a list of crimes in which computers, although perhaps not essential, usually play a large part.

In this section we'll focus on crime from the organization's viewpoint. First, we'll examine some of the more high-profile types of computer crime committed against organizations that are perpetrated from the outside. Then we'll discuss the varying motivations of people who commit these acts. Lastly, we'll briefly discuss computer crime within the organization.

OUTSIDE THE ORGANIZATION

Computer security is a big issue in business. The concern is about people stealing electronic information, accessing systems without authorization, introducing viruses into networks, defacing Web sites, to name just a few of the dangers. The Computer Security Institute (CSI) together with the FBI's Computer Intrusion Squad have conducted studies every year since 1996 to assess the extent of the security problem nationwide. The picture is grim. Online fraud is increasing ever more rapidly and financial and other con-

Figure H.2
Crimes in Which Computers Usually Play a Part

- Illegal gambling
- Forgery
- Money laundering
- Child pornography
- Hate message propagation
- Electronic stalking
- Racketeering
- Fencing stolen goods
- Loan sharking
- Drug trafficking
- Union infiltration

fidential data is falling into the hands of crooks to be sold or used on the black market. *Malware* is software designed to harm your computer or computer security, engage in criminal activity, or compromise resources in some way.

VIRUSES, WORMS, AND BOTNETS   Viruses are a type of malware. A *computer virus* or *(virus)* is software that was written with malicious intent to cause annoyance or damage. The early computer viruses depended on people exchanging infected storage media like disks. Later viruses dispensed with the need for human help. The most prevalent of these is a worm. A *worm* is a computer virus that replicates and spreads itself, not only from file to file, but from computer to computer via e-mail and other Internet traffic. A decade ago the most famous was the Love Bug worm that destroyed files but was easily detected since it changed the extensions on the files it infected.

During 2007 and 2008 the most common type of worm was a *bot,* a much more sophisticated type of worm. A *botnet* is a collection of computers that have been infected with blocks of code (called bots) that can run automatically by themselves. A computer infected with such a bot that is part of a botnet is called a *zombie* computer. The computers get infected when the bot sends out copies of itself to other machines. A malicious botnet can:

- Collect e-mail addresses from the machines it infects as the Damballa botnet did.
- Distribute vast amounts of e-mail as the Storm botnet did.
- Lie dormant to be used at a later date by the crooks—this is perhaps the most frightening aspect of botnets.

The Storm botnet started in early 2007 and wreaked havoc with massive amounts of spam until September 2008. One example was what was called the "World War III" scam that sent false messages announcing the start of World War III. The main objective of the Storm botnet was to create zombies that could be rented out to spammers who would then use those machines to serve spam to the rest of us.

YouTube was also a target. Millions of e-mails told recipients to look at a YouTube video that featured them. When the unsuspecting user clicked on the link, the malicious Web page tried to infect the user's computer.

At its height the Storm botnet had about 500,000 zombies under its control. As detection programs became widely used, that number dropped to an estimated 47,000 in late 2008. The United States has the most botnet-infected computers with 18 percent of all zombie computers. Storm eventually became a victim of its own success in that it became so well publicized that it couldn't operate effectively. The last observed activity of the Storm bot was in September 2008.

One interesting feature of Storm was its ability to launch DDos attacks against anti-virus researchers. A Distributed Denial-of-Service (DDoS) attack is where hackers overwhelm a computer system or network with so many requests that it goes down (discussed in more detail later in this chapter). How can your computer become infected? One way is through a malicious Web site you visit. It comes through your browser. This is possible because when you visit any Web page, not just the bad ones, you may get content from many different sources, i.e. third-party ads, maps, online videos, etc. The extraordinary array of features that you can build into your Web site increases the complexity of the Web browser. Each one of these components can cause you to be vulnerable to attack. However, as attractive to the bad guys as it is to infect individual computers, it's much more effective to infect Web servers. The more sophisticated infections can get thousands of servers at once. Mostly, the objective of such attacks is to redirect visitors to the attacker's server.

In early 2009 the big story was the Conficker worm that could be called the successor to the Storm worm. There were various permutations of the Conficker worm. One version, for example, installed fake security software that popped up a bogus security warning telling you that you needed to install Spyware Protect 2009. The only way to stop the pop-ups was to pay $50 for a useless program. As with the Storm virus, Conficker infected machines for spammers. Another of Conficker's features was to block you from getting to Microsoft's Windows update site.

Experts were worried about what else Conficker might do. One fear was that some sort of attack would be launched on the infected zombies on April 1, 2009. However, that date passed without incident. In all, about 10 million PCs are estimated to have been infected by Conficker. Since one infected machine can infect a whole network, the evil spread rapidly.

STUXNET   In 2010 the Stuxnet worm came to light. Stuxnet represents a new level in the development of worms because it was such a finely honed target seeker. The worm, which was transported from computer to computer using a USB stick, was designed to attack Iran's nuclear fuel enrichment centrifuges and send them spinning out of control while making the readout screens indicate that everything was working the way it was supposed to. The worm secretly recorded the normal readings and played those back while it did its other work. The worm infected Windows computers and then hid itself, but did nothing to most of the computers that it infected. It only activated when it encountered computers running Step 7, the software that runs the Siemens motors controlling the centrifuges, called PLCs or programmable logic controllers (see Figure H.3). Even then it only attacked equipment made by two specific manufacturers, one Iranian and one Finnish, and didn't go into operation until 33 or more pieces of equipment were running in the plant at a speed above a certain threshold.

Another interesting feature of Stuxnet was that if it made it onto a computer connected to the Internet it downloaded the latest version of itself. Experts believe that Stuxnet was designed and released by a well-funded group, possibly working in conjunction with one or more governments. The worm spread to other countries including India, Indonesia, and United Arab Emirates.

Stuxnet was not the first worm to attack a nuclear plant. The Slammer worm infected the monitoring system of a nuclear power plant in Ohio, but fortunately it did not pose a safety hazard. Again, this worm was introduced to the system via the corporate network using a SUB stick. Slammer had none of the sophistication of Stuxnet, but it highlighted a vulnerability in the system. What makes Stuxnet of great concern to computer security experts is that it represents a new kind of threat where the software that runs various types of machinery, turbines in power stations, for example, or oil pipelines, can be compromised.

In 2011, along with concerns about Stuxnet, phishing attacks and other types of malware became even more numerous. PandaLabs reported that about 40 new malware programs were created every minute during the first quarter of 2011. On a different front, two loosely knit groups, Anonymous and LulzSec, came on the scene and blurred the line between hacktivism and criminality. LulzSec, which is a play on geekspeak for LOL or laugh out loud, and Anonymous portray themselves as consumer champions pointing out vulnerabilities in systems that have a lot of personal data. However the groups crossed the line when they published the information they found on their hacking expeditions. LulzSec is believed to have breached Sony's Playstation system, shutting it down for a month or so, and published personally identifiable information on Sony's servers. The group also penetrated organizations such as RSA Security, the U.S. Department of Defense, the International Monetary Fund, the European Space Agency, Citigroup, and SEGA using distributed denial-of-service (DDoS) attacks. Several members of both groups have been arrested in various parts of the world.

How Stuxnet Spreads
Experts who have disassembled the code of the Stuxnet worm say it was designed to target a specific configuration of computers and industrial controllers, likely those of the Natanz nuclear facility in Iran.

Initial Infection
Stuxnet can enter an organization through an infected removable drive. When plugged into a computer that runs Windows, Stuxnet infects the computer and hides itself.

Update and Spread
If the computer is on the Internet, Stuxnet may try to download a new version of itself. Stuxnet then spreads by infecting other computers, as well as any removable drives plugged into them.

Final Target
Stuxnet seeks out computers running Step 7, software used to program Slemens controllers. The controllers regulate motors used in centrifuges and other machinery. While the computers in a secure facility may not be on a network, they can be infected with a removable drive. After infecting a controller, Stuxnet hides itself. After several days, It begins speeding and slowing the motors to try to damage or destory the machinery. It also sends out false signals to make the system think everything is running smoothly.

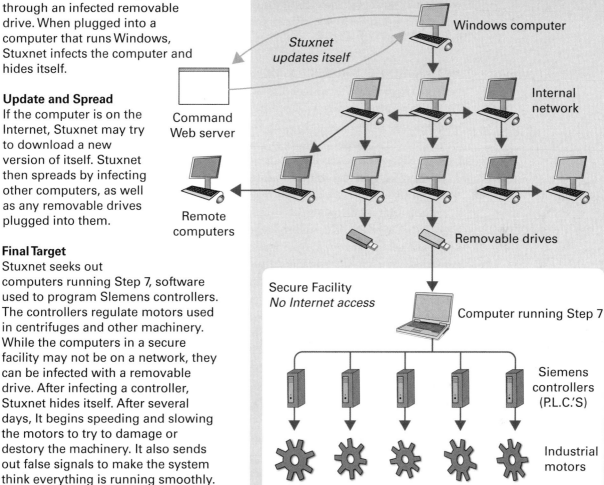
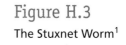

Figure H.3
The Stuxnet Worm[1]

STAND-ALONE VIRUSES   In any given month, between 200 and 300 viruses are traveling from system to system around the world, seeking a way in to spread mayhem.[2] And they're getting more deadly. Whereas the Love Bug worm was a Visual Basic script virus (i.e., it needed Visual Basic to run), the latest worms can stand alone and run on any computer that can run Win32 programs (Windows 98 or later versions). Examples are SirCam, Nimda, and Klez. Nimda adds JavaScript to every home page on the server it infects, then passes it on to visitors to the site. Viruses of this independent type are very numerous.

The Klez virus is actually a family of worms that introduced a new kind of confusion into the virus business. They spoof e-mail addresses. *Spoofing* is the forging of the return address on an e-mail so that the e-mail message appears to come from someone other than the actual sender. Previous worms went to the recipient from the infected sender's computer and contained the infected person's return e-mail address. The worm found recipient addresses in the infected computer's address book.

Klez goes a step further and uses the address book to randomly find a return address as well as recipient addresses. The result is that people who are not infected with the virus get e-mail from the irate recipients and spend time looking for a virus they may not have. Even worse, some of the virus-laden e-mails look as though they came from a technical support person, leading an unsuspecting victim to open them, believing them to be safe.

TROJAN HORSE VIRUSES   A type of virus that doesn't replicate is a Trojan-horse virus. A ***Trojan horse virus*** hides inside other software, usually an attachment or download. The principle of any Trojan horse software is that there's software you don't want hidden inside software you do want. For example, Trojan horse software can carry the ping-of-death program that hides in a server until the originators are ready to launch a DoS attack to crash a Web site.

Key logger software is usually available in Trojan horse form, so that you can hide it in e-mail or other Internet traffic. ***Key logger,*** or ***key trapper, software*** is a program that, when installed on a computer, records every keystroke and mouse click. Key logger software is used to snoop on people to find out what they're doing on a particular computer. In a small school district in Missouri, cybercriminals smuggled a key logger program onto a computer in the administrative offices of the School District Supervisor. The computer was the one used by the bookkeeper who handled all transactions with the bank. With the key logger the crooks were able to get the ID and passwords to the school district's bank accounts. Before a bank official noticed unusual activity in the accounts, $200,000 was transferred elsewhere in amounts less than $10,000 each. Transfers of $10,000 or more must be reported, so criminals keep the amounts below that. You can find out more about key logging in Chapter 8.

MISLEADING E-MAIL   One type of misleading e-mail is a virus hoax. This is e-mail sent intending to frighten people about a virus threat that is, in fact, bogus. People who get such an alert will usually tell others, who react in the same way. The virus is nonexistent, but the hoax causes people to get scared and lose time and productivity. Within companies the losses can be very severe since computer professionals must spend precious time and effort looking for a nonexistent problem.

Following are some general guidelines for identifying a virus hoax.[3]

- Urges you to forward it to everyone you know, immediately.
- Describes the awful consequences of not acting immediately.
- Quotes a well-known authority in the computer industry.

These are signs that the e-mail is not meant to help but to cause harm. If you get such an e-mail, delete it immediately.

Another type of misleading e-mail is designed to get people to actually take action that results in setting a virus loose or to do something that will disrupt the functioning of their own computers. The first step is usually to make people believe that they have inadvertently e-mailed a virus to others. They get a message (maybe it purports to come from Microsoft) that they have sent out a virus and that they need to run an attached program or delete a file to fix the problem. They then do what the e-mail says believing it to be genuine, and furthermore, they e-mail everyone they sent messages to telling them about the problem. The recipients e-mail the people in their address books and so on. Be advised that Microsoft *never* sends out attachments in any official e-mail in a public mass mailing. It's possible that Microsoft may e-mail you warning you of a problem, but it will only indicate where you can download a file to take care of it. Before you delete a file from your computer, which may be an important system file without which your computer can't function, ask someone who knows or check out the various Web sites that keep up with the latest viruses, like www.symantec.com.

DENIAL-OF-SERVICE ATTACKS   Many organizations have been hit with denial-of-service attacks. *Denial-of-service (DoS) attacks* flood a server or network with so many requests for service that it slows down or crashes. The objective is to prevent legitimate customers from getting into the site to do business. There are several types of DoS attacks. A DoS attack can come from a lone computer that tries continuously to access the target computer, or from many, perhaps even thousands, of computers simultaneously. The latter is called a distributed denial-of-service attack and is considerably more devastating.

DISTRIBUTED DENIAL-OF-SERVICE ATTACKS   *Distributed denial-of-service (DDos) attacks* are attacks from multiple computers that flood a server or network with so many requests for service that it slows down or crashes. A common type is the Ping of Death, in which thousands of computers try to access a Web site at the same time, overloading it and shutting it down. A ping attack can also bring down the firewall server (the computer that protects the network), giving free access to the intruders. E*Trade, Amazon.com, and Yahoo!, among others, were victims of this nasty little game in the early days. The process is actually very simple (see Figure H.4).

The plan starts with the hackers planting a program in network servers that aren't protected well enough. Then, on a signal sent to the servers from the attackers, the program activates and each server "pings" every computer. A ping is a standard operation that networks use to check that all computers are functioning properly. It's a sort of roll call for the network computers. The server asks, "Are you there?" and each computer in turn answers, "Yes, I'm here." But the hacker ping is different in that the return address of the are-you-there? message is not the originating server, but the intended victim's server. So on a signal from the hackers, thousands of computers try to access E*Trade or Amazon.com, to say "Yes, I'm here." The flood of calls overloads the online companies' computers and they can't conduct business.

For many companies, a forced shutdown is embarrassing and costly but for others it's much more than that. For an online stockbroker, for example, denial-of-service attacks can be disastrous. It may make a huge difference whether you buy shares of stock today or tomorrow. And since stockbrokers need a high level of trust from customers to do business, the effect of having been seen to be so vulnerable is very bad for business.

MALWARE BOTS AND ROOTKITS   A vital component of the increase in the spread of viruses and denial-of-service attacks is the use of bots. A *bot* is a computer program that runs automatically. Bots (the term comes from robot) can perform all sorts of tasks, both good and evil. In Chapter 4, Decision Support, Analytics, and Artificial Intelligence, you saw how bots take the form of intelligent agents, finding information and automatically performing computer-related tasks. Two examples are bots or intelligent agents that continuously monitor networks to find a problem before it knocks out the network and shopping bots that find products and services on the Internet for you.

However, there's another class of bots—the kind that are used for fraud or sabotage. In *Extended Learning Module E, Network Basics,* you learned that bots (software robots) can be used to break into computer systems. Having placed the unauthorized code into a computer, attackers set up servers that are used for such things as distributing illegal copies of movies, music, and software. These compromised machines may be used to

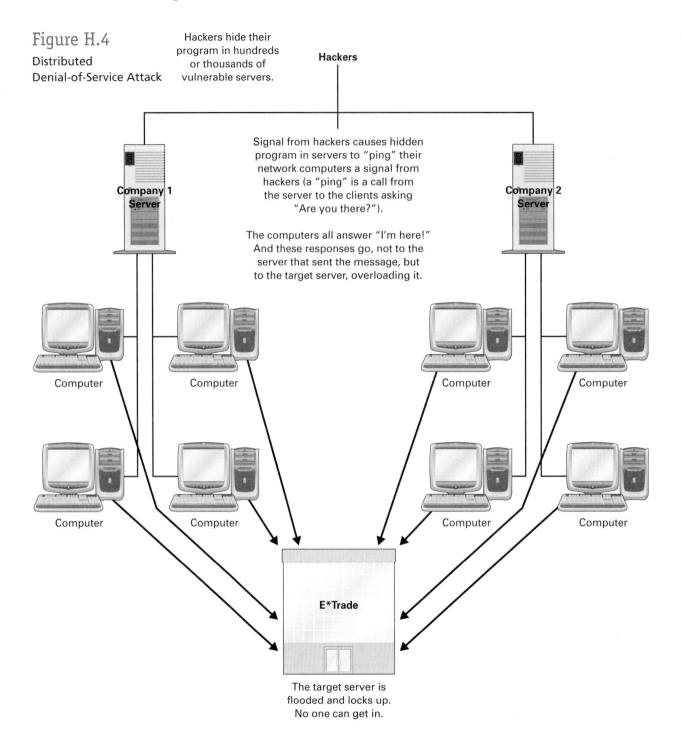

Figure H.4

Distributed
Denial-of-Service Attack

Hackers hide their
program in hundreds
or thousands of
vulnerable servers.

Hackers

Signal from hackers causes hidden
program in servers to "ping" their
network computers a signal from
hackers (a "ping" is a call from
the server to the clients asking
"Are you there?").

The computers all answer "I'm here!"
And these responses go, not to the
server that sent the message, but
to the target server, overloading it.

Company 1
Server

Company 2
Server

Computer

Computer

Computer

Computer

Computer

Computer

Computer

Computer

E*Trade

The target server is
flooded and locks up.
No one can get in.

distribute kits for breaking into other computers. Malware bots are designed to be controlled by an attacker to perform unauthorized work over some period, like sending out spam or becoming part of a denial-of-service attack. Estimates are that about three-quarters of all spam mailings come from this source.

A ***malware bot*** is a bot that is used for fraud, sabotage, DoS attacks, or some other malicious purpose. It allows an unauthorized user to take control of a host computer without the victim's knowledge or permission. The term *bot* is sometimes used to mean a compromised machine, i.e., a computer that has been compromised with a bot. Bot-infected computers are also called ***zombies*** or ***drones.***

Malware bot activity has become very sophisticated over the past few years and there is a whole underground society in the bad bot business. The lowest level of the underground comprises the people who find vulnerable machines and install bad bots. The next level up are *bot herders*. Bot herders assemble battalions of bot-infected computers and sell this network of bots or botnet to people who are called fraudsters. A *botnet* is a network of malware-infected computers. Bot herders typically sell their networks for about $1 per machine, but the price can go up to $100 per system, per month, for access to a major organization that has lots of valuable information like customer and employee data. The fraudsters, in turn, use the botnet to steal this customer and employee data along with intellectual property, and anything else of value that they can get access to. Computers in organizations as varied as the Department of Defense and Colton School District in California have been compromised. Here are two other examples:

- In early November 2006, the computer of a water plant worker in Harrisburg, Pennsylvania, was invaded by a bot which then spread to the organization's server, which was hijacked into becoming part of a botnet that was then used to send out spam.[4]
- One Sunday morning in 2005, the Seattle's Northwest Hospital & Medical Center computer system was very slow and documents wouldn't print. The next day things got worse as lots of strange things started happening. The operating-room doors stopped opening, doctors' pagers wouldn't work, and computers in the intensive care unit shut down. It was all the result of a botnet attack. Three teenagers in California managed to infect a single computer with a bad bot. The code spread and soon all the computers in the network had become part of a botnet. The hospital had to wipe several hard drives clean and reinstall software at a cost of $150,000. The oldest of the teenagers, who was 19, was sentenced to 37 months in federal prison and ordered to pay compensation to the hospital.[5]

Malware bots can infect a computer in any one of a number of ways including operating system or application vulnerabilities, e-mail, instant messaging, and computer viruses. One very effective way of commandeering computers is to use a *rootkit*. It's hard to detect and even when detected, it's hard to remove. A rootkit is a Trojan-horse type program that is activated when you start your computer. It carries code that, once inside, can do whatever it was programmed to do.

A **rootkit** is software that gives you administrator rights to a computer or network and its purpose is to allow you to conceal processes, files, or system data from the operating system. It can be used to carry code to perform virtually any type of malicious activity. It can take full control of a system and use that computer or network for spam, denial-of-service, or spyware, and, more chillingly, create a "backdoor" into the system for the attacker, who can then commandeer the system to be part of a botnet.

An attacker exploits an operating system vulnerability to get a rootkit onto your computer. A rootkit is hard to detect since it runs while the operating system is starting and looks to the operating system like it belongs.

Probably the most widely publicized example of a rootkit was the one that Sony put into CDs and DVDs as part of a copy protection scheme in 2005. It got onto your computer when you played the disc and was then exploited by hackers.

WEB DEFACING

Web defacing is a favorite sport of some of the people who break into computer systems. They replace the site with a substitute that's neither attractive nor complimentary. Or perhaps they convert the Web site to a mostly blank screen with an abusive or obscene message, or the message may just read "So-and-so was here." In essence, Web site defacing is electronic graffiti, where a computer keyboard and mouse take the place of a paint spray can. The *USA Today* Web site was once a victim. The *USA Today* Web site was attacked in July 2002, causing the newspaper to shut down the whole site for three hours to fix the problem. The hackers replaced several news stories on the site with bogus stories that were full of spelling errors. One story said that the Pope had called Christianity "a sham." The phony stories were only on the site for 15 minutes before they were spotted and the site was taken offline.[6]

CYBER WAR

Richard A. Clarke, government security expert, has defined **cyber war** as "actions by a nation-state to penetrate another nation's computers or networks for the purposes of causing damage or disruption."[7] The difference between cyber war and hacktivism or cyber terrorism (see definitions below) is that cyber war is perpetrated by one nation on another. It's a better-organized, better-funded, more targeted attack on national infrastructure.

The Department of Defense has said that a cyber attack that cripples the U.S. power grid and/or government and/or financial systems will very likely be the next Pearl Harbor. Intrusions in the last few years have compromised some of the most crucial systems in the Pentagon. These included surveillance technologies and satellite communications systems. The defense industry is also vulnerable and its networks have suffered penetrations of military systems such as missile tracking systems and drone aircraft.

LEARNING OUTCOME 2

THE PLAYERS

Who's spreading all this havoc? The answer is hackers. This is the popular name for people who break into computer systems. **Hackers** are knowledgeable computer users who use their knowledge to invade other people's computers. There are several categories of hackers, and their labels change over time. The important thing to note in the following discussion is that the motivation and reasons for hacking are as many and varied as the people who engage in it.

THRILL-SEEKER HACKERS   *Thrill-seeker hackers* break into computer systems for entertainment. Sometimes, they consider themselves to be the "good guys" since they expose vulnerabilities and some even follow a "hackers' code." Although they break into computers they have no right to access, they may report the security leaks to the victims. Their thrill is in being able to get into someone else's computer. Their reward is usually the admiration of their fellow hackers. There's plenty of information on the Web for those who want to know how to hack into a system—about 2,000 sites offer free hacking tools, according to security experts.

WHITE-HAT HACKERS   The thrill-seeker hackers used to be called white-hat hackers. But lately, the term *white-hat* is being increasingly used to describe the hackers who legitimately, with the knowledge of the owners of the IT system, try to break in to find and fix vulnerable areas of the system. These **white-hat hackers,** or **ethical hackers** are computer security professionals who are hired by a company to break into a computer system, so as to find security lapses. These hackers are also called counter hackers, or penetration testers.

BLACK-HAT HACKERS   *Black-hat hackers* are cyber vandals. They exploit or destroy the information they find, steal passwords, or otherwise cause harm. They deliberately cause trouble for people just for the fun of it. They create viruses, bring down computer systems, and steal or destroy information.

A 16-year-old black-hat hacker was sentenced to detention for six months after he hacked into military and NASA networks. He caused the systems to shut down for three weeks. He intercepted more than 3,000 e-mails and stole the names and passwords of 19 defense agency employees. He also downloaded temperature and humidity control software worth $1.7 billion that helps control the environment in the international space station's living quarters.[8]

CRACKERS *Crackers* are hackers for hire and are the people who engage in electronic corporate espionage and other profitable ventures. This can be a pretty lucrative undertaking, paying up to $1 million per gig. Typically an espionage job will take about three weeks and may involve unpleasant tasks like dumpster diving to find passwords and other useful information and "social engineering." *Social engineering* is conning your way into acquiring information that you have no right to. Social engineering methods include calling someone in a company and pretending to be a technical support person and getting that person to type in a login and password, sweet talking an employee to get information, and for sophisticated jobs, perhaps even setting up a fake office and identity.

HACKTIVISTS *Hacktivists* are politically motivated hackers who use the Internet to send a political message of some kind. The message can be a call to end world hunger, or it can involve an alteration of a political party's Web site so that it touts another party's candidate. It can be a slogan for a particular cause or some sort of diatribe inserted into a Web site to mock a particular religious or national group.

Hacktivism, in the form of Web defacing, is becoming a common response to disagreements between nations. For example, hackers in Iraq and the United States have traded intrusions during the Iraq War. Such attacks are common in the Middle East between Israel and Saudi Arabia and other Arab states. A popular target of hacktivists is companies that are located in regions of conflict but are based in some other country.

CYBERTERRORISTS Since the September 11, 2001, terrorist attacks on New York and the Pentagon, officials have become increasingly worried about the threat of *cyberterrorists*. This group of hackers, like the hacktivists, is politically motivated, but its agenda is more sinister. A *cyberterrorist* is one who seeks to cause harm to people or destroy critical systems or information. Possible targets of violent attacks would be air traffic control systems and nuclear power plants, and anything else that could harm the infrastructure of a nation. At a less lethal level, cyberterrorist acts would include shutting down e-mail or even part of the Internet itself, or destroying government records, say, on social security benefits or criminals.

In 2000 a disgruntled employee took over a water-treatment plant in Australia and released more than 200,000 gallons of sewage into parks, rivers, and the grounds of the Hyatt hotel. According to the Central Intelligence Agency, cyberattacks have interrupted power in multiple regions of the world. During the last part of 2008 and the early part of 2009, the U.S. government spent $17 billion in repairing cyber damage. Government officials believe that the attacks came from outside the United States. Another $17 billion is earmarked to protect the networks from further attack.[9]

SCRIPT KIDDIES *Script kiddies* or *script bunnies* are people who would like to be hackers but don't have much technical expertise. They download click-and-point software that automatically does the hacking for them.

The concern about script kiddies, according to the experts, apart from the fact that they can unleash viruses and denial-of-service attacks, is that they can be used by more sinister hackers. These people manipulate the script kiddies, egging them on in chat rooms, encouraging and helping them to be more destructive.

Digital Forensics

LEARNING OUTCOME 3

Digital forensics experts are called in to help solve crimes of all kinds from white collar fraud and traffic accidents to terrorist activities and political scandals. They investigate information that they collect from computer hard disk drives, smartphones and other cell phones, flash drives, CDs, and DVDs and build a picture of the crime or incident. Some high profile cases where electronic evidence has been crucial are listed below:

- In 2007, a disturbed student went on a killing rampage and in the space of two hours, in two separate attacks, killed 32 people and wounded 25 others before killing himself. To try to understand what had happened, authorities collected his electronic devices, such as his computer and cell phone, and pieced together a profile of the young man from the information they found.

- In 2009 a big rig truck driver killed a Buffalo mother of two when he was watching pornography while driving and didn't see her broken-down parked car. Police forensics experts found the evidence on his computer, leading to his arrest and being charged with second degree manslaughter.

- In Fort Collins, Colorado, parents of six-year-old Falcon Heene reported that a helium balloon had floated up into the atmosphere with their son on board. The balloon landed about 12 miles outside the Denver airport after traveling about 50 miles. When the balloon came down and the boy was not on board authorities launched a massive search believing that the boy had fallen out. Later, on the basis of evidence found by computer forensics experts, it was established that the story was a hoax and that the boy had been hiding in the attic all the time. The parents went to jail after costing taxpayers 2 million dollars.

- A Missouri auto parts store owner pled guilty to conspiring to help a terrorist network. He admitted to sending more than $23,000 to al Qaeda and performing other tasks. He communicated with others in the network through steganography, where messages are hidden inside other messages. The FBI in Kansas City cracked the code and secured evidence against him.

- In 2010 the University of Kansas athletic department announced an internal investigation into the multi-million-dollar ticket scalping scam perpetrated by several employees over a number of years where they diverted ticket sales for their own profit. The ticket director at the university controlled the computer that would have detected the theft if she hadn't changed the settings.

  Investigators found damning e-mails including one where the director of ticket operations promised eight free tickets to a neighbor who complained that work being done on the ticket operations director's home was causing him grief and a soggy lawn. The perpetrators went to jail.

Law enforcement has been turning to digital forensics for several years now to help solve crime. The Federal Bureau of Investigation has fourteen Regional Computer Forensics Laboratories with 224 forensic examiners who have processed more than 3,000 terabytes of information which is the equivalent of three million copies of the *Encyclopedia Britannica*. Their work is not confined to the 57,000 hard disks they worked on in 2010—they're also examined innumerable digital cameras, smartphones, wireless storage devices, and various other storage components.[10]

Of course, the FBI and other law enforcement agencies are not the only organizations that use digital forensics. And not all digital forensics companies investigate criminal cases. Many work on property cases, where a company believes that an employee is secretly copying and perhaps selling proprietary information such as schematics, customer lists, financial statements, product designs, or notes on private meetings. Other investigations involve domestic disputes, labor relations, and employee misconduct cases.

Digital forensics is the collection, authentication, preservation, and examination of electronic information (often for presentation in court). Electronic evidence can be found on any type of computer storage media, such as hard disks, smartphones, CDs, flash cards, USB devices, etc. But investigators have had cases that involved rather unusual media such as the black boxes used by the railroad that record information about trains and the black boxes on cranes that might yield clues as to why a crane collapsed. Forensics can even be applied to such systems as the daVinci Surgical System, which is a robot used by hospitals where mechanical arms do the actual surgery while the surgeon operates the controls (see photo). The daVinci system has a hard disk that stores video clips, records of who logged on, and other data. If someone were to erase a file that contained evidence of an error that occurred during surgery, an investigator could find remnants of that file.

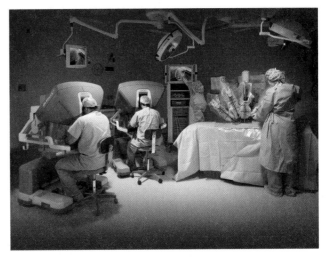

In the da Vinci system, the surgeon sits at a viewfinder (left) and remotely manipulates probes and instruments on actuator arms over the operating table.

There are two basic motivations for engaging in digital forensics. The first is to gather and preserve evidence to present in court. The second is to establish what activities have occurred on a computer, often for the purpose of dispute settlement. Evidentiary standards differ for criminal and civil cases. In criminal cases, the standard is beyond a reasonable doubt. In civil cases, it's the preponderance of evidence. Perhaps the situation doesn't involve the legal system at all. It could be that you have an employee that you suspect has been using the company's computer system to gamble online. In this case your proof can be lower, perhaps just enough to reprimand or fire the person while reducing the risk of being named in a wrongful termination lawsuit.

In a well-conducted digital forensics investigation, there are two major phases: (1) collecting, authenticating, and preserving electronic evidence; and (2) analyzing the findings.

THE COLLECTION PHASE

The collection phase consists of two steps: getting physical access to where information is stored and creating a forensic image copy.

PHYSICAL ACCESS Since getting physical access to the computer and related items is necessary, the digital forensics team collects computers, cell phones, CDs and DVDs, printouts, post-it notes, and so on and takes them back to the lab. This process is similar to what police do when investigating crime in the physical world: collecting hair, clothing fibers, bloodstained articles, papers, and anything else that they think might be useful. The crime investigators usually take these potential clue carriers with them and secure them under lock and key, where only authorized personnel may have access, and even they must sign in and out. This is to preserve the "chain of custody" of the evidence.

Digital forensics experts use the same kind of protocol. To conduct a thorough investigation, they first take digital photos of the surrounding environment and start developing extensive documentation. Then they start collecting anything that might store information. The hard disk is an obvious place to look, but digital forensics investigators also collect any other media where information might be stored. See Figure H.5 for a partial list of places where evidence, called artifacts, can be found.

Cell phones, of which there are almost as many in the world as there are people, are another obvious source of informational artifacts. When you have your phone on it's constantly in communication with nearby cell towers so that a call can be handed off to the base station receiving the strongest signal from your phone, and as you move, your change in location is being recorded. In urban areas with a lot of towers, a phone's location can be tracked almost to the block. If your phone has GPS capabilities, your exact location can pinpointed in real time. If the phone photos are geotagged (i.e. include the location where the photo was taken) there may be a wealth of information there. Phones with passwords may stop the investigator examining the phone, but if you back up your phone files on your computer that copy is not pass-worded. Cell phones are very useful in discovering who is talking to whom. When an investigation is announced, it's likely that the people involved in the fraud will start a flurry of phone calls to others involved. The list of recent calls as well as any texts or voicemail messages can be very revealing.

Since there are so many people using cell phones, it stands to reason that some of them are using them to commit crime. The list of cell phone crimes includes much of the illegal activity that's possible with computers (or without them) and some that's unique to cell phones. Some examples are

- Illegal drug deals.
- Stealing data and storing it on a cell phone.
- Using a cell phone to fraudulently obtain goods and services. A variation on this theme is stealing subscriber information and using it to create duplicate accounts which are then used to purchase goods from the Internet using the original subscribers' accounts. These crimes are particularly prevalent in Europe and Japan, where people use their cell phones to buy snacks and drinks out of vending machines, pay parking tickets, make credit payments, and engage in a host of other types of mobile commerce.

Figure H.5

Where You Might Find Electronic Evidence

Hard drives
CD's and DVD's
USB drives
Flash memory cards like SD cards
Backup media
Voice mail
Cell phones
Electronic calendars
MP3 players and iPods
Scanners
Photocopiers that usually have hard disks nowadays
Fax machines
Xbox system

- On a vastly more serious scale, cell phones have been used by terrorists to set off explosives. This happened in Madrid in 2004 when bombs went off in commuter trains; at Hebrew University in Jerusalem, in 2002, when seven people died; and in Bali outside a night club in 2002 and in the Jakarta Marriott Hotel.[11]

As well as electronic media, investigators collect any other potentially helpful items, especially passwords, for use in case any of the files they come across are encrypted or otherwise difficult to access. Passwords that are written down are often stored very near the computer, making it easy for forensics experts—and thieves—to find them. Other items that might be useful include address books and business cards of associates or contacts of the person being investigated.

AUTHENTICATION AND PRESERVATION.   Step two of the collection process is to make a forensic image copy of all the information. A *forensic image copy* is an exact copy or snapshot of the contents of an electronic medium. It is sometimes referred to as a bit-stream image copy. To get a forensic image copy, specialized forensic software copies every fragment of information, bit-by-bit, on every storage medium—every hard disk, every CD, every USB drive, every flash card, and every cell phone involved in the investigation. Hard disk drives today hold upward of 2 terabytes and even a CD holds about half a gigabyte. That can amount to the equivalent of hundreds of millions of printed pages. The copying alone can take a long time since the chain of custody must be protected.

To get a forensic image copy of a hard disk and other computer media contents, investigators physically remove the hard disk from the computer. If the suspect computer is off, they don't turn it on, because Windows performs hundreds of changes to files. Access dates change, and so do temporary files, and so on. So, once turned on, the hard drive is no longer exactly the same as it was when it was shut down. Thus, opposing counsel could argue that this is not the same hard disk that the suspect used.

Having removed the hard disk, investigators connect it to a special forensics computer that can read files but can't write or rewrite any medium. Another tool that forensic experts use is a write blocker that permits read commands but not write commands. This allows you to gather information from a drive without changing or deleting any information on the original source. There are both hardware and software write blockers. The software types are usually specific to a particular operating system while hardware write blockers work with any operating system and plug into USB or Firewire ports.

Investigators prefer to remove storage devices like hard disks, but if that's not possible, they copy the contents in place using cables. Then they use forensic software like FTK (Forensic Tool Kit) or EnCase to extract a forensic image copy of the original medium without changing the files in any way.

How do we know that nothing changed on any media during the entire investigation from the time they were seized? That's the question that opposing counsel will ask the digital forensics expert on the witness stand. So, during the collection phase and, later, the analysis phase, the investigators have to make sure that evidence to be used in a trial could not have been planted, deleted, or changed. This is a basic evidentiary rule for all court proceedings.

In a digital forensics investigation, experts use an authentication process so that they can show sometime in the future—perhaps even five or six years later—that no entry or file changed in the interim. They do this by generating an authentication code (unique identifier or checksum value) for each file and/or each medium. There are three such authentication coding systems in wide use: The *MD5 hash value,* the SHA-1, and the SHA-2 hash values. These codes are mathematically generated strings of letters and digits and each code is unique to an individual file or disk at a specific point in time. The authentication codes are based on the contents of the file or medium and any change in content will change the authentication code.

Hash values are seemingly meaningless sets of characters. For example, a hash value could be the sum of the ISBNs and the number of pages in all the books on a bookstore shelf. The result, which would be a mixture of ISBN codes and quantities of pages, would be meaningless for anything except identification. If a book, or even a page, were added to or removed from the shelf the hash total would change, so the contents of the shelf could be shown not to be the same as they were when the hash value was originally computed. Similarly, adding so much as one space to a Word document on a disk will change the authentication code. Authentication codes are the electronic equivalent of DNA for people. The probability of two hard disks with different contents having the same MD5 hash value is 1 in 10 to the power of 38: that's 1 with 38 zeros after it. You would actually have better odds of winning the Powerball lottery 39 times in your lifetime than you would of finding two hard disks with different contents having the same MD5 hash values. SHA hash values are even stronger, since the character string is longer; however, the MD5 is accepted by most organizations as strong enough. Figure H.6 shows a screen from the Forensic Tool Kit (FTK) that has an MD5 hash value and an SHA-1 hash value for the Internet/chat files directory on the medium being examined.

Burglars have been known to check their Facebook pages while conducting a robbery and that information, putting them in the burgled home at a precise time has been used. So, an obvious place to look for information about a person nowadays is social networking sites. Facebook would be a good place to start. More than three-quarters of people who have Facebook pages don't restrict who can access their photo albums and 81 percent don't restrict who can see their recent activity, which has updates that record

Figure H.6

MD5 and SHA-1 Hash Values for the Forensic Tool Kit (FTK) Program

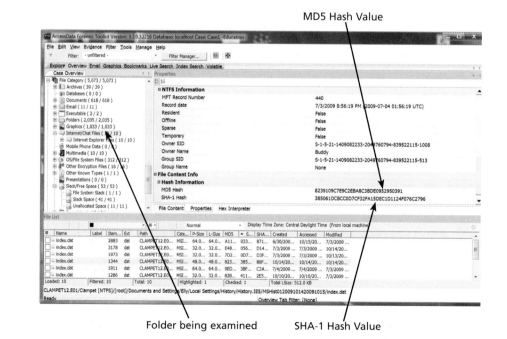

where the person is at a certain time using geo-location tools, according to a survey by Webroot. Webroot is an anti-virus and anti-spyware company. When you use Facebook, temporary files are stored on your hard disk that are not readily apparent. They don't show up when you search through folders and there's a wealth of information in those files. The files contain information on Facebook ID numbers and who they were in contact with. You can even do a reverse search and put in an ID number to get the user's name. It's also possible to re-create the threads of chat sessions.

THE ANALYSIS PHASE

The second phase of the investigation is the analysis phase when the investigator follows the trail of clues and builds the evidence into a story. The analysis phase consists of the recovery and interpretation of the information that's been collected and authenticated.

RECOVERY   Digital forensics experts use a variety of software tools to recover information. They usually use specialized digital forensics programs like Forensic Tool Kit (FTK) or EnCase. With these programs investigators can find a wealth of information on storage media. They can find deleted files pretty easily and files with extensions that don't match the file format (e.g. an image file with the extension .xlxs). If a deleted file has been overwritten, it's very possible that fragments of that file remain in ***unallocated space,*** i.e. space that is marked as being available for storage. See Figure H.7 showing a file fragment in unallocated space.

In Figure H.8 you can see some of the files that can be recovered from storage media with forensic software. A program like FTK can pinpoint a file's location on the disk, its creator, the date it was created, the date of last access, and sometimes the date it was deleted as well as formatting and notes embedded or hidden in a document.

A digital forensics program can find and display all the images on a storage device so that you don't have to look in separate places and by different extensions. In Figure H.8 you can see that FTK has collected images together in a separate folder and you can examine that folder to see what pictures are on the disk and where they are stored.

Digital forensics experts use a lot of other software too. For example, they might use something like Internet Evidence Finder (IEF) or NetAnalysis that search a hard drive

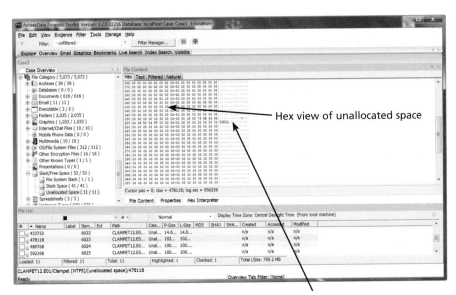

Figure H.7

File Fragment in Unallocated Space in the Forensic Took Kit (FTK) Program

Figure H.8

Collection of Images on a Hard Drive from the Forensic Tool Kit(FTK) Program

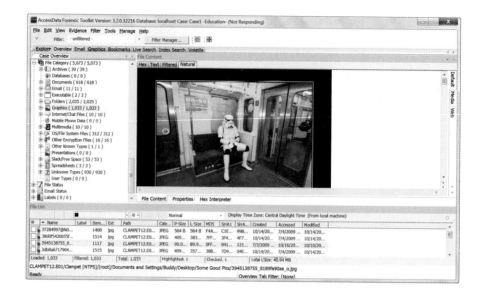

for Internet-related artifacts. Of course, also stored on the hard disk is information about where the computer user went on the Web. Every graphic image you view on the Internet is copied to your hard disk, usually without your knowledge. But also available are copies of Facebook Chat, Facebook E-mail, Google Talk, Hotmail Webmail, Twitter status updates, Firefox artifacts and on and on. Experts will often use two similar recovery packages on the same data to confirm results, known as dual tool verification.

E-mail comes in many formats and various e-mail conversion programs like Transend and Aid4Mail convert these formats into a form that the digital forensics investigator can work with easily. These programs allow you to search for specific terms in e-mails and attachments and show only those that are relevant. For videos, there's VLC media player which is a free and open source multimedia player that will play most multimedia files as well as DVDs, CDs, and streaming video files.

Live Analysis   It's not always possible, or advisable, to collect information when a computer is off. For one thing, you will lose the information in volatile storage, i.e. RAM. Therefore, the forensic team has to gather the information it needs while the system is still running. This is called a live analysis. *Live analysis* is the term used to describe an examination of a system while it is still running. Live analysis may be necessary under certain circumstances such as:

- If the company hosts a Web site that takes customer orders. In this situation a complete shutdown would cost the company precious business, and a judge might consider such action as an "undue burden" on the company.
- If information that is needed is in RAM and the examiner pulls the plug that information will be lost. So in this case it would actually be better for the forensic experts to get data from a computer that's still running. For example, if someone is caught red-handed using a computer for some illicit activity it might be much better to get a memory dump from the system rather than pull the plug which would wipe out the contents of volatile RAM.
- If the user is using a whole disk encryption program, like BitLocker that comes with Windows 7 or Guardian Edge, turning off a computer will trigger the encryption process and a password will then be required to access the data.
- With hard disk storage now in the terabyte range, it's simply too wasteful to copy all the data when only a small portion of it is relevant to the investigation. Under these circumstances, it may be acceptable to extract only certain well-defined portions.

In a live analysis, the examiner doesn't make a forensic image of the disk, and therefore, there's no MD5 or SHA hash value. This is a big disadvantage should you need to make a case in court. All you have is a momentary snapshot of what's going on within that system. On the plus side, examiners can glean information from memory and on processes and services that are running and also on open ports on the computer. The collection would usually start with memory, which is the most volatile, and then proceed on to swap file (used in virtual memory) and network processes, and other volatile areas. Live forensics is often used to determine whether an event has occurred. Data can be collected from memory on the video card and on the network card as well as the contents of RAM.

Helix, which is freeware, is often used for this purpose. It's Linux-based and provides a utility that allows the examiner to download to a PDF, which is not easily changeable, detailing what the examiner did in the correct sequence and what tools were used. This provides some assurance that the examiner did what was necessary and followed proper procedure.

One of the new problems facing digital forensics experts is the problem of access to cloud computing data. The data may be stored outside the country making access to it problematic if not impossible. Even if you use a cloud computing provider based in this country (like Gmail, Hotmail, Google Docs, or Dropbox) the company may outsource actual storage of the data to a company that operates on the other side of the world. Since laws are applicable only to particular geographical jurisdictions, the legal complications can be a nightmare.

Cell Phones   At the end of 2010 there were just over 303 million cell phones in the United States, where the population is just over 310 million people. Considering the flexibility of today's cell phones, especially smartphones, they can be great sources of information for investigative bodies. There's much more information on smartphones than calls sent and received. A modern smartphone is a combination of many devices, such as phone, personal digital assistant, still and video digital cameras, music and video players, game console, and resources traditionally available on a larger computer such as Web access, e-mail access, and word processing and spreadsheet capabilities.

See Figure H.9 for a list of some of the information stored on cell/smartphones. Many smartphones use MicroSD cards and there may be information there too.

Phone book with phone numbers, addresses, work and home contact information
Subscriber, equipment, and service provider identifiers
Calendar
To-do list
Phone number log with recently incoming and outgoing calls and missed calls
E-mail
Web activity with bookmarks and cached Web pages
Text messages and multimedia messages
Voice mail
Electronic documents
Last active location and other networks encountered
Graphics, photos, and videos
Cookies
Instant messages
GPS fixes, locations, and journeys

Figure H.9
Recoverable Cell Phone Information

The big problem with doing forensic investigations on smartphones is that, unlike computers, over 90 percent of which run Windows, Smartphones run a whole range of software that varies from company to company and even phone to phone. The first decision that an expert may have to make is whether or not to turn the phone off. Leaving it on will run the battery down and make it susceptible to an e-mail "bomb" that floods the phone's memory with messages that wipe out previous calls and messages. Putting the phone in a metal-mesh shielding bag to block signals would avoid the bomb problem but will drain the battery more quickly because the phone will boost its transmitting power to try to reach a cellphone tower. Turning the phone off may cause problems later because the phone may have a password that will prevent access. To know what cables to use will necessitate having the model number, which is usually stored under the battery and removing it to see the number will then kill the power to the phone.

No one forensic tool will retrieve all information from all smartphones but there are several programs on the market that will copy information from phones. Most of these are not specifically designed for forensic investigation so they don't have the safeguards, like hash values, against data tampering that specialized tools do. Many of the tools available are synchronization tools that people use to transfer stored information between phones.

GSM (Global System for Mobile Communications) phones have SIM cards. GSM is the most common type of phone outside the United States and is used by some companies within the United States. Apart from storing the phone number and other authentication information it acts as a secondary storage area of contacts, text messages, and other artifacts. Deleting a message from the SIM card only marks it as deleted and does not remove it until the space is needed.

INTERPRETATION   As with all evidence, the analysis of the electronic clues and the assembling of the pieces into a credible and likely scenario of what happened are very important. Much of the information may come from recovered deleted files, currently unused disk space, and deliberately hidden information of files. Following is a discussion, not necessarily exhaustive, of places where information can be found on a magnetic hard disk.

Information is written all over a disk, not only when you save a file, but also when you create folders, print documents, repartition the disk, and so on. System and application software alike continually create temporary files resulting in space and file locations being rearranged. Leftover information stays on the disk until another file writes over it, and is often recoverable with forensic software.

Deleted Files and Slack Space   It's difficult to get rid of information on a magnetic hard disk completely. When you delete a file it's not gone. What actually happens is the file is marked as deleted, meaning that that space is available to accept new information. The actual information in the file is not affected at all by the delete action.

If you delete a file from the hard disk it goes into the Recycle Bin and you recover it later from there. In the case of a removable medium, like a USB flash drive, it's a little harder, but not much since you can get the file back with one of any number of utility programs.

When you mark a file as deleted, the space is freed up for use by some other file. So, another file may shortly be written to that space. However, it's not quite that straightforward. The operating system divides storage space into sectors of bytes or characters. The sectors are grouped into clusters. A file is assigned a whole number of clusters for storage, whether it completely fills the last cluster or not. This storage allocation method usually leaves unused portions of clusters. This is analogous to writing a three and one-half page report. So, the fourth page is allocated to the report but not completely used. If the previously stored file (the deleted one) was bigger and used that last part of the space, then the remnants of the deleted file remain and can be recovered using the appropriate software. The space left over at the end of the file to the end of the cluster is called *slack space,* and information left from previous files can be recovered by forensic software.

Solid-state hard drives (SSDs) are based on flash memory and do not function in the same way as magnetic hard drives. Flash memory is not divided into the traditional blocks of bytes, but is instead in pages of 2 KB, 4 KB or larger. Rewriting a block at the operating system level will not necessarily put the data back in the same place. The information may be remapped to avoid wear in certain spots or to avoid failing pages. Each page can be erased and rewritten only a limited number of times (up to 10,000 or so). Hard drive sectors can be rewritten millions of times. SSD information can be erased very quickly—typically in seconds—and the data is more thoroughly wiped than it would be in one pass on a magnetic drive. While this is a very desirable feature from the point of view of the owner of the data, it's causing nightmares among digital forensics experts who are struggling with this new medium and have to develop some new approaches.

System and Registry Files   The operating system manages the hardware and software of your computer and lets your application software access hardware without your having to know how all the various types of hardware function. As one of its many functions, the operating systems controls virtual memory. Virtual memory is hard disk space that is used when RAM is full. Details of virtual memory activity are stored in system files. For example, if you have several applications running and you're instant messaging someone, that exchange may be stored on the hard disk without your knowing it simply because there wasn't room for it in RAM.

The registry on your computer is a multidimensional database structure that is part of the operating system. Registry files contain a wealth of information including preferences for users of the system, settings for the hardware, system software, installed programs, and a list of all the USB devices that were ever attached to the system. Even if you uninstall a program, remnants of the install process remain in the registry file. Thus, if someone uses a wiping program like CCleaner that clears out artifact areas and unallocated space, and then uninstalls the program, the fact that it was once installed is still accessible. Windows keeps track of programs that were run on the computer in its UserAssist Key registry file. With a freeware program like UserAssist you can display these entries along with last execution date and time.

Unallocated Disk Space   If your hard disk gets a lot of use, it's probable that each sector has had information put onto it many times. The operating system is always moving files around, and if you changed a Word file and resaved it, the previous version is marked as deleted and the space becomes unallocated. *Unallocated space* is the set of clusters that have been marked as available to store information, but have not yet received a file or files. Unallocated space may still contain some or all of a file marked as deleted. Until the new information takes up residence, the old information remains. The bigger the hard disk, the longer it usually takes for old space to be used.

Unused Disk Space   Unused space results from rearranging disk space. For example, when a hard drive is repartitioned, the new partitioning may not use all the space on the hard disk. So, again, those unused portions are not overwritten. The partition table and other operating system information are stored on their own tracks and are not visible under normal circumstances, but may have once stored a Word document. To be able to see the fragments of files tucked away in these tracks you need forensic software.

Erased Information   By now you may be asking whether it's possible to completely erase information from a storage medium. It is possible, but you need to know what you're doing. You can get disk-wiping programs that erase information from a disk by writing nonsense information over the previous contents. However, wiping a disk takes many hours. Even then you're not necessarily safe, for three reasons:

- A single overwrite may not erase the information completely. It must usually be written over multiple times. Government agencies have specific policies in place as to how many wipes are required.
- Some programs keep track of what was deleted and by whom, and that record is viewable if you know where to look.
- Disk-wiping programs vary greatly in which parts of the hard disk they clean. For most of them, you have to change the settings to reach certain parts of the disk. Some claim to go through the wipe process multiple times but that still doesn't erase the areas that the software isn't set to erase. Also keep in mind that if people are trying to erase information because of some illicit activity, traces may still be left of the information they're trying to discard, and unless they're very careful, they'll leave traces of their attempts to wipe the disk. At the very least, they'll most likely leave a record in the Registry that they installed the wiping program.

ANALYTICS IN FORENSICS

So far we've been concentrating on the mechanics of what's on information devices such as computers, smartphones, etc. But there's a very important movement in digital forensics toward forensics analytics. You read a lot about analytics in Chapters 3 and 4 and here you will see another example of where those same methods are applicable.

Most of the fraud, and certainly the high-dollar fraud, in the corporate world is perpetrated by insiders. It's estimated that about two-thirds of the fraud that is uncovered comes to light by means of a tip or by accident. The internal auditor or fraud investigative community is always looking for ways to detect and even predict fraud. About 80 percent of communications within organizations is unstructured as in e-mail, documents, presentations, Web content, text messages, chat sessions, calendar entries, and so on.

The Fraud Triangle, as proposed by Dr. Donald Cressey in the 1950s, is useful for getting a handle on the most likely culprits. Fraud Triangle Analytics can be helpful in predicting who in the company is more likely to commit fraud as well as in finding the fraud and the culprits. The Fraud Triangle as shown in Figure H.10 is used in analyzing the e-mail content of employees.[12] The Fraud Triangle incorporates three scores: the O-Score which is a measure of the opportunity available to an employee; the P-Score which assigns a numeric value to the incentive or pressure an employee might be under; and the R-Score which represents the employee's level of rationalization. The ACFE (Association of Certified Fraud Examiners) and Ernst and Young have put together thousands of keywords that correspond to each of these three points in the triangle and they have found that these keywords start appearing in e-mails when fraud is being contemplated or planned and that the words correlate to the presence of the three pressure points. Some of these words are shown in Figure H.11.

The analysis of perhaps millions of e-mails allows investigators to narrow down the field of people likely to commit fraud, and then the exploration can concentrate on a small number of probable suspects. The presence of high O-, P-, and R–Scores does not necessarily mean that fraud has been committed or that the person with the high scores is a perpetrator, but it gives examiners a way of approaching massive amounts of unstructured data. The traditional controls that are in place concentrate on structured accounting documents and there are far fewer of those.

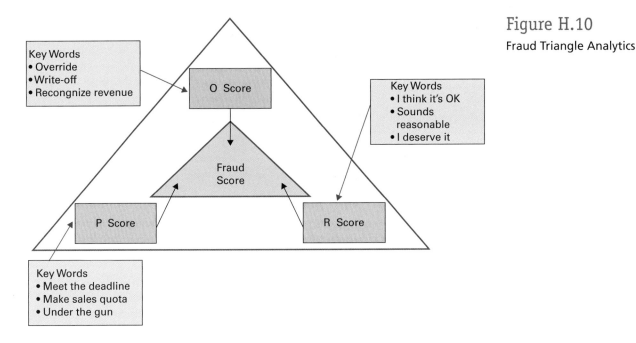

Figure H.10

Fraud Triangle Analytics

E-mails and other communications can be analyzed with text analytics that can answer questions such as who is talking to whom (social networks analytics); what they are saying (semantic analytics); and the time period during which the communications take place (time series analysis).

All investigations, whether criminal or civil, include a survey of social networking sites and other publically available sources. For example, suppose someone is suing a grocery store claiming that they got hurt in a fall and can't work because of the injury. Investigators might look on that person's Facebook page and if there's a recent photo there of the person waterskiing that would be pretty good evidence that the injury was not as bad as reported.

Modern computer forensics goes a step beyond that and includes semantic analysis of all available information structured and unstructured. Businesses investigating fraud would use three approaches: computer forensics, forensic accounting, and analytics.

Ingenium is software that does latent semantic analysis, also known as concept searching. This means that it can search for your meaning rather than just terms that match exactly. For example, if you type in "house" as a search term, the software will search for

Opportunity	Incentive/Pressure	Rationalization
Correct	Problem	Deserve
Conditional	Clarify	Owe me
Discount	Revise	Get back
Miscount	Sorry	Figure out
Override	Meet the deadline/quota	Sounds reasonable
Special fees	Don't leave a trail	Don't get paid enough
Side commission	Only a timing difference	Company can afford it

Figure H.11

Keywords Compiled by Ernst & Young and the Association of Certified Fraud Examiners

Figure H.12

Modern Computer
Forensics Involves More
than Just What's on the
Hard Disk

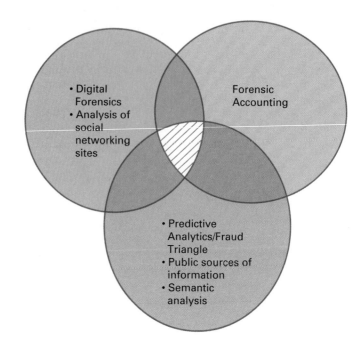

cottage, hut, domicile, home, property, estate, holdings, manor, housing, mansion, cabin, bungalow, chalet, lodge, residence, dwelling, abode, residence, habitat, apartment, etc. It uses a neural network to find other terms that are close in meaning to your search term. You can learn more about neural networks in Chapter 4, Analytics, Decision Support, and Artificial Intelligence.

Other more mundane analysis methods can still be very revealing. Examining lists of mail drops like at Mailboxes Etc., P.O. Boxes, and FedEx Kinkos and matching those to a list of vendors could be useful in a case where goods have been disappearing from a warehouse. Comparing Social Security numbers (SSN) with those on the death index or searching for an SSN that is not consistent with the Social Security Administration's method of assigning numbers where there's a state code, a region code, and a date-related number may indicate a fraudulent identity.

All these methods together—computer and cell phone examination, social networking site analysis, public information sources, semantic analysis, predictive analytics identifying high risk employees—help digital forensics investigators build a story of how fraud was conceived and perpetrated and who the people were who engaged in it (see diagram in Figure H.12).

LEARNING OUTCOME 4 ## ANTI-FORENSICS

Because of high-profile digital forensics cases, people nowadays understand more about how data is stored on computer storage media and how it can be accessed by forensic software. As a result, a new branch of the digital forensics industry is growing fast—the anti-forensics industry. Some of the tools now available that make it hard or impossible to trace user activity or access the data in files were not specifically intended to defeat law enforcement probes; rather they are there mainly to help computer owners to protect themselves and their data. For example, encryption is a very good way to protect the data on your notebook computer so that if it's stolen, the thief can't get the data. Another is keeping deleted files out of the Recycle Bin, so that someone can't recover your files easily. Others, however, products with names such as EvidenceEiminator, are clearly intended to keep the bad guys from getting caught.

Anti-forensic tools fall into three categories:

1. Configuration settings—included in your operating system, browser, and applications like Word and Excel.
2. Third-party tools—utility software on the market that performs specific tasks.
3. Forensic defeating software developed to remove or change the sort of data that forensics experts look for.

CONFIGURATION SETTINGS This category includes the *Shift + Delete* option that you can use instead of simple *Delete* so that the file is not listed in the Recycle Bin. However, if you use this bypass option you still leave a special signature that digital forensics experts can find. In Windows there are several options that mask user activity, like renaming the file with a different extension. This is probably the simplest, and most easily detected, way of deliberately hiding a file. Say you had an Excel file that had calculations you didn't want anyone to know about. You could name the file Space Needle. jpg. It would then appear in Windows Explorer in the list of files as an image file, with the name implying that it's just a vacation photo or something else equally innocuous. If you click on that file, Windows will try to load it with the default .jpg viewer, and of course, it won't load. What digital forensic experts usually do is load the file into a program that accommodates many file formats. This way, you save a lot of time trying to load the renamed file into lots of different types of software. Even more helpful is having a forensic tools like EnCase that actually flag files with extensions that don't match the contents and also show files in their true formats.

Another thing you can do would be to use the option that clears out virtual memory so that any RAM data that was temporarily stored on the hard disk for use by the processor is removed when the system no longer needs it. Enabling this option, however, will make your system shutdown much slower. The *Defrag* option rearranges data on your hard disk and overwrites deleted files. *Disk Cleanup,* listed as an option in the Properties of the C:\drive, lets you delete ActiveX controls and Java applets (little blocks of code that generate Web page content) that you downloaded automatically and without realizing it from Web sites you visit.

Internet Explorer has similar features like the option to clear temporary Internet files when you close the browser. Another one is the option to clear the history file so that your Internet surfing activity is not easy to find.

When creating a Word or Excel file, you could use a very small font or make the characters the same color as the background. Plug-ins are available for Word to remove hidden data and to redact a document. **Redacting** means blacking out portions of the document, usually to protect confidential information, so that it cannot be recovered later. The redacted portion of the document has black bars covering the selected text and the text is no longer there.

Office lets you password protect files so that when someone tries to open the file a pop-up window asks for the password. Unless you know the password, you won't be able to read the file. Forensic software can sometimes view the contents of a file without opening the file, eliminating the effectiveness of many types of password protection. And of course there are very effective third-party password cracking programs available, although not as part of the operating system.

THIRD-PARTY TOOLS There are lots of these utility programs. For example, there are some that alter your registry—the file that logs installations of hardware and software. Another type hides Excel files inside Word documents and vice versa. This does not protect files from an experienced examiner. Others change the file properties in

Windows like the creation date or the extension. Still another type can split files, password protecting and encrypting parts of the file or storing parts in different places on the storage medium.

Probably the best known type of third-party tools are the wiping programs that overwrite the disk, effectively obliterating the information that was there before. They work well enough to clean a hard disk that you may be giving away to someone, but, depending on the actual software, there may be lots of fragments that digital forensics experts can still recover.

There are lots of encryption programs available that protect files so that even if someone manages to get them, it won't be any good because they're not readable without the decryption key. *Encryption* scrambles the contents of a file so that you can't read it without the right decryption key. Often investigators can find the decryption key in a password file or on a bit of paper somewhere around the keyboard. Password cracking programs can find passwords very easily (alarmingly easily, in fact). They have dictionaries of words from multiple languages, so whole words from any widely used language are not hard to crack. Some people put a digit or two on the front or back of a word. That doesn't fool password-cracking programs at all.

Using images to hide data is another way of protecting information. This is called steganography. *Steganography* (see Figure H.13) is the hiding of information inside other information. Paper money is a good example of steganography. If you hold a dollar bill up to the light you'll see a watermark. The watermark image is hidden inside the other markings on the bill, but it can be seen if you know what to do to see it.

A very useful tool, but a hardware/software combination this time, is a *U3 Smart drive* which looks like and is a USB flash drive, but it stores and can launch and run software on any computer. You can have all the software and files you need on the U3

Figure H.13

Steganography Hides a File in an Image

You can't see the parts of the picture that were changed to encode the hidden message. You'll only be able to access the hidden file when you put the right password into a pop-up window.

and plug it into any computer, and it can take over computer resources like the CPU, screen, and keyboard—nothing gets stored on the hard disk of the computer you're using, and you can have all your own programs—even your own wallpaper—on the screen. All cache, cookie items go to the U3 and it runs it own programs. This works because it appears to your computer to be a CD and so Windows AutoPlay feature automatically runs the U3 LaunchPad which is the U3's own user interface. It works very similarly to the Windows interface. You can get a large range of software for a U3 device.

One of the most effective ways to evade detection for someone who is doing something illicit like accessing child pornography is to use a U3 Smart device since it can be plugged into virtually any computer and leaves no trace of the user or the user's activity. Other methods are detailed below.

FORENSIC DEFEATING SOFTWARE In addition to the utilities that could arguably be acquired for personal privacy or protection purposes, there is software that makes no secret of its purpose to fool investigators. One type removes residual data—data left when files are deleted and the space is partially overwritten. Other software is designed to erase cache memory, cookies, Internet files, Google search history, and so forth. Some programs are aimed at specific forensic software. EnCase is the usual target because of its standing as the most popular and most accepted software in the industry. Of course, if you're doing something illegal and there are records of it on your computer, for example, if you're keeping track of drug dealing, you could also use any or all of the tools provided by Windows or the utilities supplied by third parties.

Even given all these tools and more, it's not as easy as it may sound to hide your activity on a computer. First, not all programs function as advertised, or as fully as promised. Second, very few people have the knowledge and skill to completely hide their tracks. Third, the installation of third-party utilities or forensic defeating software or even operating system settings can be detected and can indicate intent to hide something.

A final note on the use of software to evade detection by law enforcement: If you find yourself in litigation and use such tools to get rid of information you believe may be incriminating and then claim that it was never there, you might be in for a rude awakening. The law says that "any product used to circumvent discovery" may be taken as consciousness of guilt. Even though the documents are not available, during the court hearing the inference may be made that you had them and that, by destroying them, you have shown yourself to be guilty. So, being able to determine that such tools have been used is almost as good as finding the evidence itself. This line of reasoning has often been used in cases of illegal distribution of movies and music.

Who Needs Digital Forensics Investigators?

Digital forensics is widely used wherever and whenever the investigation of electronically stored files is warranted, such as:

- In the military, both as part of national security intelligence gathering and analysis and for internal investigations of military personnel.
- In law enforcement, when the FBI, state investigatory agencies, and local police departments need to gather electronic evidence for criminal investigations.
- Inside corporations or not-for-profit organizations, when conducting internal audits, for example, or investigating internal incidents.
- In consulting firms that specialize in providing digital forensic services to corporations and law enforcement.

Digital forensics experts work both proactively, educating and warning people about possible problems, and reactively, when they're called in to help in response to an incident. The need for such expertise is growing, especially considering that it is estimated that 93 percent of all information is generated in digital form. Since computing and investigative techniques are improving continuously, digital forensics experts need a forum to exchange ideas and information (see Figure H.14).

PROACTIVE DIGITAL FORENSICS EDUCATION FOR PROBLEM PREVENTION

Companies are increasingly providing proactive education for two reasons: first, to educate employees on what to do and not to do with computer resources and why; and second, to teach employees what to do if they suspect wrongdoing, and how not to make things worse by destroying evidence.

People who use computers every day are often not very knowledgeable about what, when, and how information is stored on computers. For example, many corporations have strict policies on how long e-mails will be kept on the system (or in the form of backups). Usually the period of time is about 60 days. You might decide to save your e-mails on your hard disk so that you'll have them indefinitely. This might not be wise since the reason that companies have this policy is that should the company find itself involved in litigation, all electronic information, including e-mail, may be discoverable. That is, the company may have to hand it over to opposing counsel. The more there is, the more it costs to collect, organize, and deliver it.

The second reason for providing some education in computer forensics has to do with conducting internal investigations properly. Say a company wants to file a complaint with law enforcement about the suspected illegal activity of an employee. Before law enforcement can look into the situation, however, it needs to have sufficient cause to

Figure H.14

Professional Organizations and Standards

Professional organizations exist that support digital forensic experts in doing their jobs. The organizations below provide interaction between members who share information, experience, and methods. Such organizations also provide ethical guidelines and certification.

- IACIS (International Association of Computer Investigation Specialists) is open to law enforcement personnel and sets standards and guidelines for computer forensic investigations.

- ACFE (Association of Certified Fraud Examiners) focuses on serving those who investigate fraud. Members include people in law enforcement, auditors, accountants, and digital forensic experts.

- The HTCIA (High Technology Crime Investigation Association) is open to law enforcement and corporate investigators alike and facilitates the sharing of resources among its members.

A group called the Sedona Conference Working Group on Electronic Document Production published *The Sedona Principles: Best Practices, Recommendations & Principles for Addressing Electronic Document Production*. The document, the first draft of which emerged in 2003, is a new set of standards pertaining to properly conducting a digital forensic investigation. These principles were developed by lawyers, consultants, academics, and jurists to address the many issues involved in antitrust suits, intellectual property disputes, and other types of complex litigation.

do so. It can happen that in collecting relevant information the company inadvertently contaminates or destroys the "crime scene." The result may be that law enforcement can't prosecute after all because of lack of evidence.

REACTIVE DIGITAL FORENSICS FOR INCIDENT RESPONSE

Companies need digital forensics, in a reactive mode, to track what employees have been doing with company resources. You saw in Chapter 8 that employees may be using the Internet to such an extent during working hours that their productivity is affected, and the level of personal traffic on the company network may be such that people who are actually working are slowed down. This is just one example of misuse of the company computer system. The evidence of such misappropriation of computer resources can be found on the system itself—on individual client computers and on the servers.

A second reason for reactive digital forensics is changes in laws and government regulations and new laws passed as a consequence of recent corporate crime and misbehavior, probably the most important being the Sarbanes-Oxley Act of 2002, signed into law by President Bush. Known as "Sarbanes-Oxley," the law requires companies to (1) implement extensive and detailed policies to prevent illegal activity within the company and (2) respond in a timely manner to investigate illegal activity.

The act expressly states that executives must certify that their financial statements are accurate. They will be held criminally liable for fraudulent reporting, removing the insulation that executives previously had of being able to say that they didn't know about misstatements. Sarbanes-Oxley also specifically requires publicly traded companies to provide anonymous hotlines so that employees and others can report suspicious activity.

The provision that suspicious activity must be investigated in a timely manner in many instances automatically requires digital forensics. In earlier litigation, courts have determined that computer-stored evidence is crucial to the proper investigation of alleged corporate fraud. Add to that the fact that delay in investigating alleged wrongdoing meets with severe penalties and that courts impose severe sanctions on those judged guilty of destroying evidence including electronic information.

A DAY IN THE LIFE

The career of a digital forensics expert can be very rewarding and satisfying. But it can also mean spending long hours carefully poring over the contents of hundreds of files looking for the clue that will unravel the mystery and show what actually happened. It also means being able to explain to lawyers, judges, juries and other noncomputer people what the evidence is and what it means. You also need to be able to keep your cool since "dispute resolution" usually means someone is aggrieved or scared and such feelings are often expressed as anger. People can even turn violent during an investigation—some have gone as far as rigging their computers with explosives to thwart an investigation.

Lanny Morrow is a digital forensics and data mining expert with the Forensics and Valuation Services division of BKD, LLP, one of the largest accounting firms in the United States. He's an experienced forensics expert who has all the abilities necessary to succeed as an investigator along with years of experience. He has solved many cases while working with a list of clients that includes for-profit and nonprofit organizations; litigants in civil suits; and defendants and plaintiffs in criminal proceedings. Following are two examples from his case files.

The first involves MySpace. A high-school girl posted on MySpace her account of her own molestation by her father. Her shocked friends told their parents about her plight and the parents alerted the authorities, who initiated an investigation. The girl's parents were deeply distressed and vigorously disputed the claim. They cooperated fully in the investigation, handing over family computers and cell phones to Lanny who began the process of finding the truth.

- He found multiple drafts of the text that the girl posted on MySpace describing the incident. The date stamps showed that they had been created before the rape was alleged to have taken place.
- Further examination revealed e-mails and chat logs where the girl expressed resentment at being grounded by her parents for attending a party without permission. In her communications, the girl stated her intention and explained her plan to get even.
- Lastly, Lanny found cell phone text messages and e-mails from her friends offering pledges to corroborate her story along with suggestions of details to include in the fictitious report.

As often happens, when presented with the overwhelming evidence of her lies, the girl admitted that she had made up the whole story to get revenge on her parents. She then had to explain to her teachers and peers what she had done and why. The friends who were co-conspirators in the plan were also identified and had some explaining of their own to do.

The second case involved three employees who filed a civil case against their former employer alleging wrongful termination. They had been fired on the basis of inadequate performance in their jobs and when company executives were notified of the lawsuit they hired Lanny to see if he could find evidence that the employees' performance on the job was inadequate and the termination was, therefore, justified. Since the employees' jobs all involved heavy use of the company's computer system, Lanny and his team went to work right away and what they found was very revealing

- They used EnCase's Timeline feature to generate a profile of computer usage by each of the employees. This report shows, down to the second, when a computer was being used and what it was being used to do. The analysis showed large gaps during working hours indicating that the employees had taken extended breaks.
- Furthermore, they found files that revealed that one of the employees was using the company's time and resources to run her own business on the side. It was later established that she had taken office supplies home for her private use.
- An analysis of the activity on the computer of another one of the complainants established that she had spent up to three hours a day, during business hours, surfing the Net, often participating in eBay auctions, and had routinely spent all morning e-mailing her friends and family.
- The third employee spent a large portion of his work time gambling online.

All in all, over an extended period, the three employees had spent only about one-third of their working hours doing what they were being paid to do. To cover their tracks they delegated their tasks to other employees who believed that this was standard operating procedure. After the investigation was over the office managers were also fired for allowing such conduct and because it came to light during the investigation that one of them had been having an affair with one of the fired employees. Examination of the manager's own computer confirmed the relationship.

SUMMARY: STUDENT LEARNING OUTCOMES REVISITED

1. **Define computer crime and list three types of computer crime that can be perpetrated from inside and three from outside the organization.** *Computer crime* is a crime in which a computer, or computers, played a significant part in its commission. Crimes perpetrated outside the organization include

   - *Computer viruses*
   - *Denial-of-service (DoS) attacks*
   - *Malware bots*
   - Web defacing
   - *Trojan-horse virus*

   Crimes perpetrated inside the organization include

   - Fraud
   - Embezzlement
   - Harassment

2. **Identify the seven types of hackers and explain what motivates each group.** *Hackers* are knowledgeable computer users who use their knowledge to invade other people's computers. The seven types are

   - *Thrill-seeker hackers,* who are motivated by the entertainment value of breaking into computers
   - *White-hat hackers,* who are hired by a company to find the vulnerabilities in its network
   - *Black-hat hackers,* who are cyber vandals and cause damage for fun
   - *Crackers,* who are hackers for hire and are the people who engage in electronic corporate espionage
   - *Hacktivists,* who are politically motivated hackers who use the Internet to send a political message of some kind
   - *Cyberterrorists,* who seek to cause harm to people or destroy critical systems or information for political reasons
   - *Script kiddies* or *script bunnies,* who would like to be hackers but don't have much technical expertise

3. **Define digital forensics and describe the two phases of a forensic investigation.** *Digital forensics* is the collection, authentication, preservation, and examination of electronic information for presentation in court. Electronic evidence can be found on any type of computer storage medium. A computer forensic investigation has two phases: (1) collecting, authenticating, and preserving electronic evidence; and (2) analyzing the findings. The collection phase consists of

   - Getting physical access to the computer and any other items that might be helpful
   - Creating a *forensic image copy* of all storage media

- Authenticating the forensic image copy by generating an *MD5 hash value,* that, when recalculated at a later date will be exactly the same number, as long as nothing at all on the storage medium has changed in any way
- Using forensic hardware that can read storage media but cannot write to them
- Using forensic software that can find deleted, hidden, and otherwise hard-to-access information

The analysis phase consists of

- Finding all the information and deducing what it means
- Assembling a crime story that fits the information that has been discovered

4. **Describe what is meant by anti-forensics and give an example of each of the three types.** Anti-forensics is a name for tools that mask or eliminate traces of user activity on a computer. The three types are:

   1. Configuration settings—included in your operating system, browser, and applications like Word and Excel. An example is Shift + Delete to bypass the Recycle Bin.
   2. Third-party tools—utility software on the market that performs specific tasks. An example is encryption software.
   3. Forensic defeating software developed to remove or change the sort of data that forensics experts look for. An example is software that changes creation and access dates on files.

5. **Describe two ways in which businesses use digital forensics.** Corporations use computer forensics for proactive education and for reactive incident response. Education serves to explain to employees what they should and should not do with computer resources and also how to conduct an internal computer forensic investigation. Incident response involves uncovering employee wrongdoing and preserving the evidence so that action can be taken.

■ KEY TERMS AND CONCEPTS

■ SHORT-ANSWER QUESTIONS

1. In what two ways are computers used in the commission of crimes or misdeeds?
2. What constitutes a computer crime?
3. What kind of software is a computer virus?
4. How does a denial-of-service attack work?
5. What is the effect of a virus hoax?
6. What is the difference between the Klez family of viruses and previous worms?
7. What is a white-hat hacker?
8. What do crackers do?
9. Is there a difference between a cyberterrorist and a hacktivist? If so, what is it?
10. What is digital forensics?
11. What is anti-forensics?
12. What is live analysis?

■ ASSIGNMENTS AND EXERCISES

1. **FIND DIGITAL FORENSICS SOFTWARE** On the Web there are many sites that offer digital forensics software. Find five such software packages and for each one answer the following questions:

- What does the software do? List five features it advertises.
- Is the software free? If not, how much does it cost?
- Is there any indication of the software's target market? If so, what market is it (law enforcement, home use, or something else)?

2. **WHAT EXACTLY ARE THE SEDONA PRINCIPLES?** Figure H.14 mentioned the *Sedona Principles.* These 14 principles were developed by lawyers, consultants, academics, and jurists to address the many issues involved in antitrust suits, intellectual property disputes, and other types of complex litigation.

   Write a report on the stipulations of the *Sedona Principles.* Do some research and find out exactly what the *Sedona Principles* suggest. Here's the first one to get you started:

   1. Electronic data and documents are potentially discoverable under Fed.R. Civ. P. 34 or its state law equivalents. Organizations must properly preserve electronic data and documents that can reasonably be anticipated to be relevant to litigation.

   Be sure to explain in your paper any legal terms, such as "discoverable," which appears in the 1st principle above, and "spoliation," in the 14th principle.

3. **THE INTERNATIONAL ANTI-CYBERCRIME TREATY** Find out what the provisions of the international anti-cybercrime treaty are and how they will affect the United States. One of the concerns that will have to be addressed is the issue of whether laws of one country should apply to all. For example, if certain sites are illegal in Saudi Arabia, should they be illegal for all surfers? Or if Germany has a law about hate language, should a German or a U.S. citizen be extradited to stand trial for building a neo-Nazi Web site? What do you think?

4. **DOES THE FOURTH AMENDMENT APPLY TO COMPUTER SEARCH AND SEIZURE?** The U.S. Department of Justice's Computer Crime and Intellectual Property Section has an online manual to guide digital forensics experts through the legal requirements of the search and seizure of electronic information. It's available at www.cybercrime. gov/searchmanual.htm and has a section on "Reasonable Expectation of Privacy." There are four subsections: general principles, reasonable expectation of privacy in computers as storage devices, reasonable expectation of privacy and third-party possession, and private searches. Read and summarize these four subsections.

EXTENDED LEARNING MODULE I

BUILDING AN E-PORTFOLIO

Student Learning Outcomes

1. Describe the types of electronic résumés and specify when each is appropriate.

2. Discuss networking strategies you can use during a job search.

3. Explain how self-assessment is valuable to résumé writing.

4. Use the Internet to research career opportunities and potential employers.

5. Develop powerful job search e-portfolio content.

6. Document effective Web site structure and design components.

7. Create a job search e-portfolio Web site and place it on an Internet server.

Extended Learning Module I provides you with hands-on instructions for the most appropriate way to build an e-portfolio, an electronic resume that you publish on the Web in the hope of attracting potential employers. Important issues also cover aspects of building a strong objective statement and using strong action verbs to describe yourself and your accomplishments.

Extended Learning Module I can be found on the book's Web site at www.mhhe.com/haag.

EXTENDED LEARNING MODULE J

IMPLEMENTING A DATABASE WITH MICROSOFT ACCESS

Student Learning Outcomes

1. Identify the steps necessary to implement the structure of a relational database using the data definition language provided by Microsoft Access.

2. Demonstrate how to use the data manipulation subsystem in Access to enter and change information in a database and how to query that information.

3. Explain the use of the application generation subsystem in Access to create reports and data entry screens.

Introduction

A few short years ago, you could have performed a search of Monster.com and found literally hundreds of job postings requiring knowledge of Excel, spreadsheet software. Today, most companies *expect* you to know Excel—it's no longer a skill that will help you get a job; it's a necessity for evening getting an interview.

Today, the competitive advantage for many people seeking employment is a knowledge of database management system software, of which Microsoft Access is the most popular.

Some of the jobs that require familiarity with database management software are shown below:

• Senior Financial Analyst	• Senior Accountant
• Material Control Specialist	• Managed Care Analyst
• Property Administrator	• Loan Servicing Auditor
• Regulatory Specialist	• Quality Assurance Inspector
• Payroll Coordinator	• Regional Sales Manager
• Claim Associate	• Product Requirements Analyst
• Compensation Manager	• Quantitative Market Researcher
• Policy Analyst	• Merchandising Specialist
• Service Team Leader	• Marketing Manager

If you look carefully at the above list, you'll see that not a single job title is IT-specific. Rather, they represent job openings in such areas as finance, logistics, retail sales, health care, and marketing. If you read *Extended Learning Module K, Careers in Business,* you'll find that every single business area covered—accounting, finance, hospitality and tourism management, management, marketing, production and operations management, and real estate and construction management—lists database management as an IT skill you should pursue to be a success in those areas.

That's why we wrote this learning module—because a knowledge of database management system software can help you in your professional career. While it might not in and of itself help you land that really great job (who knows, perhaps it will), your work responsibilities will most probably include some forms of information management. Database management system software can you help you manage that information.

Solomon Enterprises Database

In Chapter 3 we discussed the important role that databases play in an organization. We followed that with *Extended Learning Module C,* in which you learned how to design the correct structure of a relational database. That module includes four primary steps. They are:

1. Define entity classes and primary keys.
2. Define relationships among the entity classes.
3. Define information (fields) for each relation (the terms *relation* and *table* are often used to refer to a file in the context of a database).
4. Use a data definition language to create your database.

In *Extended Learning Module C,* you followed the process through the first three steps above. In this module, we'll take you through the fourth step—using a data definition language to create your database—by exploring the use of Microsoft Access, today's most popular personal database management system package (it comes as part of Microsoft's Office Pro suite).

We'll also show you how to use Microsoft Access's data manipulation subsystem, including how to enter and change information and build queries; and how to use the application generation subsystem to create reports and input forms.

In Figure J.1 (on this page and the next) we've recreated the complete Solomon Enterprises database structure we defined in *Extended Learning Module C.* If it has been a while since you covered that module, we suggest that you review it before creating the database.

LEARNING OUTCOME 1

IMPLEMENTING THE STRUCTURE OF THE SOLOMON ENTERPRISES DATABASE

As we said previously, you can't simply start typing information into a database as you can when you create a document with Word or a workbook with Excel. You must first define the correct structure of the database (see *Extended Learning Module C*), and then create the structure of the database by creating its data dictionary before entering any information. The ***data dictionary*** contains the logical structure for the information in a database. It includes a description of each relation (also called a *table* or *file*) and each piece of information in each relation.

Figure J.1

The Database Structure
We'll Be Implementing

CONCRETE TYPE RELATION

Concrete Type	Type Description
1	Home foundation and walkways
2	Commercial foundation and walkways
3	Premier speckled (with smooth gravel aggregate)
4	Premier marble (with crushed marble aggregate)
5	Premier shell (with shell aggregate)

CUSTOMER RELATION

Customer Number	Customer Name	Customer Phone	Customer Primary Contact
1234	Smelding Homes	3333333333	Bill Johnson
2345	Home Builders Superior	3334444444	Marcus Connolly
3456	Mark Akey	3335555555	Mark Akey
4567	Triple A Homes	3336666666	Janielle Smith
5678	Sheryl Williamson	3337777777	Sheryl Williamson
6789	Home Makers	3338888888	John Yu

EMPLOYEE RELATION

Employee ID	Employee Last Name	Employee First Name	Date of Hire
123456789	Johnson	Emilio	2/1/1985
435296657	Evaraz	Antonio	3/3/1992
785934444	Robertson	John	6/1/1999
984568756	Smithson	Allison	4/1/1997

SUPPLIER RELATION

Supplier ID	Supplier Name
412	Wesley Enterprises
444	Juniper Sand & Gravel
499	A&J Brothers
999	N/A

TRUCK RELATION

Truck Number	Truck Type	Date of Purchase
111	Ford	6/17/1999
222	Ford	12/24/2001
333	Chevy	1/1/2002

Figure J.1

The Database Structure
We'll Be Implementing
(continued)

ORDER RELATION

Order Number	Order Date	Customer Number	Delivery Address	Concrete Type	Amount	Truck Number	Driver ID
100000	9/1/2004	1234	55 Smith Lane	1	8	111	123456789
100001	9/1/2004	3456	2122 E. Biscayne	1	3	222	785934444
100002	9/2/2004	1234	55 Smith Lane	5	6	222	435296657
100003	9/3/2004	4567	1333 Burr Ridge	2	4	333	435296657
100004	9/4/2004	4567	1333 Burr Ridge	2	8	222	785934444
100005	9/4/2004	5678	1222 Westminster	1	4	222	785934444
100006	9/5/2004	1234	222 East Hampton	1	4	111	123456789
100007	9/6/2004	2345	9 W. Palm Beach	2	5	333	785934444
100008	9/6/2004	6789	4532 Lane Circle	1	8	222	785934444
100009	9/7/2004	1234	987 Furlong	3	8	111	123456789
100010	9/9/2004	6789	4532 Lane Circle	2	7	222	435296657
100011	9/9/2004	4567	3500 Tomahawk	5	6	222	785934444

RAW MATERIAL RELATION

Raw Material ID	Raw Material Name	QOH	Supplier ID
A	Water	9999	999
B	Cement paste	400	412
C	Sand	1200	444
D	Gravel	200	444
E	Marble	100	499
F	Shell	25	499

BILL OF MATERIAL RELATION

Concrete Type	Raw Material ID	Unit
1	B	1
1	C	2
1	A	1.5
2	B	1
2	C	2
2	A	1
3	B	1
3	C	2
3	A	1.5
3	D	3
4	B	1
4	C	2
4	A	1.5
4	E	2
5	B	1
5	C	2
5	A	1.5
5	F	2.5

Figure J.2

The First Step in Creating
a Database

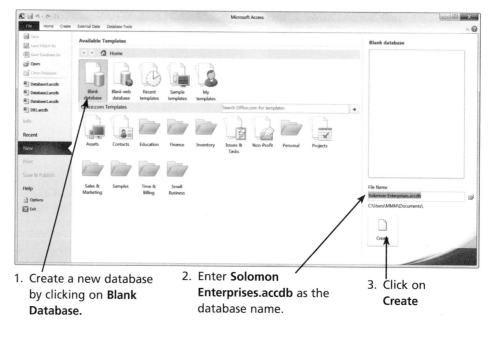

1. Create a new database
by clicking on **Blank
Database.**

2. Enter **Solomon
Enterprises.accdb** as the
database name.

3. Click on
Create

To create a database using Microsoft Access, we performed the following steps (see Figure J.2). We will assume you already have Microsoft Access open.

1. Click on **Blank Database** in the upper left corner of the screen.
2. Enter **Solomon Enterprises.accdb** as the database name.
3. Click on **Create.**

Throughout this module, we will include numerous steps and screen captures (labeled according to the step) for clarification.

After we followed these steps, we got the upper left screen in Figure J.3. Now that we've created a blank database with the name **Solomon Enterprises.accdb,** we're ready to define the structure of the database.

There are two main ways to create the data dictionary for e relation: in Datasheet View; and in Design View. They both achieve the same result. We'll do so using the Design View. The upper left screen in Figure J.3 allows you to create a relation in Datasheet View. To switch to Design View, click on **View** in the upper left corner of the screen and then click on **Design View** (the upper right Screen in Figure J.3). Access will ask you for a file name (the lower left screen in Figure J.3), and we entered *Raw Material* (and clicked on **OK**) because that is the first relation we're going to work with. Access then presented us with the lower right screen in Figure J.3, which is the Design View for the *Raw Material* relation.

IMPLEMENTING THE *RAW MATERIAL* RELATION STRUCTURE

In the lower right screen in Figure J.3, Access will now allow us to enter field names, data types, and descriptions (the last is optional) for the *Raw Material* relation. We'll also be entering some information in the **Field Properties** box in the lower portion of the screen. That area shows the various field properties for whatever field we have selected in the top portion of the screen.

Once you have entered all that information for a given relation, you save that structure and repeat the process until you've created the structure for each relation in your database. We'll do that for three of the relations in Solomon's database.

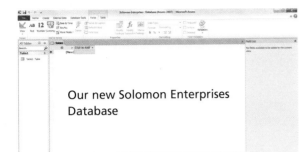

Our new Solomon Enterprises Database

This is Datasheet View. To create a data dictionary in Design View, click on **View** and then **Design View.**

Before creating a data dictionary in Design View, you must first provide a table name. We did so with *Raw Material.*

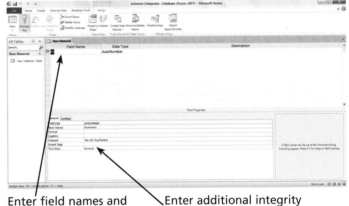

Enter field names and data types here.

Enter additional integrity constraints in **Field Properties.**

Figure J.3

The First Step in Defining the Structure for Each Relation

To start, let's implement the structure for the *Raw Material* relation within **Solomon Enterprises.accdb.** The *Raw Material* relation has four fields: *Raw Material ID, Raw Material Name, QOH,* and *Supplier ID.* As you can see in the lower right screen in Figure J.3, Access assumes that the first field name is *ID* and that its Data Type is **AutoNumber,** meaning that the first record will have an ID of 1, the second will have an ID of 2, and so on. If this is the format you want for the first field, you can accept it and move to defining the second field.

But we want the first field name to be *Raw Material ID* and its data type to be text (all numbers and characters). To implement that, we clicked in the first row of the **Field Name** column, deleted *ID,* and entered *Raw Material ID.* We then moved to the **Data Type** for that field (by using the tab key), clicked on the pull down arrow, and selected **Text.** The result of those actions is shown in the screen in Figure J.4. Now, take a look at the **Field Properties** in that screen. The **Field Size** defaults to 255 characters, which we changed to 1 because our *Raw Material IDs* range from A to F, one single character.

We also changed **Required** to Yes because we want to require that each raw material have a *Raw Material ID.* That is an example of an integrity constraint. *Integrity constraints* are rules that help ensure the quality of information. And we also changed **Allow Zero Length** to *No,* which again requires that something is entered in the *Raw Material ID* when a new record is added. The result of our changes is shown in the screen in Figure J.4.

To complete creating the structure of the *Raw Material* relation, we then clicked in the second row in the **Field Name** column and proceeded to enter the field names and data types for the three remaining fields of *Raw Material Name, QOH,* and *Supplier ID.* The screen showing the final structure of the Raw Material relation is shown in Figure J.5.

Figure J.4

Creating vthe *Raw Material* Relation Structure

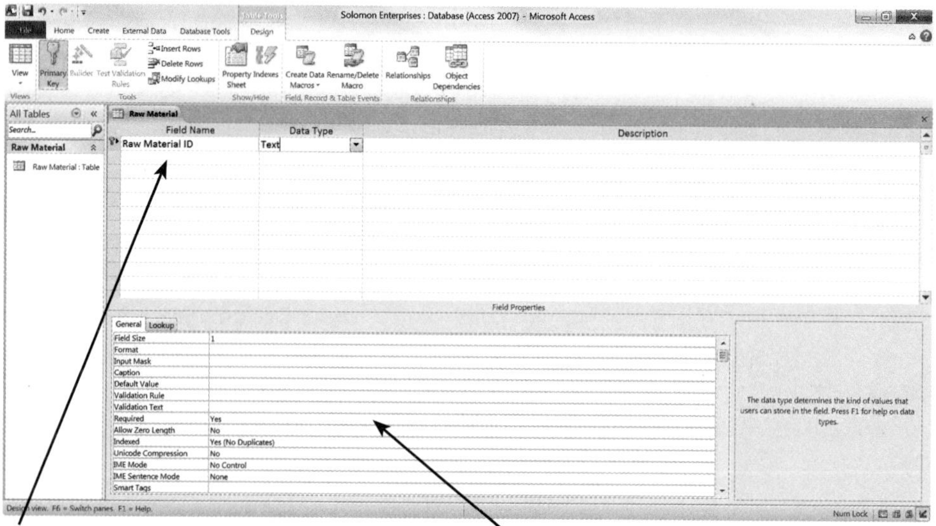

Raw Material ID with a **Data Type** of **Text**.

Raw Material ID with various integrity constraints.

When creating the data dictionary entries for both *QOH* and *Supplier ID,* we chose **Number** as the data type and set **Decimal Places** to zero in the **Field Properties** box. For *Supplier ID,* we also changed **Required** to Yes because we want to know which supplier is providing a given *Raw Material.* These are more examples of integrity constraints that Access will now enforce for us.

Access defaults to identifying the first field as the primary key. A ***primary key*** is a field (or group of fields in some cases) that uniquely describes each record. In our case,

Figure J.5

The Final Structure for the *Raw Material* Relation

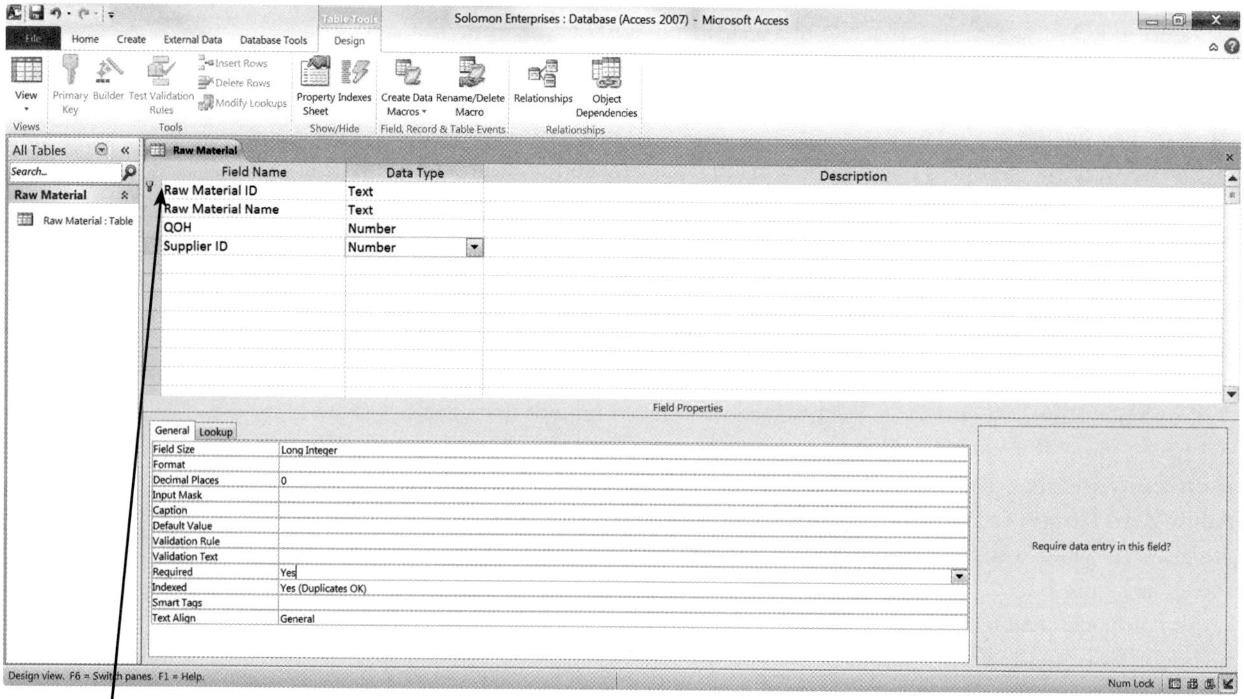

Raw Material ID is the primary key, identified by the **key** icon next to the field row.

the *Raw Material ID*, which we placed in the first field, is the primary key. If you need to change that, position the cursor in the line of the appropriate primary key field and click on the **Primary key** button in the menu area.

To save the structure (which you'll need to do if you make any changes), click on the **Save** button (the disk icon) in the upper left corner of the screen.

IMPLEMENTING THE *CONCRETE TYPE* RELATION STRUCTURE

To develop the structures of the remaining relations, you simply follow the process outlined in the previous section. Let's now create the structure for the *Concrete Type* relation. To create the *Concrete Type* relation using the Design View (you can have the Design View open for the *Raw Material* relation from the previous task), click on **Create** in the menu and then click on the **Table** button.

You will once again see a blank and unnamed table in Datasheet View. Click on the **View** button, select **Design View,** enter a new table name (*Concrete Type* in this instance), and click on **OK.** What you will then see is a screen identical to the lower right screen in Figure J.3 on page 477 that we used to create the *Raw Material* relation, only now we're creating the *Concrete Type* relation.

In Figure J.6, you can see that we entered the field names of *Concrete Type* and *Type Description*. *Concrete Type* is also the name of the table, and that's fine if it suits your purpose. *Concrete Type* is a numeric field (**Number**) and *Type Description* is a text field. *Concrete Type* is the primary key field as you can see by the Key icon to the left of the field name.

Specifically, for each we made some additional modifications to their field properties as follows:

- *Concrete Type*
  - **Decimal Places** = zero
  - **Required** = Yes

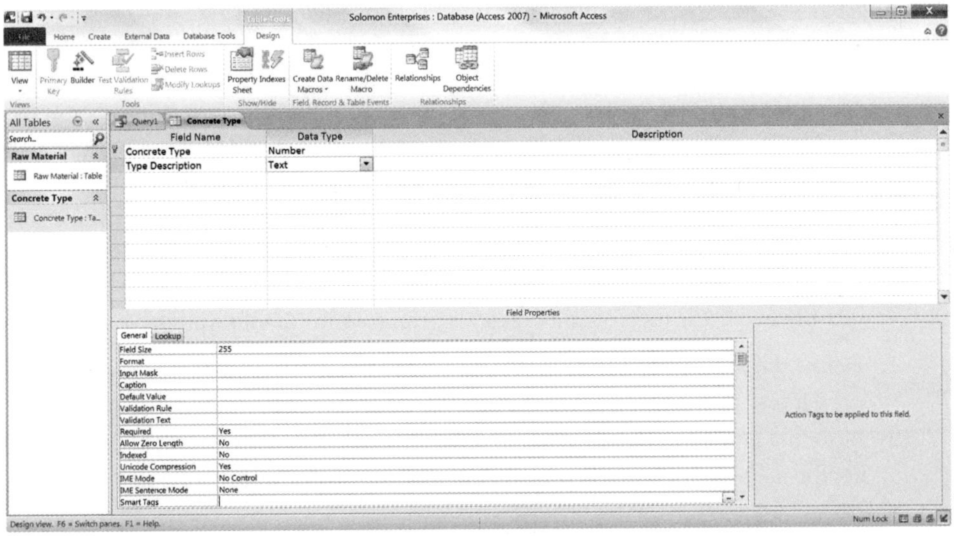

Figure J.6

Creating the *Concrete Type* Relation Structure

Figure J.7

Creating the *Bill of Material* Relation Structure

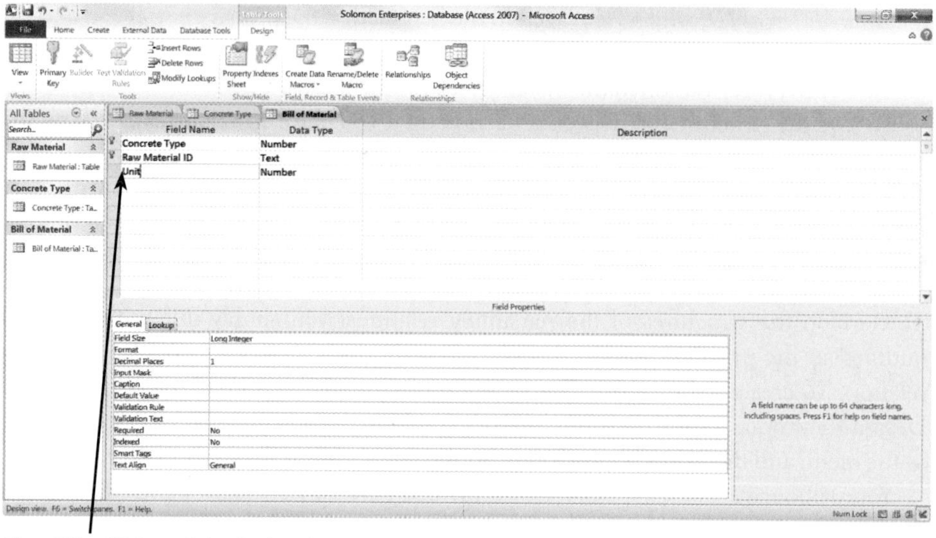

The *Bill of Material* relation is a composite relation, meaning that it has two fields (*Concrete Type and Raw Material ID*) making up the primary key.

- *Type Description*
  - **Required** = Yes
  - **Allow Zero Length** = No

We did this to further enforce integrity constraints within the database. We then saved this table structure by clicking on **Save**—the disk icon—in the upper left portion of the screen.

IMPLEMENTING THE *BILL OF MATERIAL* RELATION STRUCTURE

The last relation that we'll cover here is that of the *Bill of Material* relation. As you can see in Figure J.7, we've entered all the field names and their types.

This relation is a little different from the rest because it has a composite primary key. A **composite primary key** consists of the primary key fields from the two intersecting relations. An **intersection relation** (sometimes called a **composite relation**) is a relation you create to eliminate a many-to-many relationship. In *Extended Learning Module C,* we created the *Bill of Material* relation to eliminate the many-to-many relationship that existed between *Concrete Type* and *Raw Material.* So, the *Bill of Material* relation has a primary key composed of two fields: the primary key *Concrete Type* from the *Concrete Type* relation and the primary key *Raw Material ID* from the *Raw Material* relation. The primary key of the *Bill of Material* relation is a composite primary key. Make sure that you define *Concrete Type* and *Raw Material ID* exactly as you did in the previous tables.

To identify two fields that together create a primary key, we followed these steps:

1. Define the basic structure of the relation by entering the field names and their properties.
2. Move the pointer to the column immediately to the left of the first field name of the composite primary key (the pointer will turn into an arrow pointing to the right).
3. Click on that row and don't unclick.

Relation	Notes
Customer	*Customer Number:* Primary key, Number, no decimals, required entry *Customer Name:* Text, required entry *Customer Phone:* Text (so you can add parentheses around the area code and a dash if you wish), required entry (optional for our purposes) *Customer Primary Contact:* Text, required entry (optional for our purposes)
Employee	*Employee ID:* Primary key, Number, no decimals, required entry *Employee Last Name:* Text, required entry (optional for our purposes) *Employee First Name:* Text, required entry (optional for our purposes) *Date of Hire:* Date/Time, required entry (optional for our purposes)
Supplier	*Supplier ID:* Primary key, Number, no decimals, required entry *Supplier Name:* Text, required entry (optional for our purposes)
Truck	*Truck Number:* Primary key, Number, no decimals, required entry *Truck Type:* Text, required entry (optional for our purposes) *Date of Purchase:* Date/Time, required entry (optional for our purposes)
Order	*Order Number:* Primary key, Number, no decimals, required entry *Order Date:* Date/Time, required entry *Customer Number:* Number, no decimals, required entry *Delivery Address:* Text, required entry (optional for our purposes) *Concrete Type:* Number, no decimals, required entry *Amount:* Number, no decimals, required entry *Truck Number:* Number, no decimals, required entry *Driver ID:* Number, no decimals, required entry

4. Drag the pointer so that the second field in the composite primary key is also highlighted.
5. Unclick.
6. Click on the **Primary Key** button.

The Key icon will appear next to each of the two fields, identifying that together they make up a composite primary key.

You now need to create the relation structures for *Employee, Order, Supplier, Truck,* and *Customer*. We'll leave that task to you. However, you can use Figure J.8 as a reference guide as it provides notes concerning data types, keys, and the like for each field in those relations.

Figure J.9
Primary and Foreign Key
Logical Ties

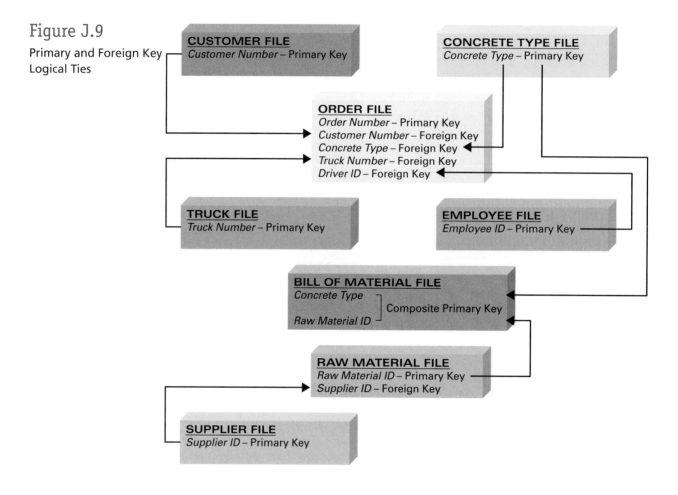

Defining Relationships within the Solomon Enterprises Database

So far, we've created the structure of the relations for our database. In other words, we specified the names and types of the field in each of the tables. As you can see, the process is very different from creating a word processing document or a workbook. We haven't yet entered any information into our database. We have one last structural issue to take care of, and that is to define how all the relations or files relate to each other.

Recall from our discussions in Chapter 3 and *Extended Learning Module C* that you can create relationships among the various tables by identifying foreign keys. A *foreign key* is a primary key of one file (relation) that appears in another file (relation). See Figure J.9 for the logical ties between primary and foreign keys.

Note that all the foreign keys have the same names as the primary keys in the original tables, except for *Employee ID,* which becomes *Driver ID* in the *Order* relation.

It's vitally important that you establish the relationships between primary and foreign keys. That way, the DBMS can enforce integrity constraints and disallow inconsistent information being entered. For example, when we specify that *Supplier ID* is a foreign key (from the *Supplier* relation) in the *Raw Material* relation, the DBMS will not allow us to enter a *Supplier ID* in the *Raw Material* relation that does not appear as a primary

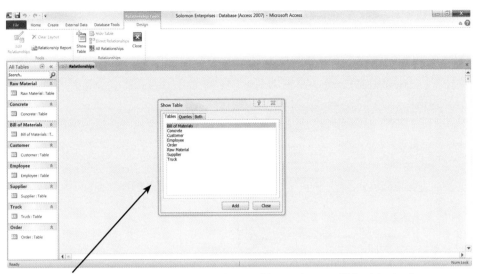

When you first start this process, the **Relationships** palette will be blank. As you highlight each relation and click on the **Add** button in the **Show Table** box, the relation will appear on the palette.

key in the *Supplier* relation. This makes business sense: You can't get raw material from a supplier who doesn't exist.

Prior to creating these relationships, you need to close all tables that you have open. You can easily right click on a tab and select **Close.** Then, to create these relationships, which means telling Access which fields are foreign keys, you click on the **Database Tools** in the menu area and then click on the **Relationships** button. You'll then see the screen in Figure J.10. Notice that it lists all of the relations in our database. When you first start this process, the palette in the background is blank. To identify the relationships, you must make each relation appear on the palette. To do this, simply highlight each relation name and click **Add.** When you have all the tables on the palette, click on the **Close** button to make the **Show Table** box disappear. When all the tables are on the palette, you're ready to identify how all the tables relate to each other.

To do this (and you must follow this process exactly), we clicked on and dragged each primary key to its respective foreign key counterpart and dropped it there. Once you drop the primary key onto its foreign key counterpart, you'll see the Edit Relationships box (see Figure J.11 on the next page). In that box, we clicked on **Enforce Referential Integrity** and then **Create.**

When you drag and drop a primary key onto a foreign key, Microsoft Access assumes that the relationship is one-to-many (1:M). That is, a primary key may appear many times as a foreign key, and a foreign key must appear once and only once as a primary key. If you perform the process in reverse (dragging and dropping the foreign key onto a primary key), the relationship will be reversed (M:1), which is not what you want.

You also need to turn on the enforcement of referential integrity. By doing so, your DBMS will make sure that when you enter a foreign key in a relation it matches one of the primary keys in the other relation. Figure J.11 shows the **Edit Relationships** box we got when we dragged and dropped *Raw Material ID* from the *Raw Material* relation onto *Raw Material ID* in the *Bill of Material* relation. We also clicked on **Enforce Referential Integrity** and **Create** and got the connecting lines you see between the other pairs of relations.

In Figure J.11, you can see many instances of a line connecting the primary key in one relation to the foreign key in another. Let's look first at the relationship between the

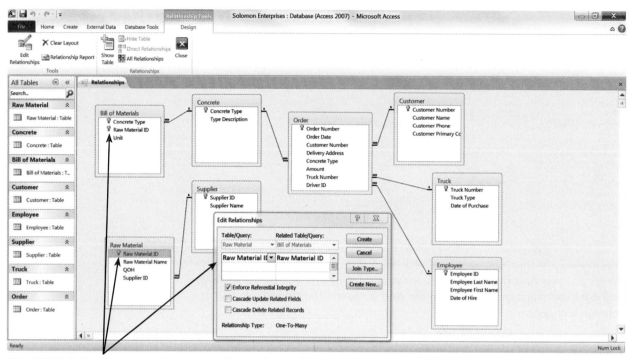

This **Edit Relationship** box is the result of dragging and dropping *Raw Material ID* from the *Raw Material* relation onto the *Bill of Material* relation. As a general rule, you should turn on **Enforce Referential Integrity** to protect your database from inconsistent data. Then, click on the **Create** button and you get the connecting line.

Figure J.11

Defining Relationships
for the Solomon
Enterprises Database

Supplier and *Raw Material* relations where Access shows a connecting line between *Supplier* and *Raw Material* with a 1 near the *Supplier* relation and an infinity symbol (∞) near the *Raw Material* relation. Likewise, a *Supplier ID* that appears in the *Raw Material* relation can appear only one time in the *Supplier* relation. Also note that the foreign key can have a different name than the primary key, as, for example, *Employee ID* in the *Employee* relation becomes *Driver ID* in the *Order* relation. This is quite permissible, and how you name the field depends on your context.

Once we completed this process, we clicked on **Save** (the disk button) to save the relationships and then closed the **Relationships** box.

Entering Information into the Solomon Database

LEARNING OUTCOME 2

Finally, we're ready to begin entering information to populate the tables. We've defined the structure for each relation in the Solomon Enterprises database, and we've defined the relationships among the tables. See Figure J.12 for the Design View of the *Supplier* relation that we created in the same manner as the *Concrete Type* relation.

To enter information, you simply double-click on the table name in the list of tables on the far left (see the upper left screen in Figure J.13 on the next page). Does it matter which relation you start with when entering information? It does if you've chosen to enforce referential integrity when you created the relationships among the relations. We can't enter information into the *Raw Material* relation yet because we need to put in a

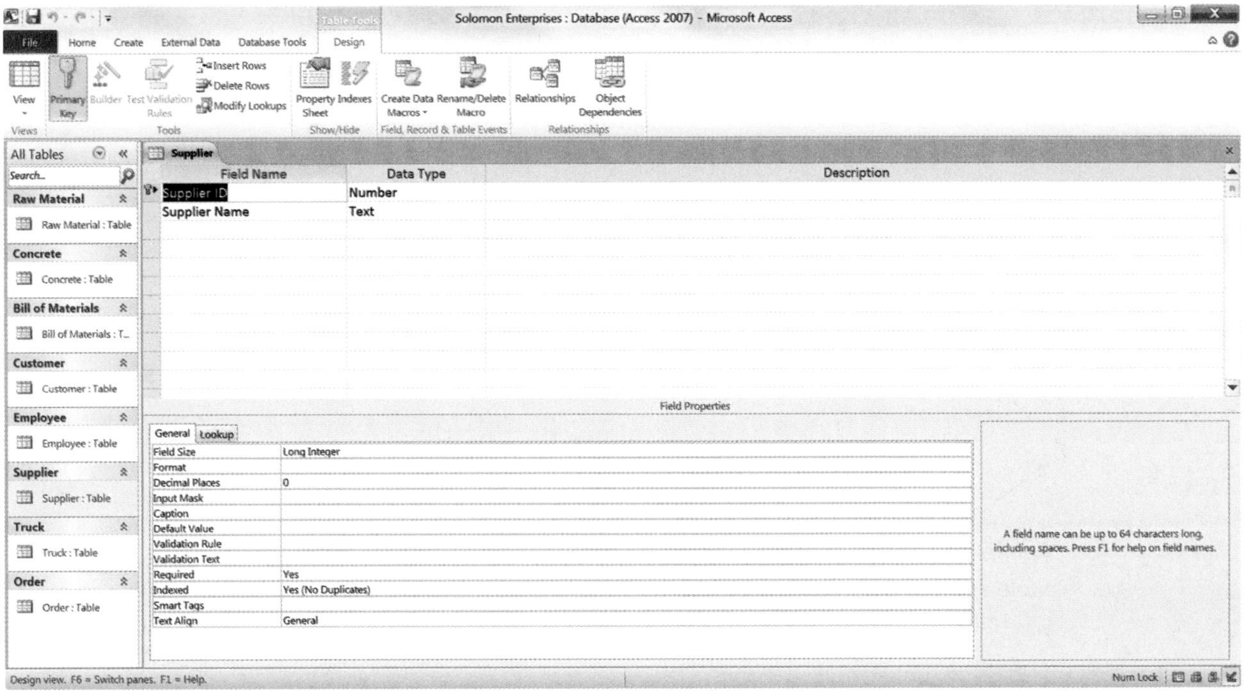

Figure J.12

Design View of the Structure of the *Supplier* Relation

Supplier ID for each row and we've not yet entered the *Supplier ID* information into the *Supplier* relation. Therefore, if we try to put a *Supplier ID* into the *Raw Material* relation that is not in the *Supplier* relation, referential integrity will be violated and Access will display an error alert and not allow us to continue.

Before entering information into those relations that have foreign keys, you must first enter information into those tables with primary keys that show up as foreign keys in other tables. So, we must complete the information entry for the *Concrete Type, Customer, Employee, Supplier,* and *Truck* relations before populating the *Raw Material, Bill of Material,* and *Order* relations.

In the lower right screen in Figure J.13, you can see that we have opened the *Supplier* relation and are now ready to begin entering information. After typing in the appropriate information into each field, we used the **Tab** key to get to the next field or row. Once we entered all the information (see the lower right screen in Figure J.13), and closed the tab for the *Supplier* table, the information was automatically saved by Access. We can then move on to entering information into the other relations.

Next, we'll populate the *Raw Material* relation, which has *Supplier ID* as a foreign key. In the screen on the left of Figure J.14 you can see that we've already entered some of the information; however, as the error message shows, we put in an incorrect *Supplier ID* (445 instead of 444). When we established the relationship between the *Raw Material* and *Supplier* relations, we chose the **Enforce Referential Integrity** option, so Access won't allow us to enter a *Supplier ID* in the *Raw Material* relation that doesn't already exist in the *Supplier* relation. That's why we got the dialog box informing us of the problem. If we click on **OK,** Access will give us a chance to fix the problem. If we don't fix the problem and we try to exit this window (see the screen on the right in Figure J.14), Access will alert us with a new box telling us that the incorrect information will not be saved (although the good information will).

Figure J.13

Entering Information
into the *Supplier* Relation

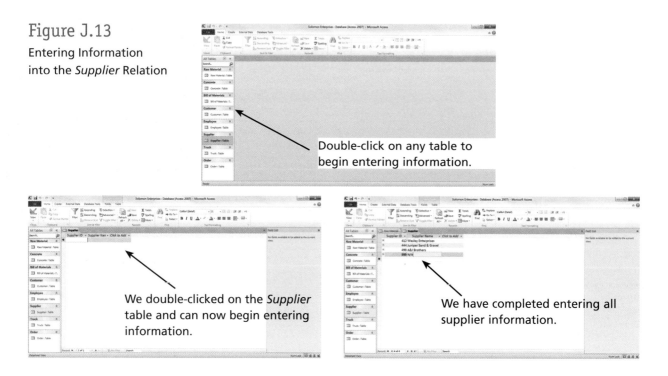

Double-click on any table to
begin entering information.

We double-clicked on the *Supplier*
table and can now begin entering
information.

We have completed entering all
supplier information.

Up to this point, we've entered the information into the *Supplier* and *Raw Material* relations. The process is identical for entering information into the other relations. But you do need to keep in mind the order in which you enter information into the other relations. You will need to enter information into those relations first whose primary keys will appear as foreign keys in other relations.

You should now enter all the information into the remaining relations just as we have done for the *Supplier* and *Raw Material* relations. We suggest you enter information into the other relations in the order below:

1. *Concrete Type*
2. *Customer*
3. *Employee*
4. *Truck*

Figure J.14

Encountering an Integrity
Error While Entering
Information

Because we entered a *Supplier* ID (445) that doesn't exist in the supplier relation, Access will not allow us to continue.

If you try to close the information entry window, Access will allow you to change the information or save the good information without the bad.

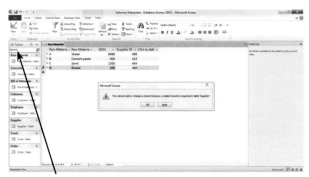

While in Datasheet View, you can change the structure of a relation only by clicking on **View** and then **Design View**.

In Design View, you can change the structure of a table.

Figure J.15

Changing the Structure of a Relation

5. *Bill of Material*

6. *Order*

The first four are interchangeable in terms of ordering as are the bottom two.

CHANGING THE STRUCTURE OF INFORMATION IN RELATIONS

If you want to change the information in any of the relations or the structure of any of the relations, you can do so quite easily. However, you need to be careful about deleting fields that you used to establish relationships between pairs of tables.

The simpler task is to add, change, or delete records in a relation. To add a record, you simply open the relation and add the new information at the bottom. Recall that to open a relation you double-click on its name in the list of tables on the left of the Access screen. To change information in a field, click on the appropriate field and make the change. To delete a record, highlight the record (row) you want deleted and press the **Delete** key on the keyboard.

To change the structure of a relation, you'll need to open the Design View for the relation. To do this, first open the relation by double-clicking on its name. What Access will present to you is the table in Datasheet View (the left screen in Figure J.15). To switch to Design View, click on the **View** button and select **Design View.** Access will show you the Design View of the table and you can then make the necessary changes to the -structure of that relation (see the right screen in Figure J.15).

Creating a Simple Query Using One Relation

The easiest way to create a query is to use a query-by-example tool. A *query-by-example (QBE) tool* helps you graphically design the answer to a question. Suppose, for example, that we wanted to see a list of all the names of all the raw materials and the IDs of the associated suppliers for each raw material. All that information is located in the *Raw Material* relation, making it a relatively simple query requiring the use of only a single relation. Realize, of course, that our Solomon database is small and the query doesn't make much

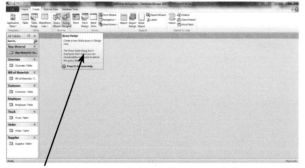

1. To create a query, click on **Create** and then **Query Design**.

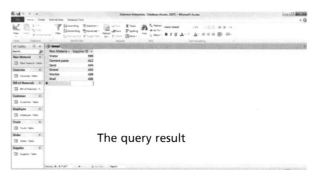

2. Select the appropriate table name, click on **Add,** and then close the box.

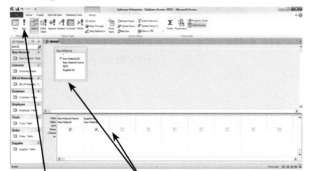

4. Click on the exclamation point (**Run**) to see the result of query.

3. Now, drag and drop *Raw Material Name* and *Supplier ID* from the *Raw Material* table to the QBE grid.

The query result

Figure J.16

Creating a Simple Query Using One Relation

sense since you could easily open the *Raw Material* relation and see the information you want. However, the objective is to demonstrate the use of a QBE tool. In the next section, we'll create a more complicated query. But first let's look at a simple query.

To create a simple query using only the *Raw Material* relation, perform the following steps (see Figure J.16):

1. Click on **Create** in the menu area and then **Query Design** in the button bar area.
2. In the **Show Table** dialog box, select the appropriate relation name, click on **Add,** and then close the **Show Table** dialog box.
3. Drag and drop the fields that you want in the query results into the QBE grid.
4. Click on the exclamation point (**Run**) in the button bar.

As you can see in Figure J.16, we followed that process by selecting the *Raw Material* relation, and dragging and dropping *Raw Material Name* and *Supplier ID* into the QBE grid. Once we clicked on the exclamation point button, Access returned a list of raw materials along with the ID of the supplier for each item.

If we wanted to be able to use this query at a later time, we could save the query, giving it a unique name such as *Raw Materials and Suppliers.* Then, the next time we need that information, we could simply open up that query in the Datasheet View (the view that shows the information) rather than having to start from scratch creating the query.

SIMPLE QUERY WITH A CONDITION (CONDITIONAL QUERY)

Creating a query with only one relation is pretty simple. So, let's add another requirement to our query. Let's say we wanted to see which raw materials from which suppliers

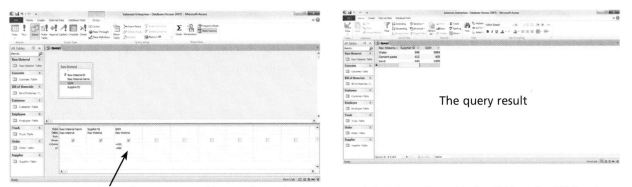

To create a conditional query, we add *QOH* from the *Raw Material* table and specify "= 400" or "> 400" in the **Criteria** fields.

Figure J.17

A Conditional Query Using One Relation

we have in quantities of 400 or more units. This is a conditional query because it will return a result based on some condition. This conditional query requires an extra couple of steps in the process we just outlined.

In Figure J.17, you can see that we again selected only the *Raw Material* relation since it contains all the information we need. However, this time we also dragged and dropped *QOH* into the QBE grid. Within the QBE grid, we added two important items of information to the query.

The first was to unselect the **Show** parameter. By doing so, we tell Access that we want to use *QOH* as part of the query, but that we don't want it to show in the query result. The second is to enter "=**400**" (without the quotation marks) in the **Criteria** parameter and then "**>400**" (again, without quotes) right below. In doing this, we're telling Access that we want to see only those raw materials that we have in quantities equal to 400 (first **Criteria** line) or greater than 400 (the **or** line). As you can see in the right screen of Figure J.17, Access provides information for only three raw materials, all of which Solomon has quantities on hand of 400 or more units. Also note that the *QOH* field does not show.

If you were looking for suppliers of Gravel, you would put "Gravel" (with or without quotation marks) into the **Criteria** box associated with *Raw Material Name,* but you must be sure to spell it correctly. The capitalization doesn't matter but the right letters (and digits and spaces, if applicable) in the right places do.

Creating an Advanced Query Using More than One Relation

What about queries that require information residing in two or perhaps several different relations? Access can handle those too. We just have to tell it where to get the information and make sure that the tables that need to reference each other have relationships already defined. For example, say we wanted to put the *Supplier Name* instead of the *Supplier ID* into a query that shows *Raw Material ID* and *Raw Material Name* and where Solomon Enterprises gets these items. We would need the *Raw Material* relation and also the *Supplier* relation and would want Access to take the *Supplier ID* from the *Raw Material* relation and match it to the *Supplier ID* in the *Supplier* relation to find the correct *Supplier Name.*

The previous query would involve two tables. But Access can handle information from many tables in one query, so let's look at a more complex example. Say the accounts receivable manager at Solomon is trying to sort out a problem with order numbers. So, the manager wants to know the following information:

- All order numbers
- Date of orders
- Where the goods were delivered
- The contact person at the delivery destination
- Which truck was involved in each delivery
- Who drove the delivery truck

We need to start by determining which relations to use. The fields we need are in the *Order, Customer, Employee,* and *Truck* relations. So these are the ones we'll use.

Table	Fields
Order	Order Number
	Order Date
	Delivery Address
Customer	Customer Primary Contact
Employee	Employee Last Name
Truck	Truck Type

We'll follow the same set of steps as we did when creating the simple query using one relation and make some modifications along the way to generate a more complex report (see Figure J.18).

1. Click on **Create** in the menu area and then **Query Design** in the button bar area.
2. In the **Show Table** dialog box, select the appropriate relation names (*Customer, Order, Employee,* and *Truck*), clicking on **Add** each time, and then close the **Show Table** dialog box. Here, as the tables that are linked by primary and foreign keys appear in the palette, they are joined by lines with the 1 beside the table that has the primary key and the infinity symbol (∞) near the table that has the foreign key. These symbols are showing you the 1:M relationships.
3. Drag and drop the fields that you want from the appropriate relation into the QBE grid in the order that you want.
4. Click on the exclamation point (**Run**) in the button bar.

And that's it. It's not significantly more difficult than using just one relation. The critical part in using multiple tables in a query is to make sure that the tables are linked correctly. Creating queries is not all that difficult using a QBE tool such as we have been doing in the previous three query examples. You simply need to take some time and practice creating queries. So, take some time here before learning how to create reports to create some queries. Below, we've listed some queries you can perform. Once you perform them, compare your results with a classmate to ensure that both of you are performing the query correctly.

1. Show all customers by only *Customer Number*, *Customer Name*, and *Customer Primary Contact*.

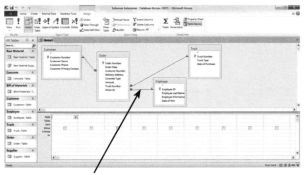

2. From the **Show Table** box, select the appropriate tables-*Customer, Order, Employee,* and *Truck.*

3. Drag and drop *Order Number, Order Date, Delivery Address, Customer Primary Contact, Employee Last Name,* and *Truck Type into* the QBE grid.

4. Click on the Exclamation Point **(Run)** button to execute the query.

The query result

Figure J.18

Creating an Advanced Query Using More than One Relation

2. Show all orders by only *Order Number, Delivery Address, Amount,* and *Truck Number.*

3. Show all raw materials by only *Raw Material ID, Raw Material Name,* and *QOH.*

4. Show the following information for all raw materials: *Raw Material ID, Raw Material Name,* and *Supplier Name.*

5. Show the following information for all orders: *Order Number, Delivery Address, Amount,* and *Driver ID.*

6. Show the following information for all concrete types: *Concrete Type, Type Description, Raw Material ID,* and *Unit.*

7. Show the following information for all orders that have more than 4 for *Amount: Order Number, Order Date, Delivery Address,* and *Truck Number.*

8. Show the following information for all orders using *Truck Number* 111: *Order Number, Order Date,* and *Delivery Address.*

Generating a Simple Report

LEARNING OUTCOME 3

Now that you know how to create a database and construct queries, let's see about making the output look better. The fundamental difference between tables (or queries) and reports is that a report is designed for human consumption; that is, it has the information

1. To create a report, click on **Create** and then **Report Wizard.**

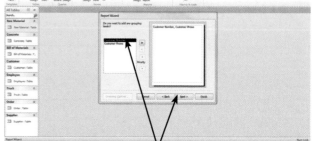

2. Select the *Customer* table.

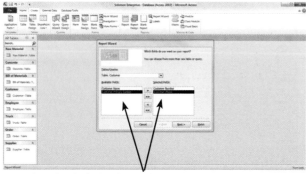

3. Select both fields by clicking on each and clicking on the >.

4. Choose grouping: We don't need grouping in this report so click on **Next.**

Figure J.19

Creating a Report Using One Relation

arranged so that it looks nice and is easy to read. The output includes headings and footers, and usually includes page numbers and the date of the report.

We'll start with a fairly simply example. As was the case with tables and queries, you can create a report using the Design View or the appropriate wizard. We're going to use the report wizard first to create a simple report and then a more complex one that we will modify using the Design View.

Let's say we want a report showing all our customers' names and phone numbers. This involves only one table, since both of the fields we want are in the *Customer* relation. To create this report, we followed the steps below (see Figure J.19 on this page and J.20 on the next page):

1. Click on **Create** in the menu area and then click on the **Report Wizard** button.
2. Choose tables and/or queries: This screen lets you choose which table or query you want to show in your report. We selected **Table: Customer** in the **Tables/ Queries** box.
3. Choose fields: In this screen you can choose the fields you want from the tables and/or queries you chose in the previous step. So, under **Available Fields,** we selected *Customer Name* and clicked on the greater-than sign (>) to the right. Next, we selected *Customer Phone* and clicked once more on the greater-than sign (>).
4. Grouping: This screen allows you to specify grouping of information. Here we accepted the default by clicking on **Next >.**
5. Sorting: This screen allows you to specify sorting of information. We chose not to sort so we clicked on **Next >.**

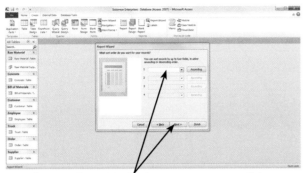

5. Select sorting: We don't want to sort so click on **Next**.

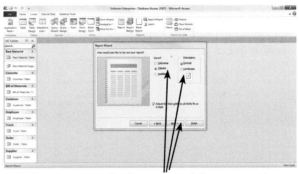

6. Select layout and orientation of the report: To accept the default, click on **Next**.

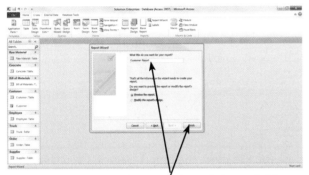

7. Enter a report heading and then click on **Finish**.

The completed report

Figure J.20

Creating a Report Using One Relation

6. Layout and orientation of the report: This screen allows you to select layout and page orientation. Again, we accepted the default and clicked on **Next** >.

7. Report header: This screen allows us to enter a title for the report. So, we entered "Customer Report" (without the quotation marks) in the title box and clicked on **Finish**.

8. The report: The report shows all customers and their phone numbers along with the settings that were selected in the wizard steps (see Figure J.20).

The completed report shows the two fields of information we requested in the style we chose in a more polished form than you get by simply printing a query with the same two fields.

You can change the report by using either the **Design View** or the **Layout View**. **Layout View** works best when you need to change the look and feel of a report. For example, you can rearrange fields or change their sizes. In contrast, **Design View** gives you control over every facet of your report. For example, you can add text boxes that display the date and time that you ran a report. In this report we will use the **Layout View** which is the simpler of the two and in the next report we will use the **Design View**.

1. Click on **Close Print Preview** to get to the other views (see Figure J.21).

2. Click on **View** and **Layout View**.

3. Now you can click on the headings or an item of data and you will be able to quickly change the position or the size of the headings and the data.

Figure J.21

Changing the look of the report in layout view

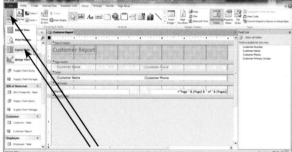

Click on the **Close Print Preview.**

Go to **View** and choose **Layout View.**

Now you can move the report elements and change the look of the report.

Generating a Report with Grouping, Sorting, and Totals

Now that we know the basic procedures, let's see how we can generate a more complex report. Look again at the *Supply Chain Management* report from *Extended Learning Module C* on page 370. It has groupings of the raw materials that go into each type of concrete along with totals for the number of units for each type of concrete.

We'll use the same process as we did with the *Customer Report*, but we'll do more than just accept default options as we proceed through the steps. The first thing to note about our *Supply Chain Management* report is that it requires more than one table. In fact, from the *Concrete Type* relation, we need *Concrete Type* and *Concrete Description*; from the *Raw Material* relation we need *Raw Material ID* and *Raw Material Name*; from the *Bill of Material* relation we need the *Unit* field; and from the *Supplier* relation we need *Supplier ID* and *Supplier Name*. We could choose each table in turn and then select the fields from each one that we need. Instead, we'll first construct a query using all these relations, then transform the result of the query into a report. The process is the same one we used in the *Creating an Advanced Query Using More than One Relation* section on page 489 in the text. We named the new query *Supply Chain Query*.

Once we have our query ready, we're ready to generate the report. Here are the steps (see Figures J.22 and J.23 that follow on the next two pages).

1. Click on **Create** in the menu area and then click on the **Report Wizard** button.

2. Choose tables and/or queries: In the **Tables/Queries** box, select **Query: Supply Chain Query.**

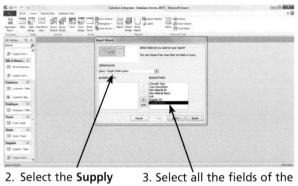

2. Select the **Supply Chain** query.

3. Select all the fields of the **Supply Chain** query.

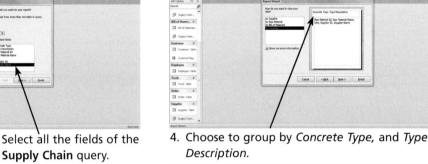

4. Choose to group by *Concrete Type*, and *Type Description*.

5. We don't want any further grouping so click on **Next**.

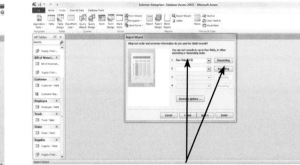

6. Choose *Raw Material ID* to sort on and change the ordering from **Ascending** to **Descending**.

Figure J.22

Creating a Report with, Grouping, Sorting, and Totals

3. Choose fields: Under **Available Fields,** select all fields in the query by clicking on the double greater-than sign (**>>**).

4. Top-level grouping: The next screen allows us to choose the ordering of information for presentation, also known as "grouping information." You'll notice in Figure J.22, in the top right-hand screen, that Access has already preselected a grouping for us. As it happens, Access has done the groupings we want (by *Concrete Type* and *Type Description*), so we accepted the default and clicked on **Next >**.

5. Further grouping: The next screen lets you specify groups within the top grouping of *Concrete Type*. Since we don't want any subgrouping, we clicked on **Next >**.

6. Sorting: Next we have a chance to sort our information. Here we'll specify that the raw material information appear in alphabetical order based on *Raw Material ID*. Since water is the least significant of the raw materials, in the sense that it's freely available, we chose to put it last in the list. Therefore, we clicked in box 1 and used the arrow button to bring *Raw Material ID* into the box. Then we clicked on the **Ascending** key to change it to **Descending.**

7. Totaling: The sorting screen that we saw above also has a **Summary Options** button. We clicked on that and chose to **Sum** *Units* and to show **Detail and Summary.** Then we clicked on **OK** and **Next >**.

8. Overall structure of report: Here we accepted **Stepped,** the default **Layout,** and **Portrait** as the page **Orientation.** Lastly, we clicked on **Next >**.

9. Style of report: Here we can choose from various report styles. We chose **Office** and then clicked on **Next >**.

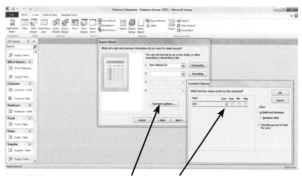

7. Click on **Summary Options** and check the **Sum** box for *Unit*.

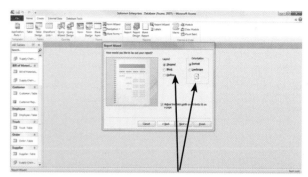

8. Choose the desired report layout and orientation.

9. Enter the report heading and click on **Finish**.

10. The completed report as generated by the **Report Wizard**.

Figure J.23

Creating a Report with Groupings, Sorting, and Totals

10. Report heading: Here we entered "Supply Chain Management Report" (without the quotation marks) for the heading and clicked on **Finish.**

11. The report: Here the report shows all the information from the wizard steps.

Look at the final screen in Figure J.23. You can see that all the information we wanted is there, grouped and sorted as we specified. The problem is that the presentation isn't aesthetically pleasing. See Figure J.24 for a closer look. Note the column headings. They appear incomplete and seem to be overlapping each other. The concrete *Type Description* entries are truncated. The word "Sum" is far away from the number. Some of the names of suppliers are truncated. The report has a *Grand Total* which we don't need since it makes no sense in this context.

We can fix these things and implement other presentation enhancements by using Design View of the report. So, while still seeing the *Supply Chain Management* report on screen, we right-clicked on the **Supply Chain Management Report** tab and selected **Design View** (see Figure J.25). The Design View screen divides the report into the following sections: *Page Header, Concrete Type Header* (as specified in step 7 of the report generation process), *Detail, Concrete Type Footer* (as specified in step 6), *Page Footer,* and *Report Footer.* By clicking on the boxes within these dividers, we can change their text, font, color, size, position, etc.

PAGE HEADER   In Figure J.26 you can see that we moved down the divider between the *Page Header* and the *Concrete Type Header* to allow room to make the individual headers deeper. That allows the words to spread over two lines and avoids the overlapping. We also spaced out the headers so that they are distributed more evenly over the page. We changed the header *Type Description* to read *Concrete Type Description*

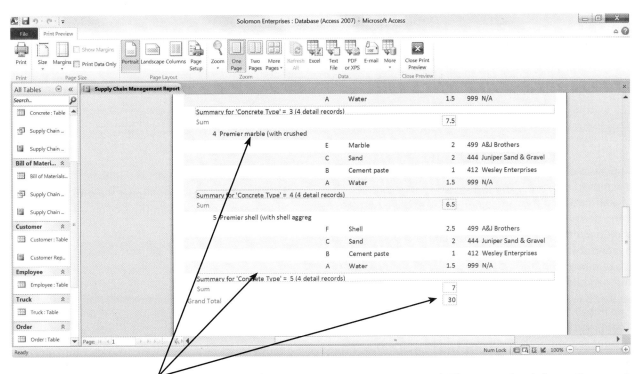

This report doesn't look good. Descriptions of the concrete types are truncated. The report has information we don't want like the *Summary line* and a *Grand Total* that makes no sense in this context.

Figure J.24

The *Supply Chain Management* Report Generated by the Report Wizard

to make it more readable. Additionally, we centered the words in the headers to make the headers look better.

To see the effect of our changes in the report, we clicked on **Views** and selected **Report View** (Figure J.26). We toggled back and forth between **Design View** and **Report View** to see the effect of our changes as we made them.

CONCRETE TYPE HEADER   In Figure J.27 you can see the changes we made to the *Concrete Type Header* section. We moved *Concrete Type* to the left and shrank the size of the text box to line up with the header. We also moved *Type Description* over a little to the right.

Figure J.25

The *Supply Chain Management* Report in Design View

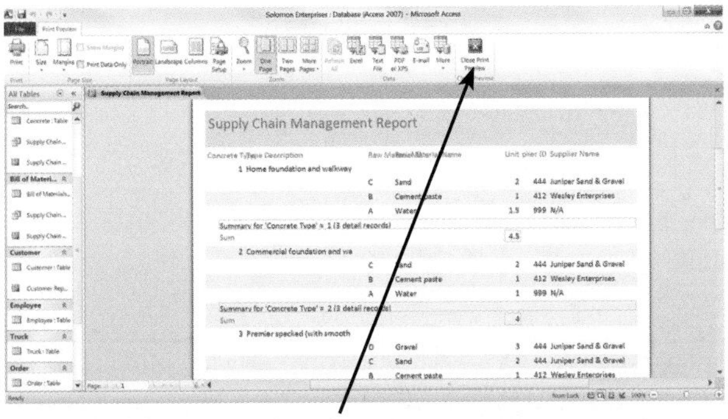

Close this view of the report by clicking on **Close Print Preview.**

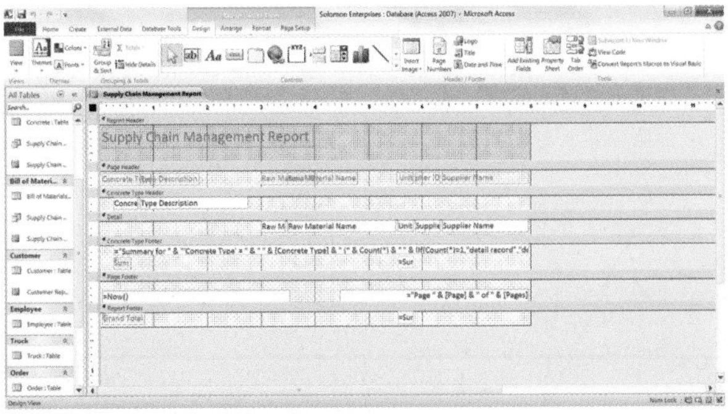

This is the report in **Design View.** It shows the divisions of the report and the formatting. This view allows us to make changes to the report.

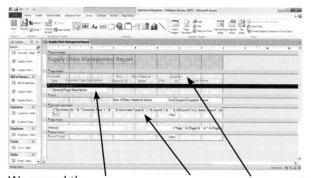

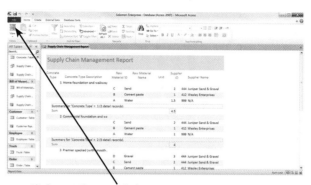

We moved the divider between the page header and the *Concrete Type* header down to make more room for the page headers.

We increased the length of *Concrete Type Description* and evened out the spacing between the headers.

We changed the shape and size of the header boxes to put some of the headers on two lines, and centered each header.

Click on **View** and then **Report View** to see the adjustments we made in the Design View.

Figure J.26

Changing the **Page Header** Section of the Report

DETAIL   In the *Detail* section, the only changes we made were to center the information in the *Raw Material ID*, *Unit*, and *Supplier ID* fields (see Figure J.28). We achieved this by following the same set of steps that we did to center *Concrete Type* in the *Concrete Type Header* section.

CONCRETE TYPE FOOTER   The top box in the *Concrete Type Footer* section of the report in Design View shows details of the summary lines of the report and shows the *Concrete Type* and the number of records for each type of concrete. We removed that by right-clicking on the box and selecting **Delete**, and you can see the result in Figure J.29. We changed the contents of the **Sum** label box to "Total Units" written in red font, and then moved it close to where the total value appears. We also changed the color of the font in the box with the total value — the one with "=Sum([Unit])." We moved both of these boxes so they look better in the report.

PAGE AND REPORT FOOTERS   In the *Page Footer* section, the box with "=Now()" is the command that places the date at the bottom of each page of our report. The box to the right keeps track of the current page and the total number of pages.

Figure J.27

Changing the **Concrete Type Header** Section of the Report

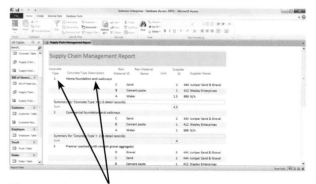

Move *Concrete Type* to the left and shrink the size of the box to place it directly under its header. Move *Type Description* to the right a little bit.

The data for *Concrete Type* should now be lined up under the header *Concrete Type* as is the data for the *Concrete Type Description*.

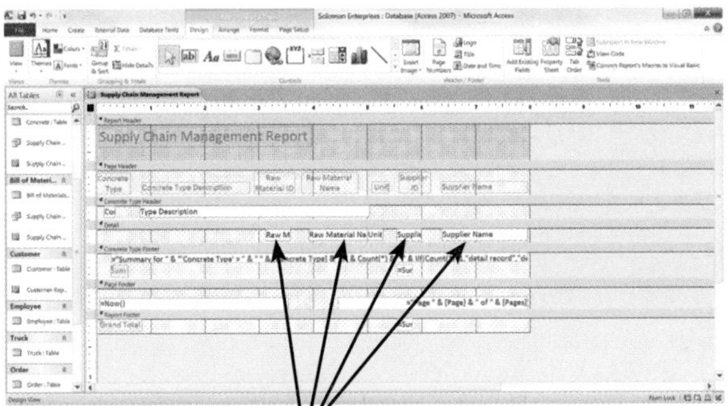

Move the elements of the detail line so that they line up with their respective headers.

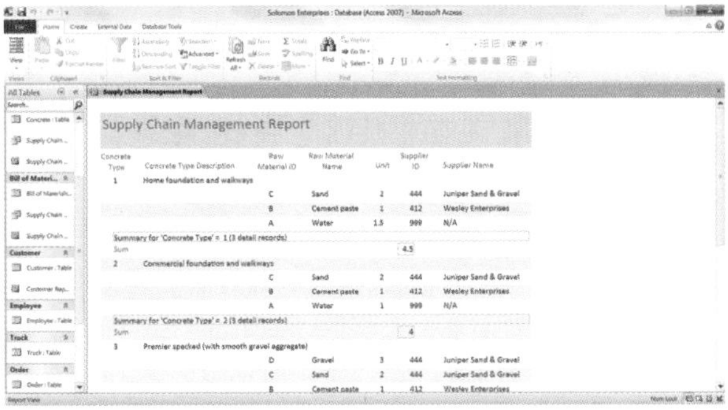

The realigned report

Figure J.28

Changing the **Detail** Section of the Report

The first box in the *Report Footer* section puts the label "Grand Total" at the end of the report, and the box to the right places the grand total value of all the units in the report at the end of the report. This doesn't make any sense in our context, so we can delete both of these grand total boxes.

Figure J.29 shows the revised *Supply Chain Management Report.* It's much tidier, more informative, and more pleasing to the eye. You can do much more with reports in the Design View. You can put in totals, averages, and lots of other things. We'll leave this for you to investigate on your own.

Creating a Data Input Form

Our last task in this database is to design an input form to simplify the task of entering new information. Let's create an input form for new orders. It's actually quite simple. Here are the steps (see Figure J.30):

1. Click on the *Order* table on the left side of the screen.
2. Click on **Create** in the menu and then click on the **Form** button.

Access then presented us with the input form you see in Figure J.30. It's not exactly pretty, but its ready for use. You can move through the records with the arrow keys across the bottom. When you reach the end of the list of records, you'll get a blank input form.

You can also change the structure of the form by right-clicking on the **Order** tab and then selecting **Design View.** It will be similar to the Design View for working with

Figure J.29

Changing the *Concrete Type* *Footer* Section of the Report

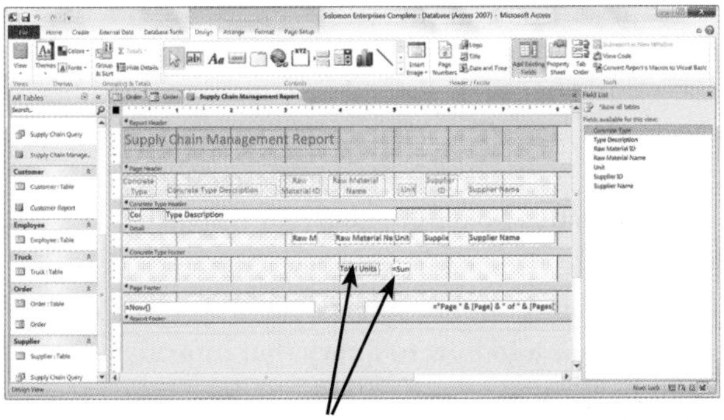

Delete the *Summary line.* Change *Sum to Total Units,* change its color and move this label closer to its data.

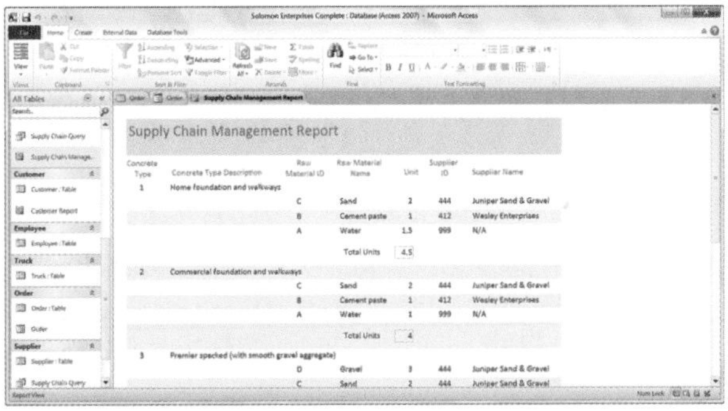

The completed report

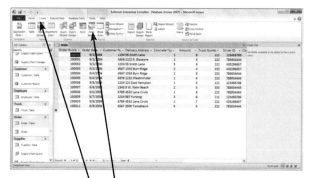

To create a data input form, click on **Create** and then **Form**.

The completed data input form

Figure J.30

Creating an Input Form

reports. And you have similar functionality — you can make field areas longer or shorter, change text colors, add and remove fields and labels, and so on.

That ends or brief tour of Microsoft Access. It's not really that difficult a package to learn. The most difficult part is correctly defining the structure of your database. Actually implementing your design in Access is comparatively simple after that. We recommend once again that you reread *Extended Learning Module C* if you intend to become a designer as well as a user of database applications. "Using" is the easy part; "designing" is the challenging part.

SUMMARY: STUDENT LEARNING OUTCOMES REVISITED

1. **Identify the steps necessary to implement the structure of a relational database using the data definition language provided by Microsoft Access.**
   Using a data definition language to implement a database is the fourth and last step in designing a database. It first requires that you use the data dictionary to create the structure of each table, assigning each one a primary key, and defining what type of information the fields will hold, how large they will be, and many other properties. The ***data dictionary*** contains the logical structure for the information in a database. A ***primary key*** is a field (or group of fields in some cases) that uniquely defines each record. A ***composite primary key*** consists of the primary key fields from two ***intersecting relations.*** An intersection relation (sometimes called a ***composite*** relation) is a relation you create to eliminate a many-to-many relationship.

   You must also define the relationships among the tables, including their foreign keys. A ***foreign key*** is a primary key of one file (relation) that appears in another file (relation). You must also consider ***integrity constraints***—rules that help ensure the quality of the information. For this you use the *Enforce Referential Integrity* feature of Access to stipulate that no information may be entered as a foreign key unless that information already exists as a primary key.

2. **Demonstrate how to use the data manipulation subsystem in Access to enter and change information in a database and how to query that information.**
   When the tables and their fields have been defined and the relationships between pairs of tables have been established, you can enter information into the tables. Then you can construct queries to view the information in multiple

ways, i.e., you can ask questions of the information. The simplest way to do this is to use Access's QBE tool. *A query-by-example (QBE) tool* helps you graphically design the answer to a question.

3. **Explain the use of the application generation subsystem in Access to create reports and data entry screens.** To create professional-looking reports you must use the report generator in the application generation subsystem of Access. It allows you to present information with page headers and footers, and grouping, sorting, and totaling of information. Similarly, to create an easy-to-use method of entering information into tables, you create input forms. This is also part of the application generation subsystem of Access.

KEY TERMS AND CONCEPTS

Composite primary key, 480
Data dictionary, 474
Foreign key, 482
Integrity constraint, 477

Intersection (composite) relation, 480
Primary key, 478
Query-by-example (QBE) tool, 487

ASSIGNMENTS AND EXERCISES

1. **ENTER NEW EMPLOYEE INFORMATION** It's likely that Solomon Enterprises would need to enter the information for a new employee. Create a new input form to enter Employee ID, Employee Last Name, Employee First Name, and Date of Hire. Design the form so that the information appears in tabular form and has Sandstone background.

2. **WHAT ARE THE INGREDIENTS FOR PREMIER MARBLE CONCRETE?** Write a query to show how many units of each raw material are in concrete type 4. Print out the name of the concrete type, its ID, the name of the raw material (not its ID), and the number of units of each of the raw materials.

3. **INVENTORY REPORT** Create a report that shows how many units Solomon Enterprises has of each of the raw materials. Don't include water (hint: you want all *Raw Material* fields that do not equal *water*). Choose your own layout and page orientation.

4. **SORT QUERY INFORMATION** The Datasheet view of a query allows you to sort the information in that query. Try this out with the *Order* relation. Download the Solomon Enterprises database from the Web site that supports this text: www.mhhe.com/haag. (Select XLM/J. The name of the file is **XLMJ_**

Solomon_Enterprises.accdb.) Click on the **Queries** tab and open the **Order** relation in Datasheet view. Sort the table alphabetically on *Employee Last Name*. Place your cursor anywhere in the column you want to sort by (in this case *Employee Last Name*), and click on the sort-ascending button. It has an "A" above a "Z" with an arrow pointing downwards.

5. **FILTER QUERY INFORMATION** You can request Access to show you any other occurrences of a data item that is in the same column. Use the same file you needed for question 4 above. You can download it from the Web site for this text: www.mhhe.com/haag. (Select XLM/J. The name of the file is **XLMJ_Solomon_ Enterprises.accdb.**) Filter the information so that only those records in which the truck is a Ford appear. To do this click in the Truck Type column on any one of the occurrences of Ford. Then, click on the Filter by Selection button (that's the button in the button bar with the funnel and a lightning strike). You will instantly see only the three records where the truck is a Ford. To return the data to its previous state, click on Remove Filter button (that's the button that has the funnel without any other symbol). If you click on this button again, it will reapply the filter.

EXTENDED LEARNING MODULE J

IMPLEMENTING A DATABASE WITH MICROSOFT ACCESS

Student Learning Outcomes

1. Identify the steps necessary to implement the structure of a relational database using the data definition language provided by Microsoft Access.

2. Demonstrate how to use the data manipulation subsystem in Access to enter and change information in a database and how to query that information.

3. Explain the use of the application generation subsystem in Access to create reports and data entry screens.

Module J presents hands-on instructions concerning how to implement a database using Microsoft Access including building tables, creating queries, building simple reports, creating customized reports, and creating input forms.

The version of the module printed in the book demonstrates how to implement a database in Access using Office 2010. If you have and use Office 2007 or an earlier version, you can find this same module in that version of Office on the Web site that accompanies the text at www.mhhe.com/haag.

EXTENDED LEARNING MODULE K

CAREERS IN BUSINESS

Student Learning Outcomes

1. Identify the career field and business specialization in which you are interested.

2. Provide typical job titles and descriptions for your career field.

3. List and describe the IT skills you need to gain while in school.

Extended Learning Module K provides an overview of job titles and descriptions in the fields of accounting, finance, hospitality and tourism management, information technology, management, marketing, productions and operations management, and real estate and construction management including what IT skills you should acquire to be successful in each field.

Extended Learning Module K can be found on the book's Web site at www.mhhe.com/haag.

EXTENDED LEARNING MODULE L

BUILDING WEB SITES WITH FRONTPAGE

Student Learning Outcomes

1. Describe the different kinds of Web sites that you can build using FrontPage.

2. Describe the different ways to navigate in FrontPage.

3. Explain the different FrontPage views.

4. Describe and build a Web site using FrontPage.

5. Describe and build a Web page using FrontPage.

6. Demonstrate the method used to insert a graphic into a Web page using FrontPage.

7. Describe and create the different types of hyperlinks available in FrontPage.

8. Create a list and a table in a Web page using FrontPage.

9. Define the benefits of using themes when developing a Web page.

Extended Learning Module L provides hands-on instructions for building a Web site using Microsoft's Web authoring software FrontPage. Like Extended Learning Module F, you'll learn how to incorporate such things as list, images, and links. You'll also learn much more in this module as FrontPage truly enhances your ability to create a Web page that takes advantage of many of today's exciting Web features.

Extended Learning Module L can be found on the book's Web site at www.mhhe.com/haag.

EXTENDED LEARNING MODULE M

PROGRAMMING IN EXCEL WITH VBA

Student Learning Outcomes

1. Explain the value of using VBA with Excel.

2. Define a macro.

3. Build a simple macro using a Sub procedure and a Function procedure.

4. Describe an object.

5. Explain the difference between a comment, a variable, and a constant.

6. List the various Visual Basic Application data types and operators.

7. Describe and build a macro that uses the *If-Then-Else, For-Next, Do-Until, Do-While,* and *Select Case* structures.

Extended Learning Module M covers the basics of learning how to write macros (short programs) in Excel using VBA, Visual Basic for Applications. It covers how to use the Visual Basic Editor (VBE), how to use the macro recorder, and how to write procedures, functions, if-then structures, and loops.

GLOSSARY

1-tier infrastructure the most basic setup because it involves a single tier on a single machine.

2-tier infrastructure the basic client/server relationship.

3-tier infrastructure the most common approach used for Web applications today.

3D printer printer that can produce solid, three-dimensional objects.

3G third generation standard for mobile devices; its download speed usually varies from just under 1 Mbps (Megabits, or millions of bits, per second) to just over 2 Mbps.

4G fourth generation standard and can be up to 10 times faster than 3G.

A

Abandoned registrations number of visitors who start the process of completing a registration page and then abandon the activity.

Abandoned shopping carts the number of visitors who create a shopping cart and start shopping and then abandon the activity before paying for the merchandise.

Abandon rate the percentage of callers who hang up while waiting for their call to be answered.

Accuracy usually measured inversely as *error rate*, or the number of errors per thousand (or million) that a system generates.

Ad hoc (nonrecurring) decision decision you make infrequently (perhaps only once) and for which you may even have different criteria for determining the best solution for each time.

Ad-supported derives revenue by selling advertising space, much like the concept of an affiliate program.

Adult sexting sexting between two consenting adults.

Adware software to generate ads that installs itself on your computer when you download some other (usually free) program from the Web.

Affiliate program an arrangement made between two e-commerce sites that directs viewers from one site to the other.

Agent-based modeling way of simulating human organizations using multiple intelligent agents, each of which follows a set of simple rules and can adapt to changing conditions.

Agent-based technology (software agent) a small piece of software that acts on your behalf (on behalf of another piece of software) performing tasks assigned to it.

Agile methodology a form of extreme programming that aims for customer satisfaction through early and continuous delivery of useful software components.

Analysis phase of the systems development life cycle involves end users and IT specialists working together to gather, understand, and document the business requirements for the proposed system.

Analytics the science of fact-based decision making.

Anonymous Web browsing (AWB) service hides your identity from the Web sites you visit.

Anti-spyware software utility software that detects and removes spyware and other unwanted software that can track every electronic move you make.

Antivirus software detects and removes or quarantines computer viruses.

Application generation subsystem of a DBMS contains facilities to help you develop transaction-intensive applications.

Application software the software that enables you to solve specific problems or perform specific tasks.

Arithmetic logic unit (ALU) a component of the CPU that performs arithmetic, as well as comparison and logic operations.

Artificial intelligence (AI) the science of making machines imitate human thinking and behavior.

ASCII (American Standard Code for Information Interchange) the coding system that most personal computers use to represent, process, and store information.

Augmented reality the viewing of the physical world with computer-generated layers of information added to it.

Automatic speech recognition (ASR) a system that not only captures spoken words but also distinguishes word groupings to form sentences.

Autonomous agent software agent that can adapt and alter the manner in which it attempts to achieve its assigned task.

Average speed to answer (ASA) the average time, usually in seconds, that it takes for a call to be answered by an actual person.

B

Back office system used to fulfill and support customer orders.

Backup the process of making a copy of the information stored on a computer.

Bandwidth capacity of the communications medium, refers to the amount of information that a communications medium can transfer in a given amount of time.

Bar code scanner reads information that is in the form of vertical bars, where their width and spacing represent digits (often used in point-of-sale [POS] systems in retail environments).

Basic formatting tag HTML tag that allows you to specify formatting for text.

Benchmarking a process of continuously measuring system results, comparing those results to optimal system performance (benchmark values), and identifying steps and procedures to improve system performance.

Benchmarks baseline values a system seeks to attain.

Binary digit (bit) the smallest unit of information that your computer can process.

Biochip a technology chip that can perform a variety of physiological functions when inserted into the human body.

Biometrics the use of physiological characteristics—such as your fingerprint, the blood vessels in the iris of your eye, the sound of your voice, or perhaps even your breath—to provide identification.

Biometric scanner scans some human physical attribute, like your fingerprint or iris, for security purposes.

Biomimicry learning from ecosystems and adapting their characteristics to human and organizational situations.

Black-hat hacker a cyber vandal.

Bluetooth a standard for transmitting information in the form of short-range radio waves over distances of up to 30 feet, used for purposes such as wirelessly connecting a cell phone or a PDA to a computer.

Bot computer program that runs automatically.

Botnet network of malware-bot infected computers.

Broadband connection that is a high-bandwidth (high-capacity) telecommunications line capable of providing high-speed Internet service.

Broadband (home) router a device to connect several computers together to share a DSL or cable Internet connection in a home or small office.

Browser-safe colors 215 colors that can be viewed by all browsers and computers.

Business continuity plan a step-by-step guideline defining how the organization will recover from a disaster or extended disruption of its business processes.

Business intelligence (BI) collective information about your customers, your competitors, your business partners, your competitive environment, and your own internal operations that gives you the ability to make effective, important, and often strategic business decisions.

Business requirement a detailed set of knowledge worker requests that the system must meet to be successful.

Business to Business (B2B) e-commerce when a business sells products and services to customers who are primarily other businesses.

Business to Consumer (B2C) e-commerce when a business sells products and services to customers who are primarily individuals.

Business to Government (B2G) e-commerce occurs when a business sells products and services to a government entity.

Buyer agent or shopping bot an intelligent agent on a Web site that helps you, the customer, find the products and services you want.

Buyer power in Porter's Five Forces Model it is high when buyers have many choices from whom to buy, and low when their choices are few.

Byte a group of eight bits that represents one natural language character.

C

Cable modem a device that uses your TV cable to deliver an Internet connection.

Call center metrics measure the success of call center efforts.

Capacity planning determines your projected future IT infrastructure requirements for new equipment and additional network capacity.

Cat 5 (Category 5) cable a better-constructed version of twisted-pair phone cable.

CAVE (cave automatic virtual environment) a special 3-D virtual reality room that can display images of other people and objects located in other CAVEs all over the world.

CD-R (compact disc—recordable) an optical or laser disc that you can write to one time only.

CD-ROM (compact disc—read-only memory) an optical or laser disc whose information cannot be changed. A CD stores up to 800 Meg of information.

CD-RW (compact disc—rewritable) an optical or laser disc on which you can save, change, and delete files as often as you like.

Central processing unit (CPU) the hardware that interprets and executes the system and application software instructions and coordinates the operation of all the hardware.

Chief information officer (CIO) responsible for overseeing every aspect of an organization's information resource.

Chief privacy officer (CPO) responsible for ensuring that information is used in an ethical way and that only the right people have access to certain types of information such as financial records and payroll.

Chief security officer (CSO) responsible for the technical aspects of ensuring the security of information such as the development and use of firewalls, intranets, extranets, and anti-virus software.

Chief technology officer (CTO) responsible for overseeing both the underlying IT infrastructure within an organization and the user-facing technologies (such as CRM systems).

Choice the third step in the decision-making process where you decide on a plan to address the problem or opportunity.

Class contains information and procedures and acts as a template to create objects.

Clickstream a stored record about your Web surfing session, such as which Web sites you visited, how long you were there, what ads you looked at, and what you bought.

Click-through a count of the number of people who visit one site, click on an ad, and are taken to the site of the advertiser.

Client/server infrastructure (client/server network) a network in which one or more computers are servers and provide services to the other computers, called clients.

Cloud computing technology model in which any and all resources—application software, processing power, data storage, backup facilities, development tools, literally everything—are delivered as a set of services via the Internet.

Coaxial cable (coax) one central wire surrounded by insulation, a metallic shield, and a final case of insulating material.

Cold site a separate facility that does not have any computer equipment but is a place where the knowledge workers can move after the disaster.

Collocation facility available to a company that rents space and telecommunications equipment from another company.

Communications medium the path, or physical channel, in a network over which information travels.

Communications protocol (protocol) a set of rules that every computer follows to transfer information.

Communications satellite microwave repeater in space.

Communications software helps you communicate with other people.

CompactFlash (CF) card a flash memory card that is slightly larger than a half-dollar, with a capacity of up to 6 gigabytes.

Competitive advantage   providing a product or service in a way that customers value more than what the competition is able to do.

Competitive intelligence (CI)   business intelligence focused on the external competitive environment.

Component-based development (CBD)   a general approach to systems development that focuses on building small self-contained blocks of code (components) that can be reused across a variety of applications within an organization.

Composite primary key   consists of the primary key fields from the two intersecting relations.

Computer crime   a crime in which a computer, or computers, played a significant part.

Computer network (network)   two or more computers connected so that they can communicate with each other and share information, software, peripheral devices, and/or processing power.

Computer virus (virus)   software that is written with malicious intent to cause annoyance or damage.

Conditional formatting   highlights information in a cell that meets some criteria you specify.

Connectivity software   enables you to use your computer to dial up or connect to another computer.

Constant   a named element whose value doesn't change.

Consumer to Business (C2B) e-commerce   when an individual sells products and services to a business.

Consumer to Consumer (C2C) e-commerce   when an individual sells products and services to other individuals.

Consumer to Government (C2G) e-commerce   when an individual sells products and services to a government entity.

Control unit   the component of the CPU that directs what happens in your computer, sends to RAM for instructions and the information it needs.

Conversion rate   the percentage of potential customers who visit your site who actually buy something.

Cookie   a small record deposited on your hard disk by a Web site containing information about you.

Copyright   the legal protection afforded an expression of an idea, such as a song, video game, and some types of proprietary documents.

Cost-per-thousand (CPM)   sales dollars generated per dollar of advertising, commonly used to make the case for spending money to appear on a search engine.

CPU cache   a type of memory on the CPU where instructions called up by the CPU wait until the CPU is ready to use them.

CPU clock   a sliver of quartz that beats at regular intervals in response to an electrical charge.

CPU (machine) cycle   consists of retrieving, decoding, and executing the instruction, then returning the result to RAM, if necessary.

Cracker   a hacker for hire; a person who engages in electronic corporate espionage.

Crash-proof software   utility software that helps you save information if your system crashes and you're forced to turn it off and then back on again.

Critical success factor (CSF)   a factor simply critical to your organization's success.

CRM analytics   the analysis of CRM data to improve functions such as sales force automation and customer service and support.

Crossover   the process within a genetic algorithm where portions of good outcomes are combined in the hope of creating an even better outcome.

Crowdsourcing   when businesses provide technologies that enable people (i.e., crowds)—instead of a designated paid employee—to create, modify, and oversee the development of a product or service.

CRT   a monitor that looks like a traditional television set.

CRUD (Create, Read, Update, Delete)   the four procedures, or ways, a system can manipulate information.

Customer relationship management (CRM) system   uses information about customers to gain insights into their needs, wants, and behaviors in order to serve them better.

Custom Filter function   allows you to hide all the rows in a list except those that match criteria, besides "is equal to," that you specify.

Cyberterrorist   one who seeks to cause harm to people or destroy critical systems or information.

D

Data   raw facts that describe a particular phenomenon.

Data administration   the function in an organization that plans for, oversees the development of, and monitors the information resource.

Data administration subsystem   of a DBMS helps you manage the overall database environment by providing facilities for backup and recovery, security management, query optimization, concurrency control, and change management.

Database   a collection of information that you organize and access according to the logical structure of that information.

Database administration   the function in an organization that is responsible for the more technical and operational aspects of managing the information contained in organizational information repositories (databases, data warehouses, and data marts).

Database management system (DBMS)   helps you specify the logical organization for a database and access and use the information within a database.

Data definition subsystem   of a DBMS helps you create and maintain the data dictionary and define the structure of the files in a database.

Data dictionary   contains the logical structure for the information in a database.

Data management   component of a DSS that performs the function of storing and maintaining the information that you want your DSS to use.

Data manipulation subsystem   of a DBMS helps you add, change, and delete information in a database and query it for valuable information.

Data mart   a subset of a data warehouse in which only a focused portion of the data warehouse information is kept.

Data-mining agent   an intelligent agent that operates in a data warehouse discovering information.

Data-mining tool   a software tool you use to query information in a data warehouse.

Data warehouse a logical collection of information—gathered from many different operational databases—used to create business intelligence that supports business analysis activities and decision-making tasks.

DBMS engine accepts logical requests from the various other DBMS subsystems, converts them into their physical equivalent, and actually accesses the database and data dictionary as they exist on a storage device.

Decision support system (DSS) a highly flexible and interactive IT system that is designed to support decision making when the situation includes nonstructured element.

Demand aggregation the combining of purchase requests from multiple buyers into a single larger order, which justifies a discount from the business.

Denial-of-service (DoS) attack floods a server or network with so many requests for service that it slows down or crashes.

Design the second step in the decision-making process, where you consider possible ways of solving the problem, filling the need, or taking advantage of the opportunity.

Design phase of the systems development life cycle builds a technical blueprint of how the proposed system will work.

Desktop computer the type of computer that is the most popular choice for personal computing needs.

Desktop publishing software extends word processing software by including design and formatting techniques to enhance the layout and appearance of a document.

Development phase of the systems development life cycle takes all your detailed design documents from the design phase and transforms them into an actual system.

Differentiation (in Porter's three generic strategies) offering a product or service that is perceived as being "unique" in the marketplace.

Digital camera captures still images or video as a series of 1s and 0s.

Digital dashboard displays key information gathered from several sources on a computer screen in a format tailored to the needs and wants of an individual knowledge worker.

Digital forensics the gathering, authentication, examination, and analysis of electronic information for presentation in court.

Digital still camera digitally captures still images in varying resolutions.

Digital Subscriber Line (DSL) a high-speed Internet connection using phone lines, which allows you to use your phone for voice communications at the same time.

Digital video camera captures video digitally.

Digital wallet both software and information—the software provides security for the transaction and the information includes payment information (for example, the credit card number and expiration date) and delivery information.

Direct materials materials that are used in production in a manufacturing company or are placed on the shelf for sale in a retail environment.

Disaster recovery cost curve charts (1) the cost to your organization of the unavailability of information and technology and (2) the cost to your organization of recovering from a disaster over time.

Disaster recovery plan a detailed process for recovering information or an IT system in the event of a catastrophic disaster such as a fire or flood.

Disintermediation use of the Internet as a delivery vehicle, whereby intermediate players in a distribution channel can be bypassed.

Disk optimization software utility software that organizes your information on your hard disk in the most efficient way.

Distributed agent software agent that works on multiple distinct computer systems.

Distributed denial-of-service (DDoS) attack attack from multiple computers that floods a server or network with so many requests for service that it slows down or crashes.

Distributed infrastructure involves distributing the information and processing power of IT systems via a network.

Distribution chain the path followed from the originator of a product or service to the end consumer.

Domain name (technical name for a Web site address) identifies a specific computer on the Web and the main page of the entire site.

Dot pitch the distance between the centers of a pair of like-colored pixels.

Drone bot-infected computer.

DS3 a high-speed business network circuit running at 44.736 Mbps.

DVD-R or DVD + R (DVD—recordable) a high-capacity optical or laser disc to which you can write one time only.

DVD-ROM a high-capacity optical or laser disc whose information cannot be changed.

DVD-RW or DVD + RW (depending on the manufacturer) a high-capacity optical or laser disc on which you can save, change, and delete files.

E

E-book reader (e-book device or e-reader) portable computer designed specifically for reading digitized books and periodicals.

Effectiveness refers to doing the right thing.

Efficiency doing something right (e.g., in the least time, at the lowest cost, with the fewest errors, etc.).

E-gallery electronic gallery of works that demonstrates your skills.

Electronic Bill Presentment and Payment (EBPP) a system that sends bills (usually to end consumers) over the Internet and provides an easy-to-use mechanism (such as clicking on a button) to pay them if the amount looks correct.

Electronic check a mechanism for sending money from your checking or savings account to another person or organization.

Electronic commerce (e-commerce) commerce, but it is commerce accelerated and enhanced by IT, in particular the Internet.

Electronic data interchange (EDI) the direct computer-to-computer transfer of transaction information contained in standard business documents, such as invoices and purchase orders, in a standard format.

Electronic job market consists of employers using Internet technologies to advertise and screen potential employees.

Electronic marketplace (e-marketplace) an interactive business providing a central space where multiple buyers and sellers can engage in e-commerce and/or other e-commerce business activities.

Electronic portfolio (e-portfolio)   collection of Web documents used to support a stated purpose such as demonstrating writing, photography, or job skills.

E-mail (electronic mail) software   enables you to electronically communicate with other people by sending and receiving e-mail.

Encapsulation   information hiding.

Encryption   scrambles the contents of a file so that you can't read it without having the right decryption key.

Enterprise resource planning (ERP) system   software system for business management, supporting areas such as planning, manufacturing, sales, marketing, distribution, accounting, finance, human resource management, project management, inventory management, service and maintenance, transportation, and e-business.

Entity class   a concept—typically people, places, or things—about which you wish to store information and that you can identify with a unique key (called a primary key).

Entity-relationship (E-R) diagram   a graphic method of representing entity classes and their relationships.

Entry barrier   a product or service feature that customers have come to expect from organizations in a particular industry and that must be offered by an entering organization to compete and survive.

Ethernet card   the most common type of network interface card.

Ethical (white-hat) hacker   a computer security professional who is hired by a company to break into its computer system, so as to find security lapses.

Ethics   the principles and standards that guide our behavior toward other people.

Expandability   refers to how easy it is to add features and functions to a system.

Expansion bus   the set of pathways along which information moves between devices outside the motherboard and the CPU.

Expansion card (board)   a circuit board that you insert into the expansion slot on the motherboard and to which you connect a peripheral device.

Expansion slot   a long skinny socket on the motherboard into which you insert an expansion card.

Expert system (knowledge-based system)   an artificial intelligence system that applies reasoning capabilities to reach a conclusion.

External information   describes the environment surrounding the organization.

Extraction, transformation, and loading (ETL)   a three-step process that includes: (1) extracting needed data from its sources, (2) transforming the data into a standardized format, and (3) loading the transformed data into a data warehouse.

Extranet   an intranet that is restricted to an organization and certain outsiders, such as customers and suppliers.

Extreme programming (XP) methodology   breaks a project into tiny phases and developers cannot continue on to the next phase until the first phase is complete.

F

F2b2C (Factory to business to Consumer)   e-commerce business model in which a consumer communicates through a business on the Internet that directly provides product specifications to a factory that makes the customized and personalized product to the consumer's specifications and then ships it directly to the consumer.

Facial recognition software   software that provides identification by evaluating facial characteristics.

Fair Use Doctrine   allows you to use copyrighted material in certain situations.

Feature analysis   captures your words as you speak into a microphone, eliminates any background noise, and converts the digital signals of your speech into phonemes (syllables).

Feature creep   occurs when developers add extra features that were not part of the initial requirements.

File transfer protocol (ftp)   communications protocol that allows you to transfer files of information from one computer to another.

Filter function   filters a list and allows you to hide all the rows in a list except those that match criteria you specify.

Financial cybermediary   an Internet-based company that makes it easy for one person to pay another person or organization over the Internet.

Financial EDI (financial electronic data interchange)   an electronic process used primarily within the Business to Business e-commerce model for the payment of purchases.

Firewall   software and/or hardware that protects a computer or network from intruders.

Firewire (IEEE 1394 or I-Link) port   fits hot-swap, plug-and-play Firewire connectors and you can connect up to 63 Firewire devices to a single Firewire port by daisy-chaining the devices together.

First call resolution (FCR)   the percentage of calls that can be resolved without having to call back.

First-mover advantage   being the first to market with a competitive advantage and thus having a significant impact on gaining market share.

Five Forces Model   helps business people understand the relative attractiveness of an industry and the industry's competitive pressures.

Flash memory card   has high-capacity storage units laminated inside a small piece of plastic.

Flash memory device (jump drive, thumb drive)   a flash memory storage device that is small enough to fit on a key ring and plugs directly into the USB port on your computer.

Flat-panel display   thin, lightweight monitor that takes up much less space than a CRT.

Focus   (in Porter's three generic strategies) focusing on offering products and services (1) to a particular market segment or buyer group, (2) within a segment of a product line, and/or (3) to a specific geographic market.

Foreign key   a primary key of one file (relation) that appears in another file (relation).

Forensic image copy   an exact copy or snapshot of the contents of an electronic medium.

Friendly fraud   identity theft when the victim knows the person who stole his/her identity.

Front office system   the primary interface to customers and sales channels.

FrontPage   Web authoring software.

Ftp (file transfer protocol) server   maintains a collection of files that you can download.

Function procedure   a VBA macro that returns a single value.

Fuzzy logic   mathematical method of handling imprecise or subjective information.

G

Game controller   used for gaming to better control screen action.

Gamepad   a multifunctional input device with programmable buttons, thumb sticks, and a directional pad.

Gaming wheel   a steering wheel and foot pedals for virtual driving.

Garbage-in garbage-out (GIGO)   if the information coming into your decision-making process is in bad form (i.e., garbage-in), you'll more than likely make a poor decision (garbage-out).

Gas plasma display   sends electricity through gas trapped between two layers of glass or plastic to create a screen image.

Genetic algorithm   an artificial intelligence system that mimics the evolutionary, survival-of-the-fittest process to generate increasingly better solutions to a problem.

Geographic information system (GIS)   a decision support system designed specifically to analyze spatial information.

Gigabyte (GB or Gig)   roughly 1 billion bytes.

Gigahertz (GHz)   the number of billions of CPU cycles per second that the CPU can handle.

Glove   an input device that captures and records the shape and movement of your hand and fingers and the strength of your hand and finger movements.

Goal Seek   works backward from an objective to compute an unknown value.

Good-enough technology economy   marked by the lack of seeking perfection, focusing rather on getting "good enough" products out the door, often allowing them to evolve and improve over time through user feedback.

Government to Business (G2B) e-commerce   when a government entity sells products and services to businesses.

Government to Consumer (G2C) e-commerce   the electronic commerce activities performed between a government and its citizens or consumers including paying taxes, registering vehicles, and providing information and services.

Government to Government (G2G) e-commerce   either (1) the electronic commerce activities performed within a single nation's government or (2) the electronic commerce activities performed between two or more nations' governments including providing foreign aid.

Graphics software   helps you create and edit photos and art.

H

Hacker   a knowledgeable computer user who uses his or her knowledge to invade other people's computers.

Hacktivist   a politically motivated hacker who uses the Internet to send a political message of some kind.

Haptic interface   uses technology to add the sense of touch to an environment that previously had only visual and auditory elements.

Hard disk   magnetic storage device with one or more thin metal platters or disks that store information sealed inside the disk drive.

Hardware   the physical devices that make up a computer (often referred to as a computer system).

Hardware key logger   a hardware device that captures keystrokes on their journey from the keyboard to the motherboard.

Heading tag   HTML tag that makes certain information, such as titles, stand out on your Web site.

Headset (head-mounted display)   a combined input and output device that (1) captures and records the movement of your head, and (2) contains a screen that covers your entire field of vision.

Help desk   a group of people who respond to knowledge workers' questions.

Hidden job market   the collective term used to describe jobs that are not advertised.

Holographic device   a device that creates, captures, and/or displays images in true three-dimensional form.

Holographic storage device   stores information on a storage medium that is composed of 3-D crystal-like objects with many sides or faces.

Horizontal e-marketplace   an electronic marketplace that connects buyers and sellers across many industries, primarily for MRO materials commerce.

Horizontal market software   application software that is general enough to be suitable for use in a variety of industries.

Hot site   a separate and fully equipped facility where the company can move immediately after the disaster and resume business.

Hot swap   an operating system feature that allows you—while your computer is running—to unplug a device and plug in a new one without first shutting down your computer.

HR analytics   the analysis of human resource or talent management data for such purposes as work-force capacity planning, training and development, and performance appraisal.

HTML document   a file that contains your Web site content and HTML formatting instructions.

HTML tag   specifies the formatting and presentation of information on a Web site.

Hub   a device that connects computers together and passes messages by repeating all network transmissions to all the other computers.

Hypertext markup language (HTML)   the language you use to create a Web site.

Hypertext transfer protocol (http)   the communications protocol that supports the movement of information over the Web.

I

Identity theft   the forging of someone's identity for the purpose of fraud.

Image scanner   captures images, photos, text, and artwork that already exist on paper.

Implant chip   a technology-enabled microchip implanted into the human body that stores important information about you (such as your identification and medical history) and that may be GPS-enabled to offer a method of tracking.

Implementation   the final step in the decision-making process where you put your plan into action.

Implementation phase of the systems development life cycle distributes the system to all the knowledge workers and they begin using the system to perform their everyday jobs.

Information data that have a particular meaning within a specific context.

Information agent intelligent agent that searches for information of some kind and brings it back.

Information decomposition breaking down the information and procedures for ease of use and understandability.

Information granularity the extent of detail within the information.

Information-literate knowledge worker can define what information they need, know how and where to obtain that information, understand the information once they receive it, and can act appropriately based on the information to help the organization achieve the greatest advantage.

Information partnership two or more companies cooperating by integrating their IT systems, thereby providing customers with the best of what each can offer.

Information technology (IT) any computer-based tool that people use to work with information and support the information and information-processing needs of an organization.

Information view includes all of the information stored within a system.

Infrared, IR, or IrDA (infrared data association) uses red light to send and receive information.

Infrastructure a relative term meaning "the structure beneath a structure."

Infrastructure-as-a-service (IaaS) delivery model for all the "extra" technologies necessary in a networked environment (e.g., network routers, communications servers, firewalls, anti-"you name it" software) in which you pay for the technologies on a pay-per-use basis instead of buying them outright.

Infrastructure-centric metric is typically a measure of the efficiency, speed, and/or capacity of technology.

Inheritance the ability to define superclass and subclass relationships among classes.

Inkjet printer makes images by forcing ink droplets through nozzles.

Input device tool you use to enter information and commands.

Insourcing using IT specialists within your organization to develop the system.

Instance an occurrence of an entity class that can be uniquely described with a primary key.

Integrated collaboration environment (ICE) the environment in which virtual teams do their work.

Integration testing verifies that separate systems can work together.

Integrity constraint rule that helps ensure the quality of the information.

Intellectual property intangible creative work that is embodied in physical form.

Intelligence the first step in the decision-making process where you find or recognize a problem, need, or opportunity (also called the diagnostic phase of decision making).

Intelligent agent software agent that incorporates artificial intelligence capabilities such as learning and reasoning; software that assists you, or acts on your behalf, in performing repetitive computer-related tasks.

Interface any device that calls procedures and can include such things as a keyboard, mouse, and touch screen.

Inter-modal transportation the use of multiple channels of transportation—railway, truck, boat, and so on—to move products from origin to destination.

Internal information describes specific operational aspects of an organization.

Internet a vast network of computers that connects millions of people all over the world.

Internet backbone the major set of connections for computers on the Internet.

Internet server computer computer that provides information and services on the Internet.

Internet service provider (ISP) a company that provides individuals, organizations, and businesses access to the Internet.

Interoperability the capability of two or more computing components to share information and other resources, even if they are made by different manufacturers.

Intersection relation (composite relation) a relation you create to eliminate a many-to-many relationship.

Intranet an internal organizational Internet that is guarded against outside access by a special security feature called a firewall (which can be software, hardware, or a combination of the two).

Intrusion-detection software looks for people on the network who shouldn't be there or who are acting suspiciously.

Intrusion detection system (IDS) a device that watches network traffic for intrusion attempts and reports them.

Intrusion prevention system (IPS) type of intrusion detection system (IDS) that also takes action against intrusion attempts, for example, by creating new policies in a firewall to block the source of the attack.

Invisible backlog the list of all systems that an organization needs to develop but—because of the prioritization of systems development needs—never get funded because of the lack of organizational resources.

IRC (Internet Relay Chat) server supports your use of discussion groups and chat rooms.

IT culture affects the placement structurally of the IT function within an organization and manifests the philosophical approach to the development, deployment, and use of IT within an organization.

J

Joint application development (JAD) occurs when knowledge workers and IT specialists meet, sometimes for several days, to define and review the business requirements for the system.

Joystick vertical handle with programmable buttons that controls action.

Just-in-time (JIT)   an approach that produces or delivers a product or service just at the time the customer wants it.

K

Keyboard   the most often used input device for desktop and notebook computers.

Key logger (key trapper) software   a program that, when installed on a computer, records every keystroke and mouse click.

Key performance indicator (KPI)   the most essential and important quantifiable measures used in analytics initiatives to monitor success of a business activity.

Knowledge-based system (expert system)   an artificial intelligence system that applies reasoning capabilities to reach a conclusion.

Knowledge management (KM) system   an IT system that supports the capturing, organization, and dissemination of knowledge (i.e., know-how) throughout an organization.

L

Language processing   attempts to make sense of what you're saying by comparing the word phonemes generated in step 2 with a language model database.

Laser printer   forms images using the same sort of electrostatic process that photocopiers use.

Legacy information system (LIS)   represents a massive, long-term business investment; such systems are often brittle, slow, and nonextensible.

Link (hyperlink)   clickable text or an image that takes you to another site or page on the Web.

Linux   an open-source operating system that provides a rich operating environment for high-end workstations and network servers.

Liquid crystal display (LCD)   makes the screen image by sending electricity through crystallized liquid trapped between two layers of glass or plastic.

List   a collection of information arranged in columns and rows in which each column displays one particular type of information.

List definition table   a description of a list by column.

Local area network (LAN)   a network that covers a building or buildings in close proximity, such as one campus of a university or corporation.

Location-based services (social locationing)   the use of a mobile device and its location (as determined by GPS) to check into locations such as businesses and entertainment venues, find friends and their locations, and receive rewards and take advantage of "specials" based on location.

Location mashup   a geographic information system (GIS) that displays a particular geographic area and then overlays content according to the user's desires.

Logical view   focuses on how you as a knowledge worker need to arrange and access information to meet your particular business needs.

Long Tail   refers to the tail of a sales curve—first offered by Chris Anderson, editor-in-chief of *Wired Magazine,* as a way of explaining e-commerce profitability.

Looping   repeating a block of statements or code numerous times.

Loyalty program   rewards customers based on the amount of business they do with a particular organization.

M

Mac OS   Apple's operating system.

Macro   a set of actions recorded or written by a user.

Macro language   a programming language that includes built-in commands that mimic the functionality available from menus and dialog boxes within an application.

Mailing list   discussion groups organized by area of interest.

Mail server   provides e-mail services and accounts.

Mainframe computer (mainframe)   a computer designed to meet the computing needs of hundreds of people in a large business environment.

Maintenance phase   of the systems development life cycle monitors and supports the new system to ensure it continues to meet the business requirements.

Maintenance, repair, and operations (MRO) materials (indirect materials)   materials that are necessary for running a modern corporation, but do not relate to the company's primary business activities.

Malware   software designed to harm your computer or computer security.

Malware bot   bot that is used for fraud, sabotage, DoS attacks, or some other malicious purpose.

Management information systems (MIS)   deals with the planning for, development, management, and use of information technology tools to help people perform all tasks related to information processing and management.

Marketing analytics   the analysis of marketing-related data to improve the efficiency and effectiveness of marketing efforts including product placement, marketing mix, and customer identification and classification.

Marketing mix   the set of marketing tools that your organization will use to pursue its marketing objectives in reaching and attracting potential customers.

Mashup   a combination of content from more than one source.

Mass customization   the ability of an organization to give its customers the opportunity to tailor its product or service to the customers' specifications.

Massively multiplayer online role-playing game (MMORPG)   a game in which thousands or perhaps millions of people play and interact in a robust virtual world.

M-commerce   the term used to describe electronic commerce conducted over a wireless device such as a cell phone, PDA, or notebook.

MD5 hash value   a mathematically generated string of 32 letters and digits that is unique for an individual storage medium at a specific point in time.

Megabyte (MB or M or Meg)   roughly 1 million bytes.

Memory Stick Media card   elongated flash memory card about the width of a penny developed by Sony with capacities up to 512 megabytes.

Message   how objects communicate with each other.

Metropolitan (municipal) area network (MAN)   a set of connected networks all within the same city or metropolitan area, but not in immediate proximity to each other.

Microblogging   users exchanging small bursts of information that often include links to Web sites, videos, and the like.

Microphone   captures audio for conversion into electronic form.

Microsoft Windows Vista   Microsoft's personal computer operating system in a wide range of editions including Vista Home Basic, Vista Home Premium, Vista Business, and Vista Ultimate.

Microsoft Windows XP Home   Microsoft's predecessor to Vista designed specifically for home users.

Microsoft Windows XP Professional (Windows XP Pro)   Microsoft's predecessor to Vista with enhanced features to support home users and business users.

Microwave transmission   a type of radio transmission.

Minicomputer (mid-range computer)   a computer designed to meet the computing needs of several people simultaneously in a small to medium-size business environment.

Mobile agent   software agent that can relocate itself onto different computer systems.

Mobile analytics   the analysis of data related to the use of mobile devices by customers and employees.

Mobile computing   broad general term describing your ability to use technology to wirelessly connect to and use centrally located information and/or application software.

Mobile CPU   a special type of CPU for a notebook computer that changes speed, and therefore power consumption, in response to fluctuation in use.

Mobisode   short one-minute video clips of TV shows designed for viewing on a small cell phone screen.

Model management   component of a DSS that consists of both the DSS models and the DSS model management system.

Monitoring-and-surveillance agent (predictive agent)   intelligent agent that constantly observes and reports on some entity of interest, that could, for example, be a network or manufacturing equipment.

Mouse   a pointing device that you use to click on icons or buttons.

Multi-agent system   group of intelligent agents that have the ability to work independently but must also work with each other in order to achieve their assigned task.

Multi-channel service delivery   the term that describes a company's offering of multiple ways in which customers can interact with it.

Multidimensional analysis (MDA) tool   slice-and-dice technique that allows you to view multidimensional information from different perspectives.

Multifunction printer   a printer that can scan, copy, and fax, as well as print.

MultiMediaCard (MMC)   flash memory card that looks identical to an SD card (but SD cards have copy protection built-in), is a little larger than a quarter, and is slightly thicker than a credit card.

Multimedia (HTML) résumé   a multimedia format displayed on the Web for employers to explore at their convenience.

Multi-state CPU   works with information represented in more than just two states, probably 10 states with each state representing a digit between 0 and 9.

Multitasking   allows you to work with more than one piece of software at a time.

Multi-tenancy   multiple people simultaneously using a single instance of a piece of software.

Mutation   the process within a genetic algorithm of randomly trying combinations and evaluating the success (or failure) of the outcomes.

N

Nanotechnology   a discipline that seeks to control matter at the atomic and sub-atomic levels for the purpose of building devices on the same small scale.

Near Field Communication (NFC)   a wireless transmission technology being developed primarily for cell phones to support mobile commerce (m-commerce) and other cell phone activities.

Nearshore outsourcing   contracting an outsourcing arrangement with a company in a nearby country.

Network access point (NAP)   a point on the Internet where several connections converge.

Network hub   a device that connects multiple computers into a network.

Network interface card (NIC)   an expansion card for a desktop computer or a PC card for a notebook computer that connects your computer to a network and provides the doorway for information to flow in and out.

Network service provider (NSP)   such as MCI or AT&T, owns and maintains routing computers at NAPs and even the lines that connect the NAPs to each other.

Neural network (artificial neural network or ANN)   an artificial intelligence system that is capable of finding and differentiating patterns.

Nonrecurring (ad hoc) decision   one that you make infrequently (perhaps only once) and you may even have different criteria for determining the best solution each time.

Nonstructured decision   a decision for which there may be several "right" answers and there is no precise way to get a right answer.

Normalization   process of assuring that a relational database structure can be implemented as a series of two-dimensional tables.

Notebook computer   a small, portable, fully functional, battery-operated computer.

N-tier infrastructure   balances the work of the network over several different servers.

O

Object   an instance of a class.

Objective information   quantifiably describes something that is known.

Object-oriented approach   combines information and procedures into a single view.

Object-oriented database   works with traditional database information and also complex data types such as diagrams, schematic drawings, video, and sound and text documents.

Object-oriented programming language   a programming language used to develop object-oriented systems.

Offshore outsourcing   contracting with a company that is geographically far away.

Online ad (banner ad)   small advertisement that appears on other sites.

Online analytical processing (OLAP)   the manipulation of information to support decision making.

Online training   runs over the Internet or off a CD or DVD.

Online transaction processing (OLTP)   the gathering of input information, processing that information, and updating existing information to reflect the gathered and processed information.

Onshore outsourcing   the process of engaging another company in the same country for services.

Open-source information   content that is publicly available (in a broad sense), free of charge, and most often updateable by anyone.

Open-source software   software for which the source code (how the software was actually written) is publicly available and free of charge.

Operating system software   system software that controls your application software and manages how your hardware devices work together.

Operational database   a database that supports OLTP.

Optical character reader   reads characters that appear on a page or sales tag (often used in point-of-sale [POS] systems in retail environments).

Optical fiber   uses a very thin and flexible glass or plastic fiber through which pulses of light travel.

Optical mark reader   detects the presence or absence of a mark in a predetermined spot on the page (often used for true/false and multiple choice exams answers).

Optical storage media   plastic discs on which information is stored, deleted, and/or changed using laser light.

Organic light emitting diode (**OLED**) uses many layers of organic material emitting a visible light and therefore eliminating the need for backlighting.

Output device   a tool you use to see, hear, or otherwise recognize the results of your information-processing requests.

Outsourcing   the delegation of specific work to a third party for a specified length of time, at a specified cost, and at a specified level of service.

Overall cost leadership   (in Porter's three generic strategies) offering the same or better quality product or service at a price that is less than what any of the competition is able to do.

P

Page exposures   average number of page exposures to an individual visitor.

Parallel implementation   using both the old and new system until you're sure that the new system performs correctly.

Parallel port   fits parallel connectors, which are large flat connectors found almost exclusively on printer cables.

Path-to-profitability (P2P)   a formal business plan that outlines key business issues such as customer targets (by demographic, industry,

etc.), marketing strategies, operations strategies (e.g., production, transportation, and logistics), and projected targets for income-statement and balance-sheet items.

Pattern classification   matches your spoken phonemes to a phoneme sequence stored in an acoustic model database.

PC Card   the expansion card you use to add devices to your notebook computer.

PC Card slot   the opening on the side or front of a notebook, where you connect an external device with a PC Card.

Peer-to-peer collaboration software   permits users to communicate in real time and share files without going through a central server.

Personal digital assistant (PDA)   a small handheld computer that helps you surf the Web and perform simple tasks such as note taking, calendaring, appointment scheduling, and maintaining an address book.

Personal finance software   helps you maintain your checkbook, prepare a budget, track investments, monitor your credit card balances, and pay bills electronically.

Personal information management software (PIM)   helps you create and maintain (1) to-do lists, (2) appointments and calendars, and (3) points of contact.

Personal productivity software   helps you perform personal tasks—such as writing a memo, creating a graph, and creating a slide presentation—that you can usually do even if you don't own a computer.

Personal software-as-a-service (personal SaaS)   a delivery model for personal productivity software such as Microsoft Office in which you pay for personal productivity software on a pay-per-use basis instead of buying the software outright.

Pharming   the rerouting of your request for a legitimate Web site, that is, you type in the correct address for your bank and are redirected to a fake site that collects information from you.

Phased implementation   implementing the new system in phases (e.g., accounts receivables, then accounts payable) until you're sure it works correctly and then implementing the remaining phases of the new system.

Phishing (carding or **brand spoofing)**   technique to gain personal information for the purpose of identity theft, usually by means of fraudulent e-mail.

Physical view   deals with how information is physically arranged, stored, and accessed on some type of storage device such as a hard disk.

Pilot implementation   having only a small group of people use the new system until you know it works correctly and then adding the remaining people to the system.

Pirated software   the unauthorized use, duplication, distribution or sale of copyrighted software.

Pivot table   enables you to group and summarize information.

Pixels (picture elements)   the dots that make up the image on your screen.

Planning phase   of the systems development life cycle, in which you create a solid plan for developing your information system.

Platform-as-a-service (PaaS)   a delivery model for software identical to SaaS with the additional features of (1) the ability to customize data entry forms, screens, reports, and the like and (2) access to software development tools to alter the way in which the software works by adding new modules (services) and/or making modifications to existing modules.

Plotter   form output by moving a pen across the surface of a piece of paper.

Plug and play   an operating feature that finds and installs the device driver for a device that you plug into your computer.

Plunge implementation   discarding the old system completely and immediately using the new system.

Pointing device   a device that is used to navigate and select objects on a display screen.

Pointing stick   a little rod (like a pencil-top eraser) used almost exclusively on notebook computers.

Polymorphism   to have many forms.

Pop-under ad   a form of a pop-up ad that you do not see until you close your current browser window.

Pop-up ad   small Web page containing an advertisement that appears on your screen outside the current Web site loaded into your browser.

Port   a place on your system unit, monitor, or keyboard through which information and instructions flow to and from your computer system.

Portable document format (PDF)   standard electronic distribution file format.

Portable document format (PDF) résumé   a standard electronic distribution format typically used for e-mailing.

Prediction goal   the question you want addressed by the predictive analytics model.

Prediction indicator   specific measurable value based on an attribute of the entity under consideration.

Predictive analytics   uses a variety of decision tools and techniques—such as neural networks, data mining, decision trees, and Bayesian networks—to analyze current and historical data and make predictions about the likelihood of the occurrence of future events.

Presentation software   helps you create and edit information that will appear in electronic slides.

Primary key   a field (or group of fields in some cases) that uniquely describes each record.

Privacy   the right to be left alone when you want to be, to have control over your own personal possessions, and not to be observed without your consent.

Private cloud   cloud computing services established and hosted by an organization on its internal network and available only to employees and departments within that organization.

Procedure   manipulates or changes information.

Procedure view   contains all of the procedures within a system.

Program   a set of instructions that, when executed, cause a computer to behave in a specific manner.

Programming language   the tool developers use to write a program.

Project manager   an individual who is an expert in project planning and management, defines and develops the project plan, and tracks the plan to ensure all key project milestones are completed on time.

Project milestone   represents a key date by which you need a certain group of activities performed.

Project plan   defines the what, when, and who questions of systems development including all activities to be performed, the individuals, or resources, who will perform the activities, and the time required to complete each activity.

Project scope document   a written definition of the project scope, usually no longer than a paragraph.

Proof-of-concept prototype   a prototype you use to prove the technical feasibility of a proposed system.

Prototype   a smaller-scale representation or working model of the user's requirements or a proposed design for an information system.

Prototyping   the process of building a model that demonstrates the features of a proposed product, service, or system.

PS/2 port   fits PS/2 connectors, which you often find on keyboards and mice.

Public cloud   cloud services that exist on the Internet offered to anyone and any business.

Public key encryption (PKE)   an encryption system that uses two keys: a public key that everyone can have and a private key for only the recipient.

Push technology   an environment in which businesses and organizations come to you via technology with information, services, and product offerings based on your profile.

Q

Query-and-reporting tool   similar to a QBE tool, SQL, and a report generator in the typical database environment.

Query-by-example (QBE) tool   helps you graphically design the answer to a question.

R

Random access memory (RAM)   a temporary holding area for the information you're working with as well as the system and application software instructions that the CPU currently needs.

Rapid application development methodology (RAD, rapid prototyping)   emphasizes extensive user involvement in the rapid and evolutionary construction of working prototypes of a system to accelerate the systems development process.

Recovery   the process of reinstalling the backup information in the event the information was lost.

Recurring decision   a decision that you have to make repeatedly and often periodically, whether weekly, monthly, quarterly, or yearly.

Redacting   blacking out portions of a document, usually to protect confidential information, so that it cannot be recovered later.

Relation   describes each two-dimensional table or file in the relational model (hence its name relational database model).

Relational database   uses a series of logically related two-dimensional tables or files to store information in the form of a database.

Repeater   a device that receives a radio signal, strengthens it, and sends it on.

Report generator   helps you quickly define formats of reports and what information you want to see in a report.

Request for proposal (RFP) a formal document that describes in detail your logical requirements for a proposed system and invites outsourcing organizations (or "vendors") to submit bids for its development.

Requirement recovery document a detailed document which describes (1) the distinction between critical and noncritical IT systems and information, (2) each possible threat, and (3) the possible worst-case scenarios that can result from each disaster.

Requirements definition document defines all the business requirements and prioritizes them in order of business importance.

Resolution of a printer the number of dots per inch (dpi) it produces.

Resolution of a screen the number of pixels it has.

Response time average time to respond to a user-generated event, such as a request for a report, a mouse click, and so on.

Résumé summary of your qualifications.

Reverse auction the process in which a buyer posts its interest in buying a certain quantity of items with notations concerning quality, specification, and delivery timing, and sellers compete for the business by submitting successively lower bids until there is only one seller left.

RFID (radio frequency identification) uses a microchip (chip) in a tag or label to store information, and information is transmitted from, or written to, the tag or label when the microchip is exposed to the correct frequency of radio waves.

Risk assessment the process of evaluating IT assets, their importance to the organization, and their susceptibility to threats to measure the risk exposure of these assets.

Rivalry among existing competitors in the Five Forces Model is high when competition is fierce in a market, and low when competition is more complacent.

Rootkit software that gives you administrator rights to a computer or network whose purpose is to allow you to conceal processes, files, or system data, from the operating system.

Router a device that passes network traffic between smaller subnetworks (or subnets) of a larger network.

Run-grow-transform (RGT) framework an approach in which you allocate in terms of percentages how you will spend your IT dollars on various types of business strategies.

S

Sales force automation (SFA) system automatically tracks all of the steps in the sales process.

Satellite modem modem that allows you to get Internet access from your satellite dish.

Satisficing the process of making a choice that meets your needs and is satisfactory, without necessarily being the best possible choice available.

Scalability refers to how well your system can adapt to increased demands.

Scannable (or ASCII) résumé a paper résumé without any formatting that becomes electronic when it is scanned into a computer.

Scanner used to convert information that exists in visible form into electronic form.

Scope creep occurs when the scope of the project increases beyond its original intentions.

Screenagers the term applied to the current generation of young people because they spend so much time in front of a screen.

Script bunny (script kiddie) someone who would like to be a hacker but doesn't have much technical expertise.

Search engine a facility on the Web that helps you find sites with the information and/or services you want.

Search engine optimization (SEO) improving the visibility of a Web site through the use of tags and key terms found by search engines.

Secure Digital (SD) card flash memory card that looks identical to an MMC card (but SD cards have copy protection built-in), is a little larger than a quarter, and is slightly thicker than a credit card.

Secure Electronic Transaction (SET) a transmission security method that ensures transactions are legitimate as well as secure.

Secure Sockets Layer (SSL) creates a secure and private connection between a Web client computer and a Web server computer, encrypts the information, and then sends the information over the Internet.

Selection the process within a genetic algorithm that gives preference to better outcomes.

Selfsourcing (also called end-user development) the development and support of IT systems by end users (knowledge workers) with little or no help from IT specialists.

Selling prototype a prototype you use to convince people of the worth of a proposed system.

Service level agreement (SLA) a formal contractually obligated agreement between two parties; within different environments, an SLA takes on different meanings.

Service level specification (SLS) or service level objective (SLO) supporting document to a service level agreement that clearly defines key metrics for success regarding the SLA.

Service-oriented architecture (SOA or SoA) a software architecture perspective that focuses on the development, use, and reuse of small self-contained blocks of code (called *services*) to meet all the application software needs of an organization.

Sexting the sending of sexually explicit messages and/or photos, primarily between mobile phones.

Sign-off the knowledge workers' actual signatures indicating they approve all the business requirements.

Skill words nouns and adjectives used by organizations to describe job skills which should be woven into the text of an applicant's résumé.

Slack space the space left over from the end of the file to the end of the cluster.

Smart card a plastic card the size of a credit card that contains an embedded chip on which digital information can be stored and updated.

SmartMedia (SM) card flash memory card that's a little longer than a CF card and about as thick as a credit card with capacities of up to 512 megabytes.

Smartphone cell phone with additional features such as a camera; Internet connectivity; note taking capabilities; GPS capabilities; and digital music and video players.

Social engineering   conning your way into acquiring information that you have no right to.

Social media analytics   the analysis of data related to social media use, mainly by customers or competitors, to help an organization better understand the interaction dynamics of itself with its customers and also to help an organization scan social media for competitive intelligence.

Social networking site   a site on which you post information about yourself, create a network of friends, share content such as photos and videos, and communicate with other people.

Social network system   an IT system that links you to people you know and, from there, to people your contacts know.

Software   the set of instructions that your hardware executes to carry out a specific task for you.

Software-as-a-service (SaaS)   delivery model for software in which you would pay for software on a pay-per-use basis instead of buying the software outright.

Software suite   bundled software that comes from the same publisher and costs less than buying all the software pieces individually.

Spam   unsolicited e-mail (electronic junk mail) from businesses that advertises goods and services.

Spam blocker software   utility software that filters unwanted e-mail from your inbox.

Spear phishing   phishing that is targeted to specific individuals.

Spoofing   the forging of the return address on an e-mail so that the e-mail message appears to come from someone other than the actual sender.

Spreadsheet software   helps you work primarily with numbers, including performing calculations and creating graphs.

Spyware (sneakware, stealthware)   malicious software that collects information about you and your computer and reports it to someone else without your permission.

Steganography   the hiding of information inside other information.

Storage area network (SAN)   an infrastructure for building special, dedicated networks that allow rapid and reliable access to storage devices by multiple servers.

Storage device   a tool you use to store information for use at a later time.

Storyboard   a visual representation illustrating relationships of objects on a Web page.

Structured decision   a decision where processing a certain kind of information in a specified way will always get you the right answer.

Structured query language (SQL)   a standardized fourth-generation query language found in most DBMSs.

Structure tag   HTML tag that sets up the necessary sections and specifies that the document is indeed an HTML document.

Stylus   penlike device used to write or draw on a PDA or tablet PC.

Subjective information   attempts to describe something that is unknown.

Sub procedure   computer code that performs some action on or with objects.

Supercomputer   the fastest, most powerful, and most expensive type of computer.

Supplier power   in the Five Forces Model is high when buyers have few choices from whom to buy, and low when their choices are many.

Supply chain management (SCM)   tracks inventory and information among business processes and across companies.

Supply chain management (SCM) system   an IT system that supports supply chain management activities by automating the tracking of inventory and information among business processes and across companies.

Swarm (collective) intelligence   collective behavior of groups of simple agents that are capable of devising solutions to problems as they arise, eventually leading to coherent global patterns.

Switch   a network device that connects computers and passes messages by repeating each computer's transmissions only to the intended recipient, not to all the computers connected.

Switching cost   a cost that makes customers reluctant to switch to another product or service supplier.

System availability   usually measured inversely as *downtime,* or the average amount of time a system is down and unavailable to end users and customers.

System bus   electrical pathways that move information between basic components of the motherboard, including between RAM and the CPU.

Systems development life cycle (SDLC)   a structured step-by-step approach for developing information systems.

System software   handles tasks specific to technology management and coordinates the interaction of all technology devices.

System testing   verifies that the units or pieces of code written for a system function correctly when integrated into the total system.

T

T1   a high-speed business network circuit typically used for business connections, running at speeds up to 1.544 Mbps (1.544 million bits per second).

Tablet PC   slim-line computer that is about the size of a notebook or smaller with a touchscreen and has the functional capabilities of notebook or desktop computer.

TCP/IP (Transport control protocol/Internet protocol)   the primary protocol for transmitting information over the Internet.

Technical architecture   defines the hardware, software, and telecommunications equipment required to run the system.

Technology-literate knowledge worker   person who knows how and when to apply technology.

Telecommunications device   tool you use to send information to and receive it from another person or computer in a network.

Telephone modem (modem)   a device that connects your computer to your phone line so that you can access another computer or network.

Terabyte (TB)   roughly 1 trillion bytes.

Test conditions   the detailed steps the system must perform along with the expected results of each step.

Testing phase of the systems development life cycle verifies that the system works and meets all the business requirements defined in the analysis phase.

Text analytics process of using statistical, artificial intelligence, and linguistic techniques to convert information content in textual sources—like surveys, e-mails, blogs, and social media—into structured information.

Threat of new entrants in the Five Forces Model is high when it is easy for new competitors to enter a market, and low when there are significant entry barriers to entering a market.

Threat of substitute products or services in the Five Forces Model is high when there are many alternatives to a product or service, and low when there are few alternatives from which to choose.

Thrill-seeker hacker a hacker who breaks into computer systems for entertainment.

Throughput the amount of information that can pass through a system in a given amount of time.

Tiered infrastructure (layer infrastructure) the IT system is partitioned into tiers (or layers) where each tier (or layer) performs a specific type of functionality.

Time service factor (TSF) the percentage of calls answered within a specific time frame, such as 30 or 90 seconds.

Top-level domain (TLD) extension of a Web site address that identifies its type.

Total hits number of visits to your Web site, many of which may be by the same visitor.

Touchpad the little dark rectangle that you use to move the cursor with your finger, often found on notebook computers.

Trackball similar to a mechanical mouse, but it has a ball on the top.

Traditional technology approach has two primary views of any computer-based system—information and procedures—and it keeps these two views separate and distinct at all times.

Transaction speed the speed at which a system can process a transaction.

Trojan horse software software you don't want hidden inside software you do want.

Trojan horse virus hides inside other software, usually an attachment or download.

Twisted-pair cable a bundle of copper wires used for transmitting voice or data communications; it comes in several varieties.

Twitter jockey person who focuses on Twitter to communicate with customers, sponsors, business partners, and the like.

U

U3 Smart drive looks like and is a USB flash drive, but it stores and can launch and run software on any computer.

Ubiquitous computing computing and technology support anytime, anywhere with access to all needed information and access to all business partners, both internal and external to the organization.

Unallocated space the set of clusters that have been set aside to store information, but have not yet received a file, or still contain some or all of a file marked as deleted.

Uniform resource locator (URL) an address for a specific Web page or document within a Web site.

Uninstaller software utility software that you can use to remove software from your hard disk that you no longer want.

Unique visitors the number of unique visitors to your sites in a given time.

Unit testing tests individual units or pieces of code for a system.

USB (universal serial bus) port fits small flat plug-and-play, hot-swap USB connectors, and, using USB hubs, you can connect up to 127 devices to a single USB port on your computer.

User acceptance testing (UAT) determines if the system satisfies the business requirements and enables knowledge workers to perform their jobs correctly.

User agent (personal agent) an intelligent agent that takes action on your behalf.

User documentation highlights how to use the system.

User interface management component of a DSS that allows you to communicate with the DSS.

Utility software software that provides additional functionality to your operating system software.

V

Value-added network (VAN) B2B service that offers information-sharing intermediary services between organizations based on various standards regarding the format of the information and how it will be sent and received.

Variable a place to store a piece of information.

Vertical e-marketplace an electronic marketplace that connects buyers and sellers in a given industry (e.g., oil and gas, textiles, and retail).

Vertical market software application software that is unique to a particular industry.

View allows you to see the contents of a database file, make whatever changes you want, perform simple sorting, and query to find the location of specific information.

Viewable image size (VIS) the size of the image on a monitor.

Viral marketing encourages users of a product or service supplied by a B2C e-commerce business to encourage friends to join in as well.

Virtual good nonphysical object.

Virtual private network (VPN) uses encryption to protect the confidentiality of *all* network transmissions between two endpoints.

Virtual reality a three-dimensional computer simulation in which you actively and physically participate.

Virus (computer virus) software that is written with malicious intent to cause annoyance or damage.

Visual Basic Editor (VBE) a separate application where you write and edit your Visual Basic macros.

VoIP (Voice over Internet Protocol) allows you to send voice communications over the Internet and avoid the toll charges that you would normally receive from your long distance carrier.

W

Walker   an input device that captures and records the movement of your feet as you walk or turn in different directions.

Waterfall methodology   a sequential, activity-based process in which one phase in the SDLC is followed by another from planning through implementation.

Web 2.0   so-called second generation of the Web, which focuses on online collaboration, users as both creators and modifiers of content, dynamic and customized information feeds, and many other engaging Web-based services.

Web 3.0   third-generation of the Web focused on semantics.

Web analytics   the analysis of data related to the Internet, often focusing on optimizing Web page usage.

Web authoring software   helps you design and develop Web sites and pages that you publish on the Web.

Web browser software   enables you to surf the Web.

Webcam   captures digital video to upload to the Web.

Web-centric metric   a measure of the success of your Web and e-business initiatives.

Web log   consists of one line of information for every visitor to a Web site and is usually stored on a Web server.

Web page   a specific portion of a Web site that deals with a certain topic.

Web portal   a site that provides a wide range of services, including search engines, free e-mail, chat rooms, discussion boards, and links to hundreds of different sites.

Web server   provides information and services to Web surfers.

Web site   a specific location on the Web where you visit, gather information, and perhaps even order products.

Web site address   a unique name that identifies a specific site on the Web.

Web space   storage area where you keep your Web site.

Whaling   the use of phishing targeted at senior business executives, government leaders, and other types of high-profile individuals.

White-hat (ethical) hacker   a computer security professional who is hired by a company to break into its computer system, so as to find security lapses.

Wide area network (WAN)   a set of connected networks serving areas or buildings not in immediate proximity to each other.

WiFi (wireless fidelity or IEEE 802.11a, b, or g)   a standard for transmitting information in the form of radio waves over distances up to about 300 feet.

Wiki   a Web site that allows you—as a visitor—to create, edit, change, and often eliminate content.

Wired communications media   transmit information over a closed, connected path.

Wireless access point (WAP)   a device that allows a computer to use radio waves to access a network.

Wireless communications media   transmit information through the air.

Word processing software   helps you create papers, letters, memos, and other basic documents.

Workshop training   held in a classroom environment and is led by an instructor.

World Wide Web (Web)   a multimedia-based collection of information, services, and Web sites supported by the Internet.

Worm   a type of virus that replicates and spreads itself, not just from file to file, but from computer to computer via e-mail and other Internet traffic.

X

xD-Picture (xD) card   flash memory card that looks like a rectangular piece of plastic smaller than a penny and about as thick, with one edge slightly curved.

Z

Zombie   bot-infected computer.

CHAPTER 1

1. "Declining Room Revenue," *The Denver Post,* September 12, 2010, p. K2.

2. "Declining Room Revenue," *Chicago Tribune,* at http://www.chicago-tribune.com/business/yourmoney/sns-graphics-hotel-services-gx,0,5876978.graphic, accessed March 17, 2011.

3. "Sexcerpts," *Rocky Mountain News,* March 25, 2006, p. 2E.

4. Fisch, Karl, Scott McLeod, and Jeff Bronan, "Did You Know?" You-Tube, at http://www.youtube.com/watch?v=cL9Wu2kWwSY, accessed March 18, 2011.

5. Petrecca, Laura, "More College Grads Use Social Media to Find Jobs," *USA Today,* April 5, 2011, at http://www.usatoday.com/tech/news/2011-04-04-social-media-in-job-searches.htm#, accessed May 4, 2011.

6. Kallman, Ernest, and John Grillo, *Ethical Decision Making and Information Technology* (San Francisco: McGraw-Hill, 1993).

7. Mullaney, Tim, "HBO Go Off to a Flying Start with 1 Million Downloads," *USA Today,* May 2011, at http://content.usatoday.com/communities/technologylive/post/2011/05/hbo-go-off-to-a-flying-start-with-1-million-downloads/1, accessed May 2, 2011.

8. Porter, Michael, "How Competitive Forces Shape Strategy," *Harvard Business Review,* March/April 1979.

9. Horovitz, Bruce, "Marketers Use Social Media for Valentine Promotions," *USA Today,* February 6, 2011, at http://www.usatoday.com/money/advertising/2011-02-11-vdsocial/11_ST_N.htm#, accessed March 1, 2011.

10. Carroll, Paul, and Chunka Mui, "Where Innovation Is Sorely Needed," *Technology Review,* February 1, 2011, at http://www.technologyreview.com/business/32245, accessed June 1, 2011.

11. Gomolski, Barb, "Best Practices in IT Cost Management," The Gartner Group, presentation DTS-Gartner 2008 Technology Day, January 9, 2008.

12. Rosen, Jeffrey, "The Web Means the End of Forgetting," *The New York Times,* July 21, 2010, at http://www.nytimes.com/2010/07/25/magazine/25privacy-t2.html, accessed December 11, 2010.

13. Rossiter, Joe, "More Families Choose to Have Funerals Webcast," *USA Today,* March 25, 2011, at http://www.usatoday.com/tech/news/2011-03-24-funeral-webcasts_N.htm#, accessed April 2, 2011.

14. Stoller, Gary, "After Soldiers' Video Goes Viral, More Bags Will Fly Free," *USA Today,* June 2011, at http://travel.usatoday.com/flights/story/2011/06/After-soldiers-video-goes-viral-more-bags-will-fly-free/48212264/1, accessed June 17, 2011.

15. Thanawala, Sudhin, "Man Gets Stolen Laptop Back after Tracking It," *USA Today,* June 2, 2011, at http://www.usatoday.com/tech/news/2011-06-02-stolen-laptop-tracking-software_n.htm#, accessed June 4, 2011.

16. McCarthy, Michael, "Rashard Mendenhall Fired by Champion over Osama Bin Laden Tweets," *USA Today,* May 7, 2011, at http://content.usatoday.com/communities/gameon/post/2011/05/rashard-mendenhall-fired-by-champion-over-osama-bin-laden-comments/1, accessed May 19, 2011.

17. Dobner, Jennifer, "Utah Man Used Facebook during Standoff," *USA Today,* June 22, 2011, at http://www.usatoday.com/tech/news/2011-06-22-facebook-standoff_n.htm#, accessed June 24, 2011.

18. Snider, Mike, "Senate Panel Grills Apple, Google on Tracking Technology," *USA Today,* May 11, 2011, at http://www.usatoday.com/tech/news/2011-05-10-mobile-location-tracking_n.htm#, accessed May 24, 2011.

19. Acohido, Byron, "Jobs, Apple Issue Complex Denial of iPhone Tracking," *USA Today,* April 27, 2011, at http://www.usatoday.com/tech/news/2011-04-27-apple-iphone-tracking_n.htm#, accessed May 24, 2011.

20. Acohido, Byron, "More Confusion Swirls around Google, Apple Tracking," *USA Today,* April 27, 2011, at http://www.usatoday.com/tech/news/2011-04-25-iphone-tracking.htm#, accessed May 24, 2011.

CHAPTER 2

1. Marshall, Ken, "Move to Online Causes Death of Travel Agency Jobs," Cleveland.com, October 14, 2009, at http://www.cleveland.com/pdgraphics/index.ssf/2009/10/move_to_online_causes_decline.html, accessed July 5, 2011.

2. "Configuring a 500 Percent ROI for Dell," i2 White Paper, www.i2.com/customer/hightech_consumer.cfm, accessed May 5, 2004.

3. "Frito Lay—Zero Emission Trucks," Share Green, Food & Beverage Case Studies, August 31, 2010, at http://www.sharegreen.ca/?p=3444, accessed July 6, 2011.

4. "Websmart," *BusinessWeek,* November 24, 2003, p. 96.

5. Koudal, Peter et al., "General Motors: Building a Digital Loyal Network through Demand and Supply Chain Integration," Stanford Graduate School of Business, Case GS-29, March 17, 2003.

6. "American Red Cross and Salesforce.com Meet the Magnitude of Need Created by Disasters," Salesforce.com Customer Success Stories, at http://www.salesforce.com/showcase/stories/american_redcross.jsp, accessed July 7, 2011.

7. "President Bush's Proposed FY06 Budget Represents Growth in IT Spending for Federal Government," February 8, 2005, www.bitpipe.com, accessed May 19, 2005.

8. "ERP Outsourcing Picks Up and Takes Off," www.outsourcing.com, accessed May 19, 2005.

9. Rashid, Mohammad et al., "The Evolution of ERP Systems: A Historical

Perspective," www.ideagroup.com, accessed May 11, 2004.

10. Morrison, Scott, and Geoffrey Fowler, "eBay Pushes into Amazon Turf," "*The Wall Street Journal*," March 29, 2011, at http://online.wsj.com/article/SB10001424052748704 4719045762228532935603752.html, accessed July 7, 2011.

11. Facebook, Facebook Statistics, at http://www.facebook.com/press/info.php?statistics, accessed July 6, 2011.

12. Molina, Brett, "Twitter: Serving 200 Million Tweets Daily," *USA Today*, July 4, 2011, at http://content.usatoday.com/communities/technologylive/post/2011/07/twitter-now-serving-200-million-tweets-daily/1, accessed July 6, 2011.

13. Parr, Ben, "LinkedIn Surpasses 100 Million Users," *USA Today*, March 22, 2011, at http://content.usatoday.com/communities/technologylive/post/2011/03/linkedin-surpasses-100-million-users, accessed May 26, 2011.

14. "Top 7 Social Media Sites from Mar 10 [2010] to Mar 11 [2011]," StatCounter, at http://gs.statcounter.com/#social_media-ww-monthly-201003-201103, accessed July 6, 2011.

15. Claburn, Thomas, "PepsiCo Debuts Social Vending Machine," *InformationWeek*, April 29, 2011, at http://www.informationweek.com/news/internet/retail/229402472, accessed May 2, 2011.

16. "World of Warcraft Subscriber Base Currently at 11.4 Million," Curse.com, May 9, 2011, at http://www.curse.com/articles/world-of-warcraft-news/956087.aspx, accessed July 7, 2011.

17. "Zynga," AppData, at http://www.appdata.com/devs/10-zynga, accessed July 7, 2011.

18. Horovitz, Bruce, "Retailers Turn to Facebook to Sell Their Wares," *USA Today*, May 10, 2011, at http://www.usatoday.com/money/industries/retail/2011-05-10-retailers-turn-to-facebook_n.htm#, accessed May 22, 2011.

19. Weier, Mary Hayes, "Collaboration and the New Product Imperative," *InformationWeek*, July 21, 2008, pp. 26–32.

20. Greengard, Samuel, "How to Win with Social Media," *Baseline*, March/April 2011, pp. 16–21.

21. Strauss, Steve, "Measuring the ROI of Your Social Media Efforts," *USA Today*, March 13, 2011, at http://www.usatoday.com/money/smallbusiness/columnist/strauss/2011-03-13-small-business-and-social-media_N.htm, accessed July 7, 2011.

CHAPTER 3

1. Crooks, Ross, "Music Retail: The Rise of Digital," Mint.com, November 2, 2009, at http://www.mint.com/blog/trends/music-retail-the-rise-of-digital/, accessed July 9, 2011.

2. "2010 Year-End Shipment Statistics," Recording Industry Association of America, at http://76.74.24.142/548C3F4C-6B6D-F702-384C-D25E2AB93610.pdf, accessed July 5, 2011.

3. "Driven by Data: The Importance of Building a Culture of Fact-Based Decision-Making," SAS, 2009, at http://www.sas.com/resources/whitepaper/wp_9867.pdf, accessed July 8, 2011.

4. "A New Model of Business Intelligence," Oracle, 2010, at http://www.infoworld.com/t/business-intelligenceanalytics/wp/new-model-business-intelligence-444, accessed July 8, 2011.

5. Watterson, Karen, "A Data Miner's Tools," *BYTE*, October 1995, pp. 170–72.

6. "Amway China Improves Replenishment Time by 20 Percent, Customer Satisfaction Soars to 97 Percent with SAS," SAS Institute Customer Success Stories, at http://www.sas.com/success/amwaychina.html, accessed July 11, 2011.

7. Cash, James, "Gaining Customer Loyalty," *InformationWeek*, April 10, 1995, p. 88.

8. Segall, Laurie, "Bloomberg Opens NYV Data to Entrepreneurs," CNNMoney.com, April 5, 2011, at http://money.cnn.com/2011/04/05/technology/bigapps_nyc/index.htm, accessed May 23, 2011.

9. Maselli, Jennifer, "Insurers Look to CRM for Profits," *InformationWeek*, May 6, 2002, www.informationweek.com/story/IWK20022050250007, accessed March 1, 2005.

10. "Laurentian Bank Creates Online Scoring Models for Dealer Financing," Customer Success Story from SAS Corporation, www.sas.com/success/laurentian.html, accessed April 21, 2005.

11. Corda Technologies, at http://centerview.corda.com/corda/dashboards/HumanCapitalManagement/main.dashxml#cordaDash=9, accessed July 11, 2011.

12. Kling, Julia, "OLAP Gains Fans among Data-Hungry Firms," *Computerworld*, January 8, 1996, pp. 43, 48.

13. Hutheesing, Nikhil, "Surfing with Sega," *Forbes*, November 4, 1996, pp. 350–51.

14. LaPlante, Alice, "Big Things Come in Smaller Packages," *Computerworld*, June 24, 1996, pp. DW/6–7.

15. "Information to Reporting to Smarter Operations: Performance Management at Dr. Pepper Snapple Group," IBM Customer Success Stories, at http://public.dhe.ibm.com/software/data/sw-library/cognos/pdfs/casestudies/cs_pm_at_dr_pepper_snapple_group.pdf, accessed July 12, 2011.

16. Copeland, Larry, "High-Tech Apps Help Drivers Evade Police," *USA Today*, March 21, 2011, at http://www.usatoday.com/news/nation/2011-03-21-1Ascofflaw21_ST_N.htm, accessed April 12, 2011.

17. Copeland, Larry, "Four Senators Target DUI Checkpoint Apps," *USA Today*, March 23, 2011, at http://www.usatoday.com/news/nation/2011-03-23-speedtrap23_ST_N.htm, accessed April 12, 2011.

18. Copeland, Larry, "Apple to Stop Accepting DUI Checkpoint Apps," *USA Today*, June 9, 2011, at http://www.usatoday.com/tech/news/2011-06-09-apple-DUI-checkpoints-app_n.htm#, accessed July 2, 2011.

19. Guth, Robert, "Glaxo Tries a Linux Approach," *The Wall Street*

Journal, May 26, 2010, at http://online.wsj.com/article/SB100014240 52748703341904575266583403844888.html, accessed July 12, 2011.

CHAPTER 4

1. Allen, I. Elaine, and Jeff Seaman, *Learning on Demand,* Babson Survey Research Group, The Sloan Consortium, January 2010.

2. Gambon, Jill, "A Database That 'Ads' Up," *InformationWeek,* August 7, 1995.

3. Simon, Herbert, *The New Science of Management Decisions,* rev. ed. (Englewood Cliffs, NJ: Prentice Hall, 1977).

4. Brewin, Bob, "IT Goes on a Mission: GPS/GIS Effort Helps Pinpoint Shuttle Debris," *Computerworld,* February 10, 2003, pp. 1, 6.

5. Siegel, Eric, "Driven with Business Expertise, Analytics Produces Actionable Predications," DestinationCRM.com, March 29, 2004, at http://www.destinationcrm.com/Articles/Web-Exclusives/Viewpoints/Driven-with-Business-Expertise-Analytics-Produces-Actionable-Predictions-44224.aspx?CategoryID=259, accessed July 22, 2011.

6. Nash, Kim, "Using Predictive Analytics to Tap More Profitable Customers," *CIO,* January 25, 2010, at http://www.cio.com/article/523013/Using_Predictive_Analytics_to_Tap_More_Profitable_Customers, accessed July 25, 2011.

7. Stodder, David, "Customer Insights," *InformationWeek,* February 1, 2010, pp. 35–38.

8. Grimes, Seth, "Text-Analytics Demand Approaches $1 Billion," *InformationWeek,* May 12, 2011, at http://informationweek.com/news/software/bi/229500096, accessed July 22, 2011.

9. Kay, Alexx, "Artificial Neural Networks," *Computerworld,* February 12, 2001.

10. Perry, William, "What Is Neural Network Software?" *Journal of Systems Management,* September 1994.

11. Port, Otis, "Diagnoses That Cast a Wider Net," *BusinessWeek,* May 22, 1995.

12. Baxt, William G., and Joyce Skora, "Prospective Validation of Artificial Neural Network Trained to Identify Acute Myocardial Infarction," *The Lancet,* January 6, 1997.

13. "Detecting Fakes at a Stroke," *New Scientist,* October 20, 2006.

14. Sisco, Paul, "'Authentic' Project Uses Digital Technology to Foil Forgers," *Voice of America News,* January 5, 2007.

15. Chicago Appraisers Association Web site, April 24, 2009.

16. Scanlon, Jessie, "Brand Management a la Affinnova," *BusinessWeek Online,* accessed May 11, 2009.

17. Williams, Sam, "Unnatural Selection," *Technology Review,* February 2005.

18. "M&S Uses Genetic IT to Create Best Displays," *Computer Weekly,* February 2004.

19. Totty, Patrick, "Pinpoint Members with New Data-Mining Tools," *Credit Union Magazine,* April 2002.

20. Wolinsky, Howard, "Advisa Helps Companies Get More from Their Data: Helps Managers to Understand Market," *Chicago Sun-Times,* December 20, 2000.

21. Anthes, Gary H., "Agents of Change," *Computerworld,* January 27, 2003.

22. Bonabeau, Eric, "Swarm Intelligence," O'Reilly Emerging Technology Conference, April 22–25, 2003, Santa Clara, California.

23. Ibid.

24. Kavilanz, Parija, "What's Hot for the Holidays? Google Knows," CNNMoney, October 19, 2010, at http://money.cnn.com/2010/09/16/technology/google_searches_predict_hot_holiday_trends/index.htm, accessed July 25, 2011.

25. Whiting, Rick, "Businesses Mine Data to Predict What Happens Next," *InformationWeek,* May 29, 2006, at www.informationweek.com/shared/printableArticleSrc.jhtml?articleID5188500520, accessed April 27, 2007.

26. Ferris, Nancy, "Report: IT Helps New York City's Public Hospitals Achieve Excellence," *Government Health IT,* October 17, 2008.

27. Lamont, Judith, "Decision Support Systems Prove Vital to Healthcare," *KM World,* February 2007.

CHAPTER 5

1. Yarow, Jay, and Kamelia Angelova, "Internet Advertising Ready to Take More Money Away from Newspapers," *Business Insider,* January 5, 2010, at http://www.businessinsider.com/chart-of-the-day-time-spent-vs-ad-spend-2010-1, accessed July 17, 2011.

2. The Lockheed Martin Corporation, "About Us," http://www.lockheedmartin.com/wms/findPage.do?dsp=fec&ci=4&sc=400, accessed April 22, 2007.

3. "Pourquoi Paypal est promu a un bel avenir? The C2B Revolution: Consumer Empowerment," August 27, 2005, http://c2b.typepad.com/, accessed April 22, 2007.

4. "The Top Five Hundred Sites on the Web," Alexa: The Web Information Company, at http://www.alexa.com/topsites, accessed July 20,1011.

5. Segall, Laurie, "Facebook's $600 Million Virtual Economy," CNNMoney, April 28, 2011, at http://money.cnn.com/2011/04/28/technology/facebook_credits/index.htm?iid=EAL, accessed July 19, 2011.

6. Baig, Edward, "Google Wallet App Lets You Tap to Pay with Smartphone," *USA Today,* May 26, 2011, at http://www.usatoday.com/tech/news/2011-05-26-google-payments_n.htm#, accessed July 15, 2011.

7. Goldman, David, "Google Wallet Lets You Pay with Your Phone," CNNMoney, May 26, 2011, at http://money.cnn.com/2011/05/26/technology/google_wallet/index.htm?, accessed July 16, 2011.

8. Anderson, Chris, "The Long Tail," *Wired Magazine,* October 2004, http://www.wired.com/wired/archive/12.10/tail.html, accesses April 24, 2007.

9. Anderson, Chris, *The Long Tail* (New York: Hyperion, 2006).

10. Tapsott, Don, and Anthony Williams, "Innovation in the Age of Mass Collaboration," *Bloomberg*

BusinessWeek, February 1, 2007, at http://www.business-week.com/innovate/content/feb2007/id20070201_774736.htm?chan=innovation_special+report+--+the+businessweek+wikinomics+series_the+business-week+wikinomics+series, accessed July 20, 2011.

11. Copeland, Michael, "Box Office Boffo for Brainiacs:" The Netflix Prize, CNNMoney, September 21, 2009, at http://tech.fortune.cnn.com/2009/09/21/box-office-boffo-for-brainiacs-the-netflix-prize/, accessed July 20, 2011.

12. Reisinger, Don, "Virtual Goods Revenue to Hit $7.3 Billion this Year," CNet, November 15, 2010, at http://news.cnet.com/8301-13506_3-20022780-17.html, accessed July 20, 2011.

13. Lehdonvirta, Vili, and Mirko Ernkvist, "Knowledge Map of the Virtual Economy," *InfoDev,* April 2011, at http://www.infodev.org/en/Publication.1076.html, accessed July 20, 2011.

14. Petrecca, Laura, "Crowdfunding and Peer-to-Peer Lending Help Small Businesses," *USA Today,* May 6, 2011, at http://www.usatoday.com/money/smallbusiness/2011-05-06-creative-financing-for-small-businesses_n.htm, accessed July 4, 2011.

15. Hoffman, Martin, "VW Revs Its B2B Engine," *Optimize,* March 2004, pp. 22–30.

16. Hansen, Meike-Uta, "Volkswagen Drives Supply-Chain Innovation," *Optimize,* April 2005, www.optimizemag.com/showArticle.jhtml;jesssionid=AWFTOBGTAWLIQQSNDBCSKHSCJUMEKJVN?articlelD=159904448, accessed May 29, 2005.

17. Molina, Brett, "Survey: Smartphone Purchases on the Rise," *USA Today,* June 30, 2011, at http://content.usatoday.com/communities/technologylive/post/2011/06/survey-smartphone-purchases-on-the-rise/1, accessed July 20, 2011.

18. Bustillo, Miguel, and Ann Zimmerman, "Phone-Wielding Shoppers Strike Fear into Retailers," *The Wall Street Journal,* December 15, 2010, at http://online.wsj.com/article/SB10001424052748704694004576019691769574496.html, accessed July 20, 2011.

19. Jansen, Jim, *Online Product Research,* Pew Internet Project, September 29, 2010, at http://pewinternet.org/Reports/2010/Online-Product-Research.aspx, accessed July 20, 2011.

CHAPTER 6

1. "Kodak Film Sales," Photo.net, October 4, 2010, at http://photo.net/film-and-processing-forum/00XQGG, accessed July 1, 2011.

2. Hafner, Katie, "Film Drop-Off Sites Fading Fast as Digital Cameras Dominate," *The New York Times,* October 9, 2007, at http://query.nytimes.com/gst/fullpage.html?res=9D0CE4DF103CF93AA35753C1A9619C8B63, accessed July 1, 2011.

3. Dobbib, Ben, "How Much Longer Can Photographic Film Hold On?" *USA Today,* June 4, 2011, at http://www.usatoday.com/money/industries/manufacturing/2011-06-04-film-camera-digital_n.htm, accessed July 1, 2011.

4. Hoover, J. Nicholas, "In Pursuit of New Efficiencies, Honda Drives Green IT Effort," *InformationWeek,* December 8, 2008, p. 19.

5. Roth, Sabine, "Profile of CAS Software AG," March 29, 2005, www.cas.de/English/Home.asp, accessed June 9, 2005.

6. Barnes, Cecily, "More Programmers Going 'Extreme,'" April 9, 2001, www.news.com, accessed June 1, 2005.

7. "Who Are We," www.agilealliance.org, accessed June 2, 2005.

8. Lohr, Steve, "Change the World, and Win Fabulous Prizes," *The New York Times,* May 21, 2011, at http://www.nytimes.com/2011/05/22/technology/22unboxed.html, accessed July 2, 2011.

9. Clendaniel, Morgan, "Recyclebank Crowdsources Its Business Plan to an Elite Group of Social Entrepreneurs," *Fast Company,* June 27, 2011, at http://www.fastcompany.com/1762971/recyclebank-purpose-startingbloc-business-plan, accessed July 2, 2011.

10. "Industry Associations," connextions.net/IndustryAssoc.asp, accessed June 1, 2005.

11. "Outsourcing's Next Wave," *Fortune,* July 15, 2004, www.fortune.com, accessed June 2, 2005.

12. Cohen, Peter, "Twelve Technical and Business Trends Shaping the Year Ahead," May 6, 2004, www.babsoninsight.com, accessed June 2, 2005.

13. Burk, Jeff, "Why We Picked China for Outsourcing," *Information-Week,* September 20, 2008, http://www.informationweek.com/news/global-cio/outsourcing/showArticle.jhtml?articleID=210602255, accessed February 19, 2009.

14. "Statistics Related to Offshore Outsourcing," May 2005, www.rttsweb.com, accessed June 1, 2005.

15. Asay, Matt, "The Rise of the 'Good Enough' Technology Economy," *CNET,* August 28, 2007, at http://news.cnet.com/8301-13505_3-9768204-16.html, accessed July 3, 2011.

16. Vuong, Andy, "LCD and Plasma TVs Fail Much Sooner as Manufacturers Cut Costs," *The Denver Post,* October 24, 1010, at http://www.denverpost.com/search/ci_16412838, accessed May 26, 2011.

17. Malik, Om, "What Works: The Economics of Good Enough," *GigaOM,* May 31, 2011, at http://gigaom.com/2011/05/31/economics-of-good-enough/, accessed July 4, 2011.

18. Baker, Stephen, "Why 'Good Enough' Is Good Enough," *Bloomberg BusinessWeek,* September 3, 2007, at http://www.businessweek.com/magazine/content/07_36/b4048048.htm, accessed July 2, 2011.

19. Singolda, Adam, "The Economy of Good Enough," *MediaPost,* May 11, 2011, at http://www.mediapost.com/publications/?fa=Articles.showArticle&art_aid=150332, accessed July 3, 2011.

20. "Average Length of Time Wireless Customers Keep Their Mobile Phones Increases Notably," J.D.

Power & Associates, September 23, 2010, at http://businesscenter.jdpower.com/news/pressrelease.aspx?ID=2010185, accessed July 4, 2011.

21. Parker, Penny, "Flagstaff Puts Wines on iPads," *The Denver Post,* February 8, 2011, p. 5B.

22. Canfield, Clark, "iPads Take Place Next to Crayons in Kindergarten," *USA Today,* April 13, 2011, at http://www.usatoday.com/tech/news/2011-04-13-ipads-kindergarten.htm#, accessed July 1, 2011.

23. Graham, Jefferson, "Alaska Airlines Replaces Pilot Manuals with iPads," *USA Today,* June 6, 2008, at http://www.usatoday.com/tech/news/2011-06-08-ipad-apple-manuals-airline_n.htm#, accessed July 1, 2011.

24. Horovitz, Bruce, "iPads Replacing Restaurant Menus, Staff," *USA Today,* February 16, 2011, at http://www.usatoday.com/money/industries/food/2011-02-16-ipadcafe16_ST_N.htm#, accessed May 13, 2011.

25. Levin, Alan, "iPads Fuel Flight of Paperless Planes," *USA Today,* March 18, 2011, at http://www.usatoday.com/travel/flights/2011-03-18-ipads-planes_N.htm, accessed July 1, 2011.

26. Martin, Scott, "Tablets Take PC Evolution to the Next Level," *USA Today,* March 21, 2011, at http://www.usatoday.com/tech/news/2011-03-21-ipad-vs-pc.htm#, accessed May 30, 2011.

CHAPTER 7

1. "Payment Trend Projections," *Financial Services Technology,* at http://www.usfst.com/media/article-images/article-image/FSTUS/issue-12/Payment_Trends_-_Chart_1.jpg, accessed July 13, 2011.

2. "Company Profile," www.delmonte.com, accessed May 16, 2005.

3. "Industry Implementations," www.dmreview.com, accessed May 16, 2005.

4. Hoover, J. Nicholas, "GE Puts the Cloud Model to the Test," *InformationWeek,* April 13, 2009, pp. 32–33.

5. Facebook Statistics, at http://www.facebook.com/press/info.php?statistics, accessed July 5, 2011.

6. Fowler, Geoffrey, and Scott Morrison, "Facebook Shares Server Designs," *The Wall Street Journal,* April 8, 2011, at http://online.wsj.com/article/SB10001424052748704013604576248953972500040.html, accessed July 14, 2011.

7. "The State of the Data Center," *InformationWeek,* December 18/25, 2006, p. 9.

8. Murphy, Chris, and Antone Gonsalves, "Elmo's at It Again," *InformationWeek,* December 18/25, 2006, p.21.

9. Marks, Howard, "Practical Disaster Recovery," *InformationWeek,* December 22/29, 2008, pp. 37–38.

10. Baig, Edward, "Amazon Service Lets You Store Your Music in the Clouds," *USA Today,* March 29, 2011, at http://www.usatoday.com/tech/columnist/edwardbaig/2011-03-29-amazon-cloud-based-storage.htm#, accessed July 2, 2011.

11. Graham, Jefferson, "Jobs Unveils Apple's iCloud," *USA Today,* June 6, 2011, at http://www.usatoday.com/tech/news/2011-06-06-apple-icloud_n.htm#, accessed July 2, 2011.

12. Windows Live, Microsoft.com, at http://explore.live.com/, accessed July 15, 2011.

13. "Denver Health Improves Caregiver Workflow and Saves $5.7M," ThinIdentity Corporation, http://www.thinidentity.com/helpers/uploads/ti_denverhealth_cs.pdf, accessed June 9, 2009.

CHAPTER 8

1. "Robotic Surgery in Urology," "Istanbul Center for Robotic Surgery," at http://www.istanbulrobotikcerrahi.com/robotic-surgery-in-urology.asp, accessed July 18, 2011.

2. Pliagas, Linda, "Learning IT Right from Wrong," *InfoWorld,* October 2, 2000.

3. Sweet, David, "$1.7B in Lost Work? That's March Madness," msnbc.com, March 19, 2008, at http://www.msnbc.msn.com/id/23708504/ns/business-sports_biz/t/b-lost-work-thats-march-madness/#, accessed July 30, 2011.

4. Horovitz, Bruce, "Marketers Surround March Madness with Social Media," *USA Today,* March 17, 2011, at http://www.usatoday.com/money/advertising/2011-03-17-Coke-Dove-ATT-NCAA-march-Madness.htm#, accessed July 30, 2011.

5. Fogliasso, Christine, and Donald Baack, "The Personal Impact of Ethical Decisions: A Social Penetration Theory Model," Second Annual Conference on Business Ethics Sponsored by the Vincentian Universities in the United States, New York, 1995.

6. Jones. T. M., "Ethical Decision-Making by Individuals in Organizations: An Issue-Contingent Model," *Academy of Management Review,* 1991.

7. Baase, Sara, *The Gift of Fire: Social, Legal and Ethical Issues in Computing* (Upper Saddle River, NJ: Prentice Hall, 1997).

8. Moores, Trevor, "Software Piracy: A View from Hong Kong," *Communications of the ACM,* December 2000.

9. *Eighth Annual BSA Global Software 2010 Piracy Study,* Business Software Alliance, May 2011, at http://portal.bsa.org/globalpiracy2010/downloads/study_pdf/2010_BSA_Piracy_Study-Standard.pdf, accessed July 30, 2011.

10. Rittenhouse, David, "Privacy and Security on Your PC," *ExtremeTech,* May 28, 2002, www.extremetech.com, accessed May 31, 2005.

11. O'Dell, Jolie, "How Much Does Identity Theft Cost?" *Mashable,* January 29, 2011, at http://mashable.com/2011/01/29/identity-theft-infographic/, accessed July 30, 2011.

12. Singletary, Michelle, "Identity-Theft Statistics Look Better, But You Still Don't Want to Be One," *The Washington Post,* February 9, 2011, at http://www.washingtonpost.com/wp-dyn/content/article/2011/02/09/AR2011020906064.html, accessed July 30, 2011.

13. "Data Breaches," Identity Theft Resource Center, at http://www.idtheftcenter.org/artman2/publish/lib_survey/ITRC_2008_Breach_List.shtml, accessed July 30, 2011.

14. Rashid, Fahmida, "Epsilon Data Breach to Cost Billions in Worst-Case Scenario," *eWeek*, May 3, 2011, at http://www.eweek.com/c/a/Security/Epsilon-Data-Breach-to-Cost-Billions-in-WorstCase-Scenario-459480/, accessed July 30, 2011.

15. Acohido, Byron, "Data Thieves Target E-Mail Addresses," *USA Today*, April 12, 2011, at http://www.usatoday.com/money/industries/technology/2011-04-12-epsilon-email-hackers-pfishing.htm#, accessed July 30, 2011.

16. Acohido, Byron, "Wave of Phishing Could Follow Epsilon Hack," *USA Today*, April 5, 2011, at http://www.usatoday.com/tech/news/2011-04-04-epsilon-hacking-poses-phishing-threat.htm#, accessed July 30, 2011.

17. *About Identity Theft*, The Federal Trade Commission, at www.ftc.gov/bcp/edu/microsites/idtheft/consumers/about-identity-theft.html, accessed October 3, 2011.

18. Acohido, Byron, "Gmail Hit by Cyberattacks from China," *USA Today*, June 1, 2011, at http://www.usatoday.com/tech/news/2011-06-01-gmail-under-attack-from-china_n.htm#, accessed July 30, 2011.

19. "Chinese Cyber Attacks Target German Ministers," *The Local*, June 29, 2011, at http://www.thelocal.de/sci-tech/20110629-35947.html, accessed July 30, 2011.

20. Vaught, Bobby, Raymond Taylor, and Steven Vaught, "The Attitudes of Managers regarding the Electronic Monitoring of Employee Behavior: Procedural and Ethical Considerations," *American Business Review*, January 2000.

21. Parker, Laura, "Medical-Privacy Law Creates Wide Confusion," *USA Today*, October 17–19, 2003.

22. Medford, Cassimir, "Know Who I Am," *PC Magazine*, February 7, 2000.

23. Naples, Mark, "Privacy and Cookies," *Target Marketing*, April 2002.

24. Reed, Brad, "Storm Worm, Other Botnets, Kept Spam Levels High in 2007; Spam Accounted for an Average of 80% of All E-Mail Traffic in 2007, Commontouch Reports," *Network World*, January 9, 2008.

25. Commontouch.com, accessed May 25, 2009.

26. Graven, Matthew P., "Leave Me Alone," *PC Magazine*, January 16, 2001.

27. Baase, *The Gift of Fire*.

28. Rittenhouse, "Privacy and Security on Your PC."

29. Soat, John, "IT Confidential," *InformationWeek*, June 3, 2002, p. 98.

30. Salkever, Alex, "A Dark Side to the FBI's Magic Lantern," *BusinessWeek Online*, November 27, 2001, www.businessweek.com, accessed May 24, 2005.

31. *Report to the Nations on Occupational Fraud and Abuse: 2010 Global Fraud Study*, Association of Certified Fraud Examiners, 2010, at http://www.acfe.com/rttn/rttn-2010.pdf, accessed July 31, 2011.

32. Messmer, Ellen, "Corporate Data Breach Average Cost Hits $7.2 Million," *Network World*, March 8, 2011, at http://www.networkworld.com/news/2011/030811-ponemon-data-breach.html, accessed July 31, 2011.

33. "Europe Plans to Jail Hackers," April 23, 2002, zdnet.com/2100-11105-889332.html, accessed May 31, 2005.

34. Acohido, Byron, "Personal Mobile Devices Create Security Headaches for Biz," *USA Today*, May 30, 2011, at http://www.usatoday.com/tech/products/2011-05-30-mobile-devices-in-the-workplace_n.htm#, accessed July 31, 2011.

35. Acohido, Byron, "Companies Begin to Set Policies for Mobile Devices," *USA Today*, June 23, 2011, at http://content.usatoday.com/communities/technologylive/post/2011/06/companies-begin-to-set-policies-for-mobile-devices/1, accessed July 31, 2011.

36. Meyer, Lisa, "Security You Can Live With," *Fortune*, Winter 2002.

37. "Fast Times," *Fortune*, Summer 2000.

38. Radcliff, Deborah, "Beyond Passwords," *Computerworld*, January 21, 2002.

39. "Texting: Sexting Statistics," Blogging by WordPress, at http://blog. amersol.edu.pe/texting/sexting-statistics/, accessed July 31, 2011.

40. Shorman, Jonathan, "Adult Sexting Tied to Power, 'Unlimited Partners,'" *USA Today*, June 2011, at http://yourlife.usatoday.com/sex-relationships/story/2011/06/Adult-sexting-tied-to-power-unlimited-partners/48208854/1, accessed July 31, 2011.

41. Camia, Catalina, "Pressure Builds on Rep. Weiner to Quit over Scandal," *USA Today*, June 7, 2011, at http://content.usatoday.com/communities/onpolitics/post/2011/06/anthony-weiner-resign-congress-/1, accessed July 31, 2011.

42. Molina, Brett, "Sony Launches 'Welcome Back' Program for PSN Users," *USA Today*, June 2011, at http://content.usatoday.com/communities/gamehunters/post/2011/06/sony-launches-welcome-back-program-for-psn-users/1, accessed July 31, 2011.

43. Snider, Mike, and Brett Molina, "Reputation of PlayStation, Sony Takes a Brand Hit," *USA Today*, May 10, 2011, at http://www.usatoday.com/tech/gaming/2011-05-09-playstation-reputation-takes-pounding_n.htm#, accessed July 31, 2011.

44. Molina, Brett, "First Class-Action Suit Filed over PlayStation Network Breach," *USA Today*, April 28, 2011, at http://content.usatoday.com/communities/gamehunters/post/2011/04/first-class-action-suit-filed-over-playstation-network-breach/1, accessed July 31, 2011.

45. Snider, Mike, "Sony: Credit Card Data at Risk in PlayStation Hack," *USA Today*, April 27, 2011, at http://www.usatoday.com/tech/gaming/2011-04-26-sony-playstation_n.htm#, accessed July 31, 2011.

46. Molina, Brett, and Mike Snider, "Experts: PlayStation Breach One of Largest Ever," *USA Today*, April 28, 2011, at http://www.usatoday.com/tech/gaming/2011-04-27-playstation-hack_n.htm#, accessed July 31, 2011.

47. Molina, Brett, "Sony: PlayStation Network Down 'At Least a Few More Days,'" *USA Today*, May

10, 2011, at http://content.usatoday.com/communities/gamehunters/post/2011/05/sony-playstation-network-down-at-least-a-few-more-days/1, accessed July 31, 2011.

CHAPTER 9

1. Mallenbaum, Carly, "Postal Service Lists 3,700 Branches for Possible Closing," *USA Today,* July 27, 2011, at http://www.usatoday.com/money/economy/2011-07-27-usps-post-office-closing-list_n.htm, accessed July 27, 2011.

2. "Envisioning America's Future Postal Service," United States Postal Service, Supporting Documents: Charts and Graphs: BCG Selected Slides, at http://www.usps.com/ strategicplanning/_pdf/BCG_Selected_Slides.pdf, accessed July 17, 2011.

3. Barr, Meghan, "Girl Scout Cookies Go High-Tech: Smartphone Sales," *USA Today,* March 25, 2011, at http://www.usatoday.com/tech/news/2011-03-25-girl-scouts-smartphone_N.htm#, accessed July 28, 2011.

4. "YouTube Pressroom Statistics," YouTube.com, July 28, 2011, at http://www.youtube.com/t/press, accessed July 28, 2011.

5. Adams, Nina, "Lessons from the Virtual World," *Training,* June 1995, pp. 45–47.

6. Flynn, Laurie, "VR and Virtual Spaces Find a Niche in Real Medicine," *New York Times,* June 5, 1995, p. C3.

7. Baig, Edward, "Sprint Unveils Glasses-Free 3-D Smartphone," *USA Today,* March 22, 2011, at http://content.usatoday.com/communities/technologylive/post/2011/03/sprint-unveils-galsses-free-3-d-smartphone, accessed July 28, 2011.

8. Ackerman, Evan, "Edible RFI Tags Track Your Food from Beginning to End," DVICE, May 30, 2011, at http://dvice.com/archives/2011/05/edible-rfid-tag.php, accessed July 28, 2011.

9. Emspak, Jesse, "Chips for Dinner: Edible RFID Tags Describe Your Food," *NewScientist,* June 10, 2011, at http://www.newscientist.com/blogs/onepercent/2011/06/chips-for-dinner-edible-rfid-t.html, accessed July 28, 2011.

10. Corcoran, Elizabeth, "The Next Small Thing," *Forbes,* July 23, 2001, pp. 96–106.

11. Center to Integrate Nanotechnologies, United States Department of Energy, http://cint.lanl.gov, accessed June 1, 2005.

12. Saltzman, Marc, "Put Yourself in the Movies with 'Yoostar 2,'" *USA Today,* March 20, 2011, at http://www.usatoday.com/tech/columnist/marcsaltzman/2011-03-20-yoostar_N.htm#, accessed July 28, 2011.

13. Smith, Aaron, *Smartphone Adoption and Usage,* July 1, 2011, Pew Research Center, Washington, D.C.

14. Washington, Jesse, "Digital Divide," *The Denver Post,* January 9, 2011, p. 3K.

15. *Lions on the Move: The Progress and Potential of African Economies,* June 2010, McKinsey Global Institute, Washington, DC.

EXTENDED LEARNING MODULE H

1. Broad, William J., John Markoff, and David E. Sanger, "Israeli Test on Worm Call Crucial in Iran Nuclear Delay," *New York Times,* January 15, 2011, http://www.nytimes.com/2011/01/16/world/middleeast/16stuxnet.html?pagewanted=all, accessed August 26, 2011.

2. Luhn, Robert, "Eliminate Viruses," *PC World,* July 2002.

3. Landolt, Sara Cox, "Why the Sky Isn't Falling," *Credit Union Management,* October 2000.

4. Hayes, Frank, "Botnet Threat," *Computerworld,* November 6, 2006.

5. Gage, Deborah, "How to Survive a Bot Attack," *Baseline,* January 2007.

6. "Hackers Attack *USA Today* Web Site," *Morning Sun* (Pittsburg, KS), July 13, 2002.

7. Clark, Richard A., and Robert K. Knake, *Cyber War: The Next Threat to National Security and What to Do About It* (Ecco, 2010).

8. Hulme, George, "Vulnerabilities Beckon Some with a License to Hack," *InformationWeek,* October 23, 2000.

9. Gorman, Siobhan, "Electricity Grid in U.S. Penetrated by Spies," *The Wall Street Journal,* April 8, 2009.

10. *USA Today,* http://www.usatoday.com/news/nation/2011-07-30-police-fbi-digital-detectives_n.htm, accessed August 27, 2011.

11. CNN.com, http://www.cnn.com/2004/TECH/04/04/mobile.terror, accessed August 27, 2011.

12. Torpey, Dan, Vince Walden, and Mike Sherrod, "Breaking the Status Quo in E-Mail Review," *Fraud Magazine,* May/June 2010, pp. 1–5.

EXTENDED LEARNING MODULE K (at www.mhhe.com/haag)

1. "Accounting: Salaries," *Careers-In-Accounting,* at http://www.careers-in-accounting.com/acsal.htm, accessed July 26, 2011.

2. "Salary Snapshot for Accountant Jobs," *PayScale,* July 22, 2011, at http://www.payscale.com/research/US/Job=Accountant/Salary, accessed July 26, 2011.

3. "Finance Salaries Top Expectation," *AllBusinessSchools,* at http://www.allbusinessschools.com/business-careers/finance/finance-salary, accessed July 27, 2011.

4. "Salary by Company Size for Finance Manager Jobs," *PayScale,* July 26, 2011, at http://www.payscale.com/research/US/Job=Finance_Manager/Salary/by_Company_Size, accessed July 27, 2011.

5. *World Travel & Tourism Council Progress and Priorities 2009-10,* World Travel & Tourism Council, 2011, at http://www.wttc.org/bin/pdf/original_pdf_file/pandp_final2_low_res.pdf, accessed July 27, 2011.

6. Nyheim, Peter, and Daniel Connolly, *Technology Strategies for the Hospitality Industry,* 2d ed. (Boston: Prentice Hall, 2012).

7. HVS Executive Search, *HCE Data Services 2010 North American Hospitality Compensation Exchange Hotel/*

Casino Property Report (New York: HVS International, 2010).

8. "Salary for Industry: Information Technology (IT) Services," *PayScale,* July 21, 2011, at http://www.payscale.com/research/US/Industry=Information_Technology_%28IT%29_Services/Salary, accessed July 27, 2011.

9. *2011 IT Skills and Salary Survey Report,* Global Knowledge Training, 2011, at http://images.globalknowledge.com/wwwimages/pdfs/2011_SalaryReport.pdf, accessed July 27, 2011.

10. "Occupational Employment and Wages News Release," Bureau of Labor Statistics, May 2010, at http://www.bls.gov/news.release/ocwage.htm, accessed July 27, 2011.

11. "Marketing Salaries," *Simply Hired,* July 27, 2011, at http://www.simplyhired.com/a/salary/search/q-marketing, accessed July 27, 2011.

12. "Advertising, Marketing, Promotions, Public Relations, and Sales Managers," *Occupational Outlook Handbook,* 2010-2011 Edition, Bureau of Labor Statistics, at http://www.bls.gov/oco/ocos020.htm, accessed July 27, 2011.

13. "Salary by Company Size for General/Operations Manager Jobs," *PayScale,* July 25, 2011, at http://www.payscale.com/research/US/Job=General_%2f_Operations_Manager/Salary/by_Company_Size, accessed July 27, 2011.

14. "Salary by Employer Name for Skill: Operations Management," *PayScale,* July 20, 2011, at http://www.payscale.com/research/US/Skill=Operations_Management/Salary/by_Employer, accessed July 27, 2011.

15. *Emerging Trends in Real Estate 2011,* Urban Land Institute and PricewaterhouseCoopers, October 2010, at http://www.pwc.com/us/en/asset-management/real-estate/assets/emerging-trends-real-estate-2011.pdf, accessed July 27, 2011.

16. "2010 Real Estate Compensation Survey," CEL & Associates, at http://www.celassociates.com/CompCurrentSummary.cfm, accessed July 27, 2011.

CHAPTER 2

38 © Veer

CHAPTER 7

206 ©2011 MOTOROLA MOBILITY, INC. ALL RIGHTS RESERVED

CHAPTER 9

267 (l) Keith Brofsky/Getty Images, (c) Andersen Ross/Photodisc/ Getty Images, (r) Stockbyte/Getty Images

MODULE A

323 (tl) Copyright © 2011 Sony Ericsson Mobile Communications AB. All rights reserved, (cl) Courtesy of Nintendo, (bl) Courtesy of Nikon Inc., (tr) Courtesy of Garmin, (cr) Courtesy of Epson America, Inc., (br) © 1996-2011, Amazon.com, Inc. or its affiliates; **324** (t) Copyright © 2009 Logitech. All rights reserved., (c) © Seagate Technology LLC; **326** (tl) Photo of BlackBerry® PlayBook™ tablet © 2011 Research In Motion Limited, (r) Courtesy of Apple Inc., (cl) Courtesy of Hewlett-Packard, (bl) Courtesy of Lenovo; **327** (cl) Courtesy of Hewlett-Packard, (bl) Courtesy of International Business Machines Corporation. Unauthorized use not permitted., (r) Photo Courtesy of Cray, Inc.; **335** (tl) Xbox 360 product photo Courtesy of Microsoft Corporation, (tc) Copyright © 2009 Logitech. All rights reserved., (r) Courtesy of Epson America, Inc.; **337** (tl) Courtesy of Samsung, (tr) Jose Fuste Raga/Corbis, (bl) Courtesy of Hewlett-Packard, (bc) Courtesy of Epson America, Inc., (br) uPrint © 2011. All rights reserved. uPrint is a Business Unit of Stratasys,

Inc.; **340** (tl) Courtesy of Lexar Media, Inc., (tr) Courtesy of OCZ Technology Group, Inc., (bl) Photo courtesy of Intel Corporation, (bc) Photo courtesy of Intel Corporation, (br) Courtesy of Hewlett-Packard; **344** (tl) Adafim / Alamy, (tr) Anna Yu / Alamy, (cl) Studio 101 / Alamy, (cr) RF Stock / Alamy, (b) Copyright © 2011 Yamaha Corporation of America and Yamaha Corporation. All rights reserved.; **345** Courtesy of Linksys® by Cisco

MODULE B

359 The McGraw-Hill Companies, Inc./John Flournoy, photographer

MODULE E

410 (1) Courtesy of NETGEAR Inc., (2) Photo courtesy of 3M Corporation, (3) Cummings, Pittsburg State University, (4) Copyright © 2011 D-Link Corporation/D-Link Systems, Inc.; **411** (cr) Proxim Corporation, (br) Courtesy of Linksys® by Cisco; **412** Product boxshot courtesy of Microsoft; **423** (t) Spencer Grant/PhotoEdit, (c) Mark Antman/The Image Works, (b) PhotoDisc/Getty Images

MODULE G (WEB)

G.9 (l) Courtesy of Sony Electronics Inc., (r) Brand X Pictures/ PunchStock; **G.14** (l) Brand X Pictures/PunchStock, (r) Karl Weatherly/Getty Images

MODULE H

449 Courtesy of Intuitive Surgical, Inc.

H